THE ELIZABETHAN STAGE

VOL. IV

Oxford University Press, Amen House, London E.C.4

GLASGOW   NEW YORK   TORONTO   MELBOURNE   WELLINGTON

BOMBAY   CALCUTTA   MADRAS   KARACHI   KUALA LUMPUR

CAPE TOWN   IBADAN   NAIROBI   ACCRA

THE ELIZABETHAN STAGE

BY E. K. CHAMBERS. VOL. IV

OXFORD: AT THE CLARENDON PRESS

FIRST PUBLISHED 1923
SET IN GREAT BRITAIN
AT THE UNIVERSITY PRESS, OXFORD
AND REPRINTED LITHOGRAPHICALLY
FROM SHEETS OF THE FIRST EDITION
1945, WITH CORRECTIONS 1951
REPRINTED LITHOGRAPHICALLY
BY D. R. HILLMAN & SONS LTD., FROME
1961

CONTENTS

VOLUME IV

19604

LIST OF ILLUSTRATIONS

NOTE

I HAVE found it convenient, especially in Appendix A, to use the symbol < following a date, to indicate an uncertain date not earlier than that named, and the symbol > followed by a date, to indicate an uncertain date not later than that named. Thus 1903 < > 23 would indicate the composition date of any part of this book. I have sometimes placed the date of a play in italics, where it was desirable to indicate the date of production rather than publication.

The documents from J. R. Dasent, *Acts of the Privy Council* (1890–1907), are reprinted by permission of the Controller of His Majesty's Stationery Office.

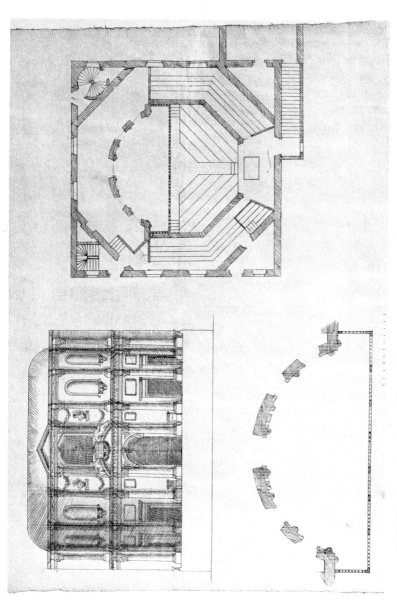

DESIGN BY INIGO JONES FOR THE COCKPIT THEATRE AT WHITEHALL

NOW IN THE LIBRARY OF WORCESTER COLLEGE OXFORD

XXIV

ANONYMOUS WORK

[HERE I bring together, giving them the same treatment as the individual works in ch. xxiii, pieces of which the authorship, as regards the whole or a large part, is unknown or conjectural. They are grouped as (A) Plays, (B) Masks, (C) Receptions and Entertainments. It has been convenient, for the sake of classification, to include in the third group a few which might alternatively have been brought into ch. xxiii under the name of a part-author or describer.]

A. PLAYS

An Alarum for London > 1600

S. R. 1600, May 27. ' Allarum to London ' is included in a memorandum of ' my lord chamberlens menns plaies Entred ' and noted as entered on this day to J. Roberts (Arber, iii. 37).

1600, May 29. ' The Allarum to London, provided that yt be not printed without further Aucthoritie.' *John Roberts* (Arber, iii. 161).

1602. A Larum for London, or The Siedge of Antwerpe. With the ventrous actes and valorous deeds of the lame Soldier. As it hath been playde by the right Honorable the Lord Charberlaine his Seruants. *For William Ferbrand.* [Prologue and Epilogue.]

Editions by R. Simpson (1872), J. S. Farmer (1912, *T.F.T.*), and W. W. Greg (1913, *M.S.R.*).

The play has been ascribed to Shakespeare by Collier, to Shakespeare and Marston by Simpson, and to Lodge by Fleay, *Shakespeare,* 291, but no serious case has been made out for any of these claims. Bullen, *Marlowe,* I, lxxiv, says that Collier had a copy with doggerel rhymes on the t.p. including the line,

> Our famous Marloe had in this a hand,

which Bullen calls ' a very ridiculous piece of forgery '.

Albion Knight > 1566

S. R. 1565–6. ' A play intituled a merye playe bothe pytthy and pleasaunt of Albyon knyghte.' *Thomas Colwell* (Arber, i. 295).

Fragment in Devonshire collection.

[The t.p. is lost, but the seventeenth-century play lists (Greg, *Masques,* xlvii) include an interlude called *Albion*. A fragment on Temperance and Humility, conjecturally assigned by Collier, i. 284, to the same play, is of earlier printing by thirty years or so (*M.S.C.* i. 243).]

Editions by J. P. Collier (1844, *Sh. Soc. Papers*, i. 55) and W. W. Greg (1910, *M. S. C.* i. 229).—*Dissertations*: M. H. Dodds, *The Date of A. K.* (1913, 3 *Library*, iv. 157); G. A. Jones, *The Political Significance of A. K.* (1918, *J. G. P.* xvii. 267).

Collier suggests that this was the play disliked at court on 31 Dec. 1559, but, as Fleay, 66, points out, that would hardly have been licensed for printing. Dodds thinks it motived by the Pilgrimage of Grace (1536–7) and written shortly after.

Alice and Alexis

A fragment (to iii. 1) of a play on the loves of Alice and Alexis, thwarted by Tanto, with an argument of the whole, is in *Douce MS.* 171 (*Bodl.* 21745), f. 48ᵛ. The date ' 1604 ' is scribbled amongst the pages. The manuscript also contains sixteenth-century accounts. There seems nothing to connect this with Massinger's *Alexius, or the Chaste Lover*, licensed by Herbert on 25 Sept. 1639 and apparently included in Warburton's list of burnt plays (3 *Library*, ii. 232, 249).

Alphonsus, Emperor of Germany > 1636

S. R. 1653, Sept. 9. ' A play called Alphonso, Emperor of Germany, by John Poole.' *H. Moseley* (Eyre, i. 428).

1654. The Tragedy of Alphonsus Emperour of Germany. As it hath been very often Acted (with great applause) at the Privat house in Black-Friers by his late Maiesties Servants. By George Chapman Gent. *For Humphrey Moseley.* [Epistle to the Reader. The B.M. copy of the play is dated ' Novemb. 29, 1653 '.]

Editions by K. Elze (1867) and H. F. Schwarz (1913), and in collections of Chapman (q.v.).

Alphonsus may reasonably be identified with the *Alfonso* given before the Queen and the Elector Palatine at the Blackfriars on 5 May 1636 (Cunningham, xxiv). The ascription on the title-page to Chapman is repeated therefrom by Langbaine who rejects that of Kirkman in 1661 and 1671 (Greg, *Masques*, xlviii) to Peele, but the intimate knowledge of German shown in the dialogue has led Elze and Ward, ii. 428, to give Chapman a German collaborator, conceivably one Rudolf Weckerlin of Würtemberg, who after a preliminary visit before 1614 settled permanently in England about 1624 and obtained political employment, which he varied with literary exercises. Later critics are inclined to reject Chapman's authorship altogether, and the case against it has been effectively put by E. Koeppel, *Quellen-Studien zu den Dramen Chapman's*, 78, and Parrott. The ascription to Peele has been revived by Robertson, *T. A.* 123, and though Parrott does not accept the full argument, he agrees in regarding the play as originally of Peele's date, possibly by him, with or without a collaborator, and drastically revised at a later period, perhaps by Weckerlin in 1636. Fleay, ii. 156, 311, also accepts Peele and identifies the play with *Harry of Cornwall*, revived by Strange's for Henslowe on 25 Feb. 1592, but, as Greg (*Henslowe*, ii. 151) points out, the character in *Alphonsus* is not Henry, but Richard of Cornwall. It must be observed that no critic has noticed the *S. R.* ascription to John Poole, which may quite well be the origin of Kirkman's ' Peele '. Who John Poole was, I do not know.

Apius and Virginia > 1567–8

S. R. 1567–8. ' A Tragedy of Apius and Virgine.' *Richard Jones* (Arber, i. 357).

1575. A new Tragicall Comedie of Apius and Virginia, Wherein is liuely expressed a rare example of the vertue of Chastitie, by Virginias constancy, in wishing rather to be slaine at her owne Fathers handes, then to be deflowred of the wicked Iudge Apius. By R. B. *William How for Richard Jones*. [Prologue and Epilogue.]

Editions in Dodsley[3, 4] (1825–76), and by J. S. Farmer (1908, *T.F.T.*) and R. B. McKerrow (1911, *M.S.R.*).

' Haphazard, the Vice ' is a character. The stage-directions name ' the stage ', ' the scaffold '. A prologue addresses ' lordings ' ; an epilogue has a prayer for the queen, nobles, and commons. The play is not controversial, but the tone is Protestant. Fleay, 61, thinks it a Westminster play of 1563–4 ; but no Westminster play of 1563–4 is on record. If Fleay means 1564–5, the Westminster play of that Christmas was *Miles Gloriosus*. There is nothing but the initials to identify the author with Richard Bower of the Chapel (q.v.), but the suggestion is more plausible than that of Wallace, i. 108, who gives the play to Richard Edwardes (q.v.), finding that the ' R. E.' subscribed to some of his manuscript poems is capable of being misread ' R. B.'.

Arden of Feversham > 1592

S. R. 1592, April 3 (Bishop of London). ' The tragedie of Arden of Feuersham and Blackwall.' *Edward White* (Arber, ii. 607). [See s.v. Kyd, *Spanish Tragedy*, for the record of a piracy of the play in 1592 by Abel Jeffes.]

1592. The Lamentable and True Tragedie of M. Arden of Feuersham in Kent. Who was most wickedlye murdered, by the meanes of his disloyall and wanton wyfe, who for the love she bare to one Mosbie, hyred two desperat ruffins Blackwill and Shakbag, to kill him. Wherin is shewed the great mallice and discimulation of a wicked woman, the vnsatiable desire of filthie lust and the shamefull end of all murderers. *For Edward White*. [Epilogue.]

1599. *J. Roberts for Edward White.*

1633. *Eliz. Allde.*

Editions by E. Jacob (1770), A. H. Bullen (1887), R. Bayne (1897, *T.D.*), J. S. Farmer (1911, *T.F.T.*), and in *Sh. Apocrypha.—Dissertations* : C. E. Donne, *Essay on the Tragedy of A. of F.* (1873) ; C. Crawford, *The Authorship of A. of F.* (1903, *Jahrbuch*, xxxix. 74 ; *Collectanea*, i. 101) ; W. Miksch, *Die Verfasserschaft des A. of F.* (1907,

Breslau diss.) ; K. Wiehl, *Thomas Kyd und die Autorschaft von . . . A. of F.* (1912, *E. S.* xliv. 356) ; H. D. Sykes, *Sidelights upon Shakespeare*, 48 (1919) ; L. Cust, *A. of F.* (1920, *Arch. Cant.* xxxiv. 101).

Jacob first claimed the authorship for Shakespeare. In spite of the advocacy of Swinburne (*Study of Sh.*, 129) modern criticism remains wholly unconvinced. The play has tragic merit, but it is not of a Shakespearian character, and it is impossible to fit its manner, before 1592, into any coherent theory of Shakespeare's development. More plausible is the case for Kyd, suggested by Fleay, ii. 28, who puts the date as far back as 1585 on quite unreliable grounds of improbable guess-work, and supported by Robertson, *T. A.* 151, and elaborately argued by Crawford and Sykes. But Boas, *Kyd*, lxxxix, thinks that the author was more likely an imitator of Kyd, and opinion remains divided. Oliphant (*M. P.* viii. 420) suggests Kyd and Marlowe, possibly with a third. The theme may also have been that of the *Murderous Michael* played at court by Sussex's in 1579.

The Birth of Hercules.   *1597 <*

[*MS.*] *B.M. Add. MS.* 28722. ' The birthe of hercules.' [Prologus Laureatus ; Mercurius Prologus ; after text, ' Testamentum poetae, ad peleum. Comoedarum pariter et histrionum princeps Peleu, tuo pro iudicio, volo hanc meam Comoediam, vel recitari, vel reticeri : hoc est : aut vivere aut mori. Scripsi, nec poeta, nec moriens : et tamen poeta moriens '. Written in one hand, with stage-directions by a second and corrections by a third and possibly a fourth, on paper datable by the watermark in 1597.]

Editions by M. W. Wallace (1903) and R. W. Bond (1911, *M.S.R.*).

This is pretty clearly a University play, and any connexion with the *Hercules* of the Admiral's men in 1595 is highly improbable. As George Peele died in 1596, it seems difficult to identify him with the Peleus of the MS. Bond thinks that ' the styles of composition and writing agree in placing a date before 1600 out of the question '.

Caesar's Revenge > *1606*

S. R. 1606, June 5. ' A booke called Julius Caesars reuenge.' *J. Wright and N. Fosbrook*, licensed by Dr. Covell and the wardens (Arber, iii. 323).

N.D. The Tragedie of Caesar and Pompey Or Caesars Reuenge. *G. E. for Iohn Wright.*

1607. . . . Priuately acted by the Studentes of Trinity Colledge in Oxford. *For Nathaniel Fosbrook and Iohn Wright.* [Re-issue with cancel t.p.]

Editions by F. S. Boas (1911, *M. S. R.*) and W. Mühlfeld (1911, 1912, *Jahrbuch*, xlvii. 132 ; xlviii. 37), and J. S. Farmer (*S. F. T.*).— *Dissertations*: T. M. Parrott, *The Academic Tragedy of C. and P.* (1910, *M.L.R.* v. 435) ; H. M. Ayres, *C. R.* (1915, *M.L.A.* xxx. 771) ; G. C. Moore Smith, *The Tragedy of C. R.* (1916, 12 *N.Q.* ii. 305).

There is no traceable connexion between this and any other of the several plays on Caesar, extant and lost, which are upon record. C. Crawford (*M. S. C.* i. 290) indicates some parallels which suggest a date of authorship between 1592 and 1596.

Charlemagne or The Distracted Emperor c. 1600

[*MS.*] *Egerton MS.* 1994. At the end is the note, ' Nella $\phi \delta \phi \nu \rho$ la B ' = ' Nella fedeltà finirò la vita '.

Editions by A. H. Bullen (1884, *O. E. P.* iii) and F. L. Schoell (1920).— *Dissertation* : F. L. Schoell, *Un Drame Élisabéthain Anonyme C* (1912, *Revue Germanique*, viii. 155).

Bullen suggests that the author was Chapman, and also thinks Tourneur or Marston conceivable. He quotes Fleay's opinion in favour of Field. Fleay, ii. 319, withdraws Field and substitutes Dekker. He identifies the play with the ' King Charlemagne ' of Peele's *Farewell* of 1589 (cf. s.v. Peele, *Battle of Alcazar*). Schoell makes an elaborate case for Chapman, and thinks that the play might be *The Fatall Love, a French Tragedy*, entered as his in *S. R.* on 29 June 1660, and included, without author's name, in Warburton's list of burnt plays (3 *Library*, ii. 231). A date later than 1584 is indicated by the use of Du Bartas's *Seconde Semaine* of that year. It may be added that the style points to *c.* 1600 rather than *c.* 1590.

Claudius Tiberius Nero > 1607

S. R. 1607, April 10 (Buck). ' A booke called the tragicall Life and Death of Claudius Tiberius Nero.' *Francis Burton* (Arber, iii. 346).

1607. The Tragedie of Claudius Tiberius Nero, Rome's greatest Tyrant. Truly represented out of the purest Records of thos⌐ Times. *For Francis Burton.* [Epistle to Sir Arthur Mannering, son of Sir George of Eithfield, Shropshire ; Verses *Ad Lectores.*]

1607. The Statelie Tragedie of Claudius Tiberius Nero . . . . *For Francis Burton.* [Another issue.]

Edition by J. S. Farmer (*S. F. T.*).

The play, which is on Tiberius, not Nero, is to be distinguished from *Nero* (1624). The epistle, not apparently by the author, says that the play's ' Father was an Academician '.

Club Law. 1599–1600

[*MS.*] St. John's College, Cambridge, MS. S. 62. [Without t.p. and imperfect ; probably identical with a MS. of the play owned by Richard Farmer.]

Edition by G. C. Moore Smith (1907). [Epilogue.]—*Dissertation* : G. C. Moore Smith, *The Date of C. L.* (1909, *M. L. R.* iv. 268).

The play is described by Fuller, *Hist. of Cambridge* (1655), 156, as given at Clare Hall in 1597–8. But J. S. Hawkins, in his edition of Ruggle's *Ignoramus* (1787), xvi, gives the alternative date 1599, and this has now been confirmed by the discovery of manuscript annals of Cambridge, probably by Fuller himself, with the entry, under the

academic year 1599–1600, ' Aula Clarensis. Club Law fabula festivis-
sima data multum ridentibus Academicis, frustra Oppidanis dolen-
tibus '. The play is a satire on the townsmen, and especially the
anti-gown mayor of 1599–1600, John Yaxley. Fuller says that the
townsmen were invited to the performance and made to sit it through,
and that they complained to the Privy Council, who first ' sent some
slight and private check to the principall Actors therein ', and then,
when pressed, said that they would come to Cambridge, and see the
comedy acted over again in the presence of the townsmen. The fact
that there is no record of these letters in the extant register of the
Council hardly disproves the substance of Fuller's story. Hawkins
ascribed the play to Ruggle (q.v.) on the authority of an eighteenth-
century memorandum.

Sir Clyomon and Clamydes c. 1570

1599. The Historie of the two valiant Knights, Syr Clyomon knight
of the Golden Sheeld, sonne to the King of Denmarke: And Clamydes
the White Knight, sonne to the King of Suauia. As it hath been sundry
times Acted by her Maiesties Players. *Thomas Creede.* [Prologue.]

Editions by W. W. Greg (1913, *M.S.R.*) and J. S. Farmer (*S.F.T.*),
and in collections of Peele.

Subtle Shift ' the vice ', Providence, and Rumour are among the
characters.

Dyce ascribed the play to George Peele on the strength of a manuscript note ' in a very old hand ' on a copy of the 1599 edition. Bullen
thinks it of earlier date than Peele. Greg agrees, regarding it as about
contemporary with *Common Conditions.* L. Kellner, in *Englische
Studien*, xiii. 187, compares the language and style at great length
with Peele's and concludes against his authorship, unless indeed he
wrote it in a spirit of parody. His arguments are challenged by
R. Fischer in *Englische Studien*, xiv. 344. Fleay, 70, assigned it, with
Common Conditions, to R. Wilson. Later (ii. 295), he substituted
R[ichard] B[ower]. He noted a parallel to Thomas Preston's *Cambyses*,
and suggested as a date 1570 or 1578, the years, according to him,
of the original production and of a revival of *Cambyses.* G. L. Kittredge, in *Journal of Germanic Philology*, ii. 8, suggests that Preston
himself was the author of *Sir Clyomon and Clamydes.* If the ' her
Maiesties Players ' of the title-page means the later company of that
name, the play, if not written, must have been revived 1583–94.
Fleay, ii. 296, further identifies it with *The Four Kings* licensed for
Henslowe (i. 103) in March 1599; but an old Queen's play would not
have needed a licence. An Anglo-German repertory of 1626 includes
a ' Tragikomödie vom König in Dänemark und König in Schweden '
(Herz, 66, 72).

Common Conditions > 1576

S. R. 1576, July 26. ' A newe and pleasant comedie or plaie after
the maner of common condycons.' *John Hunter* (Arber, ii. 301).
[Clearly ' maner ' is a misreading of the ' name ' of the t.p.]

Q$_1$, N.D. An excellent and pleasant Comedie, termed after the name of the Vice, Common Condicions, drawne out of the most famous historie of Galiarbus Duke of Arabia, and of the good and eeuill successe of him and his two children, Sedmond his sun, and Clarisia his daughter : Set foorth with delectable mirth, and pleasant shewes. *William How for John Hunter.* [T.p. adds ' The Players names ' and ' Six may play this Comedie ' ; Prologue.]

Q$_2$. Fragment, without t.p. or date, under r.t. ' A pleasant Comedie called Common Conditions '.

Editions in Brandl, 597 (1898), and by J. S. Farmer (1908, *Five Anonymous Plays*) from Q$_2$, and by Tucker Brooke (1915, *Yale Elizabethan Club Reprints,* i) from Q$_1$.

The prologue refers to the audience ' that sit in place ' and the ' actours ' that ' redy stand '. Fleay, ii. 296, suggests the authorship of Richard Bower, on grounds of style.

The Contention of York and Lancaster > 1592

S. R. 1594, March 12. ' A booke intituled, the firste parte of the Contention of the twoo famous houses of York and Lancaster with the deathe of the good Duke Humfrey and the banishement and Deathe of the Duke of Suffolk and the tragicall ende of the prowd Cardinall of Winchester, with the notable rebellion of Jack Cade and the Duke of Yorkes ffirste clayme vnto the Crowne. *Thomas Millington* (Arber, ii. 646). [Part i.]

1602, April 19. Transfer from T. Millington to T. Pavier, ' The first and Second parte of Henry the Vj^t, ij bookes ' (Arber, iii. 204). [Parts i and ii.]

1594. The First Part of the Contention betwixt the two famous Houses of Yorke and Lancaster, with the death of the good Duke Humphrey : And the banishment and death of the Duke of Suffolke, and the Tragicall end of the proud Cardinall of Winchester, with the notable Rebellion of Iacke Cade : And the Duke of Yorkes first claime vnto the Crowne. *Thomas Creede for Thomas Millington.* [Part i.]

1595. The true Tragedie of Richard Duke of Yorke, and the death of good King Henrie the Sixt, with the whole contention betweene the two Houses Lancaster and Yorke, as it was sundrie times acted by the Right Honourable the Earle of Pembrooke his seruants. *P. S. for Thomas Millington.* [Part ii.]

1600. *Valentine Simmes for Thomas Millington.* [Part i.]

1600. *W. W. for Thomas Millington.* [Part ii.]

[1619] N.D. The Whole Contention betweene the two Famous Houses, Lancaster and Yorke. With the Tragicall ends of the good Duke Humfrey, Richard Duke of Yorke, and King Henrie the sixt. Diuided into two Parts : And newly corrected and enlarged. Written by William Shakespeare, Gent. *For T.P.* [Parts i and ii, printed continuously with *Pericles,* 1619 (q.v.).]

Editions by J. O. Halliwell (1843, *Sh. Soc.*), Wright and Clark (1863–6, 1893, *Cambridge Shakespeare*), W. C. Hazlitt (1875, *Sh. Libr.*

v, vi), F. J. Furnivall and T. Tyler (1886, 1889, 1891, *Sh. Q*), and J. S. Farmer (*S. F. T.*).—*Dissertations*: E. Malone, *On the Three Parts of Hen. 6* (1821, *Variorum*, xviii. 553); R. Grant White, *On the Authorship of Hen. 6* (*Works of Sh.* 1859–65, vii); J. Lee, *On the Authorship of 2, 3 Hen. vi and their Originals* (*N.S.S. Trans.* 1875–6, 219); C. F. T. Brooke, *The Authorship of 2, 3 Hen. 6* (1912, *Trans. of Connecticut Academy*, xvii. 141).

The various claims of Marlowe, Kyd, Greene, Peele, Lodge, and Shakespeare himself to the *Contention* can only be discussed in relation to Shakespeare's revision of them as *2, 3 Henry VI*, which probably belongs approximately to the date of *1 Henry vi*, produced by Strange's on 3 March 1592.

Thomas Lord Cromwell > 1602

S. R. 1602, Aug. 11 (Jackson). 'A booke called the lyfe and Deathe of the Lord Cromwell, as yt was lately Acted by the Lord Chamberleyn his servantes.' *William Cotton* (Arber, iii. 214).

1602. The True Chronicle Historie of the whole life and death of Thomas Lord Cromwell. As it hath beene sundrie times publikely Acted by the Right Honorable the Lord Chamberlaine his Seruants. Written by W. S. *For William Jones.*

S. R. 1611, Dec. 16. Transfer from William Jones to John Browne of a 'booke called the lyfe and death of the Lord Cromwell, by W: S.' (Arber, iii. 474).

1613. . . . As it hath been sundry times publikely Acted by the Kings Maiesties Seruants. Written by W. S. *Thomas Snodham.*

1664; 1685. [Parts of F₃ and F₄ of Shakespeare.]

Editions printed by R. Walker (1734) and by T. E. Jacob (1889, *Old English Dramas*), J. S. Farmer (1911, *T.F.T.*), and in *Sh. Apocrypha*.—*Dissertation*: W. Streit, *The L. and D. of T. L. C.* (1904, Jena diss.).

The W. S. of the title-page was interpreted as William Shakespeare in Archer's play-list of 1656 (Greg, *Masques*, lx). No modern critic accepts the attribution, except Hopkinson, who thinks that the original author was Greene, and that Shakespeare revised his work. Heywood was suggested by R. Farmer, and Drayton by Fleay, *Shakespeare*, 298; *B.C.* i. 152, 160. The guesses at Wentworth Smith and William Sly rest merely on their initials.

King Darius > 1565

S. R. 1565–6. 'A playe intituled of the story of kyng Daryous beyinge taken oute of the iij^de and iiij^th chapeter of the iij^de boke of Esdras &c.'. *Thomas Colwell* (Arber, i. 298).

1565, October. A Pretie new Enterlude both pithie & pleasaunt of the Story of Kyng Daryus, Beinge taken out of the third and fourth Chapter of the thyrd booke of Esdras. *Colwell.* [On t.p. 'Syxé persons may easely play it '.]

1577. *Hugh Jackson.* [B.M. C. 34, i. 21, from Irish sale of 1906.]

Editions by J. O. Halliwell (1860), A. Brandl (1898), 359, J. S. Farmer (1907, 1909, *T. F. T.*).

The characters, other than Darius and Zorobabell, are mainly abstract, and include Iniquitie, ' the Vyce '. There is a Prolocutor.

The Dead Mans Fortune > 1591

[*MS.*] *Add. MS.* 10449. ' The plotte of the deade mans fortune.' [Probably from Dulwich.]

The text is given by Steevens, *Variorum* (1803), iii. 414 ; Boswell, *Variorum* (1821), iii. 356 ; Greg, *Henslowe Papers*, 133 ; and a facsimile by Halliwell, *The Theatre Plats of Three Old English Dramas* (1860).

The names of actors who took part in the play point to a performance by the Admiral's, about 1590–1 (cf. ch. xiii).

The Reign of King Edward the Third > 1595

S. R. 1595, Dec. 1. ' A book Intitled Edward the Third and the Blacke Prince their warres with kinge John of Fraunce.' *Burby* (Arber, iii. 55).

1596. The Raigne of King Edward the third : As it hath bin sundrie times plaied about the Citie of London. *For Cuthbert Burby.*

1599. *Simon Stafford for Cuthbert Burby.*

Editions with Shakespeare *Apocrypha*, and by E. Capel (1759–60, *Prolusiones*), F. J. Furnivall (1877, *Leopold Sh.*), J. P. Collier (1878, *Shakespeare*), G. C. Moore Smith (1897, *T. D.*), J. S. Farmer (1910, *T.F.T.*).—*Dissertations*: H. von Friesen, *Ed. iii, angeblich ein Stück von Sh.* (1867, *Jahrbuch*, ii. 64) ; J. P. Collier, *K. Edw. III, a Historical Play by W. Sh.* (1874) ; A. Teetgen, *Sh's. K. Edw. iii, absurdly called, and scandalously treated, as a ' Doubtful Play' : an Indignation Pamphlet* (1875) ; A. C. Swinburne, *On the Historical Play of K. Edw. iii* (1879, *Gent. Mag.*, 1880, &c., *Study of Sh.*) ; G. von Vincke, *K. Edw. iii, ein Bühnenstück ?* (1879, *Jahrbuch*, xiv. 304) ; E. Phipson, *Ed. iii* (1889, *N.S.S. Trans.* 58*) ; G. Liebau, *K. Ed. iii von England und die Gräfin von Salisbury* (1900, 1901), *K. Ed. iii von England im Lichte europäischer Poesie* (1901) ; R. M. Smith, *Edw. III* (1911, *J. G. P.* x. 90).

The authorship was first ascribed to Shakespeare (with that of *Edw. IV* and *Edw. II* !) in Rogers and Ley's play-list of 1656 (Greg, *Masques*, lxiv). The theory was advocated by Capell, and has received much support, largely owing to the assent of Tennyson, against whose authority, however, may be set that of Swinburne. In its latest and not altogether unplausible form, Shakespeare is regarded as the author, not of the whole play, but of i. 2 and ii, which deal with the episode of the wooing of Lady Salisbury by the king, and are possibly, although by no means certainly, due to another hand than that of the chronicle narrative, to which they are only slightly linked. The style of these scenes is not demonstrably un-Shakespearian, and they, and in less degree the play as a whole, contain many parallels with *Hen. V* and other works of the 'nineties, of which the repetition in II. i. 451 and in Sonnet XCIV of the line

Lilies that fester smell far worse than weeds

is the most striking. The controversy cannot be dealt with in detail here. Shakespeare's contribution, if any, may with most probability be assigned to the winter of 1594–5 ; but it does not follow that the original play may not have been of earlier date. No importance is to be attached to the argument of Fleay (ii. 62 ; *Shakespeare*, 282) that the use of the phrase ' Ave, Caesar ' in I. i. 164 caused its use in Greene's *Francesco's Fortunes* of 1590 (cf. App. C, no. xliii), but it is noteworthy that a play on the subject was produced, apparently under Anglo-German influence, at Danzig in 1591 (Herz, 5). Of non-Shakespearian authors, for the whole or a part of the play as extant, Marlowe is preferred by Fleay, Greene by Liebau and Robertson, and Kyd by Sarrazin.

Edward the Fourth > *1599*

S. R. 1599, Aug. 28. ' Twoo playes beinge the ffirst and Second parte of Edward the iiij[th] and the Tanner of Tamworth With the history of the life and deathe of master Shore and Jane Shore his Wyfe as yt was lately acted by the Right honorable the Erle of Derbye his seruantes.' *John Oxonbridge and John Burby* (Arber, iii. 147).

1600, Feb. 23. Transfer of Busby's interest to Humphrey Lownes (Arber, iii. 156).

1600. The First and Second Parts of King Edward the Fourth. Containing His mery pastime with the Tanner of Tamworth, as also his loue to faire mistrisse Shoare, her great promotion, fall and miserie and lastly the lamentable death of both her and her husband. Likewise the besieging of London, by the Bastard Falconbridge, and the valiant defence of the same by the Lord Maior and the Citizens. As it hath diuers times beene publikely played by the Right Honorable the Earle of Derbie his seruants. *F. K. for Humfrey Lownes and John Oxenbridge.*

1605 ; 1613 ; 1619 ; 1626.

Edition by B. Field (1842, *Sh. Soc.*).—*Dissertation* : A. Sander, *T. Heywood's Historien von König Edward iv und ihre Quellen* (1907, Jena diss.).

Sander and others date the play 1594, by an identification with the anonymous *Siege of London* revived by the Admiral's on 26 Dec. 1594. Greg (Henslowe, ii. 173) more cautiously says that the play of 1594 ' may underlie ' certain scenes of *1 Edward iv*. He regards *Edward iv*, ' on internal evidence, as unquestionably Heywood's '. This is the usual view, but Fleay, ii. 288, had doubted it. There is no external evidence for Heywood's authorship, or for any connexion between him and Derby's men. Moreover, in May 1603, he authorized Henslowe, on behalf of Worcester's, to pay Chettle and Day for ' the Booke of Shoare, now newly to be written ', also described as ' a playe wherein Shores wiffe is writen '. If this was a revision of his own

play, he would hardly have left it to others. It is fair to add that
in the previous January he had himself received payment with Chettle
for an unnamed play, which might be the same (Henslowe, ii. 234).
The ' three-mans song ' on Agincourt in iii. 2 of Part I closely resembles
Drayton's *Ballad of Agincourt* (ed. Brett, 81), and must, I think, be
his. *Jane Shore* is mentioned as a play visited by citizens in *The
Knight of the Burning Pestle* (1607), ind. 57, and ' the well-frequented
play of Shore' in *Pimlyco or Runne Red-cap* (1609). A play, apparently
on the same subject, was performed by English actors at Graz on
19 Nov. 1607 (Herz, 98).

Every Woman in Her Humour. 1607–8 ?

1609. Everie Woman in her Humor. *E. A. for Thomas Archer.*
[Prologue.]
 Editions by A. H. Bullen (1885, *O.P.* iv) and J. S. Farmer (1913,
S. F. T.).—*Dissertation*: J. Q. Adams, *E. W. I. and The Dumb Knight*
(1913, *M.P.* x. 413).
 Fleay, ii. 321, suggests a date *c.* 1602 on the ground of apparent
reference to the *Poetomachia*. But this is not conclusive, and Adams
points to the use of a song (p. 335) from Bateson's *Madrigals* (1604).
He thinks that Lewis Machin was the author, as the style resembles
that of the comic part of *The Dumb Knight* (vide s. Markham), and
two passages are substantially reproduced in the latter. If so, this
also may be a King's Revels play. Allusions on p. 270 to the ' babones '
(cf. s.v. *Sir Giles Goosecap*) and on p. 316 to the Family of Love
(cf. s.v. Middleton) are consistent with a date of 1603–8.

Fair Em c. 1590

N.D. *For T. N. and I. W.*
[In Bodleian. Greg says that this is ' considerably earlier' than 1631.
The t.p. is as in 1631. Chetwood mentions three early editions,
including one undated and one of 1619. This is not now known.]
 1631. A Pleasant Comedie of Faire Em, the Millers Daughter of
Manchester. With the loue of William the Conqueror. As it was sundry
times publiquely acted in the Honourable Citie of London, by the
right Honourable the Lord Strange his Seruants. *For John Wright.*
 Editions by R. Simpson (1878, *S. of S.* ii), J. S. Farmer (1911, *T. F. T.*),
and in collections of *Sh. Apocrypha.*—*Dissertations* : R. Simpson,
Some Plays Attributed to Sh. (1875–6, *N.S.S. Trans.* 155); K. Elze,
Nachträgliche Bemerkungen zu Mucedorus und F. E. (1880, *Jahrbuch*,
xv. 339) ; P. Lohr, *Le Printemps d'Yver und die Quelle zu F. E.* (1912).
 The play has a double plot. One theme is the contest of William
the Conqueror and the Marquess Lubeck for the loves of Princess
Blanch of Denmark and of Mariana, a Swedish captive ; the other is
the contest of Manvile, Mountney and Valingford for Em, daughter
of the Miller of Manchester. A ' ballad intituled The Miller's daughter
of Manchester ' was entered on the Stationers' Register by Henry
Carr on 2 March 1581 (Arber, ii. 390). *Fair Em* has been included

in the Shakespeare *Apocrypha* on the strength of a volume formerly in the collection of Charles II, and then in that of Garrick, in which it was bound up with *Mucedorus* and *The Merry Devil of Edmonton* and lettered ' Shakespeare, vol. i '.   On the other hand, Edward Phillips, in his *Theatrum Poetarum* (1675), assigned it to Greene.   Clearly Greene is not the author, although there are certain resemblances of situation between the play and *Friar Bacon* ; for he satirizes it in the preface to *Farewell to Folly* (*Works*, ix. 232), quoting one or two of its expressions and blaming them as borrowed out of Scripture. Of the author he says, ' He that cannot write true English without the help of clerks of parish churches will needs make himself the father of interludes ', and, ' The sexton of St. Giles without Cripple-gate would have been ashamed of such blasphemous rhetoric '. *Farewell to Folly* seems to have appeared in 1591 (cf. s.v. Greene), and *Fair Em* may perhaps therefore be dated between this pamphlet and *Friar Bacon* (*c.* 1589).   Simpson adopts the theory, which hardly deserves serious discussion, of Shakespeare's authorship.   He finds numerous (but impossible) attacks by Greene upon Shakespeare from the *Planetomachia* (1585) onwards, and thinks that Shakespeare retorted in *Fair Em*, satirizing Greene as Manvile and Marlowe as Mountney, and depicting himself as Valingford.   ' Fair Em ' herself is the Manchester stage.   In the story of William the Conqueror he finds an allusion to the travels of William Kempe and other actors in Denmark and Saxony.   Fleay, *Shakespeare Manual* (1878), 281, adopts much of this fantasy, but turns ' Fair Em ' into the Queen's company and Valingford into Peele.   In 1891 (ii. 282) he makes ' Fair Em ' Strange's company.   His minor identifications, whether of 1878 or of 1891, may be disregarded.   More plausible is his sug-gestion that the author of the play may be Robert Wilson (q.v.), which would explain the attack upon Greene (q.v.) for his *Farewell to Folly* in R. W.'s *Martin Mar-sixtus* (1591).   The suggestion that the play was the *Sir John Mandeville* revived by Strange's for Henslowe in 1592 rests on a confusion between Mandeville and Manvile, but it may have been the *William the Conqueror* similarly revived by Sussex's on 4 Jan. 1594 (Greg, *Henslowe*, ii. 151, 158).

The Fair Maid of Bristow > 1604

S. R. 1605, Feb. 8.   ' A commedy called " the fayre Mayd of Bristoe " played at Hampton Court by his Maiesties players.' *Thomas Pavier* (Arber, iii. 283).

1605. The Faire Maide of Bristow.   As it was plaide at Hampton, before the King and Queenes most excellent Maiesties. *For Thomas Pavier.*

Editions by A. H. Quinn (1902, *Pennsylvania Univ. Publ.*) and J. S. Farmer (1912, *T. F. T.*).

The court performance must have been during the Christmas of 1603–4, which was at Hampton Court.   Bullen, *Works of Day*, 10, rejects the theory of Collier that this was Day's *Bristol Tragedy*,

written for the Admiral's in May 1602, on the grounds that it is not
a tragedy and does not resemble the known work of Day. Moreover,
the King's men are not likely to have acquired an Admiral's play.

The Fair Maid of the Exchange c. 1602

S. R. 1607, April 24 (Buck). 'A booke called the faire Mayde of
the Exchaunge.' *Henry Rocket* (Arber, iii. 347).

1607. The Fayre Mayde of the Exchange. With the pleasaunt
Humours of the Cripple of Fanchurch. Very delectable, and full of
mirth. *For Henry Rockit.* [Dramatis Personae headed ' Eleauen may
easily acte this Comedie', and Prologue.]

1525. *I. L.*

1637. *A. G.*

Edition by B. Field (1845, *Sh. Soc.*).—*Dissertations* : L. A.
Hibberd, *The Authorship and Date of the Fair Maid of the Exchange*
(*M.P.* vii. 383) ; P. Aronstein, *Die Verfasserschaft des Dramas The
Fair Maid of the Exchange* (1912, *E.S.* xlv. 45).

Heywood's authorship was asserted by Kirkman in 1671 (Greg,
Masques, lxvii), denied by Langbaine in 1687, accepted by Charles
Lamb and out of respect to him by Ward, ii. 572, and is still matter
of dispute. Fleay, ii. 329, assigned it to Machin on quite inadequate
grounds. Hibberd argues the case for Heywood, and Aronstein
attempts a compromise by giving ii. 1, iv. 1, and v to Heywood and the
rest to some young academic student of Shakespeare and Jonson. The
imitations of these point to a date *c.* 1602. I do not offer an opinion.

Fedele and Fortunio or *Two Italian Gentlemen c. 1584*

S. R. 1584, Nov. 12. ' A booke entituled Fedele et Fortuna. The
deceiptes in love Discoursed in a Commedie of ij Italyan gent and
translated into Englishe.' *Thomas Hackett* (Arber, ii. 437).

1585. Fedele and Fortunio. The deceites in Loue : excellently
discoursed in a very pleasaunt and fine conceited Comoedie, of two
Italian Gentlemen. Translated out of Italian, and set downe according
as it hath beene presented before the Queenes moste excellent Maiestie.
For Thomas Hacket.

[In the Mostyn sale (1919). Epistle ' To the Woorshipfull, and very
courteous Gentleman, Maister M. R. M.A. commendeth this pleasaunt
and fine conceited comœdie ', signed M.A. ; Prologue before the
Queene ; Epilogue at the Court, signed M.A. The compiler of the
Mostyn sale catalogue says that this differs from the imperfect print
in the Chatsworth collection, containing sheets B to G only, without
t.p., epistle, prologue, or epilogue, which is the basis of the modern
editions. Both have the running title, ' A pleasant Comœdie of two
Italian Gentlemen '. Collier, iii. 60, had seen a copy with the epistle
as found in the Mostyn print, but addressed to John Heardson and
signed A.M. This has been recently found in the Huntington
collection.

Editions by P. Simpson (1909, *M.S.R.*) and F. Flügge (1909, *Archiv*, cxxiii, 45), and extracts by Halliwell (1852, *Literature of the Sixteenth and Seventeenth Centuries*, 15).—*Dissertations*: W. W. Greg, *Notes on Publications* (1909, *M.S.C.* i. 218); F. Flügge, *Fidele und Fortunio* (1912, Breslau diss.).

The epistle says ' I commende to your freendly viewe this prettie Conceit, as well for the inuention, as the delicate conueiance thereof : not doubting but you will so esteeme thereof, as it dooth very well deserue, and I hartely desire '. This praise of the ' conueiance ' (which I take to mean either ' style ' or possibly ' translation ') does not suggest that M. A. (or A. M.) was the translator. It is true that ll. 224–41 appear in *England's Helicon* (1600) signed ' Shep. Tonie ', and that this signature is often taken to indicate Munday. On the other hand, two lines of this passage also appear in *England's Parnassus* (1600, ed. Crawford, 306) over the initials S. G., which suggest Gosson. Another passage in *E.P.* (231) combines ll. 661–2 and 655–6 of the play over the signature G. Chapman. This has led Crawford (*E.S.* xliii. 203), with some support from Greg, to suggest Chapman's authorship. I do not think the suggestion very convincing, in view of the inconsistency and general unreliability of *E.P.* and the fact that Chapman's first clear appearance as a writer is ten years later, in 1594. The evidence is quite indecisive, but of Munday, Chapman, Gosson, I incline to think Gosson the most likely candidate. On the other hand, if M. R. is Matthew Roydon, he was the dedicatee of poems by Chapman in 1594 and 1595. For M. A. I hardly dare guess Matthew Arundel. In any case, the play is only a translation from L. Pasqualigo's *Il Fedele* (1576).

2 Fortune's Tennis c. 1602

[*MS.*] *Add. MS.* 10449. ' The [plott of the sec]ond part of fortun[s Tenn]is.' [A fragment, probably from Dulwich.]

The text is given by Greg, *Henslowe Papers*, 143. The actors named show that it belonged to the Admiral's, and Greg suggests that it may be Dekker's ' fortewn tenes ' of Sept. 1600. Is it not more likely to have been a sequel to that, possibly Munday's *Set at Tennis* of Dec. 1602 ?

Frederick and Basilea. 1597

[*MS.*] *Add. MS.* 10449. ' The plott of Frederick & Basilea.' [Probably from Dulwich.]

The text is given by Steevens, *Variorum* (1803), iii. 414 ; Boswell, *Variorum* (1821), iii. 356 ; Greg, *Henslowe Papers*, 135 ; and a fac-simile by Halliwell, *The Theatre Plats of Three Old English Dramas* (1860).

The play was produced by the Admiral's on 3 June 1597, and the actors named represent that company at that date (cf. ch. xiii).

George a Greene, the Pinner of Wakefield > 1593

S. R. 1595, April 1. ' An Enterlude called the Pynder of Wake-feilde.' *Cuthbert Burby* (Arber, ii. 295).

1599. A Pleasant Conceyted Comedie of George a Greene, the Pinner of Wakefield. As it was sundry times acted by the seruants of the right Honourable the Earle of Sussex. *Simon Stafford for Cuthbert Burby.*

Editions in Dodsley[1-3] (1744–1825), by W. Scott (1810, *A. B. D.* i), F. W. Clarke (1911, *M.S.R.*), and J. S. Farmer (*S.F.T.*), and in collections of Greene.—*Dissertation* : O. Mertins, *Robert Greene and the Play of G. a G.* (1885, Breslau diss.).

Sussex's men revived the play for Henslowe on 29 Dec. 1593 (Greg, *Henslowe*, ii. 158). The Chatsworth copy has on the title-page the following notes in two early seventeenth-century hands : ' Written by . . . a minister, who ac[ted] the piñers pt in it himself. Teste W. Shakespea[re] ', and ' Ed Iuby saith that the play was made by Ro. Gree[ne] '. These, though first produced by Collier, appear (*M.S.C.* i. 288) to be genuine. Greene's authorship has been very commonly accepted. Fleay, i. 264, ii. 51, supposed first Greene and Peele, then added Lodge, but, although the text has been abridged, there is no evidence of double authorship. Oliphant's suggestion (*M.P.* viii. 433) of revision by Heywood only rests on the inclusion of the play next his in the Cockpit list of 1639 (*Variorum*, iii. 159). R. B. McKerrow thinks (*M.S.C.* i. 289) that the ' by Ro. Greene ' of the note may mean ' about Ro. Greene ' as a leading incident is apparently based on an episode of Greene's life. An allusion in I. i. 42 to *Tamburlaine* gives an anterior limit of date.

Sir Giles Goosecap. *1601<>3*

S. R. 1606, Jan. 10. (Wilson). ' An Comedie called Sir Gyles Goosecap Provided that yt be printed according to the Copie wherevnto master Wilson's hand ys at.' *Edward Blount* (Arber, iii. 309).

1606. Sir Gyles Goosecappe. Knight. A Comedie presented by the Chil: of the Chappell. *John Windet for Edward Blount.*

1636. . . . A Comedy lately Acted with great applause at the private House in Salisbury Court. *For Hugh Perry, sold by Roger Bell.* [Epistle to Richard Young of Woolley Farm, Berks. Signed ' Hugh Perry '.]

Editions by A. H. Bullen (1884, *O.E.P.* iii), W. Bang and R. Brotanek (1909, *Materialien*, xxvi), J. S. Farmer (1912, *T.F.T.*), and T. M. Parrott (1914, *Chapman*, ii).—*Dissertations* : G. L. Kittredge, *Notes on Elizabethan Plays* (1898, *J.G.P.* ii. 10) ; T. M. Parrott, *The Authorship of S. G. G.* (1906, *M.P.* iv. 25).

Bullen thought the author, who is stated in Perry's epistle to be dead in 1636, might be some imitator of Chapman. Fleay, ii. 322, suggests Chapman himself. This view receives elaborate support from Parrott, and appears very plausible. As ' your greatest gallants, for men, in France were here lately' (III. i. 47) the date is after the visit of Biron in Sept. 1601 and possibly after that of Nevers in April 1602. It cannot be later than the beginning of 1603, as ' She is the best scholar of any woman, but one, in Europe ' (I. i. 140) points to Elizabeth's lifetime. Moreover, Dekker, in his *Wonderful Year* of

1603 (Grosart, i. 116), has ' Galen could do no more good, than Sir
Giles Goosecap ', and though ' goosecap ' is a known term for a booby,
e.g. in Nashe's *Four Letters Confuted* of 1592 (*Works*, i. 281), the play
seems to be responsible for the ' Sir Giles '.   The phrase ' comparisons
odorous ' in IV. ii. 64 echoes *Much Ado*, III. v. 18.   The later part of
the period 1601–3 would perhaps best fit the allusions to the Family
of Love (II. i. 263), as to which cf. s.v. Middleton's play of that name,
and to the baboons (I. i. 11), the memory of which is still alive in
Volpone (1606) and *Ram Alley* (1607–8).   Probably these had already
amused London before 1605, as on Oct. 5 of that year the Norwich
records (Murray, ii. 338) note that ' This day John Watson ironmonger
brought the Kyngs maiesties warrant graunted to Roger Lawrence
& the deputacion to the seid Watson to shewe two beasts called
Babonnes '.   So, too, Kelly, 247, has a Leicester payment of 1606
' to the Mᵣ of the Babons, lycensed to travell by the Kings warrant '.
There is a story of a country fellow who wanted to go to a market
town ' to haue seene the Baboones ' as late as J. Taylor's *Wit and
Mirth* in 1629 (Hazlitt, *Jest Books*, iii. 43).   Fleay's identifications of
Chapman himself with Clarence and Drayton with Goosecap hardly
deserve consideration.

Grim the Collier of Croydon.   1600

[Alleged prints of 1599 (Chetwood), 1600 (Ward, i. 263), and 1606
(Jacob) probably rest on no authority.]

1662. Grim the Collier of Croyden ;   Or, The Devil and his Dame :
With The Devil and Saint Dunston.   [Part of Gratiae Theatrales, or,
A choice Ternary of English plays.   Composed upon especial occasions
by several ingenious persons ;   viz. . . . Grim the Collier . . . a Comedy,
by I. T.   Never before published :   but now printed at the request of
sundry ingenious friends.   R. D. 1662, 12ᵐᵒ.]

Editions by W. Scott (1810, *A. B. D.* iii), in Dodsley⁴, viii (1876),
and by J. S. Farmer (*S. F. T.*).—*Dissertation*: H. D. Sykes, *The
Authorship of G. the C. of C.* (1919, *M. L. R.* xiv. 245).

Of I. T. nothing is known.   Greg (*Henslowe*, ii. 213) regards the
play as clearly of the sixteenth century on internal evidence, and
points out that Henslowe, on behalf of the Admiral's, paid Haughton
5s. on 6 May 1600, ' in earneste of a boocke which he wold calle the
devell & his dame '.   The entry was subsequently cancelled, and presumably Haughton transferred the play to another company.   Sykes
calls attention to analogies with *Englishmen for my Money*, which
confirm the probability of Haughton's authorship.   It is only the
ascription of 1662 to I. T. which causes hesitation.   Farmer (*Hand
List*, 19) suggests that this was John Tatham.   Grim and the Devil
both appear in the *Like Will to Like* of Ulpian Fulwell (q.v.), but
I do not understand what kind of indirect connexion Greg thinks may
have existed between Haughton's play and a possible revival of
Fulwell's by Pembroke's men in Oct. 1600.

The Famous Victories of Henry the Fifth > 1588

S. R. 1594, May 14. ' A booke intituled, The famous victories of Henrye the Fyft, conteyninge the honorable battell of Agincourt.' *Thomas Creede* (Arber, ii. 648).

1598. The Famous Victories of Henry the fifth : Containing the Honourable Battell of Agin-court : As it was plaide by the Queenes Maiesties Players. *Thomas Creede.*

1617. . . . as it was Acted by the Kinges Maiesties Seruants. *Bernard Alsop.* [Another issue of the same sheets.]

Editions by J. Nichols (1779, *Six Old Plays*, ii. 317), W. C. Hazlitt (1875, *Shakespeare's Library*, v. 321), P. A. Daniel (1887, *Sh. Q*), and J. S. Farmer (*S. F. T.*).

In *Tarlton's Jests* (ed. Halliwell for *Sh. Soc.* 24) is a story of Knell acting Henry V and Tarlton doubling the parts of the judge and the clown, which clearly refers to this play. The performance took place ' at the Bull in Bishopsgate '. Tarlton died in 1588. Fleay, 67 ; ii. 259, suggests that Tarlton was the author. Nashe in *Pierce Penilesse* (1592, *Works*, i. 213) speaks of ' *Henrie* the fifth represented on the stage '. This is obviously too early to be the new play of ' harey the V ', given thirteen times for Henslowe between 28 Nov. 1595 and 15 July 1596 by the Admiral's, in whose inventories of March 1598 Harry the Fifth's doublet and gown appear. An earlier Henslowe entry on 14 May 1592, sometimes quoted as ' harey the vth ' by Collier, is really ' harey the 6 ' (Greg, *Henslowe*, ii. 152, 177 ; *Henslowe Papers*, 121). Sykes thinks the author S. Rowley (q.v.).

Histriomastix.   1589 (?), 1599

S. R. 1610, Oct. 31 (Buck). ' A booke called, Histriomastix or the player whipte.' *Thomas Thorpe* (Arber, iii. 447).

1610. Histrio-Mastix. Or, the Player whipt. *For Thomas Thorp.*

Editions by R. Simpson (1878, *S. of S.* ii. 1) and J. S. Farmer (1912, *T. F. T.*).—*Dissertation* : F. Hoppe, *Histriomastix-Studien* (1906, Breslau diss.).

Fleay, ii. 69, gives the whole play to Marston, but the sounder view of Simpson that Marston, whose style in places is unmistakable, was only the reviser of an earlier play, is revived in the elaborate and mainly satisfactory study of Small, 67. The passages assigned by Small to Marston are ii. 63–9, 128–9, 247–79 ; iii. 179–v. 191 ; v. 234 ; vi. 259–95. I should be inclined to add v. 244–67, but to omit ii. 128–9 ; iii. 218–64 ; iv. 159–201 ; v. 61–102 ; v. 147–180 ; vi. 259–95, which may just as well belong to the original play. No doubt vi. 259–95 is an addition, constituting an alternative ending for a court performance before Elizabeth ; but this may just as well have been a contemporary as a Marstonian addition, and in fact there is no court performance at the end of the century available for it, while the attempt to find one led Fleay to the impossible theory that it was given by Derby's men. As its whole substance is a satire on professional players, it must have been both produced and revived by amateurs or boys ; and the same conclusion is pointed to by the enormous number of characters. The original matter is so full of the technical learning of the schools as to suggest an academic audience ; I think it was a University or possibly an Inns of Court, not a choir-boy, play. The theme is the cyclical progression of a state through the stages Peace, Plenty, Pride, Envy, War, Poverty, and Peace again. It is illustrated by the fortunes of a company of players, who wax insolent in prosperity, and when war comes, are pressed for soldiers. Their poet Posthaste is clearly Munday and not, as Simpson and others have vainly imagined, Shakespeare. With him is contrasted the scholar-poet, Chrisoganus, a philosopher with whom the players will have nothing to do. He seems to belong to the order of ideas connected with the scientific school of Thomas Harriott. Small thinks that the date was 1596, when there was scarcity of food, a persecution of players, and a pressing of men for service against Spain ; and that the author might be Chapman. Certainly Chapman was an early admirer of Harriott. But I disagree as to the date. The style seems to me to be that of Peele or some imitator, the attitude to the players an academic reflection of the attacks of Greene, and the political atmosphere that of the years following the Armada, when the relief of peace was certainly not unbroken by fears of renewed Spanish attempts. Impressment was not a device of 1596 alone. The only notice of it known to me in which players are known to have especially suffered is in an undated letter of Philip Gawdy, assigned by his editor to 1602 (Gawdy, 121), ' All the playe howses wer besett in one daye and very many pressed from thence, so that in all ther ar pressed ffowre thowsand besydes fyve hundred voluntaryes, and all for flaunders '. This is too late for the *proto-Histriomastix*, and probably also for the revival, but men were being pressed for foreign service as early as 1585, and again in 1588 and possibly in 1589 and 1591 (Cheyney, i. 158, 197, 219, 255 ; *Procl.* 805, 809). As to the revival, Small puts it definitely in August 1599, when a scare of a Spanish invasion, which had lasted for a month, came to a crisis in London on Aug. 7 (Stowe, *Annales*, 788 ; Chamberlain, 59 ; *Sydney Papers*, ii. 113 ; *Hist. MSS.* xv, app. v, 66), and he thinks that the words ' The Spaniards are come ! ' (v. 234) are an insertion of this date. They are not ' extra-metrical ', as Fleay says, for the passage is not in metre. There had, however, been earlier scares, e.g. in Oct. 1595 (*Sydney Papers*, i. 355 ; cf. Arber, iii. 55, 56) and in Oct. 1597 (*Edmondes Papers*, 303). The date of 1599 would agree well enough with the career of Marston, and with that of the Paul's boys, to whom the revival was probably due, although I do not agree with Small that it was their court play of 1 Jan. 1601, because I see no evidence that the court ending belongs to the revision. I take it that *Histrio-mastix* was one of the ' musty fopperies of antiquity ' with which we learn from *Jack Drum's Entertainment*, v. 112, that the Paul's boys began. The revision leaves Posthaste untouched, save for the charac-teristic Marstonian sneer of ' goosequillian ' (iii. 187). Munday of course was still good sport in 1599. But Chrisoganus is turned from a scientific into a ' translating ' scholar (ii. 63). I agree with Small

that Marston has given him Jonsonian traits, and that he intended
to be complimentary rather than the reverse. I do not know that
it is necessary to suppose that Jonson misunderstood this and took
offence, for the real offence was given by *Jack Drum's Entertainment*
in the next year. But certainly some of the ' fustian ' words put in
the mouth of Clove in *Every Man Out of His Humour*, III. i. 177 sqq.,
later in 1599 come from *Histriomastix*, and their origin is pointed by
the phrase ' as you may read in Plato's Histriomastix '. One of the
fragments of plays recited by the players contains the lines (ii. 269) :

> Come Cressida, my Cresset light,
> Thy face doth shine both day and night ;
> Behold behold thy garter blue
> Thy knight his valiant elbow wears,
> That when he shakes his furious Speare
> The foe in shivering fearful sort
> May lay him down in death to snort.

I am not convinced with Small that this belongs to the revision,
even though it seems discontinuous with the following fragment of
a Prodigal Child play. But in any case the hit at Shakespeare, if
there really is one, remains unexplained. There is nothing else which
points to so early a date as 1599 for his *Troilus and Cressida*. I note
the following parallel from S. Rowlands, *The Letting of Humors Blood
in the Head-Veine* (1600), Sat. iv :

> Be thou the Lady Cressit-light to mee,
> Sir Trollelolle I will proue to thee.

The Honest Lawyer > 1615

S. R. 1615, Aug. 14. (Taverner). ' A play called The Honest
Lawyer.' *Richard Redmer* (Arber, iii. 571). [Assigned by Redmer,
apparently at once, to Richard Woodriffe.]
1616. The Honest Lawyer. Acted by the Queenes Maiesties Seruants. Written by S. S. *George Purslowe for Richard Woodroffe.*
[Epilogue.]
Edition by J. S. Farmer (1914, *S. F.*).
A conceivable author is Samuel Sheppard (q.v.), but the absence
of extant early work by him makes a definite attribution hazardous.

How a Man may Choose a Good Wife from a Bad c. 1602

1602. A pleasant conceited Comedie, Wherein is shewed how a man
may chuse a good Wife from a bad. As it hath bene sundry times
Acted by the Earle of Worcesters Seruants. *For Mathew Law.*
1605 ; 1608 ; 1614 ; 1621 ; 1630 ; 1634.
Editions: 1824 (for Charles Baldwin), in *O. E. D.* (1825, i) and Dodsley[4]
(1876–9, ix), and by A. E. H. Swaen (1912, *Materialien*, xxxv) and
J. S. Farmer (1912, *T. F. T.*).—*Dissertations* : C. R. Baskervill, *Sources
and Analogues of H.* (1909, *M. L. A.* xxiv. 711) ; J. Q. Adams, *Thomas
Heywood and H.* (1912, *E. S.* xlv. 30).

The B.M. copy of 1602 (C. 34, b. 53) has the note 'Written by Ioshua Cooke' in ink on the title-page. Presumably the author of *Greene's Tu Quoque* (q.v.) is meant, with which Swaen, xiii, declares that the play shows 'absolutely no similarity or point of agreement'. Fleay, i. 289, suggested an ascription to Heywood on the ground of parallelisms with *The Wise Woman of Hogsdon*, and this case is elaborately and plausibly argued by Swaen and Adams. The date must be before Worcester's begin to appear in Henslowe's diary, 17 Aug. 1602. Fleay's attempt to twist its mentions of a certain 'Thomas' in the text (l. 790) into references to Heywood himself and Thomas Blackwood, the actor, is mere childishness.

Impatient Poverty (?)

S. R. 1560, June 10. '. . . nyce wantõn; impaciens poverte . . .' *John King* (Arber, i. 128).

1560. A Newe Interlude of Impacyente pouerte newlye Imprynted. *John King*. [B.M. C. 34, i. 26, from Irish sale of 1906 (cf. *Jahrbuch*, xliii. 310). Engraved t.p.; on tablet at foot 'T. R.' Thomas Petit's mark after colophon. The t.p. has also 'Foure men may well and easelye playe thys Interlude', with an arrangement of the parts.]

N.D. An new enterlude of Impacient pouerte newly Imprynted. [In Mostyn sale (1919). The t.p. has three woodcut figures. There is no imprint, but as the woodcuts are also found in W. Copland's print of *Youth* and as King's copy of *Lusty Juventus* also passed to Copland (1548–69), he was probably the printer.]

S. R. 1582, Jan. 15. Transfer from Sampson Awdeley to John Charlwood (Arber, ii. 405).

Editions by J. S. Farmer (1907, *T. F. T.*) and R. B. McKerrow (1911, *Materialien*, xxxiii).

The play has come to light since the issue of *The Mediaeval Stage*, and I therefore include it here, although it is pre-Elizabethan. The characters are Peace, Envy, Impatient Poverty (afterwards Prosperity), Conscience, Abundance, Misrule, 'Collhasarde', and a Summoner. The drama is a moral, non-controversial, and not even necessarily Protestant in tone. It sets out the mutability of the world and the defects of poverty and prosperity. The scene is a 'place', and there are allusions to Newgate and Tyburn. If the T. R. of the title-page is the same whose name is at the end of *Nice Wanton*, the play is probably not later than the reign of Edward VI; but the Summoner and allusions to penance and courts spiritual suggest an even earlier date. The final address to the 'Soueraynes' contains the following stanza:

> Let vs pray al to that lorde of great magnificence
> To send amonge vs peace rest and vnyte
> And Jesu preserue our soueraigne Quene of preclare preeminence
> With al her noble consanguynyte
> And to sende them grace so the yssue to obtayne
> After them to rule this most chrysten realme.

The form of the companion stanzas suggests that the two last lines originally rhymed, and that a line has dropped out before them. Possibly an ending originally meant for Henry VIII and Jane Seymour has been altered with a view to making it appropriate to Elizabeth. The play is offered with other pre-Elizabethan plays by the company in *Sir Thomas More*, IV. i. 42, and was also in the obsolete library of Captain Cox (*Robert Laneham's Letter*, ed. Furnivall, 30).

Jack Drum's Entertainment. 1600

S. R. 1600, Sept. 8. ' A booke Called Jack Drum's enterteynmente. A commedy as yt hathe ben diuerse tymes Acted by the Children of Paules.' *Felix Norton* (Arber, iii. 172).

1600, Oct. 23. Transfer from Norton to Richard Oliff (Arber, iii. 175).

1601. Iacke Drums Entertainment: Or the Comedie of Pasquill and Katherine. As it hath bene sundry times plaide by the Children of Powles. *For Richard Olive.* [Introduction, i.e. Induction.]

1616. . . . Newly Corrected. *W. Stansby for Philip Knight.*

1618. . . . The Actors 12 men, and 4 women. *For Nathaniel Fosbrooke.*

Editions by R. Simpson (1878, *S. of S.* ii. 125) and J. S. Farmer (1912, *T. F. T.*).

All critics have recognized the style as Marston's and some of the vocabulary is vomited in *Poetaster*; cf. Small, 93. The date is fixed to 1600 by allusions to hopes of ' peace with Spaine ', ' Kemps morice ', and ' womens yeare ' (i. 37, 45, 166). There is little doubt that the critical Brabant Senior is Jonson, and that the play is that in which he told Drummond that Marston staged him. The cuckolding of Brabant Senior is based upon a story narrated by Jonson to Drummond (Laing, 21) as one in which he had played the active, not the passive, part. If he had imparted the same story to Marston, he not unnaturally resented the use made of it. The minor identifications suggested by Fleay, ii. 74, have nothing to commend them, except possibly that of Sir Edward Fortune with Edward Alleyn, who was building the Fortune in 1600. Were not this a Paul's play, one might infer from the closing line,

> Our *Fortune* laughes, and all content abounds,

that it was given at the Fortune. Can the Admiral's have shared it with Paul's, as the Chamberlain's shared *Satiromastix* ? In iv. 37–48 Brabant Senior criticizes three ' moderne wits ' whom he calls ' all apes and guls ' and ' vile imitating spirits '. They are Mellidus, Musus, and Decius. I take them to be Marston, Middleton, and Dekker, all writers for Paul's; others take Decius for Drayton, to whom Sir John Davies applied the name, and Musus, by a confusion with Musaeus, for Chapman or Daniel. For v. 102–14, which bears on the history of the company, cf. ch. xii (Paul's).

The Life and Death of Jack Straw > 1593

S. R. 1593, Oct. 23. ' An enterlude of the lyfe and deathe of Jack Strawe.' *John Danter* (Arber, ii. 639).

1593. [Colophon, 1594]. The Life and Death of Iacke Straw, A notable Rebell in England : Who was kild in Smithfield by the Lord Maior of London. *John Danter, sold by William Barley.*

1604. *For Thomas Pavier.*

Editions in Dodsley⁴ (1874, v), and by H. Schütt (1901) and J. S. Farmer (1911, *T. F. T.*).

Fleay, ii. 153, Schütt, and Robertson, 121, all incline to suggest the authorship, whole or in part, of Peele. Schütt would date *c.* 1588, but the theme is that of T. Nelson's pageant of 1590–1, for which year a member of Walworth's company, the Fishmongers, was Lord Mayor. The text of the play is very short, with only four acts.

Jacob and Esau > 1558

S. R. 1557–8. ' An enterlude vpon the history of Jacobe and Esawe out of the xxvii chapeter of the fyrste boke of Moyses Called genyses.' *Henry Sutton* (Arber, i. 77).

1568. A newe mery and wittie Comedie or Enterlude, newely imprinted, treating vpon the Historie of Iacob and Esau, taken out of the xxvij. Chap. of the first booke of Moses, entituled Genesis. *Henrie Bynneman.*

Editions in Dodsley⁴ (1874, ii), and by J. S. Farmer (1908, *T.F.T.*).

The play must necessarily, from the date of the S. R. entry, be pre-Elizabethan, and should have been included in Appendix X of *The Mediaeval Stage.* C. C. Stopes, *Hunnis,* 265, and in *Athenaeum* (28 April 1900), claims the authorship for Hunnis; W. Bang has suggested Udall, which seems plausible. The parts of Mido and Abra point to boy-actors.

1 Jeronimo c. 1604

1605. The First Part of Ieronimo. With the Warres of Portugall, and the life and death of Don Andræa. *For Thomas Pavier.* [Dumb-shows.]

Editions by W. Scott (1810, *A.B.D.* i), in Dodsley⁴ (1874, iv), and by F. S. Boas (1901, *Works of Kyd*).—*Dissertations*: J. E. Routh, *T. Kyd's Rime Schemes and the Authorship of Soliman and Perseda and 1 J.* (1905, *M.L.N.* xx. 49); A. L. Elmquist, *Zur Frage nach dem Verfasser von 1 J.* (1909, *E.S.* xl. 309); A. Seeberger (1909, *Archiv für Stenographie,* iv. 306); K. Wiehl, *Thomas Kyd und die Autorschaft von . . . 1 J.* (1912, *E.S.* xliv. 343); B. Neuendorff, *Zur Datierung des 1 J.* (1914, *Jahrbuch,* l. 88).

The ascription by Fleay, ii. 27, and Sarrazin to Kyd is rejected on stylistic grounds by R. Fischer, *Zur Kunstentwicklung der Englischen Tragödie,* 100, with whom Boas and other writers concur. A reference to the jubilee of 1600 (I. i. 25) points to a date at the beginning of

the seventeenth century. If so, the play cannot be that revived by
Strange's for Henslowe in Feb. 1592 and given, sometimes under the
title of *Don Horatio*, and sometimes under that of the *Comedy of
Jeronimo*, during a run of, and several times on the night before, the
Spanish Tragedy (Greg, *Henslowe*, ii. 150, 154). It is, moreover, not
a comedy. It may, however, be a later version of the same theme,
motived by another revival of the *Spanish Tragedy* by the Admiral's
in 1601–2. If so, it was probably itself due, not to the Admiral's, but
to the Chamberlain's, and a piracy of their property by the Revels
boys explains the jest at ' Ieronimo *in decimo sexto* ' in the induction
to the 1604 version of Marston's *Malcontent*. It must be uncertain
whether *1 Jeronimo* was the ' Komödie vom König in Spanien und
dem Vice-Roy in Portugall ' given at Dresden in 1626 (Herz, 66, 76).

The Troublesome Reign of King John 1587< >91

1591. The Troublesome Raigne of Iohn King of England, with the
discouerie of King Richard Cordelions Base sonne (vulgarly named,
The Bastard Fawconbridge) : also the death of King Iohn at Swinstead Abbey. As it was (sundry times) publikely acted by the Queenes
Maiesties Players, in the honourable Citie of London. *For Sampson
Clarke.* There is a Second part with separate signatures and title-
page. The Second part of the troublesome Raigne of King Iohn,
conteining the death of Arthur Plantaginet, the landing of Lewes,
and the poysning of King Iohn at Swinstead Abbey. As . . . London
. . . 1591. [The text of each part is preceded by lines ' To the Gentlemen Readers ', and a head-piece, which has the initials W. D.]

1611. The First and Second Part . . . As they were (sundry times)
lately acted by the Queenes Maiesties Players. Written by W. Sh.
Valentine Simmes for John Helme. [The signatures are continuous
through both parts.]

1622. . . . as they were (sundry times) lately acted. Written by
W. Shakespeare. *Augustine Mathewes for Thomas Dewes.*

Editions by G. Steevens (1760, *T.P.* ii), J. Nichols (1779, *Six Old
Plays*, ii), W. C. Hazlitt (1875, *Sh. Libr.* v), F. G. Fleay, *King John*
(1878), F. J. Furnivall (1888, *Sh. Q*), J. S. Farmer (1911, *T.F.T.*),
F. J. Furnivall and J. Munro (1913, *Sh. Classics*).—*Dissertations* :
E. Rose, *Shakespeare as an Adapter* (*Macmillan's Magazine*, Nov.
1878) ; G. C. Moore Smith, *Sh.'s K. J. and the T. R.* (1901, *Furnivall
Miscellany*, 335) ; H. D. Sykes, *Sidelights on Shakespeare*, 99 (1919).

The authorship was assigned by Malone to Marlowe, by Pope to
Shakespeare and W. Rowley, by Fleay, ii. 53, and *King John*, 34,
to Greene, Peele, and Lodge, working on a Marlowian plot.
Furnivall and Munro accept none of these theories, and the latter
suggests a common authorship with the early *Leir*. Sykes argues
strongly for Peele. The lines prefixed to Part I begin

> You that with friendly grace of smoothed brow
> Have entertained the Scythian Tamburlaine.

They do not claim to be a prologue, and may have been added on publication. The play is not therefore necessarily later than *Tamburlaine* (*c.* 1587). But the tone is that of the Armada period. Shakespeare used the play, with which, from the booksellers' point of view, his *King John* seems to have been treated as identical.

Judith c. 1595 (?)

[*MS.*] *National Library of Wales*, Peniarth (formerly *Hengwrt*), *MS.* 508.

G. A. Jones, *A Play of Judith* (1917, *M.L.N.* xxxii. 1) describes the MS. which contains the Latin text of the *Judithae Constantia* of Cornelius Schonaeus, of which a reprint was issued in London in 1595, together with an incomplete English translation in unrhymed verse written as prose, perhaps as a school exercise, in a late sixteenth-century or early seventeenth-century hand.

A Knack to Know an Honest Man. 1594

S. R. 1595, Nov. 26. ' A booke intituled The most Rare and pleasaunt historie of A knack to knowe an honest man.' *Cuthbert Burby* (Arber, iii. 54).

1596. A Pleasant Conceited Comedie, called, A knacke to know an honest Man. As it hath beene sundrie times plaied about the Citie of London. *For Cuthbert Burby.*

Editions by H. De Vocht (1910, *M.S.R.*) and J. S. Farmer (1912, *T.F.T.*).

The play was produced by the Admiral's on 22 Oct. 1594, and twenty-one performances were given between that date and 3 Nov. 1596 (Greg, *Henslowe*, ii. 171). The text is confused and probably surreptitious.

A Knack to Know a Knave. 1592

S. R. 1594, Jan. 7. ' A commedie entitled " a Knack to knowe a knave " newlye sett fourth as it hath sundrye tymes been plaid by Ned. Allen and his Companie with Kemps applauded Merymentes of the menn of Goteham.' *Richard Jones* (Arber, ii. 643).

1594. A most pleasant and merie new Comedie, Intituled, A Knacke to knowe a knave. Newlie set foorth, as it hath sundrie tymes bene played by Ed. Allen and his Companie. With Kemps applauded Merrimentes of the men of Goteham, in receiuing the King into Goteham. *Richard Jones.*

Editions by J. P. Collier (1851, *Five Old Plays*), in Dodsley[4] (1874, vi), and by J. S. Farmer (1911, *T.F.T.*).

Strange's men produced ' the Knacke to Knowe a Knave ' on 10 June 1592, and played it seven times to 24 Jan. 1593. Henslowe usually enters it as ' the cnacke '. Fleay, 100, suggests that the *Osric*, revived by the Admiral's men on 3 and 7 Feb. 1597, may also be this play. Both Fleay, ii. 310, and Greg. *Henslowe*, ii. 156, suggest that Kempe's ' merriments ' are to be found in sc. 12, and that of the rest the romantic part may be Peele's and the moral part Wilson's.

Gayley (*R.E.C.* i. 422) would like to find in the play the comedy written by Greene and the 'young Juvenall', Nashe. The character Cuthbert Cutpurse the Conicatcher is from the pamphlet (cf. s.v. Greene) entered in S. R. on 21 April 1592, and the story of Titus Andronicus is alluded to in F₂ᵛ:

> As Titus was vnto the Roman Senators,
> When he had made a conquest on the Goths.

Leire > *1594*

S. R. 1594, May 14. ' A booke entituled, The moste famous Chronicle historye of Leire kinge of England and his Three Daughters.' *Adam Islip* (Arber, ii. 649). [Islip's name is crossed out, and Edward White's substituted.]

1605, May 8. ' A booke called " the Tragecall historie of kinge Leir and his Three Daughters &c ", As it was latelie Acted.' *Simon Stafford* (Arber, iii. 289). [Assigned the same day by Stafford with the consent of William Leake to John Wright, ' provided that Simon Stafford shall haue the printinge of this booke '.]

1605. The True Chronicle History of King Leir, and his three daughters, Gonorill, Ragan, and Cordella. As it hath bene diuers and sundry times lately acted. *Simon Stafford for John Wright.*

S. R. 1624, June 29. Transfer of ' Leire and his daughters ' from Mrs. White to E. Alde (Arber, iv. 120).

Editions by J. Nichols (1779, *S.O.P.* ii), W. C. Hazlitt (1875, *Sh. Libr.* ii. 2), W. W. Greg (1907, *M.S.R.*), S. Lee (1909, *Sh. Classics*), J. S. Farmer (1910, *T.F.T.*), R. Fischer (1914, *Quellen zu König Lear*).—*Dissertations*: W. Perrett, *The Story of King Lear* (1904, *Palaestra*, xxxv) ; R. A. Law, *The Date of King Lear* (1906, *M.L.A.* xxi. 462) ; H. D. Sykes, *Sidelights on Shakespeare*, 126 (1919).

The Queen's and Sussex's revived ' kinge leare ' for Henslowe on 6 and 8 April 1594, shortly before the first S. R. entry (Greg, *Henslowe*, ii. 162). As the play is not named in the Sussex's repertory of 1593–4, there is a presumption that it belonged to the Queen's. The authorship is quite obscure. Fleay, 90, assigns it to Lodge and Peele ; Fleay, 97, to Lodge and Greene ; Fleay, ii. 51, to Lodge and Kyd. Robertson, 176, thinks the claim for Lodge indecisive, and surmises the presence of Greene. Sykes argues for Peele. Lee hints at Rankins. The publishing history is also difficult. The entries of 1605 appear to ignore White's copyright, although this was still alive in his son's widow in 1624. Lee suggests that the Stafford-Wright enterprise was due to negotiation between Wright and White, whose apprentice he had been. The play was clearly regarded as distinct from that of Shakespeare, which was entered to N. Butter and J. Busby on 22 Nov. 1607, and it, though based on its predecessor, is far more than a revision of it. It seems a little improbable that *Leire* should have been revived as late as 1605, and the ' Tragecall ' and ' lately acted ' of the title-page, taken by themselves, would point to an attempt by Stafford to palm off the old play as Shakespeare's. But although 1605 is not an impossible date for Shakespeare's production, 1606 is on other grounds more probable.

Liberality and Prodigality. *1601*

1602. A Pleasant Comedie, Shewing the contention betweene Liberalitie and Prodigalitie. As it was playd before her Maiestie. *Simon Stafford for George Vincent.* [Prologue and Epilogue.]
Editions by J. S. Farmer (1912, *T.F.T.*) and W. W. Greg (1913, *M.S.R.*).
A reference to 'childish yeeres' in the prologue points to boy actors. The trial (l. 1261) is for an alleged crime on 4 Feb., 43 Eliz. (1601), and the next court performance after this date was on 22 Feb. 1601 by the Chapel, to which occasion the production may be assigned. Elizabeth could be described as a 'prince', so that the use of this term does not bear out Fleay, ii. 323, in assuming a revival of an Edwardian play, but the characters are mainly abstract and the style archaic for the seventeenth century, and it is conceivable that the *Prodigality* of 1567–8 had been revived.

Locrine c. *1591*

S. R. 1594, July 20. ' The lamentable Tragedie of Locrine, the eldest sonne of Kinge Brutus, discoursinge the warres of the Brittans, &c.' *Thomas Creede* (Arber, ii. 656).
1595. The Lamentable Tragedie of Locrine, the eldest sonne of King Brutus, discoursing the warres of the Britaines, and Hunnes, with their discomfiture : The Britaines victorie with their Accidents, and the death of Albanact. No lesse pleasant then profitable. Newly set foorth, ouerseene and corrected, By W. S. *Thomas Creede.* [Prologue and Epilogue.]
1664 ; 1685. [F₃; F₄ of Shakespeare.]
Editions of 1734 (J. Tonson), 1734 (R. Walker), and by R. B. McKerrow (1908, *M.S.R.*), J. S. Farmer (1911, *T.F.T.*), and in *Sh. Apocrypha.—Dissertations* : R. Brotanek (1900, *Anglia-Beiblatt,* xi. 202) ; C. Crawford, *Edmund Spenser, L. and Selimus* (1901, 9 *N.Q.* vii. 61 ; *Collectanea,* i. 47) ; W. S. Gaud, *The Authorship of L.* (1904, *M.P.* i. 409) ; T. Erbe, *Die L.-Sage* (1904) ; J. M. Robertson, *Did Sh. Write T. A. ?* (1905) ; E. Köppel, *L. und Selimus* (1905, *Jahrbuch,* xli. 193) ; A. Neubner, *König Lokrin. Deutsche Übersetzung mit literar-historischer Einleitung* (1908) ; F. G. Hubbard (*MS.* cited by J. W. Cunliffe in *C.H.* v. 84); C. A. Harper, *L. and the Faerie Queene* (1913, *M.L.R.* viii. 369).
The interpretation of the W. S. of the title-page in F₃ of 1664 as indicating Shakespeare may be accurate, but does not suggest anything more than revision for a revival, or perhaps only for the press. Some revision is proved by the allusion in the epilogue to Elizabeth,

> That eight and thirtie yeares the scepter swayd,

an allusion which was not chronologically accurate until the close of

the thirty-eighth regnal year on 16 Nov. 1596, after the play was in
print, and could hardly have been made before the beginning of that
year on 17 Nov. 1595, after it had been entered in S. R. As to the
original author, one is bound to be sceptical of the unconfirmed notice
by J. P. Collier (*Bibliographical Account*, i. 95) of an ' inscription on
an existing copy of the play . . . assigning the authorship of it to
Charles Tylney '. This, says Collier, ' is the handwriting of Sir George
Buck. He adds the information that he himself had written the
dumb shows by which it was illustrated, and that it was originally
called *Elstrild* '. Charles Tilney was a cousin of the Master of the
Revels, and was executed for complicity in the Babington plot in
1586 (Camden, *transl.* 303). The statement, if true, would give an
early date to the play, which the dumb shows and other ' Senecan '
characteristics have been supposed to confirm. Fleay, ii. 321, boldly
conjectures that the epilogue originally referred to ' eight and twentie
yeares ', and that the play was ' by ', in the sense of ' about ', Tilney,
supposing the moral drawn against ' ciuill discord ' instigated by
' priuate amours ' to point at Mary of Scots. Recent investigations,
however, concerning the relations of the play to Spenser on the one
hand, and to *Selimus* (q.v.) on the other, suggest a date not earlier
and not much later than 1591, either for the original composition of
the play, or for a very substantial revision of it. Most of the points
are well summed up by Cunliffe in *C. H.* v. 84. *Locrine* may borrow
historical facts from the *Faerie Queene* (1590) ; it does not borrow
phrases from it. It does, however, borrow phrases and whole lines,
with more than Elizabethan plagiarism, from Spenser's *Complaints*
(1591). There is also an apparent loan from Wilmot's *Tancred and
Gismund* (1591). Some of the *Complaints* passages are also borrowed
by *Selimus*, which makes similar booty both of *Locrine* itself and of
the *Faerie Queene*. I agree with Cunliffe that the evidence is clearly
in favour of *Selimus* being the later of the two plays, but am not so
certain that the second borrowing of the *Complaints* passages tells
against a common authorship of the two. It would be so, ordinarily,
but here we have to do with an abnormal plagiarist. Whoever the
author, he belongs to the school of the university wits. Marlowe is
preferred by Malone, Peele by Fleay, Ward, Gaud, and for all but
the comic scenes by Hopkinson, Greene by Brooke, Peele and Greene
by Robertson.

The London Prodigal.   1603 < > 05

  1605. The London Prodigall. As it was plaide by the Kings
Maiesties seruants. By William Shakespeare. *T. C. for Nathaniel
Butter*.
  1664 ; 1685. [F$_3$; F$_4$ of Shakespeare.]
  Editions in 1709, 1734 (J. Tonson), 1734 (R. Walker), by J. S.
Farmer (1910, *T. F. T.*), and in *Sh. Apocrypha*.
  Shakespeare's authorship is accepted by few modern critics. An
exception is Hopkinson. Fleay, *Shakespeare*, 299 ; *B. C.* i. 152, thinks
that he may have ' plotted ' the play, but that the writer is the same

as that of *Thomas Lord Cromwell,* whom he believes to be Drayton.
Perhaps he is right in regarding an allusion to service ' under the
king ' (II. i. 16) as pointing to a Jacobean date. Brooke suggests
Marston or Dekker. A play ' von einem ungehorsamen Khauffmanns
Sohn ' appears in Anglo-German repertories of 1604 and 1606 (Herz,
65, 94).

Look About You. *1599* (?)

1600. A Pleasant Commodie, Called Looke about you. As it was
lately played by the right honourable the Lord High Admirall his
seruaunts. *For William Ferbrand.*

Editions in Dodsley[4] (1874, vii), and by J. S. Farmer (1912, *T.F.T.*)
and W. W. Greg (1913, *M.S.R.*).

At the end of the play Gloucester proposes to fight the Saracens
in Portugal, and as Anthony Wadeson (q.v.) was writing *The Honourable Life of the Humorous Earl of Gloster with his Conquest of Portugal*
in June or July 1601, it has been suggested by Fleay, ii. 267, and
Greg, *Henslowe,* ii. 204, that Wadeson was also the author of *Look
About You.* The play ought itself to appear somewhere in Henslowe's
diary, and Fleay may be right in identifying it with the *Bear a Brain*
of 1599, although the only recorded payment for that play was not
to Wadeson, but to Dekker. There are reminiscences of *R.J.* II. iv. 42 ;
III. v. 221 in l. 2329, and of *1 Hen. IV,* II. iv. 295 in l. 2426.

The Rare Triumphs of Love and Fortune. *1582* (?)

1589. The Rare Triumphs of Loue and Fortune. Plaide before the
Queenes most excellent Maiestie : wherein are many fine Conceites
with great delight. *E. A. for Edward White.*

Editions by J. P. Collier (1851, Roxb. Club) and in Dodsley[4]
(1874, vi).

Fleay, ii. 26, assigns the play to Kyd on account of the similarity
of the plot to that of *Soliman and Perseda,* but this is hardly convincing. On 30 Dec. 1582 Derby's players performed *A History of
Love and Fortune* at court, for which a city and battlement were
provided by the Revels office. If the two plays were identical, as
dates and style make not improbable, the city presumably served as
a background for the scenes at court, while the battlement was used
for the presenters Venus and Fortune, who are said in Act I to be
' set sunning like a crow in a gutter '.

Love Feigned and Unfeigned (?)

[*MS.*] On first and last leaves (sig. a 1 and ii. 8 of a copy (Brit. Mus.
IB. 2172) of Johannes Herolt, *Sermones Discipuli* (1492).

Edition by A. Esdaile (1908, *M.S.C.* i. 17).—*Dissertation* : E. B.
Daw, *L. F. and U. and the English Anabaptists* (1917, *M.L.A.* xxxii.
267).

The text is a fragment, but there may have been more, as the
original fly-leaves and end papers of the volume are gone. Sir G. F.

Warner thinks the hand 'quite early seventeenth century'. The corrections in the same hand are such as rather to suggest an original composition, but may also be those of an expert copyist. Miss Daw thinks that the date of composition was in the seventeenth century, and that the play represents ideas belonging to (*a*) the Anabaptists and (*b*) the Family of Love, both of which were then active. She even suggests the possible authorship of the controversialist Edmond Jessop. Personally, I find it difficult to assign to the seventeenth century a moral written precisely in the vein of the middle of the sixteenth century, even to the notes (2, 69, 103) of action 'in place' (cf. ch. xix), and a phrase (76),

> Why stare ye at me thus I wene ye be come to se a play,

closely parallel to *Wit and Wisdom*, 12, which is probably pre-Elizabethan. The Jacobean activity of Anabaptism and Familism only revived movements which had been familiar in England from Edwardian times, were particularly vigorous in 1575, and had apparently died down during the last decade of Elizabeth's reign ; cf. for Anabaptists C. Burrage, *The Early English Dissenters* (1912), and for Familists s.v. Middleton, *Family of Love*.

The Maid's Metamorphosis. 1600

S. R. 1600, July 24 (Hartwell). 'Two plaies or thinges thone called the maides metamorphosis thother gyve a man luck and throw him into the Sea.' *Richard Oliffe* (Arber, iii. 168).

1600. The Maydes Metamorphosis. As it hath beene sundrie times Acted by the Children of Powles. *Thomas Creede for Richard Olive.* [Prologue.]

Editions by A. H. Bullen (1882, *O.E.P.* i), R. W. Bond (1902, *Lyly*, iii. 341), and J. S. Farmer (1912, *T.F.T.*).

Archer's play list of 1656 (Greg, *Masques*, lxxxvi) started an ascription to Lyly, which was probably suggested by the similarity of name to *Love's Metamorphosis*. Daniel, with Lyly as reviser, is substituted by Fleay, ii. 324 ; Day by Gosse and Bullen ; Day, with Lyly as reviser, by Bond. A limit of date is given by the reopening of Paul's in 1599, and iv. i. 157 points to the 'leape yeare' 1600. Fleay thinks that the play was performed at Anne Russell's wedding on 16 June 1600 (cf. ch. v), but, though 'three or foure Muses' dance at the end of the play, there is no indication of a mask, while the accounts of the wedding say nothing of a play.

The Marriage of Wit and Science > 1570

S.R. 1569–70. 'A play intituled the maryage of Wytt and Scyence.' *Thomas Marsh* (Arber, i. 399).

N.D. A new and Pleasant enterlude intituled the mariage of Witte and Science. *Thomas Marsh.*

Editions in Dodsley[4] (1874, ii) and by J. S. Farmer (1909, *T.F.T.*). An allegorical moral, indebted to John Redford's *Wit and Science*

(*Med. Stage*, ii. 454). Fleay, 64 ; ii. 288, 294, proposes to identify this with the *Wit and Will* played at court in 1567–8 (cf. App. B), as Will is a character.

Meleager (?)

B. Dobell, in *Athenaeum* for 14 Sept. 1901, described a MS. in his possession with the title A Register of all the Noble Men of England sithence the Conquest Created. The date of compilation is probably 1570–90. On f. 3 is the argument in English of a play headed :

> Children of Paules Play.
> Publij Ovidij Nasonis Meleager.

Presumably the play was in English also. It was classical in manner with five acts, a chorus, and dumb-shows. Act I opened with a dumb-show before Melpomene of the Fates, Althea and the burning brand. It seems distinct from the *Meleager* of W. Gager (q.v.).

The Merry Devil of Edmonton c. 1603

S. R. 1607, Oct. 22 (Buck). ' A Plaie called the Merry Devill of Edmonton.' *Arthur Johnson* (Arber, iii. 362). [*The Life and Death of the Merry Devil of Edmonton*, entered 5 April 1608, is a pamphlet by T. B.]

1608. The Merry Devill of Edmonton. As it hath beene sundry times Acted, by his Maiesties Seruants, at the Globe, on the bankeside. *Henry Ballard for Arthur Johnson*. [Prologue ; Induction.]

1612 ; 1617 ; 1626 ; 1631.

S. R. 1653, Sept. 9. 'The merry devil of Edmonton, by W^m: Shakespeare.' *H. Moseley* (Eyre, i. 429).

1655. *For William Gilbertson*.

Editions in Dodsley (1875, x), and by H. Walker (1897, *T.D.*), J. S. Farmer (1911, *T.F.T.*), J. M. Manly (1913, *R.E.C.* ii), and in collections of *Sh. Apocrypha*.

Moseley's attribution was repeated in the play lists of Archer in 1656 and Kirkman in 1661 (Greg, *Masques*, lxxxix), and the play was bound with *Mucedorus* and *Fair Em* as ' Shakespeare, vol. i ' in Charles II's library. The attempt of Fleay, ii. 313 (cf. his *Shakespeare*, 294), to show that Sir John the priest was originally called Oldcastle and gave a name to the play is too far-fetched, but it leads him to support a tradition originally based on a note by Coxeter (*Dodsley*[2], v. 247) that the author was Drayton. He puts it in 1597, apparently because Jessica calls Lancelot a ' merry devil' in *M.V.* ii. iii. 2. But the Host is pretty clearly copied from him of the *Merry Wives* (c. 1599), and allusions to the king's hunting (iv. i. 158, 186), although perhaps merely part of the historic action, might also have been topical under James I. The play existed by 1604, when it is mentioned in T. M.'s *Black Book* (Bullen, *Middleton*, viii. 36). Jonson calls it ' your dear delight ' in the prologue to *The Devil is an Ass* (1616), and it was revived at court on 3 May 1618 (Cunningham, xlv).

Minds. *1575* <

N.D. Comoedia. A worke in ryme, contayning an Enterlude of
Myndes, witnessing the Mans Fall from God and Christ. Set forth
by H. N. and by him newly perused and amended. Translated out
of Base-Almayns into English. [*No imprint or colophon.*] [Preface
to the Reader ; Prologue in dialogue.]

This is a translation of the Low German *Comoedia : Ein Gedicht
des Spels van Sinnen, anno 1575* of Henrick Niklaes, the founder of
the mystical sect known as the Family of Love (cf. s.v. Middleton).

Misogonus. *1560* < > 77

[*MS.*] In collection of the Duke of Devonshire. [By two hands, of
which one is only responsible for the t.p. and some corrections in
the text. The t.p. has the heading ' A mery and p . . . Misogonus ',
followed by the names of the speakers and ' Laurentius Barіωna
Ketthering die 20 Novembris Anno 1577 '. The text, which is apparently imperfect, stopping in iv. 4, is probably all in one other hand,
together with a prologue, at the end of which is ' Thomas Rychardes '.
The inscriptions ' Anthony Rice ' on the title-page, ' Thomas Warde
Barfold 1577 ' on the prologue-page, and ' W. Wyllm̄ ' and ' John
York Jesu ' in margins of the text, are all in later hands, some of
them not of the sixteenth century.]

Editions by A. Brandl (1898, *Q.W.D.*), J. S. Farmer (1906), and
R. W. Bond (1911, *E.P.I.*).—*Dissertation* : G. L. Kittredge, *The M.
and Laurence Johnson* (1901, *J.G.P.* iii. 335).

Brandl, following Collier, ii. 368, 378, dates the play in 1560, on
the ground of an allusion in IV. i. 131 to ' the rising rection ith north ',
i.e. the Pilgrimage of Grace of 1536, as twenty-four years before the
time of action, but it is not quite clear that the rambling dialogue of
rustics, in which the passage occurs, justifies the interpretation put
upon it ; nor is the allusion in III. ii. 3 to the weather-cock of Paul's,
set up in 1553 and destroyed in 1561, any more conclusive, as the
phrase may have become proverbial. The style might be either of
c. 1560 or, in a provincial play, of *c.* 1577, or, as Bond suggests.
a reviser of *c.* 1577 might have revised a text of ten or twelve years
earlier. For author, Fleay, 16, 58, 60, taking the piece to be that
disliked at court on 31 Dec. 1559, offered Richard Edwardes, and is
followed by Wallace, i. 111. There is nothing to suggest that the
play was ever performed at court at all. It seems more natural to
look for him, either in the Thomas Richards or in the Laurence Barjona
of the MS. Conceivably Richards might be the T. R. whose initials
appear on the prints of *Impatient Poverty* and *Nice Wanton* (cf.
Mediaeval Stage, ii. 460) in 1560. Barjona might be the name of
a converted Jew. But Kittredge regards it as an anagram of Johnson,
and points out that a Laurence Johnson matriculated at Christ's
College, Cambridge, in 1570, and took his B.A. in 1574 and his M.A.
in 1577, while a Thomas Richards of Trinity took his B.A. in 1571,
and a Thomas Ward of Jesus in 1580. A reference to Cambridge

learning (III. iii. 74) does not, of course, go far to prove Cambridge
authorship. Anyway, the Barjona of the title-page is probably the
' Laur. Bariona ' who signed, also from Kettering, the epistle to a book
called *Cometographia* on 20 Jan. 1579. It is the work of an Anglican ;
not therefore of the Laurence Johnson, who was an Oxford Jesuit.
I can add a few facts. A Laurence Jonson, with one Chr. Balam and
George Haysyll of Cambridge, made a complaint through Lord North
to the queen against the Bishop of Ely in Dec. 1575 (*S. P. D. Eliz.*
cv. 88). This is interesting, because George Haysell of Wisbech was
apparently one of Worcester's players (cf. ch. xiii) in 1583. There
is also a Laurence Johnson who on 12 June 1572 wrote to Lord
Burghley about his service in the Mint (*S. P. D. Eliz.* lxxxviii. 17);
possibly the same of whom Burghley wrote to his ' brother ' William
Herlle on 3 April 1575, that he could do nothing for him (*S. P. D. Eliz.*
ciii. 24). Finally a Laurence Johnson engraved plates in 1603 (*D. N. B.*).

Sir Thomas More c. 1596

[*MS.*] *B.M. Harleian MS.* 7368. [The wrapper is endorsed, ' The
Booke of Sir Thomas Moore ', and is in part composed of a vellum
leaf also used for that of Munday's *John a Kent and John a Cumber*.
The character of the damp stains on the two MSS. shows that they
must for some time have lain together. Two passages of the original
text have disappeared, and six passages have been inserted, on fresh
leaves or slips, to replace these and other cancelled matter. One of
these leaves appears to have been misplaced. Greg finds seven distinct
hands : (*a*) the writer of the original text, whom he has now identified
(*M. L. R.* viii. 89) with Munday ; (*b*) five contributors to the insertions,
of whom one appears also to have acted as a playhouse corrector,
another (writing 30 lines) seems clearly to be Dekker, and a third
(writing 148 lines) has been taken (v. *infra*) for Shakespeare ; (*c*) the
Master of the Revels, Edmund Tilney, who has given some directions
as censor, of which the most important, at the beginning, runs :
' Leaue out the insurrection wholy & the Cause ther off & begin with
Sʳ Tho: Moore att the mayors sessions with a reportt afterwardes off
his good service don being Shriue off London vppon a mutiny Agaynst
the Lumbardes only by A shortt reporte & nott otherwise att your
own perrilles E. Tyllney '. Whether Greg is right in calling this
a ' conditional licence ' I am not sure, but he corrects earlier writers
by pointing out that the extant insertions do not carry out Tilney's
instructions, and were probably made before the play reached him.
Although therefore the appearance of an actor's name in a s.d. suggests
that the play was cast for performance, it is not likely that it was
actually performed, at any rate in its present state.]

Editions by A. Dyce (1844, *Sh. Soc.*), A. F. Hopkinson (1902),
C. F. Tucker Brooke (1908, *Sh. Apocrypha*), J. S. Farmer (1910,
photo-facsimile in *T. F. S.*), and W. W. Greg (1911, *M. S. R.*).—*Dissertations* : R. Simpson, *Are there any extant MSS. in Sh.'s Handwriting ?* (1871,4 *N. Q.* viii. 1) ; J. Spedding, *Sh.'s Handwriting* (1872,
4 *N. Q.* x. 227), *On a Question concerning a Supposed Specimen of*

Sh.'s Handwriting (1879, *Reviews and Discussions*); B. Nicholson, *The Plays of S. T. M. and Hamlet* (1884, 6 *N. Q.* x. 423); C. R. Baskervill, *Some Parallels to Bartholomew Fair* (1908, *M. P.* vi. 109); W. W. Greg, *Autograph Plays by A. Munday* (1913, *M. L. R.* viii. 89); L. L. Schücking, *Das Datum der pseudo-Sh. S. T. M.* (1913, *E. S.* xlvi. 228); E. M. Thompson, *Shakespeare's Handwriting* (1916) and *The Autograph MSS. of Anthony Munday* (1919, *Bibl. Soc. Trans.* xiv. 325); P. Simpson, *The Play of S. T. M. and Sh.'s Hand in It* (1917, 3 *Library*, viii. 79); J. D. Wilson and others, *Sh.'s Hand in the Play of S.T.M.* (1919, *T.L.S.* 24 April onwards); W. J. Lawrence and others, *Was S.T.M. ever Acted?* (1920, *T. L. S.* 1 July onwards); M. A. Bayfield and E. M. Thompson, *Shakespeare's Handwriting* (1921, *T. L. S.* 30 June, 4 Aug.).

The play has been dated *c.* 1586 and *c.* 1596, in both of which years there were disturbances with some analogy to the ' Ill May Day ' of the plot, and an early date has been regarded as favoured by mentions (ll. 1006, 1148) of Oagle a wigmaker, since men of the name were serving the Revels Office in this and similar capacities from 1571 to 1585 (Feuillerat, *Eliz.*, *passim*), and by the appearance as a messenger in a stage-direction (Greg, p. 89) of T. Goodal, an actor traceable with Berkeley's men in 1581 and with the Admiral's or Strange's in the plot of *The Seven Deadly Sins, c.* 1590–1. But Goodal may have acted much longer, and the Admiral's men had business relations with a ' Father Ogell ' in Feb. 1600 (Greg, *Henslowe*, ii. 300). Greg, after comparing Munday's script in the play with other and better datable examples of that script, inclines to put it ' between 1596 and 1602, say 1598–1600 ', and Sir E. M. Thompson, on a further review of the same evidence, suggests 1592 or 1593. This, however, involves putting the MS. of *John a Kent and John a Cumber* (cf. ch. xxiii, s.v. Munday) back to 1590, which, although palaeographically possible, is inconsistent with evidence pointing to its production by the Admiral's in 1594. Certain parallels with *Julius Caesar* and *Hamlet* might suggest the latter part of the possible period, although the parallel suggested by Schücking with Fletcher's *The Tamer Tamed* is too slight to bear out his date of 1605–8, and the attempt of Fleay (ii. 312; *Shakespeare*, 292) to identify the play with the *Abuses* of Paul's in 1606 is guess-work. Jonson's apparent debt to *S. T. M.* in *Bartholomew Fair*, pointed out by Baskervill, is also in favour of a latish date. Obviously the mention of ' Mason among the Kings players ' (l. 1151) does not prove a Jacobean date, as Henry VIII had players. No actor of the name in either reign is known, although an Alexander Mason was marshal of the royal minstrels in 1494 (Collier, i. 45). Account must be taken of the support given by Sir E. M. Thompson to the theory of R. Simpson and Spedding that three of the added pages are in the hand of Shakespeare. This is based on a minute comparison with the few undoubted fragments, almost entirely signatures, of Shakespeare's writing. Both hands use ' the native English script ' and are ' of an ordinary type ', without marked individual character ' to any great extent ', although slight peculiarities, such as ' the use of the fine upstroke as an ornamental adjunct to certain letters ', are

common to them. The demonstration would have been more convincing had the hands been less ' ordinary ', but Sir E. M. Thompson's
authority is great, and some support is furnished by P. Simpson from
the character of the punctuation in the addition, and by J. D. Wilson
from some orthographic resemblances to the more reliable Shakespearian quartos. Sir E. M. Thompson's views are criticized in
G. Greenwood, *Shakespeare's Handwriting* (1920). If Shakespeare was
the author, the analogies between the matter of the addition and the
Jack Cade scenes of *Henry VI* would be in favour of an earlier date,
if that were possible, than 1596 or even 1594, although I should not
like to be committed to the view that Shakespeare might not have
scribbled the fragment at any time in the sixteenth century. On
a balance of the mixed literary and palaeographical evidence before
us, the safest guess seems to be 1596. As to the rest of the authorship, Dr. Greg's discoveries point to Munday, with some help from
Dekker. Fleay's argument (*Sh.* 292) for Lodge and Drayton is flimsy.
If Shakespeare had a share, the company was probably the Chamberlain's. Goodal's name proves nothing as to this.

Mucedorus > *1598 ; 1611*

1598. A most pleasant Comedie of Mucedorus, the Kings sonne of
Valentia and Amadine the Kings daughter of Arragon, with the merie
conceites of Mouse. Newly set foorth, as it hath bin sundrie times
plaide in the honorable Cittie of London. Very delectable and full of
mirth. *For William Jones.* [Arrangement of parts for eight actors ;
Induction.]

1606. *For William Jones.*

1610. . . . Amplified with new additions, as it was acted before the
Kings Maiestie at White-hall on Shroue-sunday night. By his Highness Seruants vsually playing at the Globe. Very delectable, and full
of conceited Mirth. *For William Jones.* [Arrangement of parts for
ten actors ; Prologue. Collier professes to follow a print of 1609 with
this altered title, otherwise unknown ; cf. Greg in *Jahrbuch*, xl. 104.]

1611 ; 1613 ; 1615.

S. R. 1618, Sept. 17. Transfer by Sarah, widow of William Jones,
to John Wright (Arber, iii. 632).

1618 ; 1619 ; 1621 ; 1626 ; N.D. [1629] fragm. ; 1631 ; 1634 ; 1639 ;
N.D. [1639 < > 63] ; 1663 ; 1668.

Editions by J. P. Collier (1824) and with *Shakespeare* (1878),
N. Delius (1874), in Dodsley⁴, vii (1874), Warnke-Proescholdt (1878),
J. S. Farmer (1910, *T. F. T.*), and with *Sh. Apocrypha.—Dissertations* :
R. Simpson, *On Some Plays Attributed to Sh.* (1875, *N.S.S. Trans.* 155) ;
W. Wagner, *Ueber und zu M.* (1876, *Jahrbuch*, xi. 59), *Neue Con-
jecturen zum M.* (1879, *Jahrbuch*, xiv. 274) ; K. Elze, *Noten und
Conjecturen* (1878, *Jahrbuch*, xiii. 45), *Nachträgliche Bemerkungen zu
M.* (1880, *Jahrbuch*, xv. 339), *Last Notes on M.* (1883, *E.S.* vi. 217) ;
E. Soffé, *Ist M. ein Schauspiel Sh.'s ?* (1887, Brünn Progr.) ; W. W.
Greg, *On the Editions of M.* (1904, *Jahrbuch*, xl. 95).

It is difficult to date with precision the revival for which the additions printed in the Q. of 1610 (161⁰⁄₁ ?) were written, especially as the genuineness of the Q. of 1609, in which Collier stated that he found these additions, cannot be verified, since the accounts of the Treasurer of the Chamber do not specify the exact days on which the numerous appearances of the King's men at court during the winters of 1608–9, 1609–10, and 1610–11 took place. The conjecture of Fleay (ii. 50 ; *Shakespeare*, 303) that the additions date from 1606 was largely based on a guess that they appeared in the Q. of 1606, which he had not seen. The added or altered passages are the prologue; i. 1, 2 ; iv. 1 ; parts of v. 2 ; and the final lines of the induction. The prologue wishes James security

> From blemisht Traytors, stayn'd with Periurie.

A bear is introduced in i. 2, as in *W. T.* iii. 3, and I venture to conjecture that both episodes were inspired by the successful bear in Jonson's *Mask of Oberon* on 1 Jan. 1611, to which there is also an allusion in his *Love Restored* of 6 Jan. 1612. If so, the revival must have been on Shrove Sunday, 3 Feb. 1611. In i. i. 50 Anselmo says that he was a shepherd in 'Lord Iulios Maske '. *Oberon*, however, had no shepherds proper, only satyrs and sylvans. The induction is altered to compliment James instead of Elizabeth, and the following dialogue between Comedie and Envie is introduced :

Envie.	Comedie, thou art a shallow Goose ; Ile ouerthrow thee in thine owne intent, And make thy fall my Comick merriment.
Comedie.	Thy pollicie wants grauitie ; thou art Too weake. Speake, Fiend, as how ?
Env.	Why, thus : From my foule Studie will I hoyst a Wretch, A leane and hungry Meager Canniball, Whose iawes swell to his eyes with chawing Malice : And him Ile make a Poet.
Com.	What 's that to th' purpose ?
Env.	This scrambling Rauen, with his needie Beard, Will I whet on to write a Comedie, Wherein shall be compos'd darke sentences, Pleasing to factious braines : And euery other where place me a Iest, Whose high abuse shall more torment then blowes : Then I my selfe (quicker then Lightning) Will flie me to a puisant Magistrate, And waighting with a Trencher at his backe, In midst of iollitie, rehearse those gaules, (With some additions) So lately vented in your Theator. He, vpon this, cannot but make complaint, To your great danger, or at least restraint.
Com.	Ha, ha, ha ! I laugh to hear thy folly ; This is a trap for Boyes, not Men, nor such, Especially desertfull in their doinges, Whose stay'd discretion rules their purposes. I and my faction do eschew those vices.

Fleay, with 1606 in his mind, finds here an apology for *The Fox*, thinking Jonson the raven and *Eastward Hoe* the 'trap for Boyes'. In 1610 there had been no trouble about any London play, although one in Lincolnshire had given offence. But a careful reading of the passage will show that it is no apology at all, but a boast, and an attack upon informers against the stage.

As the play had been in print since 1598, it must not be assumed that, because the King's revived it in 1610–11, it was originally a Chamberlain's play. It may have belonged to the Queen's or some other extinct company. Evidently it was a popular play, as the number of editions shows. *K. B. P.* ind. 91 tells us that Ralph has 'play'd . . . Musidorus before the Wardens of our Company'.

The ascription to Shakespeare is due to Archer's list of 1656 (Greg, *Masques*, xci) and to the inclusion of the play with *Fair Em* and *The Merry Devil of Edmonton* in a volume in Charles II's library, lettered 'Shakespeare, vol. i' (*Variorum*, ii. 682). It now receives little support, even as regards the added passages. Greene is preferred as the original author by Malone and Hopkinson, Peele by von Friesen, and Lodge by Fleay.

After the suppression of the theatres in 1642, *Mucedorus* was acted by strolling players in various parts of Oxfordshire. An accident during a performance at Witney on 3 Feb. 1654 is recorded in John Rowe, *Tragi-Comoedia. Being a brieff relation of the strange and wonderful hand of God, discovered at Witney in the Comedy acted February the third, where there were some slaine, many hurt and several other remarkable passages* (1653¾).

Either *Mucedorus* or Greene's *Alphonsus* (q.v.) may have been the play on a king of Arragon given at Dresden in 1626. It has also been suggested (Herz, 95) that *Mucedorus* influenced Pieter Hooft's Dutch pastoral *Granida* (1605).

Narcissus.   6 Jan. 1603

[*MS.*] *Bodl. MS.* 147303 (*Rawl. Poet. MS.* 212), f. 82ᵛ. 'A Twelfe Night Merriment. Anno 1602.' [Porter's speech 'at the end of supper', Wassail Song, Prologue, and Epilogue.]

Edition by M. L. Lee (1893).

The porter's name is Francis, and from some speeches and a letter composed for him, which appear in the same manuscript, it is clear that he was Francis Clark, who became porter of St. John's, Oxford, on 8 May 1601, at which house therefore the play was doubtless given. It has borrowings from *M. N. D.* and *1 Hen. IV.*

New Custom.   1558 < > 73

1573. A new Enterlude No less wittie: then pleasant, entituled new Cvstome, deuised of late, and for diuers causes nowe set forthe, neuer before this tyme Imprinted. *William How for Abraham Veale.*

Editions in Dodsley[4] (1874, iii) and by J. S. Farmer (1908, *T. F. T.*).

A moral of Protestant controversy, with typical personages, bearing allegorical names, arranged for four actors.

The final prayer is for Elizabeth, and Avarice played in the days of Queen Mary. Fleay, 64 ; ii. 294, thinks it a revised Edward VI play, on the ground of an allusion to a ' square caps ' controversy of 1550. But this was still vigorous in 1565 (cf. Parker's *Letters*, 240). Fleay also says that the *Nugize* of Captain Cox's collection (Laneham, 30) is *Mankind* (*Med. Stage*, ii. 438) in which New Gyse is a character. But *Mankind* was first printed in 1897, and probably this play is the one Laneham had in mind.

Nobody and Somebody > 1606

S. R. 1606, Jan. 8. ' The picture of No bodye.' *John Trundell* (Arber, iii. 308).

1606, March 12 (Wilson). ' A Booke called no bodie and somme bodie &c.' *John Trundell* (Arber, iii. 316).

N.D. No-Body, and Some-Body. With the true Chronicle Historie of Elydure, who was fortunately three seuerall times crowned King of England. The true Coppy thereof, as it hath beene acted by the Queens Maiesties Seruants. *For John Trundle.* [Prologue and Epilogue.]

Editions by A. Smith (1877), R. Simpson (1878, *S. of S.* i), J. S. Farmer (1911, *T. F. T.*), of the early German translation by F. Bischoff, *Niemand und Jemand in Graz im Jahre 1608* (1899, *Mitteilungen des historischen Vereins für Steiermark*, xlvii. 127), and of Tieck's translation by J. Bolte (1894, *Jahrbuch*, xxix. 4).—*Dissertation* : J. Bolte, *Eine Hamburger Aufführung von N. a. S.* (1905, *Jahrbuch*, xli. 188).

The play is probably Jacobean. There is a reference to the unwilling recipients of knighthood (l. 325), and the use of Essex's nickname for Cobham, Sycophant, as the name of a courtier, must be later than Cobham's disgrace in 1603. Simpson thought that an allusion to the misuse of the collections for rebuilding Paul's steeple (l. 754) pointed to an original date *c.* 1592, when the matter caused a scandal, but the steeple was still unbuilt in James's reign. Greg, *Henslowe*, ii. 230, revising a conjecture of Fleay, i. 293, suggests that *Albere Galles*, written by Heywood and Smith for Worcester's in Sept. 1602, may be this play, and Henslowe's title a mistake for *Archigallo*, one of the characters. The play seems to have reached Germany by 1608. A performance at Graz in that year was probably the occasion of the dedication by ' Joannes Grün Nob. Anglus ' to the archduke Maximilian of a manuscript German translation, now in the Rein library. To it is attached a coloured drawing of a bearded man in a doublet which hides his breeches, and with a book and chain in his hands. Above is written ' Nemo ' and ' Neminis Virtus ubique Laudabilis .' A version is also in the Anglo-German collection of 1620 (Herz, 66, 112).

Parnassus. 1598–1602 (?)

[*MSS.*] *Bodl. Rawlinson MS.* D. 398. 'The Pilgrimage to Parnassus', 'The Returne from Parnassus'. [1 *Parnassus* with Prologue ; 2 *Parnassus* with Stagekeeper's speech for Prologue. The
cover bears the name of 'Edmunde Rishton, Lancastrensis', who
took his M.A. from St. John's, Cambridge, in 1602.]

Halliwell-Phillipps MS. 'The Returne from Pernassus : or The
Scourge of Simony.' [3 *Parnassus*, with induction for Prologue, which
says, 'The Pilgrimage to Pernassus, and the returne from Pernassus
have stood the honest Stagekeepers in many a Crownes expence for
linckes and vizards : . . . this last is the last part of the returne from
Pernassus'.]

S. R. 1605, Oct. 16 (Gwyn). 'An Enterlude called The retourne
from Pernassus or the scourge of Simony publiquely Acted by the
studentes in Sainct Johns College in Cambridg.' *John Wright* (Arber,
iii. 304).

1606. The Returne from Pernassus : Or The Scourge of Simony.
Publiquely acted by the Students in Saint Iohns Colledge in Cambridge. *G. Eld, for Iohn Wright.* [Two issues. 3 *Parnassus* only.]

Editions of 3 *Parnassus* by T. Hawkins (1773, *O. E. D.* iii), W. Scott
(1810, *A. B. D.* i), in Dodsley⁴ (1874, ix), by E. Arber (1878) and
O. Smeaton (1905, *T. D.*), and of 1, 2, 3 *Parnassus* by W. D. Macray
(1886) and J. S. Farmer (*S. F. T.*).—*Dissertations* : B. Corney (1866,
3 *N. Q.* ix. 387) ; J. W. Hales, *The Pilgrimage to P.* (1887, *Academy*
and *Macmillan's Magazine* ; 1893, *Folia Litteraria*, 165) ; W. Lühr,
Die drei Cambridger Spiele vom P. in ihren litterarischen Beziehungen
(1900, Kiel diss.) ; E. B. Reed, *The College Element in Hamlet* (1909,
M. P. vi. 453) ; G. C. Moore Smith, *The P. Plays* (1915, *M. L. R.*
x. 162).

There are several notes of time and authorship. At the end of
1, which was 'three daies studie' (l. 3), the pilgrimage has lasted
'4 yeares' (712). Kinsader's, i. e. Marston's, *Satires* and Bastard's
Epigrams, both of 1598, are mentioned (212). The prologue to 2,
which is a 'Christmas toy' (18), deprecates the former courtesy of
'our stage' :

> Surelie it made our poet a staide man,
> Kept his proude necke from baser lambskins weare,
> Had like to have made him senior sophister.
> He was faine to take his course by Germanie
> Ere he could gett a silie poore degree.
> Hee never since durst name a peece of cheese,
> Thoughe Chessire seems to priviledge his name.
> His looke was never sanguine since that daye ;
> Nere since he laughte to see a mimick playe.

It is now seven years since the scholars started for Parnassus (62).
Gullio has been 'verie latelie in Irelande' and 'scapt knightinge'
(878), obviously with Essex in 1599. The *Epigrams* (1599) of 'one
Weaver fellow', i.e. John Weever, are alluded to (982). The prologue
to 3, also a 'Christenmas toy' (30), calls it 'an old musty show, that

hath laine this twelue moneth in the bottome of a coalehouse ' (25).
' The Authors wit ' (48) has stood ' hammering upon . . . 2 schollers some
foure (1606, whole) yeare' (37). This is the third play of a series (76) :

> In Scholers fortunes twise forlorne and dead
> Twise hath our weary play earst laboured.
> Making them Pilgrims to Pernassus hill,
> Then penning their return with ruder quill.

Belvedere (1600) is published (179) and Nashe is dead (314). The
Dominical letters are C, or for the Annunciation year D and C (1105),
and the moon is in ' the last quarter the 5 day, at 2 of the cloke and
38 minuts in the morning' (1133). These indications fit Jan. 1602
(Lühr, 15, 105). The siege of Ostend, which extended from 1601 to
1604, has begun (1333). Jonson has ' brought vp Horace giving the
Poets a pill ' (1811), and Kempe is back ' from dancing the morrice
over the Alpes ' (1823). Both events took place in 1601. It is still
Elizabeth's reign (1141).

A quite clear conclusion as to date is not possible. The calendar
references, the four years of hammering (in 3), and the probability
that the writer would try to have his allusions to literary events up
to date, suggest performances at the Christmases of 1598–9, 1599–
1600, and 1601–2. This allows for a twelve-months' delay, followed
by a good deal of revision, in the performance of 3. On the other
hand, the difference between four (in 1) and seven (in 2) years of
pilgrimage points to 1598–9, 1601–2, and 1602–3. On the whole,
I lean to the first alternative.

So far as we know, the association of Kempe with the Chamberlain's
men was out of date either in 1601 or 1602 ; conceivably he returned
to the company for a while in 1601, but he was certainly of Worcester's
in 1602.

Moore Smith thinks that the ' ruder quill ' of the prologue to 3
implies that the author of 2 and 3 was distinct from the author of
1. But the same prologue speaks clearly of a single author. Hales
took the account of his troubles in getting his degree literally, and
pointed out that foreign students at German universities were called
' Käsebettler ' and ' Käsejäger '. Moore Smith doubts, and thinks the
degree may have been given at Cambridge by the influence of William
Holland, senior fellow of St. John's, and his name glanced at in
' Germanie '. The absence alike of matriculation books and college
admission registers for the period makes identification difficult. Corney
found a copy of the print of 3 with the inscription ' To my Lovinge
Smallocke J. D.', which he thought in the same hand as the *Lansdowne MS.* of John Day's *Peregrinatio Scholastica.* Bullen was inclined
to support Day's authorship on internal grounds, but Day was a Caius
man, whose university career closed in disgrace, and is not very likely
to have written plays for St. John's some years later. And it is but
a slight connexion with Cheshire that ' dey ' means ' dairy ' in the
dialect of that county. Cheshire ought to be our clue. Charles Chester
was not, so far as I know, a writer. Hales seems to have thought

that the theatrical Beestons of London may have been connected with the Cheshire family of that name. There was a Cheshire foundation at St. John's, and Moore Smith cites a suggestion that the author may have been William Dodd, a Cheshire man, who became Scholar of St. John's in 1597, B.A. in 1599, and Fellow in 1602. The ' priviledge ' reminds me of the traditional jurisdiction of the Dutton family over minstrelsy in Cheshire (*Mediaeval Stage*, ii. 259), but I do not know whether any Dutton can be traced at St. John's.

In i. 2 of 3 Judicio is exercising the occupation of a ' corrector of the presse ', apparently in the employment of a particular printing-house, not of the licensing authorities. The house would be Danter's, who is himself introduced in i. 3 bargaining with Ingenioso to give him 40s. for a pamphlet. In iv. 3 Burbage and Kempe appear, and here is the famous passage in which Kempe says :

> ' Few of the vniuersity men pen plaies well, they smell too much of that writer *Ouid*, and that writer *Metamorphosis*, and talke too much of *Proserpina & Iuppiter*. Why heres our fellow *Shakespeare* puts them all downe, I and *Ben Ionson* too. O that *Ben Ionson* is a pestilent fellow, he brought vp Horace giuing the Poets a pill, but our fellow *Shakespeare* hath giuen him a purge that made him beray his credit.'

Fleay, *Shakespeare*, 221, suggests that the ' purge ' was the descrip-tion of Ajax in *Troilus and Cressida*, I. ii. 15, and is supported by Small, 167. If so, it was very irrelevant to its setting. The purge ought to be *Satiromastix*, and though there is nothing to indicate that Shakespeare had any responsibility for *Satiromastix*, it is just conceivable that a Cambridge man, writing before the play was assigned to Dekker in print, may have thought that he had. The allusion is clearly to Shakespeare as a writer, or one might have thought that he acted Horace-Jonson in *Satiromastix*.

Especially in 3, the writer is much occupied with contemporary literature, but this does not justify the slap-dash attempt of Fleay, ii. 347, to identify nearly all his characters with individual literary men. They are, of course, not individuals, but types, and types of university men. The most that can be said is that there may be something of Marston in Furor Poeticus, and a good deal of Nashe, with probably also a little of Greene, in Ingenioso, who ultimately takes flight, with Furor and Phantasma, to the Isle of Dogs (v. 3, 4) :

> There where the blattant beast doth rule and raigne
> Renting the credit of whom ere he please.

Il Pastor Fido > 1601

S. R. 1601, Sept. 16 (Pasfield). ' A booke called the faythfull Shepheard '. *Waterson* (Arber, iii. 192).

1602. Il Pastor Fido : Or The faithfull Shepheard. Translated out of Italian into English. *For Simon Waterson*. [Sonnets by S. Daniel and the Translator to Sir Edward Dymocke ; Epistle to the same, dated 31 Dec. 1601, and signed ' Simon Waterson '.]

1633. *For John Waterson.* [Epistle by John Waterson to Charles Dymock.]

1633. *Augustine Matthewes for William Sheares.* [Another issue.]

The preliminary matter of 1602 and 1633 is shown by Greg, *Pastoral*, 242, to point to a kinsman, but not the son, of Sir Edward Dymocke as the translator. He may be a John Dymmocke, to whom Archer's play-list of 1656 (Greg, *Masques*, xcvi) assigns in error *The Faithful Shepherdess*. The translation is from G. Battista Guarini's *Il Pastor Fido* (1590). For a Latin translation see App. L.

The Pedlar's Prophecy > 1594

S. R. 1594, May 13. ' A plea booke intituled the Pedlers Prophesie.' *Thomas Creede* (Arber, ii. 649).

1595. The Pedlers Prophecie. *Thomas Creede, sold by William Barley.* [Prologue.]

Editions by J. S. Farmer (1911, *T. F. T.*) and W. W. Greg (1914, *M. S. R.*).

The analogies of title and date of publication to *The Cobler's Prophecy* have led Fleay, ii. 283, and others to ascribe the authorship to Wilson. To me the play reads more like a belated piece of *c*. 1560–70.

Pericles c. 1607–8

See Shakespeare (ch. xxiii), except in relation to whose work the play can hardly be discussed.

Philotus > 1603

1603. Ane verie excellent and delectabill Treatise intitulit Philotus. Quhairin we may persaue the greit inconveniences that fallis out in the Mariage betwene age and zouth. *Robert Charteris, Edinburgh.* [At end are verses beginning ' What if a day or a month or a zeere ', possibly Campion's ; cf. Bullen, *Campion* (1903), 270.]

1612. A verie excellent and delectable Comedie. . . . *Andro Hart, Edinburgh.*

Editions by J. Pinkerton (1792, *Scottish Poems*, iii) and for Bannatyne Club (1835).

This has been ascribed to Robert Sempill (1530 ?–95), but merely because his play before the Regent of Scotland on 17 June 1568 (Diary of Robert Birrel in Dalyell, *Fragments of Scottish History*, 14) is not otherwise known. R. Brotanek (1898, *Festschrift zum viii allgemeinen deutschen Neuphilologentage in Wien* ; cf. *Jahrbuch*, xxxv. 302) suggests Alexander Montgomery.

The Puritan. 1606

S. R. 1607, Aug. 6 (Buck). ' A book called the comedie of " the Puritan Widowe ".' *George Elde* (Arber, iii. 358).

1607. The Puritaine Or The Widdow of Watling-streete. Acted by

the Children of Paules. Written by W. S. *G. Eld.* [Running-title
' The Puritaine Widdow '.]
    1664 ; 1685. [Parts of F_3 and F_4 of Shakespeare.]
    Editions in 1734 (J. Tonson), 1734 (R. Walker), by J. S. Farmer
(1911, *T. F. T.*), and in *Sh. Apocrypha.*
    The W. S. of the title-page was interpreted as William Shakespeare
in Archer's play-list of 1656 (Greg, *Masques*, c). The attribution is
accepted by no modern critic, and guesses at Wentworth Smith and
William Smith rest similarly on nothing but the initials. Internal
evidence points to an author who was an Oxford man, and familiar
with the plays of Shakespeare. Middleton is preferred by Fleay,
ii. 92, Bullen (*Middleton*, i. lxxix), and others ; Marston by Brooke,
who dwells on a general resemblance to *Eastward Hoe*, and seems
inclined to think that Jonson, whose *Bartholomew Fair* the play fore-
shadows, might also have contributed. The character George Pyeboard
is clearly meant for Peele, and the play uses episodes which appear
in *The Merrie Conceited Jests of George Peele Gent.* This, though the
extant print is of 1607, was entered in S. R. on 14 Dec. 1605. The
Paul's plays seem to have terminated in 1606, and Fleay points out
that an almanac allusion in III. vi. 289 is to Tuesday, 15 July, which
fits 1606. The attack on the Puritan ministers was resented in
W. Crashaw's Paul's Cross sermon of 13 Feb. 1608 (cf. App. C, no. lvi).

The Revenger's Tragedy.   1606 < > 7

S. R. 1607, Oct. 7 (Buck). ' Twoo plaies, thone called the revengers
tragedie.' *George Eld* (Arber, iii. 360).
    1607. The Revengers Tragœdie. As it hath beene sundry times
Acted, by the Kings Maiesties Seruants. *G. Eld.*
    1608. *G. Eld.*
    Editions in Dodsley$^{1-4}$ (1744–1876), and by W. Scott (1810, *A. B. D.*
ii) and A. H. Thorndike (1912, *M. E. D.*).
    The authorship is ascribed to ' Tournour ' in Archer's list of 1656
and to ' Cyril Tourneur ' in Kirkman's lists of 1661 and 1671 (Greg,
Masques, cii). Fleay, ii. 264, is sceptical, thinking the work too good
for the author of *The Atheist's Tragedy*, and inclined to suggest
Webster. Oliphant (*M.P.* viii. 427) thinks Tourneur impossible, in
view of the difference of manner, and suggests, only to reject, Middleton. E. E. Stoll, *John Webster*, 107, 212, points out that both plays
are much under the influence of Marston, and that the date may be
fixed by the borrowing of the name and character of Dandolo from
The Fawn (1606).

The True Tragedy of Richard Duke of York > 1592
See *The Contention of York and Lancaster.*

1 Richard the Second c. 1592 < > 5

[*MS.*] *Egerton MS.* 1994. The play forms a separate section of
this composite MS. It has no title-page and a few lines at the end

are missing. The handwriting is of the late sixteenth or early seventeenth century.

Editions by J. O. Halliwell (1870) and W. Keller (1899, *Jahrbuch,* xxxv. 3.—*Dissertations* : F. I. Carpenter, *Notes on the Anonymous Richard II* (1899, *Journ. Germ. Phil.* iii. 138) ; F. S. Boas, *A Seventeenth Century Theatrical Repertoire* (*Library* for July 1917).

The play deals with an earlier part of the reign than that of Shakespeare's *Richard II*. Keller concludes from a study of parallel passages that it was known to Shakespeare, and that the author knew Marlowe's *Edward II* and *2 Henry VI*. This gives a date of about 1592–5. Fleay, ii. 320, dates the play about 1591 and assigns it, for no apparent reason, to the Queen's men. Boas accepts the date 1590–5 on internal evidence, but finds the names ' George ' and ' Toby ' in the stage-directions as players of servants' parts, and supposes the MS. to belong to a seventeenth-century revival and to have been collected with others in *Egerton MS.* 1994 by the younger William Cartwright, who was one of a late King's Revels company traceable during 1629–37 (Murray, i. 279). He identifies ' George ', rather hazardously, with George Stutfield, who belonged to this company, and ' Toby ' with an Edward Tobye, who is not known to have belonged to it, but is found in 1623 among the Children of the Revels to the late Queen Anne (Murray, i. 361 ; ii. 273). My difficulty about this is that the relation of *1 Rich. II* to Shakespeare's play is so close as to make it natural to regard it as having become a Chamberlain's play, and therefore unlikely to get into the hands of either of these Revels companies. Any company might have a George. George Bryan, for example, is a possibility. Toby, no doubt, is a rarer name. Toby Mills died in 1585, but might have left a son or godson of his name.

The True Tragedy of Richard the Third > 1594

S. R. 1594, June 19. ' An enterlude entituled, The Tragedie of Richard the Third wherein is showen the Death of Edward the FFourthe with the smotheringe of the twoo princes in the Tower, with a lamentable end of Shores wife, and the Coniunction of the twoo houses of Lancaster and Yorke.' *Thomas Creede* (Arber, ii. 654).

1594. The True Tragedie of Richard the Third : Wherein is showne the death of Edward the fourth, with the smothering of the two yoong Princes in the Tower : With a lamentable endè of Shore's wife, an example for all wicked women. And lastly the conjunction and ioyning of the two noble Houses, Lancaster and Yorke. As it was playd by the Queenes Maiesties Players. *Thomas Creede, sold by William Barley.* [Induction ; Epilogue.]

Editions in *Variorum* (1821), xix. 251, and by B. Field (1844, *Sh. Soc.*) and W. C. Hazlitt (1875, *Sh. Libr.*).—*Dissertation* : G. B. Churchill, *Richard the Third up to Shakespeare* (1900, *Palaestra,* x).

Collier, *Shakespeare,* v. 342, put the play earlier than 1588 on the ground that the epilogue in praise of Elizabeth makes no mention of the Armada. But ' She hath put proud Antichrist to flight ' may pass for such a mention. Fleay, 64, dates it about 1587: in ii. 28 he says ' 1586 or late in 1585 ' as a ballad on the subject was entered on the Stationers' Register on 15 Aug. 1586; in ii. 315 he prefers 1591, regarding the play as a continuation of *The Contention between York and Lancaster*. He considers a later date as excluded by the close of the court career of the Queen's men in 1591. This, however, did not close until 1594, and the epilogue was not necessarily given at court. Churchill also thinks the play a continuation of the *Contention*, and finds influences, not very striking, of Marlowe's *Tamburlaine, Faustus*, and *Edward II*. He concludes for 1590–1. There is very little trace of any use by Shakespeare of this play for his *Richard III*.

Boswell groundlessly took the author to be that of *Locrine* (q.v.). Fleay, ii. 315, tries to divide the scenes between Lodge and Peele, and suggests that they were re-writing Kyd.

Robin Hood > 1560

S. R. 1560, Oct. 30. ' A newe playe called ——.' *William Copland* (Arber, i. 152).

N.D. A mery geste of Robyn Hoode and of hys lyfe, wyth a newe playe for to be played in Maye games very plesaunte and full of pastyme. [*Colophon*] *Imprinted at London vpon the thre Crane wharfe by Wyllyam Copland.*

N.D. *For Edward White.*

Editions in J. Ritson, *Robin Hood* (1795), ii. 199, F. J. Child, *English and Scottish Popular Ballads*, iii (1888) 114, 127, and Manly (1897), ii. 281.

The play, which deals with the episodes of Robin Hood and the Friar and Robin Hood and the Potter, is appended to a reprint of the narrative *Geste*, originally printed by Wynken de Worde. Manly assigns Copland's edition to *c.* 1550, but Arber, v. 32, to ' *c.* 1560, by the Printer's address ', and Furnivall, *Captain Cox*, to *c.* 1561. Apparently Copland is not traceable at the Three Cranes before that year and had earlier addresses. If so, I think that his anonymous entry of 1560 in the Stationers' Register may fairly be supposed to relate to *Robin Hood*.

Ruff, Cuff and Band c. 1615

[*MS.*] *Add. MS.* 23723.

S. R. 1615, Feb. 10 (Taverner). ' A booke called a Diologue betwene Ruffe Cuffe and Band &c.' *Miles Patriche* (Arber, iii. 563).

1615. A merrie Dialogue, Betwene Band, Cuffe, and Ruffe : Done by an excellent Wit, And Lately acted in a Shew in the famous Vniversitie of Cambridge. *William Stansby for Miles Partrich.*

1615. Exchange Ware at the second hand, Viz. Band, Ruffe and Cuffe, lately out, and now newly dearned vp. Or Dialogue, acted in a Shew in the famous Vniversitie of Cambridge. The second Edition. *W. Stansby for Myles Partrich.*

1661. [Title as in ed. 1.] *For F. K.*
Editions in *Harleian Miscellany*[2], x (1813), and by J. O. Halliwell
(1849, *Contributions to Early English Literature*) and C. Hindley, *Old
Book Collector's Miscellany*, ii (1872).

The Second Maiden's Tragedy.   1611

[*MS.*] *B.M., Lansdowne MS.* 807, f. 29, formerly *penes* John Warburton. [Greg distinguishes four contemporary hands : (*a*) a scribe
or copyist of the original text and certain additions on inserted slips ;
(*b*) a corrector, probably the author ; (*c*) the Master of the Revels,
Buck ; (*d*) a theatre official, who added stage-directions. The contributions of (*b*) and (*c*) are not wholly distinguishable, especially
where mere deletions are in question, as the author may, besides
literary corrections, have made others due to the hints, or known
views, of Buck as censor. The presence of a second literary corrector
is just possible. On the verso of the last leaf Buck has written : ' This
second Maydens tragedy (for it hath no name inscribed) may wth the
reformations bee acted publikely. 31 octob[r]. 1611. G. Buc.' In
later hands are the title ' The Second Maydens Tragedy ' at the beginning, and a note following Buck's endorsed licence, which originally
ran, ' The Second Maydens Tragedy October 31th 1611 By Thomas
Goffe A Tragedy indeed '. Here Goffe's name has been cancelled,
and two successive correctors have substituted, firstly, ' George
Chapman ', and then ' By Will Shakspear'. Warburton's hand is not
discernible, and the last correction was probably made after his time,
as his list of manuscript plays (3 *Library*, ii. 232) includes ' 2[d]. p[t].
Maidens Trag̃. Geo. Chapman '.]
    S. R. 1653, Sept. 9. ' The Maid's Tragedie, 2[d]. part.' *H. Moseley*
(Eyre, i. 428).
    Editions in 1824–5 (*O. E. D.* i), Chapman's *Works* (1875, iii), and
Dodsley[4] (1875, x), and by W. W. Greg (1909, *M. S. R.*).—*Disserta-
tions*: J. Phelan, *Philip Massinger* (1879, *Anglia*, ii. 47) ; A. S. W.
Rosenbach, *The Curious-Impertinent* (1902, *M. L. N.* xvii. 179) ; W.
Nicholson, *The S. M. T.* (1912, *M. L. N.* xxvii. 33).
    The play may be assigned to the King's men, in view of stage-
directions to ll. 1724, 1928, which show that ' M[r] Goughe ' played
Memphonius and ' Rich Robinson ' the Lady. Perhaps this also explains
the ascription of authorship to Thomas Goffe, which, like those to Chapman and Shakespeare, now finds no favour. Tieck, who translated the
play in his *Shakespeare's Vorschule* (1829, ii), argued for Massinger,
whose lost *Tyrant* he took the play to be. No doubt the chief character
is only entitled ' Tyrant ' in the manuscript. But the *Tyrant* has
a separate existence both in S. R. and in Warburton's list. Fleay,
ii. 331, thought that the title was originally meant to be *The Usurping
Tyrant*, and that the play was by the author of *The Revenger's Tragedy*,
generally assigned to Tourneur. Rosenbach doubts Massinger, and
thinks Tourneur's hand traceable. Swinburne seems to have suggested
Middleton.

Selimus. 1591 < > 94

1594. The First part of the Tragicall raigne of Selimus, sometime Emperour of the Turkes, and grandfather to him that now raigneth. Wherein is showne how hee most vnnaturally raised warres against his owne father Baiazet, and preuailing therein, in the end caused him to be poysoned : Also with the murthering of his two brethren, Corcut, and Acomat. As it was playd by the Queenes Maiesties Players. *Thomas Creede.* [Prologue and Conclusion.]

1638. The Tragedy of Selimus Emperour of the Turkes. Written T. G. *For John Crooke and Richard Serger.* [Re-issue of 1594 sheets with new t.p.]

Editions by A. B. Grosart (1898, *T. D.*) and W. Bang (1908, *M. S. R.*), and in collections of Greene (q.v.).—*Dissertation* : H. Gilbert, *Robert Greene's S.* (1899, Kiel diss.) ; cf. s. *Locrine.*

The T. G. of the 1638 title-page is probably meant for Thomas Goffe, the author of contemporary plays on Turkish history. He, however, was only born in 1591. Six passages from the play are assigned to Greene in R[obert] A[llot's] *England's Parnassus* (1600). This is fairly strong evidence, and Greene's authorship is supported by Grosart, Brooke (*Sh. Apocrypha*, xix), and Gilbert. Ward and Gayley (*R.E.C.* i. 420) take the opposite view. Crawford, who points out (*E.P.* xxxv, 407) that Allot is not impeccable, prefers Marlowe. Fleay, ii. 315, would divide the play between Greene and Lodge. The problem is bound up with that of the authorship of *Locrine* (q.v.), from which *Selimus* clearly borrows. It can therefore hardly be of earlier date than 1591. The Conclusion, or epilogue, promises a second part, of which nothing is known.

Soliman and Perseda c. 1589 < > 92

S. R. 1592, Nov. 20 (Bp. of London). ' The tragedye of Salamon and Perceda.' *Edward White* (Arber, ii. 622).

N.D. The Tragedye of Solyman and Perseda. Wherein is laide open, Loues constancy, Fortunes inconstancy, and Deaths Triumphs. *Edward Allde for Edward White.* [Induction.]

1599. *E. Allde for E. White.* [In some copies ' newly corrected and amended ' is stamped on the t.p.]

[1815]. [A facs. reprint, with date 1599 and imprint *Edward Allde for Edward White,* of which two copies, C. 57. c. 15 and G. 18612, are in B.M. ; cf. W. W. Greg in *M. L. Q.* iv. 188, and R. B. McKerrow, *Bibl. Evid.* 302. Some copies have ' J. Smeeton, Printer, St. Martin's Lane ' on the vº. of the t.p.]

Editions by T. Hawkins (1773, *O.E.D.* ii), in Dodsley⁴, v (1874), and by F. S. Boas (1901, *Works of Kyd*) and J. S. Farmer (*S. F. T.*).—*Dissertations* : E. Sieper (1897, *Z. f. vergleichende Litteraturgeschichte*, N. F. x) ; G. Sarrazin, *Die Verfasser von S.u.P.* (1891, *E.S.* xv. 250) ; E. Koeppel, *Beiträge zur Geschichte des elisabethanischen Dramas* (1892, *E.S.* xvi. 357) ; J. E. Routh, *T. Kyd's Rime Schemes and the Authorship of S. P.*

and 1 Jeronimo (1905, *M.L.N.* xx. 49) ; K. Wiehl, *Thomas Kyd und die Autorschaft von S. u. P.* (1912, *E.S.* xliv. 343).

Fleay, ii. 26, Sarrazin, and Boas claim the play for Kyd, partly on grounds of style, partly because the plot is an elaboration of the ' play within the play ' of *The Spanish Tragedy* (*c.* 1589), iv. 4 ; Wiehl doubts on metrical grounds. Schick (*Archiv*, xc) suggests Peele, who is said in the *Merry Conceited Jests* (Bullen, *Peele*, ii. 389) to have written, or pretended to have written, a play of *The Knight of Rhodes*, a title which would apply to *Soliman and Perseda*. Robertson, 109, 150, 166, thinks that Greene collaborated with Kyd.

Captain Thomas Stukeley. 1596

S. R. 1600, Aug. 11 (Vicars). ' Ye history of the life and Deathe of Captaine Thomas Stucley, with his Mariage to Alexander Curtis his daughter, and his valiant endinge of his life at the battell of Alcazar.' *Thomas Pavier* (Arber, iii. 169).

1605. The Famous Historye of the life and death of Captaine Thomas Stukeley. With his marriage to Alderman Curteis Daughter, and valiant ending of his life at the Battaile of Alcazar. As it hath beene Acted. *For Thomas Pavier.*

Editions by R. Simpson (1878, *S. of S.* i) and J. S. Farmer (1911, *T. F. T.*).—*Dissertations*: E. H. C. Oliphant (1905, 10 *N. Q.* iii. 301, 342, 382) ; J. Q. Adams, *C. T. S.* (1916, *J. G. P.* xv. 107).

' Tom Stucley ' is named as a stage hero by Peele in his *Farewell* (1589) ; but the present play is probably the *Stewtley* produced by the Admiral's on 11 Dec. 1596 (Greg, *Henslowe*, ii. 181). There are allusions to ' the Theatre fields ' (611) and ' her Majesty ' (752), which may only represent historic time. Although Sebastian of Portugal is a character, there is no reference to the legend of his survival, which was well known in England in 1598. Simpson regards the play as belonging to the Chamberlain's, on the ground of certain political proclivities which he chose to ascribe to that company. The text is incoherent, and several theories representing it as a contamination of two distinct plays have been promulgated. Simpson supposed that part of a play on Don Antonio has been inserted into one dealing in five acts with Stukeley's adventures in England, Ireland, Spain, Rome, and Africa respectively, and this view is elaborated by Oliphant, who attempts to disentangle several original and revising hands, including that of John Fletcher, to whom he assigns 245–335. Fleay, i. 127, thinks that Dekker made up the play for Paul's, *c.* 1600, out of *Stewtley* and a *Mahomet* by Peele. Apparently he starts from *Satiromastix*, 980, where Horace says that Demetrius Fannius ' cut an innocent Moore i' the middle, to serue him in twice ; & when he had done, made Poules-worke of it '. But surely there is a difference between making two plays out of one and making one play out of two.

1 Tamar Cham > 1592

[*MS.*] ' The plott of The First parte of Tamar Cham.' In the possession of Steevens, but now unknown.

The text is given by Steevens, *Variorum* (1803), iii. 414 ; Boswell, *Variorum* (1821), iii. 356 ; Greg, *Henslowe Papers*, 144.

The actors' names point to a performance by the Admiral's, near 2 Oct. 1602, when they bought the book from Alleyn (cf. ch. xiii). The play was produced as ' n. e.' by the same company on 6 May 1596, but probably Henslowe's ' n. e.' in this case only indicates a substantial revision, as the letters are also attached to the notice of a performance of Part ii on 11 June 1596, and Part ii had already been played as ' n. e.' by Strange's on 28 April 1592. Obviously a Part i must already have existed (Greg, *Henslowe*, ii. 155).

The Taming of A Shrew c. 1589

S. R. 1594, May 2. ' A booke intituled A plesant Conceyted historie called " the Tayminge of a Shrowe ".' *Peter Short* (Arber, ii. 648).

1594. A Pleasant Conceited Historie, called The taming of a Shrew. As it was sundry times acted by the Right honorable the Earle of Pembrook his seruants. *Peter Short, sold by Cuthbert Burby.* [Induction.]

1596. *Peter Short, sold by Cuthbert Burby.*

1607. *V. S. for Nicholas Ling.*

Editions by J. Nicholls (1779, *Six Old Plays*, i), T. Amyot (1844, *Sh. Soc.*), W. C. Hazlitt (1875, *Sh. Libr.* vi), E. W. Ashbee (1876, facs.), F. J. Furnivall (1886, *Sh. Q*), F. S. Boas (1908, *Sh. Classics*), and J. S. Farmer (*S. F. T.*).

The Admiral's and Chamberlain's revived ' the tamynge of A shrowe ' for Henslowe on 11 June 1594, shortly after the entry in S. R. (Greg, *Henslowe*, ii. 164). Presumably it belonged to the Chamberlain's, who had acquired it from Pembroke's, and the 1594 performance may have been either of the original, or of Shakespeare's revision, *The Taming of The Shrew*, for which 1594 is a plausible date. An early reference to the printed book is in Harington's *Metamorphosis of Ajax* (1596), 95, ' For the shrewd wife, read the book of Taming a Shrew, which hath made a number of us so perfect, that now every one can rule a shrew in our country, save he that hath her '. It is to be noted that, unlike *Leire* (q.v.) and *King Lear*, the two versions counted, from the copyright point of view, as one, so that the transfer of *A Shrew* to Smethwick made an entry of *The Shrew* in S. R. for the purposes of F_1 of Shakespeare unnecessary. Probably Pembroke's in their turn got the play from the earlier Admiral's or Strange's. Its date has been placed in or before 1589, because certain lines of it appear to be parodied both in Greene's *Menaphon* of that year, and in the prefatory epistle to *Menaphon* by Nashe. Some such date is confirmed by its direct imitations from Marlowe's *Tamburlaine* (*c.* 1587) and to a less extent from *Dr. Faustus* (*c.* 1588), which are collected by Boas, 93. For author, Marlowe, Kyd, Greene, and Peele have all been suggested, but, so far as we know, Marlowe did not repeat himself, and the others did not plagiarize him, in this flagrant manner. Shakespeare also is still often credited with a hand in the old play, as well as in the revision, and the problem can best be discussed in connexion with Shakespeare. Sykes gives part to S. Rowley (q.v.).

The Thracian Wonder c. 1600

1661. Two New Playes: Viz. A Cure for a Cuckold: A Comedy. The Thracian Wonder: A Comical History. As it hath been several times Acted with great Applause. Written by John Webster and William Rowley. *Tho. Johnson, sold by Francis Kirkman.* [Separate t.p. The Thracian Wonder . . . *as above.* Epistle to the Reader, signed ' Francis Kirkman '.]

Editions by C. W. Dilke (1815, *O. E. P.* vi), and in collections of Webster (q.v.).—*Dissertations*: J. le G. Brereton, *The Relation of T. W. to Greene's Menaphon* (1906, *M. L. R.* ii. 34); J. Q. Adams, *Greene's Menaphon and T. W.* (1906, *M. P.* iii. 317); O. L. Hatcher, *The Sources and Authorship of T. W.* (1908, *M. L. N.* xxiii. 16).

The ascription of the title-page is rejected by Stoll, *Webster*, 34, and modern writers generally, although Stork, *Rowley*, 61, thinks that Rowley may have added comic touches. The use of Webster's name may be due to the identity of the plot with that of William Webster's *Curan and Argentile* (1617). But William Webster took it from Warner's *Albion's England* (1586), iv. xx. From the same source Greene took it, with a change of names, for *Menaphon* (1589), and it is *Menaphon*, with another change of names, that the play follows. Brereton ascribes it to Greene himself; Hatcher thinks that the direct plagiarisms from the source and the archaistic phrase ' old Menaphon ' (iv. 2), whereas Greene's hero is a youth, point to an early sixteenth-century admirer of Greene. Adams supports the suggestion of Fleay, i. 287, that this is the *War Without Blows and Love Without Suit* written by Heywood for the Admiral's in 1598, but this is a mere guess based on Heywood's title (Greg, *Henslowe*, ii. 199). Fleay then supposed that it was revised for Queen Anne's about 1607; elsewhere (ii. 332) he supposes it a dramatization of Webster's story for Prince Charles's about 1617.

Timon c. 1581 < > 90 (?)

[*MS.*] *Dyce MS.* 52. [Epilogue. The MS. is a transcript in two hands.]

Editions by A. Dyce (1842, *Sh. Soc.*) and W. C. Hazlitt (1875, *Sh. Libr.* ii. 2).—*Dissertation*: J. Q. Adams, *The Timon Plays* (1910, *J. G. P.* ix. 506).

Greek quotations and other pedantries suggest an academic audience, but there is little indication of place or date, beyond parallels with *Pedantius*, which lead Moore Smith (*M. L. R.* iii. 143) to suggest Cambridge and *c.* 1581–90. Adams thinks that the piece may have been performed by London schoolboys, and known to Shakespeare.

Tom Tyler and his Wife > 1563

S. R. 1562–3. ' These ballettes folowynge . . . an other of Tom Tyler.' *Thomas Colwell* (Arber, i. 210).

1661. Tom Tyler and His Wife. An Excellent Old Play, As It was Printed and Acted about a hundred Years ago. The second Impression. [Prologue and ' concluding Song '. There is no imprint, but as most of the extant copies have a variant t.p. with the additional words ' Together, with an exact Catalogue of all the playes that were ever yet printed ', and as Kirkman's catalogue of 1661 is appended, he was doubtless the publisher.]

Editions by F. E. Schelling (1900, *M. L. A.* xv. 253), G. C. Moore Smith and W. W. Greg (1910, *M. S. R.*), and J. S. Farmer (1912, *T. F. T.*).

The S. R. entry may refer to a ballad based on the play, or may possibly be a loose description of the play itself. In any case there is no reason to doubt the existence of a print of about that date. The evidence of the 1661 title-page is confirmed by the entry of ' Tom tyler ' in Archer's play-list of 1656 (Greg, *Masques*, cxii). Chetwood, who cannot be relied on, gave the date as 1598, and an inaccurate reproduction of this seems to be responsible for the 1578 of other writers. The text of 1661 has been shown by C. P. G. Scott (in Schelling's introduction) to be a rendering into seventeenth-century orthography of a play whose vocabulary may be put, with decreasing certainty, within the limits 1530–80, 1540–70, and 1550–60. The prologue says that the play is ' set out by prettie boyes ', and the ' concluding Song ' has a prayer for the preservation of the queen, ' from perilous chance that hath been seen '. Fleay, ii. 295, somewhat arbitrarily thinks the Chapel ' more likely ' to have presented it than Paul's. A misinterpretation of Kirkman's list of 1661 led E. Phillips, *Theatrum Poetarum* (1675), to assign the authorship to W. Wager (*M. S. C.* i. 325).

The Trial of Chivalry c. 1600

S. R. 1604, Dec. 4 (Pasfield). ' A book called The life and Deathe of Cavaliero Dick Boyer.' *Nathaniel Butter* (Arber, iii. 277).

1605. The History of the tryall of Cheualry, With the life and death of Caualiero Dicke Bowyer. As it hath bin lately acted by the right Honourable the Earle of Darby his seruants. *Simon Stafford for Nathaniel Butter.*

1605. This Gallant Caualiero Dicke Bowyer, Newly acted. [Another issue.]

Editions by A. H. Bullen (1884, *O. E. P.* iii) and J. S. Farmer (1912, *T. F. T.*).—*Dissertation*: C. R. Baskervill, *Sidney's Arcadia and the T. of C.* (1912, *M. P.* x. 197).

Bullen thinks this may be *Love Parts Friendship*, written by Chettle and Smith for the Admiral's in 1602 ; Fleay, ii. 318, that it may be the *Burbon* brought to the Admiral's by Pembroke's in 1597, as the Duke of Bourbon is a chief personage, and also the *Cutting Dick* to which Heywood wrote additions for Worcester's in 1602 (Greg, *Henslowe*, ii. 187, 221, 231). There is, of course, no particular reason why a play by Derby's should appear in Henslowe's diary at all. They were in London in the winters of 1599–1600 and 1600–1. The only link between them and Henslowe is Heywood, if he was the author of their *Edward IV* (q.v.). Fleay, i. 289, thinks that the present play may be by the same hands. Probably the Earl of Derby himself wrote for the company.

The Trial of Treasure > *1567*

1567. A new and mery Enterlude, called the Triall of Treasure, newly set foorth, and neuer before this tyme imprinted. *Thomas Purfoot.* [Arrangement for 5 actors ; Prologue and Epilogue, headed ' Praie for all estates '.]

Editions by J. O. Halliwell (1850, *Percy Soc.* xxviii), in Dodsley[4], iii (1874), and by J. S. Farmer (1908, *T.F.T.*).—*Dissertation* : W. W. Greg, *The T. of T.*, 1567—*A Study in Ghosts* (1910, 3 *Library*, i. 28).

Greg shows that there was only one edition, not two, of 1567. The play is a non-controversial morality, and may very well date from about 1567.

1 Troilus and Cressida. 1599 (?)

[*MS.*] *Add. MS.* 10449.   [A fragmentary ' plot ' without title, probably from Dulwich.]

The text is given by Greg, *Henslowe Papers*, 142, who infers from the names of the characters that it may have been the *Troilus and Cressida* written by Chettle and Dekker for the Admiral's in April 1599. The few names of actors are not inconsistent with this (cf. ch. xiii).

The Valiant Welshman. 1610 < > *15*

S. R. 1615, Feb. 21 (Buck). 'A play called the valiant welshman.' *Robert Lownes* (Arber, iii. 564).

1615. The Valiant Welshman, Or The True Chronicle History of the life and valiant deedes of Caradoc the Great, King of Cambria, now called Wales. As it hath beene sundry times Acted by the Prince of Wales his seruants. Written by R. A. Gent. *George Purslowe for Robert Lownes.* [Epistle to the Reader ; Induction ; Epilogue.]

1663. *For William Gilbertson.*

Editions by V. Kreb (1902) and J. S. Farmer (1913, *S. F. T.*).

Borrowings from Ben Jonson's *Alchemist* (1610) require a late date, and the assertion of Fleay, i. 26, that this is *The Welshman* revived by the Admiral's on 29 Nov. 1595 may be disregarded (Greg, *Henslowe*, ii. 178). There is nothing, beyond the initials, to connect the play with Robert Armin, and Kreb would assign it to some young University man.

A Warning for Fair Women > 1599

S. R. 1599, Nov. 17. 'A warnynge for fayre women.' *William Aspley* (Arber, iii. 151).

1599. A warning for Faire Women. Containing, The most tragicall and lamentable murther of Master George Sanders of London Marchant, nigh Shooters hill. Consented vnto By his owne wife, acted by M. Browne, Mistris Drewry and Trusty Roger agents therin : with their seuerall ends. As it hath beene lately diuerse times acted by the right Honorable, the Lord Chamberlaine his Seruantes. *Valentine Sims for William Aspley.* [Induction.]

Editions by R. Simpson (1878, *S. of S.* ii) and J. S. Farmer (*S. F. T.*).

References to 'this fair circuit' and 'this Round' are inconclusive as to whether the play was produced before the Chamberlain's went to the Globe in 1599, as their earlier houses were probably also round. E. Phillips, *Theatrum Poetarum* (1675), 113, and A. Wood, *Athenae* (1691), i. 676, assign the authorship, incredibly, to Lyly. Fleay, ii. 54, conjectures Lodge ; Bullen, *O. E. P.* iv. 1, Yarington.

The Wars of Cyrus King of Persia > 1594

1594. The Warres of Cyrus King of Persia, against Antiochus King of Assyria, with the Tragicall ende of Panthæa. Played by the children of her Maiesties Chappell. *E. A. for William Blackwal.*

Editions by W. Keller (1901, *Jahrbuch*, xxxvii. 1) and J. S. Farmer (1911, *T. F. T.*).

The play, clearly influenced by *Tamburlaine*, may rest on one by Farrant (q.v.) *c.* 1578. There is no record of any court performance by the Chapel between 1584 and 1601. Fleay, ii. 322, guesses that an allusion in Nashe's *Summer's Last Will and Testament* (q. v.) points to a performance of this play at Croydon twelve months earlier. The text is disordered. A prologue 'To the audience' is inserted in Act II at 621 and refers to a chorus, but there is none. At 367 is 'Finis Actus primi ', but 'Actus Secundus ' is at 502.

The Weakest Goeth to the Wall > 1600

S. R. 1600, Oct. 23 (Pasfield). ' A booke called, the Weakest goethe to the Walles.' *Richard Oliff* (Arber, iii. 175).

1600. The Weakest goeth to the Wall. As it hath bene sundry times plaide by the right honourable Earle of Oxenford, Lord great Chamberlaine of England his seruants. *Thomas Creede for Richard Oliue.* [Dumb Show and Prologue.]

1618. *G. P. for Richard Hawkins.*

Editions by J. S. Farmer (1911, *T. F. T.*), W. W. Greg (1912, *M. S. R.*), and with *Works* of Webster (q. v.).

The ascription of the play to Dekker and Webster by E. Phillips, *Theatrum Poetarum* (1675), 116, was rejected by Langbaine (1691) and, so far as Webster is concerned, has nothing to recommend it (E. Stoll, *Webster*, 34). Ward, iii. 56, finds Dekker's humour, and Hunt, *Dekker*, 42, thinks it Chettle's, revised by Dekker. Fleay,

ii. 114, gives it to Munday, as the only known writer for Oxford's, except Oxford himself. But he is thinking of Oxford's boy company of 1580–4, not of the later company of 1601 or earlier, to whose repertory the play probably belonged, and with whom Munday is not known to have had anything to do.

Wily Beguiled. 1596 < > 1606

S. R. 1606, Nov. 12 (Hartwell). ' A booke called Wylie beguilde &c.' *Clement Knight* (Arber, iii. 333).

1606. A Pleasant Comedie, Called Wily Beguilde. The Chiefe Actors be these : A poore Scholler, a rich Foole, and a Knaue at a shifte. *H. L. for Clement Knight.* [Induction, Prologue, and Epilogue.]

N.D. ; 1623 ; 1630 ; 1635 ; 1638.

Editions by T. Hawkins (1773, *O. E. D.* iii), in Dodsley⁴, ix (1874), and by J. S. Farmer (1912, *T. F. T.*) and W. W. Greg (1912, *M. S. R.*).— *Dissertations*: J. W. Hales, *Shakespearian Imitations* (1875, *Ath.* 1875, 17 July, 4 Sept.) ; F. J. Furnivall, *Parallels* (1875, 5 *N. Q.* iv. 144) ; P. A. Daniel, *On W. B.* (1875, *Brooke's Romeus and Juliet*, xxxv, *N. S. S.*) ; E. Landsberg, *Zur Verfasserfrage des anonymen Lustspiels W. B.* (1911, *E. S.* xliii. 189).

The register of Merton College, Oxford, has for 3 Jan. 1567 the entry, ' Acta est Wylie Beguylie Comoedia Anglica nocte in aedibus Custodis per scolares, praesentibus Vicecustode, magistris, baccalaureis, cum omnibus domesticis et nonnullis extraneis ; merito laudandi recte agendo prae se tulerunt summam spem ' (Boas, 157). No connexion is traceable between this and the extant play, which Greg and Boas regard as of Cambridge origin. But it does not seem to me markedly academic. The character Lelia does not particularly suggest the Cambridge Latin *Laelia* of 1595, and the epilogue was spoken in a ' circled rounde '. The description of himself by Churms (l. 68), as ' at Cambridge a scholler, at Cales a souldier, and now in the country a lawyer, and the next degree shal be a connicatcher ', does not go far in the way of proof. This same passage fixes the date as not earlier than the Cadiz expedition of 1596 ; obviously the use of the phrase ' tricke of Wily Beguily ' in Nashe's *Have With You to Saffron Walden* of 1596 (*Works*, iii. 107) proves nothing one way or other as to date, although Dekker naturally knew the play when he described rogues and their ' knavish comedy of Wily-Beguily ' in his *Belman of London* of 1608 (*Works*, iii. 125). If the date is 1596, the authorship of Peele, suggested by the description of the prologue-speaker as ' humorous George ', although he is clearly distinct from the ' fiery Poet ', and urged by Fleay, ii. 158, and Landsberg, becomes just possible, chronologically, before his death in November of that year. But the Shakespearian imitations, although most marked of *M. V.* and earlier plays, seem also to extend to *Hamlet, M. W.,* and *T. N.,* and the right date may be *c.* 1602–6. If the production was in the ' circled rounde ' of Paul's, the quasi-academic note is explicable Sykes suggests S. Rowley (q.v.) as part author. Fleay, *Shakespeare Manual,* 272, makes an amazing attempt to interpret the play as a satire on Lyly, Lodge, Marston, Chettle, Dekker, Drayton, Middleton, Chapman, Jonson, Henslowe, the Admiral's, the Chamberlain's, the Chapel, and Paul's. In the Induction, a juggler finds the title *Spectrum* exhibited, and later, ' *Spectrum* is conueied away : and *Wily beguiled*, stands in the place of it ' (l. 46).

The Wisdom of Doctor Dodipoll.   *1599 < > 1600*

S. R. 1600, Oct. 7. ' A booke called The Wisdom of Doctor Dodepole Plaied by the Children of Paules.' *Richard Oliff* (Arber, iii. 174).

1600. The Wisdome of Doctor Dodypoll. As it hath bene sundrie times Acted by the Children of Powles. *Thomas Creede for Richard Oliue.*

Editions by A. H. Bullen (1884, *O. E. P.* iii) and J. S. Farmer (1912, *T. F. T.*).—*Dissertation*: E. Koeppel, *Sh.'s J. C. und die Entstehungszeit des anonymen Dramas The W. of D. D.* (1907, *Jahrbuch*, xliii. 210).

Fleay, ii. 155, assigned the play to Peele, chiefly on the ground that a snatch of song is from his *Hunting of Cupid* (q.v.). But Peele died in 1596, and Koeppel points out that the phrase (Bullen, p. 129), ' Then reason 's fled to animals, I see ', presupposes the existence of *Julius Caesar* (1599), III. ii. 109 :

> O judgement ! thou art fled to brutish beasts,
> And men have lost their reason.

The Wit of a Woman > *1604*

1604. A Pleasant Comoedie, Wherein is merily shewen : The wit of a Woman. *For Edward White.* [Prologue and Epilogue.]

Editions by J. S. Farmer (1912, *T. F. T.*) and W. W. Greg (1913, *M. S. R.*).

Nothing is known of the history of this prose comedy with Italian names. ' Sweet and twenty ' (l. 753) recalls *Tw. N.* II. iii. 52.

Work for Cutlers c. *1615*

S. R. 1615, July 4 (Taverner). ' A little thing called Worke for Cutlers.' *Richard Meighen* (Arber, iii. 569).

1615. Worke for Cutlers. Or, a merry Dialogue betweene Sword, Rapier, and Dagger. Acted in a Show in the famous universitie of Cambridge. *Thomas Creede for Richard Meighen and Thomas Jones.* [Epilogue.]

Editions by T. Park (1813, *Harleian Miscellany*[2], x), C. Hindley (1872, *Old Book Collector's Miscellany*, ii), A. F. Sieveking (1904).

This short dialogue is described in the epilogue as ' a Schollers Prize '. Sieveking suggests the possibility of Heywood's authorship, but an academic author is more likely.

A Yorkshire Tragedy c. *1606*

S. R. 1608, May 2 (Wilson). ' A booke Called A Yorkshire Tragedy written by Wylliam Shakespere.' *Thomas Pavier* (Arber, iii. 377).

1608. A Yorkshire Tragedy. Not so New as Lamentable and true.

Acted by his Maiesties Players at the Globe. Written by W. Shak-
speare. *R. B. for Thomas Pauier.* [Head-title: ' All's One, or, One
of the foure plaies in one, called A York-shire Tragedy.']
   1619. Omits ' Acted . . . Globe '. *For T. P.* [See ch. xxiii.]
   Editions of 1735 (J. Tonson), by W. Knight (1843, *Pictorial Sh.* vii),
J. P. Collier (1878, *Works of Sh.*), J. S. Farmer (1910, *T.F.T.*), and
in *Sh. Apocrypha.—Dissertations* : J. P. Collier (*Ath.* 1863, i. 332);
P. A. Daniel, *Notes on Sh.'s Y. T.* 1608 (*Ath.* 4 Oct. 1879) ; S. Lee,
Walter Calverley (*D.N.B.*) ; B. Dobell, *The Author of A Y. T.* (1906,
10 *N.Q.* vi. 41) ; H. D. Sykes, *The Authorship of A Y. T.* (1917,
J.G.P. xvi. 437, reprinted in *Sidelights on Shakespeare*, 77).
   This ten-scene play from a four-play bill has merit, but most modern
critics are unable to regard that merit as of Shakespearian type,
although Ward, ii. 231, finds Shakespeare's hand in some passages,
and Fleay, after wantonly guessing at Edmund Shakespeare (*Shakespeare*, 303), remained impressed (ii. 206) by the external evidence,
and thought that the play must be Shakespeare's original ending to
an earlier version of *The Miseries of Enforced Marriage*, subsequently
altered by his collaborator, George Wilkins (q. v.), to end happily.
This is ingenious, but too conjectural. The play, like that of Wilkins,
takes its material from the history of Walter Calverley, executed for
murder on 5 Aug. 1605, which is told in Stowe's *Annales* and was the
subject of contemporary pamphlets. Dobell and Sykes argue a case
on internal evidence for the authorship of Wilkins himself.

B. MASKS

Gesta Grayorum. *1594*

[*MS.*] *Harl. MS.* 541, f. 138, contains the speeches in the Shrovetide mask, probably in the hand of Francis Davison. The opening
hymn is not included, and the final hymn seems to have been added
by another hand.
   1688. Gesta Grayorum : or, the History Of the High and mighty
Prince Henry Prince of Purpoole, Arch-Duke of Stapulia and Ber-
nardia, Duke of High and Nether Holborn, Marquis of St. Giles and
Tottenham, Count Palatine of Bloomsbury and Clerkenwell, Great
Lord of the Cantons of Islington, Kentish-Town, Paddington and
Knights-bridge, Knight of the most Heroical Order of the Helmet,
and Sovereign of the Same. Who Reigned and Died, A.D. 1594.
Together with A Masque, as it was presented (by His Highness's
Command) for the Entertainment of Q. Elizabeth ; who, with the
Nobles of both Courts, was present thereat. *For W. Canning.* [Epistle
to Matthew Smyth, of the Inner Temple, signed ' W. C.' The publica-
tion is recorded in Trinity Term 1688 (Arber, *London Term Catalogues,*
ii. 230).]
   Editions in Nichols, *Elizabeth*[1, 2], iii. 262 (1807–23), and by W. W.
Greg (1914, *M.S.R.*) and B. Brown (1921).
   This is a narrative of the reign of a Christmas Prince, or Lord of

Misrule (cf. *Mediaeval Stage,* i. 417), appointed at Gray's Inn for the Christmas of 1594. The Prince was a Norfolk man, Henry Helmes, and a list of the members of the Inn who held positions at his court is given in the tract. The revels began on St. Thomas's Eve, 20 Dec., continued until Twelfth Night, were resumed at Candlemas, and again at Shrovetide, when the Prince's reign terminated.

On Innocents' Day, 28 Dec., at night, the Inner Temple were entertained, and a stage set up, but the crowd was too great for the 'inventions' contemplated, and 'it was thought good not to offer any thing of account, saving dancing and revelling with gentlewomen ; and after such sports, a Comedy of Errors (like to *Plautus* his *Menechmus*) was played by the players. So that night was begun, and continued to the end, in nothing but confusion and errors ; whereupon, it was ever afterwards called, *The Night of Errors* '. On 30 Dec. an indictment was preferred against a supposed sorcerer, containing a charge ' that he had foisted a company of base and common fellows, to make up our disorders with a play of errors and confusions ; and that that night had gained to us discredit, and itself a nickname of Errors '. Presumably the players of Shakespeare's *Comedy of Errors* were the Chamberlain's men, and the Treasurer of the Chamber's record (App. B) of a play at court by these men, as well as the Admiral's, on 28 Dec. is a slip for 27 Dec. (*M. L. R.* ii. 10).

On 3 Jan. many nobles were entertained with a show illustrating the amity of Graius and Templarius. It was followed by speeches from six ' Councellors ', advising respectively ' the Exercise of War ', ' the Study of Philosophy ', ' Eternizement and Fame, by Buildings and Foundations ', ' Absoluteness of State and Treasure ', ' Vertue, and a Gracious Government ', and ' Pass-times and Sports '. These are ascribed by Spedding, i. 342, to Francis Bacon (q.v.), a view which finds some confirmation in the fact that the Alnwick MS., many of the contents of which are by Bacon, once contained a copy of some ' Orations at Graies Inne Revells ' (Burgoyne, xii). It is amusing to note that on 5 Dec. 1594 Lady Bacon, his mother, wrote to his brother Anthony, ' I trust they will not mum nor mask nor sinfully revel at Gray's Inn ' (Spedding, i. 326). The speeches of three of the ' Councellors ', with one by the Prince, are also preserved, without ascription, in *Inner Temple Petyt MS.* 583, 43, f. 294.

On 6 Jan. appeared six Knights of the Helmet ' in a very stately mask, and danced a new devised measure ; and after that they took to them ladies and gentlewomen, and danced with them their galliards, and so departed with musick '.

On 1 Feb. the Prince visited Greenwich, and promised to return at Shrovetide. On his way back, he was met with a Latin oration by a boy at St. Paul's School.

At Shrovetide, the Prince took his mask to the court at Whitehall. The maskers were the Prince of Purpoole and his Seven Knights ; the torchbearers eight Pigmies ; the presenters Proteus, Thamesis, Amphitrite, and one of the Prince's Esquires ; the musicians two Tritons, two Nymphs, and a Tartarian Page.

The performance was upon a stage. After a hymn, the presenters made speeches setting out how the Prince and Knights were in an Adamantine Rock, to be released by Proteus, on the discovery of a Power (the Queen) of more attractive virtue. The maskers issued from the Rock, and danced ' a new devised measure, &c.' ; then took ladies, and danced ' their galliards, courants, &c.' ; then danced ' another new measure '. The Pigmies brought in eight escutcheons, with the maskers' impresses, which the Esquire presented to the Queen. The maskers then entered the rock, while another hymn was sung.

The maskers were Henry Helmes (Prince), William Cooke, Jarvis Tevery, John Lambert, Molineux, Grimes, Paylor, and Campnies.

After the mask, the courtiers danced a measure, and Elizabeth said, ' What ! shall we have bread and cheese after a banquet ? '

The maskers were presented to the Queen ' on the next day ' and praised by her. The narrative goes on to record that ' the same night ' was fighting at barriers, in which the Prince took part as a defendant with the Earl of Cumberland against the Earl of Essex and other challengers, and won the prize ; and concludes, ' Thus on *Shrove-Tuesday*, at the Court, were our sports and revels ended '. The dating is not quite clear, but it seems probable that the mask and barriers were both on the Tuesday, and the presentation on Ash Wednesday, presumably as the Queen went to chapel. Conceivably, however, the mask was on Monday, and the presentation and barriers on Tuesday. The Gray's Inn records (Fletcher, 107) note a disbursement on 11 Feb. 1595 to William Johnson and Edward Morrys, who served as the Prince's Lord Chancellor and Lord Treasurer, of 100 marks for ' the gentlemen for their sports & shewes this Shrovetyde at the court before the Queens Majestie '. There was also a levy on 8 May for the ' shewes & desports ' of sums varying from 4s. to 10s. according to status, while the public stock of the house was to contribute £30.

The speeches in the mask were apparently by Francis Davison, one of the Prince's Gentlemen Pensioners, who included in his *Poetical Rapsody* (1602), sign. D 3 v⁰, amongst Sonnets, &c., 'To his first Loue', one ' Vpon presenting her with the speech of Grayes-Inne Maske at the Court 1594, consisting of three partes, The Story of Proteus Transformations, the wonders of the Adamantine Rocke, and a speech to her Maiestie '. The *Poetical Rapsody*, sign. K 8, also contains the opening hymn of the mask, which begins ' Of Neptune's Empyre let us sing ', and ascribes it to Thomas Campion (q.v.). Whether ' The Song at the ending ', which according to Dr. Greg has been inserted in *Harl. MS.* 541 by a later hand, is also Campion's must remain doubtful. The MS. as originally written is just such a present as Davison may have sent to his mistress. A list of ' Papers lent ' by Davison in *Harl. MS.* 298 includes ' Grayes In Sportes under Sᵣ Henry Helmes. Eleaz. Hogdson '.

The Twelve Months. *1608–12*

[*MS.*] Formerly *penes* Collier, but not now among his papers in
Egerton MS. 2623.

Editions by J. P. Collier, *Five Court Masques* (1848), 131, with title
' The Masque of the Twelve Months '.

The maskers are the twelve Months ; the antimaskers Pages ; the
presenters Madge Howlet, Pigwiggen a Fairy, Beauty, Aglaia, the
Pulses, Prognostication, and Somnus ; the musicians the twelve
Spheres.

The locality is not given, but the presence of a king is contemplated.
The text is disordered, but can easily be reconstructed, as follows :
Madge Howlet, 'going up towards the King', and Pigwiggen speak
the opening dialogue (Collier, 137). The Spheres sing the first song
calling Beauty from her fort, the Heart (140). This is the scene ;
on it are plumes, ' the ensignes of the darling of the yeare, delicious
Aprill '. Beauty, Aglaia, and the Pulses, ' beating before them up
towardes the King ', speak a dialogue (131). The Pages dance an
' antemasque ' (133). Beauty and Aglaia speak a dialogue (134). The
maskers appear, and are presented by Beauty (134). The second
' antemasque ' is danced (134). Beauty and Aglaia speak a dialogue
(134). Prognostication enters, and prognosticates (135). The maskers
descend, and Beauty describes April, a prince ' lov'd of all, yett will
not love ', with a ' triple plume ' (135). After a second song, ' they
dance their entrie ' (141). Beauty and Aglaia speak a dialogue (136).
There is a third song (141). ' They dance their mayne dance : which
done, Bewty invites them to dance with the Ladies ' (137). There
is a fourth song (142). ' They dance with the Ladies, and the whole
Revells follows ' (137). Beauty calls on Somnus (140). There is
a last song (142). ' They dance their going off ' (140).

Brotanek, 346, suggests 1 Jan. 1612 as a probable date. I agree
with him that ' charming all warre from his mild monarchie ' (136)
suggests James I, although I do not think that ' our fairy King ' (137)
is necessarily a reminiscence of the *Mask of Oberon,* especially as this
fairy king is James and not Henry. In any case ' the heart of the
yeare ' (132), ' prime of this newe yeare ' (135), ' this winter nighte '
(141) do not require a performance on 1 Jan. In fact, April and not
January leads the months in the mask. I would add to Brotanek's
notes that April is clearly danced by a Prince of Wales, and that
'lov'd of all, yett will not love' fits in with the uncertainty as to
Henry's matrimonial intentions which prevailed in 1612. But he is
not very likely to have given two masks in the winter of 1611–12,
nor is there any evidence of any mask that winter except the *Love
Restored* of 6 Jan. Of course *The Twelve Months* may never have
been actually performed. I have thought that it might have been
the mask abandoned by Anne on account of the death of the Queen
of Spain in Dec. 1611 (cf. Jonson, *Love Restored*). Beauty, ' our
fairy Queene ', is said to be ' Great president of all those princely
revells ' in honour of the ' fairy King '. But the mask is danced by

men, not women, which seems to put a Queen's mask out of the question. No mask has yet been traced in the winter of 1609-10. I am afraid I must leave the date open. If Henry led the dance, his death in Nov. 1612 gives one limit. The 'antemasque' is more likely to have been introduced after than before 1608. The use of Pigwiggen as a fairy name recurs in Drayton's *Nymphidia*, published in 1627.

Mask of Flowers. 6 Jan. 1614

S. R. 1614, Jan. 21 (Nidd). 'The maske of flowers by the gent. of Graies Inne vppon Twelfe Night 1613.' *Robert Wilson* (Arber, iii. 540).

1614. The Maske of Flowers. Presented By the Gentlemen of Graies-Inne, at the Court of White-hall, in the Banquetting House, vpon Twelfe night, 1613. Being the last of the Solemnities and Magnificences which were performed at the marriage of the right honourable the Earle of Somerset, and the Lady Francis daughter of the Earle of Suffolke, Lord Chamberlaine. *N. O. for Robert Wilson.* [With Epistle to Sir Francis Bacon by I. G., W. D., T. B. These initials, presumably of Gray's Inn men, have not been identified.]

Editions in Nichols, *James* (1828), ii. 735, and H. A. Evans, *English Masques* (1897).

The maskers, in white embroidered with carnation and silver and vizards, were thirteen transformed Flowers ; the antimaskers in ' the anticke-maske of daunce ' Pantaloon, Courtesan, Swiss and his Wife, Usurer, Midwife, Smug and his Wench, Fretelyne, Bawd, Roaring Boy, Citizen, Mountebank, Jewess of Portugal, Chimney-Sweeper and his Wench ; the musicians twelve Garden Gods, also described as Priests, and in the ' anticke-maske of the song ' Miller, Wine Cooper, Vintner's Boy, Brewer, Skipper, Fencer, Pedlar, Barber ; the presenters Invierno, Primavera, Gallus the Sun's Post, Silenus, Kawasha, and attendants.

The locality was the Banqueting House, at the lower end of which was a ' travers painted in perspective ', as a city wall and gate, with temples of Silenus and Kawasha on either side. The antimasks represented a challenge, directed by the Sun, between wine and tobacco. ' The travers being drawne ' disclosed an elaborate garden sloping up to a mount and arbour (33 ft. long × 21 ft. high) with a bank of flowers before it. Upon a charm the flowers vanished to give place to the maskers, who danced their first and second measure, then took ladies, for ' measures, corantoes, durettoes, morascoes, galliards ', and then ' daunced their parting measure ', which was followed by compliments to the king and the bride and groom.

For general notices of the Somerset wedding masks, cf. s.v. Campion, *Mask of Squires.* On 23 Dec. Chamberlain wrote to Carleton (Birch, i. 282), ' Sir Francis Bacon prepares a masque to honour this marriage, which will stand him in above £2000 ; and though he have been offered some help by the House, and specially by Mr. Solicitor, Sir Henry Yelverton, who would have sent him £500, yet he would not accept it, but offers them the whole charge with the honour. Marry, his obligations are such, as well to his majesty as to the great lord and to the whole house of Howards, as he can admit no partner'. On 5 Jan. (Birch, i. 288) he briefly notes, ' Mr. Attorney's masque is for to-morrow, and for a conclusion of Christmas and these shows together '.

The records of Gray's Inn confirm Chamberlain's account, by giving no signs that any expense fell on the Inn. On a letter by Bacon which may refer to this occasion, cf. s.v. Bacon.

Osborne, *James*, 82, a not very accurate writer, speaks of a Gray's Inn mask at court, following an Anglo-Scottish quarrel between Mr. Hawley of Gray's Inn and Mr. Maxwell. Probably he has this mask, which was to honour a Scot, in mind. The quarrel was in fact over in June 1612 (Birch, i. 173). I doubt whether either this mask or the joint Gray's Inn and Inner Temple mask of 1612–13 had anything to do with it.

C. RECEPTIONS AND ENTERTAINMENTS

Coronation Triumph.   1559

S. R. 1558–9. ' The passage of the quenes maiesties Throwoute the Cytie of London.' *Richard Tottle* (Arber, i. 96).

1558 [9], Jan. 23. The Passage of our most drad Soueraigne Lady Quene Elyzabeth through the citie of London to westminster the daye before her coronacion. *Richard Tottill. Cum privilegio.*

N.D. [1604.] The Royal Passage of her Majesty from the Tower of London to her Palace of Whitehall, with all the Speaches and Devices, both of the Pageants and otherwise, together with her Majesties severall Answers, and most pleasing Speaches to them all. *S. S. for Jone Millington.*

N.D. [1604.] *S. S. for John Busby.* [Another issue.]

Editions in Nichols, *Eliz.* i. 38 (1823), and A. F. Pollard, *Tudor Tracts (England's Garner²)*, 365.

There are also accounts in Machyn, 186, and in Holinshed (1808), iv. 158. For a list of the pageants cf. ch. iv.

Bristol Entertainment.   August 1574

1575. The whole Order howe our Soveraigne Ladye Queene Eliza-beth was receyved into the Citie of Bristowe, in August, and the Speeches spoken before her presens at her Entry ; with the residue of Versis and Matter that might not be spoken (for distance of the place), but sent in a Book over the Waetter. *Thomas Marshe.* [In ' *The Firste Parte of Churchyardes Chippes, contayning Twelve seuerall Labours.* Devised and published, only by Thomas Churchyard, Gentil-man '. Epistle to Christopher Hatton.]

1578. *Thomas Marsh.*

Editions in Nichols, *Eliz.* i. 393 (1788, 1823), and by J. P. Collier (1867).

Probably Churchyard was the deviser of the entertainment, as he calls the *Chippes* 'a book of all my English verses in meter'. He says, 'Some of these Speeches could not be spoken, by means of a Scholemaister, who envied that any stranger should set forth these Shows'. *A worthie Dittie, song before the Queens Majestie at Bristow*, by D. S[and], not in the Entertainment, is in *The Paradise of Daynty Devises* (1576). Elizabeth was at Bristol 13–21 Aug. 1574 and lay at John Young's. Fame, a boy with a speech in English verse, met her at the High Cross. At the next gate were Salutation, Gratulation, and Obedient Good Will, with their verses. On 14 Aug. the Queen attended divine service at the College. On 15 and 16 Aug. the Forts of Peace and Feeble Policy were arrayed, and there were sham fights by land and sea, with speeches by Dissuasion, Persuasion, and John Roberts, who apparently wrote his own. Was he the envious schoolmaster ?

Kenilworth Entertainment.   1575

There are two descriptions :

A. By *Gascoigne*

1576. The Princelye pleasures, at the Courte at Kenelwoorth. That is to saye, The Copies of all such verses Proses, or Poeticall inuentions, and other Deuices of pleasure, as were there deuised, and presented by sundry Gentle men, before the Quenes Maiestie : In the yeare 1575. *Richard Jones.* [The unique copy is believed to have been burnt in the Shakespeare Library at Birmingham. The printer's Epistle is dated March 26, 1576.]

1587. [Part of *Collection.*]

Editions in Nichols, *Eliz.*[2] i. 486 (1823), and elsewhere (cf. Schelling, 121).

B. By *Robert Laneham*

1575. A letter : Whearin part of the entertainment untoo the Queez Majesty at Killingwoorth Castl, in Warwick Sheer in this Soomerz Progress, 1575, is signified : from a freend officer attendant in the Coourt untoo hiz freend a Citizen, and Merchaunt of London. [*No imprint or colophon.*]

Editions in Nichols, *Eliz.*[2] i. 420 (1823), by F. J. Furnivall, *Captain Cox, his Ballads and Books* (1871, *Ballad Soc.* ; 1890, *N. S. S.*), in *Sh.-Jahrbuch*, xxvii, 251 (1892), and elsewhere (cf. Furnivall, ix, clxxvi).

Elizabeth was at Kenilworth 9–27 July 1575. The diary of entertainments is given in ch. iv. The contributions of specific authors were as follows :

9 July. Speeches of Sibylla, by Williäm Hunnis ; the Porter Hercules, by John Badger ; the Lady of the Lake, by George Ferrers ; a Poet, in Latin, by Richard Mulcaster, or Mercury (?) Paten. It is

uncertain which was used ; Gascoigne prints Mulcaster's, Laneham Paten's.

11 July. Dialogue of a Savage Man and Echo, ' devised, penned, and pronounced ' by Gascoigne.

18 July. Device of the Delivery of the Lady of the Lake, by William Hunnis, with verses by Hunnis, Ferrers, and Henry Goldingham, who played Arion.

20 July. Device of Zabeta prepared by Gascoigne, but not shown.

27 July. Device of the Farewell of Silvanus, by Gascoigne.

Woodstock Entertainment.   1575

See ch. xxiii, s.v. SIR HENRY LEE.

Suffolk and Norfolk Entertainments.   August 1578

There are two contemporary descriptions :

A

S. R. 1578, Aug. 30. 'The ioyfull Receavinge of the Quenes maiestie into Norwyche.' *Henry Bynneman* (Arber, ii. 336).

N.D. The Ioyfull Receyuing of the Queenes most excellent Maiestie into her Highnesse Citie of Norwich : The things done in the time of hir abode there : and the dolor of the Citie at hir departure.   Wherein are set down diuers Orations in Latine, pronounced to hir Highnesse by Sir Robert Wood Knight, now Maior of the same Citie, and others : and certain also deliuered to hir Maiestie in writing : euery of thē turned into English.   *Henrie Bynneman.*   [Epistle by Ber[nard] Gar[ter] to Sir Owen Hopton.]

Edition in Nichols, *Eliz.* (1823), ii. 136.

B

S. R. 1578, Sept. 20. ' The enterteignement of the Quenes Maiestie in Suffolk and Norffolk ; gathered by Thomas Churchyard.'   *Henry Bynneman* (Arber, ii. 338).

N.D. A Discourse of the Queenes Maiesties entertainement in Suffolk and Norffolk :   With a description of many things then presently seene.   Deuised by Thomas Churchyarde, Gent. with diuers shewes of his own inuention sette out at Norwich : . . . *Henrie Bynneman.* [Epistle by Churchyard to Gilbert Garrard.   Adnitt (cf. s.v. Churchyard) says there were two issues with varying prefatory matter.]

Extracts in Nichols, *Eliz.* (1823), ii. 115, 128, 130, 133, 179.

A ballad and a sonnet, presumably from their titles based on A, were registered by J. Charlwood and R. Jones respectively on 24 and 31 March 1579 (Arber, ii. 349, 350).

Elizabeth was at Norwich 16–22 Aug. 1578.   The diary is as follows :

16 Aug. 1578.   Oration by Mayor at Hartford Bridge ; Speech, prepared but prevented by rain, of King Gurgunt in Town Close

near Blanch Flower Castle; Pageant of the Commonwealth, with representations of local loom industries, and speech by Garter in St. Stephen's Street; Pageant of the City of Norwich, Deborah, Judith, Esther, and Queen Martia, with the City Waits and songs by Garter and Churchyard, at entry to Market-place; Speech of a Turkish Boy by Churchyard, at Mr. Peck's door.

18 Aug. Speech of Mercury in an elaborate coach, by Churchyard.

19 Aug. Show of Chastity, with dialogue and song of Chastity, Cupid, a Philosopher, Wantonness, Riot, Modesty, Temperance, Good Exercise, and Shamefastness, by Churchyard; Oration by Minister of Dutch Church.

20 Aug. Oration by Stephen Limbert, Master of the Grammar School.

21 Aug. Shows of Water Nymphs, with speeches, and of Manhood and Desert, a contention of Manhood, Good Favour, Desert, and Good Fortune, for Lady Beauty, prepared but prevented by rain, both by Churchyard; Mask by Henry Goldingham in Privy Chamber after supper of Jupiter, Juno, Mars, Venus, Apollo, Pallas, Neptune, Diana, Mercury as presenter, Cupid, torchbearers and musicians, who marched about the chamber and made speeches and characteristic gifts, but apparently did not dance.

22 Aug. Speech and Song at St. Benet's Gate by Garter; Show of Fairies with their Queen and seven speeches, outside the gate, by Churchyard; written Oration by Mayor at departure over City boundary.

Churchyard also mentions 'speeches well sette out and a speciall device much commended' in the park of the Earl of Surrey at Kenninghall on 12 Aug.; also divers 'triumphes and devises' in Suffolk, of which he only specifies 'a shew representing the Phayries (as well as might be) . . . in the whiche shew a rich jewell was presented to the Queenes Highnesse' at Sir Thomas Kidson's house, Hengrave Hall, during 28–30 Aug. In *Churchyards Challenge* (1593) he claims 'The whole deuises pastimes and plaies at Norwich, before her Maistie', and also 'The Commedy before her Maestie at Norwich in the fielde when she went to dinner to my Lady Gerninghams' at Costessy (19 Aug.).

Fortress of Perfect Beauty. *15–16 May 1581*

S. R. 1581, July 1. 'The Tryumphe Shewed before the Quene and the Ffrenche Embassadors.' *Robert Walgrave* (Arber, ii. 396).

N.D. A brief declaratiõ of the shews, deuices, speeches, and inuentions, done & performed before the Queenes Maiestie, & the French Ambassadours, at the most valiaunt and worthye Triumph, attempted and executed on the Munday and Tuesday in Whitson weeke last, Anno 1581. Collected, gathered, penned & published, by Henry Goldwel, Gen. *Robert Waldegrave.* [Epistle by Goldwell to Rowland Brasebridge of Great Wycombe.]

Edition in Nichols, *Eliz.*[2] (1823), ii. 310.

This was a tilt, before François of Bourbon, dauphin of Auvergne, Artus de Cossé, marshal of France, and other commissioners from France, for the treaty of marriage between Elizabeth and the Duke of Anjou. The challenge was delivered by a boy in red and white, as the Queen came from Chapel on 16 April 1581. The tilt, first fixed for 24 April, was put off to 1 May, 8 May, and finally 15 May. The gallery at the end of the tilt-yard was named the Castle or Fortress of Perfect Beauty, and the challengers, the Earl of Arundel, Lord Windsor, Philip Sidney, and Fulke Greville, called themselves the Four Foster Children of Desire. They entered from the stable, with trains of followers and a Rowling Trench of printed canvas, to besiege the fortress. From this boys spoke and sang, and cannonades of perfumes were shot off, while flowers and other fancies were flung from scaling ladders. Then came twenty-one defendants, each with his 'invention' and speech. They were Henry Grey, Sir Thomas Perot, Anthony Cooke, Thomas Ratcliffe, Henry Knolles, William Knolles, Robert Knolles, Francis Knolles, Rafe Bowes, Thomas Kelwaie, George Goring, William Tresham, Robert Alexander, Edward Dennie, Hercules Meautus, Edward Moore, Richard Skipwith, Richard Ward, Edward Digbie, Henry Nowell, Henry Brunkerd. Perot and Cooke were 'both in like armour, beset with apples and fruit, the one signifying Adam and the other Eve, who had haire hung all down his helmet'. Their page was an Angel. Ratcliffe was a Desolate Knight, with a page who presented his shield. The four Knolles brothers were Sons of Despair, with Mercury for a page. The speeches of the pages are given. Each defendant ran six courses with the challengers. ' In the middest of the running came in Sir Henrie Leigh, as unknowne, and when he had broken his six staves, went out in like manner againe.' At the end of the first day the boy who gave the challenge announced a second on the morrow.

On the second day the challengers entered in a chariot ' forewearied and half overcome' with a lady representing Desire, and a consort of music. A herald made a speech for them. The defendants entered, and the tournay and barriers followed. At the end a boy clad in ash colour and bearing an olive-branch made submission of the challengers to the Queen.

Foulkes, lxiii. 49, says that a set of blank cheques for this tilt are in *Ashm. MS.* 845, f. 166.

Tilbury Visit. 1588

There are or were three accounts :

A

S. R. 1588, Aug. 10. ' The quenes visitinge the campe at Tilberye and her enterteynement there the 8 and 9 of August 1588, with condicon yat yt may be aucthorised hereafter.' *John Wolf* (Arber, ii. 495).

N.D. The Queenes visiting of the Campe at Tilsburie with her

Entertainment there. *Iohn Wolfe for Edward White.* [At end, ' T. D.', doubtless the initials of Thomas Deloney.]

Editions in A. F. Pollard, *Tudor Tracts* (*England's Garner²*), 492, and F. O. Mann, *Deloney's Works* (1912).

B

S. R. 1588, Aug. 10 (Stallard). A ioyfull songe of the Roiall Receaving of the quenes maiestie into her Campe at Tilbery : the 8 and 9 of August 1588.' *John Wolf for Richard Jones* (Arber, ii. 496). [It does not seem likely that this entry relates to Aske's book.]

C

1588. Elizabetha Triumphans. By James Aske. *Thomas Orwin for Thomas Gubbin and Thomas Newman.*

Edition in Nichols, *Eliz.* ii. 545 (1823).

The two extant narratives are discussed by M. Christy in *E.H.R.* xxxiv. 43.

Tilt-yard Entertainment.   17 Nov. 1590

See ch. xxiii, s.v. Lee.

Cowdray Entertainment.   1591

1591. The Speeches and Honorable Entertainment giuen to the Queenes Maiestie in Progresse, at Cowdrey in Sussex, by the right Honorable the Lord Montacute. *Thomas Scarlet, sold by William Wright.*

1591. The Honorable Entertainment. . . . *Thomas Scarlet, sold by William Wright.* [A different text, with a fuller description, but without the words of the songs, and inaccurately dated.]

Editions by J. Nichols, *Eliz.²* iii. 90 (1823), and R. W. Bond, *Lyly,* i. 421 (1902).

The host was Anthony Browne, first Viscount Montague. Gascoigne's mask of 1572 was also written for him. Bond assigns the present entertainment, conjecturally, to Lyly. McKerrow, 20, records that William Barley, the stationer, was brought before the High Commission for selling at Cowdray, on some date before 1598, a twopenny book relating to Her Majesty's progress.

The diary is as follows :

14 Aug. 1591. Speech by a Porter at the bridge on arrival at night.

15 Aug. Sunday : a day of rest.

16 Aug. Hunting in Park, and delivery of bow with a ditty by a Nymph.

17 Aug. Dinner at the Priory, where Lord Montague lodged, and speeches in the walks by a Pilgrim and a Wild Man, at an oak hung with Sussex escutcheons, and a ditty before hunting.

18 Aug. Speeches and ditty by an Angler and offering of fish by a Netter at a pond in the walks before hunting.

19 Aug. Dance of country people with tabor and pipe.

20 Aug. Knighting, and departure to Chichester for dinner.

Elvetham Entertainment. 1591

S. R. 1591, Oct. 1. 'The honorable entertaynement gyven to the quenes maiestie in progresse at Elvetham in Hampshire by the righte honorable the Erle of Hertford.' *John Wolf* (Arber, ii. 596).

1591. The Honorable Entertainement gieuen to the Queenes Maiestie in Progresse, at Eluetham in Hampshire, by the right Honorable the Earle of Hertford. *John Wolfe.* [There appear to be two editions or issues, (*a*) without and (*b*) with a woodcut of the pond.]

1591. . . . Newly corrected and amended. [This has a woodcut of the pond, different from that in (1) (*b*).]

Editions by J. Nichols, *Eliz.* ii. (1788), iii. 101 (1823), and R. W. Bond, *Lyly*, i. 431.

Elizabeth was at Elvetham 20–23 Sept. 1591. The host was Edward Seymour, Earl of Hertford. A Three Men's Song of Phillida and Coridon, which formed part of the Entertainment, is ascribed in *England's Helicon* (1600) and *MSS.* to Nicholas Breton. Bond ascribes the Entertainment to Lyly. An account of the amusements is in ch. iv.

Bisham, Sudeley, and Rycote Entertainments. 1592

1592. Speeches deliuered to her Maiestie this last progresse, at the Right Honorable the Lady Russels, at Bissam, the Right Honorable the Lorde Chandos at Sudley, at the Right Honorable the Lord Norris, at Ricorte. *Joseph Barnes, Oxford.* [There appear to be two issues, with slight variants.]

Editions by J. Nichols, *Eliz.*[2] iii. 130 (1823), Sir S. E. Brydges (1815), and R. W. Bond, *Lyly*, i. 471 (1902).

Bisham

The hosts were Sir Edward Hoby and his mother, Elizabeth, Dowager Lady Russell.

21 Aug. 1592. On arrival, at the top of the hill, speech by a Wild Man; at the middle of the hill, dialogue of Pan and two Virgins, Sybilla and Isabella; at the foot of the hill, ditty by Ceres and Nymphs in a harvest-cart, followed by speech and gift of crown of wheat-ears and jewel.

Sudeley

The host was Giles Brydges, third Lord Chandos.

10 Sept. 1592. Speech of old Shepherd at entry to castle.

11 Sept. Show of Apollo and Daphne, with gift of tables of verses.

12 Sept. Contemplated Presentation of High Constable of Cotswold, and Choosing of King and Queen by Shepherds, with song and dialogue of Meliboeus, Nisa, and Cutter of Cotswold—prevented by weather.

Rycote

The host was Henry, Lord Norris.

28 Sept. 1592. On arrival from Oxford, speech by an Old Gentleman [Lord Norris].

2 Oct. Music in garden, with speech by Old Gentleman, and letters containing jewels by messengers as from his sons in Ireland, Flanders, and France.

3 Oct. At departure, letter with jewel as from daughter in Jersey.

Between Sudeley and Rycote, the Queen was entertained at Oxford (cf. ch. iv) and Woodstock (cf. ch. xxiii, s.v. Sir Henry Lee).

Tilt-yard Entertainment. 17 Nov. 1595

See ch. xxiii, s.v. Peele, *Anglorum Feriae.*

Harefield Entertainment. 1602

Elizabeth was at Harefield Place, Middlesex, the house of Sir Thomas Egerton, Lord Keeper, and his wife Alice, Countess Dowager of Derby, from 31 July to 2 Aug. 1602. At the same house Milton's *Arcades* was performed before Lady Derby in 1634. Seven fragments of the entertainment have been preserved, and are printed by Nichols, *Eliz.* iii. 570, 586, and Bond, *Lyly,* i. 491. Accounts of expenditure involved, and a list of the gifts in kind contributed by Egerton's friends on this occasion are in *Egerton Papers,* 340, but the account in 342-4 is a forgery (*vide infra*).

(i) Dialogue between a Bailiff and Dairymaid, and presentation of a rake and fork to the Queen, as she entered the demesne near the dairy house.

(ii) Dialogue at the steps of the house, and presentation of a heart, by Place ' in a partie-colored roobe, like the brick house ' and Time ' with yeollow haire, and in a green roabe, with an hower glasse, stopped, not runninge '.

(iii) Verse petition accompanying gift of a robe of rainbows on behalf of St. Swithin by Lady Walsingham on Monday morning [2 Aug.].

(iv) Farewell of Place, ' attyred in black mourning aparell ' on the Queen's departure, with presentation of an anchor.

(v) Verse ' Complaint of the Satyres against the Nymphes '.

(vi) Song and speech by a Mariner, who entered the ' presence ' with a lottery box, ' supposed to come from the Carricke '.

(vii) ' The Severall Lottes ', a list of gifts and blanks, with a poesy accompanying each, and the names of the ladies who drew them. These were the Queen, the Dowager Countess of Derby, the Countesses of Derby, Worcester, and Warwick, Lady Scroope, Mistresses Nevill, Thynne, Hastinges, and Bridges, Ladies Scudamore, Francis, Knevette, and Susan Vere, Mrs. Vavissour, Ladies Southwell and Anne Clifford, Mrs. Hyde, Ladies Kildare, Howard of Effingham and Paget, Mistresses Kiddermister and Strangwidge, the Mother of the Maids, Ladies Cumberland, Walsingham, and Newton, Mrs. Wharton, Ladies Digbye and Dorothy [Hastinges] and Mrs. Anselowe. One name, ending in ' liffe ' is illegible. It may be Ratcliffe. One MS. adds three lots assigned to ' country wenches '. Most of these ladies were maids

of honour and others who came with the court ; one or two, e.g.
Mrs. Kiddermister, were country neighbours of the Egerton's.

These pieces are derived from various sources :

(*a*) A transcript made by R. Churton in 1803 of a contemporary
MS. found at Arbury, the house of Sir Roger Newdigate, to whose
family Harefield passed in 1675, contains (i)–(v) and was printed by
Nichols.

(*b*) A *Conway MS.*, printed by P. Cunningham in *Sh. Soc. Papers*,
ii. 65, contains (iii), the song from (vi), and (vii), with the heading
' The Devise to entertayne hir M^{ty} at Harfielde . . .' and the date 1602.

(*c*) The second edition (1608) of Francis Davison's *Poetical Rhapsody*
contains the speech from (vi) and (vii), with the incorrect indication
' at the Lord Chancellor's house, 1601 ', which misled Nichols into
supposing it to belong to some entertainment at York Place, the year
before that of Harefield. The item comes between two pieces by
Sir John Davies and has the initials J. D.

(*d*) The diary of John Manningham (*Harl. MS.* 5353, f. 95) contains
amongst entries of Feb. 1603 some extracts from (i) and (vii), dating
the latter in ' the last Sumer at hir M^{ties} being with the L. Keeper '.

(*e*) A contemporary MS., printed as *Poetical Miscellanies* (*Percy
Soc.* lv), 5, has (vii) dated 1602.

(*f*) *Talbot MS.* K, f. 43, in the College of Arms, contains (iv) as
given at ' Harville ' with the date ' Aug. 1602 ', and is printed by
Lodge, ii. 560.

(*g*) *B.M. Birch MS.* 4173 contains a similar copy of (iv).

On the strength of the *Poetical Rhapsody*, (vii) is generally assigned
to Sir John Davies, which hardly justified Dr. Grosart in assigning
all the pieces to him (*Works*, ii, clxxii). Bond transferred the whole
to Lyly, primarily as a conjecture, but was confirmed in his view by
finding in *Egerton Papers*, 343, a payment to ' Mr Lillyes man, which
brought the lotterye boxe to Harefield '. But the document in which
this is found, and which also contains the item ' x^{li} to Burbidges
players for Othello ', is one of Collier's forgeries (Ingleby, 261).

John Chamberlain (*Letters*, 164, 169) sent Dudley Carleton ' the
Quenes entertainment at the Lord Kepers ' on 19 Nov. 1602, and on
23 Dec. wrote that, as Carleton liked the Lord Keeper's devices so
ill, he had not cared to get Sir Robert Cecil's (cf. ch. xxiii, s.v. Cecil).

Progress from Scotland. 1603

There were several contemporary prints :

A

S. R. 1603, May 9. ' Kinge James his entrance into England.'
Burby and Millington (Arber, iii. 234).

1603. The True Narration of the Entertainment of his Royal
Majestie. *Thomas Creede for Thomas Millington.* [Epistle by T. M.
to Reader.]

Editions in Nichols, *James* (1828), i. 53, and C. H. Firth, *Stuart
Tracts (English Garner*[2]*), 11.

B

S. R. 1603, May 14. ' King James his entertainement at Theobaldes, with his welcomme to London.' *Thomas Snodham* (Arber, iii. 234).

1603. King Iames his entertainment at Theobalds : With his Welcome to London. By John Sauile. *Thomas Snodham, sold by T. Este.*

Editions in Nichols, *James* (1828), i. 135, and C. H. Firth, *Stuart Tracts*, 53.

C

S. R. 1604, Mar. 27. ' The tyme Triumphant.' *Ralph Blore* (Arber, iii. 256).

1604. The Time Triumphant, Declaring in brief the arrival of our Sovereign liege Lord, King James, into England, His Coronation at Westminster, . . . [&c.]. By Gilbert Dugdale. *By R. B.*

Editions in Nichols, *James* (1828), i. 408, and C. H. Firth, *Stuart Tracts*, 69.

D

Jonson's *Althorp Entertainment* (cf. ch. xxiii).

E

S. R. 1603, June 16. A ballad of ' Englandes sweet Comfort with the kinges entertaynmente by the Maior of Yorke '. *William White* (Arber, iii. 238).

There is also an account in Stowe, *Annales* (1631), 819. For the stages of the progress cf. App. A. Besides the device at Althorp, speeches were prepared by Dekker for the entry to London, but not used (cf. s.a. 1604).

Coronation Triumph. 1604

There are four contemporary prints :

A

S. R. 1604, Apr. 2 (Pasfield). ' The magnificent Entertainement . . . the 15 of marche 1603.' *Thomas Man junior* (Arber, iii. 258).

1604. The Magnificent Entertainment : Giuen to King Iames, Queene Anne his wife, and Henry Frederick the Prince, vpon the day of his Maiesties Tryumphant Passage (from the Tower) through the Honourable Citie (and Chamber) of London, being the 15. of March, 1603. As well by the English as by the Strangers : With the speeches and Songes, deliuered in the seuerall Pageants. Tho. Dekker. *T. C. for Tho. Man the younger.*

1604. The Whole Magnificent Entertainment. . . . And those speeches that before were publish't in Latin, now newly set forthe in English. *E. Allde for Tho. Man the younger.*

1604. *Thomas Finlason, Edinburgh.*

Editions in Nichols, *James*, i. 337, and *Somers Tracts* (1810), iii. 1.

The speeches for three of the pageants were Jonson's, and some of those for a fourth Middleton's. Two others were in Latin. But

Dekker himself probably contributed the rest. Prefixed is a dialogue intended, but not used, for James's original entry into London in 1603, which may also be assigned to Dekker.

B

Jonson's *Coronation Entertainment* (cf. ch. xxiii).

C

1604. The Arches of Triumph Erected in honor of the High and mighty prince, James, the first of that name, King of England, and the sixt of Scotland, at his Maiesties Entrance and passage through his Honorable Citty and chamber of London, vpon the 15th day of March 1603. Invented and published by Stephen Harrison Joyner and Architect: and graven by William Kip. *John Windet.* [Verses by Thomas Dekker and John Webster.]

1604. . . . *John Windet, sold by John Sudbury and George Humble.*

D

G. Dugdale's *Time Triumphant.* See s.a. 1603.

There is also an account in Stowe, *Annales*, 835, based on A. Some ballads are registered in Arber, iii. 255–7, and various verses and other illustrative materials are printed by Nichols. A list of the pageants is in ch. iv.

Entertainment of King of Denmark. 1606

There are four contemporary prints:

A

S. R. 1606, July 30 (Wilson). 'The Kinge of Denmarkes entertainement at Tilberie Hope by the kinge &c.' *Henry Robertes* (Arber, iii. 327).

1606. The Most royall and Honourable entertainement, of the famous and renowmed King, Christiern the fourth, King of Denmarke, &c. . . . With the royall passage on Thursday the 31. of July, thorough the Citty of London, and honorable shewes there presented them, and maner of their passing. By H. R. *W. Barley for H. R.* [Epistle to Sir Thomas Smith, signed 'Hen. Robarts'.]

Editions in Nichols, *James* (1828), ii. 54, and *Harleian Miscellany*, ix. 431.

B

S. R. 1606, Aug. 19 (Wilson). 'A Booke called Englandes farewell to Christian the Ffourthe kinge of Denmarke With a Relacon of suche shewes and seuerall pastymes presented to his Maiestie, as well at Courte the ffirste of Auguste as in other places since his honorable passage through the Cytie of London &c.' *William Welbye* (Arber, iii. 328).

1606. Englands Farewell to Christian the fourth, famous King of

Denmarke. By H. Roberts. *For William Welby.* [Epistle to Sir John Jolles, signed ' H. Roberts '.]
Editions in Nichols, *James* (1828), ii. 75, and *Harleian Miscellany,* ix. 440.

C

Jonson's *Entertainment of the King of Denmark* at Theobalds (cf. ch. xxiii).

D

S. R. 1606, Aug. 8 (Hartwell). ' A booke called the Kinge of Denmarkes welcomme into England &c.' *Edward Allde* (Arber, iii. 327).

1606. The King of Denmarkes welcome: Containing his arriual, abode, and entertainement, both in the Citie and other places. *Edward Allde.*
Extracts in Nichols, *James* (1828), iv. 1072.

There are also an account in Stowe, *Annales,* 885, and a *Relatio oder Erzehlung wie . . . Christianus IV, &c. im Königreich Engellandt angelanget* (1607, Hamburg). For the itinerary cf. App. A. Bond, *Lyly,* i. 505, prints a song at Theobalds on 24 July and a pastoral dialogue in Fleet Street on 31 July as possibly Lyly's.

The Christmas Prince. 1607–8

[*MS.*] *St. John's College, Oxford, MS.* ' A True and Faithfull Relation of the Risinge and Fall of Thomas Tucker, Prince of Alba Fortunata, Lord of St. John's,' &c. The writer is said (*D. N. B.*) to be Griffin Higgs, but the evidence is inadequate.
Edition [by P. Bliss], An Account of the Christmas Prince (1816, *Miscellanea Antiqua Anglicana*). Another is planned in *M. S. R.*

This is the narrative of a lordship of misrule at St. John's during the Christmas of 1607–8. The MS. includes the text of a number of plays and shows. Unfortunately Bliss omits the text of these, with the exception of one called *The Seven Days of the Week.* The others were *Ara Fortunae, Saturnalia, Philomela, Time's Complaint, Somnium Fundatoris, Philomathes, Yuletide, Ira seu Tumulus Fortunae, Periander* (an English play). Others were planned, but not given ; cf. *Mediaeval Stage,* i. 409.

Chesters Triumph. 23 April 1610

S. R. 1610, June 12 (Wilson). ' A booke called Chesters Triumph in honour of ye Prince, as it was performed vpon Saincte Georges Day 1610 in thaforesayd Citty.' *John Browne* (Arber, iii. 436).

1610. Chesters Triumph in Honor of her Prince. As it was performed vpon S. Georges Day 1610, in the foresaid Citie. *For I. B.* [The name of Robert Amerie appears at the end. A preface and one poem are by R. Davies.]
Editions in Nichols, *James,* ii. 291 (1828), and in *Chetham Soc.* publications (1844).

G. Ormerod, *Hist. of Cheshire* (1882), i. 381, gives a description of the show from a shorter account or programme in *Harl. MS.* 2150, f. 186, indexed (f. 3ᵛ) as ' Mʳ. Amory's new shew invented by him '. This is confirmed by the lines :

> Amor is loue and Amory is his name,
> That did begin this pompe and princelye game.

Camp-Bell. 29 Oct. 1609

N.D. [1609 ?] Running title : Camp-bell, or The Ironmongers Faire Field. [The only known copy (B.M. C. 33, E. 7) lacks the t.p. and sig. A. Thomas Campbell was mayor in 1609. For his grandson, James Campbell, mayor in 1629, Dekker wrote *London's Tempe, or The Field of Happines*.]

Greg, *Masques*, 21, assigns this to Munday, without stating his grounds.

London's Love to Prince Henry. 31 May 1610

1610. Londons Loue, to the royal Prince Henrie, meeting him on the Riuer of Thames, at his returne from Richmonde, with a worthie fleete of her Cittizens, on Thursday the last of May, 1610. With a breife reporte of the water Fight, and Fire workes. *Edward Allde, for Nathaniel Fosbrooke.* [Epistle to Sir Thomas Campbell, Lord Mayor.]

Edition by J. Nichols, *James*, ii. 315 (1828).

It appears from the city records that the device was by Munday, and that Richard Burbadge and John Rice of the King's men delivered the speeches as Amphion and Corinea ; cf. *Repertory*, xxix, f. 232ᵛ, and Letter Book D.D., f. 148ᵛ, quoted by Halliwell-Phillipps in *Athenaeum* (19 May 1888), Stopes, *Burbage*, 108, and C. W. Wallace in *Times* (28 March 1913). Doubtless Munday also wrote the description.

Creation of Henry Prince of Wales. 4 June 1610

S. R. 1610, June 14 (Mokett). ' A booke called, The creation of the Prince, by master Danyell Price.' *Roger Jackson* (Arber, iii. 436).

1610. The Order and Solemnitie of the Creation of the High and mightie Prince Henrie, Eldest Sonne to our sacred Soueraigne, Prince of Wales, Duke of Cornewall, Earle of Chester, &c. As it was celebrated in the Parliament House, on Munday the fourth of Iunne last past. Together with the Ceremonies of the Knights of the Bath, and other matters of speciall regard, incident to the same. Whereunto is annexed the Royall Maske, presented by the Queene and her Ladies, on Wednesday at night following. *For John Budge.* [The Mask is Daniel's *Tethys' Festival*, with a separate t.p.]

Editions in W. Scott, *Somers Tracts* (1809–15), ii. 183, and Nichols, *James* (1828), ii. 324.

The ceremonies are also described in Stowe, *Annales* (1615), 899, and in MSS. of W. Camden quoted by Nichols.

The diary is :
31 May 1610. City reception with water pageant.
4 June. Creation.
5 June. Daniel's mask.
6 June. Tilt ; fireworks ; sea-fight.

Marriage of Frederick and Elizabeth. 1613

The most important descriptions, besides the masks of Campion, Beaumont, and Chapman (q.v.), are .

A

S. R. 1613, Feb. 18 (Mokett). ' A booke called The Mariage of the twoo great prynces Ffriderick Counte Palatine and the Lady Elizabeth &c with the shewes and fierwoorkes on the Water, the maskes and Revels at the Courte.' *William Barley* (Arber, iii. 516).

1613. The Magnificent Marriage of the two great princes Frederick Count Palatine, &c. and the Lady Elizabeth, Daughter to the Imperial Majesties of King James and Queen Anne, to the Comfort of All Great Britain. Now the second time imprinted, with many new additions of the same Tryumphes, performed by the Gentlemen of the Innes of Court in the Kings Pallace at Whitehall. *T. C. for W. Barley.* [Nichols says that a manuscript copy of the first edition is in *Addl. MS.* 5767.]

Editions in W. Scott, *Somers Tracts* (1809–15), iii. 35, and Nichols, *James* (1828), ii. 536.

B

1613. Heavens Blessing and Earths Joy : or, a True Relation of the Supposed Sea-Fights and Fire-Workes as were Accomplished before the Royall Celebration of the All-beloved Marriage of the two Peerlesse Paragons of Christendome, Fredericke and Elizabeth. By John Taylor, the Water Poet. *For Joseph Hunt, sold by John Wright.* 1630. [Part of Taylor's *Works.*]

Edition in Nichols, *James* (1828), ii. 527.

C

1613. Beschreibung der Reiss : Empfahung des Ritterlichen Ordens : Volbringung des Heyraths : vnd glückliche Heimführung : Wie auch der ansehnlichen Einführung, gehaltene Ritterspiel vnd Freudenfests des Durchleuchtigsten Hochgeboren Fürsten und Herrn Friedrichen des Fünften . . . mit der . . . Princessin Elisabethen. *G. Vögelin, Heidelberg.* [Of this there is also a French translation, *Les Triomphes . . . pour le Mariage et Reception de Monseigneur le Prince Frederic V . . . et de Madame Elisabeth.* 1613.]

D

A distinct French account in *Mercure François*, iii. 72.

For other accounts, extant and lost, and verses, cf. Arber, iii. 499, 514–18; Nichols, ii. *463, 536, 601, 624; Rimbault, 161–3; M. A. Green, *Elizabeth Queen of Bohemia*, 36.

The diary is :

16 Oct. 1612. Arrival of Frederick at Gravesend.

18 Oct. Reception at Court.

29 Oct. Visit to Guildhall.

21 Dec. Investiture with Garter.

27 Dec. Betrothal.

7 Feb. 1613. Garter installation.

11 and 13 Feb. Fireworks and sea-triumph at Whitehall.

14 Feb. Wedding. Campion's mask.

15 Feb. Running at the ring. Chapman's mask.

21 Feb. Beaumont's mask.

Bristol Entertainment. 1613

[*MS.*] *Calendar* by William Adams, *penes* C. J. Harford (in 1828).

S. R. 1613, Oct. 8 (Mason). ' A booke called the Queenes Maiesties entertaynement at Bristoll.' *John Budge* (Arber, iii. 533).

1613. A Relation of the Royall, Magnificent, and Sumptuous Entertainment given to the High and Mighty Princesse Queen Anne, at the Renowned Citie of Bristoll, by the Mayor, Sheriffes, and Aldermen thereof; in the moneth of June last past, 1613. Together with the Oration, Gifts, Triumphes, Water-combats and other Showes there made. *For John Budge.* [Epistle by Robert Naile.]

Editions in *Bristol Memorialist*, No. 3 (1816), and Nichols, *James*, ii. 648 (1828).

APPENDIX A

A COURT CALENDAR

[*Bibliographical Note.*—This is primarily a list of plays, masks, and quasi-dramatic entertainments at court. The chronological evidence for the plays mainly rests upon Appendix B. Tilts and a few miscellaneous entertainments are included. And it has seemed worth while to trace the movements of the court, partly in order to locate the palaces at which the winter performances were given, partly because of the widespread use of mimetic pageantry during Elizabeth's progresses and visits abroad. For the main migrations of the household (in small capitals), the authorities here cited are confirmed by the daily or weekly indications of a much more detailed *Itinerarium* than can be printed. Additions from sources not explored by me may be possible to the record of shorter visits or even that of the by-progresses, upon which Elizabeth was not always accompanied by the full household. I have not attempted to deal so completely with the Jacobean period. The King's constant absences from court on hunting journeys are difficult to track and of no interest to dramatic history. Appendix B will show at which of the court plays he was personally present. The principal material used may be classified as follows: (*a*) The royal movements are frequently noted in ambassadorial dispatches, in private letters, notably those of Roger Manners to the Earls of Rutland (*Rutland MSS.*), of Rowland Whyte, court postmaster, to Sir Robert Sidney (*Sydney Papers*), and of John Chamberlain to Sir Dudley Carleton (*Letters*, ed. Camden Soc., and Birch, *Court of James*) and Sir Ralph Winwood (*Winwood Memorials*); and in the diaries of Henry Machyn, Lord Burghley (Haynes-Murdin, ii. 745 ; Hatfield MSS., i. 149 ; v. 69 ; xiii. 141, 199, 389, 464, 506, 596), Sir Francis Walsingham (*Camden Miscellany*, vi), and John Dee. (*b*) Collections of State and quasi-State Papers contain many dated and located documents emanating from the court, such as proclamations, privy seals, signet letters, and less formal communications from the sovereign or a secretary or other officer in attendance. Unfortunately Elizabeth's letters missive have never been collected, and many of them are unlocated. Naturally ministerial documents require handling with discretion, lest the writers should be away from court. Letters patent bear the date and location of the Chancellor's *recepi*, and the Chancellor was largely detached from the court. The sources for (*a*) and (*b*) are given in the *Bibl. Note* to ch. i. (*c*) The *Register* of the Privy Council records the localities of the meetings of that body, but it must be borne in mind that the registration was not very perfect (cf. ch. ii), and also that, although the Council ordinarily followed the court, meetings were occasionally held in Westminster or London, either at the Star Chamber or in the house of a councillor or even a citizen, when the court happened to be out of town. (*d*) Church bells were rung when the sovereign moved into or out of a parish, and the churchwardens entered the ringers' fees in their accounts. The entries in J. V. Kitto, *The Accounts of the Churchwardens of St. Martin's in the Fields, 1525–1603* (1901, cited as *Martin's*), record many comings and goings from Whitehall, but in some cases the date entered appears to be other than that of the actual ringing, either by error or because the payment was on a different day. The extracts from the accounts of St. Margaret's, Westminster (cited as *Margaret's*), in J. Nichols, *Illustrations*, i, of Lambeth in D. Lysons, *Environs of London*, i. 222, and S. Denne, *Historical Particulars of Lambeth* (1795, *Bibl. Top. Brit.* x. 185), of Fulham in T. Faulkner, *Fulham* (1813), 139, of Kingston in Lysons, *Environs*, i. 164, and of Wandsworth by C. T. Davis in *Surrey Arch. Colls.*, xviii (1903), 96, are scrappy and the year concerned is not always clear. Nichols, *Eliz.* iii. 37, gives an analogous record from the accounts of Chalk in Kent of the occasions on which the local carts were requisitioned for removes from Greenwich. (*e*) The dates and localities of knightings are given in W. A. Shaw, *The Knights of England* (1906), but many of them are from inconsistent and untrustworthy sources. (*f*) The *Chamber Accounts* (cf. App. B) contain under the annual heading ' Apparelling of Houses ' summaries of monthly bills sent in by the Gentlemen Ushers of the Chamber of their expenses while engaged in making preparations for royal visits. They yield much new information as to the houses visited, but only very approximately date the visits. And it may be that the Ushers occasionally had to prepare for a visit which never took place. Analogous information is contained in the *Declared Accounts* of the Office of Works. A single account of the Cofferer of the Household, printed by Nichols, i. 92, gives a daily record of the locality of the household throughout the progress of 1561 ; as far as I know, it is the only extant document of its kind. (*g*) J. Nichols, in his *Progresses of Elizabeth*² (1823) and *Progresses of James I* (1828), drew fully upon the contemporary printed descriptions of state entries and progresses, of which a list is given in ch. xxiv, and upon such ' gests ' of progresses (cf. ch. iv) as survive. I have been able to correct and amplify his record of houses visited to a great extent, as much of the material now available, notably the Privy Council Register and the Chamber Accounts, was not used by him, and he occasionally assumed that royal plans were carried out, when they were not. I have done what I can to identify the royal hosts and their houses, but there is more of conjecture in my lists than my query-marks quite indicate. The Chamber Accounts entries are not in chronological order. Often only a name or a locality is given, and a good deal of plotting of routes on a map has been necessary. A more thorough study of local and family histories than I have been able to undertake would doubtless add corrections and further details. Local antiquaries might well follow the lines of study opened up by E. Green, *Did Queen Elizabeth visit Bath in 1574 and 1592* (1879, *Proc. of Bath Field Club*, iv. 105), W. D. Cooper, *Queen Elizabeth's Visits to Sussex* (1852, *Sussex Arch. Colls.*, v. 190), W. Kelly, *Royal Progresses and Visits to Leicester* (1884), and M. Christy, *The Progresses of Queen Elizabeth through Essex and the Houses in which she stayed* (1917, *Essex Review*, xxvi. 115, 181). A knowledge of sixteenth- and seventeenth-century roads is useful. The Elizabethan list in W. Smith, *The Particular Description of England, 1588* (ed. H. B. Wheatley and E. W. Ashbee, 1879) is fuller than that in W. Harrison, *Description of England* (ed. *N. S. S.* ii. 107), or that described from a manuscript of *c.* 1603 by G. S. Thomson in *E. H. R.* xxxiii. 234. The seventeenth-century description of J. Ogilby, *Itinerarium Angliae* (1675) became the parent of many travellers' guides. But it does not include three private royal roads largely used in removes ; viz. the King's road by Chelsea to Richmond and Hampton Court, Theobald's Road, and a road from Lambeth Ferry to Greenwich and Eltham. Useful studies are T. F. Ordish, *History of Metropolitan Roads* (*L. T. R.* viii. 1), and H. G. Fordham, *Studies in Carto-Bibliography* (1914). Other books are given in D. Ballen, *Bibliography of Roadmaking and Roads* (1914).]

1558

Nov. 17. Accession of Elizabeth at HATFIELD.

Nov. 22. PROGRESS through Herts and Middlesex to London by Hadley (Alice Lady Stamford ?, Nov. 22-3) and Charterhouse (Lord North, Nov. 23-8).[1]

Nov. 28. TOWER OF LONDON.[2]

Dec. 5. SOMERSET HOUSE, by water.[3]

Dec. 22. WHITEHALL.[4]

1559

Jan. 6. Play (**Queen's** ?) and mask (Papists).[5]

Jan. 12. TOWER, by water.[6]

Jan. 14. Entry through London with pageants to WHITEHALL.[7]

Jan. 15. Coronation.[8]

Jan. 16. Tilt and mask (Almains and Palmers ?).

Jan. 17. Barriers.[9]

Jan. 29. Mask (Moors ?).

Feb. 5 (S.S.). Mask (Swart Rutters).

Feb. 7. Mask (Fishers).

March 21. Morris from Household feast at Mile End to court.[10]

c. March 31. Visit to Greenwich ? [11]

Apr. 25. Supper at Baynard's Castle (Earl of Pembroke).[12]

May 1. Maying on Thames at Whitehall.[13]

c. May 17. Visit to Greenwich.[14]

May 24. Mask (Astronomers) for French embassy.[15]

May 25. Baiting at palace for embassy.[16]

June 21. GREENWICH.[17]

June 25. May game from London to court.[18]

July 2. City musters and tilt at court.[19]

July 3. Visit to Woolwich, with banquet in the *Elizabeth Jonas*.[20]

July 11. Joust by pensioners and mask.[21]

July 17. PROGRESS in Kent and Surrey.[22] Dartford (July 17-18), Cobham Hall (Lord Cobham, July 18-21 <), Gillingham, Otford (July > 23-28 <), Eltham (Aug. 4), Croydon (Abp. of Canterbury, Aug. 5-6 ?) and Nonsuch (Earl of Arundel, Aug. 6-10).

[1] *P. C.* (Nov. 22, 24) ; Machyn, 179 ; Lettenhove, i. 300.

[2] Machyn, 180 ; Burghley, *Diary*.

[3] *P. C.* (Dec. 4, 5) ; Machyn, 180 ; Stowe, *Annales*.

[4] *P. C.* (Dec. 22, 23) ; *V. P.* vii. 2.   [5] Cf. ch. v.

[6] *P. C.* (Jan. 14) ; *V. P.* vii. 11 ; Machyn, 186 ; Stowe, *Annales*.

[7] Machyn, 186 ; Stowe, *Annales* ; cf. ch. xxiv.

[8] Machyn, 186 ; Nichols, i. 60 ; from *Bodl. Ashm. MS.*, 863 ; *V. P.*, vii. 11.   [9] Machyn, 187 ; *V. P.* vii. 18.   [10] Machyn, 191.

[11] *S. P. D.*   [12] Machyn, 196 ; *V. P.* vii. 80.   [13] Machyn, 196.

[14] *V. P.* vii. 84 ; Lettenhove, i. 522.

[15] Machyn, 198 ; *V. P.* vii. 91 ; cf. chh. i, v.   [16] Machyn, 198.

[17] *Sp. P.* i. 79.   [18] Machyn, 201.   [19] Machyn, 202.

[20] *C. A.* ; Machyn, 203.   [21] Machyn, 203.

[22] *C. A.* ; *S. P. F.* ; *Sc. P.* (July 28, Aug. 7) ; *Sadler Papers* (Aug. 8) ; Burghley, *Diary* ; Machyn, 204, 206.

Aug. 7. Paul's.
Aug. 10. HAMPTON COURT.[1]
Aug. 17->23. Visit to West Horsley (Lord Clinton), with mask (Shipmen and Country Maids).[2]
Sept. 28. WHITEHALL.[3]
Nov. 5. Tilt.[4]
Dec. 31. Play (**Chapel** ?) and mask (Clowns or Nusquams ?).[5]

1560

Jan. 1. Mask (Barbarians) for John Duke of Finland.[6]
Jan. 6. Masks (Patriarchs, Italian Women).
Feb. 25 (S.S.) or 26. Mask (Nusquams or Clowns ?).
Feb. 27. Masks (Diana and Nymphs, Actaeon ?).
Apr. 10. Morris and ' queen ' from London to court.[7]
Apr. 21. Tilt.[8]
Apr. 24< >27. Visit to Deptford.[9]
Apr. 28. Tilt.[10]
May 14. GREENWICH.[11]
c. May 24. Visit to Westminster ?[12]
c. May. Visit to Eltham.[13]
July 29. RICHMOND by Lambeth (Abp. Parker).[14]
Aug. 3. OATLANDS.[15]
Aug. 5-30. PROGRESS in Surrey and Hants.[16]   Sutton Place, Woking (Sir Henry Weston, Aug. 5), Farnham (Bp. Winchester, Aug. 7, 8), Rotherfield (John ? Norton), Southwick (John White), Portsmouth, Netley Castle (Aug. 12-13), Southampton (Aug. 13-16), Winchester (Aug. 16-23), Micheldever (Edmund Clerk, Aug. 23), Basing (Marquis of Winchester, Aug. 23-28), Odiham (Chidiock Paulet ?), Hartley Wintney (Sir John Mason ?), Bagshot (Sir Henry Weston ?).
Aug. 30. WINDSOR.[17]

---

[1] *Procl.* 513 ; Machyn, 206.
[2] *C. A.* ; *Procl.* 514 ; *S. P. F.* (Aug. 16 ; *S. P. D.* (Aug. 23) ; Machyn, 207 (app. Aug. 15 in error) ; Nichols, i. 75 ; Feuillerat, *Eliz.* 105. Quadra (Aug. 18, *C. D. I.* lxxxvii. 231), ' Los Embajadores de Suecia se van muy quejosos y agraviados porque creo que ha llegado á su noticia que burlaban en Palacio dellos, y la Reina mejor que los demás ' hardly bears out the interpretation of M. A. S. Hume, *Courtships of Elizabeth*, 32, that the ridicule was in a mask.
[3] *Sp. P.* i. 98 ; *Sadler Papers*, i. 462.   [4] Machyn, 216.
[5] Machyn, 221, ' the plaers plad suche matter that they wher commondyd to leyff off, and contenent the maske cam in dansyng '.
[6] Machyn, 221.   [7] Machyn, 230.   [8] Machyn, 231.
[9] *C. A.* ; Machyn, 232.   [10] Machyn, 233.
[11] Machyn, 234 ; Lodge¹, i. 313.   [12] *Procl.* 525.
[13] *C. A.*   [14] Machyn, 241 ; Parker, 120 ; *Sc. P.* i. 459.
[15] Machyn, 241 ; *Sc. P.* i. 459.
[16] *C. A.* ; *S. P. D.* (Aug. 23, 27) ; *S. P. F.* (Aug. 22, 27, 28) ; *Sc. P.* i. 475 ; Machyn, 241 ; Wright, i. 43 ; *Hatfield MSS.* xiii. 50, 142 ; Howard, 215 ; *V. H. Hants*, iii. 531.
[17] *S. P. D. Addl.* ; Lodge, i. 423.

Sept. 22 < > 30. HAMPTON COURT.[1]
c. Oct. Visit to Horsley (Lord Clinton ?).[2]
Nov. 10 < > 25. WHITEHALL.[3]
Nov. 27–> Dec. 2. Visit to Greenwich and Eltham.[4]
c. Dec. Visit to Queenborough.[5]
Christmas. **Dudley's** and **Paul's**, and masks. One of the plays was
Preston's *Cambyses.*[6]

1561

Feb. 17 (S.M.). Wrestling in ' prychyng-plase ' at court.[7]
Feb. 18, 19. Masters of fence at court.[8]
Apr. 26 < > 29. GREENWICH.[9]
June 24. River triumph. Dinner with Lord R. Dudley.[10]
July 10–Sept. 22. PROGRESS in Essex, Suffolk, Herts., Middlesex.[11]
    Tower (July 10), Charterhouse (Lord North, July 10–14) with visit
    to Strand (Sir W. Cecil, July 13), Wanstead (Lord Rich, July 14),
    Havering (July 14–19) with visits to Pyrgo (Lord John Grey,
    July 16) and Loughton Hall (Lord Darcy ?, July 17), Ingatestone
    (Sir William Petre, July 19–21), New Hall in Boreham (Earl of
    Sussex, July 21–26), Felix Hall (Henry Long ?, July 26), Colchester
    (Sir Thomas Lucas, July 26–30) with visit to Layer Marney (George
    Tuke), St. Osyth (Lord Darcy, July 30–Aug. 2), Harwich (Aug. 2–5),
    Ipswich (Aug. 5–11),[12] Shelley Hall (Philip Tilney, Aug. 11), Small-
    bridge (William Waldegrave, Aug. 11–14), Hedingham (Earl of
    Oxford, Aug. 14–19), Gosfield (Sir John Wentworth, Aug. 19–21),
    Lees (Lord Rich, Aug. 21–25), Great Hallingbury (Lord Morley,
    Aug. 25–27), Standon (Sir Ralph Sadleir, Aug. 27–30), Hertford
    (Aug. 30–Sept. 16), Hatfield ?, Enfield (Sept. 16–22).
Sept. 22. ST. JAMES'S.[13]
Oct. 28. Visit to Whitehall. Baiting and mask (Wise and Foolish
    Virgins) for French embassy.[14]

[1] *Procl.* 529 ; *S. P. F.* (Sept. 30).   [2] *C. A.*   [3] *S. P. F.* (Nov. 10, 25).
[4] *C. A.* ; *Hardwicke Papers*, i. 163 ; *Hatfield MSS.* xiii. 62.   [5] *C. A.*
[6] Christopher Playter to Mr. Kytson (J. Gage, *Hist. of Hengrave*, 180),
' at the corte new plays, which lasted almost all night—the name of the
play was huff-suff-and ruff, with other masks, both of ladies and gents '.
The only date is ' 21 Feb.', but the year can be fixed by references in
the letter to the masters of fence at court, and to *Procl.* 538 and 541 of
this winter.   [7] Machyn, 251.   [8] Machyn, 250.
[9] *S. P. F.* (Apr. 26, 29).   [10] Machyn, 261 ; *Sp. P.* i. 208.
[11] Nichols, i. 92, from Cofferer's Account in *Cott. MS. Vesp.* C. xiv ;
C. A. ; Works Account in *Lansd. MS.*, 5 ; *S. P. D.* (Aug. 9, 11) ; *S. P. F.*
(July 15, 21 ; Aug. 16, 17, 27 ; Sept. 10, 17) ; *Sc. P.* (July 13 ; Aug. 16 ;
Sept. 3, 17) ; *Procl.* 547–50 ; Rymer (July 27) ; Machyn, 263, 267 ; Parker
(Aug. 9, 12, 22) ; Wright, i. 67, 68, 69, 71 ; Hardwicke, i. 174 ; Haynes-
Murdin, ii. 752 ; *Hatfield MSS.* v. 69 ; cf. M. Christy in *Essex Review*,
xxvi. 115, 181.
[12] Fleay, 62, suggests a revival of Bale's *Kinge Johan*, the MS. of which
was found at Ipswich.   [13] Machyn, 267 ; Nichols, i. 103.
[14] Machyn, 270 ; Brantôme, i. 312 ; cf. ch. v.

Dec. 4< >14. WHITEHALL.[1]
Christmas. **Dudley's** and **Paul's.**
Dec. 27< >Jan. 3. Lord of Misrule from Temple to court.[2]

1562

Jan. 15–16. Visit to Baynard's Castle (Earl of Pembroke), with mask.[3]
Jan. 18. *Gorboduc* and mask by Inner Temple.
Feb. 1. Mask from London to court, ' and Julyus Sesar '.[4]
Feb. 2< >10 (S. T.). **Paul's.**
Feb. 10. Tilt.[5]
Feb. 14. Running at ring.[6]
June 5. GREENWICH.[7]
Sept. 16< >19. HAMPTON COURT, by Southwark.[8]
c. Oct. Visit to Oatlands.[9]
Nov. 8. SOMERSET HOUSE.[10]
Dec. 14< >21. WHITEHALL.[11]
Christmas. **Dudley's** and **Paul's.**

1563

Feb. 21 (S.S.).
June 14. GREENWICH.[12]
July 20< >Aug. 1. RICHMOND, by Lambeth.[13]
Aug. 2< >4. WINDSOR by Stanwell.[14]
1562-3. Visits to Sunninghill, Oatlands, Nonsuch (Earl of Arundel), the New Lodge, the Twelve Oaks.[15]
Christmas.[16] Two plays by unnamed companies.

[1] Parker, 156 : Wallace, ii. 65.
[2] Machyn, 273.   [3] Machyn, 275.
[4] Machyn, 276. The word ' played ', after ' Sesar ', appears to be in a modern hand ; cf. Wallace, i. 200.
[5] Machyn, 276.   [6] Machyn, 277.
[7] *Sp. P.* i. 243 ; Machyn, 284. Dasent, vii. 238, has a reference to this as ' a tyme of progresse begonne ', but there was no real progress ; cf. Somers to Throckmorton (Aug. 29, *S. P. F.* v. 269), ' The Queen has all this summer kept herself here, without accustomed progress or hunting pleasures, to attend to that whereof she shall have honour '. On the unrealized plans for a meeting with Mary of Scots and the mask devised, cf. ch. v.   [8] *C. A.* ; *S. P. D.* (Sept. 16) ; *S. P. F.* (Sept. 19).
[9] *C. A.*   [10] Machyn, 295.
[11] *S. P. D. Addl.* (Dec. 14) ; *S. P. F.* (Dec. 14) ; *Procl.* 572.
[12] Machyn, 309.
[13] *C. A.* ; *Procl.* 578, 579 ; *Rutland MSS.* (June 30) ; *S. P. F.* (Aug. 2) ; Parker, 184 (Aug. 1).
[14] *C. A.* ; *S. P. D.* (Aug. 4) ; *S. P. F.* (Aug. 4).   [15] *C. A.*
[16] Francis to Sir Thos. Chaloner (Froude, vii. 92), ' Regina tota amoribus dedita est venationibusque, aucupiis, choreis et rebus ludicris insumens dies noctesque '.

1564

Feb. 2. Play by unnamed company.

Feb. 13 (S.S.).

Apr. 23 < > May 5. RICHMOND.[1]

June 9. Three masks and ' devise with the men of armes ' for French embassy.[2]

June 28. Visit *incognita* to Baynard's Castle (Earl of Pembroke) for St. Peter's watch.[3]

June 30 < > July 5. WHITEHALL.[4]

July 5. Visit to Sackville House (Sir Richard Sackville), with play and mask.[5]

July 6. Visit to Cecil House (Sir W. Cecil) for christening of Elizabeth Cecil.[6]

July 6 < > 16. GREENWICH.[7]

July 21 or 22. WHITEHALL.[8]

c. July 27–Sept. 12. PROGRESS in Middlesex, Herts., Cambridgeshire, Hunts., Northants., Leicestershire, Bucks., and Beds.[9] Theobalds (Sir William Cecil), Enfield (July 31, Aug. 1), Hertford Castle, Aldbury (Thomas Hyde), Haslingfield (Mr. Worthington, Aug. 4–5), Grantchester (Aug. 5), Cambridge (King's College, Aug. 5–10),[10] Long Stanton (Bp. of Ely, Aug. 10), Hinchinbrook (Sir Henry Cromwell, Aug. 10),[11] Kimbolton (Thomas ? Wingfield), Boughton (Edward Montague), Launde (Henry, Lord Cromwell, c. Aug. 18), Braybrooke Castle (Sir Thomas Griffin), Dallington ? (Sir Andrew Corbett), Northampton (Mr. Crispe), Easton Neston (Sir John Fermor), Grafton, Thornton (George Tyrrell), Toddington (Sir Henry Cheyne), St. Albans (Sir Richard Lee), Great Hampden ? (Griffith Hampden), Princes Risborough ? (Mr. Penton), Shardeloes in Amersham ? (William Totehill), Harrow (Sept. 12), Osterley (Sir Thomas Gresham).

Sept. 13. ST. JAMES'S.[12]

Sept. 15. Dinner with Marchioness of Northampton at Whitehall.[13]

c. Oct.–Nov. Visits to Oatlands and Windsor.[14]

Dec. 7. WHITEHALL.[15]

Christmas. **Warwick's** (twice), **Paul's**, and **Chapel** (*Damon and Pythias ?*).

---

[1] Wright, i. 171, 172 (Apr. 23) ; *S. P. D.* (May 5) ; *S. P. F.* (May 5).

[2] Cf. ch. v.   [3] *Sp. P.* i. 366.

[4] *S. P. D.* (June 30) ; *Sp. P.* i. 368.

[5] *Sp. P.* i. 367, 385 ; Parker, 219 ; Burghley, *Diary*.

[6] Burghley, *Diary*.

[7] *S. P. D. Addl.* (July 16).   [8] *Procl.* 597 ; *Sp. P.* i. 368.

[9] *C. A.* ; *Pipe Office D. A.* (*Works*), 3202 ; *P. C.* ; *Procl.* 598 ; *S. P. F.* (Aug. 1, 8 ; Sept. 11) ; *Sp. P.* i. 373, 374, 376, 379 ; Stowe, *Annales* ; Haynes-Murdin, ii. 756 ; Nichols, i. 151, from Cambridge MSS. ; Lysons, *Magna Britannia*, i. 143, 496, 571, 627, from Lord Hampden's MSS. (year uncertain) ; Bridges, *Northants*, i. 431 (misdated 1563).

[10] For Cambridge plays cf. ch. iv.

[11] For mask at Hinchinbrook cf. ch. v.   [12] *Sp. P.* i. 376, 379.

[13] *Sp. P.* i. 381.   [14] *C. A.*   [15] *P. C.* ; *Martin's*, 218 ; *S. P. D.* (Dec. 9).

1565

Jan. **Westminster** (*Miles Gloriosus* and (?) *Heautontimorumenos*).
Jan. 7. Tilt, dance, and foot tourney at night.[1]
Feb. 2. **Paul's.**
Feb. 18. Play by **Sir Percival Hart's sons** and mask (Hunters and Muses).
March 5 (S.M.). Tilt.[2]
March 6. Tourney. Masks (Satyrs and Tilters) and play by **Gray's Inn** at supper by Earl of Leicester.[3]
Apr. 27. Visit to Earl of Leicester.[4]
May 12. Visit to Greenwich.[5]
c. June 2. Visit to Tower, with imperial ambassador, Adam Swetkowyz.[6]
June 24 < > 26. GREENWICH.[7]
July 14. WHITEHALL.[8]
July 16. Visit to Durham Place for wedding of Henry Knollys and Margaret Cave, with tourney and two masks.[9]
July 17. RICHMOND.[10]
Aug. 8. WINDSOR, by Ankerwyke (Sir Thomas Smith).[11]
c. Aug.–Sept. Visits to Sunninghill, Farnham, and Bagshot.[12]
Sept. 14. WHITEHALL. Visit to Cecilia of Sweden (Bedford House ?).[13]
c. Sept. Visit to Osterley (Sir Thomas Gresham).[14]
Oct. 7, 13. Visits to Cecilia of Sweden.[15]
Oct. 29->Nov. 2. Visit to Nonsuch (Earl of Arundel).[16]
Nov. 11. Tilt at wedding of Earl of Warwick and Lady Anne Russell.[17]
Nov. 12. Tourney.
Nov. 13. Barriers.
Christmas. **Paul's** (thrice by Jan. 3, including one at Savoy for Cecilia of Sweden) and **Westminster** (*SapientiaSolomonis*).

1566

Jan. 6. King of the Bean at court.[18]
Feb. 5. GREENWICH.[19]
Feb. 14. Visit to Baynard's Castle (Earl of Pembroke).[20]
Feb. 24–26 (S.). *Gismond of Salerne* by Inner Temple (?). Wedding of Earl of Southampton and Mary Browne, with two masks and tourney.[21]
June 28 or 29. ST. JAMES'S.[22]

---

[1] *Sp. P.* i. 403.   [2] *Sp. P.* i. 404.   [3] Cf. ch. v.   [4] *Sp. P.* i. 428.
[5] *C. A.*; *Lambeth.*   [6] *C. A.*; Burghley, *Diary*; Wright, i. 198.
[7] Stowe, *Annales* (June 24); *Sp. P.* i. 442.
[8] *Martin's*, 222; *Sp. P.* i. 446; *Procl.* 611; *P. C.* (July 15).
[9] *Sp. P.* i. 446, 451; cf. ch. v.   [10] *Martin's*, 222.
[11] *Sp. P.* i. 465; *Pepys MSS.* 67.   [12] *C. A.*
[13] *Martin's*, 222; *Sp. P.* i. 475.   [14] *C. A.*
[15] *Sp. P.* i. 487, 494.   [16] *C. A.*; *Lambeth*; *P. C.* (Oct. 29, Nov. 2).
[17] *C. A.*; Leland, *Collectanea*, ii. 666.   [18] *V. P.* vii. 374.
[19] *Martin's*, 228; *Sp. P.* i. 523.   [20] *Sp. P.* i. 526.
[21] Cf. ch. v.   [22] *Martin's*, 229; *Sp. P.* i. 564.

July 1. Wedding of Thomas Mildmay and Frances Radcliffe at Bermondsey (Earl of Sussex).[1]
July 8–Sept. 9. PROGRESS in Middlesex, Herts., Beds., Hunts., Northants., Lincs., Rutland, Warwickshire, Oxfordshire, Berks.[2] Hendon (Edward ? Herbert, July 8), Shenley (Michael Pulteney), Hatfield, Knebworth (Rowland Lytton), Bygrave (William Warren ?), Wrest (Duchess of Suffolk), Dame Ellensbury's in Houghton Conquest, Willington (John Gostwick), Bletsoe (Lord St. John), Bushmead (William Gery), Kimbolton (Thomas ? Wingfield, July 21), Leighton Bromswold, Fotheringay Castle, Apethorpe (Sir Walter Mildmay), Colly Weston (July 29, Aug. 3), Greyfriars at Stamford (Sir W. Cecil, Aug. 5), Grimsthorpe (Duchess of Suffolk), Sempringham (Lord Clinton), Irnham (Richard Thimelby), Exton (Sir James Harington), Kingscliffe, Deene (Edmund Brudenell), Dingley (Edward Griffin), Whitefriars at Coventry (Aug. 17–19),[3] Kenilworth (Earl of Leicester, Aug. 19–22), Warwick (Earl of Warwick), Charlecote (Sir Thomas Lucy, > Aug. 24), Broughton (Richard Fiennes), Woodstock (Aug. > 26–31), Oxford (Aug. 31–Sept. 6),[4] Rycote (Sir Henry Norris, Sept. 6–7), Bradenham (Lord Windsor, Sept. 7–9).
Sept. 9. WINDSOR.[5]
Sept. Visit to Bagshot (The Bush).[6]
Sept. 10 < > 17. RICHMOND.[7]
Sept. 27. WHITEHALL.[8]
Christmas. **Paul's** (twice).

1567

Jan. 10. Queen in country.[9]
Jan. 17–Feb. 1. Visits to Croydon (Abp. ?) by Lambeth (?), Nonsuch (Earl of Arundel, Jan. 21–27), and Osterley (Sir Thomas Gresham, Jan. 27–Feb. 1).[10]
Feb. 9–11 (S.). **Westminster.**
Feb. 10. Visit to Arundel House (Earl of Arundel) ?[11]
Feb. 11. **Windsor Chapel.**

[1] C. A. ; Lambeth ; cf. ch. v.
[2] C. A. ; Pipe Office D. A. (Works), 3203 ; Works Account in Rawl. MS., A. 195ᶜ ; S. P. D. (July 21) ; S. P. F. (July 29, Aug. 30, Sept. 8) ; Sp. P. i. 568, 571, 574, 577, 578 ; Margaret's ; Martin's ; Shaw, ii. 72 ; Haynes-Murdin, ii. 762 (Aug. 3, 5) ; Middleton MSS. (Hist. MSS.), 528 ; Stowe, Annales ; Burgon, Gresham, ii. 155, 212 ; Nichols, i. 192, 197, 199*, 206, 247, from Coventry records, &c. ; Plummer, Elizabethan Oxford, 115, 175, 191, 198, 205 ; Boas, 385.
[3] At the entry to Coventry the Corpus Christi pageant of the Tanners stood at St. John's Church, the Drapers at the Cross, the Smiths at Little Park Street End, the Weavers at Much Park Street (H. Craig, Two Coventry C. C. Plays, xxi, 106). The date is sometimes given as 1565 or 1567 in error.   [4] For the Oxford plays cf. ch. iv.
[5] S. P. F. (Sept. 10) ; Sp. P. i. 580.   [6] D. A. (Works).
[7] S. P. F. (Sept. 10, 17).   [8] Martin's, 229 ; Sp. P. i. 582.
[9] Sp. P. i. 609.
[10] C. A. ; Martin's, 232 ; Sp. P. i. 609, 610, 612, 613.   [11] Shaw, ii. 73.

Apr. 13. Play for Spanish embassy.[1]
June 11. RICHMOND.[2]
July 22. WINDSOR.[3]
Aug. 12 ? OATLANDS.[4]
Aug. Visit to Beddington ? (Francis Carew) by Kingston.[5]
Aug. 18< >20–30. PROGRESS or visits in Surrey and Hants. Woking, Guildford Manor (Aug. 20, 21), Loseley ? (William More), Farnham (Bp. Winchester, Aug. 24, 25, 29), Odiham, Bagshot.[6]
Aug. 30. WINDSOR.[7]
Oct. 12. HAMPTON COURT.[8]
Dec. 23. WHITEHALL.[9]
Christmas. **Rich's** (twice), **Paul's** (twice), **Westminster**. The Revels prepared eight plays this winter, *The King of Scots* (tragedy), *As Plain As Can Be*, *The Painful Pilgrimage*, *Jack and Jill*, *Six Fools*, *Wit and Will*, *Prodigality*, *Orestes* (the extant play ?), and six masks, of which two were not used.

1568

Jan. 2. Visit to Charterhouse.[10]
c. Feb. Visit to Hackney.[11]
Feb. 29–March 2 (S.). **Chapel** (tragedy) and **Windsor Chapel**.
Apr. 6. GREENWICH.[12]
July 6–12 ? Visit to Charterhouse (Duke of Norfolk).[13]
July 12–Sept. 22. PROGRESS in Essex, Middlesex, Herts., Beds., Bucks., Northants., Oxon., Berks.[14] Havering (July 13–15) with visits to Giddy Hall in Romford (Sir Anthony Cooke) and Pyrgo (Lord John Grey), Copt Hall (Thomas Heneage, July 19), Enfield (July 22, 25), Hatfield (July 30, Aug. 3, 4, 7), Knebworth (Rowland Lytton), St. Albans (Sir Ralph Rowlett, Aug. 8), Dunstable (Edward Wingate), Brickhill (Thomas Duncombe ?), Whaddon (Lord Grey), Buckingham (William Davers ? at parsonage), Easton Neston (Sir John Fermor, Aug. 14, 21), Grafton Regis, Charlton (Sir Robert

[1] *Sp. P.* i. 633: ' The hatred that this Queen has of marriage is most strange. They represented a comedy before her last night, until nearly one in the morning, which ended in a marriage, and the Queen, as she told me herself, expressed her dislike of the woman's part.'
[2] *Sp. P.* i. 644.   [3] *Sp. P.* i. 661.
[4] *Sc. P.* ii. 373; Haynes-Murdin, ii. 764.   [5] *C. A.* ('Mr. Kyrres').
[6] *C. A.*; Haynes-Murdin, ii. 764; *S. P. F.* (Aug. 20, 24); *Sc. P.* (Aug. 29); *Sp. P.* i. 672; Kempe, 265.   [7] *Sp. P.* i. 672.
[8] *Sp. P.* i. 679.   [9] *Sp. P.* i. 690; *Martin's*, 234.
[10] Nichols, i. 266, from *Privy Purse Acct.*   [11] *C. A.*
[12] *Sp. P.* ii. 21; *Martin's*, 239.
[13] *C. A.*; *Parker Letters* (July 7); Burghley, *Diary*; *S. P. F.* (July 11); *C. D. I.* xc. 98, ' Vino por el rio hasta Reder '; the translation ' Reading ' in *Sp. P.* ii. 50 is absurd; it might be Knightrider St.
[14] *C. A.*; Works Account in *Rawl. MS.* A. 195c; Burghley, *Diary*; *S. P. D.* (July 30, Aug. 8); *S. P. F.* (July 22, Aug. 21, 27); *Sc. P.* (July 22, Aug. 14); *Sp. P.* ii. 54, 57, 64, 71, 72, 74; *Syd. P.* i. 36; *Procl.* 628, 629; Shaw, ii. 73.

Lane), Bicester (Mr. More, Aug. 27), Rycote (Sir Henry Norris), Ewelme, Wallingford (Thomas Parry at College), Yattendon (Sir Henry Norris ?), Donnington Castle, Newbury (Sept. 12, 13), Aldermaston (William ? Forster), Reading (Queen's house, Mr. Stafford, Mr. Gare, Sept. 18 ?).

Sept. 22. WINDSOR.[1]
Oct. 3 < > 20. HAMPTON COURT.[2]
Dec. 26. **Rich's.**

1569

Jan. 1. **Paul's.**
Feb. 12. WHITEHALL.[3]
Feb. 22 (S.T.). **Windsor Chapel.**
May 6. GREENWICH.[4]
May 15 (?). Visit of Earl of Leicester and Odo de Coligny, Cardinal of Châtillon, to Oxford, with *The Destruction of Thebes*.[5]
July 21. RICHMOND, by Lambeth.[6]
July 29. OATLANDS.[7]
Aug. 5 < > 8–Sept. 23 or 24. PROGRESS in Surrey and Hants.[8] Chertsey (Sir William FitzWilliam ?), Woking (Aug. 9), Guildford (Aug. 10, 12), Farnham (Bp. Winchester, Aug. 14, 17, 20, 22) with visit to Kingsley (Nicholas Backhouse), Odiham, Basing (Marquis of Winchester, Aug. 27, 29 ; Sept. 1), Abbotstone (Lord St. John), Soberton (Anne, Lady Lawrence), Tichfield (Lady Southampton, Sept. 4, 6), Southampton Tower (Sept. 6 ?, 8, 9, 14), Melchet (Richard ? Audley), Mottisfont (Lord Sandys), Wherwell (Sir Adrian Poynings), Hurstbourne ? (Sir Robert Oxenbridge), Steventon (Sir Richard Pexall), The Vine in Sherborne St. John (Lady Sandys, Sept. 22), Hartley Wintney (Lady Mason), Bagshot (Sir Henry Sutton).
Sept. 23 or 24. WINDSOR.[9]
Nov. 17. Accession day first kept.[10]
c. Dec. Visit to Bisham (Lady Hoby).[11]
Dec. 27. **Windsor Chapel.**

1570

Jan. 6. **Chapel.**
Jan. 20. HAMPTON COURT.[12]

[1] *Sp. P.* ii. 73.   [2] *S. P. D.* (Oct. 3) ; Burghley, *Diary* (Oct. 20).
[3] La Mothe, i. 203.
[4] *C. A.* ; *Sp. P.* ii. 149 ; Feuillerat, *Eliz.* 124 (May 10) ; Nichols, i. 257 (May 9). The May 11 of La Mothe, i. 373, must be an error.
[5] Cf. ch. iv.
[6] *Sp. P.* ii. 178, 180. The July 27 or 28 of La Mothe, ii. 100, 133, 138, must again be an error.   [7] *Sp. P.* ii. 182.
[8] *C. A.* ; Works Accounts in *Rawl. MS.* A. 195[c] ; *S. P. F.* (Sept. 4) ; *Sc. P.* (Aug. 12, 20) ; *Sp. P.* ii. 189, 191 ; *P. C. Wales* (Aug. 22) ; Burghley, *Diary* ; *Hatfield MSS.* i. 418, 421, 435 ; Camden, 420 ; Nichols, i. 261 ; *Finch MSS.* (Aug. 9) ; *V. H. Surrey*, iii. 383 ; Lodge, i. 480, 482, 483, 485 ; La Mothe, ii. 196, 218, 223, 229, 237.
[9] Lodge, i. 483, 485 ; *S. P. F.* (Sept. 24) ; *Parker Letters* (Sept. 24).
[10] Cf. ch. i.   [11] *C. A.*   [12] *Sp. P.* ii. 228 ; *Sadler Papers* (Jan. 18).

Feb. 5 (S.S.). **Rich's.**
March 19. Visit to Ham House (Madame de Châtillon).[1]
June 18 < > 20. OATLANDS.[2]
July 16–Sept. 29. PROGRESS in Middlesex, Bucks., Beds., Oxon., and
  Berks.[3] Osterley (Sir Thomas Gresham, July 16–18), Denham (Sir
  George Peckham, July 18–19), Chenies (Earl of Bedford, July 19–
  Aug. 13), Pendley (Edmund Verney, Aug. 15–17), Toddington (Sir
  Henry Cheyne, Aug. 19, 20), Dame Ellensbury in Houghton Con-
  quest, Segenhoe in Ridgmont (Peter Grey), Wing (Sir William
  Dormer, c. Aug. 24), Eythorpe (Sir W. Dormer), Rycote (Sir Henry
  Norris, Aug. 30, Sept. 2, 6, 7), Ewelme, Reading (Sept. 17, 24–26),
  Philberds in Bray (Sir Thomas Neville).
Sept. 29. WINDSOR.[4]
Nov. 6 or 7. HAMPTON COURT.[5]
Dec. 28. **Paul's.**

1571

Jan. 6. Challenge for jousting.
Jan. 14 < > 19. SOMERSET HOUSE.[6]
Jan. 23. Visit to Bishopsgate (Sir Thomas Gresham) to open Royal
  Exchange.[7]
Jan. 20 < > 29. WHITEHALL.[8]
Feb. 25–27 (S.). **Chapel, Windsor Chapel,** and **Paul's.**
March 2. GREENWICH.[9]
March 31 < > Apr. 2. WHITEHALL.[10]
Apr. 20. Visit to St. George's Fields.[11]
Apr. 29. Queen at wedding of Marquis of Northampton and Helena
  von Snavenberg or Snachenberg.[12]
May 1–3. Tilt, tourney, barriers.[13]
June 7, 8. Visit to Osterley (Sir Thomas Gresham).[14]
c. Apr.–July. Two visits to Bermondsey (Earl of Sussex).[15]
July 7 < > 8. HAMPTON COURT.[16]
July–Aug. Visits to Horsley (Earl of Lincoln), Oatlands, Byfleet.[17]
Aug. 8 < > 12–Sept. 22. PROGRESS in Middlesex, Herts., and Essex.[18]

---

[1] *Sp. P.* ii. 239.   [2] *P. C.* (June 18, 20).
[3] *C. A.*; Works Accounts in *Rawl. MS.* A. 195[c]; *P. C.*; *S. P. D.*
(Sept. 25); *S. P. F.* (Aug. 8; Sept. 7, 26); *Procl.* 657, 658; *Finch MSS.*
(*Hist. MSS.*); Burghley, *Diary*; *Hatfield MSS.* i. 481; Wiffen, i. 474;
Digges, 5; Shaw, ii. 74; La Mothe, iii. 240, 246, 258, 264, 289.
[4] La Mothe, iii. 317; *P. C.* (Sept. 30).   [5] *P. C.* (Nov. 6, 7).
[6] *P. C.* (Jan. 14, 19); La Mothe, iii. 434.
[7] Holinshed, iii. 1224; La Mothe, iii. 443, 450, 454; *Margaret's*, 18.
[8] *P. C.* (Jan. 29).   [9] *Sp. P.* ii. 295; *Rutland MSS.* i. 91.
[10] *P. C.* (March 31); Stowe, *Annales* (Apr. 2).   [11] *Lambeth.*
[12] La Mothe, iv. 94; Rimbault, 160.
[13] Holinshed, iii. 1225; Nichols, ii. 334, from Segar; *Arch.* lxiii. 47; *Arch.
Journal,* lv. 315; lxi. 305; Clephan, 171, from *Ashm. MSS.* 837, 845; La
Mothe, iv. 88, 95.   [14] Digges, 108.
[15] *Lambeth.*   [16] *P. C.* (July 7); *S. P. F.* (July 8).
[17] *C. A.*; La Mothe, iv. 206; *Kingston.*
[18] *C. A.*; *P. C.*; *C. D. I.* xc. 492; Burghley, *Diary*; *Hatfield MSS.*

Gunnersbury, Hendon (Edward Herbert), Hatfield (Aug. 15–21), Knebworth (Rowland Lytton), Brent Pelham (Lord Morley, Aug. 26), Saffron Walden, Audley End (Duke of Norfolk, Aug. 29–Sept. 3), Horham Hall in Thaxted (Sir John Cutts, Sept. 5) with hunt in Henham Park, Lees (Lord Rich, Sept. 7, 8), Rookwood Hall in Roding Abbess (Wiston Browne), Mark Hall in Latton (James Altham, Sept. 13, 14, 17), Stanstead Abbots (Edward Bashe, Sept. 20), Theobalds (Lord Burghley, Sept. 22), Hadley (Lady Stamford), Harrow (William Wightman).

Sept. 22. ST. JAMES'S.[1]
Sept. 26. RICHMOND.[2]
Oct. 23 < > 28. GREENWICH.[3]
Dec. 12. WHITEHALL.[4]
Dec. 16 < > 23. Wedding of Earl of Oxford and Anne Cecil.[5]
Dec. 23. Wedding of Edward Somerset (Lord Herbert) and Elizabeth Hastings.[6]
Christmas. The Revels prepared six masks this winter.
Dec. 27. **Lane's** (*Lady Barbara*).
Dec. 28. **Paul's** (*Iphigeneia*).

1572

Jan. 1. **Windsor Chapel** (*Ajax and Ulysses*).
Jan. 6. **Chapel** (*Narcissus*)..
Feb. 17 (S.S.). **Lane's** (*Cloridon and Radiamanta*).
Feb. 19. **Westminster** (*Paris and Vienna*, with tourney and barriers).
Apr. 10 or 11. GREENWICH.[7]
May 5. ST. JAMES'S.[8]
c. May 25. Visit to Hampton Court (?).[9]
c. June 10. Visit to Greenwich.[10]
June 15. Baiting, and mask (Apollo and Peace) and tourney in banqueting house at Cockpit for French embassy.[11]
June 20. WHITEHALL.[12]
July 15–Sept. 28. PROGRESS in Middlesex, Essex, Herts., Beds., Bucks., Northants., Warwickshire, Oxon., Berks.[13]   Bishopsgate (Jasper

---

i. 516; v. 70; *Rutland MSS.* i. 95; Wright, i. 393; Lodge, i. 525, 527; La Mothe, iv. 245; Digges, 134, 138; Shaw, ii. 75; Hunter, *Hallamshire*, 111; Nichols, i. 280; cf. M. Christy in *Essex Review*, xxvi. 115, 181.

[1] *Rutland MSS.* i. 96.   [2] La Mothe, iv. 245; *Wandsworth*.   [3] *C. A.*, *P. C.*
[4] *Sp. P.* ii. 355; *S. P. F.* (Dec. 15, 16); *Procl.* 663 (Jan. 3). I think the *P. C.* entries of Greenwich for Dec. 25, 31 must be errors.
[5] *Hatfield MSS.* v. 70; *Rutland MSS.* i. 94–96; La Mothe, iv. 319; *Sp. P.* ii. 358. The wedding was originally planned for Theobalds in Sept. (Hunter, *Hallamshire*, 111).
[6] La Mothe, iv. 319, 321; *Sp. P.* ii. 358. Possibly Elizabeth was also at the weddings of Lords Dudley and Paget this week.
[7] La Mothe, iv. 424.   [8] La Mothe, iv. 447.
[9] *Sp. P.* ii. 393.   [10] *Martin's*, 268.
[11] Nichols, i. 305 (dating June 14), from *Lambeth MS.* 959; ii. 335, from Segar.   [12] *Martin's*, 268.
[13] *C. A.*; *P. C.* (July 31); *S. P. D.* (Aug. 10); *S. P. F.* (Aug. 22);

Fisher), Bethnal Green (Joan, Lady White), Havering (July 19, 20), Birch Hall in Theydon Bois (Edward ? Elderton), Theobalds (Lord Burghley, July 22–25) with visit to Enfield, Hatfield, Gorhambury (Sir Nicholas Bacon, July 25–28), Dunstable (Edward Wingate ?, July 28–29), Woburn (Earl of Bedford, July 29–31) with visit to Chicheley (Elizabeth Weston), Salden (John Fortescue, Aug. 1–4), Beachampton (Thomas ? Pigott), Easton Neston (Sir John Fermor, Aug. 4–8), Edgecott (William Chauncy, Aug. 10), Bishop's Itchington (Edward Fisher, Aug. 11), Warwick Castle (Earl of Warwick, Aug. 11–13), Kenilworth (Earl of Leicester, Aug. 13–16),[1] Warwick Castle (Aug. 16–18) with visit to Warwick Priory (Thomas Fisher, Aug. 16),[2] Kenilworth (Aug. 18-23), Charlecote (Sir Thomas Lucy, Aug. 23), Compton Wyniates (Lord Compton, Aug. 23), Great Tew (Henry Rainsford), Woodstock (Aug. 27, Sept. 7–19) with visit to Langley (Sir Edward Unton), Holton (Sir Christopher Browne), Ewelme, Reading (Sept. 21–28), Philberds in Bray (Sir Thomas Neville, Sept. 28).

Sept. 28. WINDSOR.[3]

c. Nov. 11. HAMPTON COURT.[4]

Christmas. **Leicester's** (thrice) and **Paul's.** The Revels prepared plays on *Theagenes and Chariclea, Perseus and Andromeda,* and *Fortune,* and a double mask (Fishermen and Fruit-wives) this winter.

1573

Jan. 1. **Windsor Chapel.**

Jan. 6. **Eton.**

c. Jan. 29. GREENWICH, by Somerset House.[5]

Feb. 1–3 (S.). **Sussex's, Lincoln's** and **Merchant Taylors** (*Perseus and Andromeda* ?).

Feb. 24–March 10. Visits to Fold in South Mimms (Mr. Waller), Islehampstead Latimer (Miles Sandys), Gorhambury (Sir Nicholas Bacon), Brockett Hall in Hatfield (John Brockett), Northiaw (Earl of Warwick), Theobalds (Lord Burghley, 8 days), and Bishopsgate (Jasper Fisher, March 7).[6]

Procl. 676 ; *Margaret's* ; *Martin's* ; *Select Committee on Public Records* (1800), ·174 ; *Sp. P.* ii. 399, 413, 417 ; *Hatfield MSS.* v. 69, xiii. 110 ; Haynes-Murdin, ii. 773 ; *Finch MSS.* (Sept. 16) ; La Mothe, v. 47, 59, 63, 65, 76, 77, 79, 84, 89, 91, 92, 99, 122, 134 ; L. Howard, 195 ; *Wilts. Arch. Mag.* xviii. 261 ; 1 Ellis, ii. 265 ; Lodge, i. 540, 542, 548, 549 ; Strype, *Sir T. Smith,* 121 ; *Zurich Letters,* ii. 211 ; Digges, 228–65 ; Nichols, i. 309, from *Warwick Corporation MSS.,* with errors.
    [1] At Kenilworth were ' such princely sports as could be devised ' (Nichols, i. 318, from Warwick *Black Book*).
    [2] At Warwick on Aug. 17 were a country dance and a show of fireworks (ibid.).   [3] Digges, 260, 263.
    [4] *Hatfield MSS.* ii. 28 ; *Sp. P.* ii. 435 ; La Mothe, v. 200.
    [5] *Martin's,* 272 (Feb. 27, 28, in error ?) ; Digges, 328 (Jan. 29) ; *P. C.* (Feb. 3) ; Feuillerat, *Eliz.* 171.
    [6] *C. A.* ; *P. C.* ; La Mothe, v. 262, 267, 270 ; *Sp. P.* ii. 467 ; Wright, i. 466 ; *Hatfield MSS.* v. 70 (misdated) ; Nichols, i. 378.

July 14–Sept. 26. PROGRESS in Surrey, Kent, and Sussex.[1] Croydon (Abp. of Canterbury, July 14–21), Orpington (Sir Percival Hart, July 21–24),[2] Otford (July 24), Knole in Sevenoaks (July 24–29), Bastead (July 29), Comfort in Birling (Lord Abergavenny, July 29–Aug. 1), Oxenheath in West Peckham ? (Sir Thomas Cotton, Aug. 1), Eridge (Lord Abergavenny, Aug. 1–7) with visit to Mayfield (Sir Thomas Gresham) ?, Bedgebury in Goudhurst (Alexander Culpepper, Aug. 7–8) by Kilndown, Hemstead in Benenden (Thomas Guildford, Aug. 8–11), Northiam (George Bishop, Aug. 11), Rye (Aug. 11–14) with visit to Winchelsea (Mr. Savage ?), Northiam (Aug. 14), Sissinghurst in Cranbrook (Richard Baker, Aug. 14–17), Boughton Malherbe (Thomas Wotton, Aug. 17–19) by Smarden, Hothfield (John Tufton, Aug. 19–21), Olantigh in Wye (Sir Thomas Kempe, Aug. 21–22), Brabourne (Sir Thomas Scott, Aug. 22), Westenhanger (Aug. 22–25), Sandgate Castle (Aug. 25), Dover, (Aug. 25–31) by Folkestone with visit to Thomas ? Fisher, Sandwich (Roger ? Manwood, Aug. 31–Sept. 3),[3] Wingham (Sept. 3), Canterbury (St. Augustine's, Sept. 3–16) with visit to Abp. Parker (Sept. 7),[4] Faversham (Sept. 16–18), Tunstall (William Cromer, Sept. 18–19), Gillingham (Sept. 19), Rochester (the Crown, Sept. 19–23) with visit to a ship, Bulley Hill (Richard Watts, Sept. 23–24), Cobham (Lord Cobham, Sept. 24), Sutton (Sept. 24), Dartford (Sept. 24–26).

Sept. 26. GREENWICH.[5]

c. Nov. Two visits to Deptford.[6]

Nov. 25. SOMERSET HOUSE, by Leicester House (?).[7]

Dec. 19. WHITEHALL.[8]

Dec. 26. **Leicester's** (*Predor and Lucia*). Mask (Lance-knights).

Dec. 27. **Paul's** (*Alcmaeon*).

Dec. 28. **Leicester's** (*Mamillia*).

1574

Jan. 1. **Westminster** (*Truth, Faithfulness, and Mercy*). Mask (Foresters and Wild Men).

Jan. 3. **Clinton's** (*Herpetulus the Blue Knight and Perobia*).

Jan. 6. **Windsor Chapel** (*Quintus Fabius*). Mask (Sages).

[1] Nichols, i. 332, 378, 548, from M. Parker, *Matthaeus*, Dering MS., and local archives; *C. A.*; *P. C.*; W. D. Cooper, *Winchelsea*, 107, and in *Sussex Arch. Coll.* v. 190, from *Acct.* of Controller of Household and local archives; Denne, *Bibl. Top. Brit.* xlv. 211; Parker Corres. 436, 437, 441, 475; *Arch. Cantiana*, vi. 43; ix. 235; xi. 199; *Zurich Letters*, ii. 221; *S. P. F.* (Sept. 15); Lodge, ii. 33; Shaw, ii. 75; La Mothe, v. 412; I Ellis, ii. 267.

[2] There was a reception at Orpington by a Nymph as Genius of the house, and a sea-fight in a bark (Hasted, i. 134).

[3] A mock sea-fight was shown at Sandwich on Sept. 1 (Nichols, i. 337, from town archives).

[4] There was a mask of Mariners at Canterbury on Sept. 7 (Feuillerat, *Eliz.* 183).   [5] Nichols, i. 351; La Mothe, v. 412.

[6] *C. A.*   [7] La Mothe, v. 454; *P. C.* (Nov. 25, 28, 29).

[8] *Martin's*, 273; *P. C.* (Dec. 19, 21).

Jan. 12. HAMPTON COURT.[1]

Feb. 2. **Merchant Taylors** (*Timoclea at the Siege of Thebes by Alexander*). Mask (Virtues) not shown.

Feb. 18–20. Visits to Earl of Lincoln and to Osterley (Sir Thomas Gresham).[2]

Feb. 21–23 (S.). Queen entertained privately by neighbours.[3]

Feb. 21. **Leicester's** (*Philemon and Philecia*).

Feb. 23. **Merchant Taylors** (*Perseus and Andromeda*). Masks (Warriors and Ladies).

March 2–3. GREENWICH, by Lambeth (Abp. Parker).[4]

June 30. RICHMOND, by Merton Abbey (Gregory ? Lovell).[5]

July 7. WINDSOR, by Stanwell and Colnbrook.[6]

July 11 < >13. **Italians.**

July 15–Sept. 25. PROGRESS in Berks., Oxon., Gloucestershire, Somerset, Wilts., Hants, and Surrey.[7] Binfield, Reading (July 15–23) with play (July 15) by **Italians,** Caversham or Rotherfield Greys (Sir Francis Knollys, July 23), Ewelme (July 23–24), Holton (Christopher Browne, July 24), Woodstock (July 24–Aug. 2), Langley (Sir Edward Unton, Aug. 2–3), Burford (Aug. 3), Sherborne (Thomas Dutton, Aug. 3–4), Sudeley Castle (Lady Chandos, Aug. 4, 5), Boddington (Mr. Denne), Gloucester (Aug. 10) with visit to Churcham ?, Frocester (George Huntley, Aug. 10–11), Iron Acton (Sir Nicholas Pointz), Berkeley Castle (Lord Berkeley, Aug. 11–12), Berkeley Hearne ?, Bristol St. Lawrence, Bristol (Sir John Young, Aug. 14–21),[8] Keynsham (Henry ? Brydges, Aug. 21), Morecroft (Stokes Croft ?, Aug. 21), Bath (Aug. 21–23), Hazelbury (John Bonham, Aug. 23), Lacock (Sir Henry Sherington, Aug. 23–28), Erlestoke (William Brouncker, Aug. 28–31), Heytesbury (Mr. Hawker, Aug. 31–Sept. 3) with visit to Longleat (Sir John Thynne, Sept. 2), Wylye ? (Lady Mervyn, Sept. 3), Wilton (Earl of Pembroke, Sept. 3–6) with visit to Clarendon Park, Salisbury (Bp.'s, Sept. 6–9) with visit to Amesbury, Winterslow (Giles Thistlethwaite ?, Sept. 9), Mottisfont (Lord Sandys, Sept. 9–10), Somborne (Henry ? Gifford, Sept. 10), Winchester (Sept. 10–13), Abbotstone (Marquis of Winchester, Sept. 13), Alresford, Herriard (George Puttenham), Odiham (Sept. 14–16), Farnham (Bp. Winchester, Sept. 15, 19), Bagshot (Sept. 24–25).

Sept. 25. OATLANDS.[9]

Oct. 1. HAMPTON COURT.[10]

---

[1] Walsingham, *Diary* ; La Mothe, vi. 8.

[2] Walsingham, *Diary* ; La Mothe, vi. 34.   [3] La Mothe, vi. 39.

[4] Walsingham, *Diary* ; *Lambeth* ; Nichols, i. 325 (misdated), 384.

[5] *C. A.* ; Walsingham, *Diary* ; La Mothe, vi. 167.

[6] *C. A.* ; Walsingham, *Diary*.

[7] *C. A.* ; *P. C.* ; Walsingham, *Diary* ; Burghley, *Diary* ; *S. P. D.* (Aug. 15) ; *S. P. F.* (July 18, 30 ; Aug. 10, 11 ; Sept. 15) ; *Zurich Letters,* ii. 258 ; A. Hall, *Life,* 57 ; Shaw, ii. 75, 76 ; Lodge, ii. 43 ; La Mothe, vi. 197, 229 ; Nichols, i. 321 (misdated 1572), 379, 392, 408 ; R. H. Gretton, *Burford Records,* 415 ; cf. E. Green in *Proc. Bath Field Club,* iv. 105.

[8] For *Bristol Entertainment* cf. ch. xxiv.

[9] Walsingham, *Diary*.   [10] Ibid.

Oct. 19–22. Visit to Nonsuch (Earl of Arundel).[1]

Christmas. *Phedrastus* and *Phigon and Lucia* rehearsed by **Sussex's**, Three masks this winter (Pilgrims, Mariners, Hobby-horses).[2]

Dec. 26. **Leicester's,** with boys.

Dec. 27. **Clinton's** (*Pretestus* ?).

1575

Jan. 1. **Leicester's** (*Panecia* ?).

Jan. 2. **Clinton's.**

Jan. 6. **Windsor Chapel** (*Xerxes* ?).

Feb. 2. **Paul's.**

Feb. 3 < > 6. RICHMOND.[3]

Feb. 13 (S.S.). **Chapel.**

Feb. 14. **Warwick's.**

Feb. 15 ? **Merchant Taylors.**

March 16. Visit to Mortlake (Dr. Dee).[4]

March 23 < > 25. ST. JAMES'S.[5]

c. Apr. (?). Visit to Osterley (Sir Thomas Gresham), by Chiswick.[6]

Apr. 20. GREENWICH.[7]

c. May 5–8. Two visits to Lady Pembroke in illness at Baynard's Castle.[8]

May 23–Oct. 10 < > 11. PROGRESS in Middlesex, Herts., Beds., Bucks., Northants., Warwickshire, Staffs., Worcestershire, Gloucestershire, Oxon., Berks.[9] Stoke Newington (John Dudley, May 23), Theobalds (Lord Burghley, May 24–June 6), Broxbourne (Sir George Penruddock), Woodhall (Sir John Butler), Hatfield (June 7–14), Luton (George Rotherham), Toddington (Lord Cheyne), Segenhoe in Ridgmont (Peter Grey), Holcutt (Richard Charnock), Chicheley (Elizabeth Weston), Grafton (June 19–July 6), Fawsley (Sir Richard Knightley), Long Itchington (Earl of Leicester, July 9), Kenilworth (Earl of Leicester, July 9–27),[10] Meriden (William Foster), Middleton (Sir Francis Willoughby), Swinfen (John Dyott ?), Lichfield (July 30–Aug. 3)[11] with visits to Beaudesert (Lord Paget) and Alrewas (Walter Griffith, July 30), Colton (Katharine, Lady Gresley), Chartley

---

[1] Walsingham, *Diary.*

[2] Some particulars of this winter's revels appear to be in *S. P. D. Eliz.* ciii. 54.   [3] Feuillerat, *Eliz.* 241 (Feb. 2) ; *P. C.* (Feb. 6).

[4] Lysons, i. 381 ; Dee, *Compendious Rehearsal* (ed. Hearne), 516.

[5] *P. C.* (March 21, 23, 25) ; *Martin's*, 284.   [6] *C. A.*

[7] *Martin's*, 284.   [8] Hunter, *Hallamshire*, 84.

[9] *C. A.* ; *P. C.* ; *P. C. Wales* (June 13, Aug. 17) ; *S. P. D.* (Aug. 21 ; Sept. 4, 12 ; Oct. 6) ; *S. P. F.* (July 12, Aug. 29, Sept. 4, 7) ; *Procl.* 693, 696 ; *Sp. P.*.ii. 492, 498 ; La Mothe, vi. 437, 442, 444, 487, 495, 498, 502 ; Haynes-Murdin, ii. 776 ; *Hatfield MSS.* ii. 99, 107, 108, 112, 116 ; v. 70 ; xiii. 142 ; Walsingham, *Diary* ; *Rutland MSS.* i. 104, 105 ; *Middleton MSS.* 538 ; Shaw, ii. 76 ; *Sydney Papers*, i. 71 ; Wright, ii. 11, 16 ; Devon, i. 119 ; *Wilts. Arch. Mag.* xviii. 261 ; *Kenilworth Entertainments* (cf. ch. xxiv) ; Nichols, i. 417, 529, 533, from local archives.

[10] For Kenilworth entertainments cf. chh. iv, xxiv.

[11] Warwick's players were at Lichfield (cf. ch. xiii).

(Lady Essex), Stafford Castle (Lord Stafford, Aug. 7, 8) with visit
to Ellenhall (Walter ? Harcourt), Chillington (John Giffard), Dudley
Castle (Lord Dudley, Aug. 12), Hartlebury Castle (Bp. of Worcester,
Aug. 12–13), Worcester (Bp. of Worcester, Aug. 13–20)[1] with visits
to Hindlip (John Habington, Aug. 16), Hallow Park (John Habing-
ton, Aug. 18) and Batenhall Park (Thomas Bromley, Aug. 19),
Elmley Bredon (Anne Daston, Aug. 20–22), Evesham ? (Aug. 21),
Campden (Thomas Smythe), Sudeley Castle (Lord Chandos), Sher-
borne (Thomas Dutton), Langley (Sir Edward Unton, Aug. 27),
Cornbury (Thomas Stafford ?, Aug. 29), Woodstock (Aug. 29–
Oct. 3) with entertainment by Sir Henry Lee,[2] Holton (Christopher
Browne), Rycote (Lord Norris, Oct. 6–8), Bradenham (Frederick
Lord Windsor), Wooburn (Sir John Goodwin), Philberds in Bray
(Sir Thomas Neville).

Oct. 10 or 11. WINDSOR.[3]
Dec. 20. HAMPTON COURT, by Colnbrook.[4]
Dec. 26. **Warwick's.**
Dec. 27. **Windsor Chapel.**
Dec. 28. **Leicester's.**

<h2 style="text-align:center">1576</h2>

Jan. 1. **Warwick's.**
Jan. 6. **Paul's.**
Feb. 2. **Sussex's.**
Feb. 6 or 7. WHITEHALL, by Sion.[5]
Feb. 27. **Italians.**
March 4 (S.S.). **Leicester's.**
March 5. **Warwick's.**
March 6. **Merchant Taylors.**
Apr. 26. GREENWICH.[6]
May 9–19. Visits to Leicester House (Earl of Leicester, May 9–10),
Osterley (Sir Thomas Gresham, May 10–12), Pyrford (Earl of Lin-
coln, May 12–15), Nonsuch (Earl of Arundel, May 15–17), Bedding-
ton (Sir Francis Carew, May 17–19).[7]
c. June 7. Visit to Hatfield.[8]
June 18. Visit to Deptford.[9]
c. June. Visit to Eltham.[10]
July 9. ST. JAMES'S.[11]
July 22 or 23. WHITEHALL.[12]
c. July. Visits to Highgate (Thomas ? Lichfield), Fold ? at Barnet
(Mr. Waller), and Hendon (Edward Herbert).[13]

There were pageants by Ralph Wyatt and Thomas Heywood at the
Cross and St. Ellen's Church, Worcester (Nichols, i. 537).
[2] Cf. ch. xxiii, s.v. Lee.   [3] Walsingham, *Diary.*
[4] *C. A.*; *Sp. P.* ii. 515.   [5] *C. A.*; Walsingham, *Diary,*
[6] Walsingham, *Diary.*   [7] Walsingham, *Diary*; Shaw, ii. 77.
[8] *Hatfield MSS.* ii. 134.   [9] *P. C.*   [10] *C. A.*
[11] Walsingham, *Diary.*   [12] *P. C.* (July 22, 23).
[13] *C. A.*, apparently (*Sp. P.* ii. 531) a false start for the progress.

July 30–Oct. 9. PROGRESS in Essex, Herts., Bucks., Berks., and Surrey.[1]
Stratford at Bow (Richard? Young, July 30), Havering (July 30–
Aug. 7) with visit to Pyrgo (Henry Grey) and hunt in Harolds
Park, Chigwell Hall (Sir John Petre, Aug. 7), Loughborough (John
Stonard, Aug. 7), Upshire? (Aug. 10), Mark Hall in Latton (James
Altham, Aug. 10–11), Hatfield Broadoak (Sir Thomas Barrington,
Aug. 11), Great Hallingbury (Lord Morley, Aug. 11–14), Stanstead
Abbots (Edward Bashe, Aug. 14–19), Hertford Castle (Aug. 19–22),
Hatfield (Aug. 24), Hertford again (Aug. 26–28), Northiaw (Earl of
Warwick, Aug. 30), St. Albans (Aug. 30–Sept. 1), Gorhambury (Sir
Nicholas Bacon, Sept. 1), Latimer (Miles Sandys, Sept. 1–3) with
visit to Chalfont St. Giles (John? Gardiner), Hedgerley (Sir Robert
Drury, Sept. 3), Windsor (Sept. 3–10) with visit to Folly John Park,
Thorpe (Richard Polsted, Sept. 10), Byfleet (Sept. 10–11), Pyrford
(Earl of Lincoln, Sept. 11–12), Guildford (Sept. 12), Loseley in
Artington (Sir William More, Sept. 12–13), Farnham (Bp. Win-
chester, Sept. 13?–20), Odiham (Sept. 20–22), Mr. Hall's (Sept. 22),
Reading (Sept. 22–Oct. 8), Rotherfield Greys (Sir Francis Knollys
Oct. 8), Hurst (Richard Ward, Oct. 8–9), Windsor (Oct. 9–12).
Oct. 12. HAMPTON COURT.[2]
Dec. 26. **Warwick's** (*Painter's Daughter*).
Dec. 27. **Howard's** (*Tooley*).
Dec. 30. **Leicester's** (*Collier*).

1577

Jan. 1. **Paul's** (*Error*).
Jan. 6. **Chapel** and **Windsor Chapel** together (*Mutius Scaevola*).
Feb. 2. **Sussex's** (*Cynocephali*).
Feb. 12. WHITEHALL.[3]
Feb. 17–19 (S.). *Cutwell* rehearsed, but not played.
Feb. 17. **Howard's** (*Solitary Knight*).
Feb. 18. **Warwick's** (*Irish Knight*).
Feb. 19. **Paul's** (*Titus and Gisippus*). Mask of children.
Feb. 26–March 3. Visit to Wanstead? (Earl of Leicester).[4]
April. Italian play before Privy Council at Durham Place.[5]
Apr. 29< >May 6. GREENWICH.[6]
May 9–10. Visit to Leicester House (Earl of Leicester).[7]
May 14–c. 25. Visits to Stoke Newington (John Dudley), Theobalds
(Lord Burghley, May 14 or 15, for 3 days), Northiaw (Earl of
Warwick), Gorhambury (Sir Nicholas Bacon, May 18–22), Fold?
at Barnet (Mr. Waller), Highgate (Thomas? Lichfield).[8]

[1] C.A.; P.C.; Walsingham, *Diary*; S.P.D. (Sept. 6, 12); S.P.F.
(Sept. 6); Sp.P.ii.533; Procl.708; Syd.P.i.392; Hatfield MSS. ii. 133;
Kempe, 490; Lodge, App. 38, 39; cf. App. B.   [2] Walsingham, *Diary*.
[3] Ibid.   [4] C.A.; Walsingham, *Diary*; Martin's, 297.   [5] C.A.
[6] P.C. (Apr. 27–29); Walsingham, *Diary* (May 6); Martin's, 297
(Apr. 26 in error).   [7] Martin's, 297.
[8] C.A.; P.C. (May 14); Birch, i. 12; Nichols, ii. 55, from Birch MS.
4100; Shaw, ii. 78; Haynes-Murdin, ii. 779; Hatfield MSS. v. 70:
Walsingham, *Diary* (May 25).

June 24. Visit to Southwark for weddings of George, Earl of Cumberland, to Margaret Russell, and Philip, Lord Wharton, to Frances Clifford.[1]

c. July. Visit to Deptford.[2]

July 19. RICHMOND, by Clapham.[3]

July 24. Visit to Isleworth (Countess of Derby).[4]

July 26. Visits to Barn Elms (Sir Francis Walsingham ?) and Mortlake Park Lodge (Earl of Leicester).[5]

Aug. 23. OATLANDS, by Hampton Court.[6]

Sept. 4–7 or 8. Visit to Pyrford (Earl of Lincoln).[7]

Sept. 12. Visit to Hanworth (Duchess of Somerset).[8]

c. Sept. Visit to Sir John Zouch.[9]

Sept. 23. WINDSOR, by Thorpe (Richard Polsted ?).[10]

c. Sept. Visit to Sunninghill.[11]

Dec. 10. HAMPTON COURT, by Staines.[12]

Dec. 26. **Leicester's.**

Dec. 27. **Chapel.**

Dec. 28. **Warwick's.**

Dec. 29. **Paul's.**

1578

Jan. 5. **Howard's.**

Jan. 6. **Warwick's.**

Feb. 2. **Sussex's.**

Feb. 9 (S.S.). **Warwick's.**

Feb. 11. **Lady Essex's** (instead of **Leicester's**).

c. Feb. Visit to Osterley (Sir Thomas Gresham).[13]

Feb. 25–27. Visit to Putney (John Lacy ?).[14]

Feb. 27–March 3 (?). Visit to Leicester House (Earl of Leicester).[15]

March 3. GREENWICH.[16]

Apr. 5 and 28. Visits to Leicester House (Earl of Leicester).[17]

May 6–16. Visits to Tottenham (Lord Compton, May 6, 7), Theobalds (Lord Burghley, May 7–10), Stanstead Abbots (Edward Bashe, May 10–12), Copt Hall (Sir Thomas Heneage, May 12–13), Wanstead (Earl of Leicester, May 13–16).[18]

[1] Wiffen, i. 508. [2] *C. A.*
[3] *C. A.*; Walsingham, *Diary*. [4] *Hatfield MSS.* ii. 157.
[5] Ibid. [6] *C. A.*; Walsingham, *Diary*.
[7] *P. C.*; Walsingham, *Diary*; *Finch MSS.* (Sept. 4); Lodge, ii. 91.
[8] *C. A.*; Walsingham, *Diary*. [9] *C. A.*
[10] *C. A.*; *S. P. F.*; Walsingham, *Diary*. [11] *C. A.*
[12] *C. A.*; Walsingham, *Diary*.
[13] *C. A.* A lost device and play at Osterley by Churchyard (cf. ch. xxiii) may belong to this visit.
[14] Walsingham, *Diary*; *Fulham*; Nichols, ii. 92.
[15] Walsingham, *Diary*.
[16] *S. P. F.*; Walsingham, *Diary*. [17] *Sp. P.* ii. 576, 581.
[18] *C. A.*; *S. P. D.* (May 8, 9, 10); *S. P. F.* (May 6, 15); Walsingham, *Diary*; *Hatfield MSS.* v. 70; *Sp. P.* ii. 582; Lodge, ii. 99. Sidney's *May Lady* entertainment may belong to this Wanstead visit or to that of 1579 (cf. ch. xxiii). For Italian tumblers in 1577–8, cf. App. B.

May 16. GREENWICH.[1]
July 11 < > 12–Sept. 23 < > 24. PROGRESS in Essex, Herts., Suffolk,
Norfolk, Cambridgeshire.[2] West Ham (Henry ? Meautys), Havering
(July 12–20), Theydon Garnon (John Branch), Mark Hall in Latton
(James Altham, July 23), Standon (Sir Ralph Sadleir, July 24),
Berden Priory (Margery Averie), Audley End (Thomas Howard,
July 26–30),[3] Barham Hall in Linton (Robert Milsent), Keddington
(Thomas Barnardiston), De Greys in Cavendish (Sir George Colt,
Aug. 1), Long Melford (Sir William Cordell, Aug. 3–5), Lawshall
(Sir William Drury, Aug. 5), Bury St. Edmunds (Aug. 5, 6), One-
house ? (Sir William Drury), Stowmarket ?,[4] Euston (Edward Rook-
wood, Aug. 10), Kenninghall (Earl of Surrey, Aug. 11, 12),[5] Bracon
Ash (Thomas Townsend, Aug. 16), Norwich (Bp. of Norwich,
Aug. 16–22) with visits to Costessey (Mary, Lady Jerningham,
Aug. 19) and Mount Surrey on Mousehold Hill (Earl of Surrey,
Aug. 20), Kimberley (Sir Roger Woodhouse, Aug. 22 or 23), Wood
Rising (Sir Robert Southwell, Aug. 24), Breckles (Francis Wood-
house), Thetford (Sir Edward Cleere, Aug. 27), Hengrave (Sir
Thomas Kitson, Aug. 28–30), Chippenham (Thomas Revett, Sept. 1),
Kirtling (Lord North, Sept. 1–3), Horseheath (Sir Giles Alington,
Sept. 4), Waltons in Ashdon (Edward Tyrell), Horham Hall in
Thaxted (Sir John Cutts, Sept. 7, 11), Manuden (Thomas Crawley),
Hadham Hall (Henry Capel, Sept. 14), Hyde Hall in Sawbridgeworth
(Henry ? Heigham), Hatfield Broadoak ? (Sir Thomas Barrington,
Sept. 15), Rookwood Hall in Roding Abbess (Wiston Browne,
Sept. 18), Theydon Bois (Mrs. Elderton) with visit to Gaynes Park
(Sir William Fitzwilliam, Sept. 19), Loughborough (John Stonard,
Sept. 21, 22), Wanstead (Earl of Leicester), Greenwich.
Sept. 25. RICHMOND.[6]
c. Dec. Visit to Hampton Court.[7]
Dec. 26. **Warwick's** (*Three Sisters of Mantua*).
Dec. 27. **Chapel.**
Dec. 28. **Sussex's** (*Cruelty of a Stepmother*).

  [1] *C. A.* ; Walsingham, *Diary* ; *S. P. F.* (May 16).
  [2] *C. A.* ; *P. C.* ; *Procl.* 724 ; *S. P. D.* (July 11, 14, 17 ; Sept. 2, 21) ;
Sp. P. ii. 607, 610 ; Shaw, ii. 78, 79 ; Haynes-Murdin, ii. 780 ; *Hatfield
MSS.* ii. 190, 192 ; xiii. 160 ; *Sydney Papers,* i. 270 ; Hatton, 93 ; Lodge,
ii. 119 ; Kempe, 248 (misdated ?) ; *Archaeologia,* xix. 283 ; Cullum,
Hawsted, 130 ; Hollingsworth, *Stowmarket,* 128 ; Nichols, ii. 111 sqq.,
from local archives ; *Entertainments* by Churchyard and Garter (cf.
ch. xxiv).
  [3] Speeches and verses sent from Cambridge to Audley End are in
G. Harvey, *Gratulationes Valdinenses* (1578).
  [4] A. G. H. Hollingsworth, *Hist. of Stowmarket* (1844), 128, 130, says
that players from Ipswich under John Corke were employed.
  [5] For devices at Kenninghall, Norwich, and Hengrave, cf. *Entertainments* by Churchyard and Garter (ch. xxiv). Blomefield, vii. 214, prints
from *Harl. MS.* 890, f. 282, verses given at Norwich with a pair of golden
spurs by William (Edward ?) Downes of Earlham.
  [6] Dee, 5 ; *S. P. D. Addl.* (Sept. 25) ; *P. C.* (Sept. 26).   [7] *C. A.*

1579

Jan. 1. **Paul's** (*Marriage of Mind and Measure*).

Jan. 4. **Leicester's** (*A Greek Maid*).

Jan. 6. **Sussex's** (*Rape of the Second Helen*).

Jan. 11. Mask (Amazons and Knights) and barriers, for Alençon's agent, M. de Simier.[1]

Jan. 22 < > 25. WHITEHALL, by Chelsea.[2]

c. Jan. 31. Visit to Hampton Court, by Putney (John Lacy).[3]

c. Jan.–Feb. Visit to Leicester House (Earl of Leicester).[4]

Feb. 1–2. Tilt and barriers for John Casimir, son of Elector Palatine.[5] Play by **Warwick's** ready, but not shown.

March 1 (S.S.). **Warwick's** (*Knight in the Burning Rock*).

March 2. **Chapel** (*Loyalty and Beauty*).

March 3. **Sussex's** (*Murderous Michael*). Device by Earls of Oxford and Surrey, Lord Thomas Howard, and Lord Windsor before French ambassador and De Simier. Morris mask prepared, but not danced.[6]

Apr. 28 or 29–May 2. Visit to Wanstead (Earl of Leicester), by Greenwich.[7]

June 24–26. Visit to Wanstead (Earl of Leicester).[8]

July 2. GREENWICH, by Lambeth.[9]

July 15–17. Visits to Gravesend and Deptford.[10]

Aug. 17–29. Private visit of Duke of Alençon to England.[11]

c. Aug. 30–31. Visit to Wanstead (Earl of Leicester).[12]

Sept. 9–27 < > Oct. 2. PROGRESS in Essex.[13] Stratford at Bow (Richard ? Young, Sept. 9), Havering (Sept. 11–14), Ingatestone (Lady Petre), New Hall in Boreham (Earl of Sussex, Sept. 17, 18), Moulsham (Sir Thomas Mildmay), Thoby (Anthony ? Berners), Brentwood (John ? Searle), Giddy Hall in Romford (Richard Cooke, Sept. 25–7), Ilford (Thomas Fanshawe, at St. Mary's Hospital ?).

Sept. 27 < > Oct. 2. GREENWICH.[14]

Dec. 22. WHITEHALL.[15]

---

[1] *Sp. P.* ii. 627, 630. [2] *C. A.*; *P. C.* (Jan. 20, 22).
[3] *C. A.*; *Procl.* 735. [4] *C. A.*
[5] Devereux, i. 170; Lodge, ii. 140, 146, 'There was never any of his cote that was able to brag of the like entertainment'.
[6] Lodge, ii. 146, 'prettier than it happened to be performed'; *Sp. P.* ii. 655, 'a grand ball, in which there were comedies and many inventions'. In the previous August (*Sp. P.* ii. 607) Oxford had declined a request of the queen to dance before Alençon's agents, 'as he did not want to entertain Frenchmen'. [7] *C. A.*; *Martin's*, 310; *Sp. P.* ii. 669, 679.
[8] *Martin's*, 310; *Sp. P.* ii. 681.
[9] *Martin's*, 310; *Lambeth* (June 2 in error).
[10] *P. C. Wales*, 192; Stowe, *Annales*.
[11] *S. P. F.* xiv. 46, 49; *V. P.* vii. 609, 611, 612, 614; *Sp. P.* ii. 690, 694; *Hatfield MSS.* ii. 293. [12] *P. C.*; Shaw, ii. 79.
[13] *C. A.*; *P. C.*; *S. P. D.* (Sept. 13, 27); *Sp. P.* ii. 697; *Hatfield MSS.* (Sept. 17); *Procl.* 740; cf. M. Christy in *Essex Review*, xxvi. 115, 181. But Nichols, ii. 285, has clearly used *two* abandoned 'gests'.
[14] *P. C.* (Oct. 2). [15] *Martin's*, 311; *P. C.* (Dec. 21, 23).

Dec. 26. **Sussex's** (*Duke of Milan and Marquis of Mantua*).
Dec. 27. **Chapel** (*Alucius*).
Dec. 28. Play by **Leicester's** ready, but not shown.

1580

Jan. 1. **Warwick's** (*Four Sons of Fabius*).
Jan. 3. **Paul's** (*Scipio Africanus*).
Jan. 6. **Leicester's.**
Jan. 15. **Strange's tumblers.**
Feb. 2. **Sussex's** (*Portio and Demorantes*).
Feb. 14 (S.S.). **Derby's** (*The Soldan and the Duke of* ——).
Feb. 16. **Sussex's** (*Sarpedon*).
c. Feb. Visit to Charterhouse.[1]
May 26 < > 29. NONSUCH, by Putney (John Lacy).[2]
c. June. Visits to Beddington (Sir Francis Carew).[3]
July 11 or 12. OATLANDS, by Molesey.[4]
c. July–Aug. Visits to Chobham (Abp. Heath, Edward ? Bray, John Wolley) and Pyrford (Earl of Lincoln).[5]
Aug. 16–20. Visit to Sunninghill, and Windsor ?[6]
c. Aug. 25–27. Visit to Woking.[7]
Sept. 13. RICHMOND, by Molesey (Thomas Brand).[8]
Sept. 17. Visit to Mortlake (Dr. John Dee).[9]
Oct. 10. Visit to Mortlake (Dr. Dee).[10]
c. Nov. Visits to Harmondsworth (Mr. Drury), Colnbrook (Henry ? Draper), Windsor, Eton College, Ditton Park, and Nonsuch.[11]
Dec. 6. WHITEHALL.[12]
Dec. 26. **Leicester's** (*Delight*).
Dec. 27. **Sussex's.**

1581

Jan. 1. **Derby's.**
Jan. 6. **Paul's** (*Pompey*). Challenge for tilt.
Jan. 22. Tilt.[13]
Feb. 2. **Sussex's.**
Feb. 5 (S.S.). **Chapel.**
Feb. 7. **Leicester's.**
March 20. ST. JAMES'S.[14]
Apr. 4. Visit to *Golden Hind* (Sir Francis Drake) at Deptford.[15]
Apr. 14. Challenge for Whitehall tilt.
Apr. 20. WHITEHALL.[16]

---

[1] *C. A.*   [2] *C. A.*; *P. C.* (May 26, 29); Lysons, i. 297.   [3] *C. A.*
[4] *C. A.*; *P. C.* (July 11); Walsingham, *Diary.*   [5] *C. A.*
[6] *C. A.*; Walsingham, *Diary.*   [7] *C. A.*; *Hatfield MSS.* ii. 340.
[8] *C. A.*; Walsingham, *Diary.*   [9] Dee, 9.   [10] Dee, 9.
[11] *C. A.*; *S. P. D.* cl. 62 (app. misdated 1581).
[12] *Martin's*, 321; Dee, 10.
[13] *M. S. C.* i. 181; *Hatfield MSS.* xiii. 199; Nichols, ii. 334, from Segar; Feuillerat, *Eliz.* 336, noting devices in the 'meane season' between challenge and tilt.   [14] *Martin's*, 329.
[15] *C. A.*; *Sp. P.* iii. 95, 101; Nichols, ii. 303.   [16] *Martin's*, 329.

Apr. 20–June 14. Commissioners for marriage with Duke of Alençon in London. Revels prepared barriers and two masks.[1]
Apr. 25. Dinner by Queen for commissioners.
Apr. 27. Dinner by Earl of Leicester for commissioners.
Apr. 30. Dinner by Lord Burghley for commissioners.
May 1. Baiting for commissioners.
May 4. Supper by Earl of Sussex for commissioners.
May 6–7. Tilt at Hampton Court for commissioners.
May 15–16. Tilt at Whitehall for commissioners.[2]
June 20. GREENWICH.[3]
June 26< >30. Visit to Eltham.[4]
July 5–8. Visits to Aldersbrook in Little Ilford ? (Nicholas ? Fuller), Loughborough (Francis Stonard), and Leyton (Mary, Lady Paulett).[5]
July 27–29. Visit to Wanstead (Earl of Leicester).[6]
c. **Sept.** Visits to Eltham and Sundridge (William Isley).[7]
Sept. 22–23. NONSUCH, by Streatham (Dr. Robert Forth).[8]
Oct. 3. Visit to Beddington (Sir Francis Carew).[9]
Oct. 4. RICHMOND.[10]
Nov. 1. Visit of Duke of Alençon to England.[11]
Nov. 16 or 17. WHITEHALL, by Putney (John Lacy).[12]
Nov. 17–19. Tilt.[13]
Christmas. The Revels prepared five plays and a mask.[14]
Dec. 26. Paul's.
Dec. 28. Strange's (activities).
Dec. 31. Chapel.

1582

Jan. 1. Barriers.[15]
Jan. Visit to Deptford for launch of *Golden Lion*.[16]
Feb. 1–17. PROGRESS in Kent at departure of Duke of Alencon. Southfleet (William ? Sedley, Feb. 1), Rochester (the Crown, Feb. 1–3), Sittingbourne (the George, Feb. 3–5), Canterbury (Sir Roger Manwood, Feb. 5–6), Sandwich (Mr. Manwood, Feb. 8), Dover (St. James), Canterbury (Feb. 12), Faversham (Feb. 13), Newington

[1] *S. P. F.* xv. 82, 115, 144, 202 ; *Sp. P.* iii. 110, 131 ; *V. P.* viii. 2–15 ; Walsingham, *Diary* ; Wright, ii. 134 ; *Remembrancia*, 487. On Apr. 6 the Queen was only thinking 'whether there are any new devices in the joust, or where a ball is to be held, or what beautiful women are to be at court' (*Sp. P.* iii. 91).   [2] Cf. chh. iv, xxiv.
[3] Walsingham, *Diary*.   [4] *Sp. P.* iii. 141, 144.
[5] *C. A.* ; Walsingham, *Diary*.
[6] *Hatfield MSS.* xiii. 200 ; *Rutland MSS.* i. 127.   [7] *C. A.*
[8] *C. A.* ; Walsingham, *Diary* ; *Rutland MSS.* i. 127.
[9] *C. A.* ; *Hatfield MSS.* xiii. 201.   [10] Walsingham, *Diary*.
[11] *S. P. F.* xv. 357 ; *Sp. P.* iii. 203 ; *V. P.* viii. 21.
[12] *C. A.* ; Walsingham, *Diary* ; Dee, 13 ; *Hatfield MSS.* xiii. 201.
[13] *Sp. P.* iii. 222 ; Clephan, 132, from *Bodl. Ashm. MS.* 845, ff. 164, 167 ; *Hatfield MSS.* xiii. 201.
[14] *S. P. F.* xv. 442, 453, 473, and *V. P.* viii. 26, note the princely entertainment of Anjou.
[15] Feuillerat, *Eliz.* 344 (table) ; Nichols, ii. 336, from Segar.   [16] *C. A.*

(Feb. 14), Rochester (Feb. 14–16) with visit to Bulley Hill (Anne ? Watts), Swanscombe (Ralph Weldon, Feb. 16), Horseman Place in Dartford (Nicholas ? Beer, Feb. 16–17).[1]

Feb. 17. GREENWICH.[2]

Feb. 26 (S.M.). Play at wedding of William Wentworth and Elizabeth Cecil.[3]

Feb. 27. **Chapel.**

c. March. Visit to Highgate (Lady Sheffield).[4]

c. Apr. Visit to Wanstead (Earl of Leicester).[5]

May 17–19. Hunting visit.[6]

May 20–22. Visit to Somerset House (Lord Hunsdon) for wedding of Sir Edward Hoby and Margaret Carey.[7]

July 10–12. NONSUCH, by Putney (John Lacy).[8]

c. July–Aug. Visit to Beddington (Sir Francis Carew).[9]

Aug. 17. OATLANDS, by Molesey (Thomas Brand).[10]

c. Aug.–Sept. Visits to Woking and Chobham (John Wolley).[11]

Sept. 1–2 <. Visit to Pyrford (Earl of Lincoln), by Byfleet (Lady Anne Askewe) ? [12]

Sept. 20. WINDSOR, by Egham (Richard Kellefet).[13]

c. Sept. Visits to Folly John, Mote Park, and Sunninghill.[14]

Dec. 26. **Chapel** (*A Game of the Cards*).

Dec. 27. **Hunsdon's** (*Beauty and Housewifery*).

Dec. 30. **Derby's** (*Love and Fortune*).

1583

Jan. 1. **Strange's** (activities).

Jan. 5. Mask by ladies and boys.

Jan. 6. **Sussex's** (*Ferrar*).

Jan. 12 < >18. RICHMOND, by Colnbrook.[15]

Feb. 10 (S.S.). **Leicester's** (*Telomo*).

Feb. 11. Visit to Barn Elms (Sir Francis Walsingham).[16]

Feb. 12. **Merchant Taylors** (*Ariodante and Genevora*).

c. March. Visit to Somerset House (Lord Hunsdon).[17]

c. Apr. 13. Wedding of Robert Southwell and Elizabeth Howard.[18]

Apr. 18. GREENWICH, by Clapham (John Worsopp).[19]

---

[1] C. A. ; P. C. (Feb. 1) ; Holinshed, iii. 1330 ; Walsingham, *Diary* ; Sp. P. iii. 280, 282 ; Hatfield MSS. ii. 500 ; S. P. F. xv. 444 (misdated), 484, 485 ; V. P. viii. 29. Apparently the Sandwich and Dover stages are for Anjou only, and Elizabeth remained at Canterbury Feb. 5–13.

[2] Walsingham, *Diary* ; P. C. (Feb. 18).

[3] Hatfield MSS. v. 70 ; S. P. D. clv. 54 ; 3 Ellis, iv. 43 ; cf. ch. vii.

[4] C. A.   [5] C. A.   [6] Sp. P. iii. 375.

[7] Rutland MSS. i. 136 ; Shaw (May 22).

[8] Hatfield MSS. xiii. 203 ; Hatton, 255 ; Lysons, i. 297.

[9] C. A.   [10] C. A. ; S. P. D. (Aug. 12, 17).   [11] C. A.

[12] C. A. ; Walsingham, *Diary*.   [13] C. A. ; Walsingham, *Diary*.

[14] C. A.   [15] C. A. ; S. P. D. Addl. (Jan. 12) ; Peck, 131 (Jan. 18)

[16] Walsingham, *Diary* ; Dee, 18 ; Lambeth.   [17] C. A.

[18] Lodge, app. 46 ; Rutland MSS. i. 149.

[19] C. A. ; Dee, 20 ; Lambeth.

May. Tilt for Count Albert of Alasco and French ambassador.[1]
May 27–31 < > June 1. Visits to Theobalds (Lord Burghley) and
Ponsbourne (Sir Henry Cock), by Edmonton (Lady Nicholas) and
Hackney (Sir Rowland Hayward).[2]
c. July. Visit to Nonsuch, by Streatham.[3]
July 30. OATLANDS, by Chelsea, Mortlake, and Sion.[4]
c. Aug. 27. Visits to Woking, Loseley (Sir William More), Guildford,
and (?) Petworth (Earl of Northumberland).[5]
c. Aug. Visits to Pyrford (Earl of Lincoln) and Sunninghill, and to
Hampton Court.[6]
c. Sept. Visits to Chobham (John Wolley) and Egham.[7]
Oct. 5. ST. JAMES'S.[8]
Nov. 25–29. Visit to Hampton Court, by Brentford (Thomas Wilkes).[9]
Dec. 20. WHITEHALL.[10]
c. Oct.–Dec. ? Visit to Arundel House (Earl of Arundel).[11]
Dec. 26. **Queen's.**
Dec. 29. **Queen's.**

1584

Jan. 1. **Oxford's** (*Campaspe* ?).
Jan. 6. **Chapel.**
? Jan. or Feb. Visits to Heneage House (Sir Thomas Heneage) and
Tower Hill (Lord Lumley).[12]
Feb. 2. **Chapel.**
March 3 (S.T.). **Queen's** and **Oxford's** (*Sapho and Phao* ?).
Apr. 20 < > May 2. GREENWICH.[13]
June 9. RICHMOND, by Stockwell.[14]
July 17 < > 21. NONSUCH.[15]
Aug. 7. OATLANDS, by Kingston (George Evelyn).[16]
c. Aug. Visit to Cobham (Robert Gavell ?).[17]
c. Sept. 2. Visits to Egham, Sunninghill, Windsor, Burley Bushes,
Bagshot (Sir Henry Weston), and Blackwater.[18]
Oct. 6 < > 10. HAMPTON COURT.[19]
c. Nov. 5. Visit to Nonsuch.[20]

[1] *Sp. P.* iii. 474.
[2] *C. A.*; *Hatfield MSS.* v. 70; xiii. 229; *Rutland MSS.* i. 150, 151;
Birch, i. 37.   [3] *C. A.*
[4] *C. A.*; *S. P. I.* (July 29, 30); *Martin's*, 349; *Margaret's*; Dee, 21;
Finch MSS.; Hatton, 346.
[5] *C. A.*; Kempe, 269; *Sussex Arch. Colls.* v. 193; *S. P. D.* clxi. 15.
[6] *C. A.*   [7] *C. A.*   [8] *Martin's*, 349; *Margaret's*; *S. P. I.* (Oct. 14).
[9] *C. A.*; *Martin's*, 349; *Remembrancia*, 407, ' for her private recreation, to take the air abroad '.   [10] *Martin's*, 350.
[11] Duke of Norfolk, *Life of Philip Earl of Arundel*, 22.
[12] Shaw, ii. 82.   [13] *S. P. F.* (Apr. 20); Peck, 149 (May 2).
[14] *C. A.*; *S. P. D.*; Shaw; *Hatfield MSS.* iii. 35.
[15] *S. P. F.* (July 17); Hatton, 382 (July 21).
[16] *C. A.*; Hatton, 388; Peck, 154.   [17] *C. A.*
[18] *C. A.*; Lodge, ii. 246.   [19] *Sc. P.* (Oct. 6); *S. P. D.* (Oct. 10).
[20] *C. A.*; *S. P. F.* xix. 92 (misdated Oct. 5 ?).

Nov. 12. ST. JAMES'S, by Putney (John Lacy).[1]
Nov. 17. Tilt.[2]
Dec. 6. Tilt.[3]
c. Dec. Visit to Arundel House.[4]
> Christmas. GREENWICH.[5]
Dec. 26. **Queen's** (*Phyllida and Corin*).
Dec. 27. **Oxford's boys** (*Agamemnon and Ulysses*).

1585

Jan. 1. **Oxford's** (activities).
Jan. 3. **Queen's** (*Felix and Philiomena*).
Jan. 6. **Queen's** (*Five Plays in One*).
Feb. 8 < >12. SOMERSET HOUSE.[6]
Feb. 21 (S.S.). **Queen's** (*Three Plays in One*), ready, but not shown.
Feb. 23. **Queen's** (' antick ' play and comedy).
Feb. 23 < >26. GREENWICH.[7]
c. March. Visit to Oatlands (?).[8]
March 26-30. Visit to Lambeth and Westminster.[9]
March 30 (?)–Apr. 3. Visits to Croydon (Abp.), Beddington (Sir Francis Carew), and Lambeth (Abp.).[10]
c. Apr. Visit to Lewisham.[11]
c. May 2. Visit to Croydon.[12]
c. June 18. Visit to Theobalds by Edmonton (Mr. Brassey) and Tottenham High Cross (Richard Martin).[13]
March–July. Tilt for M. de Campagny.[14]
July 11. Visit to Barn Elms.[15]
July 20 < >24. NONSUCH.[16]
July 27-29. Visit to Putney (John Lacy).[17]
c. Aug. 25. Visit to Wimbledon.[18]
c. Aug. Visit to Beddington (Sir Francis Carew).[19]
Sept. 26 < >Oct. 1. RICHMOND.[20]
Nov. 17-19. Visit to Westminster (Lord Admiral).[21]
Dec. 20-21. GREENWICH, by Lambeth (Lord Burgh).[22]
Dec. 26. **Queen's.**
Dec. 27. **Howard's.**

[1] C. A. ; Stowe, *Annales*. [2] 2 R. Hist. Soc. Trans. ix. 258.
[3] Ibid. 262 ; Clephan, 171, from *Bodl. Ashm. MS.* 845, f. 168.
[4] C. A. ; Duke of Norfolk, *Life of Earl of Arundel*, 193, puts this or another visit after the Earl's committal to the Tower on 25 Apr. 1585.
[5] Feuillerat, *Eliz.* 365.
[6] Ibid. ; *Martin's*, 371 ; S. P. I. (Feb. 8) ; S. P. F. (Feb. 12).
[7] *Hatfield MSS.* vi. 556.   [8] C. A.
[9] *Margaret's* ; Stowe, *Annales* (March 29).   [10] C. A. ; Hatton, 416.
[11] C. A.   [12] Hatton, 426.   [13] C. A. ; Shaw, ii. 83 ; Nichols, ii. 427.
[14] Cf. ch. xxiii (Lee).   [15] *Lambeth*.
[16] Hatton, 406 (July 20) ; S. P. D. (July 24).   [17] Lysons, i. 297.
[18] C. A. ; S. P. F. (Aug. 25).   [19] C. A.
[20] Sc. P. (Sept. 26) ; Nichols, ii. 440 (Oct. 1).
[21] C. A. ; *Rutland MSS.* i. 183 ; *Margaret's*.
[22] *Martin's*, 374 ; *Lambeth*.

1586

Jan. 1. **Queen's.**
Jan. 6. **Howard's and Hunsdon's.**
Jan. 9. **Stanley's boys** (activities).
Feb. 13 (S.S.). **Queen's.**
Feb. 26. Visit to Lambeth (Abp.).[1]
March 27–Apr. 6. Visit to Lambeth and Westminster.[2]
c. July 12. RICHMOND, by Putney (John Lacy).[3]
c. July. Visit to Hampton Court.[4]
Aug. 10. WINDSOR, by Staines.[5]
c. Sept. Visit to New Lodge.[6]
Oct. 24. RICHMOND, by Colnbrook.[7]
Dec. 20–21. GREENWICH, by Clapham and Lambeth.[8]
Dec. 26. **Queen's.**
Dec. 27. **Leicester's.**

1587

Jan. 1. **Queen's.**
Jan. 6. **Queen's.**
Feb. 26 (S.S.). **Paul's.**
Feb. 28. **Queen's.**
c. Jan.–Apr. Archery show (Arthur and Round Table) by Hugh Offley between Merchant Taylors and Mile End.[9]
Apr. 26–May 1 or 2. Visit to Croydon.[10]
May 1 or 2. NONSUCH.[11]
c. May. Visit to Beddington (Sir Francis Carew).[12]
May 25< >29. GREENWICH, by Streatham (Dr. Robert Forth).[13]
c. July 9–Aug. 13. THEOBALDS (Lord Burghley), by Hackney (Sir Rowland Hayward) and Enfield (Henry Middlemore), with visits to Waltham Forest, Cheshunt (Lord Talbot), and Northiaw (Earl of Warwick, July 20–21).[14]
Aug. 13< >20. OATLANDS, by Barnet (Mr. Waller), Harrow (William Wightman), Sion, and West Molesey (Thomas Brand).[15]
Sept. 19< >24. RICHMOND.[16]
Oct. 24. Dinner at Westminster (Lord Admiral).[17]
Nov. 17–21. Visit to Westminster (Lord Admiral) with dinner at Barn Elms (Sir F. Walsingham, Nov. 20).[18]
Nov. 18. Tilt.[19]

---

[1] *Lambeth.*   [2] *Lambeth.*
[3] *C. A.*; *P. C.* (July 10); *Hatfield MSS.* iii. 178; *Rutland MSS.* i. 199.
[4] *C. A.*   [5] *C. A.*; Nichols, ii. 460, from speech of Mayor of Windsor.
[6] *C. A.*   [7] *C. A.*; *Hatfield MSS.* iii. 182.
[8] *C. A.*; *Martin's*, 386; *Lambeth.*   [9] Nichols, ii. 529, from private MS.
[10] *C. A.*; Dasent, xv. 59, 64; *Hatfield MSS.* iii. 249.
[11] *P. C.* (May 2).   [12] *C. A.*
[13] *C. A.*; *Rutland MSS.* i. 215 (May 25); *P. C.* (May 29).
[14] *C. A.*; *P. C.*; *S. P. D.* (July 16, 18); *Rutland MSS.* i. 222; *Hatfield MSS.* iii. 270; v. 71; Devon, i. 187; Goodman, ii. 1.
[15] *C. A.*; *P. C.* (Aug. 20).   [16] *P. C.* (Sept. 19, 24).
[17] *Martin's*, 397; *Margaret's*; *Lambeth*; Gawdy, 18.
[18] Gawdy, 25; Shaw.   [19] Gawdy, 25.

Nov. 21–Dec. 6. Visit to Ely House (Sir Christopher Hatton).[1]
Dec. 6. SOMERSET HOUSE.[2]
Dec. 23. GREENWICH.[3]
Dec. 26. **Queen's.**
Dec. 28. Symons and company (? **Queen's,** activities).

1588

Jan. 1. **Paul's** (*Galathea ?*).
Jan. 6. **Queen's.**
c. Jan. 16–20. Visits to Fulham (Bp. of London), Hounslow (Thomas Crompton), Kensington (Mr. Malinge), and Lambeth (Abp.).[4]
Feb. 2. **Paul's** (*Endymion ?*).
Feb. 18 (S.S.). **Queen's.**
Feb. 20. **Evelyn's.**
Feb. 10 or 20. Show in honour of Leicester.[5]
Feb. 28. **Gray's Inn** (*Misfortunes of Arthur*).
c. Apr. 13–16. Visits to Hackney (Sir Rowland Hayward), Tottenham High Cross (Richard Martin), and Stoke Newington ? (Roger ? Townsend).[6]
Apr.–May. Visits to Erith (Thomas ? Compton), Croydon (Abp. of Canterbury), by Lewisham and Wanstead (Earl of Leicester, May 7).[7]
July 5–6. RICHMOND, by Lambeth and Stockwell.[8]
July 29. ST. JAMES'S, by Putney (John Lacy).[9]
Aug. 8–10. Visit to Tilbury camp, Ardern Hall in Horndon (Thomas Rich), and (?) Belhus in Aveley (Edward Barrett).[10]
Aug. 19. Visit to Ely House (Sir Christopher Hatton).[11]
Aug. 26. Tilt.[12]
Oct. 25. GREENWICH.[13]
Nov. 8 or 12. Salute from the *Desire* (Thomas Cavendish).[14]
Nov. 12 < >17. SOMERSET HOUSE.[15]
Nov. 17. Tilt.
Nov. 19. Tilt.[16]
Nov. 24. Visit to St. Paul's.[17]
Nov. 30. GREENWICH.[18]

[1] *Foljambe MSS.* 28 ; Gawdy, 25, 29 ; *Sc. P.* (Dec. 2).
[2] *Rutland MSS.* i. 232 ; *Hist. MSS.* vii. 520.   [3] *Rutland MSS.* i. 234.
[4] *C. A.* ; *Margaret's* ; *Lambeth* ; *Rutland MSS.* i. 236, 237.
[5] Cf. ch. xxiii (Churchyard).
[6] *C. A.* ; *P. C.* (Apr. 12, 16) ; Wright, ii. 370.   [7] *C. A.* ; Gawdy, 35.
[8] *C. A.* ; *P. C.* (July 7, 8) ; *Margaret's* ; *Lambeth*.
[9] *C. A.* ; *P.C.* (July 28, 29) ; *Rutland MSS.* i. 253 ; *Lambeth* ; *Margaret's*.
[10] *C. A.* ; Wright, ii. 387, 389 ; *Margaret's* ; *Lambeth* ; M. Christy in *E. H. R.* xxxiv. 43, quoting J. Aske, *Elizabetha Triumphans*, and T. Deloney, *The Queen's Visiting of the Camp at Tilbury* (cf. ch. xxiv).
[11] *Sp. P.* iv. 419.   [12] Ibid.
[13] *P. C.* (Oct. 26) ; *S. P. D.* (Oct. 23, 26) ; *Margaret's* (Oct. 15 in error).
[14] *Sp. P.* iv. 487 (Nov. 8) ; Arber, ii. 506 ; Nichols, ii. 544.
[15] *P. C.* (Nov. 17).   [16] *Sp. P.* iv. 494 ; Arber, ii. 508.
[17] *C. A.* ; Stowe, *Annales* ; *Sp. P.* iv. 494 ; Arber, ii. 508.
[18] *Martin's*, 407 ; *P. C.* (Dec. 1).

Dec. 21–23. RICHMOND, by Lambeth.[1]
Christmas. The Admiral's showed activities as well as plays this
   winter.
Dec. 26. **Queen's.**
Dec. 27. **Paul's.**
Dec. 29. **Admiral's.**

1589

Jan. 1. **Paul's.**
Jan. 12. **Paul's.**
c. Jan. Visit to Hampton Court.[2]
Jan. 30. WHITEHALL, by Chelsea.[3]
Feb. 9 (S.S.). **Queen's.**
Feb. 11. **Admiral's.**
May 26–28. Visit to Barn Elms (Sir Francis Walsingham).[4]
c. June 11. Visit to Highgate.[5]
June 18–19. NONSUCH, by Merton Abbey (Gregory Lovell).[6]
Aug. 10< >16. OATLANDS, by West Molesey (Thomas Brand).[7]
c. Sept. Visit to Hampton Court.[8]
Sept. 26 or 27. RICHMOND.[9]
c. Sept. Mask prepared for wedding of James VI in Scotland.[10]
Nov. 15. SOMERSET HOUSE.[11]
Nov. 17. Tilt.[12]
Dec. 2. RICHMOND, by Putney (John Lacy).[13]
Dec. 26. **Queen's.**
Dec. 28. **Paul's** and **Admiral's** (activities).

1590

Jan. 1. **Paul's.**
Jan. 6. **Paul's** (*Midas* ?).
Jan. 23–24. GREENWICH, by Lambeth.[14]
Jan. 27. Visit to Earl of Warwick (at Bedford House ?).[15]
March 1 (S.S.). **Queen's.**
March 3. **Admiral's.**
May 30 or 31–June 6. Visits to Hackney (Sir Rowland Hayward,
   Aug. 31), Waltham Forest (Sir Richard Bartlett), and Ely House
   (Sir Christopher Hatton, June 4–6).[16]

[1] *Sp. P.* iv. 504 ; *S. P. D.* (Dec. 19) ; *Margaret's.*   [2] *C. A.*
[3] Stowe, *Annales* ; *Martin's,* 411 ; Arber, v. lxxvii.
[4] *Martin's,* 411 ; *Margaret's* ; *Lambeth* ; *Fulham* ; Lodge, ii. 368, 375,
' whilst she is there may be moved to her but matter of delight and to
content her, which is the only cause of her going thither '.
[5] *Margaret's.*   [6] *C. A.* ; Lodge, ii. 379 ; *Margaret's.*
[7] *C. A.* ; *P. C.* (Aug. 10) ; *Hatfield MSS.* iii. 427 ; xiii. 416 (Aug. 10, 16).
[8] *C. A.*   [9] Dasent, xviii. 329 (Sept. 26) ; *Rutland MSS.* i. 276 (Sept. 27).
[10] Cf. ch. v.   [11] *Martin's,* 413 ; *Margaret's.*   [12] *C. A.*
[13] *C. A.* ; *Martin's,* 414 ; *Margaret's.*
[14] *Martin's,* 422 ; *P. C.* (Jan. 25).   [15] *Martin's,* 422.
[16] *C. A.* ; *P. C.* ; *Procl.* 825 ; *Margaret's* ; *Martin's* ; Lodge, app. 83.

July 28< >Aug. 6. OATLANDS, by Sydenham House (William Aubrey ?), Beddington (Sir Francis Carew), Chessington (William Harvey), and Stoke d'Abernon (Thomas Leyfield).[1]

Aug. Visit to the New Lodge.[2]

Aug. 30–31. Visit to Woking.[3]

Aug. 31< >Sept. 6. WINDSOR, by Chobham (Edward ? Bray) and Sunninghill.[4]

Sept. Visits to Ditton Park and Folly St. John Park (Mr. Norris).[5]

Nov. 8< >14. SOMERSET HOUSE, by Staines, Richmond, and Putney (John Lacy).[6]

Nov. 17, 19. Tilts.[7]

c. Nov. Visit to Sydenham Park.[8]

c. Nov. Visit to Ely House (Sir C. Hatton).[9]

c. Nov. 24. RICHMOND.[10]

Dec. 4, 14. Visits to Mortlake and East Sheen.[11]

Dec. 26. **Queen's.**

Dec. 27. **Strange's and Admiral's** (play and activities).

1591

Jan. 1. **Queen's.**

Jan. 3. **Queen's.**

Jan. 6. **Queen's.**

Feb. 11–13. GREENWICH, by Lambeth.[12]

Feb. 14 (S.S.). **Queen's.**

Feb. 16. **Strange's and Admiral's** (play and activities).

May 2< >9-20< >23. Visits to Hackney (Sir Rowland Hayward, May 9, 10), Tottenham High Cross (Sir Richard Martin), Theobalds (Lord Burghley, May 10-20), Enfield (Robert Wroth), and Havering.[13]

c. July 1. Visit to Croydon (?).[14]

July 19. Visit to Burghley House (Lord Burghley) for review of Earl of Essex's horse in Covent Garden.[15]

July 29< >Aug. 1–Sept. 27. PROGRESS in Surrey, Sussex, and Hants.[16]

---

[1] *C. A.* ; *Hatfield MSS.* iv. 52 (July 28) ; *P. C.* (Aug. 6).   [2] *C. A.*
[3] *S. P. D.* (Aug. 30) ; *P. C.* (Aug. 31) ; *Rutland MSS.* i. 283 ; Lodge, app. 83.   [4] *C. A.* ; *P. C.* (Sept. 6).   [5] *C. A.*
[6] *C. A.* ; Dasent, xx. 71, 75 (Nov. 8, 15) ; Lodge, ii. 422.
[7] Lodge, ii. 419 ; cf. ch. xxiii (Lee).   [8] *C. A.*
[9] Lodge, ii. 419 (Nov. 20), ' secretly, as she thought ', to meet the French ambassador, Viscount Turenne.
[10] Lodge, ii. 420 ; *P. C.* (Nov. 22) ; Dee, 36 (Nov. 20 in error).
[11] Dee, 37.   [12] *Syd. P.* i. 317 ; *Martin's*, 430 ; *Margaret's*.
[13] *C. A.* ; *P. C.* ; Haynes-Murdin, ii. 796 ; *Hatfield MSS.* iv. 108, 115 ; v. 71 ; *Rutland MSS.* i. 291 ; Wright, ii. 412.
[14] Lodge, app. 68.   Probably she did not go, as the letter refers to a plot to murder her there.   [15] *Hatfield MSS.* v. 71 ; Burghley, *Diary.*
[16] *C. A.* ; *P. C.* ; Burghley, *Diary* ; *Hatfield MSS.* v. 71 ; iv. 136 ; vi. 238 ; *S. P. D.* (Aug. 1, 2, 5, 31) ; Rymer, xvi. 109, 116–23 ; Kempe, 270, 305 ; G. C. Williamson, *Earl of Cumberland*, 77 ; *Procl.* 836 ; Nichols, iii. 96, 99 ; cf. W. D. Cooper in *Sussex Arch. Colls.* v. 176, 196, with some doubtful localities.

Mitcham (Margaret, Lady Blank), Nonsuch (Aug. 1, 2) with visit to Beddington (Sir Francis Carew), Leatherhead (Edmund Tilney), East Horsley (Thomas Cornwallis, Aug. 3), Clandon Park (Sir Henry Weston), Guildford (Aug. 4), Loseley (Sir William More, Aug. 5–9), Katherine Hall, Farnham (Bp. Winchester, Aug. 10–14), Bramshott (Edmund Mervyn, Aug. 14), The Holt (Lord Delawarr), Cowdray (Lord Montague, Aug. 14–20) with visit to Oseburn Priory (Lord Montague, Aug. 17),[1] West Dean (Sir Richard Lewknor, Aug. 20), Chichester (Lord Lumley, Aug. 20–22), Stanstead (Lord Lumley, Aug. 26), Portsmouth (Earl of Sussex, Aug. 26–31), Southwick (John White, Aug. 31, Sept. 1), Tichfield (Earl of Southampton, Sept. 2, 3), South Stoneham ? (John Caplen), Southampton (Sept. 5, 6), Fairthorne (Francis ? Serle), Bishop's Waltham (Bp. Winchester, Sept. 8, 9), Warnford (William Neale), Tichborne (Sir Benjamin Tichborne), Winchester (Bp.), Abbotstone (Marquis of Winchester), Wield (William Wallop), Farleigh (Sir Henry Wallop, Sept. 12, 13), Basing (Marquis of Winchester, Sept. 13–16) with visit to The Vine in Sherborne St. John ? (Lord Sandys, Sept. 18), Odiham (Edward More, Sept. 19, 20), Elvetham (Earl of Hertford, Sept. 20–23),[2] Farnham (Bp. Winchester, Sept. 23, 24) with visit to Bagshot ?, Sutton in Woking (Sir Henry Weston, Sept. 26–27).

Sept. 27. OATLANDS.[3]

Oct. 4 < >7. RICHMOND, by Hampton Court.[4]

c. Nov. 11. Visit to Ely House (Sir C. Hatton).[5]

Nov. 15 < >20. WHITEHALL.[6]

Nov. 17. Tilt.[7]

Dec. 26. **Queen's.**

Dec. 27. **Strange's.**

Dec. 28. **Strange's.**

1592

Jan. 1. **Strange's.**

Jan. 2. **Sussex's.**

Jan. 6. **Hertford's.**

Jan. 9. **Strange's.**

Feb. 6 (S.S.). **Strange's**

Feb. 8. **Strange's.**

Apr. 7–21. Visits to Hammersmith (William Payne, Apr. 7), Osterley (Lady Gresham, Apr. 7–9), Hampton Court (Apr. 12), Wimbledon (Sir Thomas Cecil, Apr. 14–17), Croydon (Abp. of Canterbury, Apr. 17–21 ?), Beddington (Sir Francis Carew, Apr. 18), Sydenham (William Aubrey, Apr. 21).[8]

Apr. 21. GREENWICH.[9]

---

[1] For *Cowdray Entertainment*, cf. ch. xxiv.

[2] For *Elvetham Entertainment*, cf. chh. iv, xxiv.   [3] Burghley, *Diary*.

[4] *C. A.* ; *Hatfield MSS.* iv. 144 (Oct. 4) ; *P. C.* (Oct. 7).

[5] *C. A.* ; *P. C.* (Nov. 15) ; Burghley, *Diary*.   [6] *C. A.* ; *P. C.* (Nov. 29).

[7] *C. A.* ; G. C. Williamson, *George Earl of Cumberland*, 108.

[8] *C. A.* ; *Hatfield MSS.* iv. 187 ; xiii. 465 ; *P. C.* (Apr. 12, 15, 16) ; *Margaret's*.   [9] *Hatfield MSS.* xiii. 465.

c. Apr.–July (?). Visit to Blackfriars (Sir George Carey).[1]
July 29–31. NONSUCH, by Mitcham (John Dent).[2]
c. Aug. 9–Oct. 9. PROGRESS in Surrey, Middlesex, Bucks., Berks.,
Wilts., Gloucestershire, and Oxon.[3] West Molesey (Thomas Brand),
Hanworth, Eastridge in Colnbrook (Ostrich Inn ?), Eton College,
Maidenhead (the Lion), Bisham (Lady Russell, Aug. 11–13),[4] John
Haynes, Hurst (Edward ? Ward), Reading (Mr. Davies, Aug. 15–19),
Burghfield (Francis ? Plowden, Aug. 19), Aldermaston (Sir Hum-
phrey Forster, Aug. 19–22), Chamberhouse in Thatcham (Nicholas
Fuller), Shaw near Newbury (Thomas Dolman, Aug. 24–26) with
hunt in Donnington Park, Hampstead Marshall (Thomas Parry,
Aug. 26–27 ?), Avington (Richard ? Choke, Aug. 27 ?), Ramsbury
(Earl of Pembroke, Aug. 27–29 ?),[5] Burderhope (Thomas Stevens,
Aug. 29), Lydiard Tregoze (Sir John St. John, Sept. 1), Down Ampney
(Anthony Hungerford, Sept. 1–2), Cirencester (Sir John Danvers,
Sept. 2–7), Rendcombe (Sir Richard Berkeley), Whittington (John
Cotton, Sept. 9), Sudeley Castle (Lord Chandos, Sept. 9–12)[6] with
visit to Alderton (Sir John Hickford), Northleach (William Dutton?),
Sherborne (William Dutton, Sept. 14–15), Taynton ? (Mr. Bray ?),
Burford (Laurence Tanfield, Sept. 15–16), Witney (James Yate,
Sept. 16–18), Woodstock (Sept. 18–23) with visit to Ditchley
(Sir Henry Lee),[7] Yarnton (Sir William Spencer, Sept. 23),
Oxford (Sept. 23–28),[8] Holton (George Browne, Sept. 28), Rycote
(Lord Norris, Sept. 28–Oct. 1),[9] Princes Risborough (John Reve
at parsonage), Hampden (Mrs. Hampden, Oct. 2, 3), Chequers in
Elsborough ? (William Hawtrey), Amersham ?, Chenies (Lady Bed-
ford, Oct. 4, 5), Latimer ? (Edwin Sandys), Denham (John Norris,
Oct. 7), Uxbridge (Francis ? Clifford), Bedfont (John Draper, Oct. 9).
Oct. 9. HAMPTON COURT.[10]
Nov. 17. Challenge for Shrovetide tilt.[11]
Dec. 26. **Pembroke's.**
Dec. 27. **Strange's.**
Dec. 31. **Strange's.**

1593

Jan. 1. **Strange's.**
Jan. 6. **Pembroke's.**
c. Jan. Visit to Chelsea (Lord Admiral).[12]

[1] *Lambeth.*   [2] *C. A.* ; *Hatfield MSS.* iv. 220.
[3] *C. A.* ; *P. C.* ; *Hatfield MSS.* iv. 224, 226, 227 ; xiii. 466 ; *S. P. D.*
(Aug. 13, Sept. 6) ; *Procl.* 851–3 ; Shaw ; Lodge, app. 69, 70 ; Birch,
i. 79 ; *Rutland MSS.* i. 302 ; Rye, 11–14 ; *Finch MSS.* (Sept. 15) ;
Nichols, *Illustrations*, 135 ; Plummer, *Elizabethan Oxford*, 249, 261 ;
Boas, 252.   [4] For *Bisham Entertainment*, cf. ch. xxiv.
[5] For a possible entertainment at Ramsbury, cf. ch. xxiii (Mary
Herbert).   [6] For *Sudeley Entertainment*, cf. ch. xxiv.
[7] For *Woodstock* (or *Ditchley*) *Entertainment*, cf. ch. xxiii, s.v. Lee.
[8] For Oxford plays, cf. ch. iv.
[9] For *Rycote Entertainment*, cf. ch. xxiv.   [10] *Hatfield MSS.* xiii. 466.
[11] Gawdy, 67.   [12] *C. A.*

Jan. 30–Feb. 1. Visit to Strand (Sir Robert Cecil), by Putney (John Lacy)?[1]
Feb. 5–14. Visit to Burghley House (Lord Burghley).[2]
Feb. 17. SOMERSET HOUSE.[3]
Feb. 25. ST. JAMES'S.[4]
Feb. 26 (S.M.). Tilt.[5]
Apr. 21. WHITEHALL.[6]
May 2–14<. Visit to Croydon (Abp.), by Streatham (Dr. Robert Forth).[7]
May 14< >22. NONSUCH.[8]
June 18< >24. OATLANDS, by Hampton Court.[9]
Aug. 1< >4. WINDSOR, by Egham (Richard Kellefet).[10]
c. Aug. Visit to Sunninghill.[11]
Nov. 17. Tilt.[12]
Dec. 1. HAMPTON COURT, by Laleham (Lawrence ? Tomson).[13]

1594

Jan. 6. **Queen's.**[14]
Feb. 10–12 (S.).
March 19. GREENWICH, by Richmond and Somerset House (Lord Hunsdon).[15]
May 29< >June 2–June 22< >July 5. Visits to Lambeth (Abp. of Canterbury), Sion (June 3), Wimbledon (Sir Thomas Cecil, June 3), Richmond, Osterley (Anne, Lady Gresham), Willesden (Mr. Payne, June 7), Highgate (Sir William Cornwallis, June 7), Hendon (Sir John Fortescue), Friern Barnet (Sir John Popham), Theobalds (Lord Burghley, June 13–23 ?), Pyneste near Waltham, Enfield (Robert Wroth), Loughborough (Francis Stonard), Hackney (Katharine, Lady Hayward).[16]

[1] C. A. ; Martin's, 451.
[2] Martin's, 451 ; P. C. (Feb. 7, 8, 11, 12, 14) ; Dee, 43.
[3] Martin's, 451.   [4] Ibid.
[5] Gawdy, 67.   [6] Martin's, 452.
[7] C. A. ; Martin's, 452 ; P. C. (May 6, 13, 14) ; S. P. D. (May 9) ; Hatfield MSS. iv. 309 (May 5).   [8] Hatfield MSS. iv. 319 (May 22).
[9] C. A. ; Procl. 861 ; P. C. (June 24).   [10] C. A. ; P. C. (Aug. 1, 4).
[11] C. A.
[12] Carey, Memoirs, 32 ; Clephan, 133, from Bodl. Ashm. MS. 1109, f. 154[v] ; Arber, ii. 640 ; G. C. Williamson, George Earl of Cumberland, 121.
[13] C. A. ; Birch, i. 137.
[14] Birch, i. 146. ' Mr. [Anthony] Standen was at the play and dancing on twelfth-night, which lasted till one after midnight, more by constraint than by choice, the earl of Essex having committed to him the placing and entertaining of certain Germans. The queen appeared there in a high throne, richly adorned, and " as beautiful ", says he, " to my old sight, as ever I saw her ; and next to her chair the earl, with whom she often devised in sweet and favourable manner ".'
[15] Hatfield MSS. xiii. 506 ; Martin's, 462.
[16] C. A. ; Haynes-Murdin, ii. 804 ; Hatfield MSS. iv. 539, 552, 558 ; v. 71 ; Martin's ; Dee, 49 ; Rutland MSS. i. 320 ; Wright, ii. 433 ; J. H. Lloyd, Highgate, 225, from Frere MS. (misdated 1593) ; Gawdy, 85.

July 12. Visit to Strand (Sir R. Cecil).[1]
Oct. 1 or 2. NONSUCH, by Camberwell (Bartholomew Scott) and Mitcham (Lady Blank).[2]
Oct. 25< >31. RICHMOND, by Combe (Thomas Vincent).[3]
Nov. 14. WHITEHALL ?, by Battersea.[4]
Nov. 17. Tilt.[5]
Nov. 27. SOMERSET HOUSE.[6]
Dec. 7. Visit to Savoy (Sir Thomas Heneage).[7]
Dec. 8. Visit to Hampton Court.[8]
Dec. 11. GREENWICH.[9]
Dec. 26. **Chamberlain's.**
Dec. 27. **Chamberlain's.**
Dec. 28. **Admiral's.**

1595

Jan. 1. **Admiral's.**
Jan. 6. **Admiral's.**
Jan. 26. Wedding of Earl of Derby and Lady Elizabeth Vere.[10] **Chamberlain's** (*Midsummer Night's Dream*) ?.
Jan. 30–Feb. 1. Visit to Burghley House (Lord Burghley).[11]
Feb. 18. ST. JAMES's, by Lambeth (Abp.).[12]
Feb. 24< >March 3. WHITEHALL.[13]
March 3 (S.M.). Mask (Proteus and the Rock Adamantine) by Gray's Inn.[14]
March 4. Tilt and Barriers.[15]
May 3. GREENWICH.[16]
Aug. 18–22. NONSUCH, by Whitehall and Mitcham (John ? Dent).[17]
c. Aug.–Oct. Visit to Beddington (Sir Francis Carew).[18]
Oct. 19< >24. RICHMOND, by Combe (Thomas Vincent).[19]
Nov. 4. Visit to Barn Elms (Earl of Essex).[20]
Nov. 14. WHITEHALL, by Putney (John Lacy).[21]

[1] *Hatfield MSS.* v. 71 ; xiii. 507 ; Haynes-Murdin, ii. 804.
[2] *C. A.* ; *Hatfield MSS.* v. 1 ; xiii. 508.
[3] *C. A.* ; *S. P. D.* (Oct. 31) ; *Sc. P.* (Oct. 25).
[4] *C. A.* ; *Hatfield MSS.* v. 19 ; *Martin's* (misdated Oct.).
[5] *C. A.* ; Arber, ii. 664.   [6] *Martin's*, 465 ; *Rutland MSS.* i. 324.
[7] Dee, 51.   [8] *C. A.* ; *S. P. I.* (Dec. 8).   [9] *Martin's*, 465.
[10] *C. A.* ; Stowe, *Annales.*
[11] *Martin's*, 471 ; cf. my paper on *The Occasion of A Midsummer Night's Dream* in *Sh. Homage*, 154. I there thought that the wedding must have been at Burghley House, but I now find that *C. A.* confirms Stowe in placing it at Greenwich, and must suppose that, after the ceremony, Elizabeth accompanied the bridal pair to Burghley House. If *M. N. D.* was produced, it may have been at either place.
[12] *C. A.* ; Nichols, iii. 38 ; *Hatfield MSS.* v. 121.
[13] *C. A.* ; *Rutland MSS.* i. 326 ; *Hatfield MSS.* v. 135, 138.
[14] Cf. ch. xxiv.   [15] *C. A.* ; *Gesta Grayorum*, 68.
[16] *Martin's*, 472.   [17] *C. A.* ; *Syd.P.* i. 344 ; Lodge, app. 78 ; *Martin's*, 472.
[18] *C. A.*   [19] *C. A.* ; *P. C.* (Oct. 19) ; Birch, i. 311.
[20] *Syd. P.* i. 357.
[21] *C. A.* ; *Syd. P.* i. 365 (misdated Nov. 25 for 15) ; *Martin's*, 473.

Nov. 17. Tilt.[1]
Nov. 27 or 28. RICHMOND.[2]
Dec. 11. Visit to Kew (Sir John Puckering).[3]
Dec. 18 or 19. WHITEHALL.[4]
Dec. 20. Visit to Huntingdon House (Lady Huntingdon).[5]
Dec. 23. RICHMOND, by Putney (John Lacy).[6]
Dec. 26. **Chamberlain's.**
Dec. 27. **Chamberlain's.**
Dec. 28. **Chamberlain's.**

1596

Jan. 1. **Admiral's.**
Jan. 4. **Admiral's.**
Jan. 6. **Chamberlain's.**
Feb. 22 (S.S.). **Chamberlain's** and **Admiral's.**
Feb. 24. **Admiral's.**
Apr. 2–3. GREENWICH, by Putney (John Lacy) and Lambeth.[7]
Apr. 8. Visit to Burghley House (Lord Burghley).[8]
c. Aug. Visit to Eltham.[9]
Oct. 1–2. NONSUCH, by Lambeth (Lord Burgh) and Mitcham.[10]
Oct. 12. RICHMOND, by Kingston (John ? Cox).[11]
Nov. 17. WHITEHALL, by Putney (John Lacy).[12] Tilt.[13]
Dec. 23. Visit to Strand (Sir R. Cecil).[14]
Dec. 26. **Chamberlain's.**
Dec. 27. **Chamberlain's.**

1597

Jan. 1. **Chamberlain's.**
Jan. 6. **Chamberlain's.**
Feb. 6 (S.S.). **Chamberlain's.**
Feb. 8. **Chamberlain's.**
Feb. 19. Visit to Chelsea (Earl of Nottingham).[15]
March. Visit to Putney (John Lacy).[16]
May 7. GREENWICH.[17]
c. July 20–22. Visit to Scadbury (Sir Thomas Walsingham), by Eltham and Chislehurst (Richard Carmarden).[18]
Aug. 17–Sept. 20. PROGRESS in Essex, Middlesex, and Herts.[19] Hackney

---

[1] *C. A.*   [2] *Syd. P.* i. 366, 369, 371 ; *Martin's,* 473.
[3] *Syd. P.* i. 376.   [4] *Syd. P.* i. 380 ; *Martin's,* 474.
[5] *Syd. P.* i. 382.
[6] *C. A.* ; *P. C.* (Dec. 28) ; *Syd. P.* i. 384 ; *Martin's,* 474.
[7] *C. A.* ; *Martin's,* 483 ; *P. C.* (Apr. 4).   [8] *Martin's,* 483.
[9] *C. A.*   [10] *C. A.* ; *Syd. P.* ii. 5, 6 ; *Martin's,* 488 ; *Margaret's.*
[11] *C. A.* ; *Hatfield MSS.* vi. 425 ; Birch, ii. 173 (Oct. 13).
[12] *C. A.* ; Wright, ii. 465.   [13] *C. A.* ; cf. ch. xxiii (Bacon).
[14] *Martin's,* 488.   [15] *Syd. P.* ii. 17 ; *Fulham.*
[16] Lysons, i. 297.   [17] *Martin's,* 496.
[18] *C. A.* ; Wright, ii. 477 (July 20) ; *Hatfield MSS.* vii. 306 (July 22).
[19] *C. A.* ; *P. C.* ; *S. P. D.* (Sept. 13) ; *Hatfield MSS.* vii. 361, 370, 378 ; *Rutland MSS.* i. 342, 343 ; iv. 209 ; Stowe, *Annales* ; Stiffkey, 141 ; Carey, *Memoirs,* 51 ; 1 Ellis, ii. 274.

(Lady Hayward), Ruckholt in Leyton (Michael Hicks, Aug. 17–19), Claybury (Thomas Knyvett, Aug. 19), Havering (Aug. 19–30) with visit to Pyrgo (Sir Henry Grey), Loughborough (Francis Stonard) with hunt at Loughton (Robert Wroth), Mrs. Bracy (Sept. 5), Theobalds (Lord Burghley, Sept. 5, 7, 9) with visit to Enfield Chase (Sir Robert Cecil) and hunt in Waltham forest (Ralph Colston's walk), Edmonton (Mr. Woodward), Highgate (Sir William Cornwallis, Sept. 13, 18, 19), Kensington (Walter Cope, Sept. 19), Putney (John Lacy, Sept. 19–20).

Sept. 20. RICHMOND.[1]

c. Oct. 20. WHITEHALL, by Putney (John Lacy) and Chelsea (Lord Delawarr).[2]

Nov. 17. Tilt.[3]

Dec. 26. **Chamberlain's.**

Dec. 27. **Admiral's.**

1598

Jan. 1. **Chamberlain's.**

Jan. 6. **Chamberlain's.** Mask (Passions) by Middle Temple.[4]

Feb. 26 (S.S.). **Chamberlain's.**

Feb. 28. **Admiral's.**

May 2. GREENWICH.[5]

July 5. Visit to Burghley House (Lord Burghley).[6]

c. July. Visit to Eltham (Hugh Miller and John Lee).[7]

c. Sept. Visit to Newington (Mr. Saunderson).[8]

Sept. 12–13. NONSUCH, by Mitcham (Dr. Julius Caesar).[9]

Sept. Visit to Beddington (Sir Francis Carew).[10]

c. Oct. 10. RICHMOND, by Kingston (George ? Evelyn).[11]

Nov. 13 or 14. WHITEHALL, by Chelsea (Earl of Shrewsbury).[12]

Nov. 17. Tilt.[13]

Dec. 26. **Chamberlain's.**

Dec. 27. **Admiral's.**

1599

Jan. 1. **Chamberlain's.**

Jan. 6. **Admiral's.**

Feb. 10. RICHMOND, by Chelsea (Earl of Shrewsbury).[14]

Feb. 18 (S.S.). **Admiral's.**

Feb. 20. **Chamberlain's.**

Apr. 3. GREENWICH, by Lambeth (Abp.).[15]

Apr. 7 (Easter Eve). Two Admiral's men at court.[16]

---

[1] C. A. ; P. C. (Sept. 21).   [2] P. C. ; Martin's, 497.   [3] C. A.
[4] Cf. ch. v.   [5] Martin's, 514 ; Rutland MSS. i. 345 (May 1).
[6] Martin's, 515.   [7] C. A.   [8] C. A.
[9] O. A. ; P. C. (Sept. 13) ; Chamberlain, 19 ; Lysons, i. 257.
[10] C. A.   [11] C. A. ; Chamberlain, 20.
[12] C. A. ; Stowe, Annales ; Martin's, 516 ; Chamberlain, 29.
[13] Chamberlain, 29.   [14] C. A. ; Martin's, 522 ; Rutland MSS. i. 351.
[15] Martin's, 523 ; P. C. (Apr. 2, 3, 4).   [16] Henslowe, i. 104.

June 25. Visit to Alice, Countess of Derby (Holborn ?), for wedding of
    Mary Hemingham.[1]
c. July. Visit to Eltham.[2]
July 27–30. Visit to Wimbledon (Thomas, Lord Burghley), by Vaux-
    hall (Sir Noel Caron).[3]
July 30. NONSUCH.[4]
Aug. 16–17. Visit to Beddington (Sir Francis Carew).[5]
c. Aug. 22. Visit to Somerset House.[6]
Sept. 4–7. Visit to Hampton Court.[7]
Oct. 3. RICHMOND, by Kingston (George ? Evelyn).[8]
c. Oct. Visit to Hampton Court.[9]
Nov. 13. WHITEHALL, by Putney (John Lacy) and Chelsea (Earl of
    Nottingham and Sir Arthur Gorges).[10]
Nov. 19. Tilt.[11]
Nov. 28. Visit to Earl of Essex at York House.[12]
Dec. 7. RICHMOND, by Putney (John Lacy).[13]
Christmas.[14]
Dec. 26. **Chamberlain's.**
Dec. 27. **Admiral's** (*Old Fortunatus ?*).

1600

Jan. 1. **Admiral's** (*Shoemaker's Holiday*).
Jan. 6. **Chamberlain's.**
Jan. 19–21. Visit to Chelsea (Earl of Nottingham).[15]
Feb. 3 (S.S.). **Chamberlain's.**
Feb. 5. **Derby's.**
Apr. 13 < >20. GREENWICH, by Lambeth.[16]
May 12. Activities, by Peter Bromvill.
May 13. Baiting.[17]
June 10. Visit to Lumley House (Lord Lumley), Greenwich.[18]

[1] Chamberlain, 52 ; Nichols, iii. 467.   [2] *C. A.*
[3] *C. A.* ; Chamberlain, 57 ; *Lambeth*.   [4] Chamberlain, 57.
[5] *Syd. P.* ii. 118.   [6] *Procl.* 903.   [7] *S. P. D.* ; *Syd. P.* ii. 119.
[8] *C. A.* ; *Syd. P.* ii. 129, 130.   [9] *C. A.*
[10] *C. A.* ; *Syd. P.* ii. 141 ; *Martin's*, 525 ; *Margaret's* ; Stowe, *Annales*.
[11] *C. A.* ; *Syd. P.* ii. 142.   [12] Devereux, ii. 92.
[13] *C. A.* ; *Syd. P.* ii. 149 ; Winwood, i. 137 ; *Martin's*, 525.
[14] *Syd. P.* ii. 155 (Jan. 5) : ' Her Majestie is in very good health, and
comes much abroad these holidayes ; for almost every night she is in the
presence, to see the ladies dawnce the old and new country dawnces, with
the taber and pipe.'   [15] *Syd. P.* ii. 161.
[16] *C. A.* ; *P. C.* (Apr. 13, 20).
[17] *Hatfield MSS.* x. 139 (May 5), ' The Queen would fain hear the French
gentleman sing and play who is so much commended, and saith if she had
been put in mind or could yet tell how to do it, she would see the gentleman who danced on the rope and is so cunning in those voltiges ' ; *Syd. P.*
ii. 194 (May 12), ' Her Maiestie is very well ; this day she appointes to
see a Frenchman doe feates upon a rope in the Conduit court. To morrow
she hath comanded the beares, the bull, and the ape, to be baited in the
tiltyard. Upon Wednesday she will have solemn dawncing.' On Peter
Bromvill, cf. App. D, No. cxxiii.   [18] *Syd. P.* ii. 201.

June 16–17. Visit to Blackfriars (Lady Russell and Lord Cobham) for wedding of Lord Herbert and Anne Russell, with mask (*The Lost Muse*).[1]

July 29. NONSUCH, by Newington (Mr. Carey).[2]

Aug. 5–6. Visit to Tooting (John Lacy).[3]

Aug. 13–16. Visit to Beddington (Sir F. Carew) and Croydon (Aug. 14).[4]

Aug. ? Visit to Kingston (George Evelyn).[5]

Aug. 24< >26. OATLANDS, by Molesey (Dorothy, Lady Edmondes).[6]

Sept. 1. Hunt at New Lodge.[7]

Sept. 4. Visit to Hanworth (William Killigrew).[8]

Sept. 9. Visit to Esher (Richard Drake).[9]

>Sept. 12. Visit to Hampton Court (Earl of Nottingham).[10]

c. Sept.–Oct. Visit to Thorpe (Mr. Bereblock).[11]

Oct. 9. RICHMOND, by Sunbury (Sir Philip Boteler).[12]

Nov. 13. WHITEHALL, by Chelsea (Earl of Shrewsbury).[13]

Nov. 17. Tilt.[14]

>Dec. 4. Visit to Sackville House (Lady Glemham).[15]

Dec. 22. Visit to Strand (Sir R. Cecil).[16]

Dec. 26. **Chamberlain's.**

Dec. 28. **Admiral's.**

1601

Jan. 1. **Paul's** and **Derby's.**

Jan. 6. **Chamberlain's, Admiral's, Derby's,** and **Chapel** (' showe ').

Feb. 2. **Admiral's.**

Feb. 22 (S.S.). **Chapel.**

Feb. 24. **Chamberlain's.**

May 1. Visit to Highgate (Sir William Cornwallis).[17]

May 2. Visit to Chelsea (Earl of Lincoln) ?[18]

May 7. GREENWICH.[19]

May 23. Visit by Lambeth.[20]

c. July. Visits to Eltham (Hugh Miller) and Blackwall.[21]

[1] Cf. ch. v.
[2] *C. A.* ; *Syd. P.* ii. 208.
[3] *C. A.* ; *Syd. P.* ii. 210.
[4] *Syd. P.* ii. 210.
[5] Nichols, iii. 489.
[6] *C. A.* ; *S. P. D.* (Aug. 23) ; *Syd. P.* ii. 208–213.   [7] *Syd. P.* ii. 213.
[8] *C. A.* ; *Syd. P.* ii. 213.
[9] *C. A.* ; *Syd. P.* ii. 213, 214.
[10] *Syd. P.* ii. 215.   [11] *C. A.*
[12] *C. A.* ; *Syd. P.* ii. 217 ; Chamberlain, 89.
[13] *C. A.* ; Stowe, *Annales* ; *Margaret's.*
[14] *C. A.* ; Winwood, i. 271, 274 ; Gawdy, 103, 105 ; cf. ch. xxiii (Clifford).
[15] *Hatfield MSS.* x. 406. A visit of 1600 to Baynard's Castle (Sir Robert Sydney) described in Harrington, i. 312, must fall between Nov. 13 and the Essex outbreak of 8 Feb. 1601, as Sydney was abroad earlier in 1600.
[16] Chamberlain, 97.
[17] *Martin's,* 546 ; *Hatfield MSS.* xi. 543, ' There is a great gest expected to come a maying hither. I wish your leisure and disposition may serve for maying '.   [18] *Hatfield MSS.* xi. 185.
[19] *Martin's,* 546.   [20] *Lambeth.*   [21] *C. A.*

Aug. 6–8. WINDSOR, by Fulham (Bp. of London), Brentford, Hanworth (William Killigrew), Staines (Bush Inn, Aug. 8).[1]

Aug. Visits to Old Windsor (William ? Meredith), Little Park, Mote Park, Folly John Park (Anthony ? Duck), and Philberds in Bray (William ? Goddard).[2]

Aug. 13. Visit to Stoke Poges (Sir Edward Coke).[3]

Aug. 28–Sept. 28. PROGRESS in Berks., Hants, and Surrey.[4] Hurst (Sir Richard Ward, Aug. 28), Reading (Mr. Davies ?, Aug. 28–Sept. 1) with visit to Caversham (Sir William Knollys),[5] Englefield (Sir Edward Norris), Aldermaston (Sir Humphrey Forster, Sept. 5), Silchester Heath (Sept. 5), Beaurepaire (Sir Robert Remington), Basing (Marquis of Winchester, Sept. 5–19), South Warnborough (Richard White, Sept. 20), Crondall (Mr. Paulet), Farnham (Bp. of Winchester, Sept. 22, 23), Seale (Lady Woodruff), Loseley (Sir George More, Sept. 23), Clandon (Sir Richard Weston), Stoke d'Abernon (Thomas ? Vincent), Absey (Epsom ?) Court (Mr. Blanden).

Sept. 28. RICHMOND.[6]

Oct. 24. WHITEHALL, by Putney.[7]

Nov. 17. Tilt.[8]

Christmas.[9] There may have been barriers.[10]

Dec. 26. **Chamberlain's.**

Dec. 27. **Chamberlain's** and **Admiral's** (with activities).

Dec. 29. Visit to Blackfriars (Lord Hunsdon), with play.[11]

1602

Jan. 1. **Chamberlain's.**

Jan. 3. **Worcester's.**

Jan. 6. **Chapel.**

Jan. 10. **Chapel.**

Feb. 14 (S.S.). **Chamberlain's** and **Chapel.**

Feb. 19. RICHMOND, by Putney (John Lacy).[12]

---

[1] *C. A.*; *Lambeth*; *Hatfield MSS.* xi. 328, 329.   [2] *C. A.* (Sept. 19).

[3] *C. A.*; *Hatfield MSS.* xi. 332; Chamberlain, 118; *S. P. D.* (Sept. 19).

[4] *C. A.*; *P. C.*; Shaw; *S. P. D.* (Aug. 27; Sept. 1, 19, 23); Stowe, *Annales*, 797; Chamberlain, 117; *Hatfield MSS.* xi. 381, 392, 394; *Carew-Cecil Corres.* 95; Goodman, ii. 22; *Remembrancia*, 286: *Rutland MSS.* i. 379, 380; *Egerton Papers*, 328.

[5] Chamberlain, 117, ' Mr. Controller made great chere, and entertained her with many devises of singing, dauncing, and playing wenches, and such like '; *Hatfield MSS.* xi. 362 (J. Herbert—R. Cecil), ' Her Majesty, God be praised, liketh her journey, the air of this soil and the pleasures and pastimes shewed her in the way, marvellous well '.

[6] *Rutland MS.* i. 380.

[7] *C. A.*; *P. C.* (Oct. 25); *Margaret's*; *Martin's*, 548.   [8] *C. A.*

[9] Chamberlain in *S. P. D.* cclxxxii, 48, ' There has been such a small court this Christmas that the guard were not troubled to keep doors at the plays and pastimes '.   [10] *Hatfield MSS.* xi. 544.

[11] *S. P. D. Eliz.* cclxxxii. 48, ' The Q: dined this day priuatly at my Ld Chamberlains; I came euen now from the Blackfriers, where I saw her at the play with all her *candidae auditrices* '; cf. ch. xiii (Chamberlain's) and *M. L. R.* ii. 12.   [12] *C. A.*; *Martin's*, 558; *Lambeth* (misdated 160⅔).

Apr. 9 or 10. Visit to Wimbledon (Lord Burghley) ?[1]
Apr. 19. GREENWICH, by Lambeth (Abp.) and Blackfriars (Lord Hunsdon).[2]
May 1. Visit to Sydmonscourt, Lewisham (Sir Richard Buckley).[3]
May 5. Visit to St. James's Park (Dorothy Lady Chandos and Sir William Knollys).[4]
c. July 15. Visit to Eltham (Sir John Stanhope, Hugh Miller, and Sir Thomas Walsingham).[5]
July 28–Aug. 10 ? PROGRESS in Middlesex and Bucks.[6] Lambeth (July 28), Chiswick (Sir William Russell, July 28), Hounslow (Mr. Whitby), Harlington (Ambrose Copinger), Harefield (Sir Thomas Egerton, July 31–Aug. 3),[7] Hitcham (Sir William Clarke, Aug. 3–9) with visit to Taplow (Sir Henry Guilford, Aug. 7), Riddings in Datchet (Richard ? Hanbury), Thorpe (Mr. Oglethorpe).
Aug. c. 10. OATLANDS.[8]
c. Aug.–Sept. Visits to Woking, Chertsey (John Hammond), Byfleet Lodge, New Lodge, and to Mr. Brooke in the forest, Mr. Bromley, and Mr. Woodward.[9]
Oct. 2 <. Visit to West Drayton (Lord Hunsdon) by Bedfont (John Draper).[10]
Oct. 8. RICHMOND.[11]
Nov. 15. WHITEHALL, by Putney (John Lacy).[12]
Nov. 17. Tilt.[13]
Dec. 6. Visit to Savoy (Sir Robert Cecil), with dialogues.[14]
Dec. 6< >23. Visits to Arundel House (Earl of Nottingham) and Blackfriars (Lord Hunsdon).[15]
Christmas.[16]
Dec. 26. **Chamberlain's.**
Dec. 27. **Admiral's.**

1603

Jan. 1. **Paul's.**
Jan. 6. **Hertford's.**

[1] *Hatfield MSS.* xii. 99.   [2] *C. A.* ; Chamberlain, 126 ; *Lambeth*.
[3] *C. A.* ; Chamberlain, 133. Lord Cumberland's May Day show of horsemen (cf. ch. xxiii) may belong to this year, or less probably 1601.
[4] *Hatfield MSS.* xii. 140 ; Chamberlain, 133.
[5] *C. A.* ; *Hatfield MSS.* xii. 226.
[6] *C. A.* ; *S. P. D.* (Aug. 4, 6, 7) ; *Martin's* ; *Fulham* ; *Hatfield MSS.* xii. 302, 305, 358 ; Lodge, ii. 552, 554 ; *Egerton Papers*, 340 ; Winwood, i. 429 ; Chamberlain, 150.   [7] For *Harefield Entertainment*, cf. ch. xxiv.
[8] *S.P.D.* (Aug. 6, 15).   [9] *C. A.*
[10] *C. A.* ; cf. Chamberlain, 152.   [11] Chamberlain, 157.
[12] *C. A.* ; Chamberlain, 162 ; *Martin's*, 561.
[13] *C. A.* ; *Hatfield MSS.* xii. 438, 459 ; Chamberlain, 163.
[14] Chamberlain, 167 ; *Hatfield MSS.* xii. 507, 560, 568 ; cf. ch. xxiii (Cecil).   [15] Chamberlain, 169.
[16] Chamberlain, 172, ' The court hath flourisht more then ordinarie ', with ' many playes ' ; *Syd. P.* ii. 262, ' Mrs. Mary [Fitton] upon St. Steuens day in the afternoon dawnced before the Queen two galliards with one Mr. Palmer, the admirablest dawncer of this tyme ; both were much commended by her Majestie ; then she dawnced with hym a corante '.

Jan. 17. Visit to Charterhouse (Lord Howard de Walden).[1]
Jan. 21. RICHMOND, by Putney (John Lacy).[2]
Feb. 2. **Chamberlain's.**
March 6 (S.S.). **Admiral's.**
March 8 (?). **Admiral's.**
March 24. *Obiit Elizabetha.* Accession of James.
Apr. 5–May 11. PROGRESS of James from Scotland.[3]   Seton (Earl of
  Wintoun, Apr. 5), Dunglass (Lord Home, Apr. 5, 6), Berwick
  (Apr. 6–8), Fenham (Sir William Read, Apr. 8), Widdrington (Sir
  Robert Carey, Apr. 8, 9), Newcastle (Robert Dudley, Apr. 9–13),
  Lumley Castle (Lord Lumley, Apr. 13), Durham Castle (Bp. of
  Durham, Apr. 13, 14), Walworth (Mrs. Jenison, Apr. 14, 15), Top-
  cliffe (William Ingleby, Apr. 15, 16), York (Lord Burghley, Apr. 16–
  18), Grimston Hall (Sir Edward Stanhope, Apr. 18, 19), Pontefract
  Castle (Apr. 19), Doncaster (Bear and Sun, Apr. 19, 20), Blyth
  (Apr. 20), Worksop (Earl of Shrewsbury, Apr. 20, 21),[4] Southwell
  (Apr. 21), Newark Castle (Apr. 21, 22), Belvoir Castle (Earl of
  Rutland, Apr. 22, 23), Burley on the Hill (Sir John Harington,
  Apr. 23), Burghley (Lord Burghley, Apr. 23–27) with another visit
  to Burley on the Hill (Apr. 25, 26), Apethorpe (Sir AnthonyMildmay,
  Apr. 27), Hinchinbrook (Sir Oliver Cromwell, Apr. 27–29), God-
  manchester (Apr. 29), Royston (Robert Chester, Apr. 29, 30),
  Standon (Thomas Sadleir, Apr. 30–May 2), Broxbourne (Henry
  Cock, May 2, 3), Theobalds (Sir Robert Cecil, May 3–7), Stamford
  Hill (May 7),[5] Charterhouse (Lord Howard de Walden, May 7–11)
  with visits to Whitehall and St. James's.
May 11. TOWER, by Whitehall.[6]
May 13. GREENWICH.[7]
May 25–27. Visits to Nonsuch by Putney, Beddington (Sir Francis
  Carew), Oatlands, and Hampton Court.[8]
c. June 12. Visits to Sion and Windsor.[9]
June 1–27. PROGRESS of Anne from Scotland.[10]   Berwick (June 3),
  Bishop Auckland ? (Bp. of Durham), York (June 11–15), Grimston
  Hall (Sir Edward Stanhope, June 15), Worksop (Earl of Shrewsbury),
  Newark, Nottingham, Wollaton (Sir Percival Willoughby, June 21),
  Ashby de la Zouch (Earl of Huntingdon, June 23), Leicester (Sir

---

[1] Chamberlain, 174.
[2] *C. A.* ; Lysons, i. 297 ; Chamberlain, 174 ; *Martin's*, 567.
[3] *Contemporary Prints* (cf. ch. xxiv) ; Stowe, *Annales* ;   Camden ;
Nichols, iii. 306 ; iv. 1054 ; Shaw ; 1 Ellis, iii. 71, 75 ; *Procl.* 943, 944 ;
S. P. D. (Apr. 21, 22, 25, 29 ; May 10) ; Hawarde, 180 ; *Egerton Papers*, 369.
[4] At Worksop were huntsmen in green with a woodman's speech
(Nichols, i. 86, from printed description).
[5] For an abandoned entertainment at Bishopsgate, cf. ch. xxiv (Dekker,
Coronation Entertainment).   [6] Stowe, *Annales* ; Shaw ; Hawarde, 181.
[7] Hawarde, 181.   [8] Hawarde, 182 ; Shaw ; Gawdy, 132.
[9] Shaw ; 2 Ellis, iii. 201, ' having vewed all his housese '.
[10] Green, 4, from *Account* of Marmaduke Darrell ;   Nichols, i. 189 ;
iv. 1056, and *Leicestershire*, i. 417 ; iii. 589 ; Kelly, *Progresses*, 318 ;
Middleton MSS. 463 ; Wiffen, ii. 70 ; 1 Ellis, iii. 73 ; Lodge, App. 108.

William Skipwith, June 23, 24), Dingley (Sir Thomas Griffin, June 24,
25), Holdenby (Christopher Hatton, June 25), Althorp (Sir Robert
Spencer, June 25-27),[1] Easton Neston (Sir George Fermor, June 27).
June 24. WINDSOR, by Hanworth (Sir William Killigrew).[2]
June 27-30. Visits to Easton Neston (June 27) meeting Anne, Grafton
(Earl of Cumberland, June 27, 28),[3] Salden in Muresly (Sir John
Fortescue), and probably Aylesbury (Sir John Packington), Hampden
(Alexander Hampden), and Great Missenden (Sir William Fleetwood).[4]
July 13 < >16. HAMPTON COURT.[5]
July 22-23. WHITEHALL, by Fulham (Bp. of London).[6]
July 25. Coronation.[7]
July 27. HAMPTON COURT.[8]
Aug. 10-Sept. 20. PROGRESS in Surrey, Hants, Berks., and Oxon.[9]
Pyrford (Sir Francis Wolley, Aug. 10), Loseley (Sir George More,
Aug. 11, 12), Farnham Castle (Bp. of Winchester, Aug. 14, 17),
South Warnborough (Sir Thomas White), Basing (Marquis of Win-
chester, Aug. 17, 22, 23), Salisbury (Bp. of Salisbury, Aug. 26-28),
Basing again (Aug. 31), Shaw (Thomas Dolman), Woodstock (Sept.
8-20) with visit to Sir Henry Lee (Sept. 15).
Sept. 20. WINCHESTER.[10]
Sept. 20 < >Oct. 6. Play.[11]
Sept. 20 < >Oct. 17.   Mask on arrival of Henry.[12]
Sept. 20 < >Oct. 17. Visits to Southampton and Isle of Wight.[13]
Oct. 20 < >24. WILTON (Earl of Pembroke).[14]
Nov. 1. Visit to Salisbury.[15]
Dec. 2. **King's** (*As You Like It ?*).
Dec. 12 < >21. HAMPTON COURT.[16]
Christmas.[17]
Dec. 26. **King's.**
Dec. 27. **King's.**
Dec. 28. **King's.**
Dec. 30. **King's.**

[1] For entertainment at Althorp, cf. ch. xxiii (Jonson).
[2] Lodge, iii. 15 ; 1 Ellis, iii. 81 ; Shaw ; Gardiner, i. 113.
[3] There were ' speeches and delicate presents ' at Grafton (Wiffen, ii. 71).
[4] Wiffen, ii. 71 ; Shaw.   [5] *S. P. D.* (July 13) ; *Procl.* 965.
[6] Stowe, *Annales*; *V.P.* x.74. [7] Stowe, *Annales*; *V.P.* x. 75. [8] *V.P.* x. 74.
[9] Nichols, i. xi, 250 (from gests in B.M. *Cole MS.* xlvi. 324) ; iv. 1059 ;
S. P. D. (Aug. 17, 22, 31 ; Sept. 11, 15) ; *Procl.* 969-71 ; Shaw ; Bradley,
ii. 180-3 ; Hawarde, 272 ; Lodge, iii. 22, 24, 26, 28, 33, 34 (' our *camp
volant*, which every week dislodgeth '), 38, App. 108, 109, 115 ; *V. P.* x. 83.
[10] Lodge, iii. 34, 36, 41.
[11] Bradley, ii. 190 (Arabella Stuart to Lord Shrewsbury), ' There was
an interlude, but not so ridiculous, as ridiculous as it was, as my letter '.
[12] Cf. ch. v.   [13] Shaw ; Beaumont in *King's MS.* cxxiv, f. 174ᵛ.
[14] Lodge, iii. 58 ; *S. P. D.* (Oct. 20) ; *Procl.* 974 (Oct. 24).
[15] Nichols, iv. 1059 ; *S. P. D.* (Nov. 1).   [16] *S. P. D.* (Dec. 21).
[17] Bradley, ii. 195, ' It is said there shall be 30 playes ', 199 ; *Wilbraham's
Journal* (*Camd. Misc.* x), 66, ' manie plaies and dances with swordes .'
One of the King's men's plays was *Fair Maid of Bristow.*

1604

Jan. 1. **King's** (two plays, one of Robin Goodfellow, *Midsummer Night's Dream* ?). Mask (Indian and Chinese Knights).[1]

Jan. 2. **Queen's.**

Jan. 4. **Prince's.**

Jan. 6. Mask.

Jan. 8. Queen's mask (*The Vision of the Twelve Goddesses*).

Jan. 13. **Queen's.**

Jan. 15. **Prince's.**

Jan. 21. **Prince's.**

Jan. 22. **Prince's.**

Jan. Tilt.[2]

Feb. 2. **King's.**

Feb. 13. Whitehall.[3]

Feb. 19 (S.S.). **King's.**

Feb. 20. **Prince's** and **Paul's** (Middleton's *Phoenix* ?).[4]

Feb. 21. **Queen's Revels.**

March 12. Tower.[5]

March 13. Lion baiting.[6]

March 15. Entry through London with pageants to Whitehall.[7]

March 29. Tilt.[8]

May 1. Visit to Highgate (Sir William Cornwallis) with Jonson's *Penates*.[9]

May 30 < > June 2. Greenwich.[10]

June 16. Visit to Ruckholt in Leyton (Michael Hicks).[11]

July 3 or 4. Whitehall.[12]

July 12–21. Visits to Oatlands (July 14–16) and Windsor (July 18, 21).[13]

July 24–Aug. 14. Progress in Herts., Hunts., and Beds., broken by Spanish visit.[14] Theobalds (Lord Cecil, July 24–29), Somersham (Sir John Cutts, > Aug. 2), Bletsoe (Lord St. John, Aug. 5–14).

Aug. 10. Arrival of Fernandez de Velasco, Constable of Castile, and other Spanish and Flemish commissioners at Somerset House.

Aug. 14. Whitehall.[15]

Aug. 19. Signature of treaty and dinner to commissioners at Whitehall, with baiting and activities.[16]

Aug. 25. Departure of Constable of Castile.

[1] Cf. ch. xxiii (Daniel, *Twelve Goddesses*).

[2] Law, *Hampton Court*, ii. 11.   [3] *Margaret's.*

[4] Gawdy, 141 (Feb. 20), 'Ther hath bene ij playes this shroftyde before the king and ther shall be an other to morrow'.   [5] *V. P.* x. 139.

[6] Stowe, *Annales.*   [7] Cf. ch. xxiv.   [8] Arber, iii. 257.

[9] Shaw; cf. ch. xxii (Jonson).   [10] Shaw (May 30, June 2).

[11] Shaw.   [12] Shaw (July 3); *S. P. D.* (July 4).

[13] *Procl.* 995; *S. P. D.* (July 14, 18); Shaw; *V. P.* x. 171.

[14] *S. P. D.* (July 28, 29, 30; Aug. 2, 6); Shaw; *V. P.* x. 171; Lodge, App. 115.

[15] 2 Ellis, iii. 207; *Egerton Papers*, 395.

[16] *C. D. I.* lxxi. 483; Rye, 117; E. Law, *Shakespeare as a Groom of the Chamber*; *V. P.* x. 175; *Gawdy MSS.* 95; Winwood, ii. 26; cf. App. B.

Aug. 20–Sept. 6 < >15. PROGRESS resumed in Herts. and Oxon.[1]
Ware (Aug. 20), Woodstock (Sept. 6), Langley.

Sept. 6 < >15. WINDSOR.[2]

Sept. 21. Visit to Eton College.[3]

Sept. 22. HAMPTON COURT.[4]

Oct. 1–6. Visit to Windsor and Easton Neston (Sir George Fermor) to meet Charles.[5]

Oct. 16. WHITEHALL.[6]

Nov. 1. **King's** (*Othello*).

Nov. 4. **King's** (*Merry Wives of Windsor*).

Nov. 23. **Prince's.**

Nov. 24. **Prince's.**

Dec. 14. **Prince's.**

Dec. 19. **Prince's.**

Dec. 26. **King's** (*Measure for Measure*).

Dec. 27. Mask for wedding of Sir Philip Herbert and Lady Susan Vere.

Dec. 28. **King's** (*Comedy of Errors*).

Dec. 30. **Queen's** (*How to Learn of a Woman to Woo*).

1605

Jan. 1. **Queen's Revels** (*All Fools*).

Jan. 3. **Queen's Revels.**[7]

Jan. 6. Creation of Charles as Duke of York. Queen's mask (*Mask of Blackness*).

Jan. 7. **King's** (*Henry V*).

Jan. 8. **King's** (*Every Man Out of His Humour*).

Jan. 9 < >14. **King's** (*Love's Labour's Lost*), at the Earl of Southampton's or Viscount Cranborne's for the Queen.[8]

Jan. 15. **Prince's.**

Jan. 22. **Prince's.**

Feb. 2. **King's** (*Every Man in His Humour*). Mask by Duke of Holst (?).[9]

Feb. 3. **King's** (play ready but not shown).

Feb. 5. **Prince's.**

Feb. 10 (S.S.). **King's** (*Merchant of Venice*).

Feb. 11. **King's** (*Spanish Maze*).

Feb. 12. **King's** (*Merchant of Venice*).

Feb. 19. **Prince's.**

Feb. 28 < >March 6. GREENWICH.[10]

[1] *S. P. D.* (Sept. 6) ; Winwood, ii. 26 ; *Gawdy MSS.* 95 ; Warton, *Hist. of Kiddington* (1815), 58 ; Shaw.
[2] *Procl.* 1001 ; *S. P. D.* (Sept. 16, 20).   [3] Shaw ; Winwood, ii. 33.
[4] *Gawdy MSS.* 96.   [5] Stowe, *Annales*, 823 ; Carey, *Memoirs*, 83.
[6] *Gawdy MSS.* 97 ; *Margaret's.*
[7] This is probably the play which concluded an entertainment by the Spanish ambassador to the Duke of Holst (Winwood, ii. 44 ; Sullivan, 26). Carleton says, ' After Dinner he came home to us, with a Play and a Banquett '.   [8] Cf. App. B (introd.).
[9] Cf. ch. xxiii (Jonson, *Blackness*).
[10] Winwood, ii. 51 ; *S. P. D.* (March 6).

March 24. Tilt.[1]
Apr. 4. Tilt.[2]
May 20. Tilt.[3]
June 3. Lion baiting in Tower.[4]
June 26. WHITEHALL.[5]
July 15. Baiting for imperial ambassador.[6]
July 16–Aug. 31. PROGRESS in Essex, Herts., Beds., Northants., Oxon.,
    and Berks.[7] Havering (July 16–18), Loughton (Sir Robert Wroth,
    July 18–20), Theobalds (Earl of Salisbury, July 20–24), Hatfield
    (July 24–26), Luton (Sir John Rotheram, July 26–27), Ampthill
    (July 27–Aug. 1), Bletsoe (Lord St. John, Aug. 1–3), Drayton (Lord
    Mordaunt, Aug. 3–6), Apethorpe (Sir Anthony Mildmay, Aug. 6–9),
    Rockingham (Sir Edward Watson, Aug. 9–12), Harrowden (Lord
    Vaux, Aug. 12–15), Castle Ashby (Lord Compton, Aug. 15–16),
    Grafton (Earl of Cumberland, Aug. 16–20), Hanwell (Sir Anthony
    Cope, Aug. 20–21), Wroxton (Sir William Pope, Aug. 21), Woodstock
    (Aug. 21–27), Oxford (Aug. 27–30),[8] Bisham (Sir Edward Hoby,
    Aug. 30–31).
Aug. 31. WINDSOR.[9]
Sept. 10 < >12. HAMPTON COURT.[10]
c. Sept. 30. WHITEHALL.[11]
Dec. 1. **Prince's.**
Christmas. Plays this winter by **King's** (ten) and **Paul's** (two).
Dec. 27. **Queen's.**
Dec. 30. **Prince's.**

1606

Jan. 1. **Prince's.**
Jan. 4. **Prince's.**
Jan. 5. Mask (*Hymenaei*) for wedding of Essex and Frances Howard.
Jan. 6. Barriers, with speeches (Truth and Opinion) by Jonson.
March 3 (S.M.). **Prince's.**
March 4. **Prince's.**
March 22. Rumoured assassination of James on visit to Woking.[12]
March 24. Tilt.[13]

[1] Winwood, ii. 54.   [2] V. P. x. 234.   [3] Lodge, iii. 162.
[4] Stowe, *Annales*.   [5] S. P. D.; Winwood, ii. 81.   [6] Stowe, *Annales*.
[7] Leland, *Collectanea*, ii. 626, from gests; Nichols, i. 517, apparently
from abandoned gests (Lodge, App. 97, 99), 518, 560; *Procl.* 1015, 1016;
S. P. D. (July 26, Aug. 5); V. P. x. 265; Shaw (July 27); Winwood,
ii. 99, 107; Lodge, iii. 171; Warton, *Life of Sir T. Pope* (1772), 413;
*Reliquiae Hearnianae*², ii. 68 (misdated 1608); and for Oxford, Camden,
Annales; Nichols, i. 530, iv. 1067, from description of Philip Stringer in
Harl. MS. 7044; A. Nixon, *The Oxford Triumph* (1605); I. Wake, *Rex
Platonicus* (1607); A. Wood, *Annals*; S. P. D. *Addl.* xxxvii. 66, 67; V. P. x.
270; Winwood, ii. 140.   [8] For plays at Oxford, cf. chh. iv, vii.
[9] Nichols, i. 518, 560, from *Marlow Accts.*
[10] S. P. D. (Sept. 10); Winwood, ii. 132.   [11] *Rutland MSS.* i. 396.
[12] Stowe, *Annales*, 882; *Procl.* 1030; V. P. x. 332; Winwood, ii. 204;
Margaret's.   [13] V. P. x. 332; Winwood, ii. 205.

March 28. Visit incognito to Guildhall for trial of Henry Garnet.[1]
May 16. GREENWICH.[2]
June 1. Challenge for tilt by Knights of the Fortunate Island, or the Lucent Pillar.[3]
June 22-23. Birth and death of Princess Sophia.
July c. 15-17. Visits to Oatlands and Farnham.[4]
July 17-Aug. 11. Visit of Christian IV of Denmark.[5] Plays (two) by King's at Greenwich.
July 18. Kings meet at Tilbury.
July 18-24. Greenwich.
July 24-28. Visit to Theobalds (Earl of Salisbury), by Blackwall and Stratford. Mask (*Solomon and Queen of Sheba*).[6]
July 24. Entertainment by Jonson.
July 28-31. Greenwich.
July 30. **Paul's** (*Abuses*).[7]
July 31. Triumph through London to Somerset House, with pageants at Great Conduit (Bower of the Muses), Little Conduit (Concord), and Fleet Conduit (Pastoral).
Aug. 1-2. Whitehall.
Aug. 2-6. Greenwich.
Aug. 4. Ringing.
Aug. 5. Tilt.
Aug. 6. Masters of defence.
Aug. 6. Visit to Richmond.
Aug. 7. Visit to Hampton Court, with play by **King's**.
Aug. 7-8. Visit to Windsor.
Aug. 8-9. Greenwich.
Aug. 9-11. Rochester (Bp. William Barlow).
Aug. 10. Dinner on *Elizabeth James* near Chatham.
Aug. 11. Farewell on *Admiral* of Denmark at Gravesend, with fireworks.
c. Aug. 17. HAMPTON COURT.[8]
Aug. PROGRESS, including Farnham (Aug. 23-24, Bp. of Winchester) and Beaulieu (Aug. 30, Earl of Southampton).[9]
Sept. 11-c. 18. Visit to Windsor.[10]
Oct. 20< >Nov. 1. WHITEHALL.[11]
Dec. 26. **King's** (*King Lear*).
Dec. 28. **Prince's**.
Dec. 29. **King's**.

[1] Winwood, ii. 205.   [2] *Margaret's*.   [3] Cf. ch. iv.
[4] S. P. D. (July 16); Shaw (July 15); Nichols, ii. 53, from Drummond (app. a day out).
[5] Nichols, ii. 54; iv. 1072, from prints (cf. ch. xxiv); Stowe, 885; Harington, i. 348; Boderie, i. 223, 226, 241, 259, 283, 297; V. P. x. 379, 383, 386, 391; Winwood, ii. 247; Birch, i. 65.   [6] Cf. ch. v.
[7] *King of Denmarkes Welcome*, 16, ' On Wednesday at night, the Youthes of Paules, commonlye cald the Children of Paules, plaide before the two Kings, a playe called *Abuses* : containing both a Comedie and a Tragedie, at which the Kinges seemed to take delight and be much pleased '.
[8] Shaw (Aug. 17).   [9] *Procl.* 1037; Shaw.   [10] Lodge, iii. 184.
[11] *Procl.* 1039; Shaw.

1607

Jan. 4. **King's.**
Jan. 6. **King's.** Mask (by Campion) for wedding of Lord Hay and Honora Denny.
Jan. 8. **King's.**
Jan. 13, 24, 30. **Prince's** (three plays).
Feb. 1. **Prince's.**
Feb. 2. **King's** (Barnes's *Devil's Charter*).
Feb. 5. **King's.**
Feb. 11. **Prince's.**
Feb. 15 (S.S.). **King's.**
Feb. 27. **King's.**
March 24. Tilt.[1]
May c. 20–24. Entry on Theobalds, with entertainment by Jonson.[2]
May 25. Tilt for Prince de Joinville. Play (*Aeneas and Dido*) at banquet by Earl of Arundel for Anne.[3]
June 12. Visit to Lord Mayor and Clothworkers.[4]
July 16. Visit to Merchant Taylors, with speech by Jonson.[5]
July 19. WINDSOR, by Oatlands ? [6]
Aug. PROGRESS in Hants and Wilts.[7] Basing (Marquis of Winchester, Aug. 5), Romsey, Beaulieu (Earl of Southampton, Aug. 10, 12), Salisbury (Aug. 14–23), and possibly Isle of Wight.
Aug. 23 < >Sept. 7. WINDSOR.[8]
Sept. 23 < >27. HAMPTON COURT.[9]
Oct. 27 < >29. WHITEHALL.[10]
Nov. 19. **Prince's.**
Dec. 26, 27, 28. **King's** (three plays).
Dec. 30. **Prince's.**

1608

Jan. 2. **King's.**
Jan. 3. **Prince's.**
Jan. 4. **Prince's.** Fireworks.[11]
Jan. 6. **King's** (two plays).
Jan. 7. **King's.**
Jan. 9. **King's.**
Jan. 10. Queen's mask (*Mask of Beauty*).
Jan. 17. **King's** (two plays).
Jan. 26. **King's.**

---

[1] Boderie, ii. 144.   [2] Boderie, ii. 253 ; *V. P.* x. 501.
[3] Boderie, ii. 247, 264, ' Et à la fin d'icelui se présenta une Tragédie d'Enée et de Didon, qui les tint jusques à deux heures après minuit '.
[4] Stowe, *Annales*, 890 ; *V. P.* x. 8 ; Nichols, ii. 133.   [5] Cf. ch. iv.
[6] *S. P. D.* ; *Margaret's* ; Shaw ; *Procl.* 1044 ; Birch, i. 68 (misdated), ' The King went home yesterday '.
[7] *S. P. D.* ; *Procl.* 1046 ; Shaw ; Winwood, ii. 328 ; Rymer, xvi. 664 ; Hunter, *Hallamshire*, 95.   [8] *S. P. D.*
[9] Shaw ; Winwood, ii. 344 ; Lodge, app. 102.
[10] Nichols, ii. 155 ; *V. P.* xi. 59.   [11] Birch, i. 69.

Feb. 2, 7 (S.S.). **King's** (two plays).
Feb. 9. Mask (by Jonson) for wedding of Viscount Haddington and Elizabeth Radcliffe.
March 24. Tilt.[1]
May 13 < >19. GREENWICH.[2]
July 1. WHITEHALL.[3]
July 7 < >14–Aug. 14 < >28. PROGRESS in Herts., Beds., and Northants.[4] Theobalds (July 14–20) with visit to Lamer in Wheathampstead (Sir John Garrard, July 19), Toddington (Lady Cheyne, July 24, 25), Grafton (Duke of Lennox, Aug. 1–3), Alderton (Sir Thomas Hesilrige, Aug. 4), Holdenby (Duke of York, Aug. 5–14) with visit to Bletsoe (Lord St. John, Aug. 5).
Aug. 14 < >28. WINDSOR.[5]
Sept. 4 < >17. HAMPTON COURT.[6]
Oct. 1 < >21. WHITEHALL.[7]
Christmas. Plays this winter by **King's** (twelve), **Queen's** (five), **Prince's** (three), and **Children of Blackfriars** (three).[8]

1609

Jan. 1. **Children of Blackfriars** (Middleton's *Trick to catch the Old One*).
Jan. 4. **Children of Blackfriars.**
Feb. 2. Queen's mask (*Mask of Queens*).
Feb. 28 (S.T.). Ringing.[9]
March 24. Tilt.[10]
Apr. 11. Visit to Durham House for opening of Britain's Burse.[11]
Apr. 18. Baiting.[12]
May 6 < >15. GREENWICH.[13]
June 23. Lion baiting in Tower.[14]
July 6. WHITEHALL.[15]
July 22. WINDSOR.[16]
July 23–Aug. 20 < >31. PROGRESS in Surrey, Hants, Wilts., Dorset.[17] Farnham (Bp. of Winchester, July 23–26), Basing (Marquis of Winchester, July 26), Beaulieu (Earl of Southampton, Aug. 3–7), Salisbury (Aug. 15, 20), Cranborne (Aug. 17–19), Tarrant.
Aug. 20 < >31. WINDSOR.[18]
Sept. 1 < >7. HAMPTON COURT.[19]
Oct. 30. WHITEHALL.[20]
Christmas. Plays this winter by **King's** (thirteen) and **Children of Whitefriars** (five).

[1] Boderie, iii. 195.   [2] Shaw; Winwood, ii. 403.   [3] *Margaret's.*
[4] Birch, i. 76; *Procl.* 1063–4; *S. P. D.* (July 14, 18, 20, 24; Aug. 10); Rymer, xvi. 673; Lodge, App. 126; Shaw; Nichols, ii. 203.
[5] *S. P. D.* (Aug. 28).   [6] *Procl.* 1065; *S. P. D.* (Sept. 17).
[7] *Procl.* 1066; *S. P. D.* (Oct. 21).
[8] Birch, i. 85 (Jan. 3), ' a dull and heavy Christmas hitherto '.
[9] *V. P.* xi. 243, 246.   [10] Birch, i. 92.   [11] Stowe, *Annales.*
[12] Birch, i. 96 (misdated Apr. 6).   [13] *Procl.* 1077, 1078, 1079.
[14] Stowe, *Annales.*   [15] *Margaret's.*   [16] Lodge, iii. 261.
[17] *S. P. D.* (July 26, Aug. 15, 20); Lodge, iii. 267, 268; Shaw (Aug. 2, 13, misdated ?); Nichols, ii. 263; Hutchins, *Dorset*, iii. 381.
[18] *S. P. D.* (Aug. 31).   [19] *S. P. D.* (Sept. 1, 7).   [20] *Margaret's.*

Dec. 26. **Prince's.**
Dec. 27. **Queen's.**
Dec. 28. **Prince's.**
Dec. 31. Challenge for barriers by Henry as Meliadus.

1610

Jan. 6. Henry's barriers, with speeches by Jonson.[1]
Jan. 7. **Prince's.**[2]
Jan. 18. **Prince's.**
Feb. 9. **Duke of York's.**
Feb. 18–20 (S.).
March 24, 27. Tilt.[3]
Apr. 20. Lion baiting in Tower.[4]
Apr. 23. Triumph for Henry at Chester.[5]
May 31–June 6. Creation of Henry as Prince of Wales.[6]
June 5. Queen's mask (*Tethys' Festival*).
June 6. Tilt, water triumph, and fireworks.[7]
June 19. Visit to Woolwich.[8]
July 24–*c.* Sept. 2. PROGRESS in Northants., Oxon., Berks., and Hants.[9]
   Bletsoe (Lord St. John, July 29), Holdenby (Duke of York, Aug. 5,
   6, 11, 12, 13, 19) with visits to Apethorpe (Sir Anthony Mildmay)
   and Kirby (Sir Christopher Hatton, Aug. 7) and Castle Ashby (Lord
   Compton, Aug. 13, 14), Grafton (Duke of Lennox, Aug. 19), Wood-
   stock (Aug. 22–25), Bisham (Sir Edward Hoby, Aug. 28), Aldershot
   (Walter Tichborne? Sept. 2).
c. Sept. 2. HAMPTON COURT.[10]
Oct. 8 < >18. WHITEHALL.[11]
Dec. 10. **Queen's** (three plays).
Dec. 12. **Duke of York's.**
Dec. 19. **Prince's.**
Dec. 20. **Duke of York's.**
Christmas. Plays this winter by **King's** (fifteen).
Dec. 27. **Queen's.**
Dec. 28. **Prince's.**

[1] Cf. ch. xxiii (Jonson).
[2] At St. James's, 10 p.m., after a supper by Henry to the players at
barriers (*Arch.* xii. 258).   [3] Nichols, ii. 287 ; *V. P.* xi. 453, 460.
[4] Nichols, ii. 307 ; Stowe, *Annales*, 895.
[5] Cf. ch. xxiv.   [6] Cf. ch. xxiv.   [7] Ibid.
[8] *Arch.* xii. 258. On June 10 a newswriter (Winwood, iii. 182) says,
' As often as he can he absents himself from the town, yet is quickly
fetched again on every occasion, which much troubles him '.
[9] *Procl.* 1095 ; *S. P. D.* (July 29 ; Aug. 5, 6, 7, 11, 13, 19, 23 ; Sept. 2) ;
Rymer, xvi. 703, 704 ; Nichols, ii. 364, and *Illustrations*, 135 ; Birch,
i. 131 ; Winwood, iii. 201, 213 ; *Rutland MSS.* i. 423 ; *V. P.* xii. 26, 41 ;
Hearne, *Reliquiae*[2], ii. 69.   [10] *Rutland MSS.* i. 423 ; *S. P. D.* (Sept. 2).
[11] *S. P. D.* (Oct. 8, 18).

1611

Jan. 1. Prince's mask (*Oberon*).
Jan. 14. **Prince's.**
Jan. 15. **Duke of York's.**
Jan. 16. **Prince's.**
Feb. 2. Queen's mask (*Love Freed from Ignorance and Folly*).
Feb. 3–5 (S.).
Feb. 3. **King's** (*Mucedorus*) ?.
Apr. 27. GREENWICH.[1]
June 26 < > July 2. WINDSOR.[2]
July 18–21. Visit to Englefield (Sir Edward Norris).[3]
July 22 < > 25–Sept. 1 < > 10. PROGRESS in Surrey, Hants, Wilts., and
   Isle of Wight.[4]   Farnham (Bp. of Winchester, July 25–8), Salisbury
   (Aug. 3, 6, 10, 13), Beaulieu (Earl of Southampton, Aug. 19, 21, 26)
   with visit to Isle of Wight (Aug. 22), Tichborne (Sir Benjamin
   Tichborne, Aug. 29), Farnham (Aug. 31), Bagshot (Sept. 1).
Sept. 1 < > 10. HAMPTON COURT.[5]
Oct. 31. WHITEHALL.[6]   **King's.**
Nov. 1. **King's** (*Tempest*).
Nov. 5. **King's** (*Winter's Tale*).
Nov. 9. **King's.**
Nov. 19. **King's.**
Dec. 16. **King's.**
Christmas.[7]
Dec. 26. Ringing.[8]   **King's** (*A King and no King*).
Dec. 27. **Queen's** (*Greene's Tu Quoque*).
Dec. 28. **Prince's.**
Dec. 29. **Prince's** (*Almanac*).
Dec. 31. **King's.**

1612

Jan. 1. Ringing.[9]   **King's** (*Twins' Tragedy*).
Jan. 5. **King's** and/or **Children of Whitefriars** (*Cupid's Revenge*).
Jan. 6. Ringing.[10]   Prince's mask (*Love Restored ?*) by gentlemen of
   the court.
Jan. 7. **King's.**
Jan. > 12–22. Visit of Anne and Henry to Greenwich.[11]

---

[1] *Margaret's.*   [2] *S. P. D.*   [3] Ibid.
[4] *Procl.* 1115 ; *S. P. D.* ; Nichols, iv. 1083.
[5] *Procl.* 1117.   [6] *S. P. D.* (Oct. 31).
[7] There is some doubt as to the dates of this winter's plays ; cf.
p. 140.   [8] Cunningham, 211.
[9] Ibid.   [10] Ibid.
[11] Ibid. ; Birch, i. 133 (Jan. 29), ' The prince went on Saturday to
Royston, called thither from his martial sports of tilt, tourney, and barrier,
which he followed so earnestly, that he was every day five or six hours
in armour. The rest of the time was spent in —— and every night a
play, in all which exercises the Lord Cranbourne attended him, keeping an honourable table all the while they were at Greenwich, and

Jan. 12. **King's and Queen's** (*Silver Age*) and/or **Duke of York's.**
Jan. 13. **King's and Queen's** (*Rape of Lucrece*).
Jan. 15. **King's.**
Jan. 19. **Lady Elizabeth's.**
Jan. 21. **Queen's.**
Jan. 23. **Queen's.**
Jan. 28. **Duke of York's.**
Feb. 2. **Queen's** (*Greene's Tu Quoque*).
Feb. 5. **Prince's.**
Feb. 9. **King's.**
Feb. 13. **Duke of York's.**
Feb. 19. **King's.**
Feb. 20. **King's** (two plays).
Feb. 23 (S.S.). **King's** (*Nobleman*).
Feb. 24. **Duke of York's** (*Hymen's Holiday or Cupid's Vagaries*).
Feb. 25. Ringing. **Lady Elizabeth's** (*Proud Maid's Tragedy*).
Feb. 28. Visit by Henry to Marquis of Winchester, with plays.[1] **King's.**
Feb. 29. **Prince's.**
March 11. **Lady Elizabeth's.**
March 24. Tilt.[2]
March 28. **King's.**
Apr. 3. **King's.**
Apr. 11. **Prince's.**
Apr. 16. **King's.**
Apr. 26. **King's,** for Duc de Bouillon ?[3]
May-June. Visits to Eltham, Wanstead (Sir Edward Phelips, June 17, 25), and Havering (Lady Oxford, June 18).[4]
c. July 9. Visit to Kensington (Sir Walter Cope).[5]
c. July 17–*c.* Sept. 1. PROGRESS in Herts., Beds., Northants., Rutland, Notts., Leicester, Oxon., Berks.[6] Theobalds (July 17), St. Albans ?, Wrest ? (Earl of Kent), Ampthill (July 23), Bletsoe (Lord St. John, July 24–27), Castle Ashby (Lord Compton, July 27–30), Kirby (Sir Christopher Hatton, July 30–Aug. 3), Apethorpe (Sir Anthony Mildmay, Aug. 3–6), Brooke (Sir Edward Noel, Aug. 6–7), Belvoir (Earl of Rutland, Aug. 7–10), Newark Castle (Aug. 10–11), Rufford Abbey (Sir George Saville, Aug. 11–14), Newstead Abbey (Sir John Byron, Aug. 14–17), Nottingham (Thurland House, Aug. 17–18), Loughborough (Aug. 18–19), Leicester (Earl of Huntingdon, Aug.

grows daily into his favour.' The plays of Jan. 12 and 13 were certainly and those of Jan. 15, 19, 21, almost certainly at Greenwich. An extant challenge to tilt of 1612 (Clephan, 133, 176, from *Harl. MS.* 4888) may be of this period.　　　　　　　　　　　　　　　[1] Birch, i. 137.
　　[2] *V. P.* xii. 329 ; Cunningham, 211.　　　　　[3] *V. P.* xii. 349.
　　[4] Birch, i. 169, 174 (June 17, ' The King has been coming and going to Eltham all the last week '), 181 ; Shaw (June 3).　　　[5] Birch, i. 187.
　　[6] Nichols, ii. 450 (from records at Leicester and Nottingham) ; iv. 1083 ; Kelly, *Progresses*, 344 (from Leicester gests) ; *S. P. D.* (July 23, 26, 28) ; *Procl.* 1123 ; Rymer, xvi. 724 ; Shaw ; Birch, i. 188, 189, 197 ; Winwood, iii. 384.

19–21), Dingley (Sir Thomas Griffin, Aug. 21–22), Holdenby (Duke of York, Aug. 22–24), Grafton (Duke of Lennox, Aug. 24–26 ?), Hanwell ? (Sir Anthony Cope), Woodstock (Prince Henry, Aug. 26–31 ?),[1] Rycote (Lord Norris, Aug. 31–Sept. 1 ?), Bisham (Sir Edward Hoby, Sept. 1 ?).

Sept. 1 < >21. WHITEHALL.[2]

Oct. 16. Arrival of Elector Palatine.[3]

Oct. 20. **Lady Elizabeth's.**[4]

Oct. 29. Visit of Elector to Lord Mayor's show.[5]

Oct. 31 or Nov. 1. Play put off for Henry's illness.[6]

Nov. 2 or 3. **Queen's Revels** (*Coxcomb*) ?.[7]

Nov. 6. Death of Henry.

Christmas. Twenty plays by **King's** this winter (Shakespeare's *1, 2 Hen. IV* (?), *J. C.*, *M. Ado* (twice), *Oth.*, *W. Tale, Tp.* ; Jonson's *Alchemist* ; Beaumont and Fletcher's *Philaster* (twice), *Maid's Tragedy, King and No King, Captain* ; Tourneur's *Nobleman* ; Niccolls's *Twins* ; Ford's *A Bad Beginning*, and *Cardenio, Merry Devil of Edmonton, Knot of Fools*).[8]

Dec. 27. Betrothal of Elector and Elizabeth.[9]

1613

Jan. 1. **Queen's Revels** (*Cupid's Revenge*).

Jan. 9. **Queen's Revels** (*Cupid's Revenge*).

Feb. 11. Fireworks.

Feb. 13. River triumph.

Feb. 14 (S.S.). Wedding of Elector and Elizabeth. Lords' mask (by Campion).

Feb. 15. Ringing. Middle Temple and Lincoln's Inn mask (by Chapman).

Feb. 16. **King's.** Mask put off.

Feb. 20. Inner Temple and Gray's Inn mask (by Beaumont).

Feb. 21. Banquet for James and the maskers.

Feb. 25. **Lady Elizabeth's** (*Dutch Courtesan*).

Feb. 27. **Queen's Revels** (*Widow's Tears*).

March 1. **Lady Elizabeth's** (*Raymond Duke of Lyons*).

March 2. **Prince Charles's** (*1 The Knaves*).

March 2–c. 4. Visit of Charles and Elector to Cambridge, with Brooke's *Adelphe* (Mar. 2) and *Scyros* (Mar. 3) by Trinity men.

March ? Visit by Frederick to Oxford.[10]

March 10. **Prince's** (*2 The Knaves*).

March 24. Tilt.[11]

---

[1] Birch, i. 197, ' The prince made the king an entertainment, with some devices, at Woodstock '.   [2] *Procl.* 1124 ; *S. P. D.* (Sept. 24).
[3] Winwood, iii. 403 ; Birch, i. 198 ; *V. P.* xii. 443 ; cf. ch. xxiv for descriptions of visit and wedding.   [4] Birch, i. 198 (cf. App. B).
[5] Winwood, iii. 406.   [6] Birch, i. 201 ; Winwood, iii. 406.
[7] Ibid.   [8] Cf. App. B.   [9] Winwood, iii. 421 ; *V. P.* xii. 473.
[10] Birch, i. 229 ; Wood, *Annals*, ii. 315.
[11] Birch, i. 238 ; *Rutland MSS.* iv. 494 ; Arber, iii. 518.

Apr. 10. Departure of Elector and Elizabeth, accompanied by James to Rochester (Apr. 13).[1]

Apr. 24–June 17. PROGRESS of Anne.[2] Hampton Court, with James, Windsor, Reading (the Friars), Caversham (Lord Knollys, Apr. 27–28),[3] Bath, Bristol (Marchioness of Winchester, June 4–8),[4] Siston (Sir Henry Billingsley, June 8), Bishop's Cannings (June 11).[5]

May 26. GREENWICH.[6]

June 8. King's (*Cardenio*) for Savoyard ambassador.

July 1–4. Visits to Hampton Court and Oatlands.[7]

c. July 8. WHITEHALL.[8]

c. July 18. WINDSOR.[9]

July 19 < >20–*c.* Aug. 21. PROGRESS in Surrey, Hants, and Wilts.[10] Farnham (Bp. of Winchester, July 20), Basing (Marquis of Winchester, July 23), Andover (July 24, 26), Lydiard (Sir Oliver St. John ?, July 27), Charlton (Earl of Suffolk, July 31), Salisbury (Aug. 5), Beaulieu (Earl of Southampton, *c.* Aug. 6 < >21).

July–Sept. Visits of Anne to Bath and Wells (Aug. 20–22).[11]

c. Aug. 21. WINDSOR.[12]

Sept. 8. WHITEHALL.[13]

c. Sept. 28. Visit to Hampton Court.[14]

Nov. 1. King's.

Nov. 4. King's.

Nov. 5. King's.

Nov. 15. King's.

Nov. 16. King's.

Dec. 12. Lady Elizabeth's (*Dutch Courtesan*).

Dec. 24 or 28. Queen's.

Dec. 26. Mask (by Campion) for wedding of Earl of Somerset and Frances Howard.

Dec. 27. King's. Challenge for tilt, with device by Jonson.

Dec. 29. Mask (*Irish Mask*) for wedding.

1614

Jan. 1. Tilt. King's.

Jan. 3. *Irish Mask* repeated.

Jan. 4. King's.

---

[1] Stowe, 1007 ; Nichols, ii. 611.

[2] Nichols, ii. 628, 643 ; Wotton, ii. 20, 22, 29 ; Winwood, iii. 454, 461 ; Birch, i. 243.   [3] For entertainment at Caversham, cf. ch. xxiii (Campion).

[4] For entertainment at Bristol, cf. ch. xxiv.

[5] For entertainment at Bishop's Cannings, cf. ch. xxiii (Ferebe).

[6] Wotton, ii. 25 (misdated).

[7] *S. P. D.* (July 1, 3, 4) ; Shaw.   [8] Winwood, iii. 468.

[9] *S. P. D.* (July 19) ; *Remembrancia*, 290 ; Birch, i. 261.

[10] *S. P. D.* (July 20, 23, 24, 26, 27, 31) ; Birch, i. 257 ; Winwood, iii. 461, 475 ; *Egerton Papers*, 462.

[11] Birch, i. 257, 275 ; *V. P.* xiii. 36 ; *Hist. MSS.* i. 107 ; *Journal of Arch. Ass.* xvi. 319. For entertainment at Wells, cf. ch. iv.

[12] Birch, i. 269.   [13] *S. P. D.* (Sept. 9) ; Birch, i. 275.

[14] *S. P. D.* ; Wotton, ii. 35.

Jan. 4. Play and two masks (one Middleton's lost *Mask of Cupid*) by City at Merchant Taylors for wedding.[1]

Jan. 5. **Queen's.**

Jan. 6. Gray's Inn mask (*Mask of Flowers*) for wedding.[2]

Jan. 10. **King's.**

Jan. 25. **Lady Elizabeth's** (*Eastward Hoe*).

Feb. 2. **King's.**

Feb. 3. Play (Daniel's *Hymen's Triumph*) for wedding of Lord Roxborough and Jean Drummond at Somerset House.

Feb. 4. **King's.** Play for Lord Mayor at Somerset House.[3]

Feb. 8. **King's.**

Feb. 10. **King's.**

Feb. 18. **King's.**

March 6 (S.S.). **King's.**

March 8. **King's.**

March 24. Tilt.[4]

June 8 < >12. GREENWICH.[5]

June 21. WHITEHALL.[6]

June 29. Visit to Richmond.[7]

July 17–23. PROGRESS in Herts., Essex, Beds., broken by Denmark visit.[8] Theobalds (July 17), The Rye in Hatfield Broadoak (Richard Francke, July 18–19), Audley End (Earl of Suffolk, July 19–21), Royston (July 21–22), Haynes (Robert Newdigate, July 22–23).

July 22. Arrival of Christian IV, King of Denmark, at Somerset House.[9]

July 24 < >30. Plays before Christian.[10]

Aug. 1. Visit to Woolwich, Rochester, and Gravesend for departure of Christian.[11]

Aug. 1–31. PROGRESS resumed in Herts., Northants., Rutland, Notts., Leicestershire, Oxon., Berks.[12] Theobalds (Aug. 1), Apethorpe (Sir Anthony Mildmay, Aug. 3–4), Burley on the Hill (Lord Harington, Aug. 4–6), Belvoir (Earl of Rutland, Aug. 6–9), Newark Castle (Aug. 9–10), Rufford Abbey (Sir George Saville, Aug. 10–15), Newstead Abbey (Sir John Byron, Aug. 15–17), Nottingham (Thurland House, Aug. 17–18), Leicester (Earl of Huntingdon, Aug. 18–19), Dingley (Sir Thomas Griffin, Aug. 19–20), Holdenby (Duke of York, Aug. 20–22), Grafton (Duke of Lennox, Aug. 22–25), Woodstock (Aug. 25–29), Oxford (Aug. 29), Rycote (Lord Norris, Aug. 29–30), Bisham (Sir Edward Hoby, Aug. 30–31).

>Sept. 11. WHITEHALL.[13]

---

[1] Cf. ch. xxiii (Middleton).   [2] Cf. ch. xxiv.   [3] Nichols, ii. 754.

[4] Nichols, ii. 759, from *Harl. MS.* 5171.

[5] Shaw; Wotton, ii. 39; Nichols, iii. 6.   [6] *C. A.*; *Procl.* 1145.

[7] Birch, i. 329.

[8] Nichols, iii. 10, from gests at Leicester; *S. P. D.* (July 14, 18, 21, 22); Shaw; Stowe, *Annales*, 1012; Birch, i. 333, 339; Camden, *Annales*; *Procl.* 1147, 1148.   [9] Birch, i. 339; *V. P.* xiii. 166.

[10] Stowe, 1012.   [11] Birch, i. 341, 342; Stowe, 1012.

[12] Nichols, iii. 20; Kelly, *Progresses*, 360; Birch, i. 343; Shaw (Aug. 25); Wood, *Annals*, ii. 319; *Egerton Papers*, 464.   [13] Birch, i. 346.

Nov. 1. **Lady Elizabeth's** (*Bartholomew Fair*).

Christmas. Plays this winter by **King's** (eight), **Queen's** (three), **Elector Palatine's** (three), **Prince's** (six).[1]

1615

Jan. 6. Household mask (*Mercury Vindicated* ?).

Jan. 8. Mask repeated.

Feb. 19–21 (S.). Mask by Spanish ambassador ? [2]

March 7–11. Visit of James and Charles to Cambridge.[3]

March 24. Tilt.[4]

May 13–15. Visit to Cambridge.

>May 21. GREENWICH.[5]

c. July 2–5. Visit to Oatlands.[6]

July 20. WINDSOR.[7]

July 21–*c.* Sept. 2. PROGRESS in Surrey, Hants, Wilts., and Dorset.[8]
Bagshot (July 22), Basing (Marquis of Winchester, July 23), Andover (July 26), Salisbury (July 28–31, Aug. 5), Lulworth Castle (Viscount Bindon, Aug. 15), Broadlands (Henry ? St. Barbe, Aug. 27), Tichborne (Sir Benjamin Tichborne, Aug. 29), Farnham (Bp. of Winchester, Aug. 31).

c. Sept. 2. WINDSOR.[9]

Sept. 2 < >Oct. 18. WHITEHALL.[10]

Dec. 17. **Queen's** at Somerset House.

Dec. 21. **King's** at Somerset House.

Christmas. Plays this winter by **King's** (fourteen), **Queen's** (four), and **Prince's** (four).

1616

Jan. 1. Household mask (*Golden Age Restored* ?).

Jan. 6. Mask repeated.

Feb. 11–13 (S.).

March 4 < >16. Visit to Royston, with play (*Susenbrotus* ?) by Cambridge men.[11]

March 25. Tilt.[12]

Apr. 23. *Obiit Gulielmus Shakespeare.*

---

[1] Birch, i. 290, ' They have plays at least every night, both holidays and working days, wherein they show great ——, being for the most part such poor stuff, that instead of delight, they send the auditory away with discontent. Indeed, our poets' brains and inventions are grown very dry, insomuch that of five new plays there is not one pleases, and therefore they are driven to furbish over their old, which stand them in best stead, and bring them most profit ' (John Chamberlain).   [2] Nichols, iii. 41.
    [3] For plays at Cambridge in March and May, see chh. iv, vii.
    [4] Birch, i. 358.   [5] *S. P. D.*
    [6] *S. P. D.* (July 3, 5) ; Shaw.   [7] Birch, i. 368.
    [8] Camden, *Annales* ; *S. P. D.* (July 23, 26, 28–31) ; Shaw ; Birch, i. 369 ; Nichols, iii. 97.   [9] Birch, i. 369.   [10] Nichols, iii. 104.
    [11] Birch, i. 395, 397 ; cf. ch. iv, App. K (*Susenbrotus*).
    [12] Birch, i. 394 ; *Rutland MSS.* iv. 508.

APPENDIX B

COURT PAYMENTS

THE body of this appendix contains extracts from the accounts of the Treasurer of the Chamber and the Office of Revels, in which expenditure on plays or masks at court is recorded. But in view of the importance of these documents as sources for the history of court entertainment, it will be well to add something about their general nature and state of preservation to what has already been said about the procedure of the Treasurer of the Chamber in ch. ii and that of the Revels Office in ch. iii.

THE AUDIT OF HOUSEHOLD ACCOUNTS

Most, but not all, of the accounts preserved are records of audit. There is, unfortunately, no systematic history of the Audit Office ; but the somewhat scrappy notices in F. S. Thomas, *The Ancient Exchequer of England* (1848), and H. Hall, *Studies in English Official Historical Documents* (1908), and *A Formula Book of English Official Historical Documents*, Part II (1909), may be supplemented for the Tudor period by the valuable study of M. D. George, *The Origin of the Declared Account* (1916, *E. H. R.* xxxi. 41). The Record Office series of *Lists and Indexes* includes lists of *Declared Accounts* (ii) and *Exchequer Accounts* (xxxv). Normally the auditing of royal expenditure was a function of the mediaeval Exchequer. The procedure was for the officer charged with incurring expenditure to appear as accountant before the Auditor-Baron and his Clerk, and produce detailed statements, known as ' particulars ', together with vouchers for sums already spent out of any ' imprest ' or advance that had been made to him, and the warrants under which his expenditure was authorized. From these the Exchequer officers prepared a ' compotus ' or balance sheet, signed it, when the balance was settled, as a record that the accountant was ' quietus ' or quit from debt to the Crown, and passed it through the King's Remembrancer to the Lord Treasurer's Remembrancer, in whose office it was enrolled by the Clerk of the Pipe on the roll of ' foreign ' or non-revenue accounts. It was then returned to the King's Remembrancer, who kept it, with the particulars and vouchers as subsidiary documents. It was a lengthy and cumbrous process. Moreover, the Lord Treasurer, like the Lord Chancellor, was one of the high officers of state whose functions came at an early date under the control of the barons, and the same motives, which led the sovereign (cf. ch. ii) to develop in the Wardrobe and Chamber an executive machinery independent of the Lord Chancellor, also led him to desire that his more private expenditure should be withdrawn from the survey of the Exchequer. Thus we find the Treasurer of the Chamber accountable (cf. ch. ii) at the end of the fifteenth century to the King alone, and in the mid-sixteenth century to the Court of Surveyors or to *ad hoc* auditors specially appointed by the King or the Privy Council. When the Court of Augmentations absorbed the Court of Surveyors in 1553, its establishment included two Auditors of Prests, and although this court was itself merged in the Exchequer under Mary, the more up-to-date methods of auditing were continued by Elizabeth's appointment in 1560, as themselves Exchequer officers, of two ' Auditores de lez Prestes et Compotorum forinsecorum nostrorum '. The main difference between the methods of the Auditors of the Prests and that of the Auditor-Baron appears to have been that the personal appearance of the accountant was no longer necessary, who now himself prepared in duplicate a balance sheet known as his Original Account, or Book of Account, of which one copy was signed after examination and returned to him as evidence of his quittance, while the other was kept by the Auditors, who based upon it a summary known as the Declared or Recorded Account, which took the place of the old *Compotus*. This also was in duplicate. Apparently the Auditors kept one copy, on paper, and sent another, on parchment, for preservation, as of record, in the Pipe Office. I understand Miss George, however, to think that the accountant was entitled to the paper copy, if he chose to pay a fee for it, which he very often did not. The amount of detail taken into the Declared Account from the Original Account varied for different offices. The Revels Declared Accounts are very summary ; those of the Treasurer of the Chamber, at any rate as regards play-payments, practically duplicates of the Original Accounts, except that, unfortunately, the names of plays, which sometimes appeared in the Original Accounts, are usually omitted. The Auditors also kept the subsidiary documents submitted with the Original Account, and became involved in a controversy, recorded in T. Fanshawe, *The Practice of the Exchequer Court* (1658), with the King's Remembrancer, who claimed that they should come to him. The King's Remembrancer did apparently see the Declared Account on its way to the Pipe Office, and enrolled it, or a further summary of it. About 1603 all the Household accounts appear to have gone before the Auditors of the Prests, except those of the Cofferer, which still followed the old course of the Exchequer. The procedures here described explain the provenance of such Household accounts as belong to the official repositories now united in the Record Office ; some others, preserved there or elsewhere, come from the private archives of the accountants themselves, being either the audit duplicates supplied to them, or office copies and drafts of their own Original Accounts, or the journals, pay books, and ledgers from which these were prepared.

CHAMBER ACCOUNTS

The following accounts appear to be extant.

(a) *Mediaeval Period.*

A few accounts and subsidiary documents of the reigns of Edward II, Edward III, and Richard II are included in the Foreign Accounts on the Great Rolls of the Exchequer (*P. R. O. Lists and Indexes*, xi. 108, 109), and in the Exchequer Wardrobe and Household Accounts

(*L. and I.* xxxv. 376, 379, 380, 382, 386, 391, 392, 396, 540). The earliest are described, with extracts, by J. C. Davies, *The First Journal of Edward II's Chamber* (*E. H. R.* xxx. 662).

(b) *Early Tudor Period.*

A number of accounts passed from the Augmentation Office to the Exchequer and were amalgamated in 1839 with others from the office of the King's Remembrancer in a series of Exchequer Accounts, Various. Here they are numbered 413 to 427. They are mainly accounts of revenue and subsidiary documents, but a few accounts of payments presented to the Record Office by the Trevelyan family have been added to the series, and with them are listed as Wardrobe and Household Accounts (*L. and I.* xxxv) some other payment accounts from the Miscellaneous Books of the Treasury of Receipt of the Exchequer, and one from the Miscellaneous Books of the Court of Augmentations. Other payment accounts are in the British Museum and in unofficial collections. It may be the case, as Newton, 359, suggests, that these or some of them were abstracted from the Records by officials of antiquarian tastes, but it must be remembered that duplicates even of audited accounts were often kept by the accountants. These accounts are generally known as The King's Books of Payments. The following can be traced :

i. *Accounts of John Heron.*

Three Books of Payments, for 1505–9, 1509–18, and 1518–21 respectively, with many royal signatures by way of audit, are now in the P. R. O. (*Misc. Books of Treasury of Receipt*, 214, 215, 216). The contents of the Henry VIII books are abstracted in Brewer, ii. 1441 ; iii. 1533. There must once have been an earlier book, for Collier, i. 49, 52, 76, gives extracts from one for 1492–1505, which he describes as ' formerly in the Chapter-house, Westminster ', as well as from the three now extant, which he describes as ' in the Chapter-house '. Possibly this was *Addl. MS.* 21480, which has been traced back (Newton, 359) through the hands of Craven Ord (a friend of Collier) and Thomas Astle to those of Peter Le Neve, a Deputy-Chamberlain of the Exchequer. But *Addl. MS.* 21481, which also came from Le Neve, is a duplicate of the R. O. books for 1505–18, and therefore *Addl. MS.* 21480 may only have been a duplicate of the missing volume. Both the *Addl. MSS.* contain the royal signatures. Craven Ord made some extracts which are now *Addl. MSS.* 7099, 7100, and to these those supplied by Astle to R. Henry, *History of Great Britain*, vi (1793), app., and those in S. Bentley, *Excerpta Historica* (1831), 85, owe their origin. Collier, i. 49, also cites a small book for 1501–2 kept (perhaps under Heron) by one Robert Fowler, which refers to parallel payments made by Thomas Trollop.

ii. *Accounts of Brian Tuke.*

A book signed monthly by Henry VIII, with some entries from 31 Dec. 1528 to 30 June 1529, but mainly covering the period from 17 Nov. 1529 to 29 Dec. 1532, was printed by N. H. Nicolas from a MS.

then in his possession as *The Privy Purse Expenses of Henry the Eighth*
(1827) and misdescribed as an account of the Treasurer of the Household. Presumably this MS. is identical with that owned by Sir O.
Bridgeman in 1634 and now *Addl. MS.* 20030. It overlaps with an
account for 1 Oct. 1528 to May 1531, presented by Sir W. C. Trevelyan
to the P. R. O. (*Exchequer Accounts, Various*, 420/11); extracts are
given in *Trevelyan Papers* (C. S.), i. 136, and an abstract in Brewer,
v. 303. Collier, i. 116, and Nicolas (*ut supra*), xxviii, give extracts
from an account for Feb. 1538 to June 1541 in the possession of the
Royal Society, presumably a duplicate of the account for the same
period in *Arundel MS.* 97, incorrectly catalogued by the B.M. as
an account of the Treasurer of the Household, and abstracted in
Brewer, xiii. 2. 524; xiv. 2. 303; xvi. 178, 698. An account for May to
Sept. 1542 in *Stowe MS.* 554 is abstracted in Brewer, xvii. 474. Collier,
i. 117, gives extracts from an account for 1543-4 in Craven Ord's
collection.

iii. *Accounts of William Cavendish.*

Account for 31 March 1547 to 31 Sept. 1549, of which extracts are
given in *Trevelyan Papers*, i. 191, ii. 13, were presented by Sir W. C.
Trevelyan to the P. R. O. (*Exchequer Accounts, Various*, 426/5, 6).
Misc. Exch. Augm. 439 for 1547-8 is referred to by Newton, 359, as
a Chamber account, and is presumably a duplicate.

iv. *Account of Edmund Felton.*

A Declared Account for 1 Apr. to 31 Dec. 1557 is in *D. A. Pipe
Office*, 541. Stopes, *Hunnis*, 145, cites a ' Compotus Marie Rither
and Edmond Felton ' for 5 and 6 Edw. VI (*Queen's Remembrancia*,
77/5) as a Chamber Account. It is doubtless a Cofferer's Account.

(c) *Elizabethan and Jacobean Periods.*

i. *Accounts in P. R. O.*

The P. R. O. contains Chamber Accounts in four forms. Original
Accounts, as submitted for audit, are in *Audit Office, Accounts Various*,
3/127-9. These are no doubt the ' very incomplete ' set from which
extracts are given by Cunningham, xxvii. So far as play-payments
are concerned, they do not appear to be more detailed than the
Declared Accounts annually drawn up from them by the auditors, of
which there are duplicate sets, both nearly complete, belonging
respectively to the Audit Office and to the Pipe Office in the Lord
Treasurer's Remembrancer's Department of the Exchequer. They
cover the terms of office of Mason (1558-66), Knollys (1566-70),
Heneage (1570-95), Killigrew (1595-6), and Stanhope (1596-1617).
From the Pipe Office series I supplemented Cunningham's extracts
in *M. L. R.* ii (1906), 1; iv (1909), 153, and give a complete record
of play-payments below. The payments are also given for 1558-85
from the Audit Office series in Wallace, i (1912), 210, and very imperfectly from the Pipe Office series for 1559-97 in Stopes, *Hunnis*, 318.
Finally, there are Enrolled Accounts in the King's Remembrancer's
Department (Scargill-Bird[1], liv). A single book for 1569-70 is in the
same Department (*Exchequer Accounts, Various*, 430/15). It appears

to be an office book, and has some original signatures by way of receipts for payments.

ii. *Accounts in British Museum.*

Harl. 1641 and 1642 are duplicates of Heneage's accounts for 1585–6 and 1593–4 as prepared for audit. *Harl.* 1644 is an office book, 1581–3, containing signatures by way of receipts for wages and the like.

iii. *Accounts in Bodleian.*

Rawlinson MS. A. 204, ff. 212, 269, contains duplicates of Stanhope's accounts for 1604–5 and 1610–11 as prepared for audit, and *Rawlinson MSS.* A. 239 and 240 (formerly *Pepys MSS.* 78 and 79) are similar duplicates of his accounts for 1612–13 and 1616–17. They are possibly office drafts, with some notes by a checking officer or an auditor, but are not signed either by accountant or auditors. Occasionally they are slightly more detailed as regards play entries than the Declared Accounts. Thus in 1610–11 and 1612–13 they give some dates of performances instead of the mere number for the season, and in 1612–13 they even give the titles of the plays. Extracts of these titles are given in Halliwell-Phillipps, ii. 87, and *N. S. S. Trans.* (1875–6) 419, and more completely below. Similar entries are given by P. Cunningham in *Sh. Soc. Papers,* ii. 123, not direct from the manuscript, but from notes taken therefrom by Vertue and Oldys. These had passed, in the case of the Oldys notes through Percy, to Steevens, and from him to Hazlewood, who had copied them, as Oldys and Steevens had done, into an interleaved Langbaine. Malone had already used Vertue's notes.

I should add that many 'declarations' or memoranda on the business of the Treasurer of the Chamber and the state of his finances from time to time are to be found in the Domestic State Papers, in Lansdowne and other B.M. MSS., and in a volume (*Lord Steward's Misc.* 301) collected by Sir J. Caesar.

REVELS ACCOUNTS

The following accounts appear to be extant :

(a) *Early Tudor Period.*

(i) *Accounts of Richard Gibson.*

Brewer, ii. 1490 ; iii. 35, 1548 ; iv. 418, 837, 1390, 1392, 1415, 1603, 3073, gives abstracts of a series of accounts, ranging from 1510 to 1530, some or all of which are presumably taken from *Miscellaneous Books of the Treasury of the Receipt of the Exchequer,* 217, 228, 229.

(ii) *Accounts of John Bridges.*

It appears from extracts given by Kempe, 69, that some accounts of John Bridges between 1539, when he became Yeoman of the Revels, and 1544, when Cawarden became Master, are at Loseley.

(iii) *Accounts of Sir Thomas Cawarden.*

Many of these are at Loseley, often in more than one copy. Kempe, 69, gives a few extracts for the last years of Henry VIII, and the most important documents for the next three reigns, ranging from

1547 to 1559, are printed by A. Feuillerat in *Materialien*, xxi and xliv, with accompanying warrants and other subsidiary documents. From 1547 to 1550 the accounts are mainly office copies of 'particular' books, setting out the details and cost of each individual revel, airing, or the like ; but for 1550–55, and again for 1555–9, the 'particular paye bookes' are brought together with summaries in two great 'Certificates' (*Loseley MSS*. 62 and 63), which relate to the Tents as well as the Revels. The second of these includes, as well as money accounts, inventories of the office stuff and notes of its employment in masking and other garments during 1555–60, and a similar record for 1550–5 is in *Loseley MS*. 112. These Certificates, although signed by the Clerk, Clerk Controller, and Yeoman, are not audited. Probably they are office copies of Original Accounts prepared for audit.

(b) *Elizabethan Period*.

Eleven Original Accounts of the Masters or Acting Masters of the Revels, with annotations by the Auditors, are in *R. O. Audit Office, Accounts Various*, 3, 907 (formerly 1213). They relate to the periods : (i) Feb. 1571–May 1572 ; (ii) June 1572–Oct. 1573 ; (iii) Nov. 1573–Feb. 1574 ; (iv) March 1574–Feb. 1575 ; (v) March 1576–Feb. 1577 ; (vi) Feb. 1578–Oct. 1579 ; (vii) Nov. 1579–Oct. 1580 ; (viii) Nov. 1580–Oct. 1581 ; (ix) Nov. 1582–Oct. 1583 ; (x) Nov. 1584–Oct. 1585 ; (xi) Nov. 1587–Oct. 1588. It will be seen that a regular annual system, starting with the opening of the season for revels at All Saints in each year, was ultimately adopted. All these accounts were printed in P. Cunningham, *Extracts from the Accounts of the Revels at Court* (1842, *Sh. Soc.*), but (ii) imperfectly and (xi) from an unaudited duplicate in the same bundle. These vagaries are corrected in the text of Feuillerat (1908, *Materialien*, xxi), who also gives an account for Nov. 1587–Oct. 1589 from *Lansd. MS*. 59, f. 38, which in part duplicates (xi), and much illustrative matter, including an estimate in some detail of the expenditure from Christmas 1563 to Shrovetide 1565 from *S. P. Dom. Eliz.* xxxvi. 22. The Audit Office series of Declared Accounts for the Revels is imperfect, but contains two, printed by Feuillerat, for the years 1581–2 and 1583–4, for which there are no Original Accounts. The Pipe Office series appears to be complete.

(c) *Jacobean Period*.

There are only two Original Accounts, for 1604–5 and 1611–12, which are printed by Cunningham. The Pipe Office Declared Accounts are complete. I have not examined those of the Audit Office. The Original Accounts for 1604–5 and 1611–12, and especially the former, have been the subject of a good deal of controversy. The facts are as follows. They were printed in 1842 by Peter Cunningham, then a clerk in the Audit Office, who described them as a separate discovery from the Elizabethan bundle, which he also printed. Twenty-six years afterwards, in 1868, he attempted to sell them to the British Museum, stating that he had found them some thirty years before 'under the vaults of Somerset House—far under the Quadrangle in a dry and lofty cellar, known by the name of the "Charcoal

Repository " '. Their official character was realized, and they were sent to the Record Office, and placed amongst the papers known as *Audit Office, Accounts Various*, 3, 908 (formerly 1214), with a note that Mr. E. A. Bond, Keeper of the Manuscripts in the British Museum, ' saw reasons for doubting the genuineness of one, at least, of these papers, from the peculiar character of the writing and the spelling '. It is probable that Bond had in mind, wholly or mainly, the play-list of the 1604–5 book, which does use some spellings, such as ' Shaxberd ' and ' aleven ', which are unusual although by no means unparalleled, and is, moreover, in a style of handwriting sufficiently different from the rest of the document to have at first sight a suspicious air. But it is an integral part of the book, occupying ff. 2, 2^v of its three small folio sheets, with other matter both on ff. 1, 1^v, and on ff. 5, 5^v, which form the second half of its sheet, and therefore, if a forged insertion, it occupies a long blank conveniently left by the original scribe just where, according to Revels practice, such a list ought to come. Bond's scepticism was shared by Sir Thomas Duffus Hardy, and although the grounds of it did not extend beyond the play-list in the 1604–5 account, the acceptance of this as a forgery naturally reflected some suspicion upon the corresponding list for 1611–12. The position, however, called for some reconsideration when, in *A Note on Measure for Measure* (1880) and subsequently in the fifth edition (1885) of his *Outlines* (ed. 9, ii. 163, 309), Halliwell-Phillipps called attention to evidence that Malone, at some date before his death in 1812, and therefore before Cunningham was born, was acquainted at least with the substance of the 1604–5 list. The Bodleian contains a number of Malone's note-books, which are believed to have been purchased from Mr. Rodd, a London bookseller, in 1838, and contain material collected after the issue of Malone's *Shakespeare* of 1790 with a view to a second edition ultimately produced by Boswell in 1821. With them were a bundle of loose scraps, which have since been mounted and bound as a supplementary volume. One of these scraps (*Malone MS.* 29, f. 19^v) consists of a list of plays headed ' 1604 & 1605 Ed^d. Tylney ', which substantially agrees with the list in the Revels book, even to the unusual spelling ' Shaxberd ', although it is clearly not a transcript of the Revels list, but merely an abstract of this, or a similar document, in an unknown hand other than Malone's. One of the plays named in the Revels book, *The Spanish Maze* of Shrove Monday, is omitted. No use of the scrap had been made by Boswell, although he prints (*Variorum*, iii. 360) extracts made by Malone from the Elizabethan Revels books, together with a letter of 7 Nov. 1791 from Sir William Musgrave, of the Audit Office, inviting Malone to inspect them, and an official memorandum on the ' State of the Books of Accounts and Records of the Master of the Revels, still remaining in the Office for Auditing the Public Accounts in 1791 '. It is, I think, inconceivable that, if the Jacobean as well as the Elizabethan books had then been discovered, no reference should have been made to them either by Musgrave or Malone, and the most probable explanation of the Bodleian scrap is that the Jacobean books turned up later, and that an abstract of the 1604–5 list was then prepared for the use of Malone. It is true that in that case the Jacobean books would naturally have been added to the ' proper presses ' which Musgrave says that he had provided for the Elizabethan ones, whereas Cunningham found the two sets apart. But as Cunningham also says that he had redeemed the Elizabethan bundle from ' a destructive oblivion ', it is possible that Musgrave's successors had been neglectful. Moreover, although the 1604–5 list does not appear in the 1821 *Variorum*, it is difficult to see on what other grounds Malone can have stated of *Othello* (*Variorum*, ii. 404), ' We know that it was acted in 1604 '. Probably, indeed, he had seen the list, before he abandoned in a note of 1800 to Dryden's *Grounds of Criticism in Tragedy* his earlier opinion that *Othello* was one of Shakespeare's latest plays. Further, there is similar indirect evidence that he had also come across the 1611–12 list. In 1808 he privately printed and in 1809 published an *Account of the . . . Tempest*, written ' some years ago '. The chief object of this was to fix an inferior date by Shakespeare's use of a pamphlet of 1610. The superior date he took for granted, saying (p. 31) ' That it was performed·before the middle of 1611, we have already seen ', and adding the foot-note ' Under a former article '. There was no former article, but in the preface Malone describes the essay as making ' a part of the Disquisition concerning the order of the plays in an enlarged form ', and no doubt the former article would have been included in the disquisition, had Malone ever completed his own work. Boswell, reprinting the essay in *Variorum*, xv. 414, altered the foot-note to refer to the essay on the Chronological Order of Shakespeare's Plays in ' vol. i '. This is in fact in vol. ii, but though Boswell here states (ii. 465) that there is evidence that the *Tempest* ' was produced in 1611 ', he does not give any evidence beyond the pamphlet of 1610. Probably he did not know everything that Malone knew. But how did Malone arrive at ' the middle of 1611 ', since the 1604–5 list does not take us beyond 1 Nov. 1611 ? I suppose he assumed that public production preceded performance at court. Later in the essay (*Variorum*, xv. 423) he says that the play ' had a being and a name in the autumn of 1611 '.

Since Halliwell-Phillipps's discovery the prevalent view, suggested by him, has been that if the lists, or at any rate that of 1604–5, are forged, the forger had before him a genuine original. More recently, however, the matter has been fully investigated by Mr. Ernest Law, who stimulated the Record Office to a minute examination of the 1604–5 document, including chemical and microscopical tests of the ink conducted by Professor J. J. Dobbie at the Government Laboratories. As a result, Mr. Law's own view that the list is genuine is confirmed by such high palaeographical authorities as Sir George Warner of the British Museum and Sir Henry Maxwell Lyte, Mr. Scargill-Bird, and other officers of the Record Office, as well as by Professor Feuillerat, than whom no one knows the Revels documents better, and Professor Wallace. Mr. Law set out the evidence and the whole history of the case in *Some Supposed Shakespeare Forgeries* (1911). His view was controverted in a review and a number of subsequent communications in the *Athenaeum* for 1911 (i. 638 ; ii. 101, 131, 421) and 1912 (i. 469,

654 ; ii. 142) by a writer using the signature ' Audi Alteram Partem ', whose rather amazing contentions Mr. Law disposed of in the same periodical (1911, ii. 297, 324, 388 ; 1912, i. 390, 470) and in *More about Shakespeare Forgeries* (1913). A recent controversy between Mrs. C. C. Stopes, Mr. Law, and Sir E. M. Thompson (*T. L. S.* 2, 23, 30 Dec. 1920; 27 Jan., 10, 24 Feb. 1921) has led to no different result.

I do not think that, in view of the palaeographical investigation, it is any longer possible to reject the genuineness of the 1604–5 list, and although that of 1611–12 has not been so minutely tested, it is pretty obviously of a piece with the ' Book ' of which it forms a part, and had it stood alone, probably no suspicion would have fallen upon it. In fact, it would really be more plausible—although this also is not in the least plausible—to take the whole documents as forgeries, than to take the lists as forged insertions in genuine accounts.

It must be added that there are some singular things about the substance of the books, with which Mr. Law does not seem to me quite to grapple. On the whole, that of 1604–5 is rather less perplexing than that of 1611–12. But the scribe has been oddly confused about his dates. On f. 1ᵛ he has written ' iijᵒ ', instead of ' ijᵒ ' for the regnal year. And at the top of f. 2 he has apparently written ' 1605 ' and then corrected it to ' 1604 '. The Queen's Revels are called by their obsolete name of ' The Boyes of the Chapell ', which is odd in an official document, but so they are, much later, in the Treasurer of the Chamber's account for 1612–13. It is more important that, while the Treasurer of the Chamber records payments for two plays to the Queen's Revels, one on 1 Jan. and the other on 3 Jan., the Revels list omits the play on 3 Jan. altogether, and instead records a performance of *Love's Labour's Lost* by the King's men ' betwin Newers Day and Twelfe Day '. No complete explanation of this is possible. The most that can be said is that there is independent evidence of a performance of *Love's Labour's Lost* in Jan. 1605, but at a date after and not before Twelfth Night. This is derived from two letters. The first is from Sir Walter Cope to Robert Cecil, Viscount Cranborne, preserved at Hatfield (*Hist. MSS.* iii. 148) and printed by Halliwell-Phillipps, ii. 83 :

' I have sent and bene all thys morning huntyng for players juglers and such kinde of creaturs, but fynde them harde to fynde ; wherfore, leavinge notes for them to seeke me, Burbage ys come, and sayes ther ys no new playe that the Quene hath not seene, but they have revyved an olde one cawled *Loves Labore lost*, which for wytt and mirthe he sayes will please her excedingly. And thys ys apointed to be playd tomorowe night at my Lord of Sowthamptons, unless yow send a wrytt to remove the corpus cum causa to your howse in Strande. Burbage ys my messenger ready attendyng your pleasure.'

The letter is undated, but endorsed ' 1604 '. Cecil's title was Viscount Cranborne from 20 Aug. 1604 to 4 May 1605. A second letter, from Dudley Carleton to John Chamberlain on 15 Jan. 1605 (*S. P. D. Jac. I*, xii. 13) gives within near limits the date of the performance. Carleton says,

' It seems we shall have Christmas all the yeare and therefore I shall never be owt of matter. The last nights revels were kept at my Lord

of Cranbornes, where the Q. with the D. of Holst and a great part of
the Court were feasted, and the like two nights before at my Lord of
Southamptons. The Temples have both of them done somewhat since
Twelftide but nothing memorable, save that it was observed on Friday
last at night the greatest part of the femal audience was the sisterhoode
of Blackfriers.'

Mr. Law (*More about S. F.* 50) rightly rejects the suggestion of
' Audi Alteram Partem ' that the ' last night ' referred to was necessarily 14 Jan., the night before the date of Carleton's letter; but
I think he is wrong in taking it as the last night of Christmas. This,
of course, was traditionally Twelfth Night, the day in 1605 of Jonson's
Mask of Blackness. But surely Carleton's whole point lies in the
exceptional prolongation of the Christmas festivities of this year
beyond Twelfth Night, and I feel clear that all the revels he here
refers to fell between 6 and 15 Jan. On 7 and 8 Jan. came *Hen. V*
and *E. M. O.* Putting the facts together, we get a performance, either
at Southampton's house or Cranborne's, between 8 and 15 Jan. of *Love's
Labour's Lost*, which the Queen had not seen before. It is not therefore at all likely that there had been another performance of the same
play at court between 1 and 6 Jan. It is true that the Queen might
by some accident have missed such a performance. But that would
not have prevented the Treasurer of the Chamber from paying for it,
whereas he would not pay for a performance ordered as part of an
entertainment given by Southampton or Cranborne. Nor would it
have been the duty of the Revels Office to attend such a performance,
which makes it rather mystifying that they should have confused it
with the second Queen's Revels performance at court some days
earlier, which it would have been their duty to attend. The vagueness
of the phrase ' betwin Newers Day and Twelfe Day ', suggesting that
the list was prepared retrospectively from memory, when the account
was made up in the autumn of 1605, may perhaps help to explain
an error. On the other hand, a forger, presumably knowing nothing
of Cope's letter, which first came to light in 1872, could hardly have
guessed at a revival of *Love's Labour's Lost* in 1605.

The discrepancies between the Revels list of 1611–12 and the
corresponding accounts of the Treasurer of the Chamber are rather
numerous. The Revels list records thirteen plays from 1 Nov. to
25 Feb. ' before the Kinges Maiestie ', including two which, although,
I suppose, ordered for the King, were in fact only given before the
Queen and Prince. The Treasurer paid for only ten plays as before
the King, and for many others before the younger members of the
royal family only, with which the Revels would not normally be
concerned. The two records agree as to 1 and 5 Nov., 26, 27, and
29 Dec., and 2, 23, and 25 Feb. On 28 Dec. the Treasurer notes
a play by the Prince's men which the Revels list does not. On 1 Jan.
the Revels list notes a play by the King's men, which the Treasurer
does not. The play on 5 Jan. is assigned by the Treasurer to the
King's men, and by the Revels list to the Whitefriars. The plays
on 12 and 13 Jan. appear from the Revels list to have been joint
performances by the King's and Queen's men, but the Treasurer notes
the play on 12 Jan. only, assigns that to the Duke of York's men,

and refers to Henry but not to the Queen as present. He also paid
for one play by the King's men before Henry, of which he does
not give the date, and which may be that of 13 Jan. Both records
note a play by the Duke of York's men on 24 Feb., but while the
Revels list does not indicate that James was absent, the Treasurer
treats the performance as one before the royal children only. I do
not know that all this is beyond the blundering of the clerks concerned, especially perhaps the Clerk of the Revels, at a time when
the functions of the office in relation to court plays had become
trivial. On the other hand, I am not clear that plays ordered by the
Queen and paid for out of her privy purse, instead of by the Treasurer
of the Chamber, may not sometimes have been produced under Revels
Office auspices; if so, some of the discrepancies might be thus
accounted for. But obviously the facts necessitate some caution in
the use of the 1611–12 list.

ABSTRACT OF PAYMENTS

I now give in tabular form an abstract of all entries in the Chamber
and Revels accounts, which enable us to establish the succession of
court performances during 1558–1616. These are arranged under years
running from Michaelmas to Michaelmas. Four columns are devoted
to the Chamber Accounts. Col. 1 records the dates of the performances, as recorded in the Declared Accounts. Any correction or
closer information as to date derivable from other sources is added
in square brackets. For the Jacobean period I also show the personages before whom the performances were given, K. standing for
James, Q. for Anne, H. for Henry, C. for Charles, E. for the Princess
Elizabeth, and F. for the Elector Palatine. Col. 2 contains the
verbatim descriptions in the accounts of the companies performing
and their payees, and in a very few cases of the nature of the performances. A few miscellaneous entries are inserted in this column.
Probably an exhaustive examination of the records of the subordinate
royal households during 1603–16 might enable a few additions to be
made. It is also possible that an occasional play, perhaps on a progress, may have been rewarded out of the Privy Purse. But the main
series of performances provided for the regular winter ' solace ' of the
sovereign appears to be fairly complete. Col. 3 shows the amounts
of the rewards. Col. 4 adds the dates of the warrants for payment
as given in the Declared Accounts and in brackets the places where
they were made out, W. for Westminster, H. for Hampton Court,
G. for Greenwich, R. for Richmond, J. for St. James's, Wi. for
Windsor. I add references to the parallel extracts of Cunningham
from the Original Chamber Accounts (C.), and to the notes of the
signing of warrants in the Privy Council Register (D.) where these
exist. A fifth column, for certain years, adds the relevant extracts
from such Revels Accounts as survive. The references are to Feuillerat's edition. Any discrepancies of importance between Chamber,
Privy Council, and Revels records are dealt with in foot-notes. The
variant dates of warrants in the ill-kept Privy Council Register are
not important.

APPENDIX B—(continued)

Performance	Payees	Amount	Warrant	Revels Accounts.
CHAMBER ACCOUNTS.				
1558-60 (*Pipe Office, Declared Accounts, Roll 541, mm. 17, 22*).				F. 34 (*1555–60*). 'ffurnisshinge of a pley by the children of the Chapple.'
—	'Quenes ... enterlude players for her hyghnes accustomed rewarde dewe vnto them at Newe yeres tyde.'	£6 13s. 4d.[1]		
—	'to players of enterludes.'	£13 6s. 8d.		F. 79 (*1558–9*). 'playes and other pastymes sett forthe and shewen in her Maiesties presence.'
1560-1 (*D. A. 541, m. 28*).				
Xmas.	'Lorde Robte Dudleyes players.'	£6 13s. 4d.	21 Jan. (W.); C. xxvii.	
Xmas	'Sebastiane Westcott Mr of the Children of Polles.'	£6 13s. 4d.	21 Jan. (W.); C. xxvii.	
1561-2 (*D. A. 541, m. 37*).				
Xmas.	'Lorde Robert Dudeleys playors,'	£6 13s. 4d.	6 Jan.	
Xmas	'Sebastiane Westcote Mr of the Children of Powles.'	£6 13s. 4d.	6 Jan.	
—	'Sebastiane Westecote Mr of the Children of Powles.'	£6 13s. 4d.	9 Mar. (W.); C. xxvii.	
1562-3 (*D. A. 541, m. 47*).				
Xmas.	'playores of the Lorde Robte Duddeley.'	£6 13s. 4d.	10 Jan. (W.); C. xxviii; D. vii. 134.	
Xmas.	'M. of the children of Poles.'[2]	£6 13s. 4d.	10 Jan. (W.); C. xxviii; D. vii. 134.	
1563-4 (*no entry in D. A.*).				F. 116. 'Charges agaynst Cristmas and Candelmas ffor iij plays at Wyndsor.'[3]

1564-5 (*D. A. 541, m. 67*).

Date		Amount	Warrant	Notes
Xmas. (2 plays).	'therle of Warwickes players.'	£13 6s. 8d.	18 Jan. (W.); C. **xxviii**; D. vii. 187.	F. 117. 'in Ienevery ffor cayrtene playes by the gramar skolle of Westmynster and the childerne of Powles.'
Xmas.	'Sebastian Westcote Mr of the Children of Powles.'	£6 13s. 4d.⁴	18 Jan. (W.); C. **xxviii**; D. vii. 187.	
2 Feb	'Sebastian Westcott Mr of the Children of Poles.'	£6 13s. 4d.	9 Mar. (W.); C. **xxviii**; D. vii. 204.	F. 116. 'Cristmas . . . for a maske and a showe and a play by the childerne of the Chaple.' [*In margin*] 'Edwardes tragedy'. F. 117. 'The xviijᵗʰ of februerie . . . for a play maid by Sir Percivall Hartts sones with a maske of huntars and diuers devisses and a rocke or hill ffor the ix musses to singe vppone with a vayne of sarsnett drawven vpp and downe before them.' F. 117. 'Shroftid [4-6 March] . . . new and diuers showes made by the gentillmen of Greys Ine.' [*In margin*] 'Gentillmenne of ye Innes of Court. Diana, Pallas.'

---

¹ This payment was by warrant of the Lord Chamberlain.
² P. C. Acts name Westcote.
³ On the unrewarded plays of 1563-4 and 1564-5. cf. ch. vii.
⁴ In P. C. Acts, by an obvious error, £7 13s. 8d.

APPENDIX B—(continued)

CHAMBER ACCOUNTS.

Performance.	Payees.	Amount.	Warrant.	REVELS ACCOUNTS.
1565-6 (*D. A. 541, m. 76*). Xmas (3 plays)	'Sebastian Westcote Mr of the Children of Powles . . . for two seuall playes . . . at the Courte . . . and one other also before her Matie at the Ladye Cecilias Lodging at the Sauoye.'	£20	3 Jan. (W.).	
1566-7 (*D. A. 541, m. 92*). Xmas (2 plays)	'Sebastyan Westcote Mr of the children of Powles.'	£13 6s. 8d.	11 Jan. (W.); D. vii. 322 (12 Jan.).	
Shrovetide (9–11 Feb.).	'John Taylor Mr of the Children of Westmr.'	£6 13s. 4d.	13 Feb. (W.); D. vii. 327.	
Shrovetide (9–11 Feb.) [11 Feb.].[1]	'Richarde Farraunte Mr of the children of Windsore.'	£6 13s. 4d.	16 Feb.; D. vii. 331 (W. 17 Feb.).	
1567-8 (*D. A. 541, mm. 102–3*). Xmas.	'John Tailer Mr of the Children at Westmr.'	£6 13s. 4d.	10 Jan. (W.).	
	'The Lord Ryches Plaiers.'	£13 6s. 8d.	11 Jan. (W.).	
Xmas (2 plays).	'Sebastian Westcote Mr of the Children of Powles.'	£13 6s. 8d.	13 Jan. (W.).	
Shrovetide (29 Feb.–2 Mar.).	'William Hunnys Mr of the Children of the Quenes Mates Chappell . . . for . . . a Tragedie.'	£6 13s. 4d.	3 Mar. (W.).	
Shrovetide.	'Richarde Ferrante Mr of the children of Windesore.'	£6 13s. 4d.	1 Mar. (W.).	F. 119. 'theis playes Tragides and Maskes . . . viz . . . seven playes, the firste namede as playne as canne be, The seconde the paynfull pliligrimage, The thirde Iacke and Iyll, The forthe sixe fooles, The fiveth callede witte and will, The sixte callede prodigallitie, The sevoenth of Orestes and a Tragedie of the Kinge of Scottes, to ye whiche belonged diuers howses, . . . as Stratoes

howse, Goblyns howse, Orestioes howse Rome, the Pallace of prosperitie Scotlande and a gret Castell one thothere side.'[2] F. 123. 'Revelles vppon Shrovesonday and Shroftuisday at nighte.'

1568-9 (*D. A. 541, m. 113*).

26 Dec.	'the Lorde Riches players.'	£6 13s. 4d.	28 Dec. (H.); C. xxix.
1 Jan.	'Sebastian Westecote mr of the Children of Powles.'	£6 13s. 4d.	2 Jan.; C. xxix.
22 Feb.	'Richard Ferraunte Scole mr of the Children of Windesore.'	£6 13s. 4d.	25 Feb. (W.); C. xxix.

1569-70 (*D. A. 541, m. 115*).

27 Dec.	'Richarde Ferrante Scholemr to the Children of Windesore.'	£6 13s. 4d.	2 Jan. (Wi.); C. xxix.
6 Jan.	'Willm Huñys mr of the children of her mates Chappell.'	£6 13s. 4d.	7 Jan. (Wi.); C. xxix.
5 Feb.	'the Lorde Riches playores.'	£6 13s. 4d.	7 Feb. (H.); C. xxix.

1570-1 (*D. A. 541, m. 127*).

28 Dec.	'Sebastian Westecote Mr of the Children of Powles.'	£6 13s. 4d.	22 Feb.
Shrovetide (25-7 Feb.) (3 plays).	'Willm Honnyes, Richarde Farraunte and Sebastian Westcote Mrs of the Children of the Q mates Chapple Royall Windsore and Powles.'	£20	28 Feb.

[1] P. C. Acts specify 'Shrove Tuesday'.

[2] Apparently one play was unrewarded.

L

APPENDIX B—(continued)

CHAMBER ACCOUNTS.

Performance.	Payees.	Amount.	Warrant.	REVELS ACCOUNTS.
1571-2 (*D. A. 541, m. 137*).				
27 Dec.	'Lawrence Dutton and his fellowes.'[1]	£6 13s. 4d.	5 Jan. (W.) ; D. viii. 61 (12 Jan.).	F. 144. 'Lady Barbara showen on Saint Iohns day at nighte by Sir Robert Lanes Men.'
28 Dec.	'Sebastian Westcott Mr of the Children of Powles.'	£6 13s. 4d.	9 Jan. (W.) ; D. viii. 62 (12 Jan.).	'Effiginia A Tragedye showen on the Innosentes daie at nighte by the Children of Powles.'
1 Jan.	'Richard Farrant gent Mr of the Children of Windsor.'	£6 13s. 4d.	5 Jan. (W.) ; D. viii. 62 (12 Jan.).	'Aiax and vlisses showen on New Yeares daie at nighte by the Children of Wynsor.'
6 Jan.	'Willm Hunnys Mr of the childer of the Chappell.'	£6 13s. 4d.	N.D. ; D. viii. 62 (12 Jan.' John' Hunnis).	'Narcisses showen on Twelfe daye at Nighte by the Children of the Chappell.'
17 Feb.	'John Greaves and Thomas Goughe servauntes to Sr Robt. Lane Knighte.'[2]	£13 6s. 8d.	26 Feb. (W.) ; D. viii. 71 (29 Feb.).	'Cloridon and Radiamanta showen on Shrove sundaye at Nighte by Sir Robert Lanes Men.'
19 Feb.	'John Billingesley.'[3]	£13 6s. 8d.	22 Feb. (W.) ; D. viii. 71 (29 Feb.).	'Paris and Vienna showen on Shrovetewsdaie at Nighte by the Children of Westminster.'
1572-3 (*D. A. 541, m. 150*).				
Xmas (3 plays).	'Therle of Leic. players.'	£30, 'videlt. for euye playe vjl xiijs iiijd and for a more rewarde by hir Mates owne comanndemt xl In all xxxl.'	1 Jan. (H.).	F. 174. Scattered entries refer to all these companies except Sussex's and to— 'the play of Cariclia', 'Theagines', 'the picture of Andromadas', 'the monster', 'the playe of fortune'.

Date	Company / Payee	Payment	Date (reference)	Notes
1 Jan.	'Richarde Farrante M^r of the children at Wyndesore.'	£6 13s. 4d.	2 Jan. (H.).	F.193. 'Predor: &Lucia, played by Therle of Leicesters servauntes vpon Saint stevens daye.'
—	'Sebastian Westecote M^r of the Cuildren of Polles.'	£6 13s. 4d.	7 Jan. (H.).	'Mamillia, playde by therle of Leicesteres seruauntes on Innosentes daye.'
6 Jan.	'Elderton and the Children of Eyton.'	£6 13s. 4d.	7 Jan. (H.).	
—	'Therle of Sussex players.'	£6 13s. 4d.	7 Feb.	
—	'Laurence Dutton s^{r}unte to therle of Lincoln.'	£6 13s. 4d.	10 Feb.	'Alkmeon, played by the Children of Powles on Saint Iohns daye.'
3 Feb.	'Mr Moncaster.'	£20, 'vi^l xiij^s iiij^d and for a more rewarde by her Ma^{tes} owne comaundem^t xiij^s vj^s viiij^d'.	10 Feb.	'Truth, flaythfullnesse, & Mercye, playde by the Children of Westminster for Elderton vpon New yeares daye.'

1573-4 (*D. A. 541, mm. 165-6*).

Date	Company / Payee	Payment	Date (reference)
Xmas (2 plays) [26, 28 Dec.]	Therle of Leicestres players.	£20, 'xiiij^l vj^s viiij^d and by waye of speciall rewarde for theyre chardges cunyng⁴ and skill shewed therein vj^l xiij^s iiij^d'.	9 Jan. (W.); D. viii. 177 (8 Jan.).
27 Dec.	'Sebastian Westcote M^r of the Children of Powles.'	£6 13s. 4d.	10 Jan. (W.); D. viii. 178.
1 Jan.	'Will$\bar{m}$ Elderton.'	£6 13s. 4d.	10 Jan. (W.); D. viii. 178.

¹ P. C. Acts describe the company as Lane's, and put the performance 26 Dec., Windsor 27 Dec., and Paul's 1 Jan.
² P. C. Acts give payees as 'Lawrence Dutton and his fellows'. Wallace, i. 213, states in error that this and the next payment are not in D.A.
³ P. C. Acts give payee as '——, Master of the Children of Westminster'.
⁴ Wallace, i. 215, reads 'cumyng' in error.

APPENDIX B—(continued)

CHAMBER ACCOUNTS.

Performance.	Amount.	Payees.	Warrant.	REVELS ACCOUNTS.
3 Jan.	£6 13s. 4d.	'Laurence Dutton and the rest of his Fellowes s[r]untes to the L Clinton.'	11 Jan. (W.); D. viii. 178 (10 Jan.).	'Herpetulus the blew knighte & perobia playde by my Lorde Klintons servantes the third of January.'
6 Jan.	£10, 'vj[l] xiij[s] iiij[d] and in respecte of his chardges coming hyther lxvj[s] viij[d].'	'Richarde Ferant Scholem[r].'	10 Jan. (W.); D. viii. 178.	'Quintus fiabius played by the Children of Wyndsor ffor M[r] ffarrant on Twelfe daye.'
2 Feb. 〉 23 Feb. 〉	£26 13s. 4d., 'xiij[l] vj[s] viij[d] and further her Mate[s] speciall rewarde for suche costes and chardges as he was at for the same xiij[l] vj[s] viij[d].'	'Richarde Moncaster.'	18 Mar. (G.); D. viii. 210.	F. 206. 'ffor Candellmas . . . Timoclia at the sege of Thebes by Alexander showen . . by M[r] Munkesters Children. F. 213. 'Percius & Anthomiris playde by Munkesters Children on Shrovetewsdaye.'
21 Feb.[1]	£10, 'vj[l] xiij[s] iiij[d] and forther by waye of her highnes rewarde for suche chardges as they had bene at for the furniture of the same lxvj[s] viij[d].'	'Therle of Leic his plaiers.'	22 Feb. (H.); D. viii. 198.	'Philemon & Philecia play by the Erle of Lecesters men on Shrove Mundaye.' F. 227. 'Italyan Players at Wynsor & Reding ...the xv[th] of July 1574.'
1574-5 (D. A. 541, m. 178). 26 Dec.	£10.	'Therle of Lecesters players.'	9 Jan.; C. xxx.	F. 239. 27 Dec. 'gloves for my Lord of Lesters boyes y[t] plaied at the coorte.' F. 244. 25 Dec. 'my Lord of Leicesters menns playe.'
1 Jan.	£6 13s. 4d.	'the Erle of Leic' players.'	9 Jan.; C. xxx.	F. 239. 1 Jan. 'chymney sweepers in my Lord of Leyces-

Date	Company	Amount	Date ; C.	Notes
27 Dec.	'the lord Clynton players.'	£6 13s. 4d.	11 Jan. ; C. xxx.	ters mennes playe & for mosse & styckes.' F. 244. 27 Dec. 'the Duttons playe.'
2 Jan.	'the lord Clinton players.'	£6 13s. 4d.	11 Jan. ; C. xxx.	
6 Jan.	'Richard Farrante mr of the children of the chapell of Wyndsor.'	£13 6s. 8d.	23 Jan. (H.) ; C. xxx.	F. 244. 'King Xerxces syster in ffarrantes playe, . . . cariage . . . for the playe . . . on twelfe nighte.'
2 Feb.	'Sebastian Westecote Mr of the Children of Powles.'	£13 6s. 8d.	16 Feb. ; C. xxxi.	
13 Feb.	'William Hunysm r of the children of her ma tes Chappell.'	£13 6s. 8d.	16 Feb. (R.) ; C. xxxi.	F. 244. 13 Feb. 'Mr Hvnnyes his playe.'
13 Feb. [15 Feb. ?].	'Richarde Moncaster.'	£13 6s. 8d., 'vjl. xiijs. iiijd and for a reward gyven by her heignes vjl. xiijs. iiijd.	17 Feb. (R.).	[F. 238. The following rehearsals took place : 14 Dec. 'my Lord Chamberlens players did show the history of Phedrastus & Phigon and Lucia together.' 18 Dec. 'my Lord of Leicesters menne showed theier matter of Panecia.' 20 Dec. 'my lord Clyntons players rehearsed a matter called Pretestus.' 21 Dec. 'the showed ij other playes.']
13 Feb. [14 Feb.].[2]	'Therle of Warwickes players.'	£10.	16 Feb. (R.) ; C. xxxi.	

[1] In view of the date in the warrant, the 'Monday' of the Revels Accounts should clearly be 'Sunday'.

[2] The D.A. give all three plays on Shrove Sunday, but Cunningham has Shrove Monday for Warwick's and omits Muncaster's, which may have been on the Tuesday, although two plays were sometimes given on the same night.

APPENDIX B—(continued)

CHAMBER ACCOUNTS.

Performance.	Payees.	Amount.	Warrant.
1575-6 (D. A. 541, mm. 195-6).			
26 Dec. } 1 Jan.	'John Dutton, Lawrence Dutton, Jerome Savage, etc. Thearle of Warwickes players.'	£20.	2 Jan. (H.); D. ix. 68.
27 Dec.	'Richard Farraunt Mr of the children of the Chappell at Wyndsore.'	£10.	30 Dec. (H.); D. ix. 67 (29 Dec.).
28 Dec.	'Thearle of Leicestre players.'	£10.	30 Dec. (H.); D. ix. 68 (29 Dec.)
6 Jan.	'Sebasten Westcott Mr of the children of Powles.'	£10.	7 Feb. (H.); D. ix. 71 (7 Jan.).
2 Feb.	'John Adams and the rest of my Lorde Chamberlaynes servaunt players.'	£10.	4 Feb. (H.); D. ix. 81 (— Jan.).
27 Feb.	'Alfruso Ferrabolle and the rest of the Italyan players.'	£10.	12 Mar. (W.).
4 Mar. ?1	'to —— Burbag and his company Servauntes to thearle of Leicester.'	£10.	14 Mar. (W.).
5 Mar.2	'Lawraunce Dutton and the rest of his company Servauntes to thrighte honourable Thearle of Warwicke.'	£10.	8 Mar. (W.); D. ix. 95 (11 Mar.).
6 Mar.	'Richard Moulcastre to hime.'	£10.	11 Mar. (W.); D. ix. 94.
[Sept.–Oct.]	'Richarde Farrant, Mr of the Children of her Maᵗᵉˢ chappell of Winsore viz. for the chardges of xv of the singinge men of the said chappell	—	11 Nov. 1577.

and sixe of the children re-payringe thither to Read-ynge at her ma^tes laste being there.'

1576-7 (*Audit Office, Declared Accounts, Roll xv, Bundle 3⁸²*) [Pipe Office copy missing].

Date	Company	Amount	Date (H.)	D.	Reference
Xmas holidays. [26 Dec.]	'Therle of Warwickes players.'	£16 13s. 4d.	20 Jan. (H.) ; 270.	D. **ix.**	F. 256, 269. 'The Paynters Daughter . . . on St Stevens daie . . . by therle of Warwickes seruauntes . . . the Duttons plaie.'
27 Dec.	'the Lord Howardes players.'	£10.	12 Jan. (H.),		F. 256. 'Toolie . . . on St. Iohn: daie . . . by the Lord Howardes seruantes.'
Xmas holidays. [30 Dec.]	'Therle of Leicesters players.'	£16 13s. 4d.	20 Jan. (H.) ; 270.	D. **ix.**	F. 256. 'The historie of the Collyer . . . on the Sundaie folowing [30 Dec.] . . . by th' erle of Leicesters men.'
Xmas holidays [1 Jan.]	'Sebastian Westcote m^r of the Children of Powles.'	£16 13s. 4d.	20 Jan. (H.) ; 270.	D. **ix.**	F. 266. 'ffor cariadge . . . for the Earle of Leicesters to the court 28° Decembris.'
Xmas holidays. [6 Jan.]	'Richard Farrante m^r of the children of the Chappell.'	£16 13s. 4d.	20 Jan. (H.) ; 270.	D. **ix.**	F. 266. 'for that their [Leicester's ?] plaie was deferred until the Sundaie folowing [30 Dec.]'³ F. 256. 'The historie of Error . . . on Newyeres daie . . . by the Children of Powles.' F. 256. 'The historye of Mutius Sceuola . . . on Twelf daie . . .'

¹ The *D. A.* give Sunday before Shrovetide, which might mean either Shrove Sunday (Mar. 4) or the preceding Sunday (Feb. 26).

² P. C. Acts name John Dutton, as well as Lawrence, and put Muncaster's play on Sunday. It is safer to follow *D. A.*

³ As the entry stands, it should refer to Warwick's, but I think it probably does refer to Leicester's.

APPENDIX B—(continued)

CHAMBER ACCOUNTS.

Performance.	Payees.	Amount.	Warrant.	REVELS ACCOUNTS.
2 Feb.	'Therle of Sussexes players.'	£16 13s. 4d.	3 Feb. (H.); D. ix. 280.	by the Children of Windsore and the Chappell.'
17 Feb.	'The Lord Howardes players.'[1]	£10.	20 Feb. (W.); D. ix. 293.	F. 256. 'The historye of the Cenofalles .. on Candelmas daie ... by the Lord Chamberleyn his men.'
18 Feb.	'Therle of Warwikes players.'	£10.	20 Feb. (W.); D. ix. 293.	F. 270. 'The Historie of the Solitarie Knight ... on Shrovesundaie . . . by the Lord Howardes seruauntes.'
17 Feb. [19 Feb.][2]	'Sebastian Westcote.'	£10.	20 Feb. (W.); D. ix. 293.	F. 270. 'The Irisshe Knyght ... on Shrovemundaie ... by the Earle of Warwick his seruauntes.'
				F. 270. 'The historye of Titus and Gisippus .. on Shrovetuysdaie ... by the Children of Pawles.'
				F. 277. Probably for a rehearsal, 'the cariadge of the partes of ye well counterfeit from the Bell in Gracious strete to St. Iohns to be performed for the play of Cutwell.'
April.	'Durham Place (an Italian playe their done before her ma^tes Privy Council).'		N.D. ['Apparelling charge.']	
1577-8 (D. A. 541, mm. 209-12).				
26 Dec.	'The Earle of Leicesters seruantes.'	£10.[3]	9 Jan. (H.); D. x. 138.	
27 Dec.	'Richarde Farrante m^r of the children of her ma^tes chappell.'	£10.	20 Jan. (H.).	

Date	Company	Amount	Reference
8 Dec.	'The Earle of Warwickes players.'	£10.	12 Jan. (H.).
30 Dec.	'Sebastian Westcott.'	£10.	31 Jan. (H.).
5 Jan.[4]	'The Lorde Howarde baron of Effingham his players.'	£10.	9 Jan. (H.); D. x. 138.
6 Jan.	'Earle of Warwickes players.'	£10.	12 Jan. (H.).
2 Feb.	'The Lorde Chamblaynes players.'	£10.	15 Mar. (G.), in duplicate, D. x. 185 (14 Mar.).
9 Feb.	'The Earle of Warwickes players.'	£10.	18 Feb. (H.).
11 Feb.	'The Countes of Essex players.'	£10.	14 Feb. (H.).
(11 Feb.)	'The Earle of Leicesters players.'	£6 13s. 4d., 'for makinge their repaire to the Courte wth their whole company and furniture to presente a playe before her matie uppon Shrovetuesdaye at nighte in consideracon of their chardgies for that purpose although the plaie by her maties commaundement was supplyed by others.'	18 Feb. (H.).

[1] P. C. Acts have Chamberlain's for Howard's.

[2] As two plays on one night are exceptional, it is safer to follow the Revels Account.

[3] The £10 payment has now become normal, but to the end of the reign is stated, usually but not invariably, as made up of £6 13s. 4d. with a 'more' sum of £3 6s. 8d., by way of Her Majesty's 'rewarde', 'speciall rewarde', or 'further liberalitie and rewarde'.

[4] The Pipe Office D. A. date Sunday, Jan. 'firste'. Jan. 5 was Sunday; the 'fifte' of A. O. (Wallace, i. 220) is right.

APPENDIX B—(continued)

Performance.	Payees.	Amount.	Warrant.	REVELS ACCOUNTS.
		CHAMBER ACCOUNTS.		
—	'for a mattres hoopes and boardes with tressells for the Italian Tumblers.'	—	N.D. [' Apparelling charge ']	
1578-9 (*D. A. 541, m. 222*).				
26 Dec.	'Therle of Warwickesrauntes.'	£10.	16 Jan. ; D. xi. 21 (R.).	F. 286. 'An Inventyon or playe of the three Systers of Mantua .. on St Stephens daie .. by thearle of Warwick his servauntes.'
28 Dec.	'ye lord Chamblaynes players.'	£10.	16 Jan. ; D. xi. 21 (R.).	F. 286. 'An history of the creweltie of A Stepmother .. on Innocentes daie .. by the Lord Chamberlaynes servauntes.'
6 Jan.	'ye sayd lord Chamblaynes srauntes.'	£10.	16 Jan. ; D. xi. 21 (R.).	F. 286. 'The historie of the Rape of the second Helene .. on Twelf daie.' F. 299. 6 Jan. 'my Lord Chamberleynes players second plaie.'
1 Jan.[1]	'ye Mr of ye Children at Pawles.'	£10.	16 Jan. ; D. xi. 21 (R.).	F. 286. 'A Morrall of the marryage of Mynde and Measure .. on the sondaie next after Newe yeares daie .. by the children of Pawles.'
4 Jan.	'Therle of Leicestres players.'	£10.	16 Jan. ; D. xi. 21 (R.)	F. 286. 'A pastorell or historie of A Greeke maide .. on the sondaie next after Newe yeares daie .. by the Earle of Leicester his servauntes.'

Date	Company	Payment	Reward	Revels	Note
5 Jan. [27 Dec.]²	'Mr Ferreunte Mr of the Children of her Mates chappell.'	£10.		16 Jan.; D. xi. 21 (R.).	F. 286. 'The historie of —— ...on St Iohns daie...by the children of the Quenes maiesties chappell.' F. 298. 27 Dec. 'for cariage of the stuffe that served the plaie for the children of the chappell to the courte and back agayne.'
(2 Feb.)	'Jerome Savage and his companye sreauntes to Therle of Warwickes.'	£6 13s. 4d., 'in consideracon of a playe wch was in readynes to have bene presented before her Matie on Candlemas night last paste'.		11 Mar.; D. xi. 81 (W. 18 Mar.).	F. 303. 'The history of —— provided to have ben shewen .. on candlemas daie .. by the Earle of Warwickes servauntes .. Being in redines at ye place to have enacted the same. But the Quenes maiestie wold not come to heare the same and therefore put of.'
1 Mar.	'therle of Warwickes sreauntes.'	£10.		13 Mar.; D. xi. 75 (W.).	F. 303. 'The history of the Knight in the Burnyng Rock ... on shrovesundaie ... by the Earle of Warwickes servauntes.'
2 Mar.	'Richarde Ferrante Mr of the children of her mates chapell.'	£10.		12 Mar.; D. xi. 70 (W.).	F. 303. 'The history of Loyaltie and bewtie .. on Shrove monday... by the children of the Quenes maiesties chappell.'
3 Mar.³	'ye lorde Chamblaynes players.'	£10.		13 Mar.; D. xi. 75 (W.).	F. 303. 'The history of murderous mychaell... on shrovetuesdaie...by the Lord Chamberleynes servauntes.'

¹ Presumably the Revels Accounts put this play on 4 Jan. in error.   ² The 27 Dec. of Revels Accounts is preferable.
³ P. C. Acts give Shrove Sunday for the Chamberlain's as well as Warwick's.

APPENDIX B—(continued)

Performance.	Payees.	Amount.	Warrant.	Revels Accounts.
1579-80 (*D. A. 542, m. 8*). 26 Dec.	'the Lorde Chamblaynes players.'	£10.	25 Feb. (W.) ; D. xi. 377 (25 Jan.).	F. 320. 'A history of the Duke of Millayn and the Marques of Mantua . . . on Sᵗ Stephens daie . . . by the lord Chamberlaynes seruauntes.'
27 Dec.	'Richarde Farrant mʳ of the children of her Maᵗᵉˢ Chappell.'	£10.	25 Jan. (W.) ; D. xi. 377.	F. 320. 'A history of Alucius . . . on Sᵗ Iohns daie . . . by the Children of her Maiesties Chappell.'
1 Jan.	'yᵉ players of the Erle of Warwicke.'	£10.	25 Jan. (W.) ; D. xi. 377.	F. 320. 'A history of the foure sonnes of ffabyous . . . on Newe Yeares daie . . . by the Earle of Warwickes seruauntes.'
3 Jan.	'Sebastian Westcote master of the children of the Churche of Sᵗ Paules.'	£10.	25 Jan. (W.) ; D. xi. 377.	F. 321. 'The history of Cipio Africanus . . . the sondaye night after newe yeares daie . . . by the Children of Pawles.'
6 Jan.	'the players of the E of Leicester.'	£10.	25 Jan. (W.) ; D. xi. 377.	F. 321. 'The history of —— . . . on Twelve-daye . . . by the Earle of Leicesters seruauntes.'
15 Jan.	'the Lorde Straunge his Tumblers . . . in consideracon of certen feates of Tumblinge by them done before her Maᵗⁱᵉ.'	£10.	25 Jan. (W.) ; D. xi. 377.	
2 Feb.	'the L. Chamblaynes players.'	£10.	23 Feb. (W.) ; D. xi. 398.	F. 321. 'The history of Portio and demorantes . . . on Candlemas daie . . . by the Lord Chamberleyns seruauntes.'

Date	Payee	Amount	Court reference	Description
16 Feb.	'the saide L. Chamberlaynes players.'	£10.	23 Feb. (W.); D. **xi.** 398.	F. 321. 'The history of Serpedon .. on Shrovetwesdaye .. by the lord Chamberleyns seruauntes.'
14 Feb.	'the players of the Erle of Derbye.'	£10.	23 Feb. (W.); D. xi. 398.	F. 321. 'The history of the —— Soldan and the Duke of —— .. on Shrovesondaye .. by the Earle of Derby his seruauntes.' [F. 326. 'Examynynge and rehersinge of dyuers plaies and choise makinge of x of them to be showen before her Maiestie.' In addition to the 8 above were the tumbling and F. 320. 'A historye of —— provided to haue bene shewen .. on Innocentes daie .. by the Earle of Leicesters seruauntes being in readynes in the place to haue enacted the same. . . . But the Queenes Maiestie coulde not come forth to heare the same/therefore put of.']

1580–1 (*D. A. 542, m. 21*).

Date	Payee	Amount	Court reference	Description
27 Dec.	'Therle of Sussex srauntes.'	£10.	14 Jan. (W.); D. xii. 321 (30 Jan.).	F. 336. 'The Earle of Sussex men. A storie of —— .. on St Iohns daie.'
1 Jan.	'Therle of Darbyes players.'	£10.	20 Jan. (W.); D. xii. 321 (30 Jan.).	F. 336. 'The Earle of Derbies men. A storie of —— .. on newe yeres daye.'

APPENDIX B—(continued)

Performance.[1]	CHAMBER ACCOUNTS.		Warrant.	REVELS ACCOUNTS.
	Payees.	Amount.		
6 Jan.	'Sebastian Wastcote m^r of the children of Powles.'	£10.	18 Jan. (W.); D. xii. 321 (30 Jan.).	F. 336. 'The children of Pawles. A storie of Pompey . . on twelf nighte.'
2 Feb.	'the Lorde Chamblaynes players.'	£10.	13 Feb. (W.); D. xii. 330 (14 Feb.).	F. 336. 'The earle of Sussex men. A storie of —— . . . on Candlemas daie.'
5 Feb. (W.)	'the M^r of the Children of the Chappell,'	£10.	14 Feb. (W.); D. xii. 330.	F. 336. 'The children of the Quenes maiesties chappell. A storie of —— . . on shrove-sondaie.'
7 Feb.	'Therle of Leicesters players.'	£10.	14 Jan. (W.); D. xii. 330 (14 Feb.).	F. 336. 'The Earle of Leicesters men. A storie of —— . . . on shrovetuesdaie.'
26 Dec.	'to them [Leicester's] more.'	£10.	14 Jan. (W.); D. xii. 321 (30 Jan.).	F. 336. 'The Earle of Leicesters men. A Comodie called delighte . . . on St Stephens daie.'
1581-2 (*D. A. 542, mm. 32-3; Harl. MS. 1644, ff. 78^v, 80^v, 81^v).*				
26 Dec.	'the M^r of the Children of Powles,'	£10.	14 Apr. (W.); D. xiii. 393 (G.).	F. 345. Table II, 'v playes'.
28 Dec.	'the Servauntes of the Lorde Straunge . . . for certen feates of activitie shewed her Matie.'	£10.	21 Jan. (W.); D. xiii. 311.	
31 Dec. 27 Feb. }	'the M^r of the Children of her mates Chappell.'	£20.	1 Apr. (G.); D. xiii. 374.	
1582-3 (*D. A. 542, mm. 44-5).*				
26 Dec. (Wi.)	'William Hunnys the m^r of the children of the chappell.'	£10.	17 Feb. (R.).	F. 349. 'A Comodie or Morrall devised on A game of the Cardes . . . on St Stephens daie . . . by the Children of her maiesties Chapple.'

27 Dec. (Wi.)	17 Feb. (R.).	£10.	'the Seruauntes of the Lorde of Hunsdon.'	F. 349. 'A Comodie of Bewtie and Huswyfery ... on St Iohns daie ... by the lord of Hundesdons seruauntes.'
30 Dec. (Wi.)	17 Feb. (R.).	£10.	'the Seruauntes of Thearle of Darby.'	F. 349. 'A Historie of Loue and ffortune ... on the sondaie ... next before newe yeares daie ... by the Earle of Derbies seruauntes.'
1 Jan. (Wi.)	17 Feb. (R.).	£13 6s. 8d.	'John Simons ... for showinge ċten ffeates of actiuitye and Tomblinge.'	F. 349. 'Sundrey feates of Tumbling and Activitie were shewed before her maiestie on Newe yeares daie at night by the Lord Straunge his seruauntes.'
6 Jan. (Wi.)	17 Feb. (R.).	£10.	'the Seruauntes of the Lorde Chamberlayne.'	F. 350. 'A historie of ffferrar ... on Twelf daie ... by the Lord Chamberleynes seruauntes.'
10 Feb. (R.)	17 Feb. (R.).	£10.	'The Seruantes of Thearle of Lecester.'	F. 350. 'A historie of Telomo ... on Shrovesondaie .. by the Earle of Leicesters seruauntes.'
12 Feb. (R.)	17 Feb. (R.).	£10.	'Richarde Mulcaster ... wth his Scholers.'	F. 350. 'A historie of Ariodante and Geneuora ... on Shrovetuesdaie ... by mr Mulcasters children.'
1583-4 (D. A. 542, m. 56). 26 Dec. } 29 Dec. } 3 Mar. }	12 Mar. (W.), paid 9 May.	£20.	'her mates seruauntes.'	F. 362. Table III, 'vj histories, one Comedie.'

¹ Both the 'Twe[f]day' of the Pipe Office and the 'Tewfday' of the Audit Office (Wallace, i. 223) D. A. are doubtless errors for 'Twelfday'. P.C. Acts have 'Twelfte Daye'.

APPENDIX B—(continued)

CHAMBER ACCOUNTS.

Performance.	Payees.	Amount.	Warrant.	REVELS ACCOUNTS.
6 Jan. ⎫ 2 Feb. ⎬	'the master of the children of her mates Chappell.'	£15.	12 Mar. (W.), paid 29 Mar.	F.365. 'A pastorall of phillyda & Choryn . . . by her highnes servauntes on St Stephens daie.'
1 Jan. ⎫ 3 Mar. ⎬	'the Erle of Oxforde his servauntes . . . paide to Johon Lilie.'	£20.	12 Mar. (W.), paid 25 Nov.	'The history of felix & philiomena . . . by her maiesties servauntes on the Sondaie next after newe yeares daye.'
1584-5 (*D. A. 542, mm. 66–8*). 26 Dec. ⎫ 3 Jan. ⎪ 6 Jan. ⎬ 23 Feb. ⎭	'Robte Willson to thuse of him selfe and the rest of her mates players.'	£40.	14 Mar. (G.).	'An invention called ffiue playes in one . . . on Twelfe daie . . . by her highnes servauntes.' 'An invention of three playes in one prepared to haue ben shewed . . . on Shroue Sondaye . . . by her maiesties servauntes. . . . But the Quene came not abroad that night.' 'An Antick play & a comodye . . . on Shrouetewsdaie . . . by her maiesties servauntes.'
27 Dec.	'Henry Evans . . . for one play . . . by the children of Therle of Oxforde.'	£6 13s. 4d.	7 Apr. (G.).	F.365. 'The history of Agamennon & Vlisses . . . by the Earle of Oxenford his boyes on St Iohns daie.'

1 Jan.	'John Symons and other his fellowes Servantes to Therle of Oxforde...for...feates of actiuitye and vawtinge.'	£10	14 Mar. (G.).	F. 365. 'Dyuers feates of Actyuytie were shewed and presented...on newe yeares daye ... by Symons and his fellowes.'

1585-6 (*D. A. 542, m. 79; Harl. MS. 1641, ff. 20^v, 21*).

26 Dec.	'her Mates players.'	£10.	31 Jan. (G.).	
27 Dec.	'the Servantes of the lo admirall.'	£10.	31 Jan. (G.).	
1 Jan.	'her Mates players.'	£10.	31 Jan. (G.).	
6 Jan.	'the Servantes of the lo: admirall and the lo Chamblaine.'	£10.	31 Jan. (G.).	
9 Jan.	'John Symondes and Mr Standleyes Boyes . . . for Tumblinge and shewinge other feates of activitie.'	£10.	31 Jan. (G.).	
13 Feb.	'her mates players.'	£10.	28 Feb. (G.); D. xiv. 20 (6 Mar.).	

1586-7 (*D. A. 542, m. 94*).

26 Dec. 1 Jan. 6 Jan. 28 Feb.	'the Quenes mates players.'	£40.	18 Mar. (G.).	
27 Dec.	'the Erle of Lecesters players.'	£10.	31 Mar. (G.).	
26 Feb.	'Thomas Giles mr of the Children of Paules.'	£10.	9 Apr. (G.); D. xv. 24.	

1587-8 (*D. A 542, mm. 108, 115*).

26 Dec. 6 Jan. 18 Feb.	'the Queenes mates players.'	£20, 'for their chardges and paines as also by waye of	20 Mar. (G.); D. xv. 425.	F. 378, 388. 'vij playes besides feattes of Activitie and other shewes by the Childeren of Poles

M

APPENDIX B—(continued)

CHAMBER ACCOUNTS.

Performance.	Payees.	Amount.	Warrant.	REVELS ACCOUNTS.
28 Dec.	'John Simons . . . for certein feates of actiuitie by him and his Companie.'	'her mates rewarde for geving their attendaunce in recitinge and playing certein playes and enterludes before her matie'. £10.	6 Mar. (G.).	her Maiesties owne servantes & the gentlemen of Grayes In.'
1 Jan. / 2 Feb. **1588-9** (*D. A. 542, mm. 125–6*).	'Thomas Giles mr of the children of Powles.'	£20.	29 Feb. (G.).	
26 Dec. / 9 Feb.	'the Quenes Mats Players.'	£20.	16 Mar. (W.) ; D. xvii. 109.	F.388. 'at Christmas Newyearstide & Twelftide there were shewed prese ·ted & enacted before her highnes fyve playes & . . . at Shrovetide there were shewed & presented before her twoe plaies All which playes were enacted by her Maiesties owne servantes the children of Paules & the Lord Admiralls men besides sondry feates of activity tumbling and Matichives.' . . . F.390, 'a paire of fflannell hose for Symmons the Tumbler'.
27 Dec. / 1 Jan. / 12 Jan.	'Tho Gyles mr of the children of Powles.'	£30.	23 Mar. (W.) ; D. xvii. 115.	
29 Dec. / 11 Feb.[1]	'the lorde Admyrall his players . . . for twoe Enterludes or playes . . . and for showinge other feates of activity and tumblinge.'	£20.	29 Feb. (W.) ; D. xvii. 90.	

1589-90 (*D. A. 542, m. 142*).

26 Dec. } 1 Mar.	'John Dutton and John Lanham her mates Sruantes for themselves and their companie.'	£20.	15 Mar.; D. xviii. 420.
28 Dec.[2]	'the Servauntes of the Lorde Admirall . . . for shewinge certen feates of activitie.' } 'the servauntes of the Lorde Admirall . . . for playinge.' }	£20.	10 Mar. (G.); D. xviii. 410.
3 Mar.			
'Christide.' [28 Dec.][3] 1 Jan. 6 Jan. }	'Thomas Giles mr of the children of Powles.'	£30.	10 Mar.; D. xviii. 410 (G.).

1590-1 (*D. A. 542, m. 155*).

26 Dec. 3 Jan. 6 Jan. 14 Feb. }	'Lawrence Dutton and John Dutton her mates players & there companye.'	£40.	7 Mar.; C. xxxii; D. xx. 327 (G., 5 Mar.).
1 Jan.	'John Laneham and his companye her mates players.'	£10.	7 Mar.; C. xxxii; D. xx. 328 (G., 5 Mar.).
27 Dec. 16 Feb. }	'George Ottewell and his companye the Lorde Straunge his players for [plays] . . . and for other feates of Activitye then also done by them.'[4]	£20.	7 Mar.; D. xx. 328 (G., 5 Mar.).

1591-2 (*D. A. 542, m. 168*).

26 Dec.	'ye Queenes mates players.'	£10.	29 Feb. (W.); D. xxii. 286 (27 Feb.).

[1] P. C. Acts give Shrove Sunday (Feb. 9). [2] P. C. Acts give 23 Dec., obviously in error.
[3] So P. C. Acts. [4] P. C. Acts do not name Ottewell, and call the company the Admiral's.

APPENDIX B—(continued)

	CHAMBER ACCOUNTS.			REVELS ACCOUNTS.
Performance.	Payees.	Amount.	Warrant.	
7 Dec. 8 Dec. 1 Jan. 9 Jan. 6 Feb. 8 Feb.	'ye seruantes of ye lo: Straunge.'	£60.	24 Feb. (W.) ; D. xxii. 264 (20 Feb.).	
2 Jan.	'ye servauntes of ye Earle of Sussex.'	£10.	20 Feb. (W.) ; D. xxii. 264.	
6 Jan.	'ye servauntes of ye Erle of Hartford.'	£10.	28 Feb. (W.) ; D. xxii. 263 (20 Feb.).	
1592-3 (*D. A. 542, m. 181*).				
26 Dec.[1] 6 Jan.	'the servantes of the Erle of Pembroke.'	£20.	11 Mar. (J.) ; D. xxiv. 113.	
27 Dec. 31 Dec. 1 Jan.	'the Servantes of the Lorde Strange.'	£30.	7 Mar. (J.) ; D. xxiv. 102.	
1593-4 (*D. A. 542, m. 194 ; Harl. MS. 1642, f. 19"*).				
6 Jan.	'her Ma^tes players,'	£10.	31 Jan.	
1594-5 (*D. A. 542, m. 208*).				
26 Dec. 28 Dec. [27 Dec. ?][2]	'To Willm̄ Kempe Willm̄ Shakespeare & Richarde Burbage seruantes to the Lord Chamḃleyne vpon the councelles warr^t dated at Whitehall xv^to Martii 1594 for twoe seuerall comedies or Enterludes shewed by them before her Matie in xp̄inas tyme laste paste viz^d vpon St Stephens daye &	£20.	15 Mar. (W.).	

Dates	Entry	Amount	Date
28 Dec. 1 Jan. 6 Jan.	Innocentes daye xiijˡ vjˢ viijᵈ and by waye of her maᵗᵉˢ Rewarde vjˡ xiijˢ iiijᵈ,' 'Edwarde Allen, Richarde Jones & John Synger, seruaunts to the Lord Admyrall.'	£30.	15 Mar. (W.).
1595-6 (*D. A. 543, m. 12*).			
26 Dec. 27 Dec. 28 Dec. 6 Jan. 22 Feb.	'John Hemynge and George Bryan sᵉruᵃⁿtes to the late Lorde Chamblayne and now sᵉruᵃⁿtes to the Lorde Hunsdon.'	£50.	21 Dec. 1596 (W.).
1 Jan. 4 Jan. 22 Feb. 24 Feb.	'Edwarde Allen and Martyn Slater seruauntes to the Lorde Admyrall.'	£40.	13 Dec. 1596 (W.).
1596-7 (*D. A. 543, m. 25*).			
26 Dec. 27 Dec. 1 Jan. 6 Jan. 6 Feb. 8 Feb.	'Thomas Pope & John Hemynges servauntes to the Lord Chambleyne.'³	£60.	27 Nov. 1597 (W.); D. xxviii. 151.
1597-8 (*D. A. 543, m. 39*).			
26 Dec. 1 Jan. 6 Jan. 26 Feb.	'John Heminges and Thomas Pope servauntes to the Lorde Chambleyne.'	£40.	3 Dec. 1598 (W.); D. xxix. 324.
27 Dec. 28 Feb.	'Robte Shawe and Thomas Downton servauntes to the Erle of Nottingham.'	£20.	3 Dec. 1598 (W.); D. xxix. 325.

¹ P. C. Acts give 27 Dec. ² Cf. p. 56. ³ Dasent reads 'Flemings'.

APPENDIX B—(continued)

CHAMBER ACCOUNTS.

Performance.	Payees.	Amount.	Warrant.
1598-9 (*D. A. 543, m. 55*).			
26 Dec. 1 Jan. 20 Feb.	'John Heminges and Thomas Pope servantes vnto the Lorde Chamberleyne.'	£30.	2 Oct. 1599 (N.) ; C. xxxii.
27 Dec. 6 Jan. 18 Feb.	'Robert Shawe and Thomas Downton servauntes to Therle of Nottingham.'	£20.	2 Oct. 1599 (N.).
1599-1600 (*D. A. 543, m. 57*).			
26 Dec. 6 Jan. 3 Feb.	'John Hemynge servaunt to the Lorde Chamberlaine.'	£30.	17 Feb. (R.); C. xxxiii; D. xxx. 89 (18 Feb.).
27 Dec. 1 Jan. 3 Feb.	'Robert Shawe servaunt to Therle of Nottingham.'[1]	£20.	18 Feb. (R.); C. xxxiii; D. xxx. 89.
[5 Feb.][2]	'Robert Browne servaunt to Therle of Darby.'	£10.	18 Feb. (R.); D. xxx. 89.
1600-1 (*D. A. 543, m. 69*).			
26 Dec. 6 Jan. 24 Feb.	'John Hemynges and Richarde Cowley servunts to the Lord Chambleine.'	£30.	31 Mar. (W.); C. xxxiii; D. xxxi. 217 (11 Mar.).
28 Dec. 6 Jan 2 Feb.	'Edwarde Allen servaunte to the Lord Admyrall.'	£30.	31 Mar. (W.); C. xxxiii.
1 Jan. 6 Jan.	'Robte Browne.'	£20.	31 Mar. (W.).
1 Jan.	'Edwarde Peers Mr of the children of Poules.'	£10.	24 June (G.); D. xxxi. 453.
6 Jan.	'Nathanyell Gyles mr of the children of the Chapple, for a showe wth musycke and speciall songes p'pared for the purpose.'	£5.	
22 Feb.	[the same] ... 'for a play'.	£10.	4 May (W.) ; C. xxxiii.

1601-2 (*D. A. 543, m. 83*).

Date	Description	Amount	Payment
26 Dec. 27 Jan. 1 Jan. 14 Feb. }	'John Hemyng[1] servaunte to the Lord Chamberleyne.'	£40.	28 Feb. (R.).
27 Dec.	'Edward Allen servaunt to the Lord Admyrall.'	£10.	28 Feb. (R.).
3 Jan.	'William Kempe and Thomas Heywoode servauntes to Therle of Worcester.'	£10.	28 Feb. (R.).
6 Jan. 10 Jan. 14 Feb. }	'Nathanyell Gyles Mʳ of the Children of her Maᵗᵉˢ Chappell.'	£30.	7 Mar. (R.).

1602-3 (*D. A. 543, mm. 95, 97*).

Date	Description	Amount	Payment
26 Dec. 2 Feb. }	'John Hemynges and the rest of his companie servauntes to the Lorde Chamberleyne.'	£20.	20 Apr. (W.) ; C. xxxiv.
27 Dec. 6 Mar. }	'Edwarde Allen servaunte to the Lorde Admyrall and the reste of his companie.'	£30.	22 Apr. (W.) ; C. xxxiv
1 Jan.	'Edward Peirs mʳ of the Children of Paules.'	£10.	31 May (G.).
6 Jan.	'Martyn Slater and his fellowes servauntes to the Erle of Hertforde.'	£10.	20 Apr.
—	'John Hassett . . . for presentinge and makinge shewe before his highnes of his skyll in vaultinge wᶜʰ he performed wᵗʰ his maᵗᵉˢ good lykinge.'[2]	£10.	29 July (H.).

---

[1] P. C. Acts have 'John' Shawe.   [2] So P. C. Acts.

APPENDIX B—(continued)

	CHAMBER ACCOUNTS.			REVELS ACCOUNTS.
Performance.	*Payees.*	*Amount.*	*Warrant.*	
1603-4 (*D.A. 543, m. 115–17*).				
2 Dec. (K.)	'John Hemyngs one of his ma^{tes} players . . . for the paynes and expences of himself and the rest of the company in comming from Mortelake in the countie of Surrie unto the courte aforesaid [at Wilton] and there p'senting before his ma^{tie} one playe.'	£30.	3 Dec. (Wilton) ; C. xxxiv.	
26 Dec. (K.) 27 Dec. (K.) 28 Dec. (K.) 30 Dec. (H.) 1 Jan. (K.) 1 Jan. (H.)	'John Hemynges one of his ma^{tes} players.'	£53.	18 Jan. (H.) ; C. xxxv.	
2 Jan. (H.) 13 Jan. (H.)	'John Duke one of the Queenes ma^{tes} players.'	£13 6s. 8d.	19 Feb. (W.) ; C. xxxv.	
4 Jan. (H.) 15 Jan. (H.) 21 Jan. (K.) 22 Jan. (H.)	'Edward Allen and Edward Juby two of the Princes Players.'	£30.	19 Feb. (W.) ; C. xxxv.	
	'Richard Burbadg one of his ma^{tes} comedians . . . for the mayntenaunce and releife of himselfe and the rest of his company being prohibited to p'sente any playes publique-	£30.	8 Feb. (H.) ; C. xxxv.	

	lie in or neere London by reason of greate perill that might growe through the extraordinary concourse and assemble of people to a newe increase of the plague till it shall please God to settle the cittie in a more p'fecte health by way of his ma^tes free gifte.		
2 Feb. (K.) ⎫ 19 Feb. (K.) ⎬ 20 Feb. (K.) ⎭	'John Hemynges one of his ma^tes players.'	£20.	29 Feb. (W.) ; C. xxxvi.
	'Edward Jubie to the use of himselfe and the rest of his company servauntes to the prince.'	£10.	17 Apr. (W.) ; C. xxxvii.
20 Feb. (K.)	'Edward Pearce m^r of the children of Powles.'	£10.	17 Apr. (W.).
21 Feb. (K.)	'Edward Kircham m^r of the children of the Queenes Ma^tes Revells.'	£10.	30 Apr. (W.) ; C xxxvii.
	[*Apparelling Charges*] 'To Augustine Phillippes and John Hemynges for thallowaunce of themselves and tenne of theire ffellowes his ma^tes groomes of the chamber, and Players for waytinge and attendinge on his ma^tes service by com̃aundemente vppon the Spanishe Embassador at Som'sette		

APPENDIX B—(*continued*)

REVELS ACCOUNTS.

CHAMBER ACCOUNTS.

Performance.	Payees.	Amount.	Warrant.
	howse the space of xviij dayes viz^d from the ixth day of Auguste 1604 vntill the xxvijth day of the same as appeareth by a bill thereof signed by the Lord Chamblayne. xxj^{li}. xij^s.'		
	'To Thomas Greene for thallow:aunce of hymselfe and tenne of his ffelowes groomes of the chamber and the Quenes Players for waytinge and attendinge vppon Countye Arrenbergh and the reste of the comyssioners at Durham howse by comaundmente the space of eighteene dayes viz^d from the ixth of Auguste 1604 vntill the xxvijth of the same as appeareth by a bill thereof signed by the Lord Chamberlayne. xix^{li}, xvj^s.'		

CHAMBER ACCOUNTS.				Bodl. Malone MS. 29, f. 69ᵛ.	REVELS ACCOUNTS.[1] Cunningham, 203; Halliwell-Phillipps, ii. 162; Law, *Sh. Forgeries*, xvi; *Audit Office, Accounts Various*, 3, 907.		The Poets wch mayd the plaies.
Performance.	Payees.	Amount.	Warrant.			1604.	
1604-5 (*D. A.* 543, mm. 136-8; Bodl. Rawlinson MS. A. 204).				1604 & 1605 Edd. Tylney			
1 Nov. (K.) 4 Nov. (K.) 26 Dec. (K.) 28 Dec. (K.) 7 Jan. (K.) 8 Jan. (K.)	'John Hemynges one of his Mats players.'	£60.	21 Jan. (W.); C. xxxvi.	Sunday after Hallowmas—Merry Wyves of Windsor perfd. by the K's players. Hallamas — in the Banquetting hos at Whitehall the Moor of Venis—perfd. by the K's players.	The Plaiers. By the Kings matis plaiers. By his Mats plaiers.	Hallamas Day being the first of Nouembar A play in the Banketinge house att Whithall called The Moor of Venis. The Sunday ffollowinge A Play of the Merry Wiues of Winsor.	Shaxberd.
				On St Stephens Night —Mesure for Mesur by Shaxberd—perfd. by the K's players.	By his Mats plaiers.	On St Stiuens Night in the Hall A Play caled Mesur for Mesur.	Shaxberd.
				On Innocents Night Errors by Shaxberd —perfd. by the K's players.	By his Mats plaiers.	On Inosents Night The Plaie of Errors.	
23 Nov. (Q.) 24 Nov. (H.)	'Edward Jubie one of the princes plaiors.'	£16 13s. 4d.	10 Dec. (W.); C. xxxvii.	On Sunday following "How to Learn of a Woman to wooe by Hewood, perfd. by the Q's players.	By the Queens Mats plaiers.	On Sunday ffollowinge A plaie cald How to Larne of a woman to wooe.	Hewood.
30 Dec. (K.)	'John Duke one of the Quenes Mates plaiers.'	£10.	19 Feb.; C. xxxvi.				
1 Jan. (K.) 3 Jan. (K.)	'Samuell Daniell and Henrie Evans . . . for . . . the Quenes Mates Children of the Re-vells.'	£20.	24 Feb. (W.); C. xxxvi.	On New Years Night—All fools by G. Chapman perfd. by the Boyes of the Chapel.	The Boyes of the Chapell.	On Newers Night A playe cauled : All Foulles.	By Georg Chapman.

¹ For a discussion of these entries, cf. p. 136.

APPENDIX B—(continued)

CHAMBER ACCOUNTS.			Warrant.	Malone MS., contd.	REVELS ACCOUNTS.	Audit Office Accounts, contd.
Performance.	Payees.	Amount.				
14 Dec. (H.) 19 Dec. (H.) 15 Jan. (H.) 22 Jan. (H.) 5 Feb. (H.) 19 Feb. (H.)	'Edward Jubie one of the princes plaiers.'	£40.	22 Feb.; C. xxxvi.	bet New yrs day & twelfth day—Loues Labour lost perfd. by the K's p.rs. On the 7th Jan. K. Hen. the fifth perfd. by the K. prs. On 8th Jan.—Every one out of his humour. On Candelmas night Every one in his humour.	By his Matis plaiers. By his Matis plaiers. By his Matis plaiers. By his Matis plaiers.	Betwin Newers Day and Twelfe day A Play of Loues Labours Lost. On the 7 of January was played the play of Henry the fift. The 8 of January A play cauled Euery on out of his Umor. On Candelmas night A playe Euery one In his Umor.
2 Feb. (K.) 10 Feb. (K.) 11 Feb. (K.) 12 Feb. (K.)	'John Heminges one of his Maᵗᵉˢ plaiers.'	£40.	24 Feb.; C. xxxvii.	On Shrove sunday 'the Marchant of Venis' by Shaxberd—perfd. by the K's Prs.—the same repeated on Shrove tuesd. by the K's Commd.'	By his Matis plaiers. By his Matis plaiers.	The Sunday following A playe provided and discharged. On Shrousunday A play of the Marthant of Venis. Shaxberd.
Feb. (K.)	'The same John Heminges.'	£10.	28 Apr.; C. xxxvii.		By his Matis players.	On Shroumonday A Tragidye of The Spanishe Maz. On Shroutusday A play cauled the Marchant of Venis againe comanded By the Kings Matie. Shaxberd.

CHAMBER ACCOUNTS.

Performance.	Payees.	Amount.	Warrant.
1605-6 (*D.A.* 543, *mm. 163, 176*).			
27 Dec. (K.)	'John Duke one of the Queenes Ma^{tes} players.'	£8 6s. 8d.	30 Apr.; C. xxxviii.
Xmas and since (K. 10 plays)	'John Hemynges one of his Ma^{tes} players.'	£100.	24 Mar.; C. xxxviii.
1 Dec. (H.) 30 Dec. (H.) 1 Jan. (K.) 4 Jan. (H.) 3 Mar. (K.) 4 Mar. (K.)	'Edward Jubie one of the Princes players.'	£50.	30 Apr.; C. xxxviii.
—(H. C. 2 plays	'Edward Kirkham one of the Mr^{es} of the Childeren of Pawles.'	£16 13s. 4d.	31 Mar.; C. xxxviii.
2 plays at G. [July–Aug. 1606] 1 play at H. [7 Aug. 1606]	(K. and K. of Denmark) 'John Heminges one of his Ma^{tes} Players.'	£30.	18 Oct.; C. xxxviii.
1606-7 (*D.A.* 543, *m. 177*).			
26 Dec. (K.) 29 Dec. (K.) 4 Jan. (K.) 6 Jan. (K.) 8 Jan. (K.) 2 Feb. (K.) 5 Feb. (K.) 15 Feb. (K.) 27 Feb. (K.)	'John Heminges one of his Ma^{tes} Players.'	£90.	30 Mar.; C. xxxix.

APPENDIX B—(continued)

	CHAMBER ACCOUNTS.			REVELS ACCOUNTS.
Performance.	Payees.	Amount.	Warrant.	
28 Dec. 13, 24, 30 Jan. 1, 11 Feb.	'Edwarde Jubye one of the princes players.'	£60.	28 Feb.; C. xxxviii.	
1607-8 (*D. A. 543, mm. 195–6*).				
26 Dec. (K.) 27 Dec. (K.) 28 Dec. (K.) 2 Jan. (K.) 6 Jan. (K. 2 plays 7 Jan. (K.) 9 Jan. (K.) 17 Jan. (K. 2 plays 26 Jan. (K.) 2 Feb. (K.) 7 Feb. (K.)	'John Hemynges one of his Mates Players.'	£130.	8 Feb. '1608 '; C. xxxviii ('1607').	
19 Nov. 30 Dec. (K. 3 Jan. H.) 4 Jan.	'Edward Juby one of the Princes Players.'	£40.	8 May; C. xxxix.	
	'John Hassett & Caleb Hassett . . . for feates of activitie by them performed upon a vaughting horse.'	£13 6s. 8d.	23 Sept.	
1608-9 (*D. A. 543, m. 214*). Xmas. (K. Q. H. C. 12 plays)	'John Hemynges one of his mates plaiers.'	£120.	5 Apr.; C. xxxix.	

— (K. H. 5 plays)	'Thomas Greene one of the Queenes Mates plaiers.'	£50.	5 Apr.
— (K. H. 3 plays)	'Edwarde Jubye one of the Princes Players,'	£30.	5 Apr. ; C. xxxix.
Xmas. (K. 2 plays)	'Robte Keyser ... for ... plaies ... by the Children of the blackfriers.'	£20.	10 Mar. (W.).
4 Jan. (H.)	'the same Robte Keyser ... for one play presented by the Children of the blackfriers before his highnes in the Cockpitt at Whitehall.'	£10.	10 Mar.
—	'John Hemynges one of his mates plaiers ... by way of his mates rewarde for their private practise in the time of infeccon that thereby they mighte be inhabled to performe their service before his Matie in Christmas hollidaies 1609,'	£40.	26 Apr. ; C. xxxix.
1609-10 (*D. A. 543, mm. 233-5*). 'before xpmas and in the tyme of the holidayes and afterwardes.' (K. Q. H. C. E. 13 plays)	'John Heminges one of the Kinges Mates players.'	£130.	2 Mar. (W.).
— (K. H. 5 plays)	'Roberte Keysar ... in the behalfe of himselfe and the reste of the Children of the Whitefryars.'	£50.	10 May (W.).

APPENDIX B—(continued)

	CHAMBER ACCOUNTS.			REVELS ACCOUNTS.
Performance.	Payees.	Amount.	Warrant.	
27 Dec. (K.)	'Thomas Greene one of the Queene Ma^tes players.'	£10.	31 Mar. (W.).	
26 Dec. (K.) 28 Dec. (K.) 7 Jan. (K.) 18 Jan. (K.) } 15 plays	'Edwarde Jubye one of the Princes Players.'	£40.	10 Mar. (W.).	
9 Feb. (C. E.)	'the sayd William Rowley.'	£6 13s. 4d.	20 Jan. 1613; C. xlii.	
— (K. Q. H.)	'John Heminges . . for himselfe and the reste of his companie beinge restrayned from publique playinge w^thin the citie of London in the tyme of infecōn duringe the space of sixe weekes in which tyme they practised pryvately for his ma^tes service.'	£30.	10 Mar. ; C. xl.	
1610-11 (*D. A. 543, mm. 249, 250, 267 ; Bodl. Rawlinson MS. A. 204*).				
10 Dec. (H. 3 plays)	'John Hemynges one of the Kinges players.'	£150.	12 Feb. ; C. xl.	
27 Dec. (K.)	'Thomas Greene one of the Quenes players . . for three severall playes before the Kinges Matie and the prince' (*D. A.*) ; 'for presentinge three severall playes before the princes highnes vppon the xth of Decemb: and St Johns daye at night 1610 before the Kinges Matie' (*Rawl. MS.*).	£30.	18 Mar. ; C. xl.	

19 Dec. ⎱ (K.)
28 Dec. ⎰
14 Jan ⎱ (K.)
16 Jan. ⎰
12 Dec. (C. E.)
20 Dec. (C. E.)
15 Jan. (C. E.)

'Edwarde Jubye one of the Princes players,'

£40.

20 Mar. ; C. xl.

'the sayd William Rowley.'

£20.

20 Jan. 1613 (W) ; C. xlii.

[Cunningham, xiii, from *Privy Purse Accounts* of Henry.]

'For makinge readie the Cocke pitt fower seuerall tymes for playes by the space of fower dayes in the month of December 1610.'

£2 10s. 8d.

2229·4

CHAMBER ACCOUNTS.

Performance.	Payees.	Amount.	Warrant.
1611–12 (*D.A. 543, mm. 267–8*).			
31 Oct. (K.) 1 Nov. (K.) 5 Nov. (K.) 26 Dec. (K.) 5 Jan. (K.) 23 Feb. (K.)	'John Hemnges...for ... the Kinges Mates seruauntes and players,'	£60.	1 June ; C. xl.

N

REVELS ACCOUNTS.¹

Cunningham, 210, from
Audit Office, Accounts Various, 3, 907.

By the Kings Players : — Hallomas nyght was presented att Whithall before ye Kinges Matie a play called the Tempest.

The Kings players : — The 5th of Nouember : A play called ye winters nightes Tayle.

The Kings players : — On St Stiuenes night A play called A King ɤ no King.

¹ For a discussion of these entries, cf. p. 140.

APPENDIX B—(continued)

CHAMBER ACCOUNTS.				REVELS ACCOUNTS. Cunningham, 210, from Audit Office, Accounts Various, 3. 907.	
Performance.	*Payees.*	*Amount.*	*Warrant.*		
9 Nov., (H. C.) 19 Nov. (H. C.) 16 Dec. (H. C.) 31 Dec. (H. C.) 7 Jan. (H. C.) 15 Jan. (H. C.) 19 Feb. (H. C.) 20 Feb. (H. C.) 28 Feb. (H. C.) 3 Apr. (H. C.) 16 Apr. (H. C.)	'the sayd John Heminges.'	£80.[1]	1 June; C. xli.	The Queens players:	St John night A play called the City Gallant.
				The Princes players.	The Sunday followinge A play called the Almanak.
				The Kings players.	On Neweres night A play called the Twines Tragedie.
				The Childern of Whitfriars.	The Sunday following A play called Cupids Reueng.
9 Feb. (H. C. E.) 20 Feb. (H.) 28 Mar. (E.) 26 Apr. (H. C. E.)	'the sayd John Heminges.'	£26 13s. 4d.	1 June; C. xli.	By the Queens players and the Kings Men.	The Sunday following [Twelfth Night] att Grinwidg before the Queen and the Prince was playd the Siluer Aiedg : and ye next night following Lucrecia.
27 Dec. (K. Q.) 2 Feb. (K. Q.)	'Thomas Greene ... for ... the Queenes Ma^{tes} servauntes.'	£20.	18 June; C. xli.	By the Queens players.	Candelmas night A play called Tu Coque.
21 Jan.[2] (H. E.) 23 Jan. (H. E.)	'the sayd Thomas Greene.'	£13 6s. 8d.	18 June; C. xli.	By the Kings players.	Shrove Sunday: A play called the Noblman.
28 Dec. (K.) 29 Dec. (K.)	'Edward Juby ... for ... the Prince highnes servauntes.'	£20.	18 June; C. xli.	By the Duck of Yorks players.	Shroue Munday: A play called Himens Haliday.
5 Feb. (H.) 29 Feb. (H.)	'the sayd Edward Juby.'	£13 6s. 8a.	18 June; C. xlii.	By the Ladye Elizabeths players.	Shroue Teuesday A play called the proud Mayds Tragedie.

11 Apr. 'last past' (E.)	'Edward Jubye ... for ... the Prynce Palatynes Servants.'[3]	£6 13s. 4d.	31 Mar. 1613; C. xlii.
25 Feb. (K.)	'Alexander Foster ... for ... the Ladye Eliz. servauntes and players ... for ... the proud Mayde.'	£10.	1 Apr.; C. xl.
19 Jan. (H. E.) 11 Mar. (H. E.)	'the sayd Alexander Foster.'	£13 6s. 8d.	1 Apr.; C. xl.
12 Jan. (H. C. E.) 28 Jan. (H. C. E.) 13 Feb. (H. C. E.) 24 Feb.[4] (H. C. E.)	'Willm Rowley ... for ... the Duke of Yorkes Servauntes and Players.'	£26 13s. 4d.	20 June (W.); C. xlii.

[Cunningham, xiv, from *Privy Purse Accounts* of Henry.]

'For makeinge readie the Cockepitt for a playe by the space of twoe dayes in the month of December 1611.' £1 14s. 4d.

'For makeing readie the Cockepitt for playes twoe severall tymes by the space of ffower dayes in the monethes of January and February 1611.' £3 10s. 8d.

1612-13 (*D. A. 544, m. 14; Bodl. Rawlinson MS. A .239, ff. 46ᵛ–48*).

8 June. 'John Hemynges ... for ... the kinges Maᵗⁱᵉˢ Players for presenting a playe before the Duke £6 13s. 4d. 9 July; C. xliii.

---

[1] The payment is for 12 plays; one date [13 Jan.?] is obviously omitted.

[2] Cunningham gives the date as 16 Jan.

[3] This item is entered in Account for 1612-13; *Rawl. MS.* gives the date.

[4] Cunningham gives this date as 18 Feb.

APPENDIX B—(continued)

REVELS ACCOUNTS.

CHAMBER ACCOUNTS.

Performance.	Payees.	Amount.	Warrant.
— (C. E. F., 14 plays)	'Savoyes Ambassadoes'; *Rawl. MS.* 'a playe ... called Cardenna', 'To him [Hemynges] more'; *Rawl. MS.* 'fowerteene severall playes, viz: one playe called ffilaster, One other called the knott of ffooles, One other Much adoe aboute nothinge, The Mayeds Tragedy, The merye dyvell of Edmonton, The Tempest, A kinge and no kinge, The Twins Tragedie, The Winters Tale, Sir John ffalstaffe, The Moore of Venice, The Nobleman, Caesars Tragedye, And on other called Love lyes a bleedinge',	£93 6s. 8d.	20 May; C. xliii.
— (K., 6 plays)	'the sayd John Heminges'; *Rawl. MS.* 'Sixe severall playes, viz: one play called a badd beginninge makes a good endinge, One other called ye Capteyne, One other the Alcumist. One other Cardenno, One other the Hotspur, And one other called Benedicte and Betteris'.	£60.	20 May; C. xliii.
2 Mar.[1] (C. E. F.) 10 Mar. (C. E. F.)	'Willm Rowley ... for ... the Prynces servantes'; *Rawl. MS.* 'One called the first parte of the Knaues ... And one other playe called the second parte of the Knaues'.	£13 6s. 8d.	7 June; C. xlii.
25 Feb. (C. E. F.) 1 Mar. (C. E. F.)	'Josephe Taylor ... for ... the Ladie Elizabeth hir servantes'; *Rawl. MS.* 'one playe called Cockle de moye ... and one other called Raymond Duke of Lyons'.	£13 6s. 8d.	28 June; C. xliii.

— (C. E. F.) [2 or 3 Nov. ?]	'Phillip Rosseter for . . . a play by the Children of the Chappell'; *Rawl. MS.* 'for . . the Children of the Queens Majestys Revels, for . . . a Commedye called the Coxcombe'.	£6 13s. 4d.	24 Nov.; C. xlii.
9 Jan. (C. E. F.) 27 Feb. (C. E. F.)	'To him more . . . for . . . two other playes by the Children of the Chappell'; *Rawl. MS.* 'one called Cupidds revenge, and the other called the Widdowes Teares'.	£13 6s. 8d.	31 May; C. xlii.
1 Jan. '1613' (K.)	'The sayd Phillip Rosseter . . for . . a play by the said Children'; *Rawl. MS.* 'called Cupides Revenge'. [Sullivan, 139, from *Accounts* of Elizabeth 29 Sept. 1612 to 25 March 1613 in *Exchequer of Receipt Misc.*, Bundle 343.]	£10.	31 May.
— [Oct. 20 p^t?] ²	'To her gracs plaiers for acting a Comedie in the Cocke pitt wᶜʰ her highnes lost to Mr Edward Sackvile on a wager.'	£5.	
1613-14 (*D. A. 544, m. 29*).			
4 Nov. (C.) 16 Nov. (C.) 10 Jan. (C.) 4 Feb. (C.) 8 Feb. (C.) 10 Feb. (C.) 18 Feb. (C.) '1614'.	'John Heminges and the rest of his fellowes his Mates servaunts the Players.'	£46 13s. 0d.³	21 June; C. xliii.

¹ The dates of the Prince's, Lady Elizabeth's, and Revels plays are given by *Rawl. MS.* but not *D. A.*

² This is probably the play of 20 Oct. in the Cockpit to which (Birch, i. 198) Elizabeth invited Frederick.

³ Both *D. A.* and Cunningham, xliii, have the error for £46 13s. 4d. Both records also date the King's men's plays of this winter as '1614' instead of '1613'.

APPENDIX B—(continued)

Performance.	CHAMBER ACCOUNTS. Payees.	Amount.	Warrant.	REVELS ACCOUNTS.
1 Nov. (K.) '1614'.				
5 Nov. (K.)				
15 Nov. (K.)				
27 Dec. (K.)	'the said John Heminges and the rest of his fellowes.'	£90.	21 June ; C. xliii.	
1 Jan. (K.)				
4 Jan. (K.)				
2 Feb. (K.)				
6 Mar. (K.)				
8 Mar. (K.)				
24 Dec.¹ (K.)	'Robte Lee and the rest of his fellowes the Queenes Ma^{tes} servauntes the Players.'	£20.	21 June (W.) ; C. xliii.	
5 Jan. (K.)	'Joseph Taylor for himselfe and the rest of his fellowes servaunts to the Lady Eliz' her grace . . . for presenting . . . a Comedy called Eastward howe.'	£10.	21 June (W.) ; C. xliv.	
25 Jan. (K.)				
12 Dec. (C.)	'To him [Taylor] more . . . for presenting . . . a comedy called the Dutch Curtezan.'	£6 13s. 4d.	21 June (W.) ; C. xliv.	
1614-15 (D.A. 544, mm. 47, 48, 65).²				
— (K. 8 plays)	'John Hemynges . . . in the behalfe of himselfe and his fellowes the Kinges ma^{tes} players.'	£80.	19 May ; C. xlii (19 May, 1613).	
— (K. 3 plays)	'Roberte Leigh.'³	£30.	25 Apr. (W.).	
— (K. 2 plays) (C.)	'Edward Juby in the behalfe of himselfe and the reste of his fellowes the Palsgraves players.'	£26 13s. 4d.	15 Apr.	

183

— (C. 6 plays) 1 Nov. (K.)	'Willm Rowley one of the Princes players,' 'Nathan ffeilde in the behalfe of himselfe and the rest of his fellowes . . . for . . . Bartholomewe Fayre'	£43 6s. 8d. £10.	17 May. 11 June; C. xliv.	[Pipe Office D.A. (Revels), 2805.] 'Canvas for tne Boothes and other necessaries for a play called Bartholmewe Faire.'
1615–16 (D.A. 544, mm. 66, 77). Between 1 Nov. and 1 Apr. (K. Q. 14 plays) — (K. 4 plays)	'John Heminges and the rest of his fellowes the Kings Mates Players.'	£140.	24 Apr. 1617.[4]	
	'Roberte Lee and his fellowes the Queenes Mates Servauntes.'	£40.	20 May (G.).	
— (C. 4 plays)	'Alexander Foster one or the Princes highnes Players,' [A. F. Westcott, *New Poems of James I*, lxxii, from *Accounts* of Anne for Apr. 1615–Jan. 1616.]	£26 13s. 4d.	29 Apr. (W.).	
17 Dec. (Q.)	'Ellis Worth one of her Mates plaiers for so much paid vnto him in the behalfe of himselfe and the rest of his fellowes of that companie for one plaie acted before her mate [at] Queenes Court.'	£10.	7 Jan.	
21 Dec. (Q.)	'John Heminge one of the Kinge Mates plaiers for so much paid vnto him in the behalfe of himselfe and the reste of his fellowes of that companie for one plaie acted before her Mate at Queenes Court.'	£10.	22 Jan.	

[1] So *D.A.*, but Cunningham's 28 Dec. is more probable.
[2] Henceforward play payments are by warrant from Lord Chamberlain, not Privy Council; cf. ch. vii.
[3] This item is entered in the Account for 1615–16.
[4] This item is entered in the Account for 1616–17.

APPENDIX C

DOCUMENTS OF CRITICISM

[There is much vain repetition in learned controversy, whether literary or ethical. I have attempted, by extract or summary, to indicate the main critical positions taken up by writers of different schools with regard to plays, and at the same time to preserve the incidental information which they furnish on points of stage history. It does not seem to me necessary to do more than cite, as of minor importance, and practically adding nothing, T. Becon, *The Catechisme* (1564, *Works*, i, f. cccccxxxii) ; E. Hake, *Merry Maidens of London* (1567), *A Touchstone for this Time* (1574), sig. G 4ᵛ ; E. Dering, *Catechisme for Householders* (1572) ; T. Brasbridge, *Poor Man's Jewel* (1578) ; R. Crowley, *Unlawful Practises of Prelates* (>1583), sig. B 3ᵛ ; N. Bownde, *Doctrine of the Sabbath* (1595), 211 ; J. Norden, *Progress of Piety* (1596, ed. *Parker Soc.*), 177 ; T. Beard, *Theatre of God's Judgments* (1597), 193, 197, 374 ; W. Vaughan, *The Golden Grove* (1600), i. 51 ; F. Hering, *Rules for the Prevention of the Sickness* (1603), sig. A 4ᵛ ; R. Knolles, *Six Books of a Commonweal* (1606, from J. Bodin, *Six Livres de la République*, 1576–8, 1601), vi. 1 ; W. Perkins, *Cases of Conscience* (1608, ed. T. Pickering), 118 ; R. Bolton, *Discourse of True Happiness* (1611), 73 ; L. Bayly, *Practice of Piety* (c. 1612, ed. Webster, 1842), 182, 190 ; O. Lake, *Probe Theologicall upon the Commandments* (1612), 267 ; J. Dod and R. Cleaver, *Exposition of the Ten Commandments* (1612) ; G. Wither, *Abuses Stript and Whipt* (1613), ii. 3 ; D. Dyke, *Michael and the Dragon* (1615), 216. Probably such references could be multiplied indefinitely ; they show how dread of the stage became a commonplace of pastoral theology. Thomas Spark's *Rehearsal Sermon* (1579) is only known from the citation of it by Munday (cf. No. xxvii, *infra*).]

i. 1489 (?). Desiderius Erasmus.

[From *Epistola* 31, to an unnamed friend (P. S. Allen, *Opus Epistolarum Des. Erasmi Roterodami*, i. 123), conjecturally dated by Mr. Allen in 1489. Erasmus more briefly commends the educational use both of Terence and Plautus in *De Ratione Studii* (1511, *Opera*, i. 521). In 1532 he edited Terence, and to the same year belongs *Epist.* 1238 (*Opera*, iii. 2, 1457), which praises the comedies without re-arguing at length the ethical controversy ; cf. W. H. Woodward, *Desiderius Erasmus concerning the Aim and Method of Education* (1904), 28, 39, 113, 164.]

Est enim in his Terentianis comoediis mirifica quaedam sermonis puritas, proprietas, elegantia ac, vt in tam antiquo comico, horroris minimum ; lepos (sine quo rustica est omnis, quantumuis phalerata, oratio) et vrbanus et salsus. Aut hoc igitur magistro aut nemine discere licebit quo pacto veteres illi Latini, qui nunc vel nobis peius balbutiunt, locuti sint. Hunc itaque tibi non modo etiam atque etiam lectitandum censeo, verumetiam ad verbum ediscendum.

Caue autem ne homuncionum istorum imperitulorum, imo liuidulorum garritus te quicquam permoueant, qui vbi in ineptissimis authoribus Florista, Ebrardo Graecista, Huguitione se senuisse viderunt, nec tantis ambagibus ex imperitiae labyrintho potuisse emergere, id vnicum suae stulticiae solatium proponunt, si in eundem errorem suum iuniores omnes pelliciant. Nefas aiunt a Christianis lectitari

Terentianas fabulas. Quam ob rem tandem quaeso ? Nihil, inquiunt,
praeter lasciuiam ac turpissimos adolescentum amores habent, quibus
lectoris animum corrumpi necesse sit. Facile vnde libet corrumpitur qui
corruptus accesserit. Syncerum nisi vas, quodcunque infundis acescit.
Itane isti religiosuli ad caetera vel vtilissima talpis caeciores, ad vnam,
si qua est, lasciuiam capreae sunt ? Imo capri ac stolidi nihil sibi
praeter nequitiam, qua sola imbuti sunt (indocti quippe iidemque
mali), rapientes, non vident quanta illic sit moralitas, quanta vitae
instituendae tacita exhortatio, quanta sententiarum venustas. Neque
intelligunt totum hoc scripti genus ad coarguenda mortalium vitia
accommodatum, imo adeo inuentum. Quid enim sunt comoediae,
nisi seruus nugator, adolescens amore insanus, meretrix blanda ac
procax, senex difficilis, morosus, auarus ? Haec nobis in fabulis,
perinde atque in tabula, proponuntur depicta ; vt, quum in moribus
hominum quid deceat, quid dedeceat, viderimus, alterum amemus
alterum castigemus. En, in Eunucho Phaedria ille ex summa con-
tinentia in summam ineptiam amore, tanquam morbo validissimo,
immutatus, adeo vt eundem esse non cognoscas ; quam pulchro
exemplo docet amorem rem esse et miserrimam et anxiam, instabilem
et prorsus insaniae turpissimae plenam. Assentatores istos, pestilens
hominum genus, Gnatonem suum, artis suae principem, spectare
iubeto. Iactabundi et sibi placentes, quales diuitum plerosque imperi-
tos videmus, Thrasonem suum spectent ac tandem cum sua magnificentia quam ridiculi sint intelligant.

Sed de his latius (quum [quae] de litteris scripsimus edemus) nostra
leges, volente quidem Deo. Ad praesentem locum satis fuerit tetigisse
comoedias Terentianas ; modo recte legantur, non modo non ad
subuertendos mores, verum etiam ad corrigendos maximopere valere,
certe ad Latine discendum plane necessarias iudicauerim. An potius
istud ex Catholicon, Huguitione, Ebrardo, Papia caeterisque ineptiori-
bus sperare iubebunt ? Mirum vero si his authoribus quis quid Latine
dicat, cum ipsi nihil non barbare locuti sint. Huiusmodi amplectatur,
qui balbutire volet ; qui loqui cupiet, Terentium dicat, quem Cicero,
quem Quintilianus, quem Hieronymus, quem Augustinus, quem Am-
brosius et iuuenes didicere et senes vsi sunt ; quem denique nemo,
nisi barbarus, non amauit.

ii. 1523–31. IOHANNES LUDOVICUS VIVES.
(a)
[From Commentary on St. Augustine, *De Civitate Dei* (1522), viii. 27.
The book was placed on the *Index Expurgatorius*, ' donec corrigatur ', and
Rainolds, *Th' Overthrow of Stage-Playes*, 161, says that this was one of
the offending passages. Vives, a Spaniard by birth, was lecturer at Louvain
1520–3, mainly in England 1523–8, and at Bruges 1528–31.]

At qui mos nunc est, quo tempore sacrum celebratur Christi morte
sua genus humanum liberantis, ludos nihil prope a scenicis illis
veteribus differentes populo exhibere, etiam si aliud non dixero satis
turpe existimabit quisquis audiet, ludos fieri in re maxime seria. Ibi
ridetur Iudas, quam potest ineptissima iactans, dum Christum prodit :

ibi discipuli fugiunt militibus persequentibus, nec sine cachinnis et actorum et spectatorum : ibi Petrus auriculam rescindit Malcho, applaudente pullata turba, ceu ita vindicetur Christi captiuitas. Et post paulum, qui tam strenue modo dimicarat, rogationibus unius ancillulae territus abnegat magistrum, ridente multitudine ancillam interrogantem, et exibilante Petrum negantem. Inter tot ludentes, inter tot cachinnos et ineptias solus Christus est serius et seuerus. Quumque affectus conatur moestos elicere, nescio quo pacto non ibi tantum, sed etiam ad sacra frigefacit, magno scelere atque impietate, non tam eorum qui vel spectant vel agunt, quam sacerdotum, qui eiusmodi fieri curant. Sed hisce de rebus loquemur forsan commodiore loco.

(b)

[From *De Tradendis Disciplinis*, iii. 6 (1531, *Opera*, vi. 328).]

After comparing the Latinity of Plautus and Terence for school purposes, he adds :

Ex vtroque cuperem resecta quae pueriles animos iis vitiis possent polluere ad quae naturae quasi nutu quodam vergimus.

(c)

[From *De Causis Corruptarum Artium*, ii. 4 (1531, *Opera*, vi. 99).]

Venit in scenam poesis, populo ad spectandum congregato, et ibi sicut pictor tabulam proponit multitudini spectandam, ita poeta imaginem quandam vitae ; vt merito Plutarchus de his dixerit, Poema esse picturam loquentem. et picturam poema tacens, ita magister est populi, et pictor, et poeta : corrupta est haec ars, quod ab insectatione flagitiorum et scelerum transiit ad obsequium prauae affectionis, vt quaecunque odisset poeta, in eum linguae ac stili intemperantia abuteretur : cui iniuriae atque insolentiae itum est obuiam, primum a diuitibus potentia sua, et opibus, hinc legibus, quibus cauebatur, ne quis in alium noxium carmen pangeret : tum inuolucris coepit tegi fabula ; paullatim res tota ad ludicra, et in vulgum plausibilia, est traducta, ad amores, ad fraudes meretricum, ad periuria lenonis, ad militis ferociam et glorias ; quae quum dicerentur cuneis refertis puerorum, puellarum, mulierum, turba opificum hominum, et rudium, mirum quam vitiabantur mores ciuitatis admonitione illa, et quasi incitatione ad flagitia, praesertim quum comici semper catastrophen laetam adderent amoribus, et impudicitiae ; nam si quando addidissent tristes exitus, deterruissent ab iis actibus spectatores, quibus euentus esset paratus acerbissimus. In quo sapientior fuit qui nostra lingua scripsit Celestinam tragicomoediam ; nam progressui amorum, et illis gaudiis voluptatis, exitum annexuit amarissimum, nempe amatorum, lenae, lenonum casus et neces violentas : neque vero ignorarunt olim fabularum scriptores turpia esse quae scriberent, et moribus iuuentutis damnosa . . . Recentiores in linguis vernaculis multo, mea quidem sententia, excellunt veteres in argumento deligendo. Nullae fere exhibentur nunc publicae fabulae quae non delectationem vtilitate coniungant.

iii. 1531. Sir Thomas Elyot.

[From *The Governour*, i. 13 (ed. H. H. S. Croft. i. 123).]

'They whiche be ignoraunt in poetes wyll perchaunce obiecte, as is their maner, agayne these verses [Horace, *Epist.* ii. 1. 126–31], sayeng that in Therence and other that were writers of comedies, also Ouide, Catullus, Martialis, and all that route of lasciuious poetes that wrate epistles and ditties of loue, some called in latine *Elegiæ* and some *Epigrammata*, is nothyng contayned but incitation to lechery.

First, comedies, whiche they suppose to be a doctrinall of rybaudrie, they be undoutedly a picture or as it were a mirrour of man's life, wherin iuell is nat taught but discouered ; to the intent that men beholdynge the promptnes of youth unto vice, the snares of harlotts and baudes laid for yonge myndes, the disceipte of seruantes, the chaunces of fortune contrary to mennes expectation, they beinge therof warned may prepare them selfe to resist or preuente occasion. Semblably remembring the wisedomes, aduertisements, counsailes, dissuasion from vice, and other profitable sentences, most eloquently and familiarely shewed in those comedies, undoubtedly there shall be no litle frute out of them gathered. And if the vices in them expressed shulde be cause that myndes of the reders shulde be corrupted : than by the same argumente nat only entreludes in englisshe, but also sermones, wherin some vice is declared, shulde be to the beholders and herers like occasion to encreace sinners.' Quotes Terence, *Eunuchus*, v. 4. 8–18, on the moral end of comedy and virtuous counsel from Plautus, *Amphitruo*, ii. 2. 17–21 ; Ovid, *Remedia Amoris*, 131–6 ; and Martial, *Epigr.* xii. 34. 'Wherfore sens good and wise mater may be picked out of these poetes, it were no reason, for some lite mater that is in their verses, to abandone therefore al their warkes, no more than it were to forbeare or prohibite a man to come into a faire gardein, leste the redolent sauours of swete herbes and floures shall meue him to wanton courage, or leste in gadringe good and holsome herbes he may happen to be stunge with a nettile. No wyse man entreth in to a gardein but he sone espiethe good herbes from nettiles, and treadeth the nettiles under his feete whiles he gadreth good herbes. Wherby he taketh no damage, or if he be stungen he maketh lite of it and shortly forgetteth it. Semblablye if he do rede wanton mater mixte with wisedome, he putteth the warst under foote and sorteth out the beste, or, if his courage be stered or prouoked, he remembreth the litel pleasure and gret detriment that shulde ensue of it, and withdrawynge his minde to some other studie or exercise shortly forgetteth it. . . . So all thoughe I do nat approue the lesson of wanton poetes to be taughte unto all children, yet thynke I conuenient and necessary that, when the mynde is become constante and courage is asswaged, or that children of their naturall disposition be shamfaste and continent, none auncient poete wolde be excluded from the leesson of suche one as desireth to come to the perfection of wysedome.'

iv. *c.* 1538 (?). Nicholas Udall.

[From Prologue to *Roister Doister* (? 1566–7).]

What Creature is in health, eyther yong or olde,
But som mirth with modestie wil be glad to use
As we in thys Enterlude shall now unfolde,
Wherin all scurilitie we utterly refuse,
Avoiding such mirth wherin is abuse :
Knowing nothing more comendable for a mans recreation
Than Mirth which is used in an honest fashion :

For Myrth prolongeth lyfe, and causeth health.
Mirth recreates our spirites and voydeth pensivenesse,
Mirth increaseth amitie, not hindring our wealth,
Mirth is to be used both of more and lesse,
Being mixed with vertue in decent comlynesse.
As we trust no good nature can gainsay the same :
Which mirth we intende to use, avoidyng all blame.

The wyse Poets long time heretofore,
Under merrie Comedies secretes did declare,
Wherein was contained very vertuous lore,
With mysteries and forewarnings very rare.
Suche to write neither *Plautus* nor *Terence* dyd spare,
Whiche among the learned at this day beares the bell :
These with such other therein dyd excell.

v. 1551. Martin Bucer.

[From *De honestis Iudis*, a section of *De Regno Christi*, presented to Edward VI by Bucer, who was then Regius Professor of Divinity at Cambridge, on 1 Jan. 1551, printed in 1557, and again in *Scripta Anglicana* (1577), ii. 54.]

Poterit iuuentus etiam exerceri agendo comoedias et tragoedias : populisque his honesta, et ad augendam pietatem non inutilis exhiberi oblectatio : sed piis, et ad regnum Christi doctis atque sapientibus viris opus fuerit, qui comoedias eas atque tragoedias componant : in quibus nimirum eiusmodi imitatio repraesentetur, consiliorum, actionum, atque euentuum humanorum, siue communium et vulgarium, vt fit in comoediis : sive singularium et qui sint maioris admirationis, quod proprium est tragoediae, quae ad certam morum correctionem, et piam conserat vitae institutionem.

Vt si comoedia repraesentetur iurgium pastorum Abrahae et Lot, atque horum a se inuicem discessio. . . . In huiusmodi comoedia tractari possent, et vtili ad piam institutionem oblectatione repraesentari, hi loci. . . . Ad eundem modum suppeditet piae comoediae vberem sane et aedificandae pietati peridoneam materiam, historia quaesitae, obtentae et adductae Isaaco sponsae Ribkae : ex hac enim historia queat describi pia parentum cura, quaerendi liberis suis religiosa connubia : fides bona et officiositas proborum seruorum. . . .

Non dissimile argumentum desumi queat et ex ea historiae de Iacobo parti qua describitur, vt metu fratris, relictis parentibus, ad Labam auunculum suum concesserit. . . .

Tragoediis, Scripturae vbique perquam copiosam offerunt materiam, historiis prope omnibus S. Patrum, regum, Prophetarum et Apostolorum inde ab Adam vsque, primo humani generis parente. Omnino enim refertae sunt hae historiae diuinis et heroicis personis, affectionibus, moribus, actionibus, euentibus quoque inexpectatis, atque in contrarium quam expectarentur cadentibus, quae Aristoteles vocat περιπετείας. Quae omnia cum mirificam vim habeant fidem in Deum confirmandi, et amorem studiumque Dei accendendi, admirationem item pietatis atque iusticiae, et horrorem impietatis, omnisque peruersitatis ingenerandi atque augendi : quanto magis deceat Christianos, ut ex his sua poemata sumant, quibus magna et illustria hominum consilia, conatus, ingenium, affectus atque casus repraesentent, quam ex impiis ethnicorum vel fabulis vel historiis ! Adhibendae autem sunt in vtroque genere poematum, comico et tragico, vt cum hominum vitia et peccata describuntur, et actione quasi oculis conspicienda exhibentur, id fiat ea ratione, vt quamuis perditorum hominum referantur scelera, tamen terror quidam in his diuini iudicii, et horror appareat peccati : non exprimantur exultans in scelere oblectatio, atque confidens audacia. Praestat hinc detrahere aliquid decoro poetico, quam curae aedificandi pietate spectatores ; quae poscit vt in omni peccati repraesentatione sentiantur, conscientiae propriae condemnatio, et a iudicio Dei horrenda trepidatio.

At dum piae et probae exhibentur actiones, in his debet exprimi quam clarissime sensus divinae misericordiae laetus, securaque et confidens, moderata tamen, et diffidens sibi exultansque in Deo fiducia promissionum Dei cum sancta et spirituali in recte faciendo voluptate. Hac enim ratione sanctorum et ingenia, et mores, et affectus, ad instaurandam in populo omnem pietatem ac virtutem, quam scitissima imitatione repraesentantur. Eum autem fructum vt Christi populus ex sanctis comoediis et tragoediis percipiant praeficiendi et huic rei erunt viri, vt horum poematum singulariter intelligentes, ita etiam explorati et constantis studii in regnum Christi : ne qua omnino agatur comoedia, aut tragoedia, quam hi non ante perspectam decreuerint agendam.

Hi quoque curabunt, ne quid leue aut histrionicum in agendo admittatur : sed omnia exhibeantur sancta quadam, et graui, iucunda tamen, sanctis duntaxat, actione : qua repraesententur non tam res ipsae, et actiones hominum, affectus et perturbationes, quam mores et ingenia : ac ita repraesententur, vt excitetur in spectatoribus studiosa imitatio : eorum autem quae secus sunt instituta et facta, confirmetur detestatio, et excitetur declinatio vigilantior.

His observatis cautionibus, poterit sane multa, nec minus ad virtutem alendam prouehendamque, vtilis ludendi materia iuuentuti praeberi, maxime cum studium et cura eiusmodi et comoediarum et tragoediarum excitata fuerit, cum lingua vernacula, tum etiam lingua Latina et Graeca. Extant nunc aliquot non poenitendae huius generis comoediae et tragoediae, in quibus, etiamsi docti mundi huius desiderent in comoediis illud acumen, eumque leporem, et sermonis venustatem, quem admirantur in Aristophanis, Terentii, Plautique fabulis : in tragoediis, grauitatem, versutiam, orationisque elegantiam, Sophoclis, Euripidis, Senecae : docti tamen ad regnum Dei, et qui viuendi Deo sapientiam discere student, non desiderant in his nostrorum hominum poematis doctrinam coelestem, affectus, mores, orationem, casusque dignos filiis Dei. Optandum tamen, vt quibus Deus plus dedit in his rebus praestare, vt id mallent ad eius gloriam explicare, quam aliorum pia studia intempestiuis reprehensionibus suis retardare : atque ducere satius, comoedias atque tragoedias exhibere, quibus si minus ars poetica, scientia tamen vitae aeternae praeclare exhibetur, quam quibus vt ingenii linguaeque cultus aliquid iuuatur, ita animus et mores impia atque foeda et scurrili mutatione conspurcantur.

vi. 1559. WILLIAM BAVANDE.

[From *A Woork of Ioannes Ferrarius Montanus touchynge the good orderynge of a Commonweale*, translated from the *De Republica bene instituenda Paraenesis*, published by Ferrarius, a Marburg jurist, in 1556.]

[Extracts] f. 81. ' The laste of all [the seven handicrafts in a commonweal] is the exercise of stage plaiyng, where the people use to repaire to beholde plaies, as well priuate as publique, whiche be set forthe partlie to delight, partlie to move us to embrace ensamples of vertue and goodnesse, and to eschue vice and filthie liuyng '. . . . f. 100ᵛ. ' *Chapter viii, Concernyng Scaffolds and Pageauntes of divers games and plaies and how farre thei be to be allowed, and set forthe in a Citee.* . . . Plaies, set foorthe either upon stages, or in open Merket places, or els where, for menne to beholde. Whiche, as thei doe sometime profite, so likewise thei tourne to great harme, if thei be not used in such sorte, as is bothe ciuill and semely in a citee, whiche wee dooe abuse, when anythyng is set foorthe openly, that is uncleanlie, unchaste, shamefull, cruell, wicked, and not standyng with honestie. . . . Soche pastimes therefore muste bee set foorthe in a commonweale, as doe minister unto us good ensamples, wherin delight and profite be matched togither. . . . It is a commendable and lawfull thing to bee at plaies, but at soche tymes as when we be unoccupied with grave and seuere affaires, not onely for our pleasure and minde sake, but that hauyng little to doe, we maie learne that, whiche shall bee our furtheraunce in vertue. . . . There shall be no Tragedie, no Comedie, nor any other kinde of plaie, but it maie encrease the discipline of good maners, if by the helpe of reason and zeale of honestie, it bee well emploied. Which then is doen, when, if thou either hearest, or seest anything committed that is euill, cruell, vilanous, and unseamely for a good manne, thou learnest thereby to beware and understandest that it is not onely a shame to committe any soche thinge but also that it shall be reuenged with euerlasting death. Contrariwise, if thou doest espie any thing dooen or saied well, manfully, temperatly, soberly, iustly, godlilye, & vertuously, thou . . . maiest labour to doe that thyself, whiche thou likest in another. . . . With whiche discrecion, who so beholdeth Tragedies, Comedies, . . . plaies of histories, holie or prophane, or any pageaunt, on stage or on grounde, shall not mispende his time. But like as a Bee of diuers floures, that be of theire owne nature of smalle vse, gathereth the swetenes of her honie : so thence gathereth he that which is commodious for the trade of his life, ioigneth it with his painfull trauaile, and declareth that soche histories and exercises bee the eloquence of the bodie.'

vii. 1563–8. ROGER ASCHAM.

[From *The Scholemaster* (1570), as reprinted in W. A. Wright, *English Works of Roger Ascham* (1904), 171. The tract, which was largely based on the teaching of Ascham's friend John Sturm, was begun as a New Year gift for Elizabeth in December 1563, and left unfinished at the author's death in 1568. The best modern edition is by J. E. B. Mayor (1863).]

The first booke teachyng the brynging vp of youth. . . . P. 185. In the earliest stage of Latin, Ascham ' would haue the Scholer brought vp withall, till he had red, & translated ouer ye first booke of [Cicero's] Epistles chosen out by *Sturmius*, with a good peece of a Comedie of *Terence* also. . . . P. 208. There be som seruing men do but ill seruice to their yong masters. Yea, rede *Terence* and *Plaut.* aduisedlie ouer, and ye shall finde in those two wise writers, almost in euery commedie, no vnthriftie yong man, that is not brought there vnto, by the sotle inticement of som lewd seruant. And euen now in our dayes *Getae* and *Daui*, *Gnatos* and manie bold bawdie *Phormios* to, be preasing in, to pratle on euerie stage, to medle in euerie matter, when honest *Parmenos* shall not be hard, but beare small swing with their masters. . . . *The second booke teachyng the ready way to the Latin tong.* . . . P. 238. Read dayly vnto him ... some Comedie of *Terence* or *Plautus* : but in *Plautus*, skilfull choice must be vsed by the master, to traine his Scholler to a iudgement, in cutting out perfitelie ouer old and vnproper wordes. . . . On *Imitatio* . . . P. 266. The whole doctrine of Comedies and Tragedies, is a perfite *imitation*, or faire liuelie painted picture of the life of euerie degree of man. . . . One of the best examples, for right *Imitation* we lacke, and that is *Menander*, whom our *Terence* (as the matter required) in like argument, in the same Persons, with equall eloquence, foote by foote did follow. Som peeces remaine, like broken Iewelles, whereby men may rightlie esteme, and iustlie lament, the losse of the whole. . . . P. 276. In Tragedies, (the goodliest Argument of all, and for the vse, either of a learned preacher, or a Ciuill Ientleman, more profitable than *Homer*, *Pindar*, *Vergill*, and *Horace* : yea comparable in myne opinion, with the doctrine of *Aristotle*, *Plato*, and *Xenophon*,) the *Grecians*, *Sophocles* and *Euripides* far ouer match our *Seneca*, in *Latin*, namely in οἰκονομίᾳ et Decoro, although *Senecaes* elocution and verse be verie commendable for his tyme.' . . . P. 284. Ascham describes some contemporary Latin tragedies. . . . P. 286. ' Of this short tyme of any pureness of the Latin tong, for the first fortie yeare of it, and all the tyme before, we haue no peece of learning left, saue *Plautus* and *Terence*, with a litle rude vnperfit pamflet of the elder *Cato*. And as for *Plautus*, except the scholemaster be able to make wise and ware choice, first in proprietie of wordes, then in framing of phrases and sentences, and chieflie in choice of honestie of matter, your scholer were better to play, then learne all that is in him. But surelie, if iudgement for the tong, and direction for the maners, be wisely ioyned with the diligent reading of *Plautus*, than trewlie *Plautus*, for that purenesse of the Latin tong in Rome, whan Rome did most florish in wel doing, and so thereby, in well speaking also, is soch a plentifull storehouse, for common eloquence, in meane matters, and all priuate mens affaires, as the Latin tong, for that respect, hath not the like agayne. Whan I remember the worthy tyme of Rome, wherein *Plautus* did liue, I must nedes honor the talke of that tyme, which we see *Plautus* doth vse. *Terence* is also a storehouse of the same tong, for an other tyme, following soone after, & although he be not so full & plentiful as *Plautus* is, for multitude of matters, & diuersitie of wordes, yet his wordes, be chosen so purelie, placed so orderly, and all his stuffe so neetlie packed vp, and wittely compassed in euerie place, as, by all wise mens iudgement, he is counted the cunninger workeman, and to haue his shop, for the rowme that is in it, more finely appointed, and trimlier ordered, than *Plautus* is. . . . The matter in both, is altogether within the compasse of the meanest mens maners, and doth not stretch to any thing of any great weight at all, but standeth chiefly in vtteryng the thoughtes and conditions of hard fathers, foolish mothers, vnthrifty yong men, craftie seruantes, sotle bawdes, and wilie harlots, and so, is moch spent, in finding out fine fetches, and packing vp pelting matters, soch as in London commonlie cum to the hearing of the Masters of Bridewell. Here is base stuffe for that scholer, that should becum hereafter, either a good minister in Religion, or a Ciuill Ientleman in seruice of his Prince and contrie : except the preacher do know soch matters to confute them, whan ignorance surelie in all soch thinges were better for a Ciuill Ientleman, than knowledge. And thus, for matter, both Plautus and Terence, be like meane painters, that worke by halfes, and be cunning onelie, in making the worst part of the picture, as if one were skilfull in painting the bodie of a naked person, from the nauell downward, but nothing else.'

viii. 1565. WILLIAM ALLEY.

[From *Miscellanea* of notes to a *Praelectio* of 1561 in Πτωχὸμνσεῖον : *The Poore Mans Librarie* (1565). On Alley, v. ch. xxiii, s.v.]

Alas, are not almost al places in these daies replenished with iuglers, scoffers, iesters, plaiers, which may say and do what they lust, be it neuer so fleshly and filthy ? and yet suffred and heard with laughing and clapping of handes.

ix. 1565–71. Richard Edwardes.

[The Prologue to *Damon and Pithias*. It appears from the title-page
that this had been ' somewhat altered ' between the production of the
play in 1565 and its publication in 1571 ; cf. ch. xxiii.]

On euerie syde, wheras I glaunce my rouyng eye,
Silence in all eares bent I playnty do espie :
But if your egre lookes doo longe suche toyes to see,
As heretofore in commycall wise, were wont abroade to bee :
Your lust is lost, and all the pleasures that you sought,
Is frustrate quite of toying Playes. A soden change is wrought.
For loe, our Authors Muse, that masked in delight,
Hath forst his Penne agaynst his kinde, no more suche sportes to
    write.
Muse he that lust, (right worshipfull) for chaunce hath made this
    change,
For that to some he seemed too muche, in yonge desires to range :
In whiche, right glad to please, seyng that he did offende,
Of all he humblie pardon craues : his Pen that shall amende :
And yet (worshipfull Audience,) thus much I dare aduouche.
In Commedies, the greatest Skyll is this, rightly to touche
All thynges to the quicke : and eke to frame eche person so,
That by his common talke, you may his nature rightly knowe :
A Royster ought not preache, that were to straunge to heare,
But as from vertue he doth swerue, so ought his woordes appeare :
The olde man is sober, the yonge man rashe, the Louer triumphyng
    in ioyes,
The Matron graue, the Harlot wilde and full of wanton toyes.
Whiche all in one course they [in] no wise doo agree :
So correspondent to their kinde their speeches ought to bee.
Which speeches well pronounste, with action liuely framed,
If this offende the lookers on, let *Horace* then be blamed,
Which hath our Author taught at Schole, from whom he doth not
    swarue,
In all suche kinde of exercise decorum to obserue,
Thus much for his defence (he sayth) as Poetes earst haue donne,
Which heretofore in Commedies the selfe same rase did ronne :
But now for to be briefe, the matter to expresse,
Which here wee shall present : is this *Damon* and *Pithias*,
A rare ensample of Friendship true, it is no Legend lie,
But a thinge once donne in deede as Hystories doo discrie,
Whiche doone of yore in longe time past, yet present shalbe here,
Euen as it were in dooynge now, so liuely it shall appeare :
Lo here in *Siracusae* thauncient Towne, which once the Romaines
    wonne,
Here *Dionysius* Pallace, within whose Courte this thing most strange
    was donne,
Which matter mixt with myrth and care, a iust name to applie,
As seemes most fit wee haue it termed, a Tragicall Commedie,

Wherein talkyng of Courtly toyes, wee doo protest this flat,
Wee talke of *Dionysius* Courte, wee meane no Court but that,
And that wee doo so meane, who wysely calleth to minde.
The time, the place, the Authours here most plainely shall it finde,
Loe this I speake for our defence, lest of others wee should be shent :
But worthy Audience, wee you pray, take thinges as they be ment,
Whose vpright Judgement wee doo craue, with heedefull eare and eye,
To here the cause, and see theffect of this newe Tragicall Commedie.

x.   1566.   LEWIS WAGER.

[From Prologue to *The Life and Repentance of Marie Magdalene* (1566) ;
cf. ch. xxiii.]

l. 10.   We and other persons haue exercised
            This comely and good facultie a long season,
        Which of some haue bene spitefully despised ;
            Wheréfore, I thinke, they can alleage no reason.
            Where affect ruleth, there good iudgement is geason.
            They neuer learned the verse of Horace doubtles,
            Nec tua laudabis studia, aut aliena reprehendes. . . .

l. 24.   I maruell why they should detract our facultie :
            We haue ridden and gone many sundry waies ;
        Yea, we haue vsed this feate at the vniuersitie ;
            Yet neither wise nor learned would it dispraise : . . .

l. 31.   Doth not our facultie learnedly extoll vertue ?
            Doth it not teache, God to be praised aboue al thing ?
        What facultie doth vice more earnestly subdue ?
            Doth it not teache true obedience to the kyng ?
            What godly sentences to the mynde doth it bryng !
            I saie, there was neuer thyng inuented,
            More worth for man's solace to be frequented.

        Hipocrites that wold not haue their fautes reueled
            Imagine slaunder our facultie to let ;
        Faine wold they haue their wickednes still concealed ;
            Therfore maliciously against vs they be set ;
            O (say they) muche money they doe get.
            Truely, I say, whether you geue halfpence or pence,
            Your gayne shalbe double, before you depart hence. . . .

l. 80.   We desire no man in this poynt to be offended,
            In that vertues with vice we shall here introduce ;
        For in men and women they haue depended :
            And therfore figuratiuely to speake, it is the vse.
            I trust that all wise men will accept our excuse.
            Of the Preface for this season here I make an ende ;
            In godly myrth to spend the tyme we doe intende.

xi. 1569. ANON.

[T. Warton, *History of Poetry*, iii (1781) 288 (ed. Hazlitt, iv. 217), ascribes to this year a 'Puritanical pamphlet without name', *The Children of the Chapel stript and whipt*, which he says was ' among Bishop Tanner's books at Oxford '. It is not, however, now traceable in the Bodleian. Warton's extracts are quoted in ch. xii, s.v. Chapel.]

xii. 1569. HENRY CORNELIUS AGRIPPA.

[From *Henry Cornelius Agrippa, of the Vanitie and uncertaintie of Artes and Sciences*, Englished by Ja[mes] San[ford] Gent. (1569), a translation of *De incertitudine et vanitate scientiarium et artium atque excellentia Verbi Dei declamatio* (1530), written in 1526 (*Opera*, ii. 1).]

' Cap. 4. Of Poetrie ' condemns it as lying. ' Cap. 20. Of the Science of stage Plaiers.' After defining the player's art and citing the discussion between Cicero and Roscius recorded by Macrobius (cf. no. xliii and ch. xi) and the banishment of players by the City of Marseilles (cf. *Mediaeval Stage*, i. 7), Agrippa concludes, ' And therefore to exercise this Arte, is not onely a dishonest and wicked occupation, but also to behold it, and therein to delite is a shameful thinge, bicause that the delite of a wanton minde is an offence. And to conclude, there was in times paste no name more infamous then stage players, and moreouer, al they that had plaide an Enterlude in the Theater, were by the lawes depriued from all honour.' Plays are briefly referred to in ' Cap. 59. Of Holy daies ' and ' Cap. 63. Of the whoorishe Arte '.

xiii. 1574. GEOFFREY FENTON.

[From *A Forme of Christian Pollicie gathered out of French* (1574). No single source has been traced and the treatise is probably a compilation.]

Book iii, ch. 7. ' Players . . . corrupt good moralities by wanton shewes and playes : they ought not to be suffred to prophane the Sabboth day in such sportes, and much lesse to lose time on the dayes of trauayle. All dissolute playes ought to be forbidden : All comicall and tragicall showes of schollers in morall doctrines, and declamations in causes made to reproove and accuse vice and extoll vertue are very profitable.' *The 7 Chapter* expands the foregoing. . . . ' Great then is the errour of the magistrate to geue sufferance to these players, whether they bee minstrels, or enterludours who on a scaffold, babling vaine newes to the sclander of the world, put there in scoffing the vertues of honest men. . . . There often times are blowen abroade the publike and secreete vices of men, sometimes shrowded under honourable personage, withe infinite other offences. . . . How often is the maiestie of God offended in those twoo or three howres that those playes endure, both by wicked wordes, and blasphemye, impudent jestures, doubtful sclaunders, unchaste songes, and also by corruption of the willes of the players and the assistauntes. Let no man obiect heare that by these publike plaies, many forbeare to doo euill, for feare to bee publikely reprehended . . . for it may be

aunswered first, that in such disguised plaiers geuen over to all sortes
of dissolucion, is not found a wil to do good, seeing they care for
nothing lesse than vertue : secondlye that is not the meane te correct
sinne. . . . Heare I reprooue not the plaies of scollers . . . Ch. 6. I wish
that in place of daunses at mariage, the time were supplied with some
comical or historical show of the auncient mariages of Abraham and
Sara, of Isaac and Rebecca, and of the two Tobies and theyr wiues,
matters honest and tending much to edify the assistauntes.'

xiv. 1575. GEORGE GASCOIGNE.

[Prologue to *The Glasse of Governement* (cf. ch. xxiii).]

What man hath minde to heare a worthie Jest,
Or seekes to feede his eye with vayne delight :
That man is much unmeete to be a guest,
At such a feaste as I prepare this night.
Who list laye out some pence in such a Marte,
Bellsavage fayre were fittest for his purse,
I lyst not so to misbestowe mine arte,
I have best wares, what neede I then shewe woorse ?
An Enterlude may make you laugh your fill,
Italian toyes are full of pleasaunt sporte :
Playne speache to use, if wanton be your wyll,
You may be gone, wyde open standes the porte.
But if you can contented be to heare,
In true discourse howe hygh the vertuous clyme,
Howe low they fall which lyve withouten feare
Of God or man, and much mispende theyr tyme :
What ryght rewardes a trustie servaunt earnes,
What subtile snares these Sycophantes can use,
Howe soone the wise such crooked guyles discernes,
Then stay a whyle : gyve eare unto my Muse.
A Comedie, I meane for to present,
No *Terence* phrase : his tyme and myne are twaine :
The verse that pleasde a *Romaine* rashe intent,
Myght well offend the godly Preachers vayne.
Deformed shewes were then esteemed muche,
Reformed speeche doth now become us best,
Mens wordes muste weye and tryed be by touche
Of Gods owne worde, wherein the truth doth rest.
Content you then (my Lordes) with good intent,
Grave Citizens, you people greate and small,
To see your selves in Glasse of Governement :
Beholde rashe youth, which daungerously doth fall
On craggy rockes of sorrowes nothing softe,
When sober wittes by Vertue clymes alofte.

XV. 1577. THOMAS WHITE.

[From *A Sermon preached at Pawles Crosse on Sunday the thirde of November 1577 in the time of the Plague*. By T. W. This was printed, according to the colophon, by F. Coldocke on 10 Feb. 1578. There are two copies in the B.M., but one has been bound in error with the title-page of an earlier sermon of 9 Dec. 1576, by the same author. T. W. was probably Thomas White, vicar of St. Dunstan-in-the-West, and later founder of Sion College and of White's Professorship of Moral Philosophy at Oxford. The sermon is sometimes claimed for Thomas Wilcox ; but he was in ecclesiastical disgrace in 1577 and unlikely to have access to Paul's Cross.]

P. 46. ' Looke but vppon the common playes in London, and see the multitude that flocketh to them and followeth them : beholde the sumptuous Theatre houses, a continuall monument of Londons pro-digalitie and folly. But I vnderstande they are nowe forbidden bycause of the plague. I like the pollicye well if it holde still, for a disease is but bodged or patched vp that is not cured in the cause, and the cause of plagues is sinne, if you looke to it well : and the cause of sinne are playes : therefore the cause of plagues are playes. . . . Shall I reckon vp the monstrous birds that brede in this nest ? without doubt I am ashamed, and I should surely offende your chast eares : but the olde world is matched, and Sodome ouercome, for more horrible enormities and swelling sins are set out by those stages, than euery man thinks for, or some would beleeue, if I shold paint them out in their colours : without doubt you can scantly name me a sinne, that by that sincke is not set a gogge : theft and whoredome ; pride and prodigality ; villanie and blasphemie ; these three couples of helhoundes neuer cease barking there, and bite manye, so as they are vncurable euer after, so that many a man hath the leuder wife, and many a wife the shreuder husband by it : and it can not other-wise be, but that whiche robbeth flatlye the Lord of all his honor, and is directly against the whole first table of his law, should make no bones of breache of the second also, which is toward our neighbour only. Wherefore if thou be a father, thou losest thy child : if thou be a maister, thou losest thy seruaunt ; and thou be what thou canst be, thou losest thy selfe that hauntest those scholes of vice, dennes of theeues, and Theatres of all leudnesse : and if it be not suppressed in time, it will make such a Tragedie, that London may well mourne whyle it is London, for it is no playing time.'

xvi. 1577. John Northbrooke.

[From *A Treatise wherein Dicing, Dauncing, Vaine playes, or Enterluds, with other idle pastimes, &c., commonly used on the Sabboth day, are reproued by the Authoritie of the word of God and auntient writers.* N.D. H. Bynneman for George Byshop. This is doubtless the 'booke wherein Dycinge, dauncinge, vaine playenge and Interludes, with other idle pastimes, &c., comonlie used on the Saboth daie are reproved', entered for Bishop in S. R. on 2 Dec. 1577 (Arber, ii. 321). A second edition was printed in 1579. Northbrooke was a Gloucester minister. The book was edited by J. P. Collier (1843, *Sh. Soc.*).]

[Summary and Extracts.] The treatise is 'made dialoguewise' between Youth and Age. *Epistles* to Sir John Yong and to The Christian and Faithful Reader, dated respectively from Bristol and Henbury. *A Treatise against Idlenes, Idle Pastimes, and Playes.* The greater part deals generally with 'ydle playes and vaine pastimes' and their relation to the Christian life. P. 82. Youth asks Age his opinion of 'playes and players, which are commonly vsed and much frequented in most places in these dayes, especiallye here in this noble and honourable citie of London'. Age condemns 'stage playes and enterludes' as 'not tollerable, nor sufferable in any common weale, especially where the Gospell is preached ; for it is right prodigalitie, which is opposite to liberalitie'. Considers 'the giftes, buildings, and maintenance of such places for players a spectacle and schoole for all wickednesse and vice to be learned in', and particularly applies this to 'those places also, whiche are made vppe and builded for such playes and enterludes, as the Theatre and Curtaine is, and other such lyke places. . . . Satan hath not a more speedie way, and fitter schoole to work and teach his desire, to bring men and women into his snare of concupiscence and filthie lustes of wicked whoredome, than those places, and playes, and theatres are ; and therefore necessarie that those places, and players, shoulde be forbidden, and dissolued, and put downe by authoritie, as the brothell houses and stewes are'. Quotes the Fathers on the offences to chastity at theatres. P. 92. Condemns the playing of 'histories out of the scriptures. By the long suffering and permitting of these vaine plays, it hath stricken such a blinde zeale into the heartes of the people, that they shame not to say, and affirme openly, that playes are as good as sermons, and that they learne as much or more at a playe, than they do at God's worde preached. . . . Many can tarie at a vayne playe two or three houres, when as they will not abide scarce one houre at a sermon. . . . I speake (alas ! with griefe and sorowe of heart) against those people that are so fleshlye ledde, to see what rewarde there is giuen to such crocodiles, whiche deuoure the pure chastitie bothe of single and maried persons, men and women, when as in their playes you shall learne all things that appertayne to craft, mischiefe, deceytes, and filthinesse, &c. If you will learne howe to bee false and deceyue your husbandes, or husbandes their wyues, howe to playe the harlottes, to obtayne one's loue, howe to rauishe, howe to beguyle, howe to betraye, to flatter, lye, sweare, forsweare, how to allure to whoredome, howe to murther, howe to poyson, howe to disobey and rebell against princes, to consume treasures prodigally, to mooue to lustes, to ransacke and spoyle cities and townes, to bee ydle, to blaspheme, to sing filthie songs of loue, to speake filthily, to be prowde, howe to mocke, scoffe, and deryde any nation . . . shall not you learne, then, at such enterludes howe to practise them ? . . . Therefore, great reason it is that women (especiallye) shoulde absent themselues from such playes.' Notes the *infamia* of *histriones*, which he translates ' enterlude players ', and refers to the statute of 1572. Expounds the heathen origin of plays. P. 101. Youth admits ' that they ought to be ouerthrowne and put downe. . . . Yet I see little sayd, and lesse done vnto them ; great resort there is daily vnto them, and thereout sucke they no small aduantage '. P. 102. ' They vse to set vp their billes vpon postes certain dayes before, to admonishe the people to make their resort vnto their theatres, that they may thereby be the better furnished, and the people prepared to fill their purses with their treasures.' P. 102. Youth concludes : ' I maruaile the magistrates suffer them thus to continue, and to haue houses builded for such exercises. . . . I maruaile much, sithe the rulers are not onely negligent and slowe herein to doe, but the preachers are as dumme to speake and saye in a pulpitte against it ' ; and Age : ' I doubt not but God will so moue the hearts of magistrates, and loose the tongue of the preachers in such godly sort (by the good deuout prayers of the faithfull) that both with the sworde and the worde such vnfruitfull and barren trees shall be cut downe '. P. 103. Youth then raises the question of scholastic plays. These Age admits. ' I think it is lawefull for a schoolmaster to practise his schollers to playe comedies, obseruing these and the like cautions : first, that those comedies which they shall play be not mixt with anye ribaudrie and filthie termes and wordes (which corrupt good manners). Secondly, that it be for learning and vtterance sake, in Latine, and very seldome in Englishe. Thirdly, that they vse not to play commonly and often, but verye rare and seldome. Fourthlye, that they be not pranked and decked vp in gorgious and sumptious apparell in their play. Fiftly, that it be not made a common exercise, publickly, for profit and gaine of money, but for learning and exercise sake. And lastly, that their comedies be not mixte with vaine and wanton toyes of loue. These being obserued, I iudge it tollerable for schollers.' *An Inuectiue against Dice-Playing* and *A Treatise against Dauncing*.

xvii. 1578. JOHN STOCKWOOD.

[From *A Sermon Preached at Paules Crosse* on 24 Aug. 1578. A reprint is in Harrison, iv. 329. John Stockwood was Master of Tonbridge Grammar School.]

P. 23. ' Wyll not a fylthye playe, wyth the blast of a Trumpette, sooner call thyther a thousande, than an houres tolling of a Bell, bring to the Sermon a hundred ? nay euen heere in the Citie, without it be at this place, and some other certaine ordinarie audience, where

shall you finde a reasonable company ? whereas, if you resorte to the
Theatre, the Curtayne, and other places of Playes in the Citie, you
shall on the Lords day haue these places, with many other that I can
not recken, so full, as possible they can throng.' P. 50. 'We
notwithstanding on the Lordes daye must haue Fayers kept, must
haue Beare bayting, Bulbayting (as if it wer a thing of necessity for
the Beares of Paris garden to be bayted on the Sunnedaye) must
haue baudie Enterludes.' P. 85. Calls on the Mayor, Sheriffs and
Aldermen as ' publike magistrates ' to keep watch against ' flocking
and thronging to baudie playes by thousandes ' on the Lord's Day,
and notes ' resorting to playes in the time of sermons a thing too
manifest '. P. 133. ' There be not many places where ye word is
preached besides the Lords day (I woulde to God there were) yet
euen that day the better parte of it is horriblie prophaned by diuellishe
inuentions, as with Lords of Misserule, Morice dauncers, Maygames,
insomuch that in some places, they shame not in ye time of diuine
seruice, to come and daunce aboute the Church, and without to haue
men naked dauncing in nettes, which is most filthie : for the heathen
that neuer hadde further knowledge, than the lighte of nature, haue
counted it shamefull for a Player to come on the stage without a slop,
and therefore amongest Christians I hope suche beastly brutishnesse
shal not be let escape vnpunished, for whiche ende I recite it, and
can tell, if I be called, where it was committed within these fewe
weekes. What should I speake of beastlye Playes, againste which
out of this place euery man crieth out ? haue we not houses of purpose
built with great charges for the maintenance of them, and that without
the liberties, as who woulde say, there, let them saye what they will
say, we will play. I know not how I might with the godly learned
especially more discommende the gorgeous Playing place erected in
the fieldes, than to terme it, as they please to haue it called, a Theatre
... I will not here enter this disputation, whether it be vtterly vnlawfull to haue any playes, but will onelye ioine in this issue, whether
in a Christian common wealth they be tolerable on the Lords day. . . .
If playing in the Theatre or any other place in London, as there are
by sixe that I know to many, be any of the Lordes wayes (which
I suppose there is none so voide of knowledge in the world wil graunt)
then not only it may, but ought to be vsed, but if it be any of the
wayes of man, it is no work for ye Lords Sabaoth, and therfore in
no respecte tollerable on that daye.' P. 137. ' For reckening with
the leaste, the gaine that is reaped of eighte ordinarie places in the
Citie whiche I knowe, by playing but once a weeke (whereas many
times they play twice and somtimes thrice) it amounteth to 2000
pounds by the yeare.'

xviii. 1578. John Florio.

[From *First Fruites* (1578), A₁, an Anglo-Italian phrase book.]

Where shal we goe ?
To a playe at the Bull, or els to some other place.
Doo Comedies like you wel ?
Yea sir, on holy dayes.
They please me also wel, but the preachers wyll not allowe them.
Wherefore, knowe you it :
They say, they are not good.
And wherfore are they vsed ?
Because euery man delites in them.
I beleeue there is much knauerie vsed at those Comedies : what thinke you ?
So beleeue I also.

xix. 1578. George Whetstone.

[From *Epistle* to William Fleetwood, dated 29 July 1578, prefixed to *Promos and Cassandra* ; cf. ch. xxiii.]

. . . I devided the whole history into two Commedies : for that, Decorum used, it would not be convayde in one. The effects of both, are good and bad : vertue intermyxt with vice, unlawful desyres (yf it were possible) queancht with chaste denyals : al needefull action (I thinke) for publike vewe. For by the rewarde of the good, the good are encowraged in wel doinge : and with the scowrge of the lewde, the lewde are feared from evil attempts : mainetayning this my oppinion with Platoes auctority. ' Nawghtinesse commes of the corruption of nature, and not by readinge or hearinge the lives of the good or lewde (for such publication is necessarye), but goodnesse (sayth hè) is beawtifyed by either action.' And to these ends Menander Plautus and Terence, themselves many yeares since intombed, (by their Commedies) in honour live at this daye. The auncient Romanes heald these showes of suche prise, that they not onely allowde the publike exercise of them, but the grave Senators themselves countenaunced the Actors with their presence : who from these trifles wonne morallyte, as the Bee suckes the honny from weedes. But the advised devises of auncient Poets, discredited with the tryfels of yonge, unadvised, and rashe witted wryters, hath brought this commendable exercise in mislike. For at this daye, the Italian is so lascivious in his commedies, that honest hearers are greeved at his actions : the Frenchman and Spaniarde folowes the Italians humor : the Germaine is too holye : for he presentes on everye common Stage, what Preachers should pronounce in Pulpets. The Englishman in this quallitie, is most vaine, indiscreete, and out of order : he fyrst groundes his worke, on impossibilities : then in three howers ronnes he throwe the worlde : marryes, gets Children, makes Children men, men to conquer kingdomes, murder monsters, and bringeth Gods from Heaven, and fetcheth Divels from Hel. And (that which is worst) their ground is not so unperfect, as their working indiscreete : not waying, so the people laugh, though they laugh them (for theyr folleys) to scorne : Manye tymes (to make mirthe) they make a Clowne companion with a Kinge : in theyr grave Counsels, they allow the advise of fooles : yea they use one order of speach for all persones : a grose *Indecorum*, for a Crowe wyll yll counterfet the Nightingales sweete voice : even so, affected Speeche doth misbecome a Clowne. For to work a Commedie kindly, grave olde men should instruct : yonge men should showe the imperfections of youth : Strumpets should be lascivious : Boyes unhappy : and Clownes should be disorderly : entermingling all these actions, in suche sorte, as the grave matter may instruct, and the pleasant delight : for without this chaunge, the attention would be small, and the likinge, lesse. But leave I this rehearsall, of the use, and abuse of Commedies : least that I check that in others, which I cannot amend in my selfe. But this I am assured, what actions so ever passeth in this History, either merry, or morneful : grave or lascivious ; the conclusion showes the confusion of Vice, and cherishing of Vertue. . . .

xx. 1579. T. F.

[From *Newes from the North. Otherwise called a Conference between Simon Certen and Pierce Plowman.* Faithfully collected and gathered by T. F. Student (1579, 1585), F₄, quoted from 1585 ed. in Stubbes, 299. There seems to be no justification for Collier's identification of T. F. with Francis Thynne.]

I call to witnesse the Theaters, Curtines, Heauing houses, Rifling boothes, Bowling alleyes, and such places, where the time is so shamefully mispent, namely the Sabaoth daies, vnto the great dishonor of God, and the corruption and vtter distruction of youth.

xxi. 1579. THOMAS TWYNE.

[From *Physic against Fortune* (1579), i. 30. This is a translation from Petrarch's *De remediis utriusque Fortunae*; but Twyne has adapted the wording to bring in the names of the London theatres.]

Joy. I am delighted with sundrie Shewes.
Reason. Perhaps with the Curteine or Theater : which two places are well knowen to be enimies to good manners : for looke who goeth thyther evyl, returneth worse. For that iourney is unknowen to the good, whiche yf any undertake uppon ignoraunce, he cannot choose but be defyled.

xxii. 1579. STEPHEN GOSSON.

[From *The Schoole of Abuse, Containing a pleasaunt inuectiue against Poets, Pipers, Plaiers, Iesters and such like Caterpillers of a Commonwelth* . . . (1579 ; S. R. 22 July 1579). A second edition appeared in 1587. There are modern reprints in *Somers Tracts*, iii (1810), 552, and by J. P. Collier (1841, *Sh. Soc.*) and E. Arber (1868, *English Reprints*). On 5 (or 16) Oct. 1579 Spenser wrote to Gabriel Harvey (Gregory Smith, i. 89, from *Two Other very Commendable Letters*, 1580) : ' Newe Bookes I heare of none, but only of one, that writing a certaine Booke, called The Schoole of Abuse, and dedicating it to Maister Sidney, was for hys labor scorned, if at least it be in the goodnesse of that nature to scorne. Suche follie is it not to regarde aforehande the inclination and qualitie of him to whome wee dedicate oure Bookes.']

[Summary and Extracts.] *Epistle to Sidney. Epistle to the Reader.*
. . . ' I take vpon mee to driue you from playes, when mine owne woorkes are dayly to be seene vpon stages, as sufficient witnesses of mine owne folly, and seuere iudges againste my selfe.' Poetry and Music are first attacked ; an apologist for Homer being likened (p. 21) ' to some of those players, that come to the scaffold with drum and trumpet to profer skirmishe, and when they haue sounded allarme, off go the peeces to encounter a shadow, or conquere a paper monster.' P. 28. ' As poetrie and piping are cosen germans : so piping and playing are of great affinity, and all three chayned in linkes of abuse.' P. 29. ' I was first instructed in the university, after drawne like a nouice to these abuses.' Criticism of the theatre by the graver Greeks and Romans and its abuses in Rome. Similar abuses have replaced ' the olde discipline of Englande '. P. 35. ' In our assemblies at playes in London, you shall see suche heauing, and shouuing, suche ytching and shouldring, too sitte by the women ; suche care for their garments, that they bee not trode on : such eyes to their lappes, that no chippes light in them : such pillowes to ther backes, that they take no hurte : such masking in their eares, I knowe not what : such giuing them pippins to passe the time : suche playing at foote saunt without cardes : such ticking, such toying, such smiling, such winking, and such manning them home, when the sportes are ended, that it is a right comedie, to marke their behauiour, to watche their conceites, as the catte for the mouse, and as good as a course at the game it selfe, to dogge them a little, or followe aloofe by the printe of their feete, and so discouer by slotte where the deare taketh soyle. If this were as well noted, as ill seene : or as openly punished, as secretly practised : I haue no doubte but the cause would be seared to dry vp the effect, and these prettie rabbets very cunningly ferretted from their borrowes. For they that lack customers al the weeke, either because their haunte is vnknowen, or the constables and officers of their parishe watch them so narrowly, that they dare not queatche, to celebrate the Sabboth, flock to theaters, and there keepe a generall market of bawdrie : not that any filthynesse in deede is committed within the compasse of that grounde, as was doone in Rome, but that euery wanton and his paramour, euery man and his mistresse, euery John and his Joan, euery knaue and his

queane, are there first acquainted and cheapen the merchandise in that place, which they pay for elsewhere as they can agree.' Players at least indirectly to blame for London's wantonness. P. 37. ' They seeke not to hurte, but desire too please : they haue purged their comedyes of wanton speaches, yet the corne whiche they sell, is full of cockle, and the drinke that they drawe, ouercharged with dregges.' Advises those who would avoid offence to avoid the theatre. The abuses are contrary to the Queen's will. P. 39. ' How often hath her Maiestie, with the graue aduise of her honorable Councell, sette downe the limits of apparell to euery degree, and how soone againe hath the pride of our harts ouerflowen the chanel ? How many times hath accesse to theaters beene restrayned, and how boldly againe haue we reentred. Ouerlashing in apparel is so common a fault, that the very hyerlings of some of our players, which stand at reuersion of vi.s by the weeke, iet vnder gentlemens noses in sutes of silke, exercising themselues too prating on the stage, and common scoffing when they come abrode, where they looke askance ouer the shoulder at euery man, of whom the Sunday before they begged an almes. I speake not this, as though euerye one that professeth the qualitie so abused him selfe, for it is well knowen, that some of them are sober, discreete, properly learned honest housholders and citizens well thought on amonge their neighbours at home, though the pryde of their shadowes (I meane those hangebyes whome they succour with stipend) cause them to bee somewhat il talked of abroade. And as some of the players are farre frome abuse : so some of their playes are without rebuke : which are as easily remembered as quickly reckoned. The twooe prose bookes plaied at the Belsauage, where you shall finde neuer a woorde without wit, neuer a line without pith, neuei a letter placed in vaine. The *Iew* and *Ptolome*, showne at the Bull, the one representing the greedinesse of worldly chusers, and bloody mindes of usurers : the other very liuely descrybing how seditious estates, with their owne deuises, false friendes, with their owne swoordes, and rebellious commons in their owne snares are owerthrowne : neither with amorous gesture wounding the eye : nor with slouenly talke hurting the eares of the chast hearers. The *Blacke Smiths daughter*, and *Catilins Conspiracies* vsually brought in to the Theater : the first contayning the trechery of Turkes, the honourable bountye of a noble minde, and the shining of vertue in distresse : the last, because it is knowen too be a pig of myne owne sow, I will speake the lesse of it ; onely giuing you to vnderstand, that the whole marke which I shot at in that woorke, was too showe the rewarde of traytors in Catilin, and the necessary gouernment of learned men, in the person of Cicero, which forsees euery danger that is likely to happen, and forstalles it continually ere it take effect. . . . These playes are good playes and sweete playes, and of al playes the best playes and most to be liked, woorthy to bee soung of the Muses, or set out with the cunning of Roscius himself, yet are they not fit for euery mans dyet : neither ought they commonly to bee shewen. Now if any man aske me why my selfe haue penned comedyes in time

paste, and inueigh so egerly against them here, let him knowe that
Semel insaniuimus omnes : I have sinned, and am sorry for my fault :
hee runnes farre that neuer turnes, better late than neuer. I gaue
my self to that exercise in hope to thriue but I burnt one candle
to seek another, and lost bothe my time and my trauell, when I had
doone.' Deprecates the excuse that plays keep idle heads occupied.
P. 42. ' These because they are allowed to play euery Sunday, make
iiii or v Sundayes at least euery weeke, and all that is doone is good
for Augustus, to busy the wittes of his people, for running a wool-
gathering, and emptie their purses for thriuing to fast.' Has shown
the abuses of players out of profane writers rather than out of the
Scriptures. Exhorts against vanity ; but, p. 44, ' if players can
promise in woordes, and performe it in deedes, proclame it in their
billes, and make it good in theaters ; that there is nothing there
noysome too the body, nor hurtfull to the soule : and that euerye
one which comes to buye their iestes, shall haue an honest neighbour,
tagge and ragge, cutte and longe tayle, goe thither and spare not,
otherwise I aduise you to keepe you thence, my selfe will beginne too
leade the daunce '. Briefly reprehends dancers, tumblers, dicers,
carders, and bowlers, and more at length fencers. *Epistle to Sir
Richard Pipe, Lord Mayor, and the Aldermen.* . . . P. 56. ' I woulde
the abuses of my Schoole were as wel knowen of you, to reformation :
as they are found out by other to their owne peril. But the fishe *Sepia*
can trouble the water to shun the nettes, that are shot to catch her :
Torpedo hath craft inough at the first touch to inchant the hooke,
to coniure the line, to bewitch the rod, and to benumme the handes
of him that angleth. Whether our players be the spawnes of such
fishes, I know not wel, yet I am sure that how many nets so euer
ther be layde to take them, or hookes to choke them, they haue ynke
in their bowels to darken the water, and sleights in their budgets, to
dry vp the arme of euery magistrate. If their letters of commendations were once stayed, it were easie for you to ouerthrow them. . . .
I doubte not but the gouernours of London will vexe mee for speaking
my minde, when they are out of their wittes, and banishe their players,
when they are beste aduised.' *Epistle to the Gentlewomen Citizens of
London.* . . . P. 58. ' It is not . . . your sober countenance, that
defendeth your credite ; nor your friends which accompany your
person, that excuse your folly ; nor your modestie at home, that
couereth your lightnesse, if you present your selues in open theaters.
. . . Though you go to theaters to se sport, Cupid may catche you
ere you departe. . . . In deede I muste confesse there comes to playes
of all sortes, old and young ; it is hard to say that all offend, yet
I promise you, I wil sweare for none.'

xxiii. *c.* 1579. Thomas Lodge.

[From a print without title-page edited by D. Laing (1853, *Sh. Soc.*) under the title of *A Defence of Poetry, Music and Stage Plays* ; part in Gregory Smith, i. 61. There can be little doubt that this is the *Honest Excuses* of Gosson's *Apology* and the suppressed work of Lodge referred to in his *Alarum* and Gosson, *P. C.* (Nos. xxx, xxxv, *infra*) ; cf. J. D. Wilson in *M. L. R.* iii. 166.]

[Summary and Extracts.] P. 3. ' There came to my hands lately a litle (would God a wittye) pamphelet, baring a fayre face as though it were the Scoole of Abuse.' Defends against Gosson poetry, music, and thirdly players, for whose art he claims both ' antiquity ' and ' use and comoditye ' as an instrument of moral criticism. P. 24. Of comedies he says, ' Tulley defines them thus, *Comedia* (saith he) is *imitatio vitae, speculum consuetudinis, et imago veritatis* '. P. 27. He has concessions to make. ' I wish as zealously as the best that all abuse of playinge weare abolished, but for the thing, the antiquitie causeth me to allow it, so it be used as it should be. I cannot allow the prophaning of the Sabaoth. I praise your reprehension in that ; you did well in discommending the abuse, and surely I wysh that folly wer disclaymed ; it is not to be admitted, it maks those sinne, which perhaps if it were not, would have binne present at a good sermon. It is in the magistrate to take away that order, and appoynt it otherwyse. But sure it were pittie to abolish that which hath so great vertue in it, because it is abused.' P. 28. He turns on the critic. ' But, after your discrediting of playmaking, you salue upon the sore somewhat, and among many wise workes there be some that fitte your vaine : The Practice of Parasites is one, which I meruel it likes you so well, since it bites you so sore. But sure in that I like your judgement, and for the rest to, I approue your wit, but for the pigg of your owne sow, (as you terme it) assuredly I must discommend your verdit : Tell me, Gosson, was all your owne you wrote there ? did you borow nothing of your neyghbours ? Out of what booke patched you out Cicero's Oration ? Whence fet you Catilin's Inuec-tiue ? . . . Beleue me I should preferr Wilson's Shorte and sweete if I were judge, a peece surely worthe prayse, the practice of a good scholler ; would the wiser would ouerlooke that, they may perhaps cull some wisedome out of a player's toye.' Assents to Gosson's rebuke of carders, dicers, fencers, bowlers, dancers, and tumblers.

xxiv. 1579. Stephen Gosson.

[From *The Ephemerides of Phialo and a short Apologie of the Schoole of Abuse* (1579 ; S. R. 7 Nov. 1579). A second edition appeared in 1586. The Apologie is reprinted by E. Arber with *The Schoole of Abuse* (1868).]

[Extracts.] *Epistle to Sidney.* . . . Sith it hath beene my fortune to bear sayle in a storme, since my first publishing the *Schoole of Abuse* . . . I can not but acknowledge my safetie, in your Worships patronage. *The Ephemerides of Phialo.* . . . I think it necessary, before I set downe the discourses of *Phialo* . . . to whippe out those

Doggs, which haue barked . . . at mee for writinge the *Schoole of Abuse*. . . . It is not long since, a friend of mine presented me with straunge newes out of *Affrick* [in margin, ' A Libell cast out against the Schoole of Abuse '] requesting me earnestly to shape them an answere. . . . I . . . unfolded the Paper, and found nothing within but guttes and garbage. . . . And had not the writer himself, which sent these newes into *England*, reuealed his name to some of his friends by whom I hearde it, I would haue iudged such a Daw to bee hacht in *Barbary*, and the tydinges that came, to be scribled in post. . . . This Doctour of *Affrike* with a straunge kinde of style begins to write thus : *To his frinds the Plaiers* . . . If Players get no better Atturnie to pleade their case, I will holde mee contented where the Haruest is harde, too take Otes of yl debters in parte of payment. . . . I intende not to aunswere him. . . . *An Apologie of the Schoole of Abuse*. . . . Such is the skirmishe of our players, who perceiuing the truthe to stand on my side as an armour of proofe ; and finding them selues vnappointed for the fielde, keepe a farre off, biting me in corners, casting out libels which are but clay, and rattle on mine armour, or tippe me on the shinnes, without farther hurt. . . . If plaiers take a little more counsel of their pillowe, they shall finde them selues to be the worste and the daungerousest people in the world. . . . If Diogenes were nowe aliue, to see the abuses that growe by playes, I beleeue hee would wyshe rather to bee a Londoners hounde than his apprentice, bicause hee rateth his dogge, for wallowing in carrion ; but rebukes not his seruaunt for resorting to playes, that are ranke poyson. . . . We perceiue not . . . that players counterfaiting a shewe to make vs merry, shoote their nettes to worke our misery ; that when *Comedie* comes vpon the stage, *Cupide* sets vpp a Springe for Wood-cockes, which are entangled ere they descrie the line, and caught before they mistruste the snare. . . . Our players, since I set out the *Schole of abuse*, haue trauailed to some of mine acquaintance of both Vniuersities, with fayre profers, and greater promises of rewardes, yf they woulde take so much paine as too write agaynst mee. . . . When neither of both Vniuersities would heare their plea, they were driuen to flie to a weake hedge, and fight for themselues with a rotten stake. . . . It is tolde mee that they haue got one in London to write certaine *Honest Excuses*, for so they tearme it, to their dishonest abuses which I reuealed. . . . How he frames his excuses, I knowe not yet, because it is doone in hudder mudder. Trueth can neuer be Falsehods Visarde, which maketh him maske without a torche and keepe his papers very secret. . . . If the Excuser be the man that is named to me, he is as famous a Clarke as *Clauitius Sabinus*, which was so troubled with a grosse conceite, and as short a memory, that euery minute he forgote the names of *Vlisses, Achilles, Priamus,* and such as he knew as well as the Begger his dishe. . . . I was determined to send you greater matters, touching the saleable toung of *Curio*, but I stay my handes till I see his booke, when I haue perusd it I will tel you more.

xxv. 1580. Anon.

[From Stationers' Register, 8 April 1580 (Arber, ii. 368). This is one of a number of ballads and pamphlets entered in April–June 1580 as a result of the earthquake on 6 April; Abraham Fleming, in his *A Bright Burning Beacon*, names eight writers on the subject besides himself, including Thomas Churchyard and Richard Tarlton. It may be that several of these improved the occasion by reproving bear-baitings and plays, as did Arthur Golding in his *A Discourse Upon the Earthquake*, but it does not appear from Golding's 'reporte' that any play-houses suffered serious damage, although Halliwell-Phillipps, i. 369, quotes Munday, *View of Sundry Examples* (1580), 'At the play-houses the people came running foorth, supprised with great astonishment', and S. Gardiner, *Doomes-day Booke* (1606), 'The earthquake . . . shaked not only the scenicall Theatre, but the great stage and theatre of the whole land'. On the contrary, the only deaths were those of two children killed 'while they were hearing a sermon' at Christ Church, Newgate, a detail which is omitted in the reprint of the 'reporte' and of some of Golding's moralizing, with an official *Order of Prayer* issued for use in parish churches (*Liturgical Services*, Parker Soc., 573).]

H. Carr, 'a ballat intituled comme from the plaie, comme from the playe: the house will fall, so people saye: the earth quakes, lett us hast awaye'.

xxvi. 1580. Anthony Munday (?).

[Entry in S. R. for Edward White on 10 Nov. 1580 (Arber, ii. 381). Collier, *S. R.* ii. 125, prints a ballad, probably forged, 'which has come down to us in MS.', and suggests that it may be the one in question. Fleay, 52, Thompson, 86, and J. D. Wilson in *M. L. R.* iv. 486, suppose the entry to refer to the 'balat against plays' ascribed to Munday (cf. ch. xxiii).]

A Ringinge Retraite Couragiouslie sounded, wherein Plaies and Players are fytlie Confounded.

xxvii. 1580. Anthony Munday (?).

[From *A second and third blast of retrait from plaies and Theaters: the one whereof was sounded by a reuerend Byshop dead long since: the other by a worshipful and zealous Gentleman now aliue: . . .* Set forth by Anglophile Eutheo (1580 ; *S. R.* 18 Oct. 1580) in Hazlitt, *E. D. S.* 97. It bears the City arms. The title recalls that of No. xxvi. J. D. Wilson (*M. L. R.* iv. 484) supports the conjectural attribution of Fleay, 51, to Munday, on the ground that the author is a converted playwright, probably identical with the one referred to in Gosson, *P. C.*, in terms resembling those applied to Munday in *A True Report of . . . M. Campion* (cf. ch. xxiii).]

[Summary and Extracts.] *Anglo-phile Eutheo to the Reader.* . . . P. 99. 'The first blast in my compt is The Schoole of abuse: a title not vnfitlie ascribed vnto plaies. For what is there which is not abused thereby? . . . that not vnfitlie they are tearmed, as of late The schoole of abuse, by one ; The schoole of Bauderie, by another ; The nest of the Diuel, and sinke of al sinne, by a third' [*in margin*, 'Mr Spark in his rehersal sermon at Paules Crosse, 29 of April, Ann. 1579']. . . . 'I cal them, A second and third blast . . . in respect of the time present, wherein none, that I knowe, besides these Autors haue written, though manie, thanked be God, in the principal places of this land haue, and dailie, yea and openlie do speake against plaies and Theaters. . . . Touching the Autor of the latter blast, thou maist coniecture who he was, but I maie not name him at this time for my promise sake ; yet this do I saie of him, that he hath bine, to vse his verie wordes, A great affecter of that vaine Art of plaie making, &c. Yea, which I ad, as excellent an Autor of those vanities, as who was best. . . . Praise God, I beseech you, for bringing this Autor, and Maister Gosson, who made the Schoole of Abuse, out of Babylon.' *A second blast of retrait.* This is translated from Salvian, *De Gubernatione Dei*, lib. vi. *A third blast of retrait.* P. 120. ' Such doubtles is mine opinion of common plaies, vsual iesting, and riming extempore that in a Christian-weale they are not sufferable. My reason is, because they are publike enimies to virtue, & religion : allurements vnto sinne ; corrupters of good manners ; the cause of securitie and carelesnes ; meere brothel houses of Bauderie : and bring both the Gospel into slander ; the Sabboth into contempt ; mens soules into danger ; and finalie the whole Common-weale into disorder.' Offers his judgement for what it is worth ; describes his experience of plays and the reasons that led him to turn from them. P. 123. ' I confess that ere this I haue bene a great affecter of that vaine art of Plaie-making, insomuch that I haue thought no time so wel bestowed, as when my wits were exercised in the inuention of those follies.' P. 125. ' What I shal speake of the abuse of plaies by my owne knowledge, I know maie be affirmed by hundreds, to whom those matters are as wel knowen as to my selfe. Some citizens wiues, vpon whom the Lord for ensample to others hath laide his hands, haue euen on their death beds with teares confessed, that they haue receiued at those spectacles such filthie infections, as haue turned their minds from chast cogitations, and made them of honest women light huswiues ; by them they haue dishonored the vessels of holines ; and brought their husbandes into contempt, their children into question, their bodies into sicknes, and their soules to the state of euerlasting damnation. . . . When I gaue my selfe first to note the abuse of common plaies . . . the Theater I found to be an appointed place of Bauderie ; mine owne eares haue heard honest women allured with abhominable speeches. Sometime I haue seen two knaues at once importunate vpon one light huswife ; whereby much quarel hath growen to the disquieting of manie. There seruants, as it is manifestlie to be prooued, haue consented to rob their maisters, to supplie the want of their harlots ; there is the practising with married wiues to traine them from their husbands, and places appointed for meeting and conference. When I had taken a note of all these abuses, & sawe that the Theater was become a consultorie house of Satan, I concluded with my selfe, neuer to imploie my pen to so vile a purpose, nor to be an instrument of gathering the wicked together.' Apologizes for pressing forward in the cause. The abuse of the Sabbath is the first thing to be put down. P. 128. ' Let therefore the Magistrate but

repel them from the libertie of plaieng on the Sabboth daie, For that
is the abuse which is generalie found fault withal, & allowed of none
but those who are altogether destitute of the feare of God, and without
conscience. To plaie on the Sabboth is but a priuiledge of sufferance,
and might with ease be repelled, were it throughlie followed. The
warrant which Magistrats have to forbid plaies is great, and passed
vnto them by such a Prince, whose auctoritie is aboue al auctorities
of earthlie gouernors. . . . Is not the Sabboth of al other daies the
most abused ? . . . Are not our eies (there) carried awaie with the
pride of vanitie ? our eares abused with amorous, that is lecherous,
filthie and abhominable speech ? Is not our tong, which was giuen
vs onelie to glorifie God withal, is not our tong there imploied to the
blaspheming of Gods holie Name ; or the commendation of that is
wicked ? Are not our hartes through the pleasure of the flesh ; the
delight of the eie ; and the fond motions of the mind, withdrawen
from the seruice of the Lord, & meditation of his goodnes ? So that
albe it is a shame to saie it, yet doubtles whosoeuer wil mark with
what multitudes those idle places are replenished, & how emptie the
Lordes sanctuarie is of his people, may wel perceaue what deuotion
we haue. . . . Alas, what folie is in you, to purchase with a penie
damnation to your selues ? . . . The Magistrate is therefore to prouide
in time a remedie to redresse the mischiefes that are like to ensue
by this common plague. . . . The Magistrates hart must be as the
hart of a Lion. He is not to shrinke in the Lordes cause, or to stand
in feare to reforme abuses of the Common-weale, because of some
particular men of auctoritie. . . . Alas, that priuate affection should
so raigne in the Nobilitie, that to pleasure, as they thinke, their
seruants, and to vphold them in their vanitie, they should restraine
the Magistrates from executing their office ! What credite can returne
to the Noble, to countenance his men to exercise that qualitie which
is not sufferable in anie Common-weale ? wheras it was an ancient
custome, that no man of Honor should reteine anie man, but such
as was excellent in some one good qualitie or other, whereby if occasion
so serued, he might get his owne liuing ? Then was euerie noble
mans house a Commonweale in it selfe : but since the reteining of
these Caterpillers, the credite of noble men hath decaied, they are
thought to be couetous by permitting their seruants, which cannot
liue of them selues, and whome for neerenes they wil not maintaine,
to liue at the deuotion or almes of other men, passing from countrie
to countrie, from one Gentlemans house to another, offering their
seruice, which is a kind of beggerie. Who in deede, to speake more
trulie, are become beggers for their seruants. For commonlie the
goodwil men beare to their lordes, makes them drawe the stringes of
their purses to extend their liberalitie to them ; where otherwise they
would not. . . . Such like men, vnder the title of their maisters or as
reteiners, are priuiledged to roaue abroad, and permitted to publish
their mametree in euerie Temple of God, and that through England,
vnto the horrible contempt of praier. So that now the Sanctuarie is
become a plaiers stage, and a den of theeues and adulterers. . . . And

trust me I am of that opinion, that the Lord is neuer so il serued as on the holie-daies. For then hel breakes loase. Then wee permit our youth to haue their swinge ; and when they are out of the sight of their maisters, such gouernment haue they of themselues, that what by il companie they meete withal, & il examples they learne at plaies, I feare me, I feare me their harts are more alienated in two houres from virtue, than againe maie wel be amended in a whole yeare.' P. 135. Players break the first commandment by profanity. P. 137. Appeal against vanities. 'Those pleasures of the stage, what are they, but the drifts of Satan ? . . . The foole no sooner showeth himselfe in his colors to make men merrie, but straightwaie lightlie there foloweth some vanitie, not onlie superfluous, but beastlie and wicked. P. 139. Whosoeuer shal visit the chappel of Satan, I meane the Theater, shal finde there no want of yong ruffins, nor lacke of harlots, vtterlie past al shame : who presse to the fore-frunt of the scaffoldes, to the end to showe their impudencie, and to be as an obiect to al mens eies. Yea, such is their open shameles behauior, as euerie man maie perceaue by their wanton gestures, wherevnto they are giuen ; yea, they seeme there to be like brothels of the stewes. For often without respect of the place and company which behold them, they commit that filthines openlie, which is horrible to be done in secret ; as if whatsoeuer they did, were warranted. For neither reuerence, iustice, nor anie thing beside can gouerne them.' The shamelessness of young men. 'Seeke to withdrawe these felowes from the Theater vnto the sermon, they wil saie, By the preacher they maie be edified, but by the plaier both edified and delighted.' P. 142. Plays are a snare to chastity, both through the examples shown on the stage, and the comments of companions on the scaffolds. 'The nature of these Comedies are, for the most part, after one manner of nature, like the tragical comedie of Calistus ; where the bawdresse Scelestina inflamed the maiden Melibeia with her sorceries.' P. 144. Examples of the intrigues 'aptlie taught in the Schoole of abuse. . . . I am sorie this schoole is not pluckt downe by the magistrate ; and the schoole-maisters banished this citie. . . . The reuerend word of God & histories of the Bible, set forth on the stage by these blasphemous plaiers, are so corrupted with their gestures of scurrilitie, and so interlaced with vncleane, and whorish speeches, that it is not possible to drawe anie profite out of the doctrine of their spiritual moralities.' P. 145. Attacks the authors of plays. 'The notablest lier is become the best Poet. . . . Our nature is led awaie with vanitie, which the auctor perceauing frames himself with nouelties and strange trifles to content the vaine humors of his rude auditors, faining countries neuer heard of ; monsters and prodigious creatures that are not ; as of the Arimaspie, of the Grips, the Pigmeies, the Cranes, & other such notorious lies. And if they write of histories that are knowen, as the life of Pompeie ; the martial affaires of Caesar, and other worthies, they giue them a newe face, and turne them out like counterfeites to showe themselues on the stage. . . . What doe they leaue behind

them ? monumentes of wanton wicked life, and doting things for men
of these latter daies. . . . But some perhaps wil saie, The noble man
delighteth in such things, whose humors must be contented, partlie
for feare, & partlie for commoditie : and if they write matters pleasant,
they are best preferred in court among the cunning heads. . . . Those
goodlie persons, if they be voide of virtue, maie wel be counted like
faire clothes ouer a foule wal; big bladers ful of wind, yet of no
waight.' P. 147. Attacks the actors. 'When I see by them
yong boies, inclining of themselues vnto wickednes, trained vp in
filthie speeches, vnnatural and vnseemlie gestures, to be brought vp
by these Schoole-masters in bawderie, and in idlenes, I cannot chuse
but with teares and griefe of hart lament. . . . And as for those stagers
themselues, are they not commonlie such kind of men in their con-
uersation, as they are in profession ? Are they not as variable in
hart, as they are in their partes ? Are they not as good practisers
of Bawderie, as inactors ? Liue they not in such sort themselues, as
they giue precepts vnto others ? doth not their talke on the stage
declare the nature of their disposition ? ' Meets divers objections.
P. 148. ' But they perhaps wil saie, that such abuses as are handled
on the stage, others by their examples, are warned to beware of such
euils, to amendment. . . . I cannot by anie means beleeue that the
wordes proceeding from. a prophane plaier, and vttered in scorning
sort, interlaced with filthie, lewde, & vngodlie speeches, haue greater
force to mooue men vnto virtue, than the wordes of truth vttered
by the godlie Preacher. . . . If the good life of a man be a better
instruction to repentance than the tong, or words, why do not plaiers,
I beseech you, leaue examples of goodnes to their posteritie ? . . .
Are they not notoriouslie knowen to be those men in their life abroade,
as they are on the stage, roisters, brallers, il-dealers, bosters, louers,
loiterers, ruffins ? . . . To conclude, the principal end of all their
interludes is to feede the world with sights, & fond pastimes ; to
iuggle in good earnest the monie out of other mens purses into
their owne handes.' P. 150. ' Some haue obiected, that by these
publique places manie forbeare to do euil for feare to be publiquelie
reprehended. And for that cause they wil saie it was tolerated in
Rome, wherein Emperors were touched, though they were present.
But to such it maie be answered, first that in disguised plaiers giuen
ouer to al sortes of dissolutenes, is not found so much as a wil to do
good, seing they care for nothing lesse than for virtue. Secondlie,
that is not a good meanes to correct sinne. For that if it be secret,
it ought not to be reuealed openlie, but by such meanes to be reformed
as Christ himselfe alloweth in his Gospel.' P. 151. ' The antiquitie
of plaieng is likewise often vsed for an argument to proue it allowable.
But the custome of euil is not to be maintained, because of antiquitie.'
P. 152. A final appeal. ' The citie Marsiles . . . would receaue into
it no stage-plaiers. . . . I would to God the Magistrates of our citie
of London would haue the like foresight. The permission of plaies
so long a time hath alreadie corrupted this citie ; and brought the
name of the citizens into slander ; the examples of Gods iudgement
is at this present an example in this citie.'

xxviii. 1581. Anon.

[Only known to me from the entry in *Catalogue of Chatsworth Library,*
iv. 49.]

A Treatise of Daunses, wherein it is showed, that they are as it
were accessories and dependants (or things annexed) to whoredom :
where also by the way is touched and proved, that Playes are ioyned
and knit together in a ranck or rowe with them.

xxix. 1581. John Rainolds.

[From *Praefatio ad Academiam Oxoniensem,* dated ' Febr. 2. 1580 ', to
Sex Theses de Sacra Scriptura et Ecclesia (1580), 30. A translation is on
p. 678 of *The Summe of the Conference between John Rainolds and John
Hart* (1584). Rainolds was Fellow of C.C.C., Oxford, 1566–86, then retired
to Queens, became Dean of Lincoln in 1593 and President of C.C.C. in
1598 ; for his share in later stage controversy cf. No. l.]

Excitate studia, paene dixeram iacentia, sed spero meliora. Ex-
tinguite Sirenes a studiis auocantes, desidiam, dulce malum : delicias,
escam Veneris : conuiuiorum luxum, vanitatem vestium, ludos
illiberales, symposia intempestiua, pestes scenicorum, Theatralia
spectacula.

xxx. 1582. Stephen Gosson.

[From *Playes Confuted in fiue Actions, Prouing that they are not to be
suffred in a Christian common weale, by the waye both the Cauils of Thomas
Lodge, and the Play of Playes, written in their defence, and other obiections
of Players frendes, are truely set downe and directlye aunsweared* (N.D. ;
S. R. 6 Apr. 1582), reprinted by Hazlitt, *E. D. S.* 157.]

[Summary and Extracts.] *Epistle to Sir Frances Walsingham.*
' So fareth it this present time with me, which giuing forth my
Defiaunce vnto Playes, am mightily beset with heapes of aduersaries.
. . . I thought it necessarye to nettle one of their Orators aboue the
rest, not of any set purpose to deface hym, because hee hath dealt
very grossely, homely, and vncharitably with me, but like a good
Surgeon to cut, & to seare, when the place requireth, for his owne
amendment. Which thinge I trust shall neither displease your honor,
nor any of the godly, in the reading, so long as the person whom
I touch is (as I heare by hys owne frendes, to hys repentance if he
can perceiue it) hunted by the heauy hand of God, and become little
better than a vagarant, looser than liberty, lighter than vanitie it
selfe.' Plays are an Augean stable to be cleansed. ' If euer so
notable a thinge bee brought to passe it must bee done by some
Hercules in the Court, whom the roare of the enimy can neuer daunt.'
Hints that this should be Walsingham. ' The Gentlemen Players
in the citie of London, are growen in such a heate, that by their
foming, their fretting, their stampinge, my frendes do perceiue how
their harts woorke, and enforce me to bring to your honor no common
fraighte, but as much as my life and securitie hereafter shall be
woorth. If the prouidence of God, who many times scourgeth a man

with the sinne that he loued, haue ordeined those players whom I fed with fancies, to be a whippe to my back, and a dagger to my brest, the fault is mine owne, the punishmente due.' *Epistle to the Universities and Inns of Court.·* P. 165. 'I was very willing to write at this time, because I was enformed by some of you which heard it with your ears, that since my publishing the *Schole of Abuse,* two Playes of my making were brought to the Stage : the one was a cast of Italian deuises, called, The Comedie of Captaine Mario : the other a Moral,. Praise at parting. These they very impudently affirme to be written by me since I had set out my inuectiue against them. I can not denie, they were both mine, but they were both penned two yeeres at the least before I forsoke them, as by their owne friends I am able to proue : but they haue got suche a custome of counterfaiting vpon the Stage, that it is growen to a habite, & will not be lefte. God knoweth, before whom to you all I doe protest, as I shall answer to him at the last day, when al hidden secrets shal be discouered, since the first printing of my Inuectiue, to this day, I neuer made Playe for them nor any other. . . . I departed from the City of London, and bestowed my time in teaching yong Gentlemen in the Countrie, where I continue with a very worshipfull Gentleman, and reade to his sonnes in his owne house. . . . As sonne as I had inueighed against Playes, I withdrewe my selfe from them to better studies, which so long as I liue I trust to follow.' *The Confutation of Playes. The First Action.* The Efficient Cause of Plays. Defends his own change of mind. P. 167. 'When I firste gaue my selfe to the studie of Poetrie, and to set my cunning abroache, by penning Tragedies and Comedies in the Citte of London : perceiuing such a Gordians knot of disorder in euery play house, as woulde neuer bee loosed without extremitie, I thought it better with Alexander to draw y[e] sword that should knappe it a sunder at one stroke, than to seeke ouernisely or gingerly to vndoe it, with the losse of my time and wante of success. This caused mee to bidde them the base at their owne gole, and to geue them a volley of heathen writers : that our diuines considering the danger of suche houses as are set vp in London against the Lord, might better them thoroughly with greater shotts.' An incomplete remedy. 'Acknowledging the mischiefe bred by playes wee hope to auoid yt by changing their day yet suffer them still to remaine amonge vs. . . . The abhominable practises of playes in London haue bene by godly preachers, both at Paules crosse, and else where so zealously, so learnedly, so loudly cried out vpon to small redresse ; that I may well say of them, as the Philosophers reporte of the moouing of the heauens, we neuer heare them, because we euer heare them.' Notes an answer to him. P. 169. 'Amongest all the fauorers of these vncircumcised Philistines, I meane the Plaiers, whose heartes are not right, no man til of late durst thrust out his heade to mayntaine there quarrell, but one, in witt, simple ; in learning, ignorant ; in attempt, rash ; in name, Lodge : whose booke, as it came not to my handes in one whole yeere after the priuy printing thereof, so I confesse, that to it, before this time, I aunswered nothing,

partlie because he brought nothing ; partlie because my hearte was
to bigge, to wrastle with him, that wanteth armes. Therefore considering with my selfe that such kinde of sōres might bee launced to
sone, I chose rather to let him ripen and breake of him selfe, that
vomiting out his owne disgrace, & being worne out of fauour among
his own friends, I might triumph in the cause & shedde no blood. . . .
Some of his acquaintance haue vaunted to cut and hewe mee, I knowe
not howe.' The Devil is the efficient cause of plays, as noted by
Tertullian. P. 171. ' And William [' Thomas ' on a cancel in some
copies] Lodge in that patchte pamphlet of his . . . confesseth openly
that playes were consecrated by the heathens to yᵉ honour of their
gods.' Expounds the policy of the Devil in the matter. P. 172.
' First hee sente ouer many wanton Italian bookes. . . . Not contented
with the number he hath corrupted with reading Italian baudery,
because all cannot reade, [he] presenteth vs Comedies cut by the same
paterne, which drag such a monstrous taile after them, as is able to
sweep whole Cities into his lap.' Argues that plays are of idolatrous
origin, and disliked by Scipio Nasica and other severer Romans.
Rome held players infamous. P. 178. ' Wherefore I beseech God
so to touch the heartes of our Magistrates with a perfite hatred
of sinne, and feare of Iudgement ; so to stirr vp some noble Scipio
in the Courte, that these daunsing Chaplines of Bacchus and all such
as set vp these wicked artes, may be driuen out of Englande.' *The
Second Action.* The Material Cause of Plays. P. 179. ' Yonge Master
Lodge thinking to iett vpon startoppes, and steale an ynche of his
hight by the bare name of Cicero, allegeth from him, yᵗ a Play is the
Schoolmistresse of life; the lookinge glasse of manners; and the image
of trueth. . . . It seemeth that Master Lodge saw this in Tullie with
other folkes eyes, and not his owne. For to my remembrance I neuer
read it in him, neither doe I thinke that Master Lodge can shewe it
me.' Cites passages of Cicero against *spectacula.* Sets down the
matter of plays. P. 180. ' The argument of Tragedies is wrath,
crueltie, incest, iniurie, murther eyther violent by sworde, or voluntary
by poyson. The persons, Gods, Goddesses, furies, fiendes, Kinges,
Quenes, and mightie men. The grounde worke of Commedies, is loue,
cosenedge, flatterie, bawderie, slye conueighance of whoredome ; The
persons, cookes, queanes, knaues, baudes, parasites, courtezannes,
lecherous olde men, amorous yong men.' Criticizes the Lodge-Cicero
metaphor in detail. Plays no schoolmistress of life. ' The beholding
of troubles and miserable slaughters that are in Tragedies, driue vs to
immoderate sorrow, heauines, womanish weeping and mourning,
whereby we become louers of dumpes, and lamentation, both enemies
to fortitude. Comedies so tickle our senses with a pleasanter vaine,
that they make vs louers of laughter, and pleasure, without any
meane, both foes to temperance. What schooling is this ? Sometime
you shall see nothing but the aduentures of an amorous knight, passing
from countrie to countrie for the loue of his lady, encountring many
a terible monster made of broune paper, & at his retorne, is so
wonderfully changed, that he can not be knowne but by some posie

in his tablet, or by a broken ring, or a handkircher, or a piece of
a cockle shell. What learne you by that ? When ye soule of your
playes is eyther meere trifles, or Italian baudery, or wooing of gentlewomen, what are we taught ? ' Aristotle forbade plays to the
young. P. 182. ' If any goodnes were to be learned at Playes
it is likely that the Players them selues which committ euery sillable
to memory shoulde profitte most . . . but the dayly experience of
their behauiour sheweth, that they reape no profit by the discipline
them selues.' Thinks Master Lodge found ' some peeuish index or
gatherer of Tullie to be a sleepe. . . . Wherein I perceiue hee is no
changeling, for he disputeth as soundly being from the vniuersitie
and out of exercise, as he did when hee was there, and at his booke.'
P. 183. Plays no glass of behaviour. Manners should not be rebuked
where no reply is possible, or before such judges as ' the common
people which resorte to Theaters being but an assemblie of Tailers,
Tinkers, Cordwayners, Saylers, olde Men, yong Men, Women, Boyes,
Girles, and such like '. The Roman law of libel restrained ' the ouerlashing of players '. P. 185. Criticizes [Wilson's] *The Three Ladies
of London* [cf. ch. xxiii] for making Love detest and Conscience allow
plays ; also a rival play of *London against the Three Ladies*. Denies
that intention either of poets or players is to profit those they rebuke.
P. 187. Plays not the image of truth. P. 188. ' In Playes either
those thinges are fained that neuer were, as Cupid and Psyche plaid
at Paules ; and a greate many Comedies more at ye Blacke friers
and in euery Playe house in London, which for breuities sake I ouer
skippe : of if a true Historie be taken in hand, it is made like our
shadows, longest at the rising and falling of the Sunne, shortest of
all at hie noone. For the Poets driue it most commonly vnto such
pointes as may best showe the maiestie of their pen in Tragicall
speaches ; or set the hearers a gogge with discourses of loue ; or
painte a fewe antickes to fitt their owne humors with scoffes & tauntes ;
or wring in a shewe to furnish the Stage when it is to bare ; when
the matter of it selfe comes shorte of this, they followe the practise
of the cobler, and set their teeth to the leather to pull it out. So
was the history of Caesar and Pompey, and the Playe of the Fabii
at the Theater, both amplified there, where the Drummes might walke,
or the pen ruffle ; when the history swelled and ran to hye for the
number of ye persons that should playe it, the Poet with Proteus
[? Procrustes] cut the same fit to his owne measure ; when it afoorded
no pompe at al, he brought it to the racke to make it serue. . . .
I may boldely say it because I haue seene it, that the Palace of
pleasure, the Golden Asse, the Œthiopian historie, Amadis of Fraunce,
the Rounde Table, baudie Comedies in Latine, French, Italian, and
Spanish, haue beene throughly ransackt to furnish the Playe houses
in London. . . . Forsooth saith the Authour of the Playe of plays
showen at the Theater, the three and twentieth of Februarie last :
They shalbe nowe purged, the matter shalbe good. . . . As for that
glosing plaie at ye Theater which profers you so faire, there is enterlaced in it a baudie song of a maide of Kent, and a little beastly

speech of the new stawled roge, both which I am compelled to burie
in silence, being more ashamed to vtter them than they.' Thinks
the minority of honest plays a trick of the devil. Repeats his points
as to the idolatrous origin of plays and the infamy of players at Rome.
The devil makes them alluring.   P. 192. ' For the eye, beeside the
beautie of the houses and the Stages, hee sendeth in Gearish apparell,
maskes, vauting, tumbling, daunsing of gigges, galiardes, morisces,
hobbihorses, showing of iudgeling castes.' *The Third Action.* The
Formal Cause of Plays. P. 195. ' The Law of God very straightly
forbids men to put on womens garments.' This is not to be explained
away as a prohibition of disguises meant to facilitate adultery, but
is absolute. P. 197. ' In Stage Playes for a boy to put one the
attyre, the gesture, the passions of a woman ; for a meane person
to take vpon him the title of a Prince with counterfeit porte, and
traine, is by outwarde signes to shewe them selues otherwise then
they are, and so with in the compasse of a lye, which by Aristotles
iudgement is naught of it selfe and to be fledde.' Admits that Gregory
Nazianzen and Buchanan wrote plays. ' To what ende ? To be Plaied
vpon Stages ? neither Players nor their friendes are able to proue
it.' Refutes another objection. P. 198. ' Let the Author of the
playe of playes & pastimes, take heede how he reason y^t action,
pronuntiation, agility of body are ye good gifts of God. *Ergo,* plaies
consisting of these cannot be euill.' Even the heathens condemned
the waste of money in spectacles. *The Fourth Action.* The Final
Cause of Plays. P. 201. The end of plays is sinful delight, as is
proved by the admissions of Menander and Terence, ' By the manner
of penning in these dayes, because the Poets send theire verses to the
Stage vpon such feete as continually are rowled vp in rime at the
fingers endes, which is plaucible to the barbarous, and carrieth a stinge
into the eares of the common people. By the obiect, because Tragedies
and Commedies stirre vp affections, and affections are naturally
planted in that part of the minde that is common to vs with brute
beastes.' Analyses the argument of the Author of the Play of Plays,
' spreading out his battel to hemme me in '. P. 202. ' He tyeth Life
and Delight so fast together, that if Delight be restrained, Life presently perisheth ; there, zeale perceyuing Delight to be embraced of
Life, puttes a snafle in his mouth, to keepe him vnder. Delight
beinge bridled, Zeale leadeth life through a wildernesse of lothsome-
nesse, where Glutte scarreth them all, chafing both Zeale and Delight
from Life, and with the clubbe of amasednesse strikes such a pegge
into the heade of Life, that he falles downe for dead vpon the Stage.
Life beinge thus fainte, and ouertrauailed, destitute of his guyde,
robbed of Delight, is readie to giue vp the Ghost, in the same place ;
then entereth Recreation, which with music and singing rockes Life
a sleepe to recouer his strength. By this meanes Tediousnesse is
driuen from Life, and the teinte is drawne out of his heade, which
the club of amasednes left behinde. At last Recreation setteth vp
the Gentleman vpon his feete, Delight is restored to him againe, and
such kinde of sportes for cullices are brought in to nourishe him, as

none but Delighte must applye to his stomache. Then time beinge
made for the benefite of Life, and Life being allowed to followe his
appetite, amongst all manner of pastimes, Life chooseth Commedies,
for his Delight, partly because Commedies are neither chargable to
ye beholders purse, nor painful to his body; partly, because he may
sit out of the raine to veiwe the same, when many other pastimes
are hindred by wether. Zeale is no more admitted to Life before he
be somewhat pinchte in the waste, to auoyde extremitie, and being
not in the end simply called Zeale but Moderate Zeale a fewe conditions are prescribed to Comedies, that the matter be purged,
deformities blazed, sinne rebuked, honest mirth intermingled, and
fitte time for the hearing of the same appointed. Moderate Zeale is
contented to suffer them, who wyneth with delight to direct life
againe, after which he triumphes ouer Death & is crowned with
eternitie.' P. 203. As Fathers and Councils ' and ye skilfulst Deuines
at this day in England which are compelled in Sermons to cry out
against them' are challenged by this playmaker, will answer him.
Distinguishes between carnal and spiritual delight. Plays bring carnal
delight, which is contrary to reason and comes of corruption. *The
Fifth Action.* The Effects of Plays. P. 211. Why should he write
against plays, when, although famous men in both universities cry
out against plays, ' none of them by printing haue taken the paines
to write any full discouery against them'? Partly because, being
young, he will be better excused than they if he ' shoulde speake but
one worde against ye sleepines of Magistrats which in this case is
necessary to be toucht '; partly because, ' hauing once already written
against playes, which no man that euer wrote playes, did, but one,
who hath changed his coppy, and turned himself like ye dog to his
vomite, to plays againe, and being falsly accused my selfe to do y^e
like, it is needfull for me to write againe '. Declares the effects of
plays. Wantonness on the stage excites the passions of the spectators.
Theatres are ' markets of bawdry '. P. 215. ' Our Theaters, and play
houses in London, are as full of secrete adulterie as they were in
Rome. . . . In the playhouses at London, it is the fashion of youthes
to go first into the yarde, and to carry theire eye through euery gallery,
then like vnto rauens where they spye the carion thither they flye,
and presse as nere to ye fairest as they can. . . . They giue them
pippines, they dally with their garmentes to passe ye time, they
minister talke vpon al occasions, & eyther bring them home to their
houses on small acquaintance, or slip into tauerns when ye plaies are
done. He thinketh best of his painted sheath, & taketh himselfe for
a iolly fellow, y^t is noted of most, to be busyest with women in all
such places.' The players are an evil in the commonwealth.
P. 215. ' Most of the Players haue bene eyther men of occupations,
which they haue forsaken to lyue by playing, or common minstrels,
or trayned vp from theire childehood to this abhominable exercise
& haue now no other way to get theire liuinge. . . . In a common-
weale, if priuat men be suffered to forsake theire calling because they
desire to walke gentleman like in sattine & veluet, with a buckler at
their heeles, proportion is so broken, vnitie dissolued, harmony con-

founded, that the whole body must be dismembred and the prince
or the heade cannot chuse but sicken. . . . Let them not looke to liue
by playes ; the little thrift that followeth theire greate gaine, is
a manifest token that God hath cursed it.' A final appeal to his
countrymen, ending, ' God is iust, his bow is bent & his arrowe drawen,
to send you a plague, if you staye too long '.

xxxi. 1583. JOHN FIELD.

[From *A godly exhortation, by occasion of the late iudgement of God, shewed
at Parris-garden, the thirteenth day of Ianuarie : where were assembled by
estimation aboue a thousand persons, whereof some were slaine ; & of that
number, at the least, as is crediblie reported, the thirde person maimed and
hurt.* Giuen to all estates for their instruction, concerning the keeping
of the Sabboth day. By Iohn Field, Minister of the word of God. . . .
Robert Waldegrave for Henry Carre, 1583. There is no entry in S. R.,
but on 21 Jan. Richard Jones and William Bartlett were imprisoned and
fined for printing ' a thing of the fall of the gallories at Paris Garden '
without licence (Arber, ii. 853). On 19 Jan. Fleetwood wrote to Lord
Burghley (*M. S. C.* i. 160, from *Lansdowne MS.* 37, f. 10 ; also in Wright,
ii. 184), ' Vpon the same day [13 Jan.] the violaters of the Sabothe were
punished by Godes providens at Paris garden and as I was writing of
these last wordes loo here is a booke sett downe vpon the same matter '.]

Epistle to the Lord Mayor, William Fleetwood, the Recorder, and
the Aldermen. Explains the address to them. A 2ᵛ. ' Is it not
a lamentable thing, that after so long preaching of the Gospell,
there should bee so great prophanation amongst vs ? that Theaters
should be full and churches be emptie ? that the streetes shoulde be
replenished, and the places of holy exercises, left destitute ? I write
not this simplie but in respect, and by comparison. . . . If you say
that this thing belongeth not vnto you, because that Parris garden
is out of your iurisdiction, yet why are these men suffered to bring
their Beares into the citie, that thereby they may gather your company
vnto them ? It were duety in you to hinder these and to take order
that none of the citie should repaire vnto such places. . . . 18ᵗʰ January
1583. Iohn Feild.' The exhortation is mainly a general call to
repentance and fear of judgement, without special reference to the
occasion. B 3. Stress is laid on abuse of the Sabbath. B 4. ' There
is no Dicing house, Bowling alley, Cock pit, or Theater, that can be
found empty. Those flagges of defiance against God, & trumpets that
are blown to gather together such company, will sooner preuail to
fil those places, then the preaching of the holy worde of God . . .
to fill Churches. Nothing can stoppe them from the same : neyther
feare of danger, losse of tyme, corruption of maners, infection of
diseases, expence of money, suspition of honestie and such like. . . .
Pounds and hundreds can be well ynough afforded, in following these
least pleasures, though euery dore hath a payment, & euery gallerie
maketh a yearely stipend : thogh euery dog hath a coller, & euery
Beare a prize, and euery cracke bring a great aduenture.' Enforces
the warning of Paris Garden. B viiᵛ. ' I wil set it down as plainly
as I can, and as truly as can be gathered from the examination of
those same common euidences, that haue fallen out. . . . You shal

vnderstand therfore (beloued Christians) that vpon the last Lords day being the thirteen day of the first month, that cruell and lothsome exercise of bayting Beares being kept at *Parrisgarden*, in the afternoone, in the time of common praiers, and when many other exercises of Religion, both of preaching and Catechizing were had in sundry places of the City, diuers Preachers hauing not long before also cryed out against such prophanations : yet (the more pitty) there resorted thither a great company of people of al sorts and conditions, that the like nomber, in euery respect (as they say) had not beene seene there a long time before. Beeing thus vngodly assembled, to so vnholy a spectacle and specially considering the time ; the yeard, standings, and Galleries being ful fraught, being now amidest their iolity, when the dogs and Bear were in the chiefest Battel, Lo the mighty hand of God vppon them. This gallery that was double, and compassed the yeard round about, was so shaken at the foundation, that it fell (as it were in a moment) flat to the ground, without post or peere, that was left standing, so high as the stake whervnto the Beare was tied. Although some wil say (and as it may be truly) that it was very old and rotten and therefore a great waight of people, being planted vpon it then was wont, that it was no maruaile that it fayled : and would make it but a light matter. Yet surely if this be considered, that no peece of post, boord, or stake was left standing : though we vrge it not as a miracle, yet it must needes be considered as an extraordinary iudgement of God, both for the punishment of those present prophaners of the Lordes day that were then, & also informe and warne vs that were abroad. In the fal of it, there were slaine fiue men and two women, that are come to knowledge, who they were and where they dwelled, to wit, *Adam Spencer* a *Felmonger*, in *Southwarke*, *William Cockram* a Baker, dwelling in *Shordich*, *Iohn Burton* Cleark, of *S. Marie Wolmers* in *Lombard streat*, *Mathew Mason*, seruant with Master *Garland*, dwelling in *Southwarke*, *Thomas Peace*, seruant with *Robert Tasker*, dwelling in *Clerken well*. The maydens names, *Alice White*, seruant to a Pursemaker without *Cripplegate*, and *Marie Harrison*, daughter to *Iohn Harrison*, being a waterbearer, dwelling in *Lombard streat*.' C iᵛ. Nowe beside these that were thus killed out right, with the flat fal of the Galleries, strangely wrunge in peeces as it were by God himselfe, it could not bee but in such confusion, there must needes come great hurt to many. Howe many carried away death, as it were in theyr bosomes, that died the same night, or some little tyme after, the Lorde knoweth. And we heare since, though we know not the iust number, that many of them are dead & buried, and namely one *Web* a Pewterer his wife that dwelt in *Limestreete* who being there sore wounded, is now gon with diuers others. Of all the multitude there, which must needes be farre aboue a thousande, it is thought by the iudgement of most people, that not the third personne escaped vnhurt ; and by some that haue made search, they esteme that there were sore hurt and maimed, aboue one hundred and fiftye persons, some hauing theyr legs and armes broken, some theyr backes, theyr bodies beeing sore brused, so that

euery way into the cittie from that time tyll towardes nine of the clocke
and past : and specially ouer *London bridge*, many were carried in
Chayres, & led betwixt their freendes, and so brought home wyth
sorrowfull and heauy heartes lyke lame cripples. They say also that
at the first, when the Scaffolde cracked (as it did once or twise) there
was a crye of *fire fire*, which set them in such a maze as was wonderfull, so that as destitute of their wits they stood styll, and could
make no shifte for them selues, till the Scaffold was made euen with
the ground. . . . Amongst the rest it is credibly reported that there
was one Woman, that beeing in the Gallery, threw downe her childe
before her, & leaped after herselfe ; and yet thankes bee to God
neyther of both had any maner of hurt, so was it with diuers others.
But it shoulde appere that they were most hurt and in danger, which
stoode vnder the Galleries on the grounde, vpon whom both the
waight of Timbre and people fel. And sure it was a miraculous worke
of God, that any one of those should haue escaped. But heere also
God shewed his power for one man falling downe into an hole as if it
had beene some sawpit, it pleased God that it was the meane of his
deliuerance, so as all things that fell vpon him did not touch him,
and by that hee was preserued, wheras two of th'other were slaine
of either side of him.' C. iii. Urges the magistrates to ' take
order especially on the Sabaoth dayes that no Cittizen or Cittizens
seruauntes haue libertie to repaire vnto any of those abuse places,
that albeit the place be without the Cittie, and by that meanes they
haue not to deale with them, yet that they keepe theyr *Beares* out,
and their straggling *Wantons* in, that they may be better occupied.
And as they haue with good commendation so far preuailed, that
vppon Sabaoth dayes these Heathenishe *Enterludes* and *Playes* are
banished, so it wyll please them to followe the matter still, that they
may be vtterly rid and taken away. For surely it is to be feared,
beesides the distruction bothe of bodye and soule, that many are
brought vnto, by frequenting the *Theater*, the *Curtin* and such like,
that one day those places will likewise be cast downe by God himselfe,
& being drawen with them a huge heape of such contempners and
prophane persons vtterly to be killed and spoyled in their bodyes.
God hath giuen them as I haue heard manye faire warninges already.
. . . January 17, 1583.'

xxxii. 1583. PHILLIP STUBBES.

[From *The Anatomie of Abuses : Contayning a Discoverie, or briefe
Summarie of such Notable Vices and Imperfections, as now raigne in many
Christian Countreyes of the Worlde : but (especiallie) in a verie famous Ilande
called Ailgna* (S. R. 1 Mar. 1583 ; eds. 1 May 1583, 16 Aug. 1583, 1584,
1585, 1595), as reprinted by F. J. Furnivall (1877-9, *N. S. S.*) ; other
reprints are by W. D. Turnbull (1836, from 1585) and J. P. Collier (1870).
Stubbes, a layman and Londoner, was author of various ballads and
pamphlets during 1581-93. A second part of *The Anatomie of Abuses*
(S. R. 7 Nov. 1583) has not been reprinted.]

[Summary and Extracts.] The book, which is ' made dialogue-wise '
between Spudeus and Philoponus, who does most of the denunciation,

is not confined to the stage, but is a comprehensive analysis of contemporary frailty. *Epistle to Phillip Earl of Arundel. Preface to
the Reader.* P. x. ' Wheras in the processe of this my booke, I haue
intreated of certen exercyses vsually practised amongest vs, as namely
of Playes and Enterludes. . . . I would not haue thee so to take mee,
as though my speaches tended to the overthrowe and vtter disliking
of all kynd of exercyses in generall : that is nothing my simple
meaning. But the particulare Abuses which are crept into euery one
of these seuerall exercyses is the only thing which I think worthie
of reprobation. For otherwise (all Abuses cut away) who seeth not
that some kind of playes, tragedies and enterluds, in their own nature
are not only of great ancientie, but also very honest and very commendable exercyses, being vsed and practised in most Christian
common weales, as which containe matter (such they may be) both
of doctrine, erudition, good example, and wholsome instruction ; and
may be vsed, in tyme and place conuenient, as conducible to example
of life and reformation of maners. For such is our grosse and dull
nature, that what thing we see opposite before our eyes, do pearce
further and printe deeper in our harts and minds, than that thing
which is hard onely with the eares. . . . But being vsed (as now
commonly they be) to the prophanation of the Lord his sabaoth,
to the alluring and inuegling of the People from the blessed word
of God preached, to Theaters and vnclean assemblies, to ydlenes,
vnthriftynes, whordome, wantonnes, drunkennes, and what not ; and
which is more, when they are vsed to this end, to maintaine a great
sort of ydle Persons, doing nothing but playing and loytring, hauing
their lyuings of the sweat of other Mens browes, much like vnto
dronets deuouring the sweet honie of the poore labouring bees, than
are they exercyses (at no hand) sufferable. But being vsed to the
ends that I haue said, they are not to be disliked of any sober and
wise Christian.' *The Maner of Sanctifiyng the Sabaoth in Ailgna.*
P. 137. ' Some spend the Sabaoth day (for the most part) in frequenting of baudie Stage-playes and enterludes.' P. 140. *Of
Stage-playes and Enterluds, with their wickednes* ' All Stage-playes,
Enterluds, and Commedies are either of diuyne or prophane matter :
If they be of diuine matter, then are they most intollerable, or rather
Sacrilegious ; for that the blessed word of God is to be handled
reuerently, grauely, and sagely, with veneration to the glorious Maiestie
of God, which shineth therin, and not scoffingly, flowtingly, and
iybingly, as it is vpon stages in Playes and Enterluds, without any
reuerence, worship, or veneration to the same. The word of our
Saluation, the price of Christ his bloud, & the merits of his passion,
were not giuen to be derided and iested at, as they be in these filthie
playes and enterluds on stages & scaffolds, or to be mixt and interlaced with bawdry, wanton shewes, & vncomely gestures, as is vsed
(euery Man knoweth) in these playes and enterludes. . . . Doo these
Mockers and Flowters of his Maiesty, these dissembling *Hipocrites*,
and flattering *Gnatoes*, think to escape vnpunished ? beware, therfore,
you masking Players, you painted sepulchres, you doble dealing

ambodexters, be warned betymes, and, lik good computistes, cast your
accompts before, what wil be the reward therof in the end, least God
destroy you in his wrath : abuse God no more, corrupt his people
no longer with your dregges, and intermingle not his blessed word
with such prophane vanities. For at no hand it is not lawfull to
mixt scurrilitie with diuinitie, nor diuinitie with scurrilitie. . . . Vpon
the other side, if their playes be of prophane matters, than tend they
to the dishonor of God, and norishing of vice, both which are damnable.
So that whither they be the one or the other, they are quite contrarie
to the Word of grace, and sucked out of the Deuills teates to nourish
vs in ydolatrie, hethenrie, and sinne. And therfore they, cariyng the
note, or brand, of GOD his curse vppon their backs, which way soeuer
they goe, are to be hissed out of all Christian kingdomes, if they wil
haue Christ to dwell amongst them.' Quotes the Fathers and ancients
against *histriones*. P. 143. ' Then, seeing that Playes were first
inuented by the Deuil, practised by the heathen gentiles, and dedicat
to their false ydols, Goddes and Goddesses, as the howse, stage, and
apparell to *Venus*, the musicke to *Appollo*, the penning to *Minerua*
and the Muses, the action and pronuntiation to *Mercurie* and the
rest, it is more than manifest that they are no fit exercyses for
a Christen Man to follow. But if there were no euill in them saue
this, namely, that the arguments of tragedies is anger, wrath, im-
munitie, crueltie, iniurie, incest, murther, & such like, the Persons
or Actors are Goddes, Goddesses, Furies, Fyends, Hagges, Kings,
Queenes, or Potentates. Of Commedies the matter and ground is
loue, bawdrie, cosenage, flattery, whordome, adulterie ; the Persons,
or agents, whores, queanes, bawdes, scullions, knaues, Curtezans,
lecherous old men, amorous yong men, with such like of infinit varietie.
If, I say, there were nothing els but this, it were sufficient to with-
draw a good christian from the vsing of them ; For so often as they
goe to those howses where Players frequent, thei go to *Venus* pallace,
& sathans synagogue [*in margin*, ' Theaters and curtaines Venus
pallaces '], to worship deuils, & betray Christ Iesus.' To say that
plays are ' as good as sermons ' is to say that ' the Deuill is equipolent
with the Lord '. P. 144. ' There is no mischief which these plaies
maintain not. For do they not norish ydlenes ? and *otia dant vitia*,
ydlenes is the Mother of vice. Doo they not draw the people from
hering the word of God, from godly Lectures and sermons ? for you
shall haue them flocke thither, thick & threefould, when the church
of God shalbe bare & emptie. . . . Do they not maintaine bawdrie,
infinit folery, & renue the remembrance of hethen ydolatrie ? Do
they not induce whordom & vnclennes ? nay, are they not rather
plaine deuourers of maydenly virginitie and chastitie ? For proofe
wherof, but marke the flocking and running to Theaters & curtens,
daylie and hourely, night and daye, tyme and tyde, to see Playes
and Enterludes ; where such wanton gestures, such bawdie speaches,
such laughing and fleering, such kissing and bussing, such clipping
and culling, Suche winckinge and glancinge of wanton eyes, and the
like, is vsed, as is wonderfull to behold. Then, these goodly pageants

being done, euery mate sorts to his mate, euery one bringes another
homeward of their way verye freendly, and in their secret conclaues
(couertly) they play the *Sodomits*, or worse. And these be the fruits
of Playes or Enterluds for the most part. And wheras you say there
are good Examples to be learned in them, Trulie so there are : if you
will learne falshood ; if you will learn cosenage ; if you will learn to
deceiue ; if you will learn to play the Hipocrit, to cogge, lye, and
falsifie ; if you will learne to iest, laugh, and fleer, to grin, to nodd,
and mow ; if you will learn to playe the vice, to swear, teare, and
blaspheme both Heauen ahd Earth : If you will learn to become
a bawde, vncleane, and to deuerginat Maydes, to deflour honest
Wyues : if you will learne to murther, slaie, kill, picke, steal, robbe,
and roue : If you will learn to rebel against Princes, to commit
treasons, to consume treasurs, to practise ydlenes, to sing and talke
of bawdie loue and venery ; if you will lerne to deride, scoffe, mock,
& flowt, to flatter & smooth : If you will learn to play the whore-
maister, the glutton, Drunkard, or incestuous person : if you will
learn to become proude, hawtie, & arrogant ; and, finally, if you will
learne to contemne GOD and al his lawes, to care nither for heauen
nor hel, and to commit al kinde of sinne and mischeef, you need to
goe to no other schoole, for all these good Examples may you see
painted before your eyes in enterludes and playes : wherfore that
man who giueth money for the maintenance of them must needs
incurre the damage of *premunire*, that is, eternall damnation, except
they repent. For the Apostle biddeth vs beware, least wee communicat with other mens sinnes ; & this their dooing is not only to
communicat with other mens sinnes, & maintain euil to the destruction
of them selues & many others, but also a maintaining of a great sorte
of idle lubbers, and buzzing dronets, to suck vp and deuoure the good
honie, wherupon the poor bees should liue.' Exhorts ' all players
& Founders of plaies and enterluds ' to leave their life. P. 146.
' Away therfore with this so infamous an art ! for goe they neuer so
braue, yet are they counted and taken but for beggers. And is it
not true ? liue they not vpon begging of euery one that comes ? Are
they not taken by the lawes of the Realm for roagues and vacaboundes?
I speak of such as trauaile the Cuntries with playes & enterludes,
making an occupation of it, and ought so to be punished, if they had
their deserts.' *Lords of Mis-rule in Ailgna. . . . The Manner of
Church-ales in Ailgna. . . . The maner of keeping of Wakesses, and
feasts in Ailgna. . . . The horrible Vice of pestiferous Dauncing, vsed
in Ailgna. . . . Of Musick in Ailgna, and how it allureth to vanitie. . . .
Beare baiting and other exercyses, vsed unlawfully in Ailgna.* P. 177.
' These Hethnicall exercyses vpon the Sabaoth day, which the Lord
hath consecrat to holy vses, for the glory of his Name, and our
spirituall comfort, are not in any respect tollerable, or to be suffered.
For is not the baiting of a Bear, besides that it is a filthie, stinking,
and lothsome game, a daungerous & perilous exercyse ? wherein
a man is in daunger of his life euery minut of an houre ; which thing,
though it weare not so, yet what exercyse is this meet for any

Christian? what christen heart can take pleasure to see one poore beast to rent, teare, and kill another, and all for his foolish pleasure? ... And, to be plaine, I thinke the Deuill is the Maister of the game, bearward and all.' *A Fearfull Example of God his Iudgement vpon the prophaners of his Sabaoth.* P. 179. Describes the accident of 13 Jan. 1583, with the page-heading, 'A wofull cry at Syrap garden'. 'So that either two or three hundred men, women, and children (by estimation), wherof seuen were killed dead, some were wounded, some lamed, and othersome brused and crushed almost to the death.' *A fearfull Iudgement of God, shewed at the Theaters.* P. 180. 'The like Iudgement (almost) did the Lord shew vnto them a litle befor, being assembled at their Theaters, to see their bawdie enterluds and other trumperies practised: For he caused the earth mightely to shak and quauer, as though all would haue fallen down; wherat the People, sore amazed, some leapt down (from the top of the turrets, pinacles, and towres, wher they stood) to the ground; wherof some had their legs broke, some their arms, some their backs, some hurt one where, some another, and many sore crusht and brused; but not any but they went away sore affraid, & wounded in conscience. And yet can neither the one nor the other fray them from these diuelish exercyses, vntill the Lorde consume them all in his wrath; *which God forbid!* The Lord of his mercie open the eyes of the maiestrats to pluck down these places of abuse, that god may be honored and their consciences disburthened.'

xxxiii. 1583. GERVASE BABINGTON.

[From *A very Fruitful Exposition of the Commandements by way of Questions and Answers* (1583), 316. More general references to the evils of plays and bear-baiting are on pp. 190, 385. Babington was Fellow of Trinity College, Cambridge, and tutor in the Earl of Pembroke's house at Wilton; he afterwards became Bishop successively of Llandaff, Exeter, and Worcester.]

These prophane & wanton stage playes or interludes: what an occasion they are of adulterie and vncleanenesse, by gesture, by speech, by conueyances, and deuices to attaine to so vngodly desires, the world knoweth with too much hurt by long experience. Vanities they are if we make the best of them. ... But I referre you to them, that vpon good knowledge of the abominations of them, haue written largely & wel against them. If they be dangerous on the day time, more daungerous on the night certainely: if on a stage, & in open courtes, much more in chambers and priuate houses. For there are manie roumes beside that where the play is, & peraduenture the strangenes of the place & lacke of light to guide them, causeth errour in their way, more than good Christians should in their houses suffer.

xxxiv. 1583 (?). Philip Sidney.

[From *The Defence of Poesie* (1595, William Ponsonby ; S. R. 29 Nov. 1594), reprinted as *An Apologie for Poetrie* (1595, Henry Olney), and with 1598 and later editions of *Arcadia*. Among many modern editions are those by E. Arber (1868), E. Flügel (1889), A. S. Cook (1890), E. S. Schuckburgh (1891), J. C. Collins (1907), and in Gregory Smith (1904), i. 148. The date 1583 is conjecturally assigned by Cook on the ground of the stylistic development since the *Arcadia* (1580–3). But any date is possible between 1579, when Gosson's *School of Abuse*, which probably stimulated it, and Spenser's *Faerie Queene*, which it mentions, appeared, and Nov. 1585, when Sidney went to the Low Countries. The book contains a general valuation of poetry, on humanistic lines, together with a criticism of English poetry in particular. Only a few pages are devoted to the drama.]

P. 44. ' Perchance it is the Comick, whom naughtie Play-makers and Stage-keepers, have iustly made odious. To the argument of abuse, I will answer after. Onely thus much now is to be said, that the Comedy is an imitation of the common errors of our life, which he representeth, in the most ridiculous and scornefull sort that may be. So as it is impossible, that any beholder can be content to be such a one. . . . So that the right vse of Comedy will (I thinke) by no body be blamed, and much lesse of the high and excellent Tragedy, that openeth the greatest wounds, and sheweth forth the Vlcers, that are couered with Tissue : that maketh Kinges feare to be Tyrants, and Tyrants manifest their tirannicall humors : that with sturring the affects of admiration and commiseration, teacheth, the vncertainety of this world, and vpon how weake foundations guilden roofes are builded. . . . But it is not the Tragedy they doe mislike : For it were too absurd to cast out so excellent a representation of whatsoeuer is most worthy to be learned.' P. 50. Answers criticisms of poetry as the ' Nurse of abuse ', &c. P. 63. Criticizes ' Our Tragedies and Comedies (not without cause cried out against) '. Even in *Gorboduc*, much more in other plays, the unities are disregarded (cf. quotations in ch. xix). ' Besides these gross absurdities, how all theyr Playes be neither right Tragedies, nor right Comedies : mingling Kings and Clownes ' in a ' mungrell Tragy-comedie. . . . Our Comedians thinke there is no delight without laughter. . . . Delight hath a ioy in it, either permanent, or present. Laughter, hath onely a scornful tickling. . . . But I haue lauished out too many wordes of this play matter. I doe it because as they are excelling parts of Poesie, so is there none so much vsed in England, and none can be more pittifully abused.'

xxxv. 1584. Thomas Lodge.

[From *An Alarum against Usurers* (1584 ; S. R. 4 Nov. 1583), edited with *Defence of Poetry* by D. Laing (1853, *Sh. Soc.*).]

[Extract from Epistle to Inns of Court.] ' About three yeres ago, one Stephen Gosson published a booke, intituled *The Schoole of Abuse*, in which having escaped in many and sundry conclusions, I, as the

occasion then fitted me, shapt him such an answere as beseemed his
discourse ; which by reason of the slendernes of the subject, (because
it was in defence of plaies and play makers) the godly and reverent
that had to deale in the cause, misliking it, forbad the publishing :
notwithstanding he, comming by a private unperfect coppye, about
two yeres since made a reply, dividing it into five sections, and in
his Epistle dedicatory, to the right honorable, Sir Frances Walsingham,
he impugneth me with these reproches, that I am become a vagarant
person, visited by the hevy hand of God, lighter than libertie, and
looser than vanitie.' He proceeds to call Gosson an ' untamed
curtail ' and an ' injurious Asinius '.

xxxvi. 1584. GEORGE WHETSTONE.

[From *A Touchstone for the Time*, printed as an ' Addition ' to *A Mirour
for Magestrates of Cyties* (1584).]

The tract is mainly on gaming. P. 24. ' The godly Divines, in
public sermons, and others in printed books, have (of late) very
sharply inveighed against Stage-plays (unproperly called, Tragedies,
Comedies, and Morals), as the springs of many vices, and the stumbling-
blocks of godliness and virtue. Truly the use of them upon the
Sabbath day, and the abuse of them at all times, with scurrility and
unchaste conveyance, ministred matter sufficient for them to blame,
and the Magistrate to reforme.'

xxxvii. 1586. WILLIAM WEBBE.

[From *A Discourse of English Poetrie* (1586), ed. Arber, 27 ; also in
Gregory Smith, i. 226. The promised expression of opinion (p. 42) is on
humanist lines.]

The profitte or discommoditie which aryseth by the vse of these
Comedies and Tragedies, which is most, hath beene long in con-
troversie, and is sore urged among us at these dayes : what I think
of the same, perhaps I shall breefely declare anon.

xxxviii. 1587. WILLIAM RANKINS.

[From *A Mirrour of Monsters : Wherein is plainely described the manifold vices & spotted enormities, that are caused by the infectious sight of
Playes, with the description of the subtile slights of Sathan, making them his
instruments.* Compiled by Wil. Rankins. Magna spes est inferni. Seene
and allowed. *I. C. for T. H.* 1587. The reference to Holywell suggests
that the author was the dramatist (cf. ch. xxiii).]

Describes the wedding of Fastus and Luxuria at the ' Chapell
Adulterinum ', near to Κοῖλοφρέαρ ' by interpretation from the Greeks
Hollow well [i.e. Holywell] where my selfe lulled in the lap of
Securitie, not long since was brought a sleepe by carelesse cogitations '.
The Chapel Adulterinum is ' the Theater and Curtine ' (4ᵛ). A
banquet and mask with torchbearers furnish an allegory of the vices
of players, and various allusions, to the fall of the Bear-garden (3),

to the 2d. payment for entrance (3ᵛ), to advertisements by drums
and trumpets (5) and bills (5ᵛ), to doorkeepers and boxholders (6ᵛ),
are commented on in marginal notes.

xxxix.   1588.   JOHN CASE.

[From *Sphaera Civitatis* (1588), a commentary on Aristotle's *Politics*
(*ad* v. 8 ; vii. 17).   A similar passage from the commentary on the *Ethics*
(iv. 8) in *Speculum Moralium Quaestionum* (1586), 183, is quoted by Boas,
228.   It is interesting to find from *The Christmas Prince*, 12 (cf.
ch. xxiv), that Case once served as lord of misrule at St. John's, Oxford.]

(a) *Lib. v, c. 8.*

Alia nunc dubitatio sequitur, Vtrum ludi chorique permittendi sunt
in ciuitate ? Memini me olim in Ethicis de his rebus obiter disputasse,
verum quoniam opportune se offert quaestio, abs re non erit eandem
paucissimis demonstrare : censeo ergo quibusdam adhibitis circum-
stantiis haec tolerari ac permitti debere ; non quod per se et vi sua
res vtiles, sed quod in moderato illorum vsu splendor comitatis (quae
virtus minima non est) manifeste apparet.   Sunt igitur ludi non inanes
et histrionicae fabulae, veneris illecebrae, sed facetae comoediae magni-
ficaeque tragaediae, in quibus expressa imago vitae morumque cernitur.
. . . Adhuc in his mores hominum depictos discere, praeclara inuenta
doctorum obseruare, temporum antiquorum caniciem cernere, vocem,
vultum, gestumque splendide componere, varios affectus et passiones
mouere, famam acquirere et comparare possumus [*in margin* : scenae
trigemina corona].   Cum ergo ex iis tot commoda existant, non solum
toleranda sed etiam iuste approbanda videntur.   Insuper antiquissimis
olim temporibus in omni praeclare instituta republica floruerunt ista :
ergo sunt licita. . . . Postremo his addi potest ratio quae est in textu,
nempe quod hoc modo potentiores viri quos timet ciuitas (coacti ad
ista edenda populo) elumbentur sedatioresque fiant.

(b) *Lib. vii, c. 17.*

Tertium est vt parentes suos liberos diligenter custodiant, et arceant
ab audiendis, videndis, spectandis, malis sermonibus, obscoenis idolis
Veneris, vanis spectaculis leuissimorum histrionum, qui plusquam
ridiculas ne dicam impias fabellas huc illuc vagabundi agunt.   Hic
opportunè monendi sunt illi, qui suos infantulos iurare et conuitiari
docent, qui simulachra Veneris intuenda, artemque amandi perdi-
scendam suis filiolis proponunt, qui denique ad theatra plena Veneris,
plena vanitatis illos non solum ire permittunt sed etiam alliciunt.
Non hic omnes ludos omnesque histriones praesertim hystoricos,
tragicos, et si placet comicos (modò sint verè faceti) condemno :
quippè Aristoteles hoc loco Theodorum quendam peritum tragoediarum actorem laudat, Cicero suum laudauit Roscium, nos Angli
Tarletonum, in cuius voce et vultu omnes iocosi affectus, in cuius
cerebroso capite lepidae facetiae habitant.

xl. 1588–90. MARTIN MARPRELATE CONTROVERSY.

[The texts of the Marprelate pamphlets have been edited by W. Pierce, *The Marprelate Tracts* (1911) ; some were reprinted earlier by E. Arber and in J. Petheram, *Puritan Discipline Tracts* (1842–60). The best accounts of this ribald controversy on Church government are E. Arber, *An Introductory Sketch to the Martin Marprelate Controversy* (1879) ; W. Pierce, *Historical Introduction to the Marprelate Tracts* (1908) ; J. D. Wilson, *The Marprelate Controversy* (1909, *C. H.* iii. 374), and *Martin Marprelate and Shakespeare's Fluellen* (1912) ; R. B. McKerrow, *Works of Nashe*, v (1910), 34, 184 ; G. Bonnard, *La Controverse de Martin Marprelate* (1916). It seems probable that Martin was a composite personality ; Sir Roger Williams, John Penry, and Job Throckmorton may all have had a share in the pamphlets. The replies were inspired by Richard Bancroft, then Canon of Westminster and a member of the High Commission. It seems clear that both Lyly and Nashe took part in them, and *Pappe with an Hatchet* may reasonably be ascribed to Lyly. Nashe has often been regarded as Pasquil, but Mr. McKerrow does not think that any of the pamphlets can be supposed with any certainty to be his ; he probably contributed to the lost plays. Of these Bonnard, 92, would distinguish five—(*a*) Martin anatomized, (*b*) the May Game of Martinism, (*c*) Martin carried to hell, as a vice, (*d*) Martin as cock, ape, and wolf, (*e*) Martin ravishing Divinity ; but (*b*) seems to be referred to as a forthcoming pamphlet rather than as a play, and of the others (*d*) and (*e*) almost certainly, and possibly all four, were episodes in the same piece. F. Bacon in his *Advertisement Touching the Controversies* (*Works*, viii. 74), written in the summer of 1589, criticizes the episcopal policy of answering like by like, and ' this immodest and deformed manner of writing lately entertained, whereby matters of religion are handled in the style of the stage '.]

(*a*)

[From *The Epistle to the Terrible Priests of the Confocation House* (Oct.–Nov. 1588), 11, 19, reprinted by E. Arber (1880) ; also by J. Petheram (1842) in *Puritan Discipline Tracts* (Martinist).]

Sohow, brother Bridges [John Bridges, Dean of Salisbury] . . . you haue bin a worthy writer as they say of a long time, your first book was a proper Enterlude, called Gammar Gurtons needle. But I think that this trifle, which sheweth the author to haue had some witte and inuention in him, was none of your doing : Because your bookes seeme to proceede from the braynes of a woodcocke as hauing neyther wit nor learning. . . . What if I should report abroad, that cleargie men come vnto their promotions by Simonie ? haue not you giuen me iuste cause ? I thinke Simonie be the bishops lacky. Tarleton tooke him not long since in Don Iohn [Aylmer] of Londons cellor.

(*b*)

[From *A Whip for an Ape : Or Martin displaied* (Apr. 1589), 53, 133, in Bond, *Lyly*, iii. 417 (Anti-Martinist).]

Now *Tarleton's* dead, the Consort lackes a vice :
For knaue and foole thou maist beare pricke and price.

   .   .   .   .

And ye graue men that answer *Martins* mowes,
   He mockes the more, and you in vaine loose times :
Leaue Apes to dogges to baite, their skins to crowes,
   And let old *Lanam* lash him with his rimes.

(c)

[From *Anti-Martinus, siue Monitio cuiusdam Londinensis, ad Adolescentes utriusque Academiae*, signed A. L. (1589; S. R. 3 July 1589), 59 (Anti-Martinist).]

Libros autem *Martini* qui legit, nihil aliud reperiet, quam perpetuatum conuitium ; sic autem vibratum, vt facile videas ad huiusmodi scurrilitates conquirendas, totam eius vitam theatris illis Londinensibus, & leuissimis scenis, vel scurrarum & nepotum circulis insidiatam.

(d)

[From *Theses Martinianae, or Martin Junior* (c. 22 July 1589), sig. D ij (Martinist).]

' There bee that affirme the rimers and stage-players to haue cleane putte you out of countenaunce . . . the stage-players, poore rogues, are not so much to be blamed, if being stage-players, that is plaine rogues (saue onely for their liueries) they in the action of dealing against Maister Martin, have gotten them many thousande eie witnesses, of their wittelesse and pittifull conceites.' The writer condoles with those who ' for one poor penny ' play ' ignominious fools for an hour or two together '. Martin may ' contemn such kennel-rakers and scullions as have sold themselves ' to be laughed at as ' a company of disguised asses '.

(e)

[From *Martins Months Minde* (Aug. 1589), in Grosart, *Nashe*, i. 164, 166, 175, 177, 180, 189 (Anti-Martinist).]

To the Reader. ' *Roscius* pleades in the Senate house ; Asses play vpon harpes ; the Stage is brought into the Church ; and vices make plaies of Churche matters. . . . These Iigges and Rimes, haue nipt the father [Martin] in the head & kild him cleane, seeing that hee is ouertaken in his owne *foolerie*. And this hath made the yong youthes his sonnes, to chafe and fret aboue measure, especiallie with the Plaiers, (their betters in all respects, both in wit, and honestie) whom sauing their *liueries* (for indeede they are hir Maiesties men, and these not so much as hir good subiects) they call *Rogues,* for playing their enterludes, and Asses for trauelling *all daie for a pennie* [*in margin,* Martin the vice condemneth the Plaiers, Eigulus, sigulum]. . . . *A true report of the death and buriall of Martin Marprelate.* . . . *Martin* . . . being . . . sundrie waies verie curstlie handled ; as . . . wormd and launced, that he tooke verie grieuouslie, to be made a *Maygame* vpon the *Stage* [*in margin,* The Theater] . . . as he saw that . . . euerie stage Plaier made a iest of him . . . fell into a feauer. . . . *Martin,* . . . calling his sonnes . . . said . . . I perceiue that euerie stage plaier, if he play the foole but two houres together, hath somewhat for his labour : and I . . . nothing. . . . [The common people are] now wearie of our state mirth, that for a penie, may haue farre better by oddes at the Theater and Curtaine, and any blind playing house euerie day. . . . In lept I . . . with . . . twittle tattles; that indeede I had learned in Alehouses, and at the Theater of Lanam and his fellowes.

. . . These gambols (my sonnes) are implements for the Stage, and
beseeme Iesters, and Plaiers, but are not fit for *Church plotters*. . . .
Afterwards ensued his bequestes, in manner and forme following . . .
Item, all my foolerie I bequeath to my good friend Lanam ; and his
consort, of whom I first had it.'

(*f*)

[From *A Countercuffe giuen to Martin Iunior* : . . . *by Pasquill of England*
(Aug. 1589), in McKerrow, *Nashe*, i. 59 (Anti-Martinist).]

The Anotamie latelie taken of him, the blood and the humors that
were taken from him, by launcing and worming him at *London* vpon
the common Stage . . . are euident tokens, that beeing thorow soust
in so many showres, hee had no other refuge but to runne into a hole,
and die as he liued, belching.

(*g*)

[From *The Protestatyon of Martin Marprelat* (1589, before 20 Oct.), 25
(Martinist).]

Then among al the rimers and stage plaiers, which my Ll. of the
cleargy had suborned against me I remember Mar-Martin, Iohn a Cant.
his hobbie-horse, was to his reproche, newly put out of the Morris,
take it how he will ; with a flat discharge for euer shaking his shins
about a May-pole againe while he liued.

(*h*)

[From *The Returne of the renowned Caualiero Pasquill of England* (*c*. 20 Oct.
1589) in McKerrow, *Nashe*, i. 82, 92, 100 (Anti-Martinist).]

Howe whorishlie Scriptures are alleaged by them, I will discouer
(by Gods helpe) in another new worke which I haue in hand, and
intituled it, *The May-game of Martinisme*. Verie defflie set out, with
Pompes, Pagents, Motions, Maskes, Scutchions, Emblems, Impreases,
strange trickes, and deuises, betweene the Ape and the Owle, the like
was neuer yet seene in Paris-garden. *Penry* the welchman is the
foregallant of the Morrice, with the treble belles, shot through the
wit with a Woodcocks bill : I woulde not for the fayrest horne-beast
in all his Countrey, that the Church of England were a cup of Methe-
glin, and came in his way when he is ouer-heated ; euery Bishopricke
woulde prooue but a draught, when the Mazer is at his nose. *Martin*
himselfe is the Mayd-marian, trimlie drest vppe in a cast Gowne, and
a Kercher of Dame *Lawsons*, his face handsomlie muffled with a Diaper-
napkin to couer his beard, and a great Nosegay in his hande, of the
principalest flowers I could gather out of all hys works. *Wiggenton*
daunces round about him in a Cotten-coate, to court him with
a Leatherne pudding, and a woodden Ladle. *Paget* marshalleth the
way, with a couple of great clubbes, one in his foote, another in his
head, & he cryes to the people with a loude voice, *Beware of the Man
whom God hath markt*. I can not yet find any so fitte to come lagging
behind, with a budget on his necke, to gather the deuotion of the
lookers on, as the stocke-keeper of the Bridewel-house of Canterburie ;

he must carrie the purse, to defray their charges, and then hee may be sure to serue himselfe. . . . Methought *Vetus Comœdia* beganne to pricke him at London in the right vaine, when shee brought foorth *Diuinitie* wyth a scratcht face, holding of her hart as if she were sicke, because *Martin* would haue forced her, but myssing of his purpose, he left the print of his nayles vppon her cheekes, and poysoned her with a vomit which he ministred vnto her, to make her cast vppe her dignities and promotions. . . . Who commeth yonder *Marforius*, can you tell me ? MARFORIUS. By her gate and her Garland I knowe her well, it is *Vetus Comœdia.* She hath been so long in the Country, that she is somewhat altred : this is she that called in a counsell of Phisitians about *Martin*, and found by the sharpnes of his humour, when they had opened the vaine that feedes his head, that hee would spit out his lunges within one yeere. . . . PASQUIL. I haue a tale to tell her in her eare, of the slye practise that was vsed in restraining of her.

(i)

[From *Pappe with an Hatchet* (1589, end of Oct.) in Bond, *Lyly*, iii. 408 (Anti-Martinist).]

Sed heus tu, dic sodes, will they not bee discouraged for the common players ? Would these Comedies might be allowed to be plaid that are pend, and then I am sure he would be decyphered, and so perhaps discouraged.

He shall not bee brought in as whilom he was, and yet verie well, with a cocks combe, an apes face, a wolfs bellie, cats clawes, &c. but in a cap'de cloake, and all the best apparell he ware the highest day in the yeare. . . .

. . . Would it not bee a fine Tragedie, when *Mardocheus* shall play a Bishoppe in a Play, and *Martin Hamman*, and that he that seekes to pull downe those that are set in authoritie aboue him, should be hoysted vpon a tree aboue all other. [*In margin*] If it be shewed at Paules, it will cost you foure pence : at the Theater two pence : at Sainct Thomas a Watrings nothing.

(k)

[From G. Harvey, *An Advertisement for Papp-Hatchett* (1589, Nov. 5), printed with *Pierces Supererogation* (1593) and in Grosart, *Harvey*, ii. 131, 213 (Philo-Martinist).]

Had I bene Martin . . . it should haue beene one of my May-games, or August triumphes, to haue driuen Officials, Commissaries, Arch-deacons, Deanes, Chauncellors, Suffraganes, Bishops and Archbishops, (so Martin would have florished at the least) to entertaine such an odd, light-headded fellow for their defence ; a professed iester, a Hick-scorner, a scoff-maister, a playmunger, an Interluder ; once the foile of Oxford, now the stale of London, and euer the Apesclogge of the presse, *Cum Priuilegio perennitatis.* . . . I am threatened with a Bable, and Martin menaced with a Comedie : . . . All you, that tender the preseruation of your good names, were best to please Pap-hatchet, and fee Euphues betimes, for feare lesse he be mooued, or some One

of his Apes hired, to make a Playe of you ; and then is your credit
quite vn-done for euer, and euer : Such is the publique reputation
of their Playes. He must needes be *discouraged*, whom they *decipher*.
Better, anger an hundred other, then two such ; that haue the Stage
at commaundement, and can furnish-out Vices, and Diuels at their
pleasure.

(*l*)

[From *An Almond for a Parrat, Or Cutbert Curry-knaues Almes* (1590,
early), in McKerrow, *Nashe*, iii. 354 (Anti-Martinist).]

Therefore we must not measure of *Martin* as he is allied to *Elderton*
or tongd like *Will Tony*, as he was attired like an Ape on the Stage,
or sits writing of Pamphlets in some spare outhouse, but as he is
Mar-Prelat of England.

(*m*)

[From *The First parte of Pasquils Apologie . . . Printed where I was,
and where I will bee readie by the helpe of God and my Muse, to send you
the May-game of Martinisme for an intermedium, betweene the first and
seconde parte of the Apologie* (2 July 1590), in McKerrow, *Nashe*, i. 135
(Anti-Martinist). It may be doubted whether *The May-game of Martinism*
ever had an existence outside the allusions to it in these pamphlets.]

And when I haue sent you the *May-game of Martinisme*, at the
next setting my foote into the styrroppe after it, the signet shall be
giuen, and the fielde fought.

xli. 1589. RICHARD (?) PUTTENHAM.

[From *The Arte of English Poesie* (1589 ; S. R. 9 Nov. 1588), edited by
E. Arber (1869) ; also in J. Haslewood, *Ancient Critical Essays*, vol. i
(1811), and in part in Gregory Smith, ii. 1. On the author, cf. ch. xxiii.]

Most of the treatise (bks. ii, iii) deals with the technicalities of
poetic structure and style, which the author sometimes illustrates
from interludes and verses of his own. Bk. i praises poetry in general,
on familiar but non-controversial humanist lines, and discusses with
some classical erudition the origin of various types of poetry, as
tragedy, comedy, and pantomime (c. 11), comedy (c. 14), tragedy
(c. 15), staging (c. 17), pastoral (c. 18). In a brief account of English
poets (c. 31) occurs : ' But the principall man in this profession at the
same time [Edward's] was Maister Edward [*sic*] Ferrys a man of no
lesse mirth and felicitie that way, but of much more skil, and magnificence in his meeter, and therefore wrate for the most part to the
stage, in Tragedie and sometimes in Comedie or Enterlude, wherein
he gaue the king so much good recreation, as he had thereby many
good rewards. . . . Of the later sort I thinke thus. That for Tragedie,
the Lord of Buckhurst and Maister Edward Ferrys for such doings
as I haue sene of theirs do deserue the hyest price : Th' Earle of
Oxford and Maister Edwardes of her Maiesties Chappell for Comedy
and Enterlude.'

xlii. 1589. Thomas Nashe.

[From an epistle *To the Gentlemen Students of Both Universities*, prefixed to Robert Greene's *Menaphon* (1589 ; S. R. 23 Aug. 1589), reprinted from ed. 1610, which has some corrections possibly by Nashe, in McKerrow, iii. 311, with valuable notes (iv. 444) upon the allusions and supposed allusions. The suggestion of Collier that *Menaphon* was originally printed in 1587 appears to be baseless. Outside the three passages quoted, Nashe praises Watson's translation of *Antigone*. McKerrow's collection of material for the critical discussion of the epistle is so full that I need only compare briefly my conclusions with his. In (i) Nashe seems to me to be criticizing (*a*) ' tragedians ', which for me are clearly ' tragic actors ', while McKerrow inclines to make them ' writers of tragedy ', and (*b*) their dramatists, who include blank-verse ' Art-masters ', which I agree with McKerrow is more likely, in view of the fact that Greene above all flourished his University degree, to mean ' masters of their art ' than ' masters of Arts ', and translating tradesmen or serving-men with no education beyond a grammar-school. The slight suggestions that Nashe may have had Marlowe especially in mind are perhaps hardly sufficient to outweigh his statement in *Have with you to Saffron Walden* (1596) that he ' neuer abusd Marloe ' ; and Marlowe was a University man, and no tradesman or serving-man. On the other hand, there is no specific praise of Marlowe with other University poets in the epistle. The whole of (i) is a precise parallel to the following lines by Thomas Brabine, also prefixed to *Menaphon*:

' Come foorth you witts that vaunt the pompe of speach,
   And striue to thunder from a Stage-mans throate :
View *Menaphon* a note beyond your reach ;
   Whose sight will make your drumming descant doate :
Players auaunt, you know not to delight ;
Welcome sweete Shepheard ; worth a Schollers sight.'

In (ii) I am rather more inclined than McKerrow to think that the ' *Nouerint* ' and the ' Kidde in *Æsop* ' may glance at Kyd, who was not one of the University group, and was a grammarian, a translator, and very likely already a serving-man. But the attempts to trace him elsewhere in the passage come to very little ; nor is one playwright only necessarily in question, so that, although the ' handfuls of Tragicall speeches ' may point to a play of *Hamlet* as already extant in 1589, the inference that Kyd was its author becomes extremely thin. In (iii) Nashe attacks the players as parasitic on the poets, in terms closely resembling those used later by Greene in his *Groatsworth of Wit* (No. xlviii). Probably Roscius is here Alleyn, and Caesar stands for the poets in general. I do not agree with Fleay, *L. of S.* 10, 99, that the epistle reflects a rivalry between the poets of the Queen's men and those of Pembroke's, who indeed did not yet exist, or any other company. The issue is between the University poets on the one hand and the players and illiterate poets on the other.]

P. 311. ' I am not ignorant how eloquent our gowned age is grown of late ; so that euery mechanicall mate abhorres the English he was borne too, and plucks, with a solemne periphrasis, his *vt vales* from the inkehorne : which I impute, not so much to the perfection of Arts, as to the seruile imitation of vainglorious Tragedians, who contend not so seriously to excell in action, as to embowell the cloudes in a speech of comparison, thinking themselues more than initiated in Poets immortality, if they but once get *Boreas* by the beard and the heauenly Bull by the deaw-lap. But heerein I cannot so fully bequeath them to folly, as their ideot Art-masters, that intrude themselues to our eares as the Alcumists of eloquence, who (mounted on the stage of arrogance) think to out-braue better pennes with the swelling bumbast of a bragging blanke verse. Indeede it may bee the ingrafted ouerflow of some kil-cow conceit, that ouercloyeth their imagination with a more than drunken resolution, being not extemporall in the inuention of any other meanes to vent their manhoode, commits the disgestion of their cholericke incumbrances to the spacious volubilitie of a drumming decasillabon. Mongst this kind of men that repose eternitie in the mouth of a Player, I can but ingrosse some deep read Grammarians, who, hauing no more learning in their skull than will serue to take vp a commoditie, nor Art in their braine than was nourished in a seruing mans idlenesse, will take vppon them to be the ironicall Censors of all, when God and Poetrie doth know they are the simplest of all. To leaue these to the mercy of their Mother tongue, that feed on nought but the crums that fall from the Translators trencher, I come (sweet friend) to thy *Arcadian Menaphon*, . . .' P. 315. 'I'le turne backe to my first text of Studies of delight, and talke a little in friendship with a few of our triuiall translators. It is a common practise now a dayes amongst a sort of shifting companions, that runne through euery Art and thriue by none, to leaue the trade of *Nouerint*, whereto they were borne, and busie themselues with the indeuours of Art, that could scarcely Latinize their neck verse if they should haue neede ; yet English *Seneca* read by Candlelight yeelds many good sentences, as *Blood is a begger*, and so forth ; and if you intreate him faire in a frostie morning, hee will affoord you whole *Hamlets*, I should say handfuls of Tragicall speeches. But O griefe ! *Tempus edax rerum*, whats that will last alwayes ? The Sea exhaled by droppes will in continuance bee drie, and *Seneca*, let blood line by line and page by page, at length must needes die to our Stage ; which makes his famished followers to imitate the Kidde in *Æsop*, who, enamoured with the Foxes newfangles, forsooke all hopes of life to leape into a newe occupation ; and these men, renouncing all possibilities of credite or estimation, to intermeddle with Italian Translations : wherein how poorely they haue plodded, (as those that are neither prouenzall men, nor are able to distinguish of Articles,) let all indifferent Gentlemen that haue trauailed in that tongue discerne by their two-pennie pamphlets : & no maruell though their home borne mediocritie bee such in this matter ; for what can bee hoped of those that thrust *Elisium* into hell, and haue not learned, so long as they haue liued in the Spheres, the iust measure of the Horizon without an hexameter ? Sufficeth them to bodge vp a blanke verse with ifs and ands, and otherwhile for recreation after their Candle-stuffe, hauing starched their beards most curiously, to make a Peripateticall path into the inner parts of the Citie, and spend two or three howers in turning ouer French *Doudie*, where they attract more infection in one minute, then they can do eloquence all daies of their life, by conuersing with any Authors of like argument.' P. 323. 'There are extant about *London* many most able men to reuiue Poetry . . . as, for example, *Mathew Roydon, Thomas Atchelow,* and *George Peele* ; the first of whom, as he hath shewed himselfe singular in the immortall Epitaph of his beloued *Astrophell*, besides many other most absolute Comike inuentions (made more publike by euery mans praise, than they can be by my speech), so the second hath more than once or twice manifested his deepe witted schollership in places of credite : and for the last, though not the least of them all, I dare commend him to all that know him, as the chiefe supporter of pleasance now liuing, the *Atlas* of Poetrie, and *primus verborum Artifex* : whose first increase, the arraignement of *Paris*, might pleade to your opinions his pregnant dexterity of wit, and manifold varietie of inuention ; where in (*me iudice*) he goeth a steppe beyond all that write. Sundry other sweete gentlemen I know, that haue vaunted their pennes in priuate deuices, and tricked vp a company of taffata fooles with their feathers, whose beauty if our Poets had not peecte with the supply of their periwigs, they might haue antickt it vntill this time vp and downe the Countrey with the King of *Fairies*, and dined euery day at the pease porredge ordinary with *Delphrigus*. But *Tolossa* hath forgot that it was sometime sacked, and beggars that euer they carried their fardels on footback : and in truth no meruaile, when as the deserued reputation of one *Roscius* is of force to enrich a rabble of counterfets ; yet let subiects for all their insolence dedicate a *De profundis* euery morning to the preseruation of their *Caesar*, least their increasing indignities returne them ere long to their iugling to mediocrity, and they bewaile in weeping blankes the wane of their *Monarchie*.'

xliii. 1590. ROBERT GREENE.

[From *Francescos Fortunes : Or, The second part of Greenes Neuer too Late* (1590), reprinted in *Works*, viii. 111. For the Roscius story, cf. No. xii and ch. xi.]

P. 129. A palmer, telling the tale of Francesco, which contains some probably autobiographical matter on the hero's writing for the stage (cf. ch. xxiii, s.v. Greene), is interrupted by a request for his ' iudgement of Playes, Playmakers and Players '. After observing that ' some for being too lauish against that facultie, haue for their satiricall inuectiues been well canuased ', he sketches the growth of comedy at Athens and Rome, where ' couetousnesse crept into the qualitie ' and ' the Actors, by continuall vse grewe not onely excellent, but rich and insolent '. This is illustrated (p. 132) by a rebuke of Cicero to Roscius, ' Why *Roscius*, art thou proud with *Esops* Crow, being pranct with the glorie of others feathers ? of thy selfe thou canst say nothing, and if the Cobler hath taught thee to say Aue Caesar, disdain not thy tutor, because thou pratest in a Kings chamber : what sentence thou vtterest on the stage, flowes from the censure of our wittes, and what sentence or conceipte of the inuention the people applaud for excellent, that comes from the secrets of our knowledge. I graunt your action, though it be a kind of mechanical labour ; yet wel done tis worthie of praise : but you worthlesse, if for so small a toy you waxe proud '. *Publius Seruilius* also bade a player ' bee not so bragge of thy silken roabes, for I sawe them but yesterday make a great shew in a broakers shop '. The palmer concludes, ' Thus sir haue you heard my opinion briefly of plaies, that Menander deuised them for the suppressing of vanities, necessarie in a common wealth, as long as they are vsed in their right kind ; the play makers worthy of honour for their Arte : & players, men deseruing both prayse and profite, as long as they wax neither couetous nor insolent '.

xliv. 1591. SAMUEL COX.

[This letter of 15 Jan. 1591 to an unknown correspondent, brother of one Mr. Lewin, occurs with other letters by Cox in the letter-book of Sir Christopher Hatton (Nicolas, *Hatton*, xxix), to whom he was secretary.]

Has his letter ' reprehending me in some sort for my·sharpness against the use of plays '. Cites view of Fathers, especially Chrysostom. Regrets present toleration of ' these dangerous schools of licentious liberty, whereunto more people resort than to sermons or prayers '. Now ' rich men give more to a player for a song which he shall sing in one hour, than to their faithful servants for serving them a whole year. . . . I could wish that players would use themselves nowadays, as in ancient former times they have done, which was only to exercise their interludes in the time of Christmas, beginning to play in the holidays and continuing until twelfth tide, or at the furthest until Ashwednesday, of which players I find three sorts of people : the first, such as were in wages with the king and played before him some time at Hallowmass, and then in the later holidays until twelfthtide, and after that, only in Shrovetide ; and these men had other trades to live of, and seldom or never played abroad at any other times of the whole year. The second sort were such as pertained to noblemen, and were ordinary servants in their house, and only for Christmas times used such plays, without making profession to be players to go abroad for gain, for in such cases they were subject to the statute against retainers. The third sort were certain artisans in good towns and great parishes, as shoemakers, tailors, and such like, that used to play either in their town-halls, or some time in churches, to make the people merry ; where it was lawful for all persons to come without exacting any money for their access, having only somewhat gathered of the richer sort by the churchwardens for their apparel and other necessaries.'

xlv. 1591. SIR JOHN HARINGTON.

[From *A Preface, or rather a Briefe Apologie of Poetrie, and of the Author and Translator*, prefixed to Harington's translation of Ariosto's *Orlando Furioso* (1591), reprinted in Gregory Smith, ii. 194.]

Harington upholds poetry on humanist lines, and answers the objections of Cornelius Agrippa. P. 209. ' The last reproofe is lightnes & wantonnes. . . . First, the Tragicall is meerly free from it, as representing onely the cruell and lawlesse proceedings of Princes, mouing nothing but pitie or detestation. The Comicall, whatsoeuer foolish playmakers make it offend in this kind, yet being rightly vsed, it represents them so as to make the vice scorned and not embraced. . . . And for Tragedies, to omit other famous Tragedies, that that was played at *S. Iohns* in Cambridge, of *Richard the 3*, would moue (I thinke) *Phalaris* the tyraunt, and terrifie all tyrannous minded men from following their foolish ambitious humors, seeing how his ambition made him kill his brother, his nephews, his wife, beside infinit others, and, last of all, after a short and troublesome raigne, to end his miserable life, and to haue his body harried after his death. Then, for Comedies, how full of harmeles myrth is our Cambridge *Pedantius* ? and the Oxford *Bellum Grammaticale* ? or, to speake of a London Comedie, how much good matter, yea and matter of state, is there in that Comedie cald the play of the Cards, in which it is showed how foure Parasiticall knaues robbe the foure principall vocations of the Realme, *videl*, the vocation of Souldiers, Schollers, Marchants, and Husbandmen ? Of which Comedie I cannot forget the saying of a notable wise counseller that is now dead, who when some (to sing *Placebo*) aduised that it should be forbidden, because it was somewhat too plaine, and indeed as the old saying is, *sooth boord is no boord*, yet he would haue it allowed, adding it was fit that *They which doe that they should not should heare that they would not.*'

xlvi. 1592. THOMAS NASHE.

[From *Pierce Penilesse his Supplication to the Diuell* (1592 ; S. R. 8 Aug. 1592), reprinted in McKerrow, i. 149.]

[Extracts.] P. 211. 'There is a certaine waste of the people for whome there is no vse, but warre : and these men must haue some employment still to cut them off. . . . To this effect, the pollicie of Playes is very necessary, howsoeuer some shallow-braind censurers (not the deepest serchers into the secrets of gouernment) mightily oppugne them. For whereas the after-noone beeing the idlest time of the day ; wherein men that are their owne masters (as Gentlemen of the Court, the Innes of the Courte, and the number of Captaines and Souldiers about *London*) do wholy bestow themselues vpon pleasure, and that pleasure they deuide (howe vertuously it skils not) either into gameing, following of harlots, drinking, or seeing a Playe : is it not then better (since of foure extreames all the world cannot keepe them but they will choose one) that they should betake them to the least, which is Playes ? Nay, what if I prooue Playes to be no extreame ; but a rare exercise of vertue ? First, for the subiect of them (for the most part) it is borrowed out of our English Chronicles, wherein our forefathers valiant acts (that haue line long buried in rustie brasse and worme-eaten bookes) are reuiued, and they themselues raised from the Graue of Obliuion, and brought to pleade their aged Honours in open presence : than which, what can be a sharper reproofe to these degenerate effeminate dayes of ours ? How would it haue ioyed braue *Talbot* (the terror of the French) to thinke that

after he had lyne two hundred yeares in his Tombe, hee should
triumphe againe on the Stage, and haue his bones newe embalmed
with the teares of ten thousand spectators at least (at seuerall times)
who, in the Tragedian that represents his person, imagine they behold
him fresh bleeding ? I will defend it against any Collian, or clubfisted
Vsurer of them all, there is no immortalitie can be giuen a man on
earth like vnto Playes. . . . All Artes to them are vanitie : and, if
you tell them what a glorious thing it is to haue *Henrie* the fifth
represented on the Stage, leading the French King prisoner, and
forcing both him and the Dolphin to sweare fealty, I, but (will they
say) what do we get by it ? Respecting neither the right of Fame
that is due to true Nobilitie deceased, nor what hopes of eternitie
are to be proposed to aduentrous mindes, to encourage them forward,
but onely their execrable luker, and fillthie vnquenchable auarice.
They know when they are dead they shall not be brought vpon the
Stage for any goodnes, but in a merriment of the Vsurer and the Diuel,
or buying Armes of the Herald, who giues them the Lyon, without
tongue, tayle, or tallents, because his maister whome hee must serue
is a Townesman, and a man of peace, and must not keepe any
quarrelling beasts to annoy his honest neighbours. In Playes, all
coosonages, all cunning drifts ouer-guylded with outward holinesse,
all stratagems of warre, all the cankerwormes that breede on the rust
of peace, are most liuely anatomiz'd : they shewe the ill successe of
treason, the fall of hastie climbers, the wretched end of vsurpers, the
miserie of ciuill dissention, and how iust God is euermore in punishing
of murther. . . . Whereas some Petitioners of the Counsaile against
them obiect, they corrupt the youth of the Cittie, and withdrawe
Prentises from theyr worke ; they heartily wishe they might bee
troubled with none of their youth nor their prentises ; for some of
them (I meane the ruder handicrafts seruants) neuer come abroade,
but they are in danger of vndoing : and as for corrupting them when
they come, thats false ; for no Play they haue, encourageth any man
to tumult or rebellion, but layes before such the halter and the
gallowes ; or praiseth or approoueth pride, lust, whoredome, prodigalitie, or drunkennes, but beates them downe vtterly. As for the
hindrance of Trades and Traders of the Citie by them, that is an
Article foysted in by the Vintners, Alewiues, and Victuallers, who
surmise, if there were no Playes, they should haue all the companie
that resort to them, lye bowzing and beere-bathing in their houses
euery after-noone. . . . Our Players are not as the players beyond
Sea, a sort of squirting baudie Comedians, that haue whores and
common Curtizens to playe womens partes, and forbeare no immodest
speech or vnchast action that may procure laughter ; but our Sceane
is more statelye furnisht than euer it was in the time of *Roscius*,
our representations honourable, and full of gallant resolution, not
consisting, like theirs, of a Pantaloun, a Whore, and a Zanie,
but of Emperours, Kings, and Princes ; whose true Tragedies
(*Sophocleo cothurno*) they do vaunt. Not *Roscius* nor *Æsope*, those
admyred tragedians that haue liued euer since before Christ was

borne, could euer performe more in action than famous *Ned Allen*. . . .
If I euer write any thing in Latine (as I hope one day I shall) not
a man of any desert here amongst vs, but I will haue vp. *Tarlton,
Ned Allen, Knell, Bentlie*, shall be made knowne to *France, Spaine*,
and *Italie* : and not a part that they surmounted in, more than other,
but I will there note and set downe, with the manner of theyr habites
and attyre.'

xlvii. 1592. ROBERT GREENE.

[From *A Quip for an Upstart Courtier : Or, A quaint Dispute between
Velvet Breeches and Cloth Breeches. Wherein is plainely set downe the
disorders in all Estates and Trades* (*Works*, xi. 205).]

A jury is being empanelled between the disputants, who represent
new and old ideals of gentry. P. 289. ' An ouerworne gentleman
attired in veluet and satin ' is followed by ' two pert Applesquires :
the one had a murrey cloth gowne on, faced down before with gray
conny, and laid thicke on the sleeues with lace, which he quaintly
bare vp to shew his white taffata hose, and black silk stockings :
a huge ruffe about his necke wrapt in his great head like a wicker
cage, a little Hat with brims like the wings of a doublet, wherein
he wore a jewell of glasse, as broad as a chancery seale : after him
followed two boies in cloakes like butterflies : carrying one of them
his cutting sword of choller, the other his dauncing rapier of delight.'
The ' ouerworne gentleman ' is a poet, the ' applesquires ' a player
and the usher of a dancing school. Velvet Breeches thinks the poet
' a proud fellow ', the others ' plaine, honest, humble men, that for
a penny or an old-cast sute of apparell will do anything. Indeed
quoth Cloth Breeches you say troth, they are but too humble, for
they be so lowly, that they be base minded : I mean not in their
lookes or apparell, for so they be peacockes and painted asses, but in
their corse of life, for they care not how they get crowns, I meane
how basely so they haue them, and yet of the two I hold the Plaier
to be the better Christian, although in his owne imagination too full
of selfe liking and selfe loue, and is vnfit to be of the Iury though
I hide and conceale his faults and fopperies, in that I haue beene
merry at his sports : onely this I must say, that such a plaine country
fellow as my selfe, they bring in as clownes and fooles to laugh at
in their play, whereas they get by vs, and of our almes the proudest
of them all doth liue. Well, to be breefe, let him trot to the stage,
for he shall be none of the Iury.'

xlviii. 1592. ROBERT GREENE.

[From *Greens Groats-worth of Wit* (1596 ; S. R. 20 Sept. 1592), reprinted
in Grosart, xii. 131, and C. M. Ingleby, *Shakespere Allusion-Books*, Part i
(1874, *N. S. S.*) ; cf. ch. xxiii, s.v. Greene.]

' *Roberto* . . . vttered his present greefe, beseeching his advuise how
he might be imployed. Why easily, quoth hee, and greatly to your
benefit : for men of my profession get by schollers their whole liuing.

What is your profession, sayd *Roberto* ? Truely sir, said he, I am
a player. A Player, quoth *Roberto*, I tooke you rather for a gentleman
of great liuing ; for if by outward habit men shuld be censured,
I tell you, you would be taken for a substantiall man. So am I where
I dwell (quoth the player) reputed able at my proper cost, to build
a Windmill. What though the worlde once went hard with mee,
when I was faine to carrie my playing Fardle a footebacke ; *Tempora
mutantur* : I know you know the meaning of it better than I, but
I thus conster it, it is otherwise now ; for my very share in playing
apparrell will not be solde for two hundred pounds. Truely (said
Roberto) it is strange, that you should so prosper in that vaine practise,
for that it seemes to me your voyce is nothing gracious. Nay then,
said the player, I mislike your iudgement : why, I am as famous for
Delphrigus, and the king of Fairies, as euer was any of my time.
The twelue labors of *Hercules* haue I terribly thundred on the stage,
and plaied three scenes of the deuill in the highway to heauen. Haue
ye so (said *Roberto* ?) then I pray you pardon me. Nay more (quoth
the player) I can serue to make a prettie speech, for I was a countrie
Author, passing at a morrall, for it was I that pende the Morral of
mans wit, the Dialogue of Diues, and for seauen yeeres space was
absolute interpreter of the puppets. But now my Almanacke is out
of date :

> *The people make no estimation,*
> *Of Morrals teaching education.*

Was not this prettie for a plaine rime extempore ? if ye will, ye shall
haue more. Nay it is enough, said *Roberto*, but how meane you to vse
mee ? Why sir, in making playes, said the other, for which you shall
be well paied, if you will take the paines. . . . Roberto, now famozed
for an Arch-plaimaking-poet, his purse like the sea sometime sweld,
anon like the same sea fell to a low ebbe ; yet seldom he wanted,
his labors were so well esteemed. Marry, this rule he kept, what euer
he fingerd aforehand, was the certaine meanes to vnbinde a bargaine ;
and being asked why he so sleightly dealt with them that did him
good ? It becomes me, sath hee, to be contrarie to the worlde : for
commonly when vulgar men recieue earnest, they doe performe ; when
I am paid any thing afore-hand, I breake my promise. . . . *To those
Gentlemen, his Quondam acquaintance, that spend their wits in making
Plaies, R. G. wisheth a better exercise, and wisdome to preuent his
extremities.* . . . Base minded men al three of you, if by my miserie
ye be not warned : for vnto none of you (like me) sought those burres
to cleaue : those Puppits (I meane) that speake from our mouths,
those Anticks garnisht in our colours. Is it not strange that I, to
whom they al haue beene beholding : is it not like that you, to whome
they all haue beene beholding, shall (were ye in that case that I am
now) be both at once of them forsaken ? Yes, trust them not : for
there is an vpstart Crow, beautified with our feathers, that with his
Tygers heart wrapt in a Players hide, supposes he is as well able to
bumbast out a blank verse as the best of you : and being an absolute
Iohannes fac totum, is in his owne conceit the onely Shake-scene in

a countrie. O that I might intreate your rare wits to be imployed in more profitable courses : & let these Apes imitate your past excellence, and neuer more acquaint them with your admired inuentions. I know the best husband of you all will neuer proue an Vsurer, and the kindest of them all wil neuer prooue a kinde nurse : yet, whilst you may, seeke you better Maisters ; for it is pittie men of such rare wits, should be subiect to the pleasures of such rude groomes. In this I might insert two more, that both haue writ against these buckram Gentlemen : but let their owne works serue to witnesse against their owne wickednesse, if they perseuer to maintaine any more such peasants. For other new commers, I leaue them to the mercie of these painted monsters, who (I doubt not) will driue the best minded to despise them : for the rest, it skils not though they make a ieast at them.' Cf. ch. xxiii, s.v. Greene.

xlix. 1592. HENRY CHETTLE.

[From *Kind-Harts Dreame. Conteining fiue Apparitions, with their Inuectiues against abuses raigning. Deliuered by seuerall Ghosts vnto him to be publisht* . . . by H. C. (N.D.). The tract was entered in the Stationers' Register (Arber, ii. 623) on 8 Dec. 1592. The Ghosts are those of Anthony Now Now a fiddler, William Cuckoe a juggler, Doctor Burcot a physician, Robert Greene, and Richard Tarlton. Greene died in Sept. 1592. The Epistle is signed by Henry Chettle (cf. ch. xxiii). The whole is reprinted by C. M. Ingleby in Part I (1874) of the *Shakspere Allusion-Books* of the New Shakspere Society.]

P. 37. *To the Gentlemen Readers.* ' About three moneths since died M. *Robert Greene,* leauing many papers in sundry Booke sellers hands, among other his Groatsworth of wit, in which a letter written to diuers play-makers, is offensiuely by one or two of them taken ; and because on the dead they cannot be auenged, they wilfully forge in their conceites a liuing Author : and after tossing it two and fro, no remedy, but it must light on me. How I haue all the time of my conuersing in printing hindered the bitter inueying against schollers, it hath been very well knowne ; and how in that I dealt, I can sufficiently prooue. With neither of them that take offence was I acquainted, and with one of them I care not if I neuer be : The other, whome at that time I did not so much spare, as since I wish I had, for that as I haue moderated the heate of liuing writers, and might haue vsde my owne discretion (especially in such a case) the Author beeing dead, that I did not, I am as sory as if the originall fault had beene my fault, because my selfe haue seene his demeanor no lesse ciuill, than he exelent in the qualitie he professes : Besides, diuers of worship haue reported his vprightnes of dealing, which argues his honesty, and his facetious grace in writting, that aprooues his Art. For the first, whose learning I reuerence, and at the perusing of *Greenes* Booke, stroke out what then in conscience I thought he in some displeasure writ : or had it beene true, yet to publish it, was intollerable : him I would wish to vse me no worse than I deserue. I had onely in the copy this share : it was il written, as sometime

Greenes hand was none of the best ; licensd it must be, ere it could bee printed, which could neuer be if it might not be read. To be breife, I writ it ouer ; and as neare as I could, followed the copy ; onely in that letter I put something out, but in the whole booke not a worde in ; for I protest it was all *Greenes,* not mine nor Maister *Nashes,* as some vniustly haue affirmed.' *Henrie Chettle.* . . . *The Dreame.* P. 43. 'There entered at once fiue personages. . . . The next, by his sute of russet, his buttond cap, his taber, his standing on the toe, and other tricks, I knew to be either the body or resemblaunce of Tarlton, who liuing, for his pleasant conceits was of all men liked, and dying, for mirth left not his like. . . . With him was the fifth, a man of indifferent yeares, of face amible, of body well proportioned, his attire after the habite of a schollerlike Gentleman, onely his haire was somewhat long, whome I supposed to be Robert Greene, maister of Artes : of whome (howe euer some suppose themselues iniured) I haue learned to speake, considering he is dead, *nill nisi necessarium.* He was of singuler pleasaunce the verye supporter, and, to no man's disgrace bee this intended, the only Comedian of a vulgar writer in this country.' P. 63. *To all maligners of honest mirth,* Tarleton *wisheth continuall melancholy.* ' Now Maisters, what say you to a merrie knaue, that for this two years day hath not beene talkt of. Wil you giue him leaue, if he can, to make ye laugh ? What, all a mort ? No merry countenance ? Nay then I see hypocrisie hath the vpper hand, and her spirit raignes in this profitable generation. Sith it is thus, Ile be a time-pleaser. Fie vppon following plaies, the expence is wondrous ; vpon players speeches, their wordes are full of wyles ; vppon their gestures, that are altogether wanton. Is it not lamentable, that a man should spende his two pence on them in an after-noone, heare couetousnes amongst them daily quipt at, being one of the commonest occupations in the countrey ; and in liuely gesture see trecherie set out, with which euery man now adaies vseth to intrap his brother. Byr lady, this would be lookt into : if these be the fruites of playing, tis time the practisers were expeld. Expeld (quoth you) ; that hath been pretily performd, to the no smal profit of the Bouling-allyes in Bedlam and other places, that were wont in the after-noones to be left empty, by the recourse of good fellows vnto that vnprofitable recreation of Stage-playing. And it were not much amisse, would they ioine with the Dicing houses to make sute againe for their longer restraint, though the sicknesse cease. Is not this well saide (my maisters) of an olde buttond cappe, that hath most part of his life liu'd vppon that against which he inueighs : Yes, and worthily.' Suppression of plays to the advantage of bawdy-houses, especially those not near Shoreditch. Discourse with a pander. P. 65. ' And you, sir, find fault with plaies. Out vpon them, they spoile our trade, as you your selfe haue proued. Beside, they open our crosse-biting, our conny-catching, our traines, our traps, our gins, our snares, our subtilties : for no sooner haue we a tricke of deceipt, but they make it common, singing Iigs, and making ieasts of vs, that euerie boy can point out our houses as they passe by.

Whither now *Tarlton* ? this is extempore, out of time, tune, and temper. . . . Thy selfe once a Player, and against Players : nay, turne out the right side of thy russet coate, and lette the world know thy meaning. Why thus I meane, for now I speake in sobernes. Euery thing hath in it selfe his vertue and his vice : from one selfe flower the Bee and Spider sucke honny and poyson. In plaies it fares as in bookes, vice cannot be reproued, except it be discouered : neither is it in any play discouered, but there followes in the same an example of the punishment : now he that at a play will be delighted in the one, and not warned by the other, is like him that reads in a booke the description of sinne, and will not looke ouer the leafe for the reward. Mirth in seasonable time taken, is not forbidden by the austerest Sapients. But indeede there is a time of mirth and a time of mourning. Which time hauing been by the Magistrats wisely obserued, as well for the suppressing of Playes, as other pleasures : so likewise a time may come, when honest recreation shall haue his former libertie. And lette *Tarleton* intreate the yoong people of the Cittie, either to abstaine altogether from playes, or at their comming thither to vse themselues after a more quiet order. In a place so ciuill as this Cittie is esteemed, it is more than barbarously rude, to see the shamefull disorder and routes that sometimes in such publike meetings are vsed. The beginners are neither gentlemen, nor citizens, nor any of both their seruants, but some lewd mates that long for innouation ; & when they see aduantage, that either Seruingmen or Apprentises are most in number, they will be of either side, though indeed they are of no side, but men beside all honestie, willing to make boote of cloakes, hats, purses, or what euer they can lay holde on in a hurley burley. These are the common causers of discord in publike places. If otherwise it happen (as it seldome doth) that any quarrell be betweene man and man, it is far from manhood to make so publike a place their field to fight in : no men will doe it, but cowardes that would faine be parted, or haue hope to haue many partakers. Nowe to you that maligne our moderate merriments, and thinke there is no felicitie but in excessiue possession of wealth : with you I would ende in a song, yea an Extempore song on this Theame, *Ne quid nimis necessarium* : but I am now hoarse, and troubled with my Taber and Pipe : beside, what pleasure brings musicke to the miserable. Therefore letting songes passe, I tell them in sadnes, how euer Playes are not altogether to be commended : yet some of them do more hurt in a day, than all the Players (by exercizing theyr profession) in an age. Faults there are in the professors as other men, this the greatest, that diuers of them beeing publike in euerie ones eye, and talkt of in euery vulgar mans mouth, see not how they are seene into, especially for their contempt, which makes them among most men most contemptible. Of them I will say no more : of the profession, so much hath *Pierce Pennilesse* (as I heare say) spoken, that for mee there is not any thing to speake. So wishing the chearefull, pleasaunce endlesse ; and the wilfull sullen, sorrow till they surfet ; with a turne on the toe I take my leaue. *Richard Tarleton.*

l. 1592–9. JOHN RAINOLDS v. WILLIAM GAGER
AND ALBERICO GENTILI.

[A controversy arising out of criticism by Rainolds on the legitimacy
of academic drama is contained in (a) Gager's *Momus* and *Epilogus
Responsiuus*, written c. Jan. 1592, spoken 8 Feb., printed with additional
matter c. May (cf. ch. xxiii, s.v. Gager, *Ulysses Redux* ; (b) Rainolds to
Thomas Thornton, 6 Feb. 1592 ; (c) Rainolds to Gager, 10 July 1592 ;
(d) Gager to Rainolds, 31 July 1592 ; (e) Rainolds to Gager, 30 May 1593 ;
(f) Gentili, *Commentatio de Professoribus et Medicis*, printed with *Ad
Titulum de Maleficis et Mathematicis Commentarius* (1593, with epistle of
26 June 1593 ; 1604) ; (g) Gentili to Rainolds, 7 July 1593 ; (h) Rainolds
to Gentili, 10 July 1593 ; (i) Gentili to Rainolds, 14 July 1593 ; (k) Rainolds
to Gentili, 5 Aug. 1593 ; (l) two further letters by Gentili and two by
Rainolds, who ends the correspondence on 12 Mar. 1594 ; (m) Gentili,
De Actoribus et Spectatoribus Fabularum non Notandis Disputatio (1599,
with epistle of 14 Oct. 1597 ; reprinted in Gronovius, *Thesaurus Antiqui-
tatum*, viii) ; (n) *Th' Overthrow of Stage-Players* (1599, no imprint, with
epistle from Printer to Reader ; 1600 ; 1629). This is a print of (c), (e),
(g), (h), (i), (k). All the twelve letters are in *Oxon. C.C.C. MS.* 352 and
some in *Queen's Coll. MS.* 359 ; a collection in *Univ. Coll. MS.* 157 is
lost, but probably added no more. Rainolds is satirized in the Queen's
College, Cambridge, play of *Fucus Histriomastix* (1623, ed. G. C. Moore
Smith, 1909), probably by Robert Ward.]

The academic controversy is fully summarized by F. S. Boas in
Fortnightly Review for August 1907 and *University Drama in the Tudor
Age* (1914), 229, together with the analysis of Gager's defence by
K. Young in *An Elizabethan Defence of the Stage* (1916, *Wisconsin
Shakespeare Studies*, 103). I only quote the reference in the Epistle
to *Th' Overthrow* of 1599 to ' Men . . . that haue not been afraied of
late dayes to bring vpon the Stage the very sober countenances,
graue attire, modest and matronelike gestures, and speaches of men
& women to be laughed at as a scorne and reproch to the world '.

li. 1597 (?). JOHN HARINGTON.

[From *A Treatise on Playe*, printed in *Nugae*, i. 191. I retain Park's
date of ' circa 1597 ', although I doubt whether it is based on anything
but a conjecture that ' this deere yeer ' (204) may be 1595 or 1597, and
the latest definite event referred to is the death of Hatton on 20 Nov. 1591.
The treatise deals mainly with gambling.]

One sayd merely that ' enterludes weare the divells sarmons, and
jesters the divells confessors ; thease for the most part disgracing of
vertue, and those not a little gracinge of vices '. But, for my part,
I commend not such sowere censurers, but I thinke in stage-playes
may bee much good, in well-penned comedies, and specially tragedies ;
and I remember, in Cambridge, howsoever the presyser sort have
banisht them, the wyser sort did, and still doe mayntayn them.

lii. 1598. FRANCIS MERES.

[From *Palladis Tamia: Wit's Treasury* (S. R. 7 Sept. 1598). The general attitude of the treatise is humanist, but it is only of value for the incidental notices and appreciations of contemporary writers given in a rather fantastic series of parallels between classical and Elizabethan literature. Fuller extracts, including some personalia on Shakespeare and other playwrights, not reprinted here, are in C. M. Ingleby, *Shakspere Allusion-Books*, Part I (1874, *N. S. S.*), 151, and Gregory Smith, ii. 308.]

Our famous and learned Lawreat masters of England would entitle our English to far greater admired excellency if either the Emperor Augustus, or Octauia his sister, or noble Mecaenas were aliue to rewarde and countenaunce them ; or if our witty Comedians and stately Tragedians (the glorious and goodlie representers of all fine witte, glorified phrase, and queint action) bee still supported and vphelde, by which meanes for lacke of Patrones (O ingratefull and damned age) our Poets are soly or chiefly maintained, countenaunced, and patronized. . . .

. . . A COMPARATIUE DISCOURSE OF OUR ENGLISH POETS WITH THE GREEKE, LATINE, AND ITALIAN POETS. . . .

. . . As Plautus and Seneca are accounted the best for Comedy and Tragedy among the Latines : so Shakespeare among the English is the most excellent in both kinds for the stage. For Comedy, witnes his *Gentlemen of Verona*, his *Errors*, his *Loue Labors Lost*, his *Loue Labours Wonne*, his *Midsummers Night Dreame*, and his *Merchant of Venice* ; For Tragedy, his *Richard the 2*, *Richard the 3*, *Henry the 4*, *King Iohn*, *Titus Andronicus*, and his *Romeo and Iuliet*. . . .

. . . These are our best for Tragedie, The Lorde Buckhurst, Doctor Leg of Cambridge, Doctor Edes of Oxford, Master Edward Ferris, the author of the *Mirror for Magistrates*, Marlow, Peele, Watson, Kid, Shakespeare, Drayton, Chapman, Decker, and Beniamin Iohnson.

As M. Anneus Lucanus writ two excellent tragedies, one called *Medea*, the other *De incendio Troiae cum Priami calamitate* : so Doctor Leg hath penned two famous tragedies, the one of *Richard the 3*, the other of *The Destruction of Ierusalem*. . . .

. . . The best for Comedy amongst vs bee Edward, Earle of Oxforde, Doctor Gager of Oxforde, Master Rowley, once a rare scholler of learned Pembrooke Hall in Cambridge, Maister Edwardes, one of Her Maiesties Chappell, eloquent and wittie Iohn Lilly, Lodge, Gascoyne, Greene, Shakespeare, Thomas Nash, Thomas Heywood, Anthony Mundye, our best plotter, Chapman, Porter, Wilson, Hathway, and Henry Chettle. . . .

As Georgius Buchananus' *Iepthae* amongst all moderne Tragedies is able to abide the touch of Aristotle's precepts and Euripedes's examples : so is Bishop Watson's *Absalon*. As . . . Watson for his *Antigone* out of Sophocles, ha[s] got good commendations : so these versifiers for their learned translations are of good note among vs . . . the Translators of Seneca's *Tragedies*, . . . As Antipater Sidonius was famous for extemporall verse in Greeke, and Ouid for his *Quicquid conabar dicere versus erat* : so was our Tarleton, of whome Doctor Case, that learned physitian, thus speaketh in the Seuenth Booke and seuenteenth chapter of his *Politikes* : *Aristoteles suum Theodoretum laudauit quendam peritum Tragœdiarum actorem, Cicero suum Roscium : nos Angli Tarletonum, in cuius voce et vultu omnes iocosi affectus, in cuius cerebroso capite lepidae facetiae habitant.* And so is now our wittie Wilson, who for learning and extemporall witte in this facultie is without compare or compeere, as, to his great and eternall commendations, he manifested in his challenge at the *Swanne* on the Banke Side.

liii.   1603.   HENRY CROSSE.

[From *Vertues Common-wealth : Or The High-way to Honour*, reprinted in A. B. Grosart, *Occasional Issues*, vii (1878), 111.]

Must the holy Prophets and Patriarkes be set vpon a Stage, to be derided, hist, and laught at ? or is it fit that the infirmities of holy men should be acted on a Stage, whereby others may be inharted to rush carelessly forward into vnbrideled libertie ? . . . Furthermore, there is no passion wherwith the king, the soueraigne maiestie of the Realme was possest, but is amplified, and openly sported with, and made a May-game to all the beholders. . . . If a man will learne to be proud, fantasticke, humorous, to make love, sweare, swagger, and in a word closely doo any villanie, for a two-penny almes hee may be throughly taught and made a perfect good scholler. . . . And as these copper-lace gentlemen growe rich, purchase lands by adulterous Playes, & not fewe of them vsurers and extortioners, which they exhaust out of the purses of their haunters, so are they puft vp in such pride and selfe-loue, as they enuie their equalles, and scorne theyr inferiours. . . . But especially these nocturnall and night Playes, at vnseasonable and vndue times, more greater euils must necessarily proceed of them, because they do not onely hide and couer the thiefe, but also entice seruants out of their maisters houses, wherby opportunitie is offered to loose fellowes, to effect many wicked stratagems. . . . To conclude, it were further to be wished, that those admired wittes of this age, Tragædians, and Comædians, that garnish Theaters with their inuentions, would spend their wittes in more profitable studies, and leaue off to maintaine those Anticks, and Puppets, that speake out of their mouthes : for it is pittie such noble giftes, should be so basely imployed, as to prostitute their ingenious labours to inriche such buckorome gentlemen.

liv.   1604–5 (?).   BEN JONSON.

[Prologue to *Every Man In His Humour*, first printed in Folio of 1616, and possibly written for a Jacobean revival.]

Though neede make many *Poets*, and some such
As art, and nature haue not betterd much ;
Yet ours, for want, hath not so lou'd the stage,
As he dare serue th'ill customes of the age :
Or purchase your delight at such a rate,
As, for it, he himselfe must iustly hate.

To make a child, now swadled, to proceede
Man, and then shoote vp, in one beard, and weede,
Past threescore yeeres : or, with three rustie swords,
And helpe of some few foot-and-halfe-foote words,
Fight ouer *Yorke*, and *Lancasters* long iarres :
And in the tyring-house bring wounds, to scarres.
He rather prayes, you will be pleas'd to see
One such, to day, as other playes should be.
Where neither *Chorus* wafts you ore the seas ;
Nor creaking throne comes downe, the boyes to please ;
Nor nimble squibbe is seene, to make afear'd
The gentlewomen ; nor roul'd bullet heard
To say, it thunders ; nor tempestuous drumme
Rumbles, to tell you when the storme doth come ;
But deedes, and language, such as men doe vse :
And persons, such as *Comœdie* would chuse,
When she would shew an Image of the times,
And sport with humane follies, not with crimes,
Except, we make 'hem such, by louing still
Our popular errors, when we know th'are ill.
I meane such errors as you'll all confesse
By laughing at them, they deserue no lesse :
Which when you heartily doe, there 's hope left, then,
You, that haue so grac'd monsters, may like men.

lv. 1607. BEN JONSON.

[From Epistle to *Volpone* (cf. ch. xxiii).]

Hence is it, that I now render my selfe gratefull, and am studious to iustifie the bounty of your act : To which, though your mere authority were satisfying, yet it being an age wherein *Poëtry* and the Professors of it heare so ill on all sides, there will a reason bee look'd for in the subject. It is certaine, nor can it with any forehead be oppos'd, that the too-much licence of *Poëtasters* in this time hath much deform'd their *Mistresse* ; that euery day their manifold and manifest ignorance doth stick vnnaturall reproches vpon her. But for their petulancy, it were an act of the greatest iniustice, either to let the learned suffer, or so diuine a *skill* (which indeed should not be attempted with vncleane hands) to fall vnder the least contempt. For if men will impartially, and not à-squint, looke toward the offices and function of a *Poët*, they will easily conclude to themselues the impossibility of any mans being the good *Poët*, without first being a good *Man*. He that is sayd to be able to informe *yong-men* to all good disciplines, inflame *growne-men* to all great vertues, keepe *old men* in their best and supreme state, or as they decline to child-hood, recouer them to their first strength ; that comes forth the Interpreter and Arbiter of *Nature*, a Teacher of things diuine no lesse than humane, a Master in manners ; and can alone, or with a few, effect the busines of Man-kind. This, I take him, is no subject for *Pride* and *Ignorance* to exercise their railing *rhetorique* vpon. But it will here be hastily answer'd, that the *Writers* of these dayes are other things ; that not onely their manners, but their natures, are inuerted, and nothing remaining with them of the dignity of *Poët*, but the abused name, which euery Scribe vsurpes ; that now, especially in *Dramatick*, or (as they terme it) Stage-*Poëtry*, nothing but Ribaldry, Profanation, Blasphemy, al Licence of offence to God, and Man, is practisd. I dare not deny a great part of this, and am sory I dare not : because in some mens abortiue *Features* (and would they had neuer boasted the light) it is ouer-true. But that all are embarqu'd in this bold aduenture for Hell, is a most vncharitable thought, and vtterd, a more malicious slander. For my particular, I can, and from a most cleare conscience, affirme, that I haue euer trembled to thinke toward the least Prophanenesse ; haue loathed the vse of such foule and vn-washd Baudr'y, as is now made the foode of the *Scene*.

lvi. 1608. WILLIAM CRASHAW.

[From *The Sermon preached at the Crosse, Feb. xiiij. 1607* (1608, 2nd ed. 1609). Crashaw was preacher at the Inner Temple and father of Richard Crashaw, the poet. The hypocrites, Nicholas Saint-Tantlings and Simon Saint-Mary-Oueries, are characters in *The Puritan* (1607). John Selden says in his *Table Talk* (1689 ; ed. Reynolds, 134), ' I never converted but two, the one was Mr. Crashaw from writing against plays, by telling him a way how to understand that place, of putting on woman's apparel, which has nothing to do with the business ' ; cf. *infra*, s.v. Selden (1616).]

P. 169. ' Now there are also besides these two great Babels, certaine other little pettie Babylons, namely, incurable sinnes amongst vs, . . .'
P. 170. ' 2. The vngodly Playes and Enterludes so rife in this nation : what are they but a bastard of Babylon, a daughter of error and confusion, a hellish deuice (the diuels owne recreation to mock at holy things) by him deliuered to the Heathen, from them to the Papists, and from them to vs ? Of this euill and plague, the Church of God in all ages can say, truly and with a good conscience, *wee would haue healed her.* [Quotes Tertullian and others.] . . . All this they are daily made to know, but all in vaine, they be children of Babylon that will not bee healed : nay, they grow worse and worse, for now they bring religion and holy things vpon the stage : no maruel though the worthiest and mightiest men escape not, when God himselfe is so abused. Two hypocrites must be brought foorth ; and how shall they be described but by these names, *Nicolas S. Antlings, Simon S. Maryoueries.* Thus hypocrisie a child of hell must beare the names of two Churches of God, and two wherein Gods name is called on publikely euery day in the yeere, and in one of them his blessed word preached euerie day (an example scarce matchable in the world) : yet these two, wherin Gods name is thus glorified, and our Church and State honoured, shall bee by these miscreants thus dishonoured, and that not on the stage only, but euen in print.' Complains of profaneness, atheism, blasphemy, and profaning of Sabbath ' which generally in the countrie is their play day '. Calls on magistrate, lest God take the matter into his own hand.

lvii. 1608 (?). Thomas Heywood.

[From *An Apology for Actors. Containing three briefe Treatises. 1. Their Antiquity. 2. Their ancient Dignity. 3. The True Use of their Quality* (1612), reprinted by William Cartwright as *The Actor's Vindication* (N.D., but according to Douce 1658) and in 1841 (*Sh. Soc.*). I think the treatise was probably written in 1607 and touched up in 1608, since (a) the series of actors named as dead ends with Sly, who died in Aug. 1608 ; (b) the Revels Office is located at St. John's, which it lost about Feb. 1608 ; (c) the frustrated Spanish landing in ' Perin ' in Cornwall ' some 12 yeares ago ' is probably the abortive Spanish attempt to burn Pendennis Castle on Falmouth Harbour, 3 miles from Penrhyn, which appears from *S. P. D. Eliz.* cclvi, 21, 40, and Dasent, xxv. 15, to have taken place in the autumn of 1595, probably in connexion with the better-known landing of 22 July 1595 in Mount's Bay. Here there is a Perranuthnoe, but this was a successful landing, resulting in serious damage to Penzance, Mousehole, and Newlyn (*Procl.* 879). There was also a raid at Cawsand Bay near Plymouth on 14 Mar. 1596 (*S. P. D. Eliz.* cclvi. 89), in which the invaders fired some houses and boats, and fled to sea on a shot being fired. But there is no ' Perin ' in Cawsand Bay. In *Journal of the Folk-Song Society*, v. 275, is recorded a tradition that ' the French once landed invading troops at Padstow Bay ; but on seeing a number of mummers in red cloaks with their hobby-horse they supposed that the English army was at hand, and fled '. This raid was at St. Eval, 3 miles west of Padstow, on 13 July 1595 (*Hatfield MSS.* v. 285), and no doubt formed part of the same expedition which reached Mount's Bay. Of course it was Spanish, not French ; the perversion is characteristic of tradition. Conceivably this episode was what Heywood had in mind, but the nearest ' Perin ', Perranporth, is some dozen miles farther west than St. Evall. Heywood was answered by I. G. in *A Refutation of the Apology for Actors* (1615), which contributes nothing new, and uses material from Gosson's *Plays Confuted* (No. xxx), with references to the long-destroyed Theatre unchanged.]

[Summary and Extracts.] P. 3. *To the Earl of Worcester.* ' I presumed to publish this unworthy worke under your gracious patronage . . . as an acknowledgement of the duty I am bound to you in as a servant.' P. 4. *To my good Friends and Fellowes the Citty-Actors.* ' That it [our quality] hath beene esteemed by the best and greatest . . . I need alledge no more than the royall and princely services in which we now live. . . . Some over-curious have too liberally taxed us . . . we may as freely (out of our plainnesse) answere, as they (out of their perversenesse) object, instancing my selfe by famous Scaliger, learned Doctor Gager, Doctor Gentiles, and others. . . . So, wishing you judiciall audiences, honest poets, and true gatherers, I commit you all to the fulnesse of your best wishes.' P. 6. *Verses* by, *inter alios*, John Webster, and by Richard Perkins, Christopher Beeston and Robert Pallant to their ' fellow '. *Book i.* P. 15. The author is ' mooved by the sundry exclamations of many seditious sectists in this age. . . . It hath pleased the high and mighty princes of this land to limit the use of certaine publicke theaters, which, since many of those over-curious heads have lavishly and violently slandered, I hold it not amisse to lay open some few antiquities to approve the true use of them.' A vision of Melpomene. Actors in antiquity. P. 20. The lives of worthies ' can no way bee so exquisitly demonstrated, nor so lively portrayed, as by action. . . . A description is only a shadow, received by the eare, but not perceived by the eye ; so lively portratuie is meerely a forme seene by the eye, but can neither shew action, passion, motion, or any other gesture to moove the spirits of the beholder to admiration : but to see a souldier shap'd like a souldier, walke, speake, act like a souldier ; to see a Hector all besmered in blood, trampling upon the bulkes of kinges ; a Troilus returning from the field, in the sight of his father Priam, as if man and horse, even from the steed's rough fetlockes to the plume on the champion's helmet, had bene together plunged into a purple ocean ; to see a Pompey ride in triumph, then a Caesar conquer that Pompey ; labouring Hannibal alive, hewing his passage through the Alpes. To see as I have seene, Hercules, in his owne shape, hunting the boare, knocking downe the bull, taming the hart, fighting with Hydra, murdering Geryon, slaughtering Diomed, wounding the Stymphalides, killing the Centaurs, pashing the lion, squeezing the dragon, dragging Cerberus in chaynes, and lastly, on his high pyramides waiting *Nil ultra*, Oh, these were sights to make an Alexander ! To turne to our domesticke hystories : what English blood, seeing the person of any bold Englishman presented, and doth not hugge his fame, and hunnye at his valor, pursuing him in his enterprise with his best wishes, and as beeing wrapt in contemplation, offers to him in his hart all prosperous performance, as if the personator were the man personated ? so bewitching a thing is lively and well-spirited action, that it hath power to new-mold the harts of the spectators, and fashion them to the shape of any noble and notable attempt. What coward, to see his countrymen valiant, would not bee ashamed of his owne cowardise ? What English prince, should hee behold the true portrature of that famous King Edward the Third, foraging France, taking so great a king captive in his owne country, quartering the English lyons with the French flower-delyce, and would not bee suddenly inflam'd with so royale a spectacle, being made apt and fit for the like atchievement. So of Henry the Fift.' The place of actors at Rome. P. 24. ' Neither Christ himselfe, nor any of his sanctified apostles, in any of their sermons, acts, or documents, so much as named them, or upon any abusive occasion touched them. . . . Since they (I say) in all their holy doctrines, bookes, and principles of divinity, were content to passe them over, as thinges tollerated and indifferent, why should any nice and over-scrupulous heads, since they cannot ground their curiousnesse either upon the Old or New Testament, take upon them to correct, controule, or carpe at that, against which they cannot finde any text in the sacred scriptures ? ' P. 25. ' Since God hath provided us of these pastimes, why may we not use them to his glory ? Now, if you aske me why were not the theaters as gorgeously built in all other cities of Italy as Rome, and why are not play-houses maintained as well in other cities of England as London ? My answere is . . . Rome was a metropolis, a place whither all the nations knowne under the sunne resorted : so is London, and being to receive all estates, all princes, all nations,

therefore to affoord them all choyce of pastimes, sports, and recreations.' Actors in Greece. The scriptural prohibition of change of
sex-costume has no reference to plays. P. 28. 'To see our youths
attired in the habit of women, who knowes not what their intents
be ? who cannot distinguish them by their names, assuredly knowing
they are but to represent such a lady, at such a tyme appoynted ?
Do not the Universities, the fountaines and well springs of all good
arts, learning, and documents, admit the like in their colledges ?
and they (I assure my selfe) are not ignorant of their true use. In
the time of my residence at Cambridge, I have seen tragedyes,
comedyes, historyes, pastorals, and shewes, publickly acted, in which
the graduates of good place and reputation have bene specially
parted.' Value of such exercises in teaching audacity in disputation
and good enunciation. The critics of acting ' a sorte of finde-faults '.
Book ii. Antiquities of the theatre, and distribution of theatres in
ancient and modern states. P. 40. ' The King of Denmarke, father
to him that now reigneth, entertained into his service a company
of English comedians, commended unto him by the honourable the
Earle of Leicester : the Duke of Brunswicke and the Landgrave of
Hessen retaine in their courts certaine of ours of the same quality. . . .
And amongst us one of our best English Chroniclers [in margin,
' Stowe '] records, that when Edward the Fourth would shew himselfe
in publicke state to the view of the people, hee repaired to his palace
at S. Johnes, where he accustomed to see the citty actors : and since
then that house, by the prince's free gift, hath belonged to the Office
of the Revels, where our court playes have beene in late daies yearely
rehersed, perfected, and corrected before they come to the publike
view of the prince and the nobility.' Famous classical actors.
P. 43. ' According to the occasion offered to do some right to our
English actors, as Knell, Bentley, Mils, Wilson, Crosse, Lanam, and
others, these, since I never saw them, as being before my time, I cannot (as an eye-witnesse of their desert) give them that applause,
which no doubt they worthily merit ; yet by the report of many
juditiall auditors their performances of many parts have been so
absolute, that it were a kinde of sinne to drowne their worths in
Lethe, and not commit their (almost forgotten) names to eternity.
Here I must needs remember Tarleton, in his time gratious with the
queene, his soveraigne, and in the people's generall applause, whom
succeeded Wil. Kemp, as wel in the favour of her majesty, as in the
opinion and good thoughts of the generall audience. Gabriel, Singer,
Pope, Phillips, Sly, all the right I can do them is but this, that,
though they be dead, their deserts yet live in the remembrance of
many. Among so many dead, let me not forget one yet alive, in his
time the most worthy, famous Maister Edward Allen. . . . I also could
wish, that such as are condemned for their licentiousnesse, might by
a generall consent bee quite excluded our society ; for, as we are
men that stand in the broad eye of the world, so should our manners,
gestures, and behaviours, savour of such government and modesty,
to deserve the good thoughts and reports of all men, and to abide

the sharpest censures even of those that are the greatest opposites to the quality. Many amongst us I know to be of substance, of government, of sober lives, and temperate carriages, house-keepers, and contributory to all duties enjoyned them, equally with them that are rank't with the most bountifull; and if amongst so many of sort, there be any few degenerate from the rest in that good demeanor which is both requisite and expected at their hands, let me entreat you not to censure hardly of all for the misdeeds of some.' On royal actors, quoting (p. 45) ' M. Kid, in his Spanish Tragedy '. *Book iii.* The quality not to be condemned because of its abuses. P. 52. ' Playing is an ornament to the citty.' It refines the language, instructs the ignorant, and teaches moral lessons. P. 54. ' Briefly, there is neither tragedy, history, comedy, morall, or pastorall, from which an infinite use cannot be gathered. I speake not in the defence of any lascivious shewes, scurrelous jests, or scandalous invectives. If there be any such I banish them quite from my patronage.' Plays have discovered murders. P. 57. ' We will prove it by a domestike and home-borne truth, which within these few years happened. At Lin, in Norfolke, the then Earl of Sussex players acting the old History of Feyer Francis ' drove a townswoman to confess the murder of her husband in circumstances parallel to those of the play. P. 58. Relates rout of Spanish raiders ' at a place called Perin in Cornwall ', though their alarm at the drum and trumpets of ' a company of the same quality some 12 yeares ago, or not so much . . . playing late in the night '. Another story of a woman who had driven a nail into her husband's brain, urged to remorse by a similar incident in ' the last part of the Four Sons of Aymon ' played by ' a company of our English comedians (well knowne) ' at Amsterdam. Summarizes the favour of many sovereigns to players. P. 60. ' The cardinal at Bruxels hath at this time in pay a company of our English comedians. . . . But in no country they are of that eminence that our's are : so our most royall and ever renoued soveraigne hath licenced us in London : so did his predecessor, the thrice vertuous virgin, Queen Elizabeth ; and before her, her sister, Queene Mary, Edward the sixth, and their father, Henry the eighth.' P. 61. ' Moreover, to this day in divers places of England there be townes that held the priviledge of their faires, and other charters by yearely stage-playes, as at Manningtree in Suffolke, Kendall in the north, and others. . . . Now, to speake of some abuse lately crept into the quality, as an inveighing against the state, the court, the law, the citty, and their governements, with the particularizing of private men's humors (yet alive) noble-men, and others : I know it distastes many ; neither do I any way approve it, nor dare I by any meanes excuse it. The liberty which some arrogate to themselves, committing their bitternesse, and liberall invectives against all estates, to the mouthes of children, supposing their juniority to be a priviledge for any rayling, be it never so violent, I could advise all such to curbe and limit this presumed liberty within the bands of discretion and government. But wise and juditiall censurers, before whom such complaints shall at any time hereafter come, wil not (I hope) impute these abuses to any transgression in us, who have ever been carefull and provident to shun the like.' P. 162. *Epistle to the publisher.* Notes the printer's faults in his *Britain's Troy*, and the pirating of his two epistles of Paris to Helen, and Helen to Paris by Jaggard [in *The Passionate Pilgrim*].

lviii. 1610. William Crashaw.

[From *A Sermon Preached in London before the right honorable the Lord Lawarre, Lord Gouernour and Captaine Generall of Virginea . . . Feb. 21, 1609 (1610).*]

P. 57. 'We confesse this action hath three great enemies : but who be they ? euen the Diuell, Papists, and Players.' P. 62. ' 3. As for Plaiers : (pardon me right Honourable and beloued, for wronging this place and your patience with so base a subiect) they play with Princes and Potentates, Magistrates and Ministers, nay with God and Religion, and all holy things : nothing that is good, excellent or holy can escape them : how then can this action ? . . . But why are the Players enemies to this Plantation and doe abuse it ? I will tell you the causes : First, for that they are so multiplied here, that one cannot liue by another, and they see that wee send of all trades to Virginea, but will send no Players, which if wee would doe, they that remaine would gaine the more at home. Secondly . . . because wee resolue to suffer no Idle persons in Virginea, which course if it were taken in England, they know they might turne to new occupations.'

lix. 1615. I. H.

[From *This World's Folly. Or A Warning-Peece discharged vpon the Wickednesse thereof. By I. H. (1615).*]

B^v–B2. 'What voice is heard in our streetes ? Nought but the squeaking out of those τερετίσματα, obscaene and light Iigges, stuft with loathsome and vnheard-of Ribauldry, suckt from the poysonous dugs of Sinne-sweld Theaters. . . . More haue recourse to Playing houses, then to Praying houses. . . . I will not particularize those *Blitea dramata* (as *Laberius* termes another sort) those *Fortune*-fatted fooles, and Times Ideots, whose garbe is the Tooth-ache of witte, the Plague-sore of Iudgement, the Common-sewer of Obscaenities, and the very Traine-powder that dischargeth the roaring *Meg* (not *Mol*) of all scurrile villanies vpon the Cities face ; who are faine to produce blinde *Impudence* [*in margin,* ' Garlicke '], to personate himselfe vpon their stage, behung with chaynes of Garlicke, as an Antidote against their owne infectious breaths, lest it should kill their Oyster-crying Audience. *Vos quoque* [*in margin,* ' Or *Tu quoque* '], and you also, who with *Scylla*-barking, *Stentor*-throated bellowings, flash choaking squibbes of absurd vanities into the nosthrils of your spectators, barbarously diuerting *Nature*, and defacing Gods owne image, by metamorphising humane [*in margin,* ' *Greenes* Baboone '] shape into bestiall forme. Those also stand within the stroke of my penne, who were wont to *Curtaine* ouer their defects with knauish conueyances, and scum off the froth of all wanton vanity, to qualifie the eager appetite of their slapping Fauorites.'

lx. 1615. J. COCKE.

[The variant texts of this character are here given from the two editions of John Stephens' essays, in each of which it is Bk. ii, char. 4, viz. (A) *Satyrical Essayes Characters and Others* (1615) and (B) *Essayes and Characters, Ironical and Instructive. The second impression* (1615), of which a reprint is in J. O. Halliwell, *Old Books of Characters* (1857), 131. Between A and B had appeared the sixth edition of *The Wife*, with the character of *An Excellent Actor* and the reference to a rival as ' the imitating Characterist ' (v. No. lxi). To this the additions in B are a rejoinder, and they are reinforced by two epistles. One is ' To the namelesse Rayler : who hath lenghthened his Excellent Actor, a most needy Caracter following the wife with a peece of dog-skin witt ; dressed ouer with oyle of sweaty Posthorse '. Here the writer, I. S., says he did ' admit a friends Satyre '. The other epistle, ' To the nameles Author of a late Character entituled, an *Excellent Actor*, following the *Wife* ', is signed by ' I. Cocke ', who says, ' witnes your gross mistaking of approued and authorised actors for counterfeit Runagates, or country Players, inueighed against by the Characterist '. Some appended verses claim for Cocke the authorship of the *Tinker*, *Apparator*, and *Almanac-maker* in *The Wife*. It seems clear that Cocke and not Stephens wrote the present character, and that *An Excellent Actor* was a reply to it. It is true that Stephens only speaks of it as ' lenghthened ' by the attack on himself, but ' lenghthened ' may mean ' pieced out ', and there is no version, long or short, in any of the five first editions of *The Wife*, while a reference to ' the sixt impression of S. Thomas Overburyes wife ' on p. 434 of B shows this was before its writers. John Stephens (cf. ch. xxiii) was a Lincoln's Inn dramatist. I cannot find a likely Cocke in the *Lincoln's Inn Admission Books* ; there is an Isaac Cox, admitted 10 Jan. 1611 (i. 154), and a John Cookes on 6 June 1614 (i. 166). Can the satirist be the John Cooke (cf. ch. xxiii) who wrote *Greene's Tu Quoque* ?]

A common Player

Is a slow Payer, seldom a Purchaser, never a Puritan. The Statute hath done wisely to acknowledg him a Rogue errant [1], for his chiefe essence is, *A daily Counterfeit* [2] : He hath beene familiar so long with out-sides, that he professes himselfe (being vnknowne) to be an apparant Gentleman. But his thinne Felt, and his silke Stockings, or his foule Linnen, and faire Doublet, doe (in him) bodily reveal the Broker : So beeing not sutable, hee proves a Motley : his mind observing the same fashion of his body : both consist of parcells and

---

[1] errant. *Om.* A. B has marginal note ' *Erratum* in the last impression '.

[2] B adds in margin, King Agesilaus teaches the respect due to common players in his answere to Callipides, who being a presumptious excellent actor ; & thinking himself not graced enough by the kings notice, as the king passed along, doth sawcily interrupt him thus ; *doth not your grace know me ?* Yes, said the king, *thou art Calipides the Player.*

remnants : but his minde hath commonly the newer fashion, and the
newer stuffe : hee would not else hearken so passionately after new
Tunes, new Trickes, new Devises : These together apparrell his braine
and understanding, whilst he takes the materialls upon trust, and is
himself the Taylor to take measure of his soules liking. Hee doth
conjecture somewhat strongly, but dares not commend a playes
goodnes,[1] till he hath either spoken, or heard the *Epilogue*[2] : neither
dares he entitle good things *Good*, unlesse hee be heartned on by the
multitude : till then hee saith faintly what hee thinkes, with a willing
purpose to recant or persist : So howsoever hee pretends to have
a royall Master or Mistresse, his wages and dependance prove him
to be the servant of the people.[3] When he doth hold conference upon
the stage ; and should looke directly in his fellows face ; hee turnes
about his voice into the assembly for applause-sake, like a Trumpeter
in the fields, that shifts places to get an eccho.[4] The cautions of his
judging humor (if hee dares undertake it) be a certaine number of
sawsie rude[5] jests against the common lawyer ; hansome conceits
against the fine Courtiers ; delicate quirkes against the rich Cuckold
a cittizen ; shadowed glaunce[6] for good innocent Ladies and Gentlewomen ; with a nipping scoffe for some honest Justice, who hath[7]
imprisoned him : or some thriftie Trades-man, who hath allowed him
no credit : always remembred, his object is, *A new play*, or *A play
newly revived*. Other Poems he admits, as good-fellowes take Tobacco,
or ignorant Burgesses give a voyce, for company sake ; as thinges
that neither maintaine nor be against him. To be a player, is to
have a *mithridate* against the pestilence ; for players cannot tarry
where the plague raignes ; and therfore they be seldome infected.[8]
He can seeme no lesse then one in honour, or at least one mounted ;
for unto miseries which persecute such, he is most incident. Hence
it proceeds, that in the prosperous fortune of a play frequented, he
proves immoderate, and falles into a Drunkards paradise, till it be
last no longer. Otherwise when adversities come, they come together :
For Lent and Shrovetuesday be not farre asunder, then he is dejected
daily and weekely : his blessings be neither lame nor monstrous ;
they goe upon foure legges, but moove slowly, and make as great
a distance between their steppes, as· between the foure Tearmes.
Reproofe is ill bestowed uppon him ; it cannot alter his conditions :
he hath bin so accustomed to the scorne and laughter of his audience,
that hee cannot bee ashamed of himselfe : for hee dares laugh in the
middest of a serious conference, without blushing.[9] If hee marries,
hee mistakes the Woman for the Boy in Womans attire, by not

---

[1] Hee . . . goodnes. A, If hee cannot beleeue, hee doth coniecture
strongly ; but dares not resolue vpon particulars.

[2] *Epilogue*. A adds : ' vnlesse he be prevented '.

[3] B, in margin, Iuxta Plautinum illud Collybisci: quin aedepol con-
ductior sum quam tragaedi aut comici.

[4] When . . . eccho. *Om.* A.   [5] sawsie rude. A, lying.

[6] glaunce. A, glaunces.   [7] hath. A, hath once.

[8] To . . . infected. *Om.* A.   [9] Reproofe . . . blushing. *Om.* A.

respecting a difference in the mischiefe : But so long as he lives unmarried, hee mistakes the Boy, or a Whore for the Woman ; by courting the first on the stage, or visiting the second at her devotions. When hee is most commendable, you must confesse there is no truth in him : for his best action is but an imitation of truth, and *nullum simile est idem.* It may be imagined I abuse his carriage, and hee perhaps may suddenly bee thought faire-conditioned : for he *playes above board.*[1] Take him at the best, he is but a shifting companion ; for hee lives effectually by putting on, and putting off. If his profession were single, hee would think himselfe a simple fellow, as hee doth all professions besides his owne : His own therefore is compounded of all Natures, all humours, all professions. Hee is politick also[2] to perceive the common-wealth[3] doubts of his licence, and therefore in spight of Parliaments or Statutes hee incorporates himselfe by the title of a brotherhood. Painting and fine cloths may not by the same reason be called abusive, that players may not be called rogues : *For they bee chiefe ornaments of his Majesties Revells.*[4] I need not multiplie his character ; for boyes and every one, wil no sooner see men of this Facultie walke along but they wil (unasked) informe you what hee is by the vulgar title.[5] Yet in the generall number of them, many may deserve a wise mans commendation : and therefore did I prefix an Epithite of *common,* to distinguish the base and artlesse appendants of our citty companies, which often times start away into rusticall wanderers and then (like Proteus) start backe again into the Citty number.[6]

lxi. 1615. JOHN WEBSTER (?).

[This Character *Of an Excellent Actor* is one of the additions made in the 6th edition (1615) to the Characters printed with Sir Thomas Overbury's *The Wife,* of which the 1st edition appeared after Overbury's death on 15 Sept. 1613. The Characters do not profess to be all from Overbury's hand, and the present one was evidently written as a reply to that of *A Common Player* (No. lx). The allusion to painting suggests that the model was Richard Burbadge. The passage *Therefore the imitating Characterist . . . flea them* was omitted in the 7th edition (1616) and in later editions, including the 9th (1616), from which the reprints in E. F. Rimbault, *Works of Overbury,* 147, and H. Morley, *Character Writings,* 86, are taken. A. F. Bourgeois, in 11 *N. Q.* x. 3, 23, gives some striking parallels of phrase between the Characters of 1615 and the work of John Webster, which may point to his authorship. Later Characters of a Player are in J. Earle, *Microcosmography* (1628, ed. A. S. West, 81), and R. M., *Micrologia* (1629, Morley, 285).]

An Excellent Actor.

Whatsoeuer is commendable in the graue Orator, is most exquisitly perfect in him ; for by a full and significant action of body, he charmes

---

[1] When . . . *board. Om.* A.   [2] also. A, enough.
[3] common-wealth. A, common-wealths.
[4] Painting . . . *Revells. Om.* A. B, in margin, I would haue the correcting Pedant goe study *Logicke.*
[5] title. A, denomination.   [6] Yet . . . number. *Om.* A.

our attention : sit in a full Theater, and you will thinke you see so
many lines drawne from the circumference of so many eares, whiles
the *Actor* is the *Center*. He doth not striue to make nature monstrous,
she is often seene in the same Scaene with him, but neither on Stilts
nor Crutches ; and for his voice tis not lower then the prompter, nor
lowder then the Foile and Target. By his action he fortifies morall
precepts with example ; for what we see him personate, we thinke
truely done before vs : a man of a deepe thought might apprehend,
the Ghosts of our ancient *Heroes* walk't againe, and take him (at
seuerall times) for many of them. Hee is much affected to painting,
and tis a question whether that make him an excellent Plaier, or his
playing an exquisite painter. Hee addes grace to the Poets labours :
for what in the Poet is but ditty, in him is both ditty and musicke.
He entertaines vs in the best leasure of our life, that is betweene
meales, the most vnfit time, either for study or bodily exercise : the
flight of Hawkes and chase of wilde beastes, either of them are delights
noble : but some think this sport of men the worthier, despight all
calumny. All men haue beene of his occupation : and indeed, what
hee doth fainedly that doe others essentially : this day one plaies
a Monarch, the next a priuate person. Heere one Acts a Tyrant, on
the morrow an Exile : A Parasite this man to night, to morow
a Precisian, and so of diuers others. I obserue, of all men liuing,
a worthy Actor in one kind is the strongest motiue of affection that
can be : for when he dies, wee cannot be perswaded any man can
doe his parts like him. Therefore the imitating Characterist was
extreame idle in calling them Rogues. His Muse it seemes, with all
his loud inuocation, could not be wak'd to light him a snuffe to read
the Statute : for I would let his malicious ignorance vnderstand, that
Rogues are not to be imploide as maine ornaments to his Maiesties
Reuels ; but the itch of bestriding the Presse, or getting vp on this
wodden Pacolet, hath defil'd more innocent paper, then euer did
Laxatiue Physicke : yet is their inuention such tyred stuffe, that like
Kentish Post-horse they can not go beyond their ordinary stage,
should you flea them. But to conclude, I valew a worthy Actor by
the corruption of some few of the quality, as I would doe gold in the
oare ; I should not mind the drosse, but the purity of the metall.

lxii. 1616. JOHN SELDEN.

[From a letter to Ben Jonson of ' 28th of Feb. 1615 ' (*Works*, ii. 1690).]

' I have most willingly collected what you wished, my notes touching
the literal sense and historical of the holy text usually brought against
the counterfeiting of sexes by apparell.' Explains it as a prohibition
of an idolatrous Palestine ritual.

lxiii. 1616. NATHAN FIELD.

[From *Feild the Players Letter to Mr Sutton, Preacher att St Mary Overs*, 1616, printed by Halliwell, *Illustrations*, 115, from *S. P. Dom. Jac. I*, lxxxix. 105. There are some slight references to the stage in Thomas Sutton's *England's First and Second Summons* (1616), 27, 195, but these are Paul's Cross sermons delivered, and in the case of the first at least printed, before he became preacher at Saint Mary Overies in 1616, and Field is probably answering something later and more pointed.]

Protests that Sutton's labour ' to hinder the Sacrament and banish me from myne owne parishe Churche ' is ' uncharitable dealing with your poore parishioners, whose purses participate in your contribucion and whose labour yow are contented to eate '. Can find nothing in the Bible, ' which I have studied as my best parte ', condemning players, nor does ' our Caesar, our David ', King James, condemn them.

APPENDIX D

DOCUMENTS OF CONTROL

[*Bibliographical Note.*—The material here collected relates to the control of the stage both by the central and, so far as London and its suburbs are concerned, by the local authorities. It is largely drawn from official sources, especially the Chancery Rolls and the Privy Council Register, and the City archives, in particular the series of *Remembrancia*, which begins in 1579 and contains copies of official correspondence between the Corporation and the Privy Council, or individual persons of honour. Something has also been contributed by the *Repertories* of the Court of Aldermen and the *Journals* of the Common Council, but these, as well as the *Liber Legum* and the *Letter Books*, which extend to 1590, probably still require further search. The nature of the Privy Council Register is described in ch. ii, and it must be borne in mind that orders relating to plays are probably missing from it, owing to *lacunae*, of which the chief are May 1559–May 1562, Sept. 1562–Nov. 1564, Dec. 1565–Oct. 1566, May 1567–May 1570, July 1572–Feb. 1573, June 1582–Feb. 1586, Aug. 1593–Oct. 1595, April 1599–Jan. 1600, Jan. 1602–May 1613. For the last of these an abstract covering 1602–10 in *Addl. MS.* 11402 is an inadequate substitute. Probably some volumes of the Register were burnt in the fire of 1619 (cf. ch. i). Many of the documents were printed by Collier, Hazlitt, Wright, and others, but in most cases more authoritative texts are available in such publications as the *Statutes of the Realm* (1810–22), J. R. Dasent, *Acts of the Privy Council* (1890–1907), J. C. Jeaffreson, *Middlesex County Records* (1888–92), W. W. Greg, *Henslowe Papers* (1907), C. C. Stopes, *Extracts from London Play Regulations* (1908, Harrison, *Description of England*, Part iv), and *Collections of the Malone Society*, vol. i (*Dramatic Records* from the *Remembrancia, Lansdowne Manuscripts, Patent Rolls*, and *Privy Council Register 1603–42*, by E. K. Chambers and W. W. Greg), and in view of the diplomatic accuracy of these I have allowed myself to make the present copies more readable by means of additional punctuation, modifications in the use of capitals, and the extension of contractions. I have also occasionally omitted an irrelevant passage or an endorsement. And I have replaced full texts by abstracts where, as in the case of the company patents, the full texts seemed to go better in other sections of this work.]

i.

[1531. Extract from *An Acte concernyng punysshement of Beggers & Vacabundes* (*22 Hen. VIII*, c. 12), printed in *Statutes*, iii. 328. The Act was continued and amended in detail in 1536 by *27 Hen. VIII*, c. 25 (*St.* iii. 558), replaced in 1547 by the more severe *1 Edw. VI*, c. 3 (*St.* iv. 5), revived in 1550 by *3 & 4 Edw. VI*, c. 16 (*St.* iv. 115), and continued in 1551–2 by *5 & 6 Edw. VI*, c. 2 (*St.* iv. 131), in 1552–3 by *7 Edw. VI*, c. 11 (*St.* iv. 175), in 1553 by *1 Mary*, c. 13 (*St.* iv. 215), and in 1563 by *5 Eliz.* c. 3 (*St.* iv. 411).]

[§ 3.] And be it farther enacted by the aucthoryte aforsayde that yf any person or persones beyng hole & myghtie in body & able to laboure, at any tyme after the sayde feast of Saynt John [24 June 1531] be taken in beggyng in any parte of this Realme, or yf any Man or Woman beyng hole & myghty in body & able to laboure havyng no lande [or] maister nor usyng any lawful marchaundyse crafte or mystery, wherby he myght gette his lyvyng after the same feast, be vagarant & can gyve none rekenyng howe he doth lefully gett his lyvyng, that than yt shalbe lefull to the Constables & all other the Kynges Officers Mynysters & Subjectes of every Towne Paryshe & Hamlet to arest the sayd Vacaboundes & ydell persons & them bryng to any of the Justices of Peace of the same Shyre or Libertie, or els to the Highe Constable of the Hundrede Rape or Wapentake wythin whyche suche persones shalbe taken ; and yf he be taken wythin any Cyte or Towen Corporate, than to be brought before the Mayre, Shereffes or Baylyffes of every suche Towne Corporate ; and that every suche Justyce of Peace, Highe Constable, Mayres, Shereffes and Baylyffes by their dyscretions shall cause every suche ydell person so to hym brought to be had to the next market Towne or other place, where the sayde Justices of Peace, Highe Constable, Mayres, Baylyffes or other Officers shall thynke most convenyent by his or there discretions & there to be tyed to the end of a Carte naked and be beten wyth Whyppes thoroughe oute the same market Towne or other place tyll his Body be blody by reason of suche whyppyng ; and after suche punysshement & whyppyng had, the person so punysshed by the dyscretion of the Justice of Peace, Highe Constable, Mayre, Sheryffes, Baylyffes & other Officers, afore whom suche person shalbe brought, shalbe enyoyned upon his othe to retourne forthewyth wythout delaye in the next & streyght waye to the place where he was borne, or where he last dwelled before the same punysshement by the space of iij yeres & there put hym selfe to laboure, lyke as a trewe man oweth to doo . . . and yf the person so whypped be an ydell person & no common begger than after suche whippyng he shall be kepte in the Stockes till he hath founde suertie to goo to servyce or elles to laboure after the dyscretion of the sayde Justice of Peace, Mayres, Shireffes, Baylyffes, Highe Constables or other suche Offycers afore whome any suche ydell person beyng no commen begger shalbe brought, yf by the dyscretion of the same Justice of Peace, Mayer, Shyreff, Bayly, Highe Constable, or other suche hedde offycer, yt be so thought convenyent & that the partie so punysshed be able to fynde suretye or elles to be ordered & sworne to repayer to the place where he was borne or where he last dwelled by the space of three yeres.

ii.

[1549, May 27. Minute of Court of Aldermen, printed in Harrison, iv. 313, from London *Repertory*, xii, f. 92.]

Amcotes, Mayor.
Wylkynson.

Item, John Wylkynson, coriour, who comenly suffreth & meynteyneth interludes & playes to be made and kept within his dwellyng house, was streyghtly commandid no more to suffer eny suche pleyes there to be kept, vpon peyne of imprysonement, &c.

iii.

[1549, July 4. Minute of Court of Aldermen, printed in Harrison, iv. 313, from London *Repertory*, xii. 1, f. 100.]

Interludes & bukler playinge.

At this courte, yt was agreyd that my Lorde Mayer, at his next repayrynge to the Lorde Chaunceler, shulde desyre his Lordeshyps ayde and advise for the steyinge of all comen interludes & pleyes within the Citie & the suburbes therof. And further, that euery of my maisters thaldermen shulde take suche ordre in their wardes with the constables, & otherwyse by their discrecion, that there be no more buckler playing suffred nor vsed within eny of their wardes duryng this besye tyme.

iv.

[1549, 7 Nov. Minute of Court of Aldermen, printed in Harrison, iv. 314, from London *Repertory*, xii. 1, f. 162ᵛ.]

Hyll, Mayor.
Enterludes.

Item, it is orderyd that the ij Secondaries of the Compters, Mr. Atkyns & Mr. Burnell, shall, accordyng to the tenour of the recognysaunce lately taken before the Lorde grete Master, & remaynyng with my Lorde Mayer, pervse all suche enterludes as hereafter shalbe pleyed by eny comen pleyr of the same within the Citie or the liberties therof, And make reporte of the same to the Lorde Mayer for the tyme beynge, And accordyng thervnto, my Lorde Mayer to suffer them to go forwarde, or to stey.

v.

[1550, 23 Dec. Minute of Court of Aldermen, printed in Harrison, iv. 314, from London *Repertory*, xii. 2, f. 294ᵛ.]

Players of interludes.

At this Courte, certein comen plaiers of interludes within this Citie were bounden by Recognisaunce as herafter insuythe :

Item, Johannes Nethe, Robertus Southyn, Robertus Drake, Robertus Peacocke, Johannes Nethersall, Robertus Sutton, Ricardus Jugler,

Johannes Ronner, Willelmus Readyng, Edmundus Stokedale, Johannes Rawlyns, Johannes Crane, Ricardus Gyrke, Johannes Radstone, Oliuerus Page, Ricardus Pokeley, Ricardus Parseley, & Willelmus Clement, recognoverunt se & eorum quemlibet, per se debere domino Regi xx li, bonis etc soluendis etc : The condicion, etc, that yf the above bounden John Nethe, Robert Southyn etc & eny and euery of them, do not at herafter play eny interlude or comen play within eny of our Soueraygn Lorde the kynges domynyons, without the especiall licence of our seid Soueraygn Lorde, or of his most honourable Councell for the tyme beyng, had & obteyned for the same, And also yf they the seid Recognytours, & euery of them, do att all & euery tyme & tymes herafter, when they or any of them shalbe, by the seid Counsell or eny of them, sent for, personally appere before the seid Counsell or some of them, that then, etc, or els etc.

vi.

[1553. City order cited from *Letter Book*, R, f. 246, in *V. H. London*, i. 295.]

Plays and interludes were forbidden before 3 p.m. on Sundays and holidays.

vii.

[1558. A reference to plays is cited from *Letter Book*, V, f. 216, in *V. H. London*, i. 322.]

viii.

[1559, April 7. Proclamation. Despatches in *V. P.* vii. 65, 71, also record this, which, however, is not preserved. It forms no part of *Procl.* 504 for peace with France, which both Machyn and Holinshed describe as proclaimed immediately before it, and which bears date 7 April. *Procl.* 503, of 22 March, prescribing Easter Sacrament in both kinds, has a clause enjoining mayors and other officers to commit to prison ' all disordred persons, that shall seke willingly to breake, either by misordred dede, or by railing, or contemptuous speach, the common peace and band of charytie ' ; but, apart from the discrepancy of dates, this seems too general in its terms to answer the descriptions.]

(a)

[Entry in *Machyn's Diary*, 193, misdated April 8.]

Bluw-mantyll dyd proclaymyd that no players shuld play no more tyll a serten tyme of no mans players ; but the mare or shreyff, balle, constabull, or odur offesers take them, lay them in presun, and the quen commondement layd on them.

(b)

[Extract from Holinshed, *Chronicle*, iii. 1184.]

The same time also [April 7] was another proclamation made under the queenes hand in writing, inhibiting that from thenceforth no plaies nor interludes should be exercised, till Alhallowes tide next insuing.

ix.

[1559, May 8.   Extract from *An Act for the Uniformity of Common Prayer and Service in the Church and Administration of the Sacraments* (*1 Eliz.* c. 2), printed in *Statutes*, iv. 1, 355.   Later clauses give concurrent power to deal with offences under the Act to justices of assize or mayors and other head officers of cities and boroughs, and to archbishops and bishops and other ordinaries by ecclesiastical process.]

It is ordained and enacted by the authority abovesaid, that if any person or persons whatsoever, after the said feast of the Nativity of St. John Baptist next coming [24 June 1559], shall in any interludes, plays, songs, rhymes, or by other open words, declare or speak anything in the derogation, depraving, or despising of the same book [of Common Prayer], or of anything therein contained, or any part thereof, . . . then every such person, being thereof lawfully convicted in form aforesaid, shall forfeit to the queen our sovereign lady, her heirs and successors, for the first offence a hundred marks.

x.

[1559, May 16.   Proclamation 509, printed in Collier, i. 166, and Hazlitt, *E. D. S.* 19.]
¶ By the Quene.

Forasmuche as the tyme wherein common Interludes in the Englishe tongue are wont vsually to be played, is now past vntyll All Hallou-tyde, and that also some that haue ben of late vsed, are not conuenient in any good ordred Christian Common weale to be suffred.   The Quenes Maiestie doth straightly forbyd all maner Interludes to be playde eyther openly or priuately, except the same be notified before hande, and licenced within any Citie or towne corporate, by the Maior or other chiefe officers of the same, and within any shyre, by suche as shalbe Lieuetenauntes for the Quenes Maiestie in the same shyre, or by two of the Justices of peax inhabyting within that part of the shire where any shalbe played.

And for instruction to euery of the sayde officers, her maiestie doth likewise charge euery of them, as they will aunswere : that they permyt none to be played wherin either matters of religion or of the gouernaunce of the estate of the common weale shalbe handled or treated, beyng no meete matters to be wrytten or treated vpon, but by menne of aucthoritie, learning and wisedome, nor to be handled before any audience, but of graue and discreete persons :   All which partes of this proclamation, her maiestie chargeth to be inuiolably kepte.   And if any shal attempt to the contrary :   her maiestie giueth all maner of officers that haue authoritie to see common peax kepte in commaundement, to arrest and enprison the parties so offendinge, for the space of fourtene dayes or more, as cause shal nede :   And furder also vntill good assuraunce may be founde and gyuen, that they shalbe of good behauiour, and no more to offende in the likes.

And further her maiestie gyueth speciall charge to her nobilitie and gentilmen, as they professe to obey and regarde her maiestie, to take good order in thys behalfe wyth their seruauntes being players, that this her maiesties commaundement may be dulye kepte and obeyed.

Yeuen at our Palayce of Westminster the xvi. daye of Maye, the first yeare of oure Raygne.

xi.

[1559, June. Lord Robert Dudley to the Earl of Shrewsbury, Lord President of the North, printed from *Heralds College Talbot MS.* E. f. 29, in Collier, i. 168 ; also in Lodge, i. 376.]

My good Lorde,

Where my servauntes, bringers hereof unto you, be suche as ar plaiers of interludes ; and for the same have the Licence of diverse of my Lords here, under ther seales and handis, to plaie in diverse shieres within the realme under there aucthorities, as maie amplie appere unto your L. by the same licence. I have thought emong the rest by my Lettres to beseche your good L. conformitie to them like wise, that they maie have your hand and seale to ther licence for the like libertye in Yorke shiere ; being honest men, and suche as shall plaie none other matters (I trust) ; but tollerable and con-venient ; whereof some of them have bene herde here alredie before diverse of my Lordis : for whome I shall have good cause to thank your L. and to remaine your L. to the best that shall lie in my litle power. And thus I take my leave of your good L. From Westm., the of June, 1559.

Your good L. assured,

R. Duddley.

To the right Honourable & my verie good Lorde, the Erle of Shrewsburie.

xii.

[1559, *c.* 13 June. Extract from *Injunctions given by the Queen's Majesty concerning both the Clergy and Laity of this Realm,* printed by Pollard, *S. F.* 13 ; in full in Gee, 46, and E. Cardwell, *Documentary Annals of the Church of England* (ed. 1844), i. 210.]

Li. Item, because there is a great abuse in the printers of bookes, which for couetousness cheefely, regard not what they print, so they may haue gaine, whereby ariseth great disorder by publication of vnfruitefull, vaine, and infamous bookes and papers, the Queenes maiestie straitlye chargeth and commaundeth, that no manner of person shall print any manner of booke or paper, of what sort, nature or in what language soeuer it be, excepte the same be firste licensed by her maiestie, by expresse wordes in writing, or by six of her priuie counsel : or be perused and licensed by the Archbishops of Canter-burie and Yorke, the Bishop of London, the Chauncelors of both Vniuersities, the Bishop being Ordinarye and the Archdeacon also of the place, where any such shal be printed or by two of them, wherof the Ordinarie of the place to be alwayes one. And that the names of such as shall allowe the same to bee added in the end of euery such worke, for a testimonie of the alowance thereof. And because many pamphlets, playes and ballads, bee oftentimes printed, wherein regarde would bee had, that nothing therein should be either heretical, seditious, or vnseemely for Christian eares : her maiestie likewise commaundeth, that no manner of person shall enterprise to print any such, excepte the same bee to him licensed by suche her maiesties Commissioners, or three of them, as be appointed in the Cittie of London, to heare and determine diuers causes Ecclesiasticall, tending to the execution of certaine statutes, made the last Parliament for vniformitie of order in Religion. And if any shall sell or vtter any maner of bookes or papers, being not licensed, as is aboue sayd : that the same partie shalbe punished by order of the saide Commissioners, as to the qualitie of the fault shalbe thought meete. And touching all other bookes of matters of religion, or pollicie, or gouernance, that hath bene printed eyther on this side the seas, or on the other side, because the diuersitie of them is great, and that there nedeth good consideration to be had of the particularities thereof, her maiestie referreth the prohibition or permission thereof, to the order whiche her sayde Commissioners within the Cittie of London shall take and notifie. According to the whiche, her maiestie straitly commaundeth all maner her subiectes, and especially the Wardens and company of Stationers to be obedient.

Prouided that these orders doe not extende to any prophane aucthors, and works in any language that hath ben heretofore commonly receiued or allowed in any of the vniuersities or schooles, but the same may be printed and vsed as by good order they were accustomed.

[From appended Articles of Enquiry for diocesan visitations.]

Item, whether you know any person in your parish . . . that hath invented, bruited, or set forth any rumours, false and seditious tales, slanders, or makers, bringers, buyers, sellers, keepers, or conveyors of any unlawful books, which might stir or provoke sedition, or maintain superstitious service within this realm, or any aiders, counsellors, procurers, or maintainers thereunto.

Item, whether any minstrels or any other persons do use to sing or say any songs or ditties that be vile or unclean, and especially in derision of any godly order now set forth and established.

xiii.

[1559, July 19. Extract from Patent for the establishment of the High Commission for ecclesiastical causes, printed by Gee, 147, from *Patent Roll, 1 Eliz.* p. 9, m. 23 dorso ; also in Cardwell, *Documentary Annals,* i. 255. There were later commissions of 20 July 1562 (heads from *S. P. D. Eliz.* xxvi. 41, in Gee, 178), 1572 (*P. R. 14 Eliz.* p. 8), 23 April 1576 (text in Strype, *Grindal*, 543), 1583 (cf. Strype, *Whitgift*, i. 268), and 1601 (text from *P. R. 43 Eliz.* p. 16, m. 37 dorso, in Rymer, xvi. 400). That of 1562 seems to have followed the model of 1559 ; those of 1576 and 1601 give a jurisdiction over seditious books similar to that of 1559, but omit the provision as to vagrants in London, which was doubtless made unnecessary by the legislation of 1572 (cf. No. xxiv).]

Elizabeth, by the grace of God, &c., to the Reverend Father in God Matthew Parker nominated Bishop of Canterbury, and Edmond

Grindall nominated Bishop of London [and others] greeting. Where at our Parliament . . . there was two Acts and Statutes made and established, the one entitled An Act for the Uniformity of Common Prayer . . . and the other entitled An Act restoring to the Crown the Ancient Jurisdiction of the State Ecclesiastical and Spiritual . . . and where divers seditious and slanderous persons do not cease daily to invent and set forth false rumours, tales, and seditious slanders, not only against us and the said good laws and statutes, but also have set forth divers seditious books within this our realm of England, meaning thereby to move and procure strife, division, and dissension amongst our loving and obedient subjects, much to the disquieting of us and our people :

Wherefore we . . . have authorized, assigned, and appointed you to be our Commissioners, and by these presents do give our full power and authority to you or six of you . . . to inquire . . . for all offences, misdoers, and misdemeanours . . . contrary to the tenor and effect of the said several Acts and Statutes, and either of them ; and also of all and singular heretical opinions, seditious books, contempts, conspiracies, false rumours, tales, seditious misbehaviours, slanderous words or showings published, invented or set forth or hereafter to be published, invented or set forth by any person or persons against us or contrary or against any the laws or statutes of this our realm, or against the quiet governance and rule of our people and subjects in any county, city, or borough or other place or places within this our realm of England, and of all and every the coadjutors, counsellors, comforters, procurers and abettors of every such offender ; and . . . to hear and determine all the premises . . . and to visit, reform, redress, order, correct and amend . . . errors, heresies, crimes, abuses, offences, contempts and enormities spiritual and ecclesiastical . . . and to inquire of and search out all ruleless men, quarrellers, vagrants and suspect persons within our city of London and ten miles compass about the same city, and of all assaults and frays done and committed within the same city and the compass aforesaid.

xiv.

[1563, Sept. 30. Precept from Lord Mayor to Aldermen, noted, apparently from *Journal, Lodge*, No. 18, f. 184, in ' Abstract of Several Orders relating to the Plague ' (*Addl. MS.* 4376, f. 52) ; cf. Creighton, i. 317]

Another to prohibit all interludes & playes during the Infection.

xv.

[1564, Feb. 23. Extract from letter of Edmund Grindal, Bishop of London, at Paul's, to Sir W. Cecil, printed *M. S. C.* i. 148, from *Lansd. MS.* 7, f. 141 ; also in Grindal, *Remains* (1843), 269 ; Wright, i. 166.]

Mr. Calfhill this mornynge shewed me your letter to him, wherin ye wishe some politike orders to be devised agaynste Infection. I thinke it verie necessarie, and wille doo myne endevour bothe by exhortation, and otherwise. I was readye to crave your helpe for that purpose afore, as one nott vnmyndefulle of the parishe.

By searche I doo perceive, thatt ther is no one thinge off late is more lyke to have renewed this contagion, then the practise off an idle sorte off people, which have ben infamouse in all goode common weales : I meane these Histriones, common playours ; who now daylye, butt speciallye on holydayes, sett vp bylles, whervnto the youthe resorteth excessively, & ther taketh infection : besydes that goddes worde by theyr impure mowthes is prophaned, and turned into scoffes ; for remedie wheroff in my iugement ye shulde do verie well to be a meane, that a proclamation wer sette furthe to inhibitte all playes for one whole yeare (and iff itt wer for ever, it wer nott amisse) within the Cittie, or 3. myles compasse, vpon paynes aswell to the playours, as to the owners off the howses, wher they playe theyr lewde enterludes.

xvi.

[1569, May 12. City precept, printed in Harrison, iv. 315, from *Journal*, xix, f. 167ᵛ.]

A precept for no playes to be played from the last day of May 1569, vntill the last day of September then next following. And also for beting clothes in wyndowes & other places next the streat. Intratur.

Forasmuch as thoroughe the greate resort, accesse and assembles of great multitudes of people vnto diuerse and seuerall Innes and other places of this Citie, and the liberties & suburbes of the same, to thentent to here and see certayne stage playes, enterludes, and other disguisinges, on the Saboth dayes and other solempne feastes commaunded by the church to be kept holy, and there being close pestered together in small romes, specially in this tyme of sommer, all not being and voyd of infeccions and diseases, whereby great infeccion with the plague, or some other infeccious diseases, may rise and growe, to the great hynderaunce of the comon wealth of this citty, and perill and daunger of the quenes maiesties people, the inhabitantes thereof, and all others repayryng thether, about there necessary affares ; . . . Thes are, in the quenes maiesties name, streightly to charge and commaund, that no mannour of parson or parsons whatsoeuer, dwelling or inhabiting within this citie of London liberties and suburbes of the same, being Inkepers, Tablekepers, Tauernours, hall-kepers, or bruers, Do or shall, from and after the last daye of this moneth of May nowe next ensuinge, vntill the last day of September then next following, take vppon him or them to set fourth, eyther openly or privatly, anny stage play or interludes, or to permit or suffer to be set fourth or played within his or there mansion howse, yarde, court, garden, orchard, or other place or places whatsoeuer, within this Cittye of London, the liberties or suburbes of the same, any mannour of stage play, enterlude, or other disguising whatsoeuer. . . . And fayle ye not heíof, as ye tender the welth of this citie, and the health of the quenes maiesties people, her highnes good fauour and pleasure, and will aunswere for the contrary at your vttermost perills. Yeouen at the guild hall of London, the xij of May, 1569. God save the Quene.

xvii.

[1571, Nov. 27. Minute of City Court of Aldermen, printed in Harrison, iv. 317, from *Repertory*, xvii, f. 236ᵛ.]

**Intratur.
Preceptes to
be made.** Item, it was ordered that preceptes shalbe made to euery of my Masters thaldermen, that they from henceforth suffre no playe or enterlude to be played within the precynctes of there seuerall wardes vpon Sondaies, holly daies, or other daie of the weke, or ells at nyght of any of the same daies, till suche tyme as other order by this courte shalbe taken in that behalf.

xviii.

[1571, Dec. 6. Minute of Court of Aldermen, printed in Harrison, iv. 318, from *Repertory*, xvii, f. 239ᵛ.]

**My Lord of
Leicesters men
licensed to playe.** Item, this daye, licence is geven to my lord of Leicesters men to playe within this Citie such matters as are alowed of to be played, at convenient howers & tymes, so that it be not in tyme of devyne service.

xix.

[1572, Jan. 3. Abstract of Proclamation for the Execution of the Laws made against Unlawful Retainers (*Procl.* 663) ; for text cf. *M. S. C.* i. 350.]

Requires justices of assise to enforce after 20 Feb. 1572 the statutes against unlawful retainers, and in particular *3 Hen. VII* (1487), c. 12, one of several statutes confirming *8 Hen. VI* (1429), c. 4, which forbade the giving of any livery of cloths or hat by a lord to other than his menials and lawyers (*R. O. Statutes of the Realm*, ii. 240, 522).

xx.

[1572, *c.* Jan. Letter to the Earl of Leicester from his Players ; cf. text in Bk. iii.]

Requests that they may be retained as ' houshold servaunts and daylie wayters ', in view of the recent proclamation (No. xix, *supra*), and may continue to have their lord's license to certify the same when they travel.

xxi.

1572, Jan. 29. Minute of Court of Aldermen, printed in Harrison, iv. 318, from *Repertory*, xvii, f. 263ᵛ.]

**My lord of
Burgauaneys
players.** Item, it is further granted at the like request [of Sir Thomas Gresham] that my lord of Burgaueneys players shall play within this Citie duringe my lordes Maiours pleasure.

xxii.

[1572. Extract from MS. *Chronologie* of William Harrison, s.a. 1572, printed in Harrison, i. liv. The entries continue to 1593, and this one was probably written after the building of the Theatre and Curtain in 1576.]

1572. Plaies are banished for a time out of London, lest the resort vnto them should ingender a plague, or rather disperse it, being alredy begonne. Would to god these comon plaies were exiled for altogether, as semenaries of impiety, & their theaters pulled downe, as no better then houses of baudrie. It is an euident token of a wicked time when plaiers wexe so riche that they can build suche houses. As moche I wish also to our comon beare baitinges vsed on the Sabaothe daies.

xxiii.

[1572, May 20. Minute of City Court of Aldermen, printed in Harrison, iv. 318, from *Repertory*, xvii, f. 316.]

The Counsells Lettres for Plaies & Commodies. Intratur.
Item, this daie, after the readyng of the Lordes of the Ouenes Maiesties most honorable Counselles Letters, written in the favor of certein persones to haue in there howses, yardes, or back sydes, being overt & open places, such playes, enterludes, commedies, & tragedies as maye tende to represse vyce & extoll vertwe, for the recreacion of the people, & therby to drawe them from sundrye worser exercyses, The matter theerof being first examyned, sene & allowed, by such discrete person or persones as shalbe by the Lord Maiour thervnto appoynted, and takyng bondes of the said houskeapars not to suffer the same playes to be in the tyme of devyne service, & vpon other condicions in the same Letters specified :

Item, it was agreed that Master Townclark shall devyse a letter for answer of thother, to be sent vnto my Lord Burleighe, signifiing to his honour, that it is thought very perillous (considering the tyme of the yere & the heat of the weather) to haue such conventicles of people by such meanes called together, wherof the greatest number are of the meanest sorte, beseching his honour, yf it maye so seame him good, to be a meane wherby the same, for a tyme, may be forborne.

xxiv.

[1572, June 29. Extract from *An Acte for the punishement of Vacabondes and for Releif of the Poore & Impotent* (14 Eliz. c. 5), printed in *Statutes*, iv. 590. The Act was continued and amended in detail by *18 Eliz.* c. 3 in 1576 (*St.* iv. 610) and continued by *37 Eliz.* c. 11 in 1584–5 (*St.* iv. 718).]

[§ 2.] . . . All & every person and persons whatsoever they bee, being above thage of fourtene yeres, being hereafter sett foorth by this Acte of Parliament to bee Roges Vacabonds or Sturdy Beggers, and bee at any tyme after the Feaste of Sainte Bartholomewe the Apostle next comming [24 Aug.] taken begging in any parte of this Realme, or taken vagrant wandring and misordering themselves contrary to the purport of this present Acte of Parliament in any part of the same, shall uppon their Apprehention be brought before one of the

Justices of the Peece or Maior or Cheef Officer of Cities Boroughes
and Townes Corporate within the Countye Cytye Boroughe or Towne
Corporate, where the Apprehention shall happen to bee . . . to bee
presentlye committed to . . . Gaole . . . or . . . Prison . . . untyll the
next Sessions of the Peace or Generall Gaole Delivery. . . . At whiche
Sessions or Gaole Delyverye yf suche person or persones bee duelye
convict of his or her Rogishe or Vacabondes Trade of Lyef . . . that
then ymmedyatlye he or shee shalbe adjudged to bee grevouslye
whipped, and burnte through the gristle of the right Eare with a hot
Yron of the compasse of an Ynche about, manifestinge his or her
rogyshe kynde of Lyef, and his or her Punyshment receaved for the
same . . . which Judgment shall also presentlye bee executed, Except
some honest person . . . wyll of his Charitye be contented presentlye
to take suche Offendour before the same Justices into his Service for
one whole yere next followinge.

[§ 4.] . . . Yf after the said Punyshment executed or Judgement
gyven, the said persone . . . do eftsones fall againe to any kynde of
Rogyshe or Vacabonde Trade of Lyef, that then the said Roge Vacabonde or Sturdy Begger from thenceforthe to be taken adjudged
& demed in all respectes as a Felon ; and shall in all Degrees receave
have suffer and forfayte as a Felon, excepte some honest person . . .
wyll . . . take him or her into his Service for two whole yeres. . . . And
yf suche Roge or Vacabounde . . . eftsones the third tyme fall againe
to a kynde of Rogyshe or Vacabounde Trade of Lyef, that then suche
Roge or Vacabound shalbe adjudged & deemed for a Felon, and suffer
paynes of Death and losse of Land and Goodes as a Felon without
Allowance or Benefyte of Cleargye or Sanctuary.

[§ 5.] . . . All and everye persone and persones beynge whole and
mightye in Body and able to labour, havinge not Land or Maister,
nor using any lawfull Marchaundize Crafte or Mysterye whereby hee
or shee might get his or her Lyvinge, and can gyve no reckninge
howe he or shee dothe lawfully get his or her Lyvinge ; & all Fencers
Bearewardes Comon Players in Enterludes & Minstrels, not belonging
to any Baron of this Realme or towardes any other honorable Personage of greater Degree ; all Juglers Pedlars Tynkers and Petye Chapmen ; whiche seid Fencers Bearewardes Comon Players in Enterludes
Mynstrels Juglers Pedlers Tynkers & Petye Chapmen, shall wander
abroade and have not Lycense of two Justices of the Peace at the leaste,
whereof one to be of the Quorum, when and in what Shier they shall
happen to wander . . . shalbee taken adjudged and deemed Roges
Vacaboundes and Sturdy Beggers.

[§ 12.] Provided alwayes, That yt shalbe lawfull to the Lord
Chauncelour or Lorde Keper of the Greate Seale of England for the
tyme beinge to make Lycence under the said Greate Seale, as heretofore hath benne accustomed, and that the said Lycence and Lycences
shall as largely extend as the Contentes of them wyll beare ; any
thing herein to the contrary in any wyse notwithstandinge.

[§ 39.] Provided alwayes, That . . . yt maye and shall be lawfull
to the Justice and Justices of Peace, Maior Baylyffes and other Head

Officers of those Cytyes, Boroughes Places and Townes Corporate where there bee Justice or Justices, to proceed to the execucion of this Acte within the Precinct and Compasse of their Liberties, in suche manner & fourme as the Justices of Peace in any Countye may or ought to doo within the same Countye by vertue of this Acte, any Matter or Thinge in this Acte expressed to the contrary therof notwithstandinge.

[§ 42.] Provided alwayes, That this Acte or any Thing therein contayned, or any aucthoritye thereby given, shall not in any wyse extend to dysheneryte prejudice or hinder John Dutton of Dutton in the Countye of Chester Esquier, his Heires or Assignes, for towching or concerninge any Libertye Priviledge Preheminence Aucthoritie Jurisdiccion or Inheritaunce which the sayd John Dutton nowe lawfully useth or hathe, or lawfully may or ought to use within the County Palatyne of Chester and the Countye of the Cyte of Chester, or eyther of them, by reason of any anncient Charteres of any Kinges of this Land, or by reason of any Prescription or other lawfull Usage or Tytle whatsoever.

XXV.

1573, July. Privy Council Minutes, printed in Dasent, viii. 131, 132.]

(a) [July 14]

A letter to the Lord Mayour of London to permitte libertie to certein Italian plaiers to make shewe of an instrument of strainge motiones within the Citie.

(b) [July 19]

A letter to the Lord Mayour to graunt libertie to certein Italians to make shewe of an instrument there, merveling that he did it not at their first request.

xxvi.

[1574, March 2. Lord Mayor and Aldermen of London to Lord Chamberlain Sussex, printed from *Cotton MS.* Roll xvi. 41, in Collier, i. 206 ; also by S. Ayscough in *Gentleman's Magazine*, lxii, 1, 412 ; Hazlitt, *E. D. S.* 23.]

Our dutie to your good L. humbly done. Whereas your Lord. hath made request in favour of one Holmes for our assent that he might have the appointment of places for playes and enterludes within this citie, it may please your L. to reteine undoubted assurance of our redinesse to gratifie, in any thing that we reasonably may, any persone whom your L. shall favor and recommend. Howbeit this case is such, and so nere touching the governance of this citie in one of the greatest matters thereof, namely the assemblies of multitudes of the Queenes people, and regard to be had to sundry inconveniences, whereof the peril is continually, upon everie occasion, to be foreseen by the rulers of this citie, that we cannot, with our duties, byside the precident farre extending to the hart of our liberties, well assent that the sayd apointment of places be committed to any private persone. For which, and other reasonable considerations, it hath long since pleased your good L. among the rest of her Majesties most honourable Counsell, to rest satisfied with our not granting to such persone as, by their most honourable lettres, was heretofore in like case commended to us. Byside that, if it might with reasonable convenience be granted, great offres have been, and be made for the same to the relefe of the poore in the hospitalles, which we hold as assured, that your L. will well allow that we prefer before the benefit of any private person. And so we committ your L. to the tuition of Almighty God. At London, this second of March, 1573.

Your L. humble

Wm. Box.	Leonell Ducket, Aldr.
Thomas Blanke.	James Haloys, Alderman.
Nicholas Woodrof.	Ambrose Nich'as, Ald.
Anthony Gamage.	Jhon Langley, Ald.
Wyllm Kympton.	Thomas Ramsey.
Wolstan Dixe.	Wyllym Lond.
John Ryvers, Maior.	John Clyffe.
Row. Hayward, Alder.	Richard Pype.
William Allyn, Alderman.	

To the most honourable our singular good Lord, the Erle of Sussex, Lord Chamberlan of the Queens most honourable Houshold.

xxvii.

[1574, March 22. Minute of Privy Council, printed from Register in Dasent, viii. 215.]

A letter to the Lord Mayour of London to advertise their Lordships what causes he hath to restraine plaies, to thintent their Lordships may the better aunswer suche as desyre to have libertye for the same.

xxviii.

[1574, May 10. Patent for Leicester's men ; cf. text in Bk. iii.]

Gives authority to perform music, and plays seen and allowed by the Master of the Revels, both in London and elsewhere, except during the time of common prayer, or of plague in London.

xxix.

[1574, July 22. Minute of Privy Council, printed from Register in Dasent, viii. 273.]

A letter to the Mayor of London to admitte the comedie plaiers to play within that Cittie and to be otherwise favorablie used.

A pasport for them to go to London, and to be well used in their voyadge.

xxx.

(a)

[1574, Nov. 15. Minute of Privy Council, printed from Register in Dasent, viii. 313.

Three letters of one effect to the Sherif and Justices of the counties of Middlesex, Essex and Surrey to restraine all plaiers and other unnecessarie assemblies, in respect of the plague, within x miles of London untill Esther next.

(b)

[1574, Nov. 15.   Extract from report on papers of W. M. Molyneux *Hist. MSS.* vii. 627).]

Letter from Lords of the Council to the Sheriff and Justices of the Peace of co. Surrey.   Ordering 'that there be no plays shewes nor any such unnecessarie assemblies vsed in that countie within ten myles of the cytie vntill Easter next vppon payne of imprisonment to such as shall in any wies offend to the contrarie ' : it having been ' found by experience that very great perill and inconveniences hath fallen vppon sondry of the queenes maiesties subjects by the sufferance of great assemblies of the people to come together at plaies and shewes neare London in this tyme of contagion and infection of the plague '.

xxxi.

[1574, c. Nov.   Extract from *An Exhortation, or Rule, sett downe by one Mr. ⟨Thomas⟩ Norton, sometyme Remembrauncer of London, wherebie the L. Maior of Lo. is to order himselfe and the Cittie*, printed by Collier, *Illustrations*, iii. 14, from a manuscript of Sir Christopher Hatton, now *Addl. MS.* 32379, f. 36, and datable by a mention of James Hawes (1574–5) as mayor.]

And one note out of place, that showld before have bene spoken : the presente time requirithe yowe to have good care and use good meanes towchinge the contagion of sickenes, that the sicke be kept from the whole, that the places of persons infected be made plaine to be knowen and the more releeved ; that sweetenes and holsomnes of publique places be provided for ; that unnecessarie and scarslie honeste resorts to plaies, to shewes to thoccasion of thronges and presse, except to the servyce of God; and especiallie the assemblies to the unchaste, shamelesse and unnaturall tomblinge of the Italion Weomen maye be avoided : to offend God and honestie is not to cease a plague.

xxxii.

[1574, Dec. 6.   Act of Common Council of London during the mayoralty of Sir James Hawes, printed *M. S. C.* i. 175, from copy in *Lansd. MS.* 20, enclosed with reply of City to Petition of Queen's men *c.* Nov. 1584 (cf. No. lxxv) ;   also in Collier, i. 208 ;   Hazlitt, *E. D. S.* 27.   I suppose that this is the record of 1574 on plays cited from *Liber Legum*, x. 363, in *V. H. London*, i. 322.]

Whearas hearetofore sondrye greate disorders and inconvenyences have benne found to ensewe to this Cittie by the inordynate hauntyinge of greate multitudes of people, speciallye youthe, to playes, enterludes, and shewes, namelye occasyon of ffrayes and quarrelles, eavell practizes of incontinencye in greate Innes, havinge chambers and secrete places adioyninge to their open stagies and gallyries, inveglynge and alleur-ynge of maides, speciallye orphanes and good Cityzens Children vnder Age, to previe and vnmete Contractes, the publishinge of vnchaste

vncomelye and vnshamefaste speeches and doynges, withdrawinge
of the Queenes Maiesties Subiectes from dyvyne service on Sonndaies
and hollydayes, at which Tymes suche playes weare Chefelye vsed,
vnthriftye waste of the moneye of the poore and fond persons,
sondrye robberies by pyckinge and Cuttinge of purses, vtteringe of
popular busye and sedycious matters, and manie other Corruptions
of youthe and other enormyties, besydes that allso soundrye slaughters
and mayheminges of the Quenes Subiectes have happened by ruines
of Skaffoldes, fframes, and Stagies, and by engynes, weapons, and
powder used in plaies ; And whear[as] in tyme of goddes visitacion
by the plaigue suche assemblies of the people in thronge and presse
have benne verye daungerous for spreadinge of Infection, and for the
same and other greate Cawses by the Aucthoritie of the honorable
Lordes maiors of this Cyttie and the aldermen their Brethern, and
speciallye uppon the severe and earneste Admonition of the Lordes
of the moste honorable Councell, with signifyenge of her maiesties
expresse pleasure and commaundemente in that behalfe, suche vse
of playes, Interludes, and shewes hathe benne duringe this tyme of
syckenes forbydden and restrayned ; And for that the lorde Maior
and his Bretheren the aldermen, together with the grave and discrete
Citizens in the Comen Councell assemblyd, doo doughte and feare
leaste vppon Goddes mercyfull withdrawinge his hand of syckenes
from vs (which god graunte !) the people, speciallye the meaner and
moste vnrewlye sorte, sheould with sodayne forgettinge of his visyta-
cion, withowte feare of goddes wrathe, and withowte deowe respecte
of this good and politique meanes that he hathe ordeyned for the
preservacion of Commen weales and peoples in healthe and good
order, retourne to the vndewe vse of suche enormyties to the greate
offence of god, the Quenes maiesties commaundementes and good
gouernaunce ; Nowe therfore, to the intent that suche perilles maie
be avoyded and the lawefull honest and comelye vse of plaies pastymes
and recreacions in good sorte onelye permitted, And good provision
hadd for the saiftie and well orderynge of the people thear assemblydd,
Be yt enacted by the Aucthoritie of this Comen Councell, That from
henceforthe no playe, Commodye, Tragidye, enterlude, nor publycke
shewe shalbe openlye played or shewed within the liberties of the
Cittie, whearin shalbe vttered anie wourdes, examples, or doynges of
anie vnchastitie, sedicion, nor suche lyke vnfytt and vncomelye matter,
vppon paine of Imprisonment by the space of xiiijten daies of all
persons offendinge in anie suche open playinge or shewinges, and v li.
for euerie suche offence ; And that no Inkeper Tavernekeper nor
other person whatsoeuer within the liberties of thys Cittie shall openlye
shewe or playe, nor cawse or suffer to be openlye shewed or played,
within the hous, yarde or anie other place within the Liberties of
this Cyttie anie playe, enterlude, Commodye, Tragidie, matter, or
shewe, which shall not be firste pervsed and Allowed in suche order
and fourme and by suche persons as by the Lorde Maior and Courte
of Aldermen for the tyme beinge shalbe appoynted, nor shall suffer
to be enterlaced, Added, mynglydd, or vttered in anie suche play,

enterlude, Comodye, Tragidie, or shewe anie other matter then suche as shalbe firste perused and allowed as ys abovesaid ; And that no person shall suffer anie plays, enterludes, Comodyes, Tragidies, or shewes to be played or shewed in his hous, yarde, or other place wheareof he then shall have rule or power, but onelye suche persons and in suche places as apon good and reasonable consideracions shewed shalbe thearvnto permitted and allowed by the lord maiour and Aldermen for the tyme beinge ; Neither shall take or use anie benifitt or Advauntage of suche permission or Allowaunces before or vntill suche person be bound to the Chamberlaine of London for the tyme beinge with suche suerties and in suche Summe and suche fourme for the keepinge of good order and avoydinge of the discordes and Inconvenyences abovesaid, as by the Lorde maior and Courte of Aldermen for the tyme beinge shall seme convenyent ; neither shall vse or execvte aine suche Lycence, or permission, at or in anie tymes in which the same for anie reasonable consideracion of syckenes or otherwise shalbe by the Lorde Maior and Aldermen by publique proclamacion or by precept to suche persons restrayned or Commaunded to staye and cease, nor in anie usuall tyme of dyvyne service in the sonndaie or hollydaie, nor receyve anie to that purpose in tyme of service to se the same, apon payne to forfeite for euerie offence v li. ; And be yt enacted that euerie person so to be lycensed or permitted shall duringe the tyme of suche Contynuaunce of suche lycens or permission paye or Cawse to be paid to the vse of the poor in hospitalles of the Cyttie or of the poore of the Cyttie visyted with sycknes, by the dyscretion of the said lorde maiour and Aldermen, suche somes and Paymentes and in suche forme as betwen the lord Maior and Aldermen for the tyme beinge on thonne partie and suche person so to be lycensed or permitted on th'other partie shalbe Agreed, apon payne that in waunte of euerie suche paymente, or if suche person shall not firste be bound with good suerties to the Chamberlayne of London for the tyme beinge for the trewe payment of suche Sommes to the poore, That then euerye suche lycence or permission shalbe vtterlye voide and euerie doinge by force or Cullour of suche lycence or permission shalbe adiudged an offence against this Acte in suche manner as if no suche lycence or permission hadd benne hadd, nor made, anie suche lycence or permission to the Contrarye Notwithstandinge ; And be yt lykewise Enacted that all Sommes and fforfeytures to be incurrydd for anie offence Against this Acte and all forfeytures of Bondes to be taken by force meane or occasyon of this Acte shalbe ymployed to the reliefe of the poore in the hospitalles of this Cittie, or the poore infected or diseased in this Cittie of London, as the lorde Maior and Courte of Aldermen for the tyme beinge shall adiudge meete to be distributed ; and that the Chamberlayne of London shall have and recover the same to the purpozies aforesaid by Bill, plainte, Accion of dett, or ynformacion to be Comenced and pursewed in his owne name in the Courte of the vtter Chamber of the Guildhall of London Called the Maioures Courte, in which svte no Essoine nor Wager of Lawe for the defendaunte shalbe Admittyd or allowed ; Provydid allwaie that this Acte (otherwise then towchinge the publishinge of vnchaste, sedycious, and vnmete matters :) shall not extend to anie plaies, Enterludes, Comodies, Tragidies, or shewes to be played or shewed in the pryvate hous, dwellinge, or lodginge of anie nobleman, Citizen, or gentleman, which shall or will then have the same thear so played or shewed in his presence for the festyvitie of anie marriage, Assemblye of ffrendes, or otherlyke cawse withowte publique or Commen Collection of money of the Auditorie or beholders theareof, reservinge alwaie to the Lorde Maior and Aldermen for the tyme beinge the Iudgement and construction Accordinge to equitie what shalbe Counted suche a playenge or shewing in a pryvate place, anie thinge in this Acte to the Contrarie notwithstanding.

xxxiii.

[1577, April 8. Robert Dudley, Earl of Leicester, to Lord Burghley, printed *M. S. C.* i. 151, from *Lansdowne MS.* 25, f. 38. The Lord Chamberlain was the Earl of Sussex. Nothing more is known of the nature or issue of Sir Jerome Bowes's suit. He was a follower of Leicester in 1571 (Stowe, *Annales*, 669), but was banished from court for slandering him between the date of this letter and Aug. 8, 1577 (*S. P. D. Add. Eliz.* xxv. 30). In 1583 he was sent as ambassador to Russia.]

My good L. I am requyred to put you in remembrance, for that Sir Ierome Boues semes that your L. hath partely forgotten that hit was her maiesties pleashr, that your L. my Chamberleyn & I shuld conferr & consider of the sute touching plays to be granted to him & certayn others, &c., which hir maiesties pleashr I brought to your L. & my Chamberleyn being together in the preuey Chamber at Hampton court. & I remember at that time we talking of that we myslyked of the perpetuytie that they sutors desiered. & this also my L. Chamberleyn him self doth well remember. Thus much I thought good at his request to remember to your L. that it ys very trew hir maiestie dyd referr the consyderacion of the sute to vs & to make report thereof accordingly. So I wyll take leue & wishe your L. perfect health, this viij of Aprill,

your L. assured frend,
R. Leycester.

xxxiv.

[1577 Aug. 1. Minute of Privy Council, printed (*bis*) from Register in Dasent, ix. 388 ; x. 4.]

A letter to the Lord Wentworth, Master of the Rolles, and Mr. Lieutenant of the Tower signifieng unto them that for thavoiding of the sicknes likelie to happen through the heate of the weather and assemblies of the people of London to playes, her Highnes' plesure is that as the Lord Mayour hath taken order within the Citee, so they immediatlie upon the receipt of their Lordships' letters shall take order with such as are and do use to play without the Liberties of the Citee within that countie, as the theater and such like, shall forbeare any more to play untill Mighelmas be past, at the least, as they will aunswer to the contrarye.

XXXV.

[1577, Oct. 5. Extract from letter (Oct. 6) of William Fleetwood, Recorder of London, to Lord Treasurer Burghley, printed in *M. S. C.* i. 152, from *Lansdowne MS.* 24, f. 196 ; also in Wright, ii. 66.]

Yesterday . . . I was at London with the Master of the Rolls at my Lord Maiors at dyner. . . . At my Lord Maiors there dyned the Master of the Rolles, Justice Sowthcot, Sir William Damsell, Mr. Levetenant, Sir Rowland Hayward, Mr. Justice Randoll, Alderman Pulliso and my self. At after dyner we heard a brabell betwene John Wotton and the Levetenuntes sonne of the one parte, and certen ffreholders of Shordyche, for a matter at the Theater. I mistrust that Wotton wilbe found in the fault although he complayned.

XXXVI.

[1578, Jan. 13. Privy Council Minute, printed in Dasent, x. 144

To the Lord Maiour of London to geve order that one Drousiano ['Dronsiano', Dasent], an Italian, a commediante and his companye, may playe within the Cittie and the Liberties of the same betwene this and the firste weeke in Lent.

XXXVII.

[1578, July 18. Extract from letter (July 21) from William Fleetwood, Recorder of London, to Lord Treasurer Burghley, printed in *M. S. C.* i. 155, from *Lansdowne MS.* 26, f. 191 ; also in Wright, ii. 86.]

Vpon Fridaye laste my Lord of London, my Lord Wentworthe and Mr. Lievetenunte (but the Master of the Rolles was absent) did assemble at my Lord Maiours, in assistaunce for good order shewed furthe the Lords lettres. Sir Thomas Gresham, the Deane of Westminster, Mr. Iustice Southcote, Sir William Damsell and others were wont to be of the nomber ; but surelie I think they were forgotten at the writinge of my Lords theire honorable lettres. . . . I shewed vnto my Lords our Assistaunts those pointes that your honour in tyme paste gave vs for good order; plaies, vnlawful games, ffensse skoles, vacaboundes and suche like to be suppressed, with a vigilant eye to the plage, to the watches, and to laye often privie searches.

XXXVIII.

[1578, Nov. 10. Minute of Privy Council, printed from Register in Dasent, x. 381.]

A letter to Mr. Doctor Fourthe, Robert Lewseye, Edward Bellingham and Barnarde Randolphe, esquiers, to restraine certen players within the Bouroghe of Southewarke and other places nere adjoyning within that part of Surreye, who by means of the alluring of the people to their plaies [plans, Dasent] doe augement the infection of the Plages in London, and if they shall not obeye their order to see them severely punished.

xxxix.

[1578, Dec. 23. Minute of Privy Council, printed from Register in Dasent, x. 435.]

A letter to the Lord Maiour and the Justices of Middlesex and Surrey requiring them to suffer the exercise of playes within the Cittie of London and without the Liberties, and to have regarde that suche orders as are prescribed for the stayeng of thinfection maie be duelie observed, so as ther growe no hurte unto the sounde in their publicque assemblies.

xl.

[1578, Dec. 24. Privy Council Minute, printed in Dasent, x. 436.]

A letter to the Lord Maiour, &c, requiring him to suffer the Children of her Majesties Chappell, the servauntes of the Lord Chamberlaine, therle of Warwicke, the Erle of Leicester, the Erle of Essex and the Children of Powles, and no companies els, to exercise playeng within the Cittie, whome their Lordships have onlie allowed thereunto by reason that the companies aforenamed are appointed to playe this tyme of Christmas before her Majestie.

xli.

[1579, March 13. Minute of Privy Council, printed from Register in Dasent, xi. 73.]

To the Lord Maiour of London to take order within the Cittie and in all other places within his jurisdiccion that there be no plaiers suffered to plaie during this tyme of Lent, untill it be after the Ester weke; and also to advertise their Lordships whose plaiers they be, and in what places they have plaied since the begynnyng of this Lent, and that this order may be observed hereafter yerelie in the Lent tyme &c.

To the Justices of Peace in Midlesex to forbidd all maner of plaiers in the Suburbs of London and other places neare adjoyning to the same, that they do not in any wise exercise the same during this tyme of Lent, and that this order may be observed hereafter yerelie during the tyme of Lent, &c.

xlii.

[1580, Feb. 21. Indictment of Middlesex jury, printed by J. C. Jeaffreson, *Middlesex County Records*, ii. xlvii.]

Midd. ss. Juratores pro domina Regina presentant quod Johannes Braynes de Shorditche in comitatu Middlesexie yoman et Jacobus Burbage de eadem yoman xxi^{mo} die Februarii anno regni Elizabethe Dei gracia Anglie Francie et Hibernie Regine fidei defensoris &c. xxii^{do} et diuersis aliis diebus et vicibus antea et postea congregauerunt et manutenuerunt illicitas assemblaciones populi ad audienda et spectanda quedam colloquia siue interluda vocata playes or interludes per ipsos Johannem Braynes et Jacobum Burbage et diuersas alias personas ignotas exercitata et practicata apud quendam locum vocatum the Theatre in Hallywell in comitatu predicto Racione cuius

quidem illicite assemblacionis populi magne affraie insultus tumultus
et quasi insurrexiones et diuersa alia malefacta et enormia per quam-
plures maledispositas personas tunc et ibidem facta et perpetrata fuere
in magnam perturbacionem pacis Domine Regine ac subuersionem
bonorum ordinis et regiminis ac ad periculum vitarum diuersorum
bonorum subditorum dicte Domine Regine ibidem existencium ac
contra pacem ipsius Domine Regine necnon contra formam statuti
inde editi et prouisi &c.

xliii.

[1580, April 12. Sir Nicholas Woodrofe, Lord Mayor, to Sir Thomas
Bromley, Lord Chancellor, printed in *M. S. C.* i. 46, from *Remembrancia,*
. 9.]

My dutie humblie done to your Lp. Where it happened on Sundaie
last that some great disorder was committed at the Theatre, I sent
for the vnder shireue of Middlesex to vnderstand the cercumstances,
to the intent that by my self or by him I might haue caused such
redresse to be had as in dutie and discretion I might, and therefore
did also send for the plaiers to haue apered afore me, and the rather
because those playes doe make assembles of Cittizens and their familes
of whome I haue charge. But forasmuchas I vnderstand that your
Lp with other of hir Maiesties most honorable Counsell haue entered
into examination of that matter, I haue surceassed to procede further,
and do humbly refer the whole to your wisdomes and graue considerations. Howbeit I haue further thought it my dutie to informe
your Lp, and therewith also to beseche to haue in your honorable
remembrance, that the players of playes, which are vsed at the
Theatre, and other such places, and tumbleres and such like are
a very superfluous sort of men, and of suche facultie as the lawes
haue disalowed, and their exersise of those playes is a great hinderaunce
of the seruice of God, who hath with his mighty hand so lately
admonished vs of oure earnest repentance. It is also great corruption
of youthe with vnchast and wicked matters, occasion of muche incontinence, practises of many ffrayes, querrells, and other disorders and
inconueniences, bisid that the assemble of terme and parliament being
at hand, against which time the most honorable Lordes haue given
vs earnest charge to haue care to auoide vncleanenesse and pestering
of the Citty, the said playes are matter of great daunger. Therefore
I humble beseche your Lp, for those and other graue considerations
that your Lp can better call to mind, it will please you that some
order be taken by commaundement from your Lp and the rest of
the most honorable Lordes that the said playes and toumbelers be
wholy stayed and forbidden as vngodlye and perilous, as well at those
places nere our liberties as within the iurisdiction of this Cittie. And
so I leaue to troble your Lp. At London this 12 of Aprill 1580.

Your Lps humble,

N: W: M.

To the right honorable my singuler good Lord the Lord Chaunceller
of England.

xliv.

1580, April–July.   Minutes of Privy Council, printed from Register in Dasent, xi. 445 ; xii. 37, 112.]

(a) [April 13]

Robert Leveson and Larrance Dutton, servantes unto the Erle of Oxford, were committed to the Mareshalsea for committing of disorders and frayes appon the gentlemen of the Innes of the Courte.

(b) [May 26]

A letter to the Lord Chiefe Justice, Master of the Rolles and Mr. Justice Southcote, to examine a matter of a certaine fraye betwene the servauntes of th'erle of Oxforde and the gentlemen of the Innes of the Courtes.

(c) [July 18]

A letter to the Master of the Rooles and the Recorder of London to take bondes of Thomas Chesson (sometime servant to therle of Oxford) for his good behavior for one yere next following, and to release him out of the prison of the Gatehowse.

xlv.

[1580, April 17.   Minute of Privy Council, printed from Register in Dasent, xi. 449.]

A letter to the Lord Wentworth and Lord Hunsdon and the rest of the Justices of Pece in the county of Middlesex that wheras the Queen's Majesty had given straight charg unto the Lord Maiour to have a speciall care to the keping cleene of the City, and to provide and prevent all soch occasions and causes as might breed or encrease any infection, forasmuche as the great resorte of people to playes ys thought to be very dangerous &c, they are required to give order that all playes may be restrained until Michelmas, and further to have a good regard to the execution of the Statute against roges and vagabondes.

xlvi.

[1580, May 13.   Minute of Privy Council, printed from Register in Dasent, xii. 15.]

A letter to the Justices of Peace of the countie of Surrey that whereas their Lordships do understand that notwithstandinge their late order geven to the Lord Maiour to forbidd all playes within and about the Cittie untill Michalmas next for avoydynge of infection, nevertheles certen players do playe sunderie daies every weeke at Newington Buttes on that parte of Surrey without the jurisdiccion of the said Lord Maior contrary to their Lordships' order ; their Lordships requier the Justices not only to enquier who they be that disobey their comaundement in that behalf, and not only to forbidd them expresly for playing in any of theis remote places nere unto the Cittie untill Michaelmas, but to have regard that within the precincte of Surrey none be permitted to play ; if any do to comitt them and to advertise, &c.

xlvii.

[1580, June 17. Sir Nicholas Woodrofe, Lord Mayor, to Lord Burghley, Lord High Treasurer, printed *M. S. C.* i. 47, from *Remembrancia,* i. 40–1.]

It may please your good Lp. Byside the continuall charge of my Dutie, hauing lately receued by your Lp. a speciall and ernest commaundement from hir Maiestie for the best meanes to be vsed that I can for preseruing the Citty from infection, I will not faile so to do my dilligence both for the cleane keping of the streates, for avoiding of Inmeates, and for keping of good orders as haue ben heretofore prescribed or that I can any way deuise, as shall ly in my power to the vttermost that I shalbe able. Howbeit, because perill may and doth commonlie growe vnto hir Maiesties Cittie and people many wayes by such meanes as we cannot reforme, I humble besech your Lp. that you wilbe meane to hir Maiestie and give the ayde of the hye autoritie of your Lp. and the rest of the most honorable Counsell for redresse of such thinges as in that behalf we finde dangerous, whereof some thinges haue doble perill, both naturarly in spreding the infection and otherwise in drawing Godes wrath and plage vpon vs, as the erecting and frequenting of howses verie infamous for incontinent rule out of our liberties and iurisdiction, also the drawing of the people from the seruice of God and from honest exersises to vnchast plaies. Some vther thinges do carrie other inconveniences, as the pestering of the Cittie with mvltitudes of people for whome we shall not be able to make prouision of vitale, fewell, and other necessaries at any reasonable prises. I haue therefore sett downe a note which I send to your Lp. hereinclosed of such matters as I do lack power to redresse, but ame constrayned to craue such further ayde and assistance, as shalbe by your Lp. thought meete in those cases. And so I leaue to troble your Lp. At London this xvijth of Iune 1580.

Your Lps. humble to comaund,

N. W. M.

To the right honorable my singuler good Lord the Lord Tresorer of England.

The 'note' enclosed includes :

'Item that haunting of playes out of the liberties be restrayned as well as within the fredome.'

xlviii.

[1581, July 10. The Privy Council to the Lord Mayor and the Justices of Middlesex and the Liberties, printed *M. S. C.* i. 49, from *Remembrancia,* i. 221. The minute of the letter is in Dasent, xiii. 128.]

After our right hartie commendacons. Whereas we haue ben credibly informed that the plage and other contagious diseases are sumwhat of late increased within the Citie of London and liberties thereto adioyning : fforasmuch as it is to be feared that the said infections will spred further, in case any great assemblies of people together, especially in this somer season, be permitted, as by former experience it hath appeared, We haue thought good to requier yowe

and euery of yowe vpon the receipte hereof to geue streight order
that no playes or enterludes be suffered to be played within the
Citie or liberties adioyning, but that fourthwith yow charge and
comaunde them to forbere and desist, vntill thende of September or
that yowe shall receaue further order from vs, whereof we pray yowe
that there be no fault. And so bid yow hartely farewell. From
Grenewich the xth of Iuly 1581.

Your louing frendes,

Thomas Bromeley Cancellarius   Thomas Sussex
Ambrose Warwicke   ffraunces Bedford
Robert Leycester   ffraunces Knowles
Henrie Sidney   Christopher Hatton.

xlix.

[1581, July 11. City order, printed in Harrison, iv. 320, without reference, probably from *Repertory*, xx.]

Stafferton com-
mitted to the
Compter.

Item, Parr Stafferton gentleman of Grayes Inne
for that he that daye brought a dysordered companye of gentlemen of the Innes of Courte &
others, to assalte Arthur Kynge, Thomas Goodale,
and others, servauntes to the Lord Barkley, & players of Enterludes
within the Cyttye, was by this Courte committed to the Compter in
Wood streete, and the said players lykewyse. And aswell the sayd
players as the sayd Parre Stafferton, weare by this Courte commanded
to set downe in wrytinge the maner how the same quarell began.

l.

[1581, July. Henry Lord Berkeley to the Lord Mayor, printed *M. S. C.*
i. 51, from *Remembrancia*, i. 224 ; but it appears from No. xlix that the
date is rather earlier than was there suggested.]

My very good Lord, ther is lately fallen owt some broile betwixt
certaine of my men and some of the Innes of the Courte, sought
onely by them. The matter, as I ame aduertised, is better knowen
to your Lp. then to my self. Whereupon ther is some of my men
comitted to warde. If by their misdemeanour they shold deserue
imprisonment, I ame most willing they shold abide it : Otherwise
behauing them selues honestly in euery respecte, as I cannot learne
the contrary, sauing that they played on the sabothe daie contrary
to your order & comaundment vnknowen to them, in respecte of
that I yelde them faultie and they them selues craue pardon. So
ame I now to desier your Lp. to sett them at libertie, whoe are vpon
going into the Countrie to auoide querrell or other inconuenience that
mought followe. And thereupon I geue my word that at any time
hereafter, if further question shall arise hereby, they shalbe fourth-
coming to answere it, and so I leaue your good Lp. to the Almightie.
From my lodgeing at Strand this presente Tuesdaie. 1581.

Your Lps assured
Henrie Berkeley.

To the right honorable the Lord Maiour of the Citie of London.

li.

[1581, July 13. Minute of City Court of Aldermen, printed in Harrison, iv. 320, from *Repertory*, xx. f. 192.]

Preceptes for playes & enterludes.

Item, yt ys orderyd that preceptes shalbe forthwith made and dyrected vnto euery Alderman of thys Cyttye, that from henceforthe durynge the pleasure of thys Courte, they suffer no playes, enterludes, tumblynges, pryces, or other suche publyque shewes, to be had or made within theyr sayde wardes, by any parson or parsons whatsoever, vntil further order shalbe taken by this Courte.

lii.

[1581, Nov. 14. Precept of Lord Mayor, printed in Harrison, iv. 320, from London *Journal*, xxi, f. 151ᵛ.]

By the Mayor.

A preceptt agaynste foote-ball playe and stage playes.

Theis shalbe streightlye to charge and commaunde you, that ye take present order. . . . And also that ye gyve streighte charge & commaundement to all thinhabitauntes within the same warde, that they doe not at anye tyme hereafter, suffer anye person or persons whatsoeuer, to sett vpp or fixe anye papers or breifes vppon anye postes, houses, or other places within your warde, for the shewe or settynge out of anye playes, enterludes, or pryzes, within this Cyttye, or the lybertyes and suburbes of the same, or to be played or shewed in anye other place or places within two myles of this Cyttie, and that if anye suche shalbe sett vp, the same presentlye to be pulled downe & defaced. Fayle you not hereof, as you will, etc. Dated the xiiijth of November, 1581.

Sebryght [Town Clerk].

liii.

1581, Nov. 18. The Privy Council to the Lord Mayor, the Recorder, and the Court of Aldermen, printed *M. S. C.* i. 50, from *Remembrancia*, i. 295. The Acts of the Council show no meeting on 18 Nov. 1581 ; cf. No. lv.]

After our hartie commendations. Whereas for auoyding the increase of infection within your citie this last somer yow receaued order from vs for the restrainte of plaies vntill Mighelmas last. For that (thankes be to god) the sicknesse is very well seised and not likely in this time of the yeare to increase ; Tendering the releife of theis poore men the players and their redinesse with conuenient matters for her highnes solace this next Christmas, which cannot be without their vsuall exercise therein ; We haue therefore thought good to requier yowe forethwith to suffer them to vse such plaies in such sort and vsuall places as hath ben heretofore accustomed, hauing carefull regard for continuance of such quiet orders in the playeng places as tofore yowe

haue had. And thus we bidd yowe hartelie farewell from the Courte
at Whitehall this xviij⁰ of Nouember 1581.

Your Louing frendes,

Edward Lincoln	Thomas Sussex	Amb: Warwick
Robert Leycester	H. Hunsdon	James Croft
Christopher Hatton		

To our very Louing frendes the Lord Maiour, mr. Sariant Fletewood
Recorder, and the Aldermen of the Cittie of London.

liv.

[1581, Nov. 25. Extract from letter of John Field to the Earl of
Leicester, printed from *Cotton MS. Titus*, B. vii, f. 22, in Collier, i. 245.]

The more Sathan rageth, the more valianter be you under the
standert of him who will not be foyled. And I humblie beseech your
honor to take heede howe you gyve your hande, either in evill causes,
or in the behalfe of evill men, *as of late you did for players to the great
greife of all the godly* ; but as you have shewed your forwardnes for
the Ministery of the Gospel, so followe that course still. Our Cyttie
hath bene well eased of the pester of those wickednesses, and abuses,
that were wonte to be nourished by those impure *interludes and playes*
that were in use—surely the schooles of as greate wickednesses as
can be. I truste your honor will herein joyne with them that have
longe, owt of the word, cryed out against them ; and I am persuaded
that if your honor knewe what sincks of synne they are, you woulde
never looke once towards them. The lord Jesus blesse you. Nov. 25,
1581.

Your good lordshippes most bounden

Jo Feilde.

lv.

[1581, Dec. 3. Minute of Privy Council, printed from Register in
Dasent, xiii. 269.]

Whereas certayne companyes of players hertofore usinge their
common excersice of playing within and aboute the Cittie of London
have of late in respect of the generall infection within the Cittie ben
restrayned by their Lordships' commaundement from playing, the
said players this daye exhibited a peticion unto their Lordships,
humblie desiring that as well in respecte of their pore estates, having
noe other meanes to sustayne them, their wyves and children but
their exercise of playing, and were only brought up from their youthe
in the practise and profession of musicke and playeng, as for that
the sicknes within the Cittie was well slaked, so as noe danger of
infection could followe by the assemblyes of people at their playes,
yt would please their Lordships therfore to grante them licence to
use their sayd exercise of playeng as heretofore they had don ; their
Lordships their upon for the consyderations aforesaid as also for that
they are to present certayne playes before the Quenes Majestie for
her solace in the Christmas tyme nowe following, were contented to

yeld unto their said humble peticion, and ordered that the Lord
Mayor of the Cittie of London should suffer and permitt them to
use and exercise their trade of playing in and about the Cittie as
they have hertofore accustomed upon the weeke dayes only, being
holy dayes or other dayes, so as they doe forbeare wholye to playe
on the Sabothe Daye, either in the forenone or afternone, which to
doe they are by this their Lordships' order expressely denyed and
forbidden.

lvi.

[1581, Dec. 24. Patent of Commission for Edmund Tilney as Master
of the Revels, printed by Feuillerat, *Eliz.* 51, from *Patent Rolls*, 1606
(*Watson's Rolls*), m. 34, No. 46 ; also by T. E. Tomlins in *Sh. Soc. Papers*,
iii (1847), 1 ; Collier, i. 247, who supposed the document to refer to the
formation of the Queen's men in 1583 ; and Halliwell-Phillipps, *Illustrations*, 114 ; cf. ch. iii and *Tudor Revels*, 62, 72.]

De Commissione
speciali pro
Edmundo Tylney
Armigero Magistro
Revellorum.

Elizabeth by the grace of God &c. To all manner
our Iustices, Maiors, Sheriffes, Bayliffes, Constables, and all other our officers, ministers, true
liege men, and subiectes, and to euery of them
greetinge. We lett you witt that we haue
aucthorised licensed and commaunded and by
these presentes do aucthorise licence and commaunde our welbeloved
Edmunde Tylney Esquire Maister of our Revells, aswell to take and
retaine for vs and in our name at all tymes from hensforth and in all
places within this our Realme of England, aswell within ffranchesies
and liberties as without, at competent wages aswell all suche and as
many painters, imbroderers, taylors, cappers, haberdashers, joyners,
carders, glasiers, armorers, basketmakers, skinners, sadlers, waggen
makers, plaisterers, fethermakers, as all other propertie makers and
conninge artificers and laborers whatsoever as our said Servant or
his assigne bearers hereof shall thinke necessarie and requisite for the
speedie workinge and fynisheinge of any exploite workmanshippe or
peece of seruice that shall at any tyme hereafter belong to our saide
office of the Revells, As also to take at price reasonable in all places
within our said Realme of England aswell within ffranchesies and
liberties as without any kinde or kindes of stuffe, ware or marchandise,
woode or coale or other fewell, tymber, wainscott, boarde, lathe,
nailes, brick, tile, leade, iron, wier, and all other necessaries for our
said workes of the said office of our Revells as he the said Edmunde
or his assigne shall thinke behoofefull and expedient from tyme to
tyme for our said seruice in the said office of the Revells together
with all carriages for the same both by land and by water as the
case shall require. And furthermore we haue by these presentes
aucthorised and commaunded the said Edmunde Tylney that in case
any person or persons, whatsoever they be, will obstinatelie disobey
and refuse from hensforth to accomplishe and obey our commaundement and pleasure in that behalfe, or withdrawe themselues from any
of our said workes vpon warninge to them or any of them given by

the saide Edmunde Tylney, or by his sufficient deputie in that behalfe
to be named, appointed for their diligent attendance and workman-
ship 'vpon the said workes or devises as to their naturall dutie and
alleigeance apperteineth, that then it shalbe lawfull vnto the same
Edmund Tilney or his deputie for the tyme beinge to attache the
partie or parties so offendinge and him or them to commytt to warde,
there to remaine without baile or mainprise vntill suche tyme as the
saide Edmunde or his deputie shall thinke the tyme of his or their
imprisonment to be punnishment sufficient for his or their saide
offences in that behalfe, and that done to enlarge him or them so
beinge imprisoned at their full libertie without any losse, penaltie,
forfaiture or other damage in that behalfe to be susteined or borne
by the said Edmunde Tilney or his saide deputie. And also if any
person or persons beinge taken into our said workes of the said office
of our Revells beinge arrested comminge or goinge to or from our
saide workes of our said office of our Revells at the sute of any person
or persons, then the said Edmunde Tilney by vertue and aucthoritie
hereof to enlarge him or them as by our speciall proteccion during
the tyme of our said workes. And also if any person or persons
beinge reteyned in our said workes of our said office of Revells haue
taken any manner of taske worke, beinge bound to finishe the same
by a certen day, shall not runne into any manner of forfeiture or
penaltie for breakinge of his day, so that he or they ymediatly after
the fynishinge of our said workes indevor him or themselues to fynishe
the saide taske worke. And furthermore also we haue and doe by
these presentes aucthorise and commaunde our said Servant Edmunde
Tilney Maister cf our said Revells by himselfe or his sufficient deputie
or deputies to warne commaunde and appointe in all places within
this our Realme of England, aswell within francheses and liberties
as without, all and euery plaier or plaiers with their playmakers,
either belonginge to any noble man or otherwise, bearinge the name
or names of vsinge the facultie of playmakers or plaiers of Comedies,
Tragedies, Enterludes or what other showes soever, from tyme to
tyme and at all tymes to appeare before him with all suche plaies,
Tragedies, Comedies or showes as they shall haue in readines or meane
to sett forth, and them to presente and recite before our said Servant
or his sufficient deputie, whom wee ordeyne appointe and aucthorise
by these presentes of all suche showes, plaies, plaiers and playmakers,
together with their playing places, to order and reforme, auctorise
and put downe, as shalbe thought meete or vnmeete vnto himselfe
or his said deputie in that behalfe. And also likewise we haue by
these presentes aucthorised and commaunded the said Edmunde
Tylney that in case if any of them, whatsoever they bee, will obstinatelie
refuse, vpon warninge vnto them given by the said Edmunde or his
sufficient deputie, to accomplishe and obey our commaundement in
this behalfe, then it shalbe lawful to the said Edmunde or his sufficient
deputie to attache the partie or parties so offendinge, and him or
them to commytt to warde, to remaine without bayle or mayneprise
vntill suche tyme as the same Edmunde Tylney or his sufficient

deputie shall thinke the tyme of his or theire ymprisonment to be
punishement sufficient for his or their said offences in that behalfe, and
that done to inlarge him or them so beinge imprisoned at their plaine
libertie, without any losse, penaltie, forfeiture or other daunger in this
behalfe to be susteyned or borne by the said Edmunde Tylney
or his deputie, Any Acte Statute Ordynance or prouision heretofore
had or made to the contrarie hereof in any wise notwithstandinge.
Wherefore we will and commaunde you and euery of you that vnto
the said Edmunde Tylney or his sufficient deputie bearer hereof in
the due execucion of this our aucthoritie and commaundement ye be
aydinge, supportinge and assistinge from tyme to tyme as the case
shall require, as you and euery of you tender our pleasure and will
answer to the contrarie at your vttermost perills. In witnesse whereof
&c, witnes our selfe at Westminster the xxiiijth day of December in
the xxiiijth yere of our raigne.

per breve de priuato sigillo.

lvii.

[1582, April 3.   Precept by Lord Mayor, printed in Nicholl, *Iron-mongers*, 128.]

By the Maior.

These shalbe straightlie to charge and command you, that forth-
withe uppon the receit hereof you call before you all the freemen of
your said companie, and give to everie one of them straightlie charge
and commandement that they or anie of them do at annye time
hereafter suffer any of ther sarvants, apprentices, journemen, or
children, to repare or goe to annye playes, peices, or enterludes, either
within the cittie or suburbs thereof, or to annye place witheout the
same, uppon payne of everie servant so offendinge, or master so
sufferinge, to be punyshed at the dyscretion of me and my brethren.
Fayle you not hereof, as you will answer the contrarie at your perill.
Geven at the Guildhall, the iij daie of Aprill, 1582.

Sebright [Town Clerk].

lviii.

[1582, April 11.   The Privy Council to the Lord Mayor, printed *M. S. C.*
i. 52, from *Remembrancia*, i. 317.   The minute of the letter, undated and
bound up before a minute of April 13 as f. 691 of the manuscript Register
among minutes of May 1582, is in Dasent, xiii. 404.]

After our hartie comendacons. Whereas heretofore for sundry good
causes and consideracons, as yow know, we haue oftentimes geuen
order for the restraint of plaies, in and about the Citie of London :
and neuerthelesse of late for honest recreation sake, in respecte that
her maiestie sometimes taketh delight in those pastimes, we thought
it not vnfitt, hauing regard vnto the season of the yere and the
Clerenes of the Citie from infection, to allowe of certaine companies
of plaiers to exercise their playeng in London, partly to the ende
they might thereby attaine to the more dexteritie and perfection in
that profession, the better to content her maiestie, whereupon we

permitted the said players to vse their playeng vntill we shold se
cause to the contrary, and foreseing that the same might he done
without impeachment of the seruice of God whereof we haue a speciall
care, we restrained them from playeng on the sabothe daye : and.
forasmucheas we suppose that their honest exercise of recreation in
playeng, to be vsed on the ordinarie S. Hollydaies after euening
prayer, as long as the season of the yere may permitt and may be
without daunger of the infection, will not be offensiue, so that if care
be had that their comodies and enterludes be looked into, and that
those which do containe mater that may bread corruption of maners
and conuersacion among the people (which we desire in any case to
haue auoided) be forbidden, whereunto we wishe yow did appointe
some fitt persones whoe maie consider and allowe of suche playes
onely as be fitt to yeld honest recreacion and no example of euell :
We haue therefore thought good to pray your Lp. to reuoke your
late inhibition against their playeng on the said hollydaies after
euening prayer, onely forbearing the Sabothe daie whollie according
to our former order. And when yow shall finde that the continuance
of the same their excercise by the increase of the sicknes and infection
shalbe dangerous, we praye your Lp. therin to geue vs knowlege
& thereupon we will presently take order for their restrainte accordinglie : Soe fare yowe hartelie well from the Court at Grenewich the
xjth of Aprill 1582.

Your louing frendes,

  E: Lyncoln: T: Sussex: A: Warwyk: R: Leycester.
  H: Hunsdon.   I: Crofte.
To our very Louing frende the Lord maior of the Citie of London.

lix.

[1582, April 13.   The Lord Mayor to the Privy Council, printed *M. S. C.*
i. 54, from *Remembrancia*, i. 319.]

My dutie humblie done to your LLps. I haue receaued significacon
of your LLps. pleasure by your letters for enlarging the restrainte of
players on holydaies in the afternone, being not the sabbat daye, so
as the same may be done after seruice and without disturbance of
comon prayer and seruice of God, which as the experience is among
vs peraduenture not made knowen to your LLps. can very hardly
be done. For thoughe they beginne not their playes till after euening
prayer, yet all the time of the afternone before they take in hearers
and fill the place with such as be therby absent from seruing God
at Chirch, and attending to serue Gods enemie in an Inne ; If for
remedie hereof I shold also restraine the letting in of the people till
after seruice in the chirche, it wold driue the action of their plaies
into very inconuenient time of night, specially for seruantes and
children to be absent from their parentes and masters attendance
and presence : Howbet the case is of more inconuenience (as I take
it) for that the plag increaseth, and the season extraordinarilie whote
and perelous for this time of yere, and in the opinion of me and my

bretheren, both more mete for the safetie of the Quenes subiectes, and more easy to be stayed by good and lawfull policie in the beginning then when it is growen to further spreding of infection, byside that the tearme being at hand, and the parlament by prorogacon not long after, I haue thought it dutie to obey your LLps. comaundement in signifieng that euen now the renewing and continuance of their exersise by the increase of siknes and infection is daungerous, prayeng your LLps. to take order for continuing the restrainte accordinglie. As touching the orders prescribed in your LLps. lettres for the maters and maner of their playes at such time as yow may hereafter enlarge them, I will according to your said direction take furder order at all times to restraine them, till their maters be perused by graue and discrete persones such as I shall require to take that peine, and till they well asure me to obey the cautions appointed in your said letters. And so I leaue to troble your LLps. At London this xiijth of Aprill 1582.

Your LLps. humble.

To the right honorable the Lords and other of the Quenes Maiesties most honorable Counsell.

lx.

[1582, July 1. Ambrose, Earl of Warwick, to the Lord Mayor and Aldermen, printed *M. S. C.* i. 55, from *Remembrancia*, i. 359.]

My Lord maiour, I ame to request yow and the rest whome it doth apperteine that they wold geue licence to my seruant John Dauid this bearer to playe his prouest prices in his science and profession of defence at the Bull in Bishopsgatestrete or some other conuenient place to be assigned within the liberties of London, and I will hartely thanke your Lp. and the rest for the fauor yow shal shew him in this behalf : So with my very hartie commendacions I wish yowe all well to fare. From the Court this first of Iuly 1582.

Your Lps. very louing frend,
Amb: Warwik.

To my verie honorable good frend the L. Maiour and the rest of the aldermen or shirefes.

lxi.

[1582, July 23. Ambrose, Earl of Warwick, to the Lord Mayor, printed *M. S. C.* i. 56, from *Remembrancia*, i. 383.]

My Lord Maiour, I cannot thinke my self frendely delt with to haue my seruante put to such publike disgrace : Yf yow had not first allowed bothe others and him to take a like course of playeng prises, I had not moued your Lp. by my former lettres nor my man shold not haue requested extraordinary fauour aboue otheres, but to repulse him and to forbid the place appointed, after allowance & publicacon of his Bills (wherein my name was also vsed) and my seruante hereby greatly charged, wanteth some part of that good and frendely consideracion, which in curtesie and common humanitie I might looke for. The Circumstances and manner of dealing geueth me cause to iudge my self hardly befrended and regarded, that a light suggestion of a Companie of lewde verlettes could so sodainely and easely carry yow awaye from a good frende to my mans great losse and discredit, and in some sort to myne owne impeachement. Yf yow be resolued that it standeth most behouefull for the good gouerment of the Citie to haue those exercises vtterly put downe and none allowed hereafter to deale in these kinde of prises, my man shall rest him self without further sute, (albeit the first and last to whome disgrace hath ben offered in this sorte :) But if others be suffered to proceade as heretofore, and they not restrained, aswell as my man, I must nedes iuge it no frendely nor indifferent maner of dealing. I pray therefore, vnlesse there be cause to the contrary and greater mater of exception, than lewde suggestions of badd persones ; (because my man refused to yealde to their disorder, and abvse of exaction) giue my man such ordinarie and indifferent fauor, that he may forthwith haue his daie and place as others of his profession. Or ells I shall haue more iust cause of vnkindnesse offered me. From the Court this xxiijth of Iuly 1582.

Your Lps. very louing frende,
Ambrose: Warwike.

To my very louing frende the Lord Maiour of London : ffrom the Courte.

lxii.

[1582, July 24. The Lord Mayor to Ambrose, Earl of Warwick, printed *M.S.C.* i. 57, from *Remembrancia*, i. 384.]

My dutie humblie done to your Lp. I ame sorry that your Lp. taketh my dealinges toward your seruant in such part, as I perceaue by your letters yow are informed. Albeit the lawe in case of fensers haue some hard exposition in some mens iugement, yet the truthe is that I did not expulse your seruant from playeng his prise, but for your sake I did geue him licence. Onely I did restraine him from playeng in an Inne which was somewhat to close for infection, and appointed him to playe in an open place of the leaden hall more fre from danger and more for his Comoditie, which licence I gaue him in open Courte, and he might well haue‘ vsed it before increace of peril by heate of the yere. But about xiiijtene daies afterward, when I thought he had taken the benefitt and effecte of my graunte, the infection growing, whereof your Lp. knoweth what earnest care I ought to haue, and how seriously bothe her maiestie and your Lp. with the rest of the most honorable haue often charged me, and for some other reasonable respectes touching my dutie, I was indede inforced to restraine him from gathering publik assemblie of people to his play within the Citie, and neuerthelesse did allowe him in the open feildes where the peril might not be so great : But verely my good Lord, whoesoeuer hath Informed yow that I haue forbidden your man and licenced other to your seruantes disgrace he doth me great wrong, for I neither haue nor intende so to doe. For bothe your Lp. and my Lord of Leycester your brother haue euer ben my honorable good Lordes, and so I haue and doe esteeme yow, and wold doe asmuche to gratefie yow or any of yours as any that hath ben in my place ; and so I beseche yow to accoumpte of me. I haue herein yet further done for your seruante what I may, that is that if he obteine lawefully to playe at the Theater or other open place out of the Citie, he hath and shall haue my permition with his companie, drumes, and shewe to passe openly throughe the Citie, being not vpon the Sondaye, which is asmuche as I maye iustefie in this season, and for that cause I haue with his owne consent apointed him Monday next. And so I humblie comitt your Lp. to the tuition of the Almightie. At London the xxiiijth of Iuly 1582.

Your Lps. humble.

To the right honorable my singular good L. my Lorde the Erle of Warwicke.

lxiii.

[1582 (?). Extract from *Orders Appointed to be Executed in the Cittie of London for Setting Rogues and Idle Persons to Worke, and for Releefe of the Poore*, printed by Hugh Singleton (N.D.). The B.M. copy (796 E. 37) is catalogued, with the date 1587, as an Act of the Court of Aldermen. C. Welch, *The City Printers (Bibl. Soc. Trans.* xiv. 191), also gives the date as 1587, and says that Singleton became City Printer on 4 Aug. 1584. Whatever the date of the print, it seems clear from No. lxxv (2) (*a*) that the order itself, or at any rate Art. 62 of it, is later than the crying of the preachers against plays and earlier than the Paris Garden accident of 13 Jan. 1583. The autumn of 1582 seems to me the most likely date. Possibly Art. 62 was alone new. Aydelotte, 70, says that the Orders which were to enforce 18 Eliz. c. 3 were originally printed in 1579 or 1580, and refers to *Journal*, xx, pt. ii, f. 325. Art. 61, and also Art. 25, which directs an inquest for ' suspect persons which . . . spend their times at bowling allies, playes, and other places unthriftily ', may belong to the earlier version.]

Art. 61. For helpe of the hospitals & Parishes in this charge all churchwardens & collectors for the poore be strayghtly charged to execute the lawe against such as come not to church, against al persons without exception, and specially against such as while they ought to be at diuine seruice, doo spend their time and their money lewdly in haunting of plaies, and other idle and wycked pastimes and exercises.

Art. 62. For as much as the playing of Enterludes, & the resort to the same are very daungerous for the infection of the plague, whereby infinite burdens and losses to the Citty may increase, and are very hurtfull in corruption of youth with incontinence & lewdnes, and also great wasting both of the time and thrift of many poore people and great prouoking of the wrath of God the ground of all plagues, great withdrawing of the people from publique prayer & from the seruice of God : and daily cryed out against by the graue and earnest admonitions of the preachers of the word of God : Therefore be it ordered that all such Enterludes in publique places, and the resort to the same shall wholy be prohibited as ungodly, and humble sute be made to the Lords that lyke prohibition be in places neere unto the Cittie.

APPENDIX D

lxiv.

[1583, Jan. 14. Extract from letter of Lord Mayor to Lord Burghley, printed *M. S. C.* i. 158, from *Lansd. MS.* 37, f. 8, and *M. S. C.*.i. 58, from letter-book copy misdated Jan. 18 in *Remembrancia,* i. 456 ; also in Wright, ii. 184, and quoted by Collier, i. 243, with inaccurate reference to *Lansd. MS.* 73.]

It maye please your Lp. to be further advertised (which I thinke you haue alredie hard) of a greate mysshappe at Parise gardeine, where by ruyn of all the scaffoldes at once yesterdaie a greate nombre of people are some presentlie slayne, and some maymed and greavouslie hurte. It giveth greate occasion to acknowledge the hande of god for suche abuse of the sabboth daie, and moveth me in Consciens to beseche your Lp. to give order for redresse of suche contempt of gods service. I haue to that ende treated with some Iustices of peace of that Countie, who signifie them selfes to haue verye good zeale, but alledge want of Comyssion, which we humblie referre to the Consideracion of your honorable wisedome. And so I leve to trowble your Lp. At London the xiiijth of Ianuarye 1582.

Your Lps. humble,
Thomas Blank Maior.

To the right honorable my singler good lorde my lorde highe Tresurer of Englande.

lxv.

[1583, Jan. 15. Extract from letter of Lord Burghley to Lord Mayor, printed *M. S. C.* i. 60, from *Remembrancia,* i. 458.]

I am also hartely sorry for the mischance, whereof I haue vnderstanding bothe by your Lps. lettres and otherwise at my being now at Westminster, mishappened at Parrise Garden on Sonday last, and althoughe I thinke your learning derely bought by the losse of so many bodies, to haue the Saboth daie so prophaned to see wilde beastes bayted, yet I think it very conuenient to haue both that and other like prophane assemblies prohibited on the Saboth daie, and if it shalbe requisite to haue such like worldly pastimes, I think some other daie within the weke meeter for those purposes, and to that ende I minde to treate with my LLs. of the Counsell, that some good order may be taken for that purpose ; wishing neuerthelesse that your Lp. in the meane time, hauing rule of the whole Citie, might thinke it conuenient to make a generall prohibition within euerie warde of that Citie and liberties, that no person vnder your comaundement shold on the Saboth daie resort to any such prophane assemblies or pastimes, which I leaue to your Lps. discretion to be considered by the aduise of the Aldermen your bretheren. From Richmond the xvth of Ianuary 1582.

Your Lps. assured louing frend,
William: Burghley.

To my very good Lord the Lord maiour of the Citie of London.

DOCUMENTS OF CONTROL 293

lxvi.

[1583, Jan. 14–Feb. 6. Notes of credentials of Worcester's men, shown at Leicester in March 1584 ; for text of entries in *Hall Papers*, cf. ch. xiii, s.v. Worcester's.]

(a) [Jan. 14]

Abstract of warrant of licence and recommendation from William Earl of Worcester.

(b) [Feb. 6]

Abstract of article in indenture of licence from Edmund Tilney, Master of the Revels.

lxvii.

[1583, April 19. ·Proclamation against Retainers (*Procl.* 768).]

This is substantially similar to *Procl.* 663 of 3 Jan. 1572 (v. No. xix).

lxviii.

[1583, April 27. The Lord Mayor to Mr. Young, a Justice of Middlesex, printed *M. S. C.* i. 62, from *Remembrancia*, i. 498. The letter referred to in the first sentence was one from the Privy Council on April 21, intimating the Queen's surprise that no plague hospital had been built outside the City (*Remembrancia*, i. 497 ; *Index*, 336). ' Ill May daie ' was that of 1517, on which a riot took place against the aliens resident in London.]

Mr. Yong. I and my brethren haue lately receiued lettres from the LLs. of the most honorable counsell for auoiding of all perills of infection, in which lettres we haue also a most ernest significaton of maiesties pleasure to that end with verie greuous charging vs with negligence and defalt. Ther ar certain fencers that haue set vp billes and meane to play a prise at the Theatre on Tuesday next, which is May eue. How manie waies the same maie be inconuenient and dangerous, specially in that they desire to passe with pomp through the citie, yowe can consider, namelie the statute against men of that facultie, the perill of infection, the danger of disorders at such assemblies, the memorie of ill May daie begon vpon a lesse occasion of like sort, the weakenesse of the place for ruine, wherof we had a late lamentable example at Paris garden. For these causes, in good discretion we haue not only not geuen them licence, but also declared to them the dangers, willing them at their perill to forbeare their passing both thorough the citie, and their whole plaieng of such prise. Now bicause yowe know how much this mater importeth the whole citie, and how from time to time the LLs. of the counsell haue willed the iustices of the cowntie geue assistance for auoideng of such perills, we pray yowe hartely, in confidence of your good diligence in her maiesties seruice and the safetye of this citie, that yowe will both looke vnto it your self, and so deale with the rest of the iustices, that no such prise be suffred, or assemblie had, specially in this time of infection and those daies of speciall danger, considering also the like danger in plaies at that place. And so praieng yowe to remember that, if we be blamed for suffering, we must say that we admonished yowe of it in time, I bid yowe hartelie ffarewell. At the Guildhall this xxvijth of Aprill 1583.

Your louing freind.

lxix.

[1583, May 3. The Lord Mayor to Sir Francis Walsingham, Secretary, printed *M. S. C.* i. 63, from *Remembrancia*, i. 538.]

It may please your honor. According to oure dutie, I and my bretheren haue had care for staye of infection of the plage and published orders in that behalfe, which we intend god willing to execute with dilligence. Among other we finde one very great and dangerous inconuenience, the assemblie of people to playes, beare bayting, fencers, and prophane spectacles at the Theatre and Curtaine and other like places, to which doe resorte great multitudes of the basist sort of people ; and many enfected with sores runing on them, being out of our iurisdiction, and some whome we cannot discerne by any dilligence ; and which be otherwise perilous for contagion, biside the withdrawing from Gods service, the peril of ruines of so weake byldinges, and the auancement of incontinencie and most vngodly confederacies, the terrible occasion of gods wrathe and heauye striking with plages. It auaileth not to restraine them in London, vnlesse the like orderes be in those places adioyning to the liberties, for amendment whereof I beseche your honor to be meane to the most honorable Counsel, and the rather I ame to make that humble sute, for that I wold be lothe to susteine hir maiesties heauie displeasure, when such forren and extraordinarie occasions shalbe aboue all our habilities by any dilligence or foresight to redresse it. And so I leaue to troble your honor. At London this 3 of May 1583.

Your honours to comaund.

To the right honorable Sir Frances Walsingham knight, principal Secretarie to the Quenes most excellent Maiestie.

lxx.

[1583, July 3. The Lord Mayor to the Privy Council, printed *M. S. C.* i. 64, from *Remembrancia*, i. 520. In reply to a letter of June 30, calling attention to the neglect of the statutes and orders for the maintenance of archery (*Remembrancia*, i. 519 ; *Index*, 16).]

My dutie humbly done to your LLps. I and my brethren haue receiued your honourable letters, for execution of the lawes for maintenance of archerie and restraineng of vnlawfull games. We must acknowledge your honourable and godly consideracion and for our partes do accordingly intend to call the wardens of those pore companies, at whose suite your lettres were obteined, and both to vse their aduise and diligence and to adde our owne good meanes and indeuours that your LLps. good meaninges maie take effect, and the lawes be executed with such good circumspection and reasonable orders, as haue ben founde requisite for the good gouernance of the youth in this citie. Vpon the occasion of your LLps. said lettres reciting the vse of vnlawfull games to be to the hinderance of the vse of archerie and of the maintenance of those honest artificors, We ar humbly to pray [your] LLps. to haue in your honorable remembrance how much not only the said vse of archerie and maintenance of good artes ar decaied by the assemblers to vnlawfull spectacles, as barebaiting, vnchast enterludes and other like, but also infection therby increased, affraies, actes and bargaines of incontinencie and thefte, stolen contractes and spoiling of honest mens children, the withdrawing of people from seruice of God, and the drawing of godes wrath and plages vpon vs, whereof god hath in his iudgement shewed a late terrible example at Paris garden, in which place in great contempt of god the scaffoldes ar new builded, and the multitudes on the Saboath daie called together in most excessiue number. These thinges ar obiected to vs, both in open sermons at Poules crosse and elsewhere in the hearing of such as repaire from all partes of to our shame and grief, when we cannot remedie it. The reproch also to vs as the sufferers and mainteiners of such disorders is published to the whole world in bokes. We herewith moued, as becomieth vs in conscience and in regard of our honestie and credites not to be accompted senselesse of the feare of God and of our duties to her maiestie and the preseruacion of her subiectes in our charge, haue endeuoured, and your good fauours concurring will more endeuour, our selues for redresse of such enormities within our iurisdiction, specially on the Sabbat and daies appointed for comon praier. Which our trauailes shall yet be vaine and to no effect without your honourable help and assistance. It may therfore please your good Lps. both to geue your allowance of our proceding in such reformacion within our liberties, and to send your Lps. lettres of request and comandement to the Iustices of the cownties and gouernours of precinctes adioining to this citie to execute like orders as we shall do for the honour of god and seruice of her maiestie. And so beseching your Lps. that I may haue your resolucion herein I leaue to troble your honours. At London this iijd of Iulie 1583.

Your LLps. humble.

To the right honourable the Lordes and other of the Quenes maiesties most honorable Counsell.

lxxi.

[1583, Nov. 26. The Privy Council to the Lord Mayor, printed *M. S. C.* i. 66, from *Remembrancia*, i. 554.]

After our hartie comendacons to your good Lp. Forasmuch as (God be thanked) there is no suche infection within that citie at this presente, but that hir maiesties playeres may be suffered to playe within the liberties as heretofore they haue done, especially seeing they are shortly to present some of their doeinges before hir maiestie, we haue thought good at this present to pray your Lp. to geue order, that the said players may be licenced so to doe within the Citie and liberties betwene this and shroftyde next; so as the same be not done vpon sondaies, but vpon some other weke daies, at conuenient times. And so prayeng yowe that thereof there be no defaulte, We bid yowe right hartely farewell. From St Iames the xxvjth of Nouember 1583.

Your very louing frendes,

Tho: Bromeley: cancellarius: William Burghley
Fra: Bedford: He: Hunsdon   Fra: Knollys:
Chr. Hatton: Fra: Walsingham:

To our verie louing frende the L. Maiour of the Citie of London.

lxxii.

[1583, Nov. 28. Abstract of City licence, given by C. W. Wallace in *Nebraska University Studies*, xiii. 11.]

I shall later publish in extenso a licence granted by the City to the Queen's men, dated 28 Nov. 1583, wherein we learn for the first time that the twelve chosen actors were 'Robert Wilson, John Dutton, Rychard Tarleton, John Laneham, John Bentley, Thobye Mylles, John Towne, John Synger, Leonell Cooke, John Garland, John Adams, and Wyllyam Johnson', and that their playing places were to be 'at the sygnes of the Bull in Bushoppesgate streete, and the sygne of the Bell in Gratioustreete and nowheare els within this Cyttye' for the time being.

lxxiii.

[1583, Dec. 1. Sir Francis Walsingham, Secretary, to the Lord Mayor, printed *M. S. C.* i. 67, from *Remembrancia*, i. 553.]

My very good L. Vnderstanding that vpon the receipte of my Ls. letters written lately vnto yow in the behalf of hir maiesties players, your Lp. interpreteth the licence geuen them therin to extend onely to holy daies and not to other weke daies, I haue therefore thought good, being partlie priuie to their LLps. meaning signified in their letters, to explane more plainely their pleasures herein to your Lp., whoe, considering in their graue wisdomes that without frequent exercise of such plaies as are to be presented before hir maiestie, her seruantes cannot conueniently satisfie hir recreation and their owne duties, were therefore pleased to directe their letters vnto yowe, that vpon the weke daies and worke daies at conuenient times your Lp. wold geue order that they might be licenced betwene this and Shrouetide to exercise their playes and enterludes (sondaies onely excepted and such other daies wherein sermons and lectures are comonly vsed). I pray your Lp. therefore that from hence fourthe yow will suffer them to haue the benefite of this libertie accordinglie, as without the which they shall not be able to doe that which is expected at their handes for hir maiesties seruice and contentacion, whereunto I know your Lp. will rather yelde your best ayde and furtherance, than any the least impediment or interruption, which I wishe may be effectually manifested by your especiall licence to be graunted to this ende to those hir maiesties seruantes with all fauorable regard and expedition. And so I comitt your Lp. to the grace of God. From the Courte at St. Iames the first of December 1583.

> Your Lps. very assured louing frende,
>> Fra: Walsingham.

To my very good Lord the Lord maiour of the Citie of London.

lxxiv.

[1584, June 18. Extracts from letter of William Fleetwood to Lord Burghley, printed *M. S. C.* i. 163, from *Lansd. MS.* 41, f. 31 ; also in Wright, ii. 226.]

Right honorable and my very good Lo. Vpon Whit Sondaye there was a very good Sermond preached at the New churche yard nere bethelem, wherat my Lo. Maiour was with his bretherne, and by reason no playes were the same daye all the citie was quiet. . . .

Vpon Mondaye night I retorned to London and found all the wardes full of watchers. The cause thereof was for that very nere the Theatre or Curten at the tyme of the Playes there laye a prentice sleping vpon the Grasse, and one Challes *al.* Grostock dyd turne vpon the Too vpon the belly of the same prentice, whervpon the apprentice start vp and after wordes they fell to playne bloues ; the companie encressed of bothe sides to the nosmber of v^c at the least. This Challes exclaimed and said that he was a gentelman and that the apprentise was but a Rascall ; and some there were litell better then rooges that tooke vpon theym the name of gentilmen and said the prentizes were but the skomme of the worlde. Vpon these trobles the prentizes began the next daye, being Twesdaye, to make mutines and assembles, and dyd conspire to have broken the presones & to have taken furthe the prentizes that were imprisoned ; but my Lo. and I having intelligens thereof apprensed .iiij. or .v. of the chieff conspirators, who are in Newgate and stand Indicted of theire lewd demeanors.

Vpon Weddensdaye one Browne, a serving man in a blew coat, a shifting fellowe having a perrelous witt of his owne, entending a spoile if he cold have browght it to passe, did at Theatre doore querell with certen poore boyes, handicraft prentises, and strook some of theym, and lastlie he with his sword wondend and maymed one of the boyes vpon the left hand ; where vpon there assembled nere a ml. people. This Browne dyd very cuninglie convey hym selff awaye, but by chaunse he was taken after and browght to mr. Humfrey Smithe, and because no man was able to charge hym he dismissed hym, and after this Browne was browght before mr. Yonge, where he vsed hym selff so connynglie and subtillie, no man being there to charge hym, that there also he was demised. And after I sent a warraunt for hym, and the Constables with the deputie at the Bell in Holbourne found hym in a parlor fast locked in, and he wold not obeye the warraunt, but by the meane of the hoost he was conveyed a waye, and then I sent for the hoost and caused hym to appere at Newgat

at the Sessions of Oier and determiner, where he was committed
vntill he browght furth his gest. The next daye after he browght
hym forthe, and so we Indicted hym for his misdemeanour. This
Browne is a commen Cossiner, a thieff, & a horse stealer, and colloreth
all his doynges here abowt this towne with a sute that he haithe in
the lawe agaynst a brother of his in Staffordshire. He resteth now
in Newgate. . . .

Vpon Weddensdaye, Thursdaye, Frydaye and Satterdaye we dyd
nothing els but sitt in commission and examine these misdemeanors ;
we had good helpe of my lord Anderson and mr. Sackforthe.

Vpon Sonndaye my Lo. sent ij Aldermen to the Court for the
suppressing and pulling downe of the Theatre and Curten. All the
LL. agreed therevnto, saving my Lord Chamberlen and mr. Viz-
chamberlen, but we obteyned a lettre to suppresse theym all. Vpon
the same night I sent for the quenes players and my Lo. of Arundel
his players, and they all willinglie obeyed the LL. lettres. The
chiefestes of her highnes players advised me to send for the owner
of the Theater, who was a stubburne fellow, and to bynd hym. I dyd
so ; he sent me word that he was my Lo. of Hunsdons man, and
that he wold not come at me, but he wold in the mornyng ride to
my lord ; then I sent the vndershereff for hym and he browght hym
to me ; and at his commyng he stowtted me owt very hastie ; and
in the end I shewed hym my Lo. his mrs. hand and then he was
more quiet ; but to die for it he wold not be bound. And then
I mynding to send hym to prison, he made sute that he might be
bound to appere at the Oier & determiner, the which is to morrowe ;
where he said that he was suer the Court wold not bynd hym being
a Counselers man. And so I have graunted his request, where he
shalbe sure to be bound or els ys lyke to do worse.

lxxv.

[c. 1584, Nov. (1) Petition of the Queen's Players to the Privy Council,
and (2) Answer of the Corporation of London enclosing the Act of
Common Council of 6 Dec. 1574 (No. xxxii), printed *M. S. C.* i. 168, from
Lansd. MS. 20, f. 23 ; also in part by Strype in his edition of Stowe's
Survey (1720), i. 292 ; Collier, i. 208 ; Hazlitt, *E. D. S.* 27. The documents
are bound up out of order in the Lansdowne volume, the Act of 1574
being Art. 10 and (1) being inserted as Art. 12 between the two parts of
(2) which are the reply to it. Each article is officially endorsed in pencil
with the date 1575, and the same date is assigned by the printed *Catalogue
of the Lansdowne Manuscripts* (1819) to Arts. 10, 12, and 13. This has
misled Collier and nearly all subsequent historians of the stage into a belief
that players were expelled from the City more or less permanently in 1575,
and that this expulsion led to the building of the Theatre and the Curtain
in 1576. The difficulty due to the description of the petitioners as the
Queen's men is met by Collier with a suggestion that ' perhaps the Earl
of Leicester's servants might so call themselves after the grant of the
patent in May 1574 ', and by Fleay, 46, with an assertion that ' the whole
body of then existing men actors who were going to perform at Court at
Christmas (Warwick's, Leicester's, Howard's) ' were meant. I called attention to the true bearing of the documents in a review of T. F. Ordish,
Early London Theatres in the *Academy* for 24 Aug. 1895, but the mis-

conception still exists ; it is found, for instance, in Thompson, 41. The facts, however, are correctly given in Gildersleeve, 171. It is clear from that part of the Corporation's Answer which Collier suppressed that the real date of the Lansdowne documents is later than the ' ruine at Parise garden ', which was on 13 Jan. 1583 (cf. No. lxiv), and it must also be later than the establishment of the Queen's men in March 1583, and their first performances at court in the winter of 1583–4. The petition was, on the face of it, written at the beginning of a winter, and the most natural interpretation would place it in the winter of 1584. It might conceivably be 1585. There is no reference to it in the Acts of the Privy Council, and it probably belongs to the period of the missing register between June 1582 and Feb. 1586. Unfortunately, the *Remembrancia* also have a gap between March 1584 and Jan. 1587. It will be observed that the Lansdowne papers are not, as they stand, complete, since they lack the Articles sent with the players' Petition, and also the printed Act of Common Council sent by the Corporation (No. lxiii). Strype says that the proposed Remedies were adopted, but it is doubtful whether he had any evidence other than the Lansdowne MS. itself.]

(1)

To the Right Honorable the Lordes of her Maiesties
Privie Counsell:

In most humble manner beseche your LLp. your dutifull and daylie Orators the Queenes Maiesties poore Players. Wheras the tyme of our service draweth verie neere, so that of necessitie wee must needes haue excercise to enable vs the better for the same, and also for our better helpe and relief in our poore lyvinge, the season of the yere beynge past to playe att anye of the houses without the Cittye of London, as in our articles annexed to this our Supplicacion maye more att large appeere vnto your LLp: Our most humble peticion ys thatt yt maye please your LLp. to vowchsaffe the readinge of these few Articles, and in tender Consideracion of the matters therin mentioned, contayninge the verie staye and good state of our Lyvinge, to graunt vnto vs the Confirmacion of the same, or of as manye or as much of them as shalbe to your Honors good Lykinge, And therwith all your LLp: favorable letters vnto the L. Mayor of London to permitt vs to excercise within the Cittye accordinge to the articles, and also thatt the said lettres maye contayne some order to the Justices of Middlesex as in the same ys mentioned, wherbie as wee shall cease the Continewall troublinge of your LLp. for your often lettres in the premisses. So shall wee daylie be bownden to praye for the prosperous preservation of your LLp. in honor helth and happines long to Continew.

Your LLp: most humblie bownden and daylie Orators,
her Maiesties poore Players.

[Endorsed] Queens Players their Petition.

(2) (a)

It may please your good Lp.

The orders in London whereunto the players referr them are misconceaued, as may appeare by the two actes of comon Counsell which I send yow with note ☞ directing to the place.

The first of these actes of Comon counsell was made in the maraltie
of Hawes xvij° Regine, and sheweth a maner how plaies were to be
tollerated and vsed, althoughe it were rather wished that they were
wholly discontinued for the causes appearing in the preamble ; which
is for that reason somewhat the longer.

Where the players reporte the order to be that they shold not play
till after seruice time, the boke ['fo. 8° ' added in margin] is otherwise ; for it is that they shal not onely not play in seruice time, but
also shal not receue any in seruice time to se the same ; for thoughe
they did forbeare beginning to play till seruice were done, yet all the
time of seruice they did take in people ; which was the great mischef
in withdrawing the people from seruice.

Afterward when these orders were not obserued, and the lewd maters
of playes encreasced, and in the haunt vnto them were found many
dangers, bothe for religion, state, honestie of manners, vnthriftinesse
of the poore, and danger of infection &c, and the preachers dayly
cryeng against the L. maiour and his bretheren, in an Act of Common
Counsel for releafe of the poore which I send yowe printed, in the
Article 62 the last leafe, is enacted as there appeareth, by which
there are no enterludes allowed in London in open spectacle, but in
priuate howses onely at marriages or such like, which may suffise,
and sute is apointed to be made that they may be likewise banished
in places adioyning.

Since that time and namely upon the ruine at Parise garden, sute
was made to my LLs. to banishe playes wholly in the places nere
London, according to the said lawe. Letters were obtained from my
LLs. to banishe them on the sabbat Daies.

(b)
Now touching their petition and articles

Where they pretend that they must haue exercise to enable them
in their seruice before her maiestie :

It is to be noted that it is not conuenient that they present before
her maiestie such playes as haue ben before commonly played in open
stages before all the basest assemblies in London and Middlesex, and
therfore sufficent for their exercise and more comely for the place
that (as it is permitted by the sayd lawes of common counsell) they
make their exercise of playeng only in priuate houses.

Also it lyeth within the dutiefull care for her Maiesties royal persone,
that they be not suffred, from playeing in the throng of a multitude
and of some infected, to presse so nere to the presence of her maiestie.

Where they pretend the mater of stay of their lyuing :

It hath not ben vsed nor thought meete heretofore that players
haue or shold make their lyuing on the art of playeng, but men for
their lyuings vsing other honest and lawfull artes, or reteyned in
honest seruices, haue by companies learned some enterludes for some
encreasce to their profit by other mens pleasures in vacant time of
recreation.

Where in the first article they require the L. Maiors order to continue for the times of playeing on hollydaies :

They missreport the order. For all those former orders of toleration are expired by the last printed act of common Counsell.

Also if the toleration were not expired, they do cautelously omitt the prohibition to receiue any auditoire before common prayer be ended. And it may be noted how vncomely it is for youth to runne streight from prayer to playes, from Gods seruice to the Deuells.

To the second article.

If in winter the dark do cary inconuenience, and the short time of day after euening prayer do leaue them no leysure, and fowlenesse of season do hinder the passage into the feldes to playes, the remedie is ill conceyued to bring them into London, but the true remedie is to leaue of that vnnecessarie expense of time, wherunto God himself geueth so many impediments.

To the third.

To play in plagetime is to encreasce the plage by infection : to play out of plagetime is to draw the plage by offendinges of God vpon occasion of such playes.

But touching the permission of playes vpon the fewnesse of those that dye in any weke, it may please you to remember one special thing. In the report of the plage we report only those that dye, and we make no report of those that recouer and cary infection about them either in their sores running or in their garmentes, which sort are the most dangerous. Now, my Lord, when the number of those that dye groweth fewest, the number of those that goe abrode with sores is greatest, the violence of the disease to kill being abated. And therfore while any plage is, though the number reported of them that dye be small, the number infectious is so great that playes are not to be permitted.

Also in our report, none are noted as dyeing of the plage except they haue tokens, but many dye of the plage that haue no tokens, and sometime fraude of the searchers may deceiue. Therfore it is not reason to reduce their toleration to any number reported to dye of the plage. But it is an vncharitable demaund against the safetie of the Quenes subiectes, and per consequens of her persone, for the gaine of a few, whoe if they were not her maiesties seruants shold by their profession be rogues, to esteme fifty a weke so small a number as to be cause of tolerating the aduenture of infection.

If your Lp. shal think resonable to permit them in respect of the fewnesse of such as dye, this were a better way. The ordinarie deaths in London, when there is no plage, is betwene xl. and l. and commonly vnder xl., as our bokes do shew. The residue or more in plage time is to be thought to be the plage. Now it may be enough if it be permitted, that when the whole death of all diseases in London shal by ij or iij wekes together be vnder l. a weke, they may play (*obseruatis alioqui obseruandis*) during such time of death vnder l. a weke.

Where they require that only her maiesties servants be permitted to play :

It is lesse eiuell than to grannt moe.   But herin if your Lp. will so allow them, it may please you to know that the last yere when such toleration was of the Quenes players only, all the places of playeing were filled with men calling themselues the Quenes players. Your Ls. may do well in your lettres or warrants for their toleration to expresse the number of the Quenes players and particularly all their names.

The remedies.

That they hold them content with playeing in priuate houses at weddings etc. without publike assemblies.

If more be thought good to be tolerated : that then they be restrained to the orders in the act of common Counsell tempore Hawes.

That they play not openly till the whole death in London haue ben by xx daies under 50 a weke, nor longer than it shal so continue.

That no playes be on the sabbat.

That no playeing be on holydaies but after euening prayer : nor any receiued into the auditorie till after euening prayer.

That no playeing be in the dark, nor continue any such time but as any of the auditorie may returne to their dwellings in London before sonne set, or at least before it be dark.

That the Quenes players only be tolerated, and of them their number and certaine names to be notified in your Lps. lettres to the L. Maior and to the Iustices of Middlesex and Surrey.   And those her players not to diuide themselues into seueral companies.

That for breaking any of the orders, their toleration cesse.

lxxvi.

[1586, May 11.   Minutes of Privy Council, printed from Register in Dasent, xiv. 99, 102.]

A letter to the Justices of Surrey that according to suche direction as hath ben geven by their Lordships to the Lord Maior to restraine and inhibite the use of plaies and interludes in publique places in and about the Cittie of London, in respect of the heat of the yeere now drawing on, for th'avoyding of the infection like to grow and increase by th'ordinarie assemblies of the people to those places, they ar also required in like sorte to take order that the playes and assemblies of the people at the theater or anie other places about Newington be forthwith restrained and forborne as aforesaid, &c.

A letter to the Lord Maiour ; his Lordship is desired, according to his request made to their Lordships by his letters of the vijth of this present, to geve order for the restrayning of playes and interludes within and about the Cittie of London, for th'avoyding of infection feared to grow and increase this time of sommer by the comon assemblies of people at those places, and that their Lordships have taken the like order for the prohibiting of the use of playes at the theater and th'other places about Newington out of his charge.

lxxvii.

[1586, June 23. Extract from *The newe Decrees of the Starre Chamber for orders in printinge*, printed by Arber, ii. 807, from *S. P. D. Eliz.* cxc. 48.]

4. *Item* that no person or persons shall ymprynt or cawse to be ymprinted, or suffer by any meanes to his knowledge his presse, letters, or other Instrumentes to be occupyed in pryntinge of any booke, work, coppye, matter, or thinge whatsoever, Except the same book, woork, coppye, matter, or any other thinge, hath been heeretofore allowed, or hereafter shall be allowed before the ymprintinge thereof, accoruinge to thorder appoynted by the Queenes maiesties *Iniunctyons*, And been first seen and pervsed by the Archbishop of Canterbury and Bishop of London for the tyme beinge or any one of them (The Queenes maiesties Prynter for somme speciall service by her maiestie, or by somme of her highnes pryvie Councell therevnto appoynted, and such as are or shalbe pryviledged to prynte the bookes of the *Common Lawe* of this Realme, for such of the same bookes as shalbe allowed of by the Twoo Chief Justices, and Chief Baron for the tyme beinge, or any twoo of them onely excepted). Nor shall ymprynt or cause to be ymprinted any book, work or coppie against the fourme and meaninge of any Restraynt or ordonnaunce conteyned or to be conteyned in any statute or lawes of this Realme, or in any Iniunctyon made, or sett foorth by her maiestie, or her highnes pryvye Councell, or against the true intent and meaninge of any Letters patentes, Commissions or prohibicons vnder the great seale of England, or contrary to any allowyd ordynaunce sett Downe for the good governaunce of the Cumpany of Staconers within the Cyttie of London, vppon payne to haue all such presses, letters, and instrumentes as in or about the pryntinge of any such bookes or copyes shalbe employed or vsed, to be defaced and made vnserviceable for ymprintinge forever. And vppon payne also that euery offendour and offendours contrarye to this present Artycle or ordynaunce shalbe dishabled (after any such offence) to vse or exercise or take benefytt by vsinge or exercisinge of the art or feat of ympryntinge. And shall moreover sustayne ymprysonment Six moneths without Bayle or mayneprise.

Clause 6 empowers the Stationers Company to seize offending books and bring offenders before the ' highe Comissioners in causes Ecclesyastycall or some three or more of them, whereof the sayd Archbishop of Cánterbury or Bishop of London for the tyme beinge to be one '.

lxxviii.

[1587, Jan. 25. Anon. to Secretary Sir Francis Walsingham, printed from *Harl. MS.* 286, f. 102, in Collier, i. 257. A partial copy by T. Birch is in *Addl. MS.* 4160, No. 53.]

The daylie abuse of Stage Playes is such an offence to the godly, and so great a hinderance to the gospell, as the papists do exceedingly rejoyce at the bleamysh thearof, and not without cause ; for every day in the weake the players billes are sett up in sondry places of the cittie, some in the name of her Majesties menne, some the Earl of Leic^r, some the E. of Oxford, the Lo. Admyralles, and dyvers others ; so that when the belles tole to the Lectorer, the trumpetts sound to the Stages, whereat the wicked faction of Rome lawgheth for joy, while the godly weepe for sorrowe. Woe is me ! the play howses are pestered, when churches are naked ; at the one it is not possible to gett a place, at the other voyde seates are plentie. The profaning of the Sabaoth is redressed, but as badde a custome entertayned, and yet still our long suffering God forbayreth to punishe. Yt is a wofull sight to see two hundred proude players jett in their silkes, wheare five hundred pore people sterve in the streets. But yf needes this mischief must be tollerated, whereat (no doubt) the highest frownith, yet for God's sake (Sir) lett every Stage in London pay a weekly pention to the pore, that *ex hoc malo proveniat aliquod bonum* : but it weare rather to be wisshed that players might be used, as Apollo did his lawghing, *semel in anno.* . . . Nowe, mee thinks, I see your honor smyle, and saye to your self, theise things are fitter for the pullpit, then a souldiers penne ; but God (who searcheth the hart and reynes) knoweth that I write not hipocritically, but from the veary sorrowe of my soule.

lxxix.

[**1587, May 7.** Minute of Privy Council, printed from Register in Dasent, **xv. 70.**]

A letter to the Lord Maiour of the Citie of London that whereas their Lordships were given to understand that certaine outrages and disorders were of late committed in certaine places and theaters erected within that Citie of London or the suburbes of the same, where enterludes and comedies were usuallie plaied, and for that the season of the yeare grew hotter and hotter, it was to be doubted least by reason of the concorse of people to such places of common assemblies there might some danger of infeccion happen in the Citie, their Lordships thought it expedient to have the use of the said interludes inhibited both at the theaters and in all other places within his jurisdiccion, and therefore required him accordinglie to take presente order for the stayinge of the same, charginge the plaiers and actors to cease and forbeare the use of the said places for the purpose of playinge or shewinge of anie such enterludes or comedies untill after Bartholomew tide next ensuinge.

A like letter to the same effecte to the Master of the Rolles.

A like letter to the like effecte to the Justices of Surrie.

lxxx.

[**1587, Oct. 29.** Minute of Privy Council, printed from Register in Dasent, **xv. 271.**]

A letter to the Justices of Surry that whereas thinhabitauntes of Southwark had complained unto their Lordships declaring that th'order by their Lordships sett downe for the restrayning of plaies and enterludes within that countie on the Saboath Daies is not observed, and especiallie within the Libertie of the Clincke and in the parish of St. Savours in Southwarke, which disorder is to be ascribed to the negligence of some of the Justices of Peace in that countie ; they are required to take suche stricte order for the staying of the said disorder as is allreadie taken by the Lord Maiour within the Liberties of the Cittie, so as the same be not hereafter suffred at the times forbidden in any place of that countie.

A letter to the Justices of Middlesex that forasmuch as order is taken by the Lord Maiour within the precinctes of the Cittie for the restrayninge of plaies and interludes on the Saboath Daie, according to such direccion as hath been heretofore given by their Lordships in that behalfe, they are required to see the like observed and kept within that countie, aswell in anie places priviledged as otherwise.

lxxxi.

[1587, Nov. 23. Minute of City Court of Aldermen, printed in Harrison, iv. 322, from *Repertory*, xxi, f. 503^v.]

Item yt is ordered that Sir Rowland Haywarde, Sir George Barne, Knight, Mr. Martyn, Mr. Harte, Mr. Allott, Aldermen, shall repayre to the right honorable the LL. and others of her Maiesties most honorble Pryuye Councell & to move theyre honours for the suppressinge of playes and interludes within this Cittye and the libertyes of the same.

lxxxii.

[1589, Nov. 6. Sir John Harte, Lord Mayor, to Lord Burghley, printed *M. S. C.* i. 180, from *Lansd. MS.* 60, f. 47 ; also in Collier, i. 265 ; Hazlitt, *E. D. S.* 34.]

My very honourable good L. Where by a lettre of your Lps. directed to mr. Yonge it appered vnto me, that it was your honours pleasure I sholde geue order for the staie of all playes within the Cittie, in that mr. Tilney did vtterly mislike the same. According to which your Lps. good pleasure, I presentlye sente for suche players as I coulde here of, so as there appered yesterday before me the L. Admeralles and the L. Straunges players, to whome I speciallie gaue in Charge and required them in her Maiesties name to forbere playinge, vntill further order mighte be geuen for theire allowance in that respecte : Whereupon the L. Admeralles players very dutifullie obeyed, but the others in very Contemptuous manner departing from me, went to the Crosse keys and played that afternoon, to the greate offence of the better sorte that knewe they were prohibited by order from your L. Which as I might not suffer, so I sent for the said Contemptuous persons, who haueing no reason to alleadge for theire Contempt, I coulde do no lesse but this evening Comitt some of them to one of the Compters, and do meane according to your Lps. direction to prohibite all playing, vntill your Lps. pleasure therein be further

knowen. And thus resting further to trouble your L., I moste humblie
take my leaue. At London the Sixte of Nouember 1589.

Your Lps. moste humble,

John Harte, maior.

To the righte honorable my very good Lorde, the Lorde highe
Tresaurer of Englande.

lxxxiii.

[1589, Nov. 12. Minute of Privy Council, printed from Register in
Dasent, xviii. 214.]

At the Starre Chamber 12⁰ Novembris, 1589.

A letter to the Lord Archbishop of Canterbury that whereas there
hathe growne some inconvenience by comon playes and enterludes
in and about the Cyttie of London, in [that] the players take upon
themselves to handle in their plaies certen matters of Divinytie and
of State unfitt to be suffred, for redresse whereof their Lordships
have thought good to appointe some persones of judgement and
understanding to viewe and examine their playes before they be
permitted to present them publickly. His Lordship is desired that
some fytt persone well learned in Divinity be appointed by him to
joyne with the Master of the Revells and one other to be nominated
by the Lord Mayour, and they joyntly with some spede to viewe
and consider of suche comedyes and tragedyes as are and shalbe
publickly played by the companies of players in and aboute the Cyttie
of London, and they to geve allowance of suche as they shall thincke
meete to be plaied and to forbydd the rest.

A letter to the Lord Mayour of London that whereas their Lordships
have already signified unto him to appointe a sufficient persone
learned and of judgement for the Cyttie of London to joyne with the
Master of the Revelles and with a divine to be nominated by the
Lord Archebishop of Canterbury for the reforming of the plaies daylie
exercised and presented publickly in and about the Cyttie of London,
wherein the players take uppon them without judgement or decorum
to handle matters of Divinitye and State ; he is required if he have
not as yet made choice of suche a persone, that he will so doe forthwith, and thereof geve knowledge to the Lord Archebishop and the
Master of the Revells, that they may all meet accordingly.

A letter to the Master of the Revelles requiring him [to join] with
two others the one to be appointed by the Lord Archbishop of
Canterbury and the other by the Lord Mayour of London, to be men
of learning and judgement, and to call before them the severall
companies of players (whose servauntes soever they be) and to require
them by authorytie hereof to delyver unto them their bookes, that
they maye consider of the matters of their comedyes and tragedyes,
and thereuppon to stryke oute or reforme suche partes and matters
as they shall fynd unfytt and undecent to be handled in playes, bothe
for Divinitie and State, comaunding the said companies of players,
in her Majesties name, that they forbeare to present and playe pub-

lickly anie comedy or tragedy other then suche as they three shall have seene and allowed, which if they shall not observe, they shall then knowe from their Lordships that they shalbe not onely sevearely punished, but made [in]capable of the exercise of their profession forever hereafter.

lxxxiv.

[1591, July 25. Minute of Privy Council, printed from Register in Dasent, xxi. 324.]

A letter to the Lord Maiour of the Cyttie of London and the Justices of Midlesex and Surrey. Whereas heretofore there hathe ben order taken to restraine the playinge of enterludes and playes on the Sabothe Daie, notwithstandinge the which (as wee are enformed) the same ys neglected to the prophanacion of this daie, and all other daies of the weeke in divers places the players doe use to recyte theire plaies to the greate hurte and destruction of the game of beare baytinge and lyke pastymes, which are maynteyned for her Majesty's pleasure yf occacion require. These shalbe therefore to require you not onlie to take order hereafter that there maie no plaies, interludes or commodyes be used or publicklie made and shewed either on the Sondaie or on the Thursdaies, because on the Thursdayes those other games usuallie have ben allwayes accustomed and practized. Whereof see you faile not hereafter to see this our order dulie observed for the avoydinge of the inconveniences aforesaid.

lxxxv.

[1592, Feb. 25. The Lord Mayor to John Whitgift, Archbishop of Canterbury, printed *M. S. C.* i. 68, from *Remembrancia*, i. 635.]

Our most humble dueties to your Grace remembred. Whereas by the daily and disorderlie exercise of a number of players & playeng houses erected within this Citie, the youth thearof is greatly corrupted & their manners infected with many euill & vngodly qualities, by reason of the wanton & prophane divises represented on the stages by the sayed players, the prentizes & seruants withdrawen from their woorks, & all sorts in generall from the daylie resort vnto sermons & other Christian exercises, to the great hinderance of the trades & traders of this Citie & prophanation of the good & godly religion established amongst vs. To which places allso doe vsually resort great numbers of light & lewd disposed persons, as harlotts, cutpurses, cuseners, pilferers, & such lyke, & thear, vnder the collour of resort to those places to hear the playes, divise divers evill & vngodly matches, confederacies, & conspiracies, which by means of the opportunitie of the place cannot bee prevented nor discovered, as otherwise they might bee. In consideration whearof, wee most humbly beeseach your Grace for your godly çare for the refourming of so great abuses tending to the offence of almightie god, the prophanation & sclaunder of his true religion, & the corrupting of our youth, which are the seed of the Church of god & the common wealth among vs, to voutchsafe

vs your good favour & help for the refourming & banishing of so
great evill out of this Citie, which our selves of loong time though
to small pourpose have so earnestly desired and endeavoured by all
means that possibly wee could. And bycause wee vnderstand that
the Q. Maiestie is & must bee served at certen times by this sort of
people, for which pourpose shee hath graunted hir lettres Patents to
Mr. Tilney Master of hir Revells, by virtue whearof hee beeing
authorized to refourm exercise or suppresse all manner of players,
playes, & playeng houses whatsoeuer, did first licence the sayed
playeng houses within this Citie for hir Maiesties sayed service, which
beefore that time lay open to all the statutes for the punishing of
these & such lyke disorders. Wee ar most humbly & earnestly to
beeseach your Grace to call vnto you the sayed Master of hir Maiesties
Revells, with whome allso wee have conferred of late to that pourpose,
and to treat with him, if by any means it may bee devised that
hir Maiestie may bee served with these recreations as hath ben
accoustomed (which in our opinions may easily bee don by the privat
exercise of hir Maiesties own players in convenient place) & the Citie
freed from these continuall disorders, which thearby do growe, &
increase dayly among vs. Whearby your Grace shall not only benefit
& bynd vnto you the politique state & government of this Citie,
which by no one thing is so greatly annoyed & disquieted as by
players & playes, & the disorders which follow thearvpon, but allso
take away a great offence from the Church of god & hinderance to
his ghospell, to the great contentment of all good Christians, specially
the preachers, & ministers of the word of god about this Citie, who
have long time & yet do make their earnest continuall complaint
vnto vs for the redresse hearof. And thus recommending our most
humble dueties and service to your Grace wee commit the same to
the grace of the Almightie. From London the 25th of February, 1591.
                    Your Graces most humble.
To the right reuerend Father in God my L. the Archbisshop of Cantur-
bury his Grace.

lxxxvi.

[1592, March 6. The Lord Mayor to Archbishop Whitgift, printed
M. S. C. i. 70, from *Remembrancia*, i. 646. Whitgift's letter, here referred
to, does not appear to be in the *Remembrancia*.]

My humble duety to your Grace remembred. I received your graces
letter, wherain I vnderstood the contents of the same, & imparted
the same presently to my Brethren the Aldermen in our common
Assembly, who togither with my self yeld vnto your Grace our most
humble thancks for your good favour & godly care over vs, in voutch-
safing vs your healp for the removing of this great inconvenience
which groweth to this Citie by playes & players. As toutching the
consideracion to bee made to Mr. Tilney, and other capitulations that
ar to passe beetwixt vs, for the better effecting & continuance of this
restraint of the sayed playes in & about this Citie, wee have appointed
certein of our Brethren the Aldermen to conferre with him forthwith,

pourposing to acquaint your Grace with our agreement & whole
proceeding hearin as occasion shall requier. And thus recommending
my humble duety and seruice to your Grace I commit the same to
the grace of the Almightie. From London the 6. of March, 1591.

Your Graces most humble.

To the right reverend Father in God the L. Archbishop of Canterbury
his Grace.

lxxxvii.

[1592, March 18. Minute of City Court of Aldermen, printed in Harrison,
iv. 322, from *Repertory*, xx, f. 345.]

Mr. Tilney to be
treated for re-
straynte of plays.
Item yt is ordered that Sir Richard Martyn
Knighte and William Horne grocer, shall treate
with Tilney Esquire Maister of the Revells for
some good order to be taken for the restrayning
of the playes and enterludes within this citie.

lxxxviii.

[1592, March 22. Extracts from records of the Court of the Guild of
Merchant Taylors of London, printed in C. M. Clode, *Early History of the
Guild of Merchant Taylors* (1888), i. 236.]

' A precepte directed frome the Lord Mayor to this Companie
shewinge to the Companie the great enormytie that this Citie sus-
teyneth by the practice and prophane exercise of players and playinge
howses in this Citie, and the corrupcion of youth that groweth thereupon, invitinge the Companie by the consideration of this myscheyfe
to yeilde to the paymente of one Anuytie to one Mr. Tylney, mayster
of the Revelles of the Queene's house, in whose hands the redresse
of this inconveniency doeth rest, and that those playes might be
abandoned out of this citie.'

' An Assemblye hereon the xxijth of March (1591), beinge our Master's
view daye after they came downe frome dynner out of the Gallarie,'
took the precept into consideration and determined, ' albeit the
Companie think yt a very good service to be performed yet wayinge
the damage of the president and enovacion of raysinge of Anuyties
upon the Companies of London what further occasions yt may be
drawne unto, together with their great chardge otherwyse which this
troublesome tyme hath brought, and is likely to bringe, they thinke
this no fitt course to remedie this myscheife, but wish some other
waye were taken in hand to expell out of our Citye so generall a contagion of manners and other inconveniency, wherein if any endevour
or travile of this Companie might further the matter they would
be readye to use their service therein. And this to be certified as
the Companies answere if yt shall apeare by conference with
other Companies that the precepte requireth necessarilie a returne
of the Companies certificate, and answere in this behalf.'

lxxxix.

[1592, June 12. Extract from a letter of Sir William Webbe, Lord Mayor, to Lord Burghley, printed *M. S. C.* i. 187, from *Lansd. MS.* 71, f. 28, and *M. S. C.* i. 70, from a letter-book copy misdated 'May 30' in *Remembrancia*, i. 662.]

My humble duety remembred to your good L. Beeing informed of a great disorder & tumult lyke to grow yesternight abowt viij of the clock within the Borough of Southwark, I went thither with all speed I could, taking with mee on of the Sherifes, whear I found great multitudes of people assembled togither, & the principall actours to bee certain servants of the ffeltmakers gathered togither out of Barnsey street & the Black fryers, with a great number of lose & maisterles men apt for such pourposes. Whearupon having made proclamation, & dismissed the multitude, I apprehended the chief doers and authors of the disorder, & have committed them to prison to bee farther punished, as they shall bee found to deserve. And having this morning sent for the Deputie & Constable of the Borough with Divers other of best credit, who wear thear present, to examine the cause & manner of the disorder, I found that it began vpon the serving of a warrant from my L. Chamberlain by on of the Knight Mareschalls men vpon a feltmakers servant, who was committed to the Mareschallsea with certein others, that were accused to his L. by the sayed Knight Mareschalls men without cause of offence, as them selves doe affirm. For rescuing of whome the sayed companies assembled themselves by occasion & pretence of their meeting at a play, which bysides the breach of the Sabboth day giveth opportunitie of committing these & such lyke disorders. The principall doers in this rude tumult I mean to punish to the example of others. Whearin also it may please your L. to give mee your direction, if you shall advise vpon anything meet to bee doon for the farther punishment of the sayed offenders.

XC.

[1592, June 23. Extract from Privy Council Minute, printed by Dasent, xxii. 549. The main purpose of the letter is to require a 'watch' at midsummer, as certain apprentices were expected to renew the recent disorder in Southwark (cf. No. lxxxix). The Lord Mayor had already been charged, and letters also went to the Justices of Surrey for the precincts of Newington, Kentish Street, Bermondsey Street, the Clink, Paris Garden, and the Bankside, and to those of other places near the City, including Lord Cobham for the Blackfriars.]

A letter to the Master of the Rolles, Sir Owen Hopton, knight, John Barnes and Richard Yonge, esquiours. . . .
Moreover for avoidinge of theis unlawfull assemblies in those quarters, yt is thoughte meete you shall take order that there be noe playes used in anye place neere thereaboutes, as the Theator, Curtayne, or other usuall places where the same are comonly used,

nor no other sorte of unlawfull or forbidden pastymes that drawe together the baser sorte of people, from hence forth untill the feast of St. Michaell.

xci.

[1592, June 23. Privy Council Minute, printed by Dasent, xxii. 549.]

A letter to the Earle of Darbye. Whereas wee are informed that there are certaine May gaimes, morryce daunces, plaies, bearebaytinges, ales and other like pastimes used ordinarilye in those counties under your Lordship's Lieutenancye on the Sondaies and Hollydaies at the tyme of Divine service and other Godlie exercyses, to the disturbance of the service, and bad example that those kinde of pastimes should be used in such sorte and at suche tyme when men do assemble togeather for the hearinge of God's worde and to joyne in Common praiers, which sportes are moste ordinarilye used at those undue seasons by such as are evill affected in religion, purposlie by those meanes to drawe the people from the service of God, and to disturbe the same. Theis shalbe therefore to praie your. Lordship by vertue hereof to give knowledge not onlie to the Byshop of that Dioces of this common and unsufferable disorder, but to give speciall direction to all the Justices in theire severall divisions by all meanes to forbid and not to suffer theis or the like pastimes to be in anye place whatsoever on the Sondaie or Holydaie at the tyme of Divine service. And yf notwithstandinge this straite prohibicion and speciall order taken, any shall presume to use the saide sportes or pastimes in the tyme [of] services, sermons or other Godlye exercyses, you shall cause the favorers, mayntainers or cheife offenders to be sent up hether to answere this theire contentions and lewde behaviour before us.

xcii.

[c. 1592, c. July. Undated documents, printed by Greg, *Henslowe Papers*, 42, from *Dulwich MS*. i. 16–18 ; also in Collier, *Alleyn Memoirs*, 33–6. I agree with Greg (cf. Henslowe, ii. 52) that 1592 is a more likely date than 1593, during the whole of the long vacation of which plague ruled. We have not the terms of the Surrey inhibition of 23 June 1592 (cf. No. xc), but it may have made an exception for Newington Butts. If so, the documents can hardly be later than July, as the plague was increasing by 13 Aug. (Dasent, xxiii. 118). But Greg tacitly assumes that no earlier year than 1592 can be in question, and as against this, cf. vol. i, p. 359. I think that 1591 is a conceivable alternative, as Strange's (q.v.) were probably at the Rose by the spring of that year. There is no corroborative evidence, indeed, of any inhibition in 1591. But do the documents point to a general inhibition ? The inference from (b) is that houses other than the Rose were open.]

(a)

[Petition from Strange's men to the Privy Council.]

To the right honorable our verie good Lordes, the Lordes of her maiesties moste honorable privie Councell.

Our dueties in all humblenes remembred to your honours. Forasmuche (righte honorable) oure Companie is greate, and thearbie our chardge intollerable, in travellinge the Countrie, and the Contynuaunce thereof wilbe a meane to bringe vs to division and seperacion, whearebie wee shall not onelie be vndone, but alsoe vnreadie to serve her maiestie, when it shall please her highenes to commaund vs, And for that the vse of our plaiehowse on the Banckside, by reason of the passage to and frome the same by water, is a greate releif to the poore watermen theare, And our dismission thence, nowe in this longe vacation, is to those poore men a greate hindraunce, and in manner an vndoeinge, as they generallie complaine, Both our and theire humble peticion and suite thearefore to your good honnours is, That youe wilbe pleased of your speciall favour to recall this our restrainte, and permitt vs the vse of the said Plaiehowse againe. And not onelie our selues But alsoe a greate nomber of poore men shalbe especiallie bounden to praie for yor Honours.

Your honours humble suppliantes,
The righte honorable the Lord Straunge
his servantes and Plaiers.

(*b*)

[Petition from the Watermen of the Bankside to Lord Admiral Howard.]

To the right honnorable my Lorde Haywarde Lorde highe
Admirall of Englande and one of her maiesties moste
honnorable previe Counsayle.

In most hvmble manner Complayneth and sheweth vnto your good Lordeshipp, your poore suppliantes and dayly Oratours Phillipp Henslo, and others the poore watermen on the bancke side. Whereas your good L. hathe derected your warrant vnto hir maiesties Justices, for the restraynte of a playe howse belonginge vnto the saide Phillipp Henslo one of the groomes of her maiesties Chamber, So it is, if it please your good Lordshipp, that wee your saide poore watermen have had muche helpe and reliefe for vs oure poore wives and Children by meanes of the resorte of suche people as come vnto the said playe howse, It maye therefore please your good L. for godes sake and in the waye of Charetie to respecte vs your poore water men, and to give leave vnto the said Phillipp Henslo to have playinge in his saide howse duringe suche tyme as others have, according as it hathe byne accustomed. And in your honnors so doinge youe shall not onely doe a good and a Charitable dede, but also bynde vs all according to oure dewties, with oure poore wives and Children dayly to praye for your honnor in muche happynes longe to lyve.

Isack Towelle.   William Dorret, master of her maiestes barge.
[Fifteen signatures or marks of royal watermen and others follow.]

(*c*)

[Warrant from the Privy Council for the reopening of the Rose.]

Wheareas not longe since vpon some Consideracions we did restraine the Lorde Straunge his servauntes from playinge at the Rose on the banckside, and enioyned them to plaie three daies at Newington

Butts, Now forasmuch as wee are satisfied that by reason of the tediousnes of the waie and that of longe tyme plaies haue not there bene vsed on working daies, And for that a nomber of poore watermen are therby releeved, Youe shall permitt and suffer them or any other there to exercise them selues in suche sorte as they haue don heretofore, And that the Rose maie be at libertie without any restrainte, solonge as yt shalbe free from infection of sicknes, Any Comaundement from vs heretofore to the Contrye notwithstandinge : ffrom.

To the Justices Bayliffes Constables and others to whome yt shall Apperteyne.

xciii.

[1593, Jan. 28. Minute of Privy Council, printed from Register in Dasent, xxiv. 31.]

A letter to the Lord Maiour and Aldermen of the cittie of London. Forasmuch as by the certificate of the last weeke yt appeareth the infection doth increase, which by the favour of God and with your diligent observance of her Majesty's comandementes and the meanes and orders prescribed to be put in execution within the cittie of London maie speedelie cease. Yeat for the better furderance therof we thinke yt fytt that all manner of concourse and publique meetinges of the people at playes, beare-baitinges, bowlinges and other like assemblyes for sportes be forbidden, and therefore doe hereby requier you and in her Majesty's name straightlie charge and commande you forthwith to inhibite within your jurisdiction all plaies, baiting of beares, bulls, bowling and any other like occasions to assemble any nombers of people together (preacheing and Devyne service at churches excepted), wherby no occasions be offred to increase the infection within the cittie, which you shall doe both by proclamacion to be published to that ende and by spetiall watche and observacion to be had at the places where the plaies, beare-baitinges, bowlinges and like pastimes are usually frequented. And if you shall upon the publicacion finde any so undutifull and disobedient as they will notwithstanding this prohibition offer to plaie, beate beares or bulles, bowle, &c., you shall presentelie cause them to be apprehended and comitted to prison, there to remaine untill by their order they shalbe dismissed. And to the end the like assemblies within the out liberties adjoyning to the cittie [may be prohibited], we have given direction to the Justices of the Peace and other publique officers of the counties of Middelsex and Surrey to hold the like course, not onlie within the said liberties but also within the distance of seven myles about the cittie, which we doubte not they will carefullie see to be executed, as you for your partes within the cittie will doe the like, in reguarde of her Majestie's comandement, the benefitt of the cittie and for the respectes alreadie signified unto you.

Two other letters of the like tenour written to the Justices of the Peace within the counties of Surrey and Middelsex for the prohibition of like assemblies in the out liberties and within seven miles of the cittie of either countie.

xciv.

[1593, April 12. Minute of City Court of Aldermen, printed in Harrison, iv. 322, from *Repertory*, xxiii, f. 50ᵛ.]

Elders of the Councell. Bearebaitinge and plaies.

Item, yt is ordered that Sir Richarde Martyn, Knighte, and Master Saltonstall, aldermen, shall repayre to the righte honourable the Lordes and others of her Maiesties most honorable Pryuey Counsell, towching the presente suppressinge of bearebaitinge, bowling alleyes, and such like prophane exercises within this Cytie, and the libertyes thereof, and other places neare adioyninge. And Christofer Stubbes to warne them, etc.

xcv.

[1593, April 29. Privy Council Minute, printed Dasent, xxiv. 209.]

An open warrant for the plaiers, servantes to the Erle of Sussex, authorysinge them to exercyse theire qualitie of playinge comedies and tragedies in any county, cittie, towne or corporacion not being within vijᵉⁿ miles of London, where the infection is not, and in places convenient and tymes fitt.

xcvi.

[1593, May 6. Privy Council Minute, printed Dasent, xxiv. 212 ; cf. text in Bk. iii.]

Gives authority to Strange's men, notwithstanding inhibition of plays in London, to perform in towns seven miles from London or court, at their most convenient times and places, except during times of divine prayer.

xcvii.

[1594, Feb. 3. The Privy Council to Sir Cuthbert Buckle, Lord Mayor, printed *M. S. C.* i. 72, from *Remembrancia*, ii. 6.]

For restraint of playes.

After our very hartie commendations to your L. Whearas certein infourmation is given that very great multitudes of all sorts of people do daylie frequent & resort to common playes lately again set vp in & about London, whearby it is vpon good cause feared that the dangerous infection of the plague, by Gods great mercy and goodnes well slaked, may again very dangerously encrease and break foorth, to the great losse and preiudice of hir Maiesties Subiects in generall & especially to those of that Citie, of whose safetie & well doing hir Highnes hath alwayes had an especiall regard, as by the last years experience by lyke occasions & resort to playes it soddainly encreased from a very little number to that greatnes of mortallitie which ensued. Wee thearfore thought it very expedient to require your L. foorthwith to take strait order that thear bee no more publique playes or enterludes exercised by any Compaine whatsoever within the compas of five miles distance from London, till vpon better lykelyhood and assurance

of health farther direction may bee giuen from vs to the contrary.
So wee bid your L. very hartily farewell. From the Court at Hampton.
the 3. of February. 1593.

Your L. very louing friends,

Io: Cant.	Io. Puckering.	C. Howard.
Th. Buckhurst.	R. Cecyll.	I. Fortescue.

To our very good L. mr. Alderman Buckle L. Maior of the Citie of
London.

xcviii.

[1594, May 10. Minute of City Court of Aldermen, printed in Harrison,
iv. 323, from *Repertory*, xxiii, f. 220.]

Countess of Warwicks playes.

Item yt is ordred that Mr. Saltonstall, Mr. Soame, Mr. Weoseley,
Mr. Barnham, and Mr. Houghton, aldermen, or any others [?] of
them, calling unto them Richard Wright, gentleman, shall consider
of a cawse recommended to this courte by the right honorable the
Countys of Warwicke concerning playes, And to make reporte to this
courte of their doings therein. And George Foster to warne them to
meet together and to attend on them.

xcix.

[*c.* 1594, July–Oct. Extract from Articles submitted to the Privy
Council against the increase of the plague and for the relief of poor people,
printed *M. S. C.* i. 202, from *Lansd. MS.* 74, f. 75. The date 1593 is
assigned in the *Catalogue of Lansdowne MSS.*, but the document seems
to be related to No. c.]

That for avoydinge of great concourse of people, which causeth
increase of thinfection, yt were convenient, that all Playes, Bearebaytinges, Cockpittes, common Bowlinge alleyes, and suche like
vnnecessarie assemblies should be suppressed duringe the tyme of
infection, for that infected people, after theire longe keepinge in, and
before they be clered of theire disease and infection, beinge desirous
of recreacion, vse to resort to suche assemblies, where throughe heate
and thronge, they infecte manie sound personnes.

c.

[*c.* 1594, July–Oct. Extract from Orders, suggested by the Privy
Council, to be set down by the Lord Mayor and Aldermen. These are
undated, but appear to be the ' breif ' of orders sent with a letter of the
Privy Council, also undated, but addressed to Sir Richard Martin, who
was Lord Mayor from July to Oct. 1594. Both documents are printed
in *M. S. C.* i. 206, 211, from *Lansd. MS.* 74, ff. 69, 71.]

Interludes and plaies.

If the increase of the sicknes be feared, that Interludes and plaies
be restreyned within the libertyes of the Cyttye. . . .
. . . That all maisterlesse men who lyve idelie in the Cyttye without

any lawfull calling, frequenting places of common assemblies, as Interludes, gaming howses, cockpittes, bowling allies, and such other places, maie be banished the Cyttye according to the lawes in that case provyded.

ci.

[1594, Oct. 8. Henry Lord Hunsdon, Lord Chamberlain, to Sir Richard Martin, Lord Mayor, printed *M. S. C.* i. 73, from *Remembrancia*, ii. 33. The document is misdescribed in the *Index* to *Remembrancia*, 353, as referring, not to ' my nowe companie ', but to ' the new company '.]

For players to bee suffred to play with in London.

After my hartie comendacions. Where my nowe companie of Players haue byn accustomed for the better exercise of their qualitie, & for the seruice of her Maiestie if need soe requier, to plaie this winter time within the Citye at the Crosse kayes in Gracious street. These are to requier & praye your Lo. (the time beinge such as, thankes be to god, there is nowe no danger of the sicknes) to permitt & suffer them soe to doe ; The which I praie you the rather to doe for that they haue vndertaken to me that, where heretofore they began not their Plaies till towardes fower a clock, they will now begin at two, & haue don betwene fower and fiue, and will nott vse anie Drumes or trumpettes att all for the callinge of peopell together, and shalbe contributories to the poore of the parishe where they plaie accordinge to their habilities. And soe not dowting of your willingnes to yeeld herevnto, vppon theise resonable condicions, I comitt yow to the Almightie. Noonesuch this viijth of October 1594.

Your lo. lovinge freind,

H. Hounsdon.

To my honorable good freind Sir Richard Martin knight Lo: mayour of the Citie of London.

cii.

[1594, Nov. 3. The Lord Mayor to Lord Burghley, printed *M. S. C.* i. 74, from *Remembrancia*, ii. 73. The theatre was doubtless the Swan.]

Langley intending to erect a niew stage on the Banckside & against playes.

My humble duetie remembred to your good L. I vnderstand that one Francis Langley, one of the Alneagers for sealing of cloth, intendeth to erect a niew stage or Theater (as they call it) for thexercising of playes vpon the Banck side. And forasmuch as wee fynd by daily experience the great inconuenience that groweth to this Citie & the government thearof by the sayed playes, I haue embouldened my self to bee an humble suiter to your good L. to bee a means for vs rather to suppresse all such places built for that kynd of exercise, then to erect any more of the same sort. I am not ignorant (my very good L.) what is alleadged by soom for defence of these playes, that the people must haue soom kynd of recreation, & that policie requireth to divert idle heads & other ill disposed from other woorse practize by this kynd of exercize.

Whearto may bee answeared (which your good L. for your godly wisedom can far best iudge of) that as honest recreation is a thing very meet for all sorts of men, so no kynd of exercise, beeing of itself corrupt & prophane, can well stand with the good policie of a Christian Common Wealth. And that the sayed playes (as they are handled) ar of that sort, and woork that effect in such as ar present and frequent the same, may soon bee decerned by all that haue any godly vnderstanding & that obserue the fruites & effects of the same, conteining nothing ells but vnchast fables, lascivious divises, shifts of cozenage, & matters of lyke sort, which ar so framed & represented by them, that such as resort to see & hear the same, beeing of the base & refuse sort of people or such yoong gentlemen as haue small regard of credit or conscience, draue the same into example of imitation & not of avoyding the sayed lewd offences. Which may better appear by the qualitie of such as frequent the sayed playes, beeing the ordinary places of meeting for all vagrant persons & maisterles men that hang about the Citie, theeues, horsestealers, whoremoongers, coozeners, connycatching persones, practizers of treason, & such other lyke, whear they consort and make their matches to the great displeasure of Almightie God & the hurt and annoyance of hir Maiesties people, both in this Citie & other places about, which cannot be clensed of this vngodly sort (which by experience wee fynd to bee the very sinck & contagion not only of this Citie but of this whole Realm), so long as these playes & places of resort ar by authoritie permitted. I omit to trouble your L. with any farther matter how our apprentices and servants ar by this means corrupted & induced hear by to defraud their Maisters, to maintein their vain & prodigall expenses occasioned by such evill and riotous companie, whearinto they fall by these kynd of meetings, to the great hinderance of the trades & traders inhabiting this Citie, and how people of all sorts ar withdrawen thearby from their resort vnto sermons & other Christian exercise, to the great sclaunder of the ghospell & prophanation of the good & godly religion established within this Realm. All which disorders hauing observed & found to bee true, I thought it my duetie, beeing now called to this publique place, to infourm your good L., whome I know to bee a patrone of religion & lover of virtue & an honourable a friend to the State of this Citie, humbly beeseaching you to voutchsafe mee your help for the stay & suppressing, not only of this which is now intended, by directing your lettres to the Iustices of peace of Middlesex & Surrey, but of all other places, if possibly it may bee, whear the sayed playes ar shewed & frequented. And thus crauing pardon for this ouer much length I humbly take my leaue. From London the 3. of November. 1594.

Your L. most humble.

To the right honourable my very good L. the L. high Treasurer of England.

318 APPENDIX D

ciii.

[1595, Sept. 13. The Lord Mayor and Aldermen to the Privy Council, printed *M. S. C.* i. 76, from *Remembrancia*, ii. 103.]

Toutching the putting doune of the plaies at the Theater & Bankside which is a great cause of disorder in the Citie :

Our humble duty remembred to your good LL. & the rest. Wee haue been bold heartofore to signify to your HH: the great inconvenyence that groweth to this Cytie by the common exercise of Stage Plaies, whear in wee presumed to be the more often & earnest suters to your HH: for the suppressing of the said Stage Plaies, aswell in respect of the good government of this Cytie, (which wee desire to be such as her Highnes & your HH: might be pleased thearwithall), as for conscience sake being perswaded (vnder correccion of your HH. Iudgment) that neither in policye nor in religion they ar to be permitted in a Christian Common wealthe, specially being of that frame & making as vsually they are, & conteyning nothing but profane fables, Lasciuious matters, cozonning devizes, & other vnseemly & scurrilous behaviours, which ar so sett forthe, as that they move wholy to imitacion & not to the avoyding of those vyces which they represent, which wee verely think to bee the cheef cause, aswell of many other disorders & lewd demeanors which appeer of late in young people of all degrees, as of the late stirr & mutinous attempt of those fiew apprentices and other servantes, who wee doubt not driew their infection from these & like places. Among other inconveniences it is not the least that the refuse sort of evill disposed & vngodly people about this Cytie haue oportunitie hearby to assemble together & to make their matches for all their lewd & vngodly practizes : being also the ordinary places for all maisterles men & vagabond persons that haunt the high waies to meet together & to recreate themselfes. Whearof wee begin to haue experienc again within these fiew daies, since it pleased her highnes to revoke her Comission graunted forthe to the Provost Marshall, for fear of whome they retired themselfes for the time into other partes out of his precinct, but ar now retorned to their old haunt & frequent the Plaies (as their manner is) that ar daily shewed at the Theator & Bankside : Whearof will follow the same inconveniences whearof wee haue had to much experienc heartofore, ffor preventing whearof wee ar humble suters to your good LL: & the rest to direct your lettres to the Iustices of peac of Surrey & Middlesex for the present stay & finall suppressing of the said Plaies, aswell at the Theator & Bankside as in all other places about the Cytie. Whearby wee doubt not but, the oportunytie & very cause of so great disorders being taken away, wee shalbe able to keepe the people of this Cytie in such good order & due obedienc, as that her highnes & your HH: shalbe well pleased & content thearwithall. And so most humbly wee take our Leaue. From London the xiijth of September. 1595.

Your HH: most humble.

To the right honourable the LL: & others of her Maiesties most honourable privy Counsell.

civ.

[1596, July 22. Privy Council Minute, printed Dasent, xxvi. 38.]

Letters to the Justices of Middlesex and Surrey to restrayne the players from shewing or using anie plaies or interludes in the places usuall about the citty of London, for that by drawing of muche people together increase of sicknes is feared.

cv.

[1596, c. Sept. Extract from letter of T. Nashe to William Cotton, printed with facsimile by McKerrow, *Nashe*, v. 194, from *Cotton MS. Julius*, C. iii, f. 280. Internal evidence bears out the ' T. Nashe ' subscribed in a nineteenth-century hand. The original signature has gone, but the top of ' N ' was declared to be visible by Collier, who printed the letter in *H. E. D. P.* (1831), i. 303 ; it is also in Grosart, *Nashe*, i. lxi. The date is suggested by an allusion to the return of Essex from Cadiz on 10 Aug. 1596, and the beginning of term on 9 Oct. 1596. Allusions to Harington's *Metamorphosis of Ajax* (S. R. 30 Oct. 1596) might point to a rather later date, but Harington's dedication is dated 3 Aug. 1596, and the first issue may not have been registered.]

Sir this tedious dead vacation is to mee as vnfortunate as a terme at Hertford or St. Albons to poore cuntry clients or Iack Cades rebellion to the lawyers, wherein they hanged vp the L. cheife iustice. In towne I stayd (being earnestly inuited elsewhere) vpon had I wist hopes, & an after harvest I expected by writing for the stage & for the presse, when now the players as if they had writt another Christs tears, ar piteously persecuted by the L. Maior & the aldermen, & howeuer in there old Lords tyme they thought there state setled, it is now so vncertayne they cannot build vpon it.

cvi.

[1596, Nov. Petition by Inhabitants of Blackfriars to Privy Council, printed by Halliwell-Phillipps, i. 304, from undated copy assignable by the handwriting to c. 1631 in *S. P. D. Eliz.* cclx. 116. The date is given by No. cvii ; cf. Bk. iv, s.v. Blackfriars. The document has been suspected as a forgery, but is probably genuine, although it is odd to find Lord Hunsdon as a signatory, since one would have supposed that he could influence James Burbage through his son Richard, who was one of Hunsdon's players. Collier, who first produced it, misdated it 1576, and used it to support a theory that the Blackfriars was built in 1576 (i. 219). Curiously enough, he used it again for 1596 (i. 287), and added to it an alleged counter-petition by the Chamberlain's men, now in *S. P. D. Eliz.* cclx. 117, which is certainly a forgery. Hunsdon was not Chamberlain in Nov. 1596.]

To the right honorable the Lords and others of her Majesties most honorable Privy Councell,—Humbly shewing and beseeching your honors, the inhabitants of the precinct of the Blackfryers, London, that whereas one Burbage hath lately bought certaine roomes in the same precinct neere adjoyning unto the dwelling houses of the right

honorable the Lord Chamberlaine and the Lord of Hunsdon, which
romes the said Burbage is now altering and meaneth very shortly to
convert and turne the same into a comon playhouse, which will grow
to be a very great annoyance and trouble, not only to all the noble-
men and gentlemen thereabout inhabiting but allso a generall inconvenience to all the inhabitants of the same precinct, both by reason
of the great resort and gathering togeather of all manner of vagrant
and lewde persons that, under cullor of resorting to the playes, will
come thither and worke all manner of mischeefe, and allso to the
great pestring and filling up of the same precinct, yf it should please
God to send any visitation of sicknesse as heretofore hath been, for
that the same precinct is allready growne very populous ; and besides,
that the same playhouse is so neere the Church that the noyse of the
drummes and trumpetts will greatly disturbe and hinder both the
ministers and parishioners in tyme of devine service and sermons ;—
In tender consideracion wherof, as allso for that there hath not at
any tyme heretofore been used any comon playhouse within the same
precinct, but that now all players being banished by the Lord Mayor
from playing within the Cittie by reason of the great inconveniences
and ill rule that followeth them, they now thincke to plant them
selves in liberties ;—That therefore it would please your honors to
take order that the same roomes may be converted to some other
use, and that no playhouse may be used or kept there ; and your
suppliants as most bounden shall and will dayly pray for your Lordships in all honor and happines long to live.   Elizabeth Russell,
dowager ; G. Hunsdon ; Henry Bowes ; Thomas Browne ; John
Crooke ; William Meredith ; Stephen Egerton ; Richard Lee ; . . .
Smith ; William Paddy ; William de Lavine ; Francis Hinson ; John
Edwards ; Andrew Lyons ; Thomas Nayle ; Owen Lochard ; John
Robbinson ; Thomas Homes ; Richard Feild ; William Watts ; Henry
Boice ; Edward Ley ; John Clarke ; William Bispham ; Robert
Baheire ; Ezechiell Major ; Harman Buckholt ; John Le Mere ; John
Dollin ; Ascanio de Renialmire ; John Wharton.

cvii.

[1596, Nov.   Extract from Petition of c. Jan. 1619 from Constables
and Inhabitants of Blackfriars to Lord Mayor and Aldermen, printed in
M. S. C. i. 90, from *Remembrancia*, v. 28 ; cf. Bk. iv, s.v. Blackfriars.]

Sheweth That whereas in Nouember 1596, diuers both honorable
persons and others then inhabitinge the said precinct, made knowne
to the Lordes and others of the privie Counsell, what inconveniencies
where likelie to fall vpon them, by a common Playhouse which was
then preparinge to bee erected there, wherevpon their Honours then
forbadd the vse of the said howse, for playes, as by'the peticion and
indorsemente in aunswere thereof may appeare.

cviii.

[1597, May 6. Privy Council Minute, printed Dasent, xxvii. 97.]

A letter to the High Sheriff of Suffolk, William Foorth, John Gurdall and —— Clopton, esquires. We do understand by your letter of the third of this instant of a purpose in the towne of Hadley to make certaine stage playes at this time of the Whitson holydaies next ensuinge, and thether to draw a concourse of people out of the country thereaboutes, pretending heerein the benefit of the towne, which purpose we do utterly mislike, doubting what inconveniences may follow thereon, especially at this tyme of scarcety, when disordred people of the comon sort wilbe apt to misdemeane themselves. We do therefore require you straightly to prohibite the officers and all others in the towne of Hadley not (*sic*) to goe forward with the sayd playes and to cause the stage prepared for them to be plucked downe, letting them know that they are to obey this our order as they will answere it at their perill. We thanck you for the care you take to keepe the country in good order. And so, &c.

cix.

[1597, July 28. The Lord Mayor and Aldermen to the Privy Council, printed *M. S. C.* i. 78, from *Remembrancia*, ii. 171.]

To the Lords against Stage playes.

Our humble dutyes remembred to your good LL. & the rest. Wee haue signifyed to your HH. many tymes heartofore the great inconvenience which wee fynd to grow by the Common exercise of Stage Playes. Wee presumed to doo, aswell in respect of the dutie wee beare towardes her highnes for the good gouernment of this her Citie, as for conscience sake, beinge perswaded (vnder correction of your HH. iudgment) that neither in politie nor in religion they are to be suffered in a Christian Commonwealth, specially beinge of that frame & matter as vsually they are, conteining nothinge but prophane fables, lascivious matters, cozeninge devises, & scurrilus beehaviours, which are so set forth as that they move wholie to imitation & not to the auoydinge of those faults & vices which they represent. Amonge other inconveniences it is not the least that they give opportunity to the refuze sort of euill disposed & vngodly people, that are within and abowte this Cytie, to assemble themselves & to make their matches for all their lewd & vngodly practices ; being as heartofore wee haue fownd by th'examinaton of divers apprentices & other seruantes whoe have confessed vnto vs that the said Staige playes were the very places of theire Randevous appoynted by them to meete with such otheir as wear to ioigne with them in theire designes & mutinus attemptes, beeinge allso the ordinarye places for maisterles men to come together & to recreate themselves. For avoyding whereaof wee are now againe most humble & earnest sutours to your honours to dirrect your lettres aswell to our selves as to the Iustices of peace of Surrey & Midlesex for the present staie & fynall suppressinge of the saide Stage playes, aswell at the Theatre, Curten, and banckside, as in all other places in and abowt the Citie, Wheareby wee doubt not but, th'opportunitie & the very cause of many disorders beinge taken away, wee shalbee more able to keepe the worse sort of such evell & disordered people in better order then heartofore wee haue been. And so most humbly wee take our leaves. From London the xxviijth of Iulie. 1597.

Your HH most humble.

The inconueniences that grow by Stage playes abowt the Citie of London.

1. They are a speaciall cause of corrupting their Youth, conteninge nothinge but vnchast matters, lascivious devices, shiftes of Coozenage, & other lewd & vngodly practizes, being so as that they impresse the very qualitie & corruption of manners which they represent, Contrary to the rules & art prescribed for the makinge of Comedies eauen amonge the Heathen, who vsed them seldom & at certen sett tymes, and not all the year longe as our manner is. Whearby such as frequent them, beinge of the base & refuze sort of people or such young gentlemen as haue small regard of credit or conscience, drawe the same into imitacion and not to the avoidinge the like vices which they represent.

2. They are the ordinary places for vagrant persons, Maisterles men, thieves, horse stealers, whoremongers, Coozeners, Conycatchers, contrivers of treason, and other idele and daungerous persons to meet together & to make theire matches to the great displeasure of Almightie God & the hurt & annoyance of her Maiesties people, which cannot be prevented nor discovered by the Gouernours of the Citie for that they are owt of the Citiees iurisdiction.

3. They maintaine idlenes in such persons as haue no vocation & draw apprentices and other seruantes from theire ordinary workes and all sortes of people from the resort vnto sermons and other Christian exercises, to the great hinderance of traides & prophanation of religion established by her highnes within this Realm.

4. In the time of sicknes it is fownd by experience, that many hauing sores and yet not hart sicke take occasion hearby to walk abroad & to recreat themselves by heareinge a play. Whearby others are infected, and them selves also many things miscarry.

CX.

[1597, July 28. Privy Council Minute, printed Dasent, xxvii. 313.]

A letter to Robert Wrothe, William Fleetwood, John Barne, Thomas Fowler and Richard Skevington, esquires, and the rest of the Justices of Middlesex nerest to London. Her Majestie being informed that there are verie great disorders committed in the common playhouses both by lewd matters that are handled on the stages and by resorte and confluence of bad people, hathe given direction that not onlie no plaies shalbe used within London or about the citty or in any publique place during this tyme of sommer, but that also those play houses that are erected and built only for suche purposes shalbe plucked downe, namelie the Curtayne and the Theatre nere to Shor-

ditch or any other within that county. Theis are therfore in her
Majesty's name to chardge and commaund you that you take present
order there be no more plaies used in any publique place within
three myles of the citty untill Alhalloutide next, and likewyse that
you do send for the owners of the Curtayne Theatre or anie other
common playhouse and injoyne them by vertue hereof forthwith to
plucke downe quite the stages, gallories and roomes that are made
for people to stand in, and so to deface the same as they maie not
be ymploied agayne to suche use, which yf they shall not speedely
perform you shall advertyse us, that order maie be taken to see the
same don according to her Majesty's pleasure and commaundment.
And hereof praying you not to faile, we, &c.

The like to Mr. Bowier, William Gardyner and Bartholomew Scott,
esquires, and the rest of the Justices of Surrey, requiring them to
take the like order for the playhouses in the Banckside, in Southwarke
or elswhere in the said county within iijͤ miles of London.

cxi.

[1597, Aug. 15. Privy Council Minute, printed Dasent, xxvii. 338.]

A letter to Richard Topclyfe, Thomas Fowler and Richard
Skevington, esquires, Doctour Fletcher and Mr. Wilbraham. Uppon
informacion given us of a lewd plaie that was plaied in one of the
plaiehowses on the Bancke Side, contanynge very seditious and
sclanderous matter, wee caused some of the players to be apprehended and comytted to pryson, whereof one of them was not only
an actor but a maker of parte of the said plaie. For as moche as
yt ys thought meete that the rest of the players or actors in that
matter shalbe apprehended to receave soche punyshment as theire
leude and mutynous behavior doth deserve, these shalbe therefore
to require you to examine those of the plaiers that are comytted,
whose names are knowne to you, Mr. Topclyfe, what ys become of
the rest of theire fellowes that either had their partes in the devysinge
of that sedytious matter or that were actors or plaiers in the same,
what copies they have given forth of the said playe and to whome,
and soch other pointes as you shall thincke meete to be demaunded
of them, wherein you shall require them to deale trulie as they will
looke to receave anie favour. Wee praie you also to peruse soch
papers as were fownde in Nash his lodgings, which Ferrys, a Messenger of the Chamber, shall delyver unto you, and to certyfie us
th'examynacions you take. So, &c.

cxii.

[1597, Oct. 8. Privy Council Minute, printed Dasent, xxviii. 33. A
note dates the actual signing of the warrants on Oct. 3.]

A warrant to the Keeper of the Marshalsea to release Gabriell
Spencer and Robert Shaa, stage-players, out of prison, who were of
lat comitted to his custodie.

The like warrant for the releasing of Benjamin Johnson.

cxiii.

[1598, Feb. 9. Extract from *An Acte for punyshment of Rogues Vaga-bondes and Sturdy Beggars* (*39 Eliz.* c. 4, printed in *Statutes*, iv. 899). The Act was continued, subject as regards John Dutton to legal proof of his claim, by *43 Eliz.* c. 9, in 1601 (*St.* iv. 973).]

[§ 1.] From and after the Feaste of Easter next comminge [16 April 1598], all Statutes heretofore made for the punyshment of Rogues Vagabondes or Sturdy Beggers . . . shall . . . be utterly repealed. . . .

[§ 2.] All Fencers Bearewardes common Players of Enterludes and Minstrelles wandring abroade (other than Players of Enterludes belonging to any Baron of this Realme, or any other honorable Personage of greater Degree, to be auctoryzed to play, under the Hand and Seale of Armes of such Baron or Personage) . . . shalbe taken adjudged and deemed Rogues Vagabondes and Sturdy Beggers, and shall susteyne such Payne and Punyshment as by this Acte is in that behalfe appointed.

[§ 3.] Every person which is by this presente Acte declared to be a Rogue Vagabonde or Sturdy Begger, which shalbe . . . taken begging vagrant wandering or mysordering themselves in any part of this Realme . . . , shall uppon their apprehension by thappoyntment of any Justice of the Peace Constable Hedborough or Tythingman of the same County Hundred Parish or Tything where suche person shalbe taken, the Tythingman or Headborow being assisted therein with thadvise of the Minister and one other of that Parrish, be stripped naked from the middle upwardes and shall be openly whipped untill his or her body be bloudye, and shalbe forthwith sent from Parish to Parish by the Officers of every the same, the nexte streighte way to the Parish where he was borne, if the same may be knowen by the Partyes confession or otherwyse ; and yf the same be not knowen, then to the Parish where he or she last dwelte before the same Punyshment by the space of one whole yeare, there to put him or her selfe to labour as a true Subject ought to do ; or not being knowen where he or she was borne or last dwelte, then to the Parish through which he or she last passed without Punyshment.

[§ 4.] Yf any of the said Rogues shall appeare to be dangerous to the inferior sorte of People where they shalbe taken, or otherwyse be such as will not be reformed of their rogish kinde of lyfe by the former Provisions of this Acte, . . . it shall and may be laufull to the said Justices of the Lymittes where any such Rogue shalbe taken, or any two of them, whereof one to be of the Quorum, to commit that Rogue to the House of Correccion, or otherwyse to the Gaole of that County, there to remaine untill their next Quarter Sessions to be holden in that County, and then such of the same Rogues so committed, as by the Justices of the Peace then and there presente or the most parte of them shalbe thought fitt not to be delivered, shall and may lawfully by the same Justices or the more parte of them be banysshed out of this Realme. . . . And if any such Rogue so banyshed as aforesaid shall returne agayne into any part of this

Realme or Domynion of Wales without lawfull Lycence or Warrant so to do, that in every such case such Offence shalbe Felony, and the Party offending therein suffer Death as in case of Felony.

[§ 10.] Reserves privileges of John Dutton.

cxiv.

[1598, Feb. 19. Privy Council Minute, printed Dasent, xxviii. 327.]

A letter to the Master of the Revelles and Justices of Peace of Middlesex and Surrey. Whereas licence hath bin graunted unto two companies of stage players retayned unto us, the Lord Admyral and Lord Chamberlain, to use and practise stage playes, whereby they might be the better enhabled and prepared to shew such plaies before her Majestie as they shalbe required at tymes meete and accustomed, to which ende they have bin cheefelie licensed and tollerated as aforesaid, and whereas there is also a third company who of late (as wee are informed) have by waie of intrusion used likewise to play, having neither prepared any plaie for her Majestie nor are bound to you, the Masters of the Revelles, for perfourming such orders as have bin prescribed and are enjoyned to be observed by the other two companies before mencioned. Wee have therefore thought good to require you uppon receipt heereof to take order that the aforesaid third company may be suppressed and none suffered heereafter to plaie but those two·formerlie named belonging to us, the Lord Admyrall and Lord Chamberlaine, unles you shall receave other direccion from us. And so, &c.

cxv.

[1598, May 1. Abstract from Vestry records of St. Saviour's, Southwark, by W. Rendle, *Bankside*, vi, in Harrison, ii, App. i.]

It had been ordered, May 1, 1598, that Mr. Langley's new buildings shall be viewed—they were near to the Paris Garden play-house—and that Mr. Henslowe and Jacob Meade shall be moved for money for the poor on account of the play-houses.

cxvi.

[1598, July 19. Extract from Vestry records of St. Saviour's, Southwark, printed in *Variorum*, iii. 452, and by W. Rendle, *Bankside*, v, in Harrison, ii, App. i.]

It is ordered at this vestrye that a petition shal be made to the bodye of the councell concerninge the play houses in this pareshe, wherein the enormeties shal be showed that comes therebye to the pareshe, and that in respect thereof they may be dismissed and put down from playing, and that iiij or ij of the churchwardens, Mr. Howse, Mr. Garlonde, Mr. John Payne, Mr. Humble, or ij of them, and Mr. Russell and Mr. Ironmonger, or one of them, shall prosecute the cause with a collector of the Boroughside and another of the Bankside.

cxvii.

[1600, Jan. 12. Warrant from Charles Howard, Earl of Nottingham, Lord Admiral, printed by W. W. Greg, *Henslowe Papers*, 49, from *Dulwich MS*. i. 27 ; also by Collier, *Alleyn Memoirs*, 55.]

Weareas my Servant Edward Allen (in respect of the dangerous decaye of that Howse which he and his Companye haue nowe, on the Banck, and for that the same standeth verie noysome for resorte of people in the wynter tyme) Hath thearfore nowe of late taken a plott of grounde neere Redcrossestreete London (verie fitt and convenient) for the buildinge of a new Howse theare, and hath prouided Tymber and other necessaries for theffectinge theareof, to his greate chardge : Forasmuche as the place standeth verie convenient for the ease of People, and that her Maiestie (in respect of the acceptable Service, which my saide Servant and his Companie haue doen and presented before her Highenes to her greate likeinge and Contentment, aswell this last Christmas as att sondrie other tymes) ys gratiouslie moued towardes them, with a speciall regarde of fauor in their proceedinges : Theis shalbe thearefore to praie and requier youe, and everie of youe, To permitt and suffer my saide Servant to proceede in theffectinge and finishinge of the saide New howse, without anie your lett or molestation, towardes him or any of his woorkmen. And soe not doubtinge of your observacion in this behalf, I bidd youe right hartelie farewell. Att the Courte, at Richmond, the xijth of Januarye, 1599.

Notingham.

To all & euery her maiesties Justices & other Ministers, and Officers, within the Countye of Middlesex, & to euery of them, And to all others whome it shall Concerne :

cxviii.

[1600, March 9. Privy Council Minute, printed Dasent, xxx. 146.]

A letter to Sir Drew Drewry, knight, William Waad, esquier, Clerke of the Councell, Thomas Fowler, Edward Vaughan and Nicholas Collyns, esquires, Justices of the Peace in the countie of Middlesex. Wee are given to understand by our very good Lord the Lord Willoughby and other gentlemen and inhabitauntes in the parishe of St. Giles without Creplegate that there is a purpose and intent in some persons to erect a theatre in White Crosstreete, neere unto the Barres in that parte that ys in the countie of Middlesex, wherof ther are to manie allreadie not farr from that place, and as you knowe not longe sithence you receaved spetiall direction to pluck downe those and to see them defaced, therefore yf this newe erection should be suffered yt would not onlie be an offence and scandall to divers, but a thinge that would greatly dysplease her Majestie. These are therefore to will and require you in any case to take order that no soche theatre or plaie-howse be built there, or other howse to serve for soche use, both to avoide the many inconveniences that therby

are lyklie to ensue to all the inhabitantes, and the offence that would
be to her Majestie, haveinge heretofore given sufficient notice unto you
of the great myslyke her Highnes hath of those publicke and vayne
buildinge[s] for soche occacions that breed increase of base and lewde
people and divers other disorders. Therefore wee require you not to
faile forthwith to take order that the foresaid intended buildinge
maie be staied, and yf any be begone, to see the same quite defaced.
So, &c.

<h3 style="text-align:center">cxix.</h3>

[1600, March 28. Extract from Vestry records of St. Saviour's, Southwark, printed in *Variorum*, iii. 452, and by W. Rendle, *Bankside*, v, in
Harrison, ii, App. i.]

It is ordered that the churchwardens shall talk with the players
for tithes for their playhouses within the liberty of the Clinke, and
for money for the poore, according to the order taken before my
lords of Canterbury and London and the Master of the Revels.

<h3 style="text-align:center">cxx.</h3>

[1600, April 1. Abstract of entry in Roll of the General Sessions of
the Peace for Middlesex, printed by J. C. Jeaffreson, *Middlesex County
Records*, i. 260. The proclamation referred to must, I suppose, be the old
one of 1559 (No. x). I do not know of any Star Chamber order about
plays, but it is quite possible that one was made in 1597, and not recorded
in the Council Registers, as the Star Chamber had its own Clerk, distinct
from those of the Privy Council.]

Recognizance . . . of John Wolf of Eastsmithfield, co. Midd.
Stationer, in the sum of forty pounds ; The condition of the recognizance being ' that, whereas the abovebounden John Wolf hathe
begun to erecte and builde a Playhowse in Nightingale Lane near
East Smithefeilde aforesaid contrary to Her Majesties proclamacion
and orders sett downe in Her Highenes Court of Starrchamber. If
therefore the said John Wolf do not proceede anie further in buildinge
or erectinge of the same playhowse, unless he shall procure sufficient
warrant from the Rt. Honourable the Lords of Her Majesties most
honourable Privye Councill for further . . . then this recognizaunce
to be void or els to remaine in full force.'

<h3 style="text-align:center">cxxi.</h3>

[*c.* 1600, April. Certificate of the Inhabitants of Finsbury to the Privy
Council, printed by W. W. Greg, *Henslowe Papers*, 50, from *Dulwich MS.*
i. 28 ; also by Collier, *Alleyn Memoirs*, 58.]

To the righte honorable the Lordes and others of her
maiesties most honorable privie Councell :

In all humblenes, wee the Inhabitantes of the Lordshipp of Fynisburye, within the parrishe of St. Gyles without Creplegate, London,
doe certifie vnto your honnours, That wheare the Servantes of the

right honorable Earle of Nottingham haue latelie gone aboute to erect
and sett vpp a newe Playehowse within the said Lordshipp, Wee
could be contented, that the same might proceede and be Tollerated
(Soe it stande with your honnours pleasuers) ffor the reasons and
Causes followeinge.

First because the Place appoynted oute for that purpose Standeth
very tollerable, neere vnto the ffeildes, and soe farr distant and remote
frome any person or Place of accompt, as that none cann be Annoyed
thearbie :

Secondlie because the Erectours of the saied howse are contented
to give a very liberall porcion of money weekelie, towardes the releef
of our Poore, The nomber & necessity whereof is soe greate that the
same will redounde to the contynuall comfort of the saied Poore :

Thirdlie and lastlie wee are the rather Contented to accept this
meanes of releif of our Poore, because our Parrishe is not able to
releeue them, neither hath the Justices of the Sheire taken any order,
for any Supplie oute of the Countrye, as is enioyned by the late Acte
of Parliamente :

[Twenty-seven signatures follow.]

[Endorsed] The Certificate of the Inhabitantes of the Lordship of
Fynisburye of theire Consent to the Tolleracion of the Erection of
a newe Plaiehowse theare.

cxxii.

[1600, April 8. Privy Council to the Justices of Middlesex, printed by
W. W. Greg, *Henslowe Papers*, 51, from *Dulwich MS.* i. 29 ; also by Collier,
Alleyn Memoirs, 57.]

After our hartie comendacions. Whereas her Maiestie (haveinge
been well pleased heeretofere at tymes of recreacion with the services
of Edward Allen and his Companie, Servantes to me the Earle of
Nottingham, wheareof, of late he hath made discontynuance) hath
sondrye tymes signified her pleasuer, that he should revive the same
agayne : Forasmuche as he hath bestowed a greate some of money,
not onelie for the Title of a plott of grounde, scituat in a verie remote
and exempt place neere Goulding lane, theare to erect a newe house,
but alsoe is in good forwardnes aboute the frame and woorkmanshipp
theareof ; the conveniencie of which place for that purpose ys testified
vnto vs vnder the handes of manie of the Inhabitantes of the Libertie
of Fynisbury, wheare it is, and recomended by some of the Justices
them selves. Wee thearfore havinge informed her Maiestie lykewise
of the decaye of the house, wherein this Companye latelie plaied,
scituate vppon the Bancke, verie noysome for the resorte of people
in the wynter tyme, haue receaued order to requier youe to Tollerate
the proceedinge of the saide New howse neere Goulding lane, and doe
heerbye requier youe and everie of youe to permitt and suffer the
said Edward Allen to proceede in theffectinge and finishinge of the
same Newe howse, without anie your lett or interrupcion, towardes
him, or anye of his woorkmen, the rather because an other howse

is pulled downe, in steade of yt. And soe, not doubtinge of your conformitye heerin, wee comitt youe to God. Frome the Courte at Richmond the viijth of Aprill 1600.

Your lovinge frendes

Notingham
G Hunsdon
Ro: Cecyll

To the Justices of Peace of the Countye of Middlesex especially of St. Gyles without Creplegate, and to all others whome it shall Concerne.

cxxiii.

[1600, May 15. Privy Council Minute, printed Dasent, xxx. 327. Bromvill had performed at court on 12 May (cf. App. A).]

An open letter to the Justices of Peace in the countie of Surrey, and to all others her Majesty's officers and lovinge subjectes in that county or burrough of Southwark to whome yt shall appertain, &c. Whereas the bearer Peter Bromvill hath bene recommended unto her Majestie from her good brother the French Kinge and hath shewed some feates of great activity before her Highnes, her Majestie ys pleased to afforde him her gratious favor and leave to exercyse and shewe the same in soch publicke place as maie be convenient for soche exercyses. and shewes, and because for the present he hath made choice of a place called the Swann, in old Parys Garden, beinge the howse of Francis Langley, these shalbe to let you understand her Majesty's good pleasure in his behalfe, and to require you not onlie to permytt him there to shewe his feates of activitye at convenient tymes in that place without let or interrupcion, but to assyst him (as there shalbe occacion) that no abuse be offered him.

Postscript of Mr. Secretary's hand. It ys not meant that he shall exercyse upon any Sabothe day.

cxxiv.

[1600, June 22. Order of the Privy Council, printed *M.S.C.* i. 80, from *Remembrancia*, ii. 188 ; also by Dasent, xxx. 395, and Halliwell-Phillipps, i. 307, from minute in Council Register. The examiner's note at the end is by one of the Clerks of the Council. The original draft of the order has been altered in the Register, and there is a marginal note by Thomas Smith that ' the alteracion and interlyning of this order was by reason that the said order after the same was entred in the Booke came againe in question and debate, and the said interlyninge and amendementes were sett downe according to the laste determinacion of their Lordships '. Evidently the interlineations were important, and they are therefore marked below with square brackets, although of course they do not appear as such in the *Remembrancia* copy, which agrees substantially with the final draft in the Register. Dasent found the cancelled passages in the Register illegible.]

Whereas diuers Complaintes haue bin heretofore made vnto the Lordes and others of hir Maiesties privie Counsaile of the manifold abuses and disorders that haue growen and doe Continew by occasion of many howses erected & emploied in and aboute the Cittie of London for common Stage Plaies. And nowe verie latelie, by reason of some Complainte exhibited by sondrie persons against the buildinge of the like house in or nere Goldinge Lane by one Edward Allen, a seruant of the right honorable the Lo: Admirall, the matter, aswell in generalitie touchinge all the said houses for Stage Plaies and the vse of playenge, as in particuler concerninge the said house now in hand to be builte in or neere Goldinge Lane, hath bin brought into question & Consultacion amonge

An order sett downe by the lordes and others of hir Maiesties pruiye Councell the 22 of Iune 1600 to re-strain the excessiue number of Plaie howses & the imoderate vse of Stage plaies in & about the Cittye.

theire LL. Forasmuch as yt is manifestlie knowne and graunted that the multitude of the said houses and the misgouerment of them hath bin made and is dailie occasion of the idle riotous and dissolute livinge of great numbers of people, that leavinge all such honest and painefull Course of life, as they should followe, doe meete and assemble there, and of maine particuler abuses and disorders that doe there vppon ensue. And yet neuerthelesse yt is Considered that the vse and exercise of suche plaies, not beinge euill in yt self, may with a good order and moderacion be suffered in a well gouerned estate, and that, hir Maiestie beinge pleased at some times to take delighte and recreacion in the sight and hearinge of them, some order is fitt to bee taken for the allowance and mainteinance of suche persons, as are thoughte meetest in that kinde to yeald hir Maiestie recreacion and delight, & consequentlie of the howses that must serue for publique playenge to keepe them in exercise. To the end therefore, that bothe the greatest abuses of the plaies and plaienge houses maye be redressed, and the vse and moderacon of them retained, The Lordes and the rest of hir Maiesties privie Councell, withe one and full Consent, haue ordered in manner and forme as followeth.

First, that there shall bee about the Cittie two howses and noe more allowed to serue for the vse of the Common Stage plaies, of the which howses one shalbe in Surrey in that place which is Commonlie called the banckside or there aboutes, and the other in Midlesex. And foras muche as there Lordshippes haue bin enformed by Edmond Tylney Esquire, hir Maiesties seruant and Master of the Reuells, that the howse now in hand to be builte by the said Edward Allen is not intended to encrease the number of the Plaiehowses, but to be in steed of an other, namelie the Curtaine, Which is either to be ruined and plucked downe or to be putt to some other good vse, as also that the scituacion thereof is meete and Conuenient for that purpose. Yt is likewise ordered that the said howse of Allen shall be allowed to be one of the two howses, and namelie for the house to be alowed in Middlesex, [for the Companie of Plaiers belonging to the L: Admirall], soe as the house Called the Curtaine be (as yt is pretended) either ruinated or applied to some other good vse. And for the other allowed to be on Surrey side, whereas [there Lordshipps are pleased to permitt]

to the Companie of players that shall plaie there to make there owne
Choice which they will haue [of diuers houses that are there], Choosinge
one of them and noe more, [And the said Companie of Plaiers, being
the Seruantes of the L. Chamberlen, that are to plaie there haue made
choise of the house called the Globe, yt is ordered that the said house
and none other shall be there allowed]. And especiallie yt is forbidden
that anie stage plaies shalbe plaied (as sometimes they haue bin) in
any Common Inn for publique assemblie in or neare about the Cittie.

Secondlie, forasmuche as these stage plaies, by the multitude of
houses and Companie of players, haue bin too frequent, not seruing
for recreacion but inviting and Callinge the people daily from there
trad and worke to mispend there time, It is likewise ordered that the
two seuerall Companies of Plaiers assigned vnto the two howses
allowed maie play each of them in there seuerall howse twice a weeke
and noe oftener, and especially that they shall refraine to play on
the Sabboth daie, vppon paine of imprisonment and further penaltie,
and that they shall forbeare altogether in the time of Lent, and likewise at such time and times as anie extraordinarie sicknes or infeccion
of disease shall appeare to be in and about the Cittie.

Thirdlie, because these orders wilbe of litle force and effecte vnlesse
they be dulie putt in execucion by those to whome yt appertaineth
to see them executed, It is ordered that seuerall Coppies shall be
sent to the L. Mayor of London, and to the Iustices of the Peace of
the Counties of Middlesex and Surrey, and that Lettres should be
written vnto them from there Lordshipps, straightlye Charginge them
to see the execucion of the same, as well by Committinge to prison
the owners of Plaiehouses and players as shall disobey & resist these
orders, as by anie other good and lawfull meanes that in there discretion they shall finde expedient, And to certifie there Lordshipps from
time to time, as they shall se Cause, of there proceedinges therein.

Examinatum per Tho: Smithe.

CXXV.

[1600, June 22. Minute of Privy Council for letters conveying No. cxxiv, printed by Dasent, xxx. 411, and Halliwell-Phillipps, i. 308, from Council Register.]

Letter of this tenour to the Lord Maiour of London, the Justices
of the Peace of the counties of Midlesex and Surrey. By occasion
of some complaintes that of late have bin made vnto us of the multitude of houses servinge for common stage-playes in and aboute the
citty of London, and of the greate abuses and disorders growen by
the overmuch haunte and resorte of many licentious people vnto
those houses and places, we have entred into consideracion of some
fitt course to be taken for redresse of the saide disorders by suppressing
dyvers of those houses and by some restrainte of the imoderate use
of the plaies. For which cause wee have sett downe certaine orders
to be duely henceforth observed and kept, a copy whereof we sende
you hereinclosed, and have sent the like to the Lord Maiour of London

and to the Justices of the Peace of Middlesex. But as wee have donne our partes in prescribinge the orders, so unlesse you perfourme yours in lookinge to the due execution of them wee shall loose our labour and the wante of redresse must be imputed unto you and others unto whome it apperteyneth, and therefore wee doe hereby authorize and require you to see the said orders to be putt in execucion and to be continued, as you do wish the amendement of the aforesaide abuses and will remove the blame thereof from your selves. And so, &c.

cxxvi.

[1601, March 11. Privy Council Minute, printed Dasent, xxxi. 218.]

A letter to the Lord Mayour requiring him not to faile to take order the playes within the cyttie and the liberties, especyally at Powles and in the Blackfriers, may be suppressed during this time of Lent.

cxxvii.

[1601, May 10. Privy Council Minute, printed Dasent, xxxi. 346.]

A letter to certaine Justices of the Peace in the county of Middlesex. Wee do understand that certaine players that use to recyte their playes at the Curtaine in Moorefeildes do represent upon the stage in their interludes the persons of some gentlemen of good desert and quallity that are yet alive under obscure manner, but yet in such sorte as all the hearers may take notice both of the matter and the persons that are meant thereby. This beinge a thinge very unfitte, offensive and contrary to such direccion as have bin heretofore taken that no plaies should be openly shewed but such as were first perused and allowed and that might minister no occasion of offence or scandall, wee do hereby require you that you do forthwith forbidd those players to whomsoever they appertaine that do play at the Courtaine in Moorefeildes to represent any such play, and that you will examine them who made that play and to shew the same unto you, and as you in your discreccions shall thincke the same unfitte to be publiquely shewed to forbidd them from henceforth to play the same eyther privately or publiquely, and yf upon veiwe of the said play you shall finde the subject so odious and inconvenient as is informed, wee require you to take bond of the cheifest of them to aunswere their rashe and indiscreete dealing before us. So, &c.

cxxviii.

[1601, Dec. 31. Minute of letter from Privy Council to Justices of Middlesex and Surrey, printed by Dasent, xxxii. 466, and Halliwell-Phillipps, i. 309, from Council Register.]

Two letters of one tenour to the Justices of Middlesex and Surrey. It is in vaine for us to take knowledg of great abuses and disorders complayned of and to give order for redresse, if our directions finde no better execution and observation then it seemeth they do, and wee must needes impute the fault and blame thereof to you or some of you, the Justices of the Peace, that are put in trust to see them executed and perfourmed, whereof wee may give you a plaine instance in the great abuse contynued or rather encreased in the multitude of plaie howses and stage plaies in and about the cittie of London.

For whereas about a yeare and a half since (upon knowledge taken of the great enormities and disorders by the overmuch frequentinge of plaies) wee did carefullie sett downe and prescribe an order to be observed concerninge the number of playhowses and the use and exercise of stage plaies, with lymytacion of tymes and places for the same (namely that there should be but two howses allowed for that use, one in Middlesex called the Fortune and the other in Surrey called the Globe, and the same with observacion of certaine daies and times as in the said order is particularly expressed), in such sorte as a moderate practice of them for honest recreation might be contynued, and yet the inordinate concourse of dissolute and idle people be restrayned, wee do now understande that our said order hath bin so farr from takinge dew effect, as in steede of restrainte and redresse of the former disorders the multitude of play howses is much encreased, and that no daie passeth over without many stage plaies in one place or other within and about the cittie publiquelie made.

The default of perfourmance of which our said order we must in greate parte the rather impute to the Justices of the Peace, because at the same tyme wee gave earnest direction unto you to see it streightly executed, and to certifie us of the execution, and yet we have neither understoode of any redresse made by you, nor receaved any certificate at all of your proceedinges therein, which default or omission wee do now pray and require you foorthwith to amende, and to cause our said former order to be putt duely in execution, and especiallie to call before you the owners of all the other play howses (excepting the two howses in Middlesex and Surrey aforementioned), and to take good and sufficient bondes of them not to exercise, use or practise, nor to suffer from henceforth to be exercised, used or practized any stage playinge in their howses, and if they shall refuse to enter into such bondes, then to comitt them to prison untill they shall conforme themselves. And so, &c.

cxxix.

[1601, Dec. 31. Minute of letter from Privy Council to Lord Mayor and Aldermen of London, printed by Dasent, xxxii. 468, and Halliwell-Phillipps, i. 308, from Council Register; also in *M. S. C.* i. 83, from letter-book copy in *Remembrancia*, ii. 187.]

A letter to the Lord Maiour and Aldermen of London. Wee have receaved a letter from you renewing a complaint of the great abuse and disorder within and about the cittie of London by reason of the multitude of play howses and the inordinate resort and concourse of dissolute and idle people daielie unto publique stage plaies, for the which information, as wee do commende your Lordship because it betokeneth your care and desire to reforme the disorders of the cittie, so wee must lett you know that wee did muche rather expect to understand that our order (sett downe and prescribed about a yeare and a half since for reformation of the said disorders upon the like complaint at that tyme) had bin duelie executed, then to finde the same disorders and abuses so muche encreased as they are. The blame whereof, as wee cannot but impute in great part to the Justices of the Peace or somme of them in the counties of Middlesex and Surrey, who had speciall direction and charge from us to see our said order executed for the confines of the cittie, wherein the most part of those play howses are scituate, so wee do wishe that it might appeare unto us that any thinge hath bin endeavoured by the predecessours of you, the Lord Maiour, and by you, the Aldermen, for the redresse of the said enormities, and for observation and execution of our said order within the cittie.

Wee do therefore once againe renew heereby our direction unto you (as wee have donne by our letters to the Justices of Middlesex and Surrey) concerninge the observation of our former order, which wee do praie and require you to cause duelie and dilligentlie to be put in execution for all poyntes thereof, and especiallie for th'expresse and streight prohibition of any more play howses then those two that are mentioned and allowed in the said order, charging and streightlie comaunding all suche persons, as are the owners of any the howses used for stage plaies within the cittie, not to permitt any more publique plaies to be used, exercised or shewed from hencefoorth in their said howses, and to take bondes of them (if you shall finde it needefull) for the perfourmaunce thereof, or if they shall refuse to enter into bonde or to observe our said order, then to committ them to prison untill they shall conforme themselves thereunto. And so praying you, as your self do make the complaint and finde the ennormitie, so to applie your best endeavour to the remedie of the abuse, wee bidd, &c.

CXXX.

[1602, March 31. The Privy Council to the Lord Mayor, printed *M.S.C.* i. 85, from *Remembrancia*, ii. 189.]

After our verey hartie Commendacions to your Lp. We receaued your lettre, signifieinge some amendment of the abuses or disorders by the immoderate exercise of Stage plays in and about the Cittie, by meanes of our late order renued for the restraint of them, and with all shewinge a speciall inconvenience yet remayneinge, by reason that the seruants of our verey good L. the Earle of Oxford, and of me the Earle of Worcester, beinge ioyned by agrement togeather in on Companie (to whom, vpon noteice of her Maiesties pleasure at the suit of the Earle of Oxford, tolleracion hath ben thaught meete to be graunted, notwithstandinge the restraint of our said former Orders), doe not tye them selfs to one certaine place and howse, but do chainge there place at there owne disposition,

A lettre to the L. Maior for the Bores head to be licensed for the plaiers.

which is as disorderly and offensiue as the former offence of many
howses. And as the other Companies that are alowed, namely of me
the L. Admirall and the L. Chamberlaine, be appointed there certaine
howses, and one and noe more to each Companie. Soe we doe
straightly require that this third Companie be likewise to one place.
And because we are informed the house called the Bores head is the
place they haue especially vsed and doe best like of, we doe pray
and require yow that that said howse, namely the Bores head, may
be assigned onto them, and that they be verey straightlie Charged
to vse and exercise there plaies in noe other but that howse, as they
will looke to haue that tolleracion continued and avoid farther displeasure. And soe we bid your Lp. hartely farewell, from the Court
at Ritchmond the last of March, 1602.

Your lordshippes verey lovinge friendes,

T Buckurst	Notingham
E Worcester.	W: Knowlis
Ihon Stannop:	Ro: Cecyll.
Io: fortescu.	I: Herbert.

cxxxi.

[1603, March 19.   Abstract of Privy Council Minute, printed Dasent,
xxxii. 492, from *Addl. MS.* 11402.]

Letters to the Lord Mayor and Justices of Middlesex and Surrey
for the restraint of stage-plaies till other direction be given.

cxxxii.

[1603, May 7.   Extract from *Procl.* 944, printed, with 'in their lewd'
for 'Enterludes', in Strype, *Annals*, iv. 528.]

And for that we are informed that there hath beene heretofore
great neglect in this kingdome of keeping the Sabbath-day : For
better observing of the same, and avoyding all impious prophanation,
we do straightly charge and commaund, that no Beare-bayting, Bulbayting, Enterludes, Common Playes, or other like disordered or
unlawful Exercises, or Pastimes, be frequented, kept, or used at any
time hereafter upon the Sabbath-day.

cxxxiii.

[1603, May 19.   Patent for King's men ; cf. text in Bk. iii.]

Gives authority to perform plays at the Globe and in convenient
places in towns elsewhere.

cxxxiv.

[1604, Feb. 4.   Patent for Children of the Queen's Revels ; cf. text
in Bk. iii.]

Gives authority to perform plays approved by Samuel Daniel in
the Blackfriars or other convenient place.

CXXXV.

[1604, April 9. Privy Council to Lord Mayor of London and Justices of Middlesex and Surrey, printed by W. W. Greg, *Henslowe Papers*, 61, from contemporary copy in *Dulwich MS.* i. 39 ; also in Collier, *Alleyn Memoirs*, 66 ; Halliwell-Phillipps, *Illustrations*, 115, *Outlines*, i. 310. The abstract of the lost Council Register in *Addl. MS.* 11402 has the note (f. 93^v) ' 9 Ap. 1604 A lettre to the lo: Mayor & the Iustices of Surrey & Middlesex to suffer the players to playe againe Lent being past &c ' (Dasent, xxxii. 511 ; *M. S. C.* i. 371).]

After our hart[ie commendacions] to your [Lo.] Wheras the kings maiesties Plaiers have given ty[   ] hyghnes good service in ther Quallitie of Playinge, and for as much Lickwise as they are at all times to be emploied in that Service, whensoever they shalbe Comaunded, we thinke it therfore fitt, the time of Lent being now Passt, that your L. doe Permitt and suffer the three Companies of Plaiers to the King, Queene, and Prince publicklie to Exercise ther Plaies in ther severall and vsuall howses for that Purpose, and noe other, viz. The Globe scituate in Maiden lane on the Banckside in the Countie of Surrey, the Fortun in Golding Lane, and the Curtaine in Hollywell in the Cowntie of Midlesex, without any lett or interuppion in respect of any former Lettres of Prohibition heertofore written by vs to your Lo. Except there shall happen weeklie to die of the Plague Aboue the Number of thirtie within the Cittie of London and the Liberties therof. Att which time we thinke it fitt they shall Cease and forbeare any further Publicklie to Playe, vntill the Sicknes be again decreaced to the saide Number. And so we bid your Lo. hartilie farewell. From the Court at Whitehalle the ixth of Aprille, 1604.

Your very Loving ffrends

Nottingham
Suffock
Gill Shrowsberie
Ed Worster
W: Knowles
J: Stanhopp

To our verie good L. the Lord Maior of the Cittie of London and to the Justices of the Peace of the Counties of Midlesex and Surrey. L. Maiore.

CXXXVI.

[1604, July 7. Extracts from *An Acte for the Continuance and Explanation of the Statute made in the 39 yeere of the Raigne of our late Queene Elizabeth, intituled An Acte for Punishmente of Rogues, Vagabondes and Sturdie Beggers* (*1 Jac. I*, c. 7), printed in *Statutes*, iv. 1024. The Act was amended in detail by 7 *Jac. I*, c. 4, in 1610 (*St.* iv. 1159).]

[§ 1.] Whereas by [*39 Eliz.* c. 4] . . . it was enacted, That all persons callinge themselves Scholers goinge aboute begginge, all Seafaringe men pretending losse of their Shippes or Goods on the Sea, goinge aboute the Countrie begginge, all idle persons goinge aboute in any Countrie, either begginge, or usinge any subtile Crafte or

unlawfull Games or Playes, or fayninge themselves to have knowledge in Phisiognomie Palmestry or other like craftye Science, or
pretendinge that they can tell Destinies Fortunes or such other like
fantasticall Imaginations ; all persons that be, or utter themselves
to be Proctors Procurers Patent Gatherers or Collectors for Gaoles
Prisons or Hospitals ; all Fencers Bearwardes common Players of
Enterludes, and Minstrels wandringe abroad, (other then Players of
Enterludes belonginge to any Baron of this Realme, or any other
honourable Personage of greater Degree, to be authorized to play
under the Hande and Seale of Armes of such Baron or Personage)
shalbe taken adjudged and deemed as Rogues Vagabondes and Sturdie
Beggers, and shall suffer such Paine and Punishment as in the said
Acte is in that behalfe appointed, as by the same Acte more at large
is declared ; Sithence the making of which Acte divers Doubtes and
Questions have bene moved and growen by diversitie of Opinions
taken in and upon the letter of the said Acte : For a plaine Declara-
tion whereof be it declared and enacted, That from henceforthe no
Authoritie to be given or made by any Baron of this Realme or any
other honourable Personage of greater Degree, unto any other person
or persons, shall be availeable to free and discharge the saide persons,
or any of them, from the Paines and Punishmentes in the saide
Statute mentioned, but that they shall be taken within the Offence
and Punishment of the same Statute.

[§ 3.] Amends *39 Eliz.* c. 4, § 4, which provided for banishment of
dangerous rogues, by providing for branding and setting to labour
in place of settlement ; a second offence to be felony, without benefit
of clergy.

[§ 6.] Continues *39 Eliz.* c. 4 as amended.

[§ 8.] Reserves privileges of John Dutton.

CXXXvii.

[1604, Oct. 13. Letter of Assistance from the Duke of Lennox for his
players, printed by W. W. Greg from *Dulwich MS.* i. 40, in *Henslowe
Papers*, 62 ; also in Collier, *Alleyn Memoirs*, 69.]

Sir I am given to vnderstand that youe haue forbidden the Companye of Players (that call themselues myne) the exercise of their
Playes ; I praie youe to forbeare any such course against them, and
seeing they haue my License, to suffer them to continue the vse of
their Playes ; and vntill you receaue other significacion from me of them,
to afforde them your favoure and assistance. And so I bidd youe hartely
farewell. From Hampton Courte the xiijth of October, 1604.

Your loving freende

Lenox.

To all maiors, Justeses of peas, Shreefes, Balifes, Constabells and all
other his highnes officers and lofing subiects to whome it shall or
may in any wise appertaine.

[*Addressed*] To my loving freend Mr. Dale esqr. and all other Justeses
whatsoeuer.

cxxxviii.

[N.D. *c.* 1604. Draft royal licence for Queen Anne's men; cf. text in Bk. iii.]

Gives authority ιo perform plays, when the plague-list in London and the liberties thereof falls to thirty, in the Curtain and Boar's Head, and in convenient places in towns elsewhere.

cxxxix.

[1605, Oct. 5. Abstract of Privy Council Minute, printed *M. S. C.* i. 371, from *Addl. MS.* 11402, f. 107.]

A lettre to the Lord Mayor to forbidde Stage plaies & to take order that the infectede bee kept in their howses, &c.
Like lettres to the Iustices of the peace of Middlesex & Surrey.

cxl.

[1605, Dec. 15. Abstract of Privy Council Minute, printed *M. S. C.* i. 372, from *Addl. MS.* 11402, f. 109.]

Lettres to the Lord Mayor, the Iustices of Middlesex and Surrey to suffer the Kings the Queens and the Princes Players, to play & recite their enterludes at their accustomed places.

cxli.

[1606, March 7. Signet warrant from Queen Anne for her players; cf. text in Bk. iii.]

Gives authority to perform plays in London and other towns, except during divine service, and requires assistance of justices.

cxlii.

[1606, April 30. Patent for Prince Henry's men; cf. text in Bk. iii.]

Gives authority to perform plays at the Fortune and in convenient places in towns elsewhere, with a proviso saving the authority, power, privileges, and profits of the Master of the Revels.

cxliii.

[1606, May 27. *An Acte to Restraine Abuses of Players* (3 *Jac. I*, c. 21), printed in *Statutes*, iv. 1097; also in Hazlitt, *E. D. S.* 42.]

For the preventing and avoyding of the greate Abuse of the Holy Name of God in Stageplayes, Interludes, Maygames, Shewes, and such like; Be it enacted by our Soveraigne Lorde the Kinges Majesty, and by the Lordes Spirituall and Temporall, and Commons in this present Parliament assembled, and by the authoritie of thē same, That if at any tyme or tymes, after the end of this present Session of Parliament, any person or persons doe or shall in any Stage play,

Interlude, Shewe, Maygame, or Pageant jestingly or prophanely speake or use the holy Name of God or of Christ Jesus, or of the Holy Ghoste or of the Trinitie, which are not to be spoken but with feare and reverence, [? such person or persons] shall forfeite for everie such Offence by hym or them committed Tenne Pounds, the one moytie thereof to the Kinges Majestie, his Heires and Successors, the other moytie thereof to hym or them that will sue for the same in any Courte of Recorde at Westminster, wherein no essoigne, Proteccion or Wager of Lawe shalbe allowed.

cxliv.

[1607, April 12. The Lord Mayor to the Earl of Suffolk, Lord Chamberlain, printed *M. S. C.* i. 87, from *Remembrancia*, ii. 283.]

Concerninge the Infection of the Plague.

My humble dutie remembred to your good Lp: Whereas it pleaseth god that the Infeccion of sicknes is for theis two or three weekes of late somewhat increased in the Skirtes and Confines of this Cittie, and by the vntymely heate of this season may spreade further then can hereafter be easelie prevented, My humble desier is that your Lp: for the preventinge of soe great a danger will vouchsafe your honourable favour in two speciall pointes concerninge this Matter. First in restrayninge such comon Stage Plaies, as are Daylie shewed and exercised and doe occasion the great Assembleis of all sortes of people in the suburbes and partes adioyninge to this Cittie, and cannot be continiewed but with apparant daunger of the encrease of the sicknes. Secoundly, Whereas it appeareth by the Certificate that the said Skirtes and out Partes of the Cittie are more subiecte to the Infection then any other Places. That your Honours will please to give order to the Iustices of Middlesex to put in due execution such ordenances as are formerly by your Lordshippes recomended vnto them in this behalfe, especially that there may be a better care hade of White Chappell, Shorditch, Clarken-Well and such other remote Partes then formerly hath ben accustomed. And that there may some speciall Officers be appointed to see good order kept and obserued in those Places, where there is noe Iustice of Peace resident or nere there biwaies to looke to the same. Which beinge accordingly performed in the out Skirtes of this Cittie, My desier is that your Lp: will rest satisfied and assuered of oure carefullnes here within the Cittie and Lyberties thereof to the vtmost of our Indeauour, as is fittinge a matter of such Consequence. And soe most humblie I take my leaue And rest

Aprill 12, 1607.   Your Lps: most humble.

To the right honourable my very good Lo: the Earle of Suffolke Lo: Chamberlaine of his Maiesties House.

cxlv.

[1608, Dec. 20. Entry in Gaol Delivery Register of Justices for Middlesex, printed by J. C. Jeaffreson, *Middlesex County Records*, ii. 47.]

Recognizances, taken before Sir William Waad knt. J.P., Lieutenant of the Tower of London, of Daniel Hitch of Whitechappell yeoman and James Waters of Eastsmythfeilde ironmounger, in the sum of ten pounds each, and of William Claiton of Eastsmythfeilde victualler, in the sum of twenty pounds ; For the appearance of the said William Claiton at the next Session of the Peace, to answer for sufferinge playes to bee played in his house in the night season.

cxlvi.

[1609, April 15. Patent for Queen Anne's men ; cf. text in Bk. iii.]

Gives authority to perform plays at the Red Bull and Curtain and in convenient places in towns elsewhere, with a proviso saving the authority, power, privileges and profits of the Master of the Revels.

cxlvii.

[1610, Jan. 4. Patent for the Children of the Queen's Revels ; cf. text in Bk. iii.]

Gives authority to perform plays in the Whitefriars or other convenient place.

cxlviii.

[1610, March 30. Patent for the Duke of York's men ; cf. text in Bk. iii.]

Gives authority to perform plays in houses and about London and in convenient places in towns elsewhere, with proviso saving the authority, power, privilege and profit of the Master of the Revels.

cxlix.

[1611, April 27. Patent for the Lady Elizabeth's men ; cf. text in Bk. iii.]

Gives authority to perform plays in houses in and about London and in convenient places in towns elsewhere, with proviso saving the authority, power, privilege and profit of the Master of the Revels.

cl.

[1612, Oct. 1. Order at General Session of the Peace for Middlesex held at Westminster, printed from Sessions Rolls in J. C. Jeaffreson, *Middlesex County Records*, ii. 83.]

An Order for suppressinge of Jigges att the ende of Playes—Whereas Complaynte have [*sic*] beene made at this last Generall Sessions, that by reason of certayne lewde Jigges songes and daunces vsed and accustomed at the play-house called the Fortune in Gouldinglane,

divers cutt-purses and other lewde and ill disposed persons in greate
multitudes doe resorte thither at th'end of euerye playe, many tymes
causinge tumultes and outrages wherebye His Majesties peace is often
broke and much mischiefe like to ensue thereby, Itt was hereuppon
expresselye commaunded and ordered by the Justices of the said
benche, That all Actors of euerye playhouse within this cittye and
liberties thereof and in the Countye of Middlesex that they and euerie
of them utterlye abolishe all Jigges Rymes and Daunces after their
playes, And not to tollerate permitt or suffer anye of them to be
used vpon payne of ymprisonment and puttinge downe and suppressinge of theire playes, And such further punishment to be inflicted
upon them as their offences shall deserve, And that if any outrage
tumult or like disorder as aforesaid should be committed or done,
that then the partyes so offending should forthwith be apprehended
and punished accordinge to their demeritt. For the better suppressinge
of which abuses and outrages, These are to will and require you and
in His Majesties name streightelye to charge and commaunde you
that you diligently and stryctlye looke vnto the performaunce of the
same order, And that if either the players do persiste and contynewe
their sayd Jigges daunces or songes as aforesayd or any disordered
persons doe committ or attempt any violence or outrage in or about
the sayd playe-houses, That then you apprehend all and euerie such
person of either kind so offendinge and forthwith bringe them before
me or some other of his Majesties Justices of Peace to answeare their
contemptes and further to be dealt [with] as to Justice shall appertayne.—By the Court. S. P. Reg.

cli.

[1612, Nov. 8. The Privy Council to the Lord Mayor, printed *M. S. C.*
i. 88, from *Remembrancia*, iii. 64.]

From the Lordes,   After our very hartie Commendacions to your
for the suppressinge   Lordshipp. Whereas it hath pleased the Al-
of Stage plaies,   mightie God to take awaie the most Noble and
Bearebaytinges   Worthie Prince of Wales, to the exceedinge greate
and idle shewes,   sorrowe and Greef, aswell of theire Maiesties, as
vpon the death of   of all theire deere and lovinge Subiectes. And
Prince Henry.   that these tymes doe not suite with such playes
and idle shewes, as are daily to be seene in and neere the cittie of
London, to the scandall of Order and good governement at all occasions when they are most tollerable. As wee haue allreadie addressed
lettres to the Iustices of peace of Middlesex and Surrey for the suppressinge of any playes or shewes whatsoever within those Counties,
soe wee doe hereby require your Lpp. to take speedie and speciall
order for the prohibitinge of all Playes, shewes, Bearebaytinges, or
any other such sighte, within that cittie and liberties thereof, and
vtterlie to restraine the vse and exercise thereof, vntill you shall
receave further order from vs. And if you shall finde anie person
offendinge therein, to commytt him or them to Prison without fauour

or connyvauncie, and to acquainte vs therewith. And soe wee bidd
your Lordshipp Hartelie farewell. From Whitehall the viijth of
November, 1612.

Your Lps. verie loving Frindes,

T. Ellesmorc Cancellarius.   H: Northampton: T. Suffolk:
E. Wotton: Stanhop.

clii.

[1613, Jan. 11. Patent for the Elector Palatine's men ; cf. Bk. iii, and
text in *M. S. C.* i. 275.]

Gives authority to perform plays at the Fortune and in convenient
places in towns elsewhere, with proviso saving the authority, power,
privileges and profits of the Master of the Revels.

cliii.

[1613, July 13. Extract by Sir Henry Herbert from an office-book of
Sir George Buck, printed in *Variorum*, iii. 52, and Adams, *Herbert* 42.]

For a license to erect a new play-house in the White-friers, &c. £20.

cliv.

[1615, March 29. Minute of Privy Council, printed from Register in
M. S. C. i. 372 ; also in Collier, i. 380.]

A warrant to John Sentie one of the Messingers. Whereas John
Hemminges, Richard Burbidge, Christopher Beeston, Robert Lee,
William Rowley, John Newton, Thomas Downton, Humphry Ieffs
with others Stageplayers in and about the Citty of London have
presumed notwithstanding the commaundement of the Lord Chamberlayne signified vnto them by the Master of the Revells to play this
prohibited time of Lent. Theese are therefore to will and commaund
yowe to make your repayre vnto the persons abouenamed, and to
charge them in his Maiesties name to make their appearance heere
before vs of his Maiesties Privie Councell on ffriday next at 8 of the
Clocke in the forenoone without any excuse or delay. And in the
meane time that neither they, nor the rest of their Company presume
to present any Playes or interludes, as they will answere the contrary
at their perills.

clv.

[1615, June 3. Patent for erectiou of Porter's Hall ; cf. text in Bk. iv.]

Gives authority to the patentees of the Queen's Revels to build
a play-house for the Queen's Revels, at Porter's Hall in Blackfriars,
and for the performance of plays by the Queen's Revels, Prince
Charles's men, and the Lady Elizabeth's men therein.

clvi.

[1615, July 13. Patent for the Children of the Queen's Chamber of Bristol; cf. text in Bk. iii.]

Gives authority for the performance of plays in houses in Bristol and in convenient places in towns elsewhere, with proviso saving the authority, power, privilege and profit of the Master of the Revels.

clvii.

[1615, Sept. 26. Minute of Privy Council, printed from Register in *M. S. C.* i. 372; also in Chalmers, 463; *Variorum*, iii. 493.]

Whereas Complaint was made to this Boarde by the Lord Mayour and Aldermen of the Cittie of London That one Rosseter, and others havinge obtayned lycense vnder the great Seale of Englande for the buildinge of a Play house haue pulled downe a great Messuage in Puddle wharfe, which was sometimes the house of the Ladie Sanders within the Precinct of the Blackfryers, are now erectinge a Newe Playhouse in that place, to the great prejudice and inconvenience of the Gouerment of that Cittie : Their Lordships thought fitt to send for Rosseter to bringe in his Lettres Patentes, which beinge seene, and pervsed by the Lord Chief Iustice of Englande fforasmuch as the Inconveniences vrged by the Lord Mayour and Aldermen were many, and of some consequence to their Goverment. And specially for that the said Play house would adioyne soe neere vnto the Church in Blackfryers, as it would disturbe, and interrupt the Congregacion at divine Service vpon the weeke dayes : And that the Lord Chiefe Iustice did deliver to their Lordships, That the Lycence graunted to the said Rosseter did extende to the buildinge of a Playhouse without the liberties of London, and not within the Cittie. It was this day ordered by their Lordships, That there shalbe noe Play house erected in that place, And that the Lord Mayour of London shall straitly prohibit, and forbidd the said Rosseter and the rest of the Patentees, and their workemen to proceede in the makeinge, and convertinge the said Buildinge into a Play house : And if any of the Patentees or their workemen shall proceede in their intended buildinge contrary to this their Lordships Inhibicion, that then the Lord Mayour shall committ him or them soe offendinge, vnto Prison and certefie their Lordships of their contempt in that behalfe. Of which their Lordships order the said Rosseter, and the rest are to take notice, and conforme themselves accordingly as they will aunsweare to the contrary at their perrilles.

Ordered at the Sessions next before.

clviii.

[1616, July 16. Warrant by William Earl of Pembroke, Lord Chamberlain, printed by Murray, ii. 343, from copy recorded in Mayor's Court Books of Norwich.]

Whereas Thomas Swynnerton and Martin Slaughter beinge two of the Queens Maiesties company of Playors hauinge separated themselves from their said Company, have each of them taken forth

a severall exemplification or duplicate of his maiesties Letters patente
graunted to the whole Company and by vertue therof they severally
in two Companies with vagabonds and such like idle persons, haue
and doe vse and exercise the quallitie of playinge in diuerse places
of this Realme to the great abuse and wronge of his Maiesties Subjects
in generall and contrary to the true intent and meaninge of his
Maiestie to the said Company And whereas William Perrie haueinge
likewise gotten a warrant whereby he and a certaine Company of
idle persons with him doe travel and play under the name and title
of the Children of his Maiesties Revels, to the great abuse of his
Maiesties service And whereas also Gilberte Reason one of the prince
his highnes Playours hauing likewise separated himselfe from his
Company hath also taken forth another exemplification or duplicate
of the patent granted to that Company and liues in the same kinde
& abuse And likewise one Charles Marshall, Homfry Jeffes and
William Parr : three of Prince Palatynes Company of Playours
haueinge also taken forthe an exemplification or duplicate of the
patent graunted to the said Company and by vertue thereof liue
after the like kinde and abuse Wherefore to the [end that] such idle
persons may not be suffered to continewe in this course of life These
are therefore to pray, and neatheless in his Maiesties name to will
and require you vpon notice giuen of aine of the said persons by the
bearer herof Joseph More whome I haue speciallye directed for that
purpose that you call the said parties offendours before you and
therevpon take the said seuerall exemplifications or duplicats or other
ther warrants by which they vse ther said quallitie from them, And
forthwith to send the same to me And also that you take goode and
sufficient bonds of any of them to appeare before me at Whitehall
at a fixt daye to answeare ther said contempte and abuses whereof
I desire you not to fayle And these shalbe your sufficient warrant
in that behalfe Dated at the Courte at Theobalds this 16th day of
July in the fowertenth yeare of the raigne of our soueraigne Lord
the Kings Maiestie of England ffrance and Irelande and of Scotland
the nine and fortieth 1616.

Pembrook.

To all Justices of peace Maiours Sheriffs Baliffs Constables and other
his Maiesties officers to whome it may appertayne.

clix.

[1616, Oct. 4. Abstract of entries in Process Book for General Sessions
of the Peace for Middlesex, printed by J. C. Jeaffreson, *Middlesex County
Records*, ĥ. 235.]

Amongst memoranda of process against a large number of persons,
charged with neglecting to work or contribute for the repair of the
highways, appears this memorandum, touching the Red Bull theatre,
' Christofer Beeston and the rest of the players of the Redd Bull are
behinde five pounds, being taxed by the bench 40s. the yeare by theire
owne consentes '.

clx.

[1617, Jan. 27. Minute of Privy Council, printed from Register in *M. S. C.* i. 374 ; also in Chalmers, 463 ; *Variorum*, iii. 494.]

A letter to the Lord Mayor of London. Whereas his Maiestie is informed that notwithstanding diverse Commaundementes and prohibicions to the contrary there bee certaine persons that goe about to sett vp a Play howse in the Black ffryaers neere vnto his Maiesties Wardrobe, and for that purpose have lately erected and made fitt a Building, which is allmost if not fully finished, Youe shall vnderstand that his Maiesty hath this day expressly signifyed his pleasure, that the same shalbee pulled downe, so as it bee made vnfitt for any such vse, whereof wee Require your Lordshipp to take notice, and to cause it to bee performed accordingly with all speede, and therevpon to certify vs of your proceedinges. And so, &c.

APPENDIX E

PLAGUE RECORDS

[*Bibliographical Note.*—Early accounts of the vital statistics of the plague are J. Graunt, *Natural and Political Observations upon the Bills of Mortality* (1662, 1665, 1676) ; *Reflections on the Weekly Bills of Mortality* (1665, two eds.) ; J. Bell, *London's Remembrancer* (1665). Modern studies are C. Creighton, *History of Epidemics in Britain* (1891) ; C. H. Hull, *The Economic Writings of Sir William Petty* (1899, with reprint of Graunt's *Observations*) ; W. J. Simpson, *A Treatise on Plague* (1905). Murray, ii. 171, discusses *The Relation of the Plague to the Closing of the Theatres.* The ultimate material consists largely of the weekly bills of mortality returned for each London parish and published by the City authorities. In these the deaths from plague were separately stated. They were probably prepared throughout our period, at any rate from the plague of 1563. On 14 July 1593 John Wolf entered in the Stationers' Register (Arber, ii. 634) a licence to print ' the billes, briefes, notes and larges gyven out for the sicknes weekly or otherwise '. The only complete bill extant is one for 20 Oct. 1603 (*Political Tracts*, 1680, in Guildhall Library), but summaries of the weekly totals are available for 1563–6 (J. Gairdner, *Three Fifteenth-Century Chronicles*, 123, 144), 1578–83 (Creighton, i. 341, from *Hatfield MSS.*), 1593 (Hull, ii. 426, from Graunt; *vide infra*), 1597–1600 (Hull, ii. 432, from *Ashmolean MS.* 824), 1603 (Hull, ii. 426, from Graunt ; Scaramelli in *V. P.* x. 33 sqq.), 1604 (Nicolo Molin in *V. P.* x. 132 sqq.), 1606–10 (Creighton, i. 494, from Bell). During the sixteenth century the bills appear normally to have covered 108 or 109 parishes wholly or partly within the City jurisdiction, but on 4 Aug. 1593 Westminster, St. Katherine's, St. Giles, Southwark, Shoreditch, and other suburbs were ordered exceptionally to make returns to the Lord Mayor (Dasent, xxiv. 442). On 14 July 1603 the normal list was extended to include eleven suburban parishes, and in 1606 another was added, making 121 in all. But the important areas of Westminster, Lambeth, Newington, Stepney, Hackney, Islington, and Rotherhithe remained uncovered. Moreover, the suburban figures seem from the print of 1603 to have been recorded separately, and those in Bell's pamphlet are shown by a comparison of his entry for 12 May 1636 with that in Herbert's Office-Book (*Variorum*, iii. 239) to relate only to the City and liberties. The returns for this area were probably the basis for play restraints in the seventeenth century (cf. Bk. ii, ch. x). The bills seem to have been issued on Thursdays, with figures for the seven days ending on the day of issue.]

I give all facts indicating any epidemic condition of plague such as would affect the performance of plays. The play restraints cited are in App. D.

1560. Trinity term was adjourned to Michaelmas on 24 May (*Procl.* 525), but plague is not named as the reason.

1563. Plague was brought about June by English troops from Havre. The deaths were above 30 from 3 July to 7 Jan. 1564, and reached 1,828 on 1 Oct. Stowe, *Annales*, 656, gives the totals as 17,404 from 108 City parishes, and 2,732 from 11 suburban parishes; Camden (tr.), 83, as 21,130 from 121 parishes. Michaelmas term was adjourned to Hilary on 21 Sept. (*Procl.* 582), and Hilary term transferred to Hertford on 10 Dec. (*Procl.* 583). Plays were restrained on 30 Sept.

1564–6. The bills show no plague deaths over 30.

1568. Some precautions were taken in the City and Westminster against plague (Creighton, i. 318, 338).

1569. Further precautions were taken on 27 March (Creighton, i. 338) and plays restrained on 31 May until 30 Sept. There was in fact plague in September and October (Creighton, i. 338; La Mothe, ii. 249, 287; *Sp. P.* ii. 193, 203). Michaelmas term was deferred on 28 Sept. (*Procl.* 642) and adjourned to Hilary on 23 Oct. (*Procl.* 644). Access to court was restrained on 3 Oct. (*Procl.* 643).

1570. There was plague in July and August (*Hatfield MSS.* i. 476; *Sp. P.* ii. 262, 270, 273; Creighton, i. 338). Michaelmas term was deferred on 24 Sept. (*Procl.* 658).

1572. Harrison reports a restraint of plays for fear of plague. There is no other evidence.

1573. Plague appeared in the autumn (Creighton, i. 339). The Lord Mayor's feast was suppressed (*Remembrancia*, 38).

1574. Michaelmas term was deferred on 1 Oct. (*Procl.* 691). The plague deaths on 28 Oct. were 65 (Holinshed, iii. 1240). The Lord Mayor's feast was suppressed (Dasent, viii. 303). Plays were restrained on 15 Nov. until Easter.

1575. There was plague in Westminster, but apparently none in London (Creighton, i. 340). Michaelmas term was deferred on 26 Sept. (*Procl.* 696).

1576. There was plague in the Tower on 13 July (Dasent, ix. 163). Michaelmas term was deferred on 29 Sept. (*Procl.* 708).

1577. There was plague in August, September, and November (Dasent, x. 22, 35, 40, 86). Plays were restrained on 1 Aug. to Michaelmas. Michaelmas term was deferred on 16 Sept. (*Procl.* 719), and further on 15 Oct. (*Procl.* 722).

1578. The plague deaths were over 30 in nearly every week from 17 April to 18 Dec., reaching 280 on 2 Oct., and totalling 3,568 for the year. The Lord Mayor's feast was suppressed and the precautions against infection revised (Dasent, x. 339, 386, 413). Michaelmas term was deferred on 22 Sept. (*Procl.* 724) and 20 Oct. (*Procl.* 725), and adjourned on 14 Nov. to Hilary (*Procl.* 729). Plays were restrained on 10 Nov. and the restraint removed on 23 Dec.

1579. The plague deaths were below 30 in each week, totalling 629 for the year.

1580. The plague deaths were not above 8 in any week, totalling 128 for the year, but plays were restrained from 17 April to Michaelmas, and other precautions taken (*Remembrancia,* 329).

1581. There was plague in the latter part of the year, with deaths over 30 from 17 Aug. to 2 Nov., reaching 107 on 5 Oct., and totalling 987 for the first forty-five weeks of the year ; the figures for the last seven weeks are missing. The precautions were revised (Creighton, i. 319). Plays were restrained on 10 July and the restraint removed on 18 Nov. Michaelmas term was deferred on 21 Sept. (*Procl.* 760), and other precautions taken (*Remembrancia,* 331).

1582. There was some plague during the year (*Remembrancia,* 332), with deaths over 30 from 26 July to 27 Dec., reaching 216 on 25 Oct. and totalling 2,976 for fifty-one recorded weeks of the year. Play were restrained, probably with the assent of the Privy Council, although the Register is missing. Michaelmas term was deferred on 18 Sept. (*Procl.* 764), and transferred to Hertford on 8 Oct. (*Procl.* 765).

1583. The plague deaths were over 30 from 3 to 31 Jan., after which the record fails. But precautions continued (*Remembrancia,* 335). A restraint of plays was terminated on 26 Nov.

1584. There is no evidence of plague, but the dispute of this year suggests that the summer restraint of recent years had been repeated.

1585. There is no evidence of plague or restraint.

1586. There is no evidence of plague, other than a precautionary restraint of 11 May.

1587. There was a similar precautionary restraint on 7 May.

1588–91. There is no evidence of plague or even of precautionary restraints.

1592. The first notice of plague is on 13 Aug., when it was daily increasing (Dasent, xxiii. 118), and there is ample evidence of its seriousness to the end of the year (ibid., 136, 177, 181, 183, 203, 220, 230, 231, 241, 273, 274, 276, 365 ; Birch, *Eliz.* i. 87 ; Creighton, i. 351). A new 'booke of orders and remedies' was recommended by the Council (Dasent, xxiii. 203) on 19 Sept. to the Kent justices. This is doubtless the *Orders Thoughte Meete by her Maiestie and her privie Counsell to be executed* of which several prints (1592, 1593, 1603, N.D.) exist. It is for provincial use, and has no special reference to the restraint of plays. Plays had been under restraint for other reasons than plague since 23 June. The mayoral feast was suppressed on 11 Oct. (Dasent, xxiii. 232). Access to Hampton Court was restrained on 12 Oct. (*Procl.* 854). Michaelmas term was deferred and finally transferred for a short session to Hertford on 21 Oct. (*Procl.* 852, 855, 856). There appear to be no statistics of deaths; those ordinarily given belong to 1593 (*vide infra*). Suitors were still excluded from court on 13 Dec. (Dasent, xxiii. 365), but thereafter there was some recovery, and the records in Henslowe, i. 15, show that plays were permitted from 29 Dec. to 1 Feb. 1593, although no formal order is extant.

1593. This was a year of continuous plague (Creighton, i. 352). The Privy Council warned the Lord Mayor on 21 Jan. that the increase of deaths after some weeks of diminution required care (Dasent, xxiv. 21), and the Register shows preoccupation with the subject up to August, when the record fails (ibid., 31, 163, 209, 212, 252, 265, 284, 342, 343, 347, 373, 400, 405, 413, 442, 443, 448, 472). Plays were restrained on 28 Jan. Trinity term was deferred on 28 May and Michaelmas term transferred for a short session to St. Albans on 24 Sept. (*Procl.* 860, 865, 866). Bartholomew Fair (24 Aug.) was strictly limited (*Procl.* 863). Access to court at Nonsuch was restrained on 18 June and at Windsor on 15 Sept. (*Procl.* 861, 864). The statistics of deaths are puzzling. Stowe, *Annales*, 766, gives for the period from 29 Dec. 1592 (Friday) to 20 Dec. 1593 (Thursday) 8,598 in all and 5,390 from plague within the walls, and 9,295 in all and 5,385 from plague in the liberties, totalling 17,893 in all and 10,775 from plague. Camden (tr.), 423, gives a corresponding total of 17,890. A marginal note to the printed bill of 1603 gives for weeks ending 20 Dec. 1592 (Wednesday) to 23 Dec. 1593 (Sunday) 25,886 in all and 15,003 from plague. Here are two divergent computations for the same period, one of which deserts the Thursdays, to which we know that earlier and later weekly bills related. Both are more or less contemporary records. On the other hand, a series of broadsheets (cited in Hull, ii. 426), followed by a table appended to Graunt's *Observations* (ibid.), give nearly the same figures (25,886 and, not 15,003, but 11,503) as the totals of weekly figures for the period from 17 March (Friday) to 22 Dec. (Friday), not of 1593, but of 1592, and Graunt adopts these figures for March to Dec. 1592 in the text of his *Observations* (Hull, ii. 363), while he adopts 17,844 and 10,662, which are approximately Stowe's figures, for 1593. As a matter of fact, the weekly figures given do not add up exactly to 25,886 and 11,503; I make them (as does Hull, ii. 427) 26,407 and 11,106; Creighton, i. 354, makes the larger figure 25,817. Finally, the anonymous *Reflections on the Bills of Mortality* (1665) give 25,886 and 11,503 as the totals for 13 March (Tuesday) to 18 Dec. (Tuesday), not of 1592, but of 1593 again. The authority of these *Reflections* is not great, and there is a discrepancy between the period they take and that taken in the 1603 bill. But I do not see how the detailed weekly figures of the broadsheets can belong to 1592. The plague deaths are 3 on 17 March and 31 on 24 March. For the rest of the year they only fall below 30 on 31 March, 7 April, 5 May, and finally on 22 Dec. They reach 41 on 28 April, 58 on 26 May, and climb to 118 on 30 June. There is a big jump to 927 on 7 July; they get to a maximum of 983 on

4 Aug. and thereafter decline, dropping below 100 from 24 Nov. and ending with 71 on 15 Dec. and 39 on 22 Dec. These figures cannot apply to 1592, when plague only made its appearance about August. On the other hand, the figures for 4 Aug. (1,503 and 983) and 29 Sept. (450 and 330) do not tally exactly, although they do in general effect, with the 1,603 and 1,135 given as ‘the greatest that came yet’ in Henslowe’s letter of Aug. 1593, or the 1,100 to 1,200 from plague, representing an abatement in two weeks of 435, in his letter of 28 Sept. (*H. P.* 37, 40). On the whole, however, I think that all the figures before us relate to 1593 and not 1592, and that the ascription of the detailed tables to 1592 is due to the fact that they begin with 17 March 159⅔. Graunt similarly (Hull, ii. 378) quotes 1593 and 1594, where he clearly means 1594 and 1595. The discrepancies between Stowe and the tables are probably due to the different number of parishes covered by different computations. If the larger figures relate to an area wider than that of City and liberties (cf. the P. C. order of 4 Aug. 1593 cited in the *Bibl. Note*), we perhaps get also an answer to the view of Creighton, i. 354, and Hull, ii. 427, that they are neither of 1592 nor 1593, but altogether spurious as representing an impossibly high rate of general mortality for sixteenth-century London, even when allowance is made for the unscientific nature of the ‘plague-tokens’ as a diagnosis and the consequent increase in plague-time of deaths ascribed to other causes.

1594. As in 1592–3, the diminution of plague in December allowed of a short winter play season. Henslowe, i. 16, records plays from 26 Dec. to 6 Feb. A restraint was ordered on 3 Feb. It was still thought necessary to inhibit access to court on 21 April (*Hatfield MSS.* iv. 514), but the plague deaths for the year were only 421 (Graunt in Hull, ii. 378 ; Bell, *London's Remembrancer*). Plays began tentatively in April and May and regularly in June (Henslowe, i. 17). The systematization of City precautions was under consideration in the autumn.

1595. There were only 29 plague deaths (Graunt, in Hull, ii. 378 ; Bell, *London's Remembrancer*).

1596. Plays were restrained for fear of infection on 22 July, but there is no other evidence of plague.

1597–1600. The tables show no plague deaths above 4 in any week.

1601–2. There is no evidence of plague.

1603. Plague broke out during April (*V. P.* x. 33). Precautions were already being taken on 18 April (*Remembrancia,* 337). Plays had been restrained during the illness of Elizabeth on 19 March and probably not resumed. The terms of the patent to the King's men on 19 May imply an existing restraint. The epidemic was a bad one ; for an account of it, cf. Creighton, i. 474, and Dekker, *The Wonderful Year* (1603, *Works,* i. 100). The coronation was shorn of its entry and other splendours, and speedy resort to the country enjoined (*Procl.* 961, 964, 967). Bartholomew and other fairs were suppressed or put off (*Procl.* 964, 968). Trinity term was deferred on 23 June

(*Procl.* 957) and Michaelmas term deferred on 16 Sept. and transferred to Winchester on 18 Oct. (*Procl.* 970, 973). Stowe, *Annales*, 857, gives the total deaths in the City and liberties as 38,244, including 30,578 from plague. Creighton, i. 478, calculates from the weekly tables that with the addition of those suburbs for which records are available, these figures must be increased to 42,945 and 33,347. The report of 60,000 deaths, which Nicolo Molin (*V. P.* x. 126) found hard to believe, was obviously an exaggeration. The weekly plague bill for the City and liberties reached 30 on 26 May, 43 on 9 June, and rose very rapidly from the end of the month, reaching a maximum of 2,495, with 542 for the recorded suburbs, on 1 Sept. On 22 Dec. the plague deaths for City, liberties, and the suburbs henceforward included in the City lists (120 parishes in all) was still 74. Nicolo Molin's statements on 5 Dec. that the plague had almost disappeared, and on 15 Dec. that it was never mentioned (*V. P.* x. 124, 126), must have been optimistic.

1604. Nicolo Molin (*V. P.* x. 132 sqq.) records the totals of the bills (probably a week or so late) in despatches from 26 Jan. to 23 Oct. He gives 15 on 26 Jan. and 27 for the City only on 8 Feb., and thereafter 20 is only reached in a few weeks of May, August, and September ; 30 never. On 23 Oct. there had only been 6 in the last fortnight, and 'as that is nothing out of the common, I will not make any further reports on this subject' (*V. P.* x. 190). A play restraint was removed on 9 April, but the reason given was the expiration of Lent, and it is not impossible that the theatres may have been open before Lent, which began on 22 Feb. The warrant of 8 Feb., however, for a special royal subsidy to the King's men (App. B) suggests that they were still unable to perform in public on that date.

1605. Creighton, i. 493, says there was 'not much' plague ; but a letter of 12 Oct. (Winwood, ii. 140) notes a 'sudden rising of the sickness to thirty a week', followed by some abatement, and there was a restraint of plays for infection on 5 Oct. which was removed on 15 Dec.

1606. This was a year of plague. The deaths reached 33 on 10 July and 50 on 17 July, rose to a maximum of 141 on 2 Oct., and remained, but for one or two weeks, above 40 to 4 Dec. and above 30 to the end of the year. The total, for 121 parishes, was 2,124. Michaelmas term was adjourned on 23 Sept. (*Procl.* 1038) and access to court restrained on 1 Nov. (*Procl.* 1039). There is no record of a specific order for the restraint of plays ; possibly it was automatic as a result of the play-bill.

1607. During the first half of the year the plague deaths were under 30, except for 38 on 1 Jan., 33 on 5 Feb., 30 on 12 March, 33 on 19 March, and 43 on 30 April. They increased in the autumn, passing 30 on 9 July and 40 on 23 July, to a maximum of 177 on 24 Sept. After 19 Nov. they fell below 30. The total for the year was 2,352. As early as 12 April the City, unjustified as yet by the plague bill, asked for a restraint of plays. Access to court was restrained on 2 Nov. (*Procl.* 1050).

1608. The plague deaths were under 30 until 28 July, when they rose to 50 ; for the rest of the year they were over 40, with a maximum of 147 on 29 Sept. and a total of 2,262. The King's men practised privately for about eight weeks this winter (App. B).

1609. The plague of this year, the heaviest since 1603, is recorded in Dekker's *Work for Armourers* (1609, *Works*, iv. 96). The deaths were over 30, and, with four exceptions, over 40 up to 30 Nov., with a maximum of 210 on 21 Sept. and a total of 4,240. Michaelmas term was deferred on 22 Sept. (*Procl.* 1085). The King's men practised privately for six weeks this winter (App. B).

1610. The plague deaths were between 30 and 40 on 28 Dec. 1609 and on 4 and 18 Jan. 1610 ; then under 30 to 28 June, passing 30 on 5 July and 40 on 12 July, and remaining there during most of the rest of the year, with a maximum of 99 on 30 Aug. and a total of 1,803. They fell below 40 on 29 Nov. and below 30 on 6 Dec.

1611-16. Plague was absent from London (Creighton, i. 496).

APPENDIX F

THE PRESENCE-CHAMBER AT GREENWICH

[Entry for 27 Aug. 1598 in *Pauli Hentzneri J. C. Itinerarium Germaniae, Galliae, Angliae, Italiae* (1629) 200. The first edition is of 1612. A translation by R. Bentley was printed by Horace Walpole in 1757.]

Venimus deinde, ad Arcem Regiam, Grönwidge seu Grunwidge, vulgo dictam. . . . Postquam hanc arcem ingressi sumus, ex mandato summi Cubiculariorum Praefecti, quod Dn. Daniel Rogerius impetraverat, in Cameram Praesentationis, undiquaque tapetis preciosis exornatam, (Pavimentum vero, uti in Anglia moris est, foeno erat constratum) quam Regina, quando in sacellum ad preces ire vult, transire solet ; Ad ianuam stabat nobilis quidam vestibus holosericis amictus, et catena aurea cinctus, qui Comites, Barones, Nobiles et alios utriusque sexus, Reginam adire cupientes, ad eandem deducebat ; (erat tum forte dies Dominicus, quo Magnates plaerumque Reginam invisere solent) in Camera, quam dixi, praestolabantur Reginam, Episcopi, Cantuariensis et Londinensis, Consiliarii, Officiarii, et nobiles magno numero. Postea cum hora precum instaret, Regina ex suo conclavi prodiit, tali cum comitatu ; Praeibant Nobiles, Barones, Comites, et Equites Ordinis Periscelidis, omnes splendide vestiti, et capite detecto ; Proxime antecedebant duo, alter qui sceptrum Regni, alter qui gladium in vagina rubra aureis liliis distincta, reconditum cuspide sursum versa portabat, inter quos medius procedebat, Magnus Angliae Cancellarius, sigillum Regni in marsupio holoserico rubro gerens ; Hos sequebatur Regina, aetatis, uti rumor erat, lxv annorum, magna cum Maiestate, facie oblonga et candida, sed rugosa, oculis parvis, sed nigris et gratiosis, naso paululum inflexo, labiis compressis, dentibus fuliginosis (quod vitium ex nimio saccari usu, Anglos contrahere verisimile est) inaures habens duas margaritis nobilissimis appensis, crinem fulvum sed factitium ; Capiti imposita, erat parva quaedam corona, quae ex particula auri celeberrimae illius tabulae Lunaeburgensis, facta esse perhibetur ; pectore erat nuda, quod Virginitatis apud Anglos Nobiles signum est ; Nam maritatae sunt tectae ; Collum torques gemmis nobilissimis refertus circumdabat ; manus erant graciles, digiti longiusculi, statura corporis mediocris ; in incessu magnifica, verbis blanda et humanissima ; induta forte tum temporis erat veste serica alba, cuius oram margaritae preciosissimae fabarum magnitudine decorabant, toga superiniecta ex serico nigro, cui argentea fila admista, cum cauda longissima, quam Marchionissa pone sequens a posteriori parte elevatum gestabat ; Collare habebat oblongum, vice catenae, gemmis et auro fulgens ; Tum, cum tali in pompa et magnificentia incederet, nunc cum hoc, mox cum alio loquebatur, perhumaniter, qui vel legationis vel alterius rei causa eo venerant, utens nunc materno, nunc Gallico, nunc Italico idiomate ; Nam, praeterquam quod Graece, et Latine eleganter est docta, tenet ultra iam commemorata idiomata, etiam Hispanicum, Scoticum, et Belgicum ; Omnes illam alloquentes, pedibus flexis id faciunt, quorum aliquos interdum manu elevare solet ; Hos inter forte tum erat, Baro quidam Bohemus, Gulielmus Slawata nomine, Reginae literas offerens, cui manum dextram, chirotheca detracta, annulis et lapidibus preciosissimis splendentem porrexit osculandam, quod maximum insignis clementiae signum est ; In transitu, quocunque faciem vertit, omnes in genua procidunt ; Sequebatur Gynaeceum ex Comitissis, Baronissis, et Nobilibus foeminis, summa pulchritudine et forma excellentibus constans, et maxima ex parte, vestimentis albicans ; Ab utroque latere comitabantur eam Satellites nobiles cum hastis deauratis, quorum quinquaginta sunt numero ; In praeambulo Sacelli, quod huic atrio contiguum est, porriguntur ipsi libelli supplices, quos benignissime accipit, unde tales fiunt acclamationes ; God save the quene Elisabeth, hoc est, Deus salvet Reginam Elisabetham ; Ad quae populo sic ipsa respondet ; I thancke you myn good peupel, id est, Ago tibi gratias popule mi bone ; In sacello habebatur excellens Musica, qua finita una cum precibus, quae vix ultra dimidiam horam durabant, Regina eadem magnificentia et ordine, quo antea discesserat, redibat, et ad prandium se conferebat. Interea vero dum sacris intererat, vidimus illi apparari mensam hac adhibita solemnitate ; Primo Nobilis quidam atrium ingressus, sceptrum manu tenebat, adiunctum sibi habens alium quendam Nobilem cum mappa, qui ambo cum ter summa cum veneratione genua flexissent, alter ad mensam propius accedens, eam mappa insternebat ; quo facto, rursus poplite flexo discedebant ; veniebant post hos alii duo, quorum alter rursum cum sceptro, alter cum salino, orbe, et pane aderat, qui cum, uti priores, ter genua incurvassent, et res modo dictae mensae impositae essent, eadem omnino cum ceremonia abivere. Venit tandem Virgo quaedam Comitissa, uti affirmabatur, eximiae pulchritudinis, vestita veste serica alba, cui erat adiuncta nobilis matrona, cultrum praegustatorium ferens, quae ter summo cum decore in pedes provoluta,

postea ad mensam accessit, orbes sale et pane abstersit, tanta cum
veneratione, ac si Regina ipsa praesens fuisset ; cumque paululum
commorata ad mensam esset, venerunt satellites Regii, omnes capite
nudi, sagis rubris induti, quibus in postica parte erant affixae rosae
aureae, singulis vicibus xxiv missus ferculorum, in patinis argenteis
et maxima ex parte deauratis, adferentes ; Ab his nobilis quidam,
ordine cibos accepit, et mensae imposuit ; Praegustatrix vero, cuilibet
satelliti, ex eadem, quam ipsemet attulerat, patina, buccellam de-
gustandam praebuit, ne aliqua veneni subesset suspicio ; Dum satellites isti, qui centum numero procera corporis statura, et omnium
robustissimi ex toto Angliae Regno, ad hoc munus summa cura
deliguntur, supradictos cibos adportarent, erant in Aulae area xii
Tubicines, et duo Tympanistae, qui tubis, buccinis, et tympanis
magno sonitu per sesqui horam clangebant ; Caeremoniis autem,
modo commemoratis, circa mensam absolutis, aderant illico virgines
aliquot nobiles, quae singulari cum veneratione, cibos de mensa
auferebant, et in interius et secretius Reginae cubiculum asportabant ;
Eligere ibi Regina solet quos vult, caeteri pro Gynaeceo servantur ;
Prandet et coenat sola paucis astantibus, atque nullus admittitur,
neque peregrinus, neque Regni quoque incola, nisi rarissime, et quidem
ex singulari magnatis alicuius intercessione.

APPENDIX G

SERLIO'S TRATTATO SOPRA LE SCENE

[Extract from Sebastiano Serlio's *Architettura* (1551), being the text of
ff. 26ᵛ–31ᵛ of *Il secondo libro di Perspettiva*, which also contain five woodcuts, representing (*A*) the *profilo* or section of a stage (f. 26ᵛ), (*B*) the *pianta*
or ground-plan of the same stage (f. 27ᵛ), (*C*), (*D*), (*E*) elevations of a *scena
comica* (f. 28ᵛ), *scena tragica* (f. 29ᵛ), and *scena satyrica* (f. 30). An English
translation, through the ' Dutch ', of the five books of the *Architettura*
was published in 1611, having been entered in the Stationers' Register
by Thomas Snodham on 14 Dec. 1611 (Arber, iii. 473). Each book has
a separate imprint, *London Printed for Robert Peake and are to be sold
at his shop neere Holborne conduit, next to the Sunne Tauerne. Anno Dom.
1611*. Each has also a colophon, with slight variants ; that of the fifth
book, which alone names the printer, is *Here endeth the fift Booke : And
this also is the end of the whole worke of Sebastian Serlius ; Translated out
of Italian into Dutch, and out of Dutch into English, at the charges of Robert
Peake. Printed at London, by Simon Stafford. 1611. B. W.* I do not
know whether B. W. conceals the name of a translator. Robert Peake,
who also signs an Epistle to Prince Henry, prefixed to the first book, was
not a stationer, but a serjeant painter to James. In this translation the
Treatise of Scenes occupies ff. 23ᵛ–27 of Bk. ii, ch. 3. The title of this
book is *The second Booke of Architecture, made by Sebastian Serly, entreating
of Perspectiue, which is, Inspection, or looking into, by shortening of the
sight*. The woodcuts are reproduced, with some modifications, especially
in details of heraldic decoration.]

[f. 26ᵛ] Per che ne la seguente carta io trattaro delle Scene e
de Theatri che a nostri tempi si costumano, onde sara difficile a

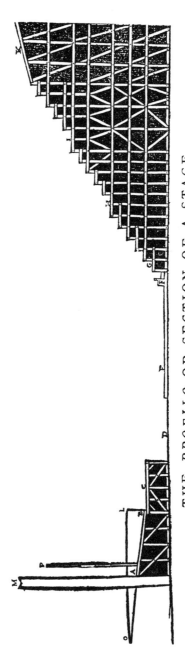

THE *PROFILO* OR SECTION OF A STAGE

(*A*)

comprendere doue et come si debbia porre l' orizonte delle scene, per
essere diuerso modo dalle regole passate, ho voluto far prima questo
profilo, accio che la pianta in sieme col profilo l' un per l' altro si
possino intendere ; ma sara perho bene a studiare prima su la pianta,
et se quelle cose non si intenderanno ne la pianta, recorrere al profilo
doue meglio s' intendera. Primieramente donque io cominciaro dal
suolo dauanti : loquale sara a l' altezza de l' occhio et voglio que sia
piano et e segnato C, et da B fin a l' A sara lo suolo leuato dalla
parte de A la nona parte ; et quel diritto piu grosso sopra del qual
e M dinota lo muro nel capo della sala. Quel diritto piu sottile doue
e P sara lo pariete della scena cioe l' ultimo. Il termine doue e l' o e
l' orizonte. La linea di punti che viene ad essere aliuello da L a O
doue essa finira nel pariete vltimo della scena, iui sara l' orizonte,
loqual pero seruira solamente per quel pariete, et questa linea sara
quella che sara sempre orizonte, alle faccie de i casamenti che saranno
in maiesta. Ma quelle parti de i casamenti che scurtiano lo suo
orizonte sara quel piu lontano segnato O. Et e ben ragione se i casamenti in effetto han dua facie, lequai spettino a dua lati, che anchora
habbino dua orizonti ; et questo e quanto al profilo della scena. Ma
lo proscenio si e quella segnata D : la parte E rappresenta l' hor-
chestra leuata da terra mezzo piede. Doue si vede F sonno le sedie
de piu nobili. Li primi gradi segnati G saran per le donne piu nobili,
et salendo piu ad alto le men nobili vi si metterano. Quel luoco piu
spacioso doue e H e vna strada, e cosi la parte I vn altra strada
onde fra l' una e l' altra quei gradi saranno per la nobilita de gli huomini. Dal I in su li gradi che vi sonno, li men nobili si metteranno.
Quel gran spacio segnato K sara per la plebe, et sara magiore et
minore secondo la grandezza del luoco ; et lo Theatro, et la scena
ch' io feci in Vicenza, furono circa a questo modo, et de l' un corno
a l' altro del Theatro era da piedi ottanta, per essere questo fatto in
vn gran cortile, doue trouai magior spacio, che doue era la scena per
essere quella appoggiata ad vna loggia. Li armamenti et ligature de
i legnami furono nel modo dimostrato qui auanti, et per esser questo
Theatro senza appoggio alcuno, io volsi (per magior fortezza) farlo
ascarpa nella circonferentia di fori.

Trattato sopra le Scene.

[f. 27] Fra l' altre cose fatte per mano de gli huomini che si possono
mirare con gran contentezza d' occhio et satisfationi d' animo : e (al
parer mio) il discoprirsi lo apparato di vna scena, doue si vede in
picol spacio fatto da l' arte della Perspettiua superbi palazzi, amplis-
simi tempij, diuersi casamenti, et da presso, e di lontano, spaciose
piazze ornate di varii edificij, dritissime e longhe strade incrociate
da altre vie, archi triomphali, altissime colonne, pyramide, obelischi,
et mille altre cose belle, ornate d' infiniti lumi, grandi, mezzani,
et piccoli, secondo che l' altre lo comporta, liquali sono cosi
arteficiosamente ordinati, che rappresentano tante gioie lucidis-
sime, come saria Diamanti, Rubini, Zafiri, Smeraldi, et cose

simili. Quiui si vede la cornuta et lucida Luna leuarsi pian piano; et essersi inalzata, che gli occhi de i spettatori non l'han veduta muouersi: in alcune altre si vede lo leuare del sole, et il suo girare, et nel finire della comedia tramontar poi con tale artificio che molti spettatori di tal cosa stupiscono; con l'artificio a qualche bon proposito si vedera descendere alcun Dio dal cielo, correre qualche Pianeta per l'aria, venir poi su la scena diuersi intermedij richissimamente ornati, liuree di varie sorti con habiti strani, si per moresche come per musiche. Tal'hor si vede strani animali entro de i quali son huomini, et fanciulli, atteggiando, saltando, et correndo cosi bene, che non e senza merauiglia de riguardanti, le quai tutte cose dan tanto di contentezza a l'hocchio, et a l'animo, che cosa materiale, fatta da l'arte, non si potria imaginare piu bella; et di quelle cose poi che siamo in proposito de l'arte della perspettiua, io ne trattaro alquanto. Pure quantunque questo modo di perspettiua di ch'io parlaro sia diuerso dalle regole passate, per essere quelle imaginate sopra li parieti piani: et questa per essere materiale et di rilieuo e ben ragione a tenere altra strada. Primieramente per il commune vso si fa vn suolo leuato da terra quanto l'hocchio nostro; cioe dalla parte dauanti et di dietro si fa piu alto la nona parte, partendo in noue parti tutto il piano, et vna di quelle. Sia leuato il detto suolo dalla parte di drieto verso l'orizonte, et sia ben piano et forte per causa delle moresche. Questa pendentia io l'ho trouata commoda con la esperientia, perche in Vicenza (citta molto ricca et pomposissima fra l'altre d'Italia) io feci vno Theatro, et vna scena di legname, perauentura, anzi senza dubio, la magiore che a nostri tempi si sia fatta, doue per li merauigliosi intermedij che vi accadeuano, cioe carette, Elefanti, et diuerse moresche, io volsi che dauanti la scena pendente vi fosse vn suolo piano, la latitudine del quale fu piede xij, et in longitudine piedi lx, doue io trouai tal cosa ben commoda, et di grande aspetto. Questo primo suolo essendo piano, lo suo pauimento non vbidiua a l'orizonte, ma li suoi quadri furono perfetti, et al cominciare dal piano pendente tutti quei quadri andauano a l'orizonte ilche con la sua debita distantia sminui. Et perche alcuni han posto l'orizonte a l'ultimo pariete che termina la scena, il qual e necessario metterlo sul proprio suolo al nascimento di esso pariete, doue dimostra che tutti li casamenti se adunano, io mi sono imaginato di trapassare piu la con l'orizonte, la qual cosa mi e cosi bene reuscita, che a fare tal cose ho sempre tenuto questa strada, et cosi consiglio coloro che di tal arte se diletterano, a tener questo camino, come nella seguente carta dimostraro, et come ne ho trattato qui adietro nel profilo del Theatro, et della Scena. Et perche gli apparati delle comedie sono di tre maniere, cioe la Comica, la Tragica, et la Satyrica, io trattaro al presente de la comica, i casamenti della quale voglion essere di personagi priuati, liquali apparati per la maggior parte si fanno al coperto in qualche sala, che nel capo di essa vi sia camere per la commodita de i dicitori, et iui si fa lo suolo come qui piu a dietro io dissi, e ne dimostrai lo suo profilo, et qui auanti dimostrero la pianta. Primieramente la parte c e quel suolo

(B)

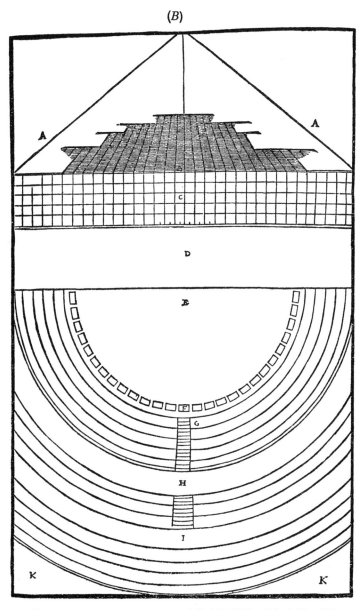

THE *PIANTA* OR GROUND-PLAN OF
A STAGE

piano et poniam caso che vn quadro sia dua piedi, et medesimamente
quegli del piano pendente son dua piedi per ogni lato, et e segnato
B ; e (come ho detto nel profilo) io non intendo di mettere l' orizonte
al pariete vltimo de la scena, ma quanto sara dal principio di esso
piano B fin al muro sia trapassato altro tanto di la dal muro con
l' orizonte ; et quelle dua linee di punti dinotano lo muro in capo
di essa sala, e cosi tutti li casamenti et altre cose haueranno piu
dolcezza ne i scurcij, doue tirati tutti li quadri ad esso orizonte, et
diminuiti secondo la sua distantia, si leuaran su li casamenti, li quali
son quelle linee grosse sul piano, per diritto, et per trauerso ; et
questi tai casamenti io li ho sempre fatti di telari, sopra liquali ho
poi tirato tele, facendogli le sue porte in faccia et in scurtio secondo
le occasioni, et ancho ci ho fatto alcune cose di basso rilieuo di legnami
che han aiutato molto le pitture, come al suo loco ne trattaro. Tutto
lo spacio da li telari al muro segnati A seruiranno per li dicittori,
et sempre lo pariete vltimo vuol essere discosto dal muro almen dua
piedi, accio li diccitori possino passar coperti ; dipoi quanto si trouera
alto l' orizonte, sia tanto alzato vn termino al principio del piano
B che sara L et da li a l' orizonte sia tirata vna linea chi e di punti,
laquale sara al liuello, et doue questa ferira nel vltimo pariete : iui
sara l' orizonte di esso pariete : et non seruira perho ad altro telaro :
ma la detta linea sia vna cosa stabile, perche questa seruira a tutti
quei telari che saranno in maiesta, per trouare le grossezze di alcune
cose, ma lo primo orizonte di la dal muro seruira a tutti li scurcij
de i casamenti. Et perche a far questo saria necessario a rompere
esso muro, ilche non si puo fare, io ho sempre fatto vno modello
piccolo di cartoni et legnami, ben misurato et traportato poi in grande
di cosa in cosa giustamente con facilita. Ma questa lettione forsi ad
alcuno sara difficile, nondimeno sara necessario faticarsi nel far de
modelli et esperientie, che studiando trouara la via. Et perche le
sale (per grande che siano) non son capaci di Theatri, io nondimeno,
per accostarmi quanto io possi agli antichi, ho voluto di esso Theatro
farne quella parte che in vna gran sala possi capere. Perho la parte
D seruira per proscenio. La parte circolare segnata E sara l' orchestra
leuata vn grado dal proscenio, intorno laquale son sedie per li piu
nobili, che son F ; li gradi primi G son per le donne piu nobili ; la
parte H e strada et cosi la parte I. Gli altri gradi son per li huomini
men nobili, fra liquali vi son scale per salire piu agiatamente. Quei
luochi spaciosi segnati K saran poi per la plebe et saranno magiori
o minori secondo li luochi, et come il luoco sara magiore, lo Theatro
prendera piu della sua perfetta forma.

Della Scena Comica.

[f. 28] Quanto alla dispositione de i Theatri, et delle Scene circa alla pianta io ne ho trattato qui adietro, hora delle scene in perspettiua ne trattaro particularmente, et perche (com' io dissi) le scene si fanno di tre sorte, cioe la Comica per rappresentar comedie, la Tragica per le tragedie, e la Satyrica per le satyre, questa prima sara la Comica, i casamenti della quale vogliono essere di personaggi privati, come saria di cittadini auocati, mercanti, parasiti, et altre simili persone.

(C)

ELEVATION OF A *SCENA COMICA*

Ma sopra il tutto che non vi manchi la casa della Rufiana ne sia senza hostaria, et uno tempio vi e molto necessario. Per disporre li casamenti sopra il piano detto suolo, io ne ho dato il modo piu adietro, si nel leuare i casamenti sopra li piani, come nella pianta delle scene massime, come et doue si dee porre l' orizonte. Niente-dimeno accio che l' huomo sia meglio instrutto circa alle forme de i casamenti, io ne dimostro qui a lato vna figura, laquale potra essere vn poco di luce a chi di tal cosa vorra dilettarsi. Pur in questa essendo cosi picola non ho potuto osseruare tutte le misure. Ma

solamente ho accennato alla inuentione per aduertir l' huomo a saper
fare elettione di quei casamenti che posti in opera habbino a reuscir
bene come saria un portico traforato, dietro del quale si vegga vn
altro casamento come questo primo, li archi delquale son di opera
moderna. Li poggiuoli (altri dicono pergoli ; altri Renghiere) hanno
gran forza nelle faccie che scurzano, et cosi qualche cornice che li
suoi finimenti vengono fuori del suo cantonale, tagliati intorno et
accompagnati con l' altre cornice dipinte, fanno grande effetto ; cosi
le case che han gran sporto in fuori riusciscono bene, come l' hostaria
della luna qui presente ; et sopra tutte le altre cose si de fare elettione
delle case piu piccole, et metterle dauanti, accio che sopra esse si
scuoprano altri edificii, come si vede sopra la casa della Ruffiana,
l' insegna della quale sono li rampini, o vogliam dire hami, onde per
tal superiorita della casa piu adietro viene a rappresentar grandezza,
et riempisse meglio la parte della scena, che non farebbe diminuendo,
se le summita delle case diminuissero l' una dopo altra ; et benche
le cose qui disegnate habbino vn lume solo da vn lato, nondimeno
tornano meglio a dargli il lume nel mezzo : perciocce la forza de
i lumi si mette nel mezzo, pendenti sopra la scena, et tutti quei
tondi, o quadri, che si veggono per gli edificii sono tutti i lumi artificiati di varii colori transparenti : de i quali daro il modo da fargli
ne l' estremo di questo libro.   Le finestre che sono in faccia sara
bene a mettergli de lumi di dietro, ma che siano di vetro, et ancho
di carta ouero di tela dipinta torneran bene. Ma s' io volessi scriuere
di tutti gli aduertimenti che mi abbundano circa a tal cose, io sarei
forsi tenuto prolisso, perho io le lassaro nel' intelletto di coloro che
in tal cose si voranno essercitare.

Della Scena Tragica.

[f. 29] La Scena Tragica sara per rappresentare tragedie. Li casamenti d' essa vogliono essere di grandi personagi ; perciocce gli
accidenti amorosi, et casi inopinati, morte violenti et crudeli (per
quanto si lege nelle tragedie antiche, et ancho nelle moderne) sonno
sempre interuenute dentro le case de signori, duchi, o gran principi,
imo, di Re ; et perho (come ho detto) in cotali apparati non si fara
edificio che non habbia del nobile : si come se dimostra nella seguente
figura, entro la quale (per esser cosa piccola) non ho potuto dimostrare
quei grandi edificij Regij et signorili, che in vn luogo spatioso si
potrebbono fare.   Ma basti solamente a l' Arcitetto che in torno
a cose simili si vorra essercitare, per hauer vn poco di luce circa alla
inuentione, et dipoi secondo li luochi et anchora li sugietti sapersi
accommodare ; et (come ho detto nella scena comica) sempre si de
fare elettione di quelle cose che tornano meglio a riguardanti, non
hauendo rispetto a mettere vn edificio piccolo dauanti ad vno grande,
per le gia dette ragioni. Et perche tutte le mie scene ho fatte sopra
li telari, ci sonno tal volta alcune difficulta, che e ben necessario
a seruirsi del rilieuo di legname, come quello edificio al lato sinistro,
li pilastri del quale posano sopra vn basamento con alcuni gradi. In
questo caso sara da fare il detto basamento di basso rilieuo, leuato
sopra lo piano, et poi si faran li due telari, cioe quello in faccia, et

quello in scurtio ; et stano solamente fin alla summita del parapetto, che e sopra li primi archi. Hora perche gli archi secondi se ritirano per dar luoco al parapetto, cosi li dua telari di sopra si ritiraranno : di maniera che tal opera verra bene, et quello ch'io dico di questo edificio se intende anchora de gli altri, quando qualche parti si ritire-ranno, massimamente di quei casamenti che sono qua dauanti. Ma quando tai cose fussero di lontano, vn telaro solo seruiria, facendo tutte le parti ben lineate, et ben colorite. Circa alli lumi artificiati,

(D)

ELEVATION OF A *SCENA TRAGICA*

s'e detto a bastanza nella scena comica. Tutte le superficie sopra li tetti, come saria camini, campanili, et cose simili (benche quiui non vi siano) se faranno sopra vna tauola sottile, tagliati intorno, ben lineati et coloriti. Similmente qualche statue finte di marmo o di bronzo si faranno di grosso cartone, o pur di tauola sottile, ben ombregiate et tagliate intorno ; poi si metteranno alli suoi luochi, ma siano talmente disposti, et lontani che i spettatori non le possino vedere per fianco. In queste Scene, benche alcuni hanno dipinto qualche personagi che rappresentano il viuo, come saria vna femina ad vn balcone, o drento d'una porta, etiamdio qualche animale, queste cose non consiglio che si faccino, perche non hanno il moto et pure rappresentano il viuo ; ma qualche persona che dorma a bon proposito, ouero qualche cane o altro animale che dorma, perche non hanno il moto. Anchora si possono accomodare qualche statue, o altre cose finte di marmo, o d' altra materia, o alcuna hystoria, o fabula dipinta sopra vn pariete, che io lodaro sempre si faccia cosi. Ma nel rappresentare cose viue lequali habbino il moto, ne l' estremo di questo libro ne trattaro, et daro il modo come s' abbino a fare.

(E)

ELEVATION OF A *SCENA SATYRICA*

Della Scena Satyrica.

[f. 30] La Scena Satyrica e per rappresentar satyre, nelle quali se riprendono (anzi vero se mordeno) tutti coloro che licentiosamente viuono, et senza rispetto nelle satyre antiche erano quasi mostrati a dito gli huomini viciosi et mal viuenti. Perho tal licentia si puo comprendere che fusse concessa a personaggi che senza rispetto par- lassero, come saria a dire gente rustica, percioche Vitruuio trattando delle scene, vuole che questa sia ornata di arbori, sassi, colli, montagne, herbe, fiori, et fontane, vuole anchora che vi siano alcune capanne alla rustica, come qui appresso se dimostra. Et perche a tempi nostri queste cose per il piu delle volte si fanno la inuernata, doue pochi arbori et herbe con fiori se ritrouano, si potran bene artificiosamente fare cose simili di seta lequali saranno anchora piu lodate che le naturali ; percioche, cosi come nelle Scene Comiche et Tragiche se imitano li casamenti et altri edificij, con l'artificio della pittura, cosi anchora in questa si potran bene imitare gli arbori et l'herbe co fiori. Et queste cose quanto saranno di maggior spesa tanto piu lodeuoli saranno, perche (nel vero) son proprie di generosi magnanimi, et richi signori, nemici della bruta Auaritia. Questo gia vidiro gli occhi mei in alcune scene ordinate da l'intendente Architetto Girolamo Genga, ad instantia del suo padrone Francesco Maria Duca di Vrbino, doue io compresi tanta liberalita nel prence, tanto giuditio et arte l'Architetto, et tanta bellezza nelle cose strutte, quanto in altra opera fatta da l'arte che da me sia stata veduta giamai. (O Dio immortale) che magnificentia era quella di veder tanti arbori et frutti, tante herbe et fiori diuersi, tutte cose fatte di finissima seta di variati colori, le ripe et i sassi copiosi de diuerse conche marine, di limache et altri animaletti, di tronchi di coralli di piu colori, di matre perle, et di granchi marini inserti ne i sassi, con tanta diuersita di cose belle ; che a volerle scriuere tutte, io sarei troppo longo in questa parte. Io non diro de i satyri, delle Nymphe, delle syrene, et diuersi monstri o animali strani, fatti con tal artificio, che aconzi sopra gli huomini et fanciulli secondo la grandezza loro, et quelli, andando et mouendosi secondo la sua natura, rappresentauano essi animali viui. Et se non ch'io sarei troppo prolisso, io narrarei gli habiti superbi di alcuni pastori, fatti di ricchi drappi d'oro et di seta, foderati di finissime pelle d'animali seluatichi. Direi anchora de i vestimenti d'alcuni pescatori, liquali non furono men ricchi de gli altri, le rete de i quali erano di fila d'oro fino, et altri suoi stromenti tutti dorati. Direi di alcune pastorelle et Nymphe, gli habiti delle quali sprezauano l'Auaritia. Ma io lassaro tutte queste cose ne gli intelletti de i giudiciosi Architetti : liquali faranno sempre di queste cose, quando trouaranno simili padroni conformi alle lor voglie, gli et donanti piena licentia, con larga mano, di operare tutto quello che vorranno.

Di Lumi arteficiali delle Scene.

[f. 31] Ho promesso piu adietro negli trattati delle scene, di dare il modo come si fanno i lumi artificiali di variati colori transparenti ; perche primieramente diro del colore celeste, il quale rappresenta il zafiro et ancho assai piu bello. Prendi vn pezzo di sale ammoniaco, et habbi vn bacile da barbiere o altro vaso di ottone, mettendogli drento vn detto di aqua. Poi questo pezzo di sale va ben fregando nel fondo, et intorno questo bacile, tanto che'l se consumi tutto : agiungendoli de l'aqua tuttauia, et quando vorrai piu quantita di questa aqua, et che'l colore sia piu bello, fa maggiore la quantita del sale ammoniaco. Fatto adonque vno bacile pieno di questa aqua falla passare per il feltro in vno altro vaso, et questa sara di color

celeste bellissimo. Ma volendolo piu chiaro vi agiungerai de l' aqua
pura, cosi di questo sol colore ne farai di molti piu chiari et piu scuri
quanto vorrai ; et se di questa medesima aqua zafrina vorrai fare
colore di Smeraldo, mettili drento alquanto di zaffarano, tanto piu
o meno, secondo che la vorrai piu oscura o piu chiara. Di queste
cose non ti do le proportioni ; ma con la esperientia ne farai di piu
forte o chiare o pur oscure. Se vorrai fare del colore di Rubino, se
sarai in luoco doue siano vini vermigli carichi di colore et chiaretti :
questi faranno di rubin maturi et gai cioe acerbi, et se non hauerai
de vini, prendi del vergine tagliato in pezzeti, mettendolo in vna
caldara piena d' aqua, con alquanto di alume di rocha, et la farai
bolire spiumandola, et poi passare pel feltro, et agiungendoli aqua
pura se vorrai colore piu chiaro ; et se vorai colore di Balasso, il
vino goro, bianco, et vermiglio insieme, fara tal colore. Cosi anchora
li vini bianchi piu et meno carichi faran colore de Griso passo, et di
Thopasso. Ma (senza dubio alcuno) l' aqua pura passata pel feltro
contrafara li Diamanti. Pure, per farli, sara necessario adoperare
alcune forme in punta, et in tauola, et alla fornace de i vetri fare
delle bozze che prendano tal forma, et quelle impire d' aqua. Ma
il modo de disporre questi colori transparenti sara questo. Sara di
dietro alle cose dipinte, doue anderanno questi colori, vna tauola
sottile traforata nel modo che saran compartiti questi lumi, sotto
laquale sara un' altra tauola per sostenere le bozze di vetro piene
di queste aque ; poi dette bozze si metteranno con la parte piu curua
appoggiate a quei buchi, et bene assicurate che non caschino per
i strepiti delle moresche ; et dietro le bozze si mettera vno cesendelo,
overo lampada, accio lo lume sia sempre equale ; et selle bozze verso
la lampada saranno piane anzi concaue, riceueranno meglio la luce,
et li colori saranno piu transparenti, cosi anchora per quei tondi
liquali saranno in scurtio sara da fare le bozze di quella sorte. Ma
se accadra tal fiata vn lume grande et gagliardo, sara da metterui
di dietro vna torza, dopo laquale sia vn bacile da barbiere ben lucido
et nuovo, la reflettione del quale fara certi splendori, come di raggi
del sole. Et se alcuni luochi saranno quadri come mandola, o altre
forme, si prendera delle piastre di vetri di variati colori posti a quei
luochi col suo lume di dietro. Ma questi lumi non saran (perho)
quelli che alluminenanno la scena, percioche gran coppia di torze si
metteno pendente dauanti alla scena. Si potra anchora su per la
scena mettere alcuni candelieri con torze sopra, ed anchora sopra essi
candelieri vi sia vn vaso pieno di acqua, drento laquale metterai vn
pezzo di camphora, loquale ardendo fa bellissimo lume, et e odorifero.
Alcuna fiata accadera a dimostrare qualche cosa che abbruscia (sia
che si voglia) ; si bagnara benissimo di aqua vite della piu potente,
et apizatogli lo fuoco con vna candeletta : ardera per vn pezzo. Et
ben che quanto alli fuochi si potra dire assai piu, voglio questo sia
basteuole per presente. Ma parliamo di alcune cose lequali sono di
gran diletto a spettatori. Mentre la scena e vota de dicitori, potra
l' architetto hauer preparato alcune ordinanze di figurette, di quella
grandezza che si ricercara dove hauranno a passare, et queste saranno

di grosso cartone colorite et tagliate intorno, lequali posaranno sopra vn regolo di legno a trauerso la scena, doue sia qualche arco, fatto sopra il suolo vno incastro a coda di Rondina, entro lo quale si mettera detto regolo ; et cosi pianamente vna persona dietro al detto arco le fara passare, et tal fiata dimostrare che siano musici con istrumenti et voci, onde dietro alla scena sara vna musica a somissa voce. Tal volta fara correre vn squadrone di gente chi a piedi et chi a cauallo, lequali con alcune voci o gridi sordi, strepiti di tamburi, et suono di trombe, pascono molto gli spettatori. Et se tal volta accadera che vno Pianeta, o altra cosa per aria si vegga passare, sia ben dipinta quella cosa in cartone et tagliata intorno ; poi dietro la scena (cioe a gli vltimi casamenti) sia tirato a trauerso vn filo di ferro sottile, et con alcuni aneletti in esso filo attacati dietro il cartone, nel quale sia un filo negro, et da l' altro lato sara vna persona che pian piano lo tirara a se, ma sara di forte lontano, che ne l' uno ne l' altro filo sara veduto. Tal fiata accadera tuoni, lampi et folgori a qualche proposito ; li tuoni cosi si faranno. Sempre (come ho detto) le scene si fanno nel capo di vna sala, sopra laquale gli e sempre vn suolo, sopra del quale si fara correre vna grossa balla di pietra, laquale fara bene il tuono. Lo lampo cosi si fara. Sara vno dietro alla scena in luoco alto, hauendo nella mano vna scatoletta, entro laquale vi sia polue di vernice : et il coperchio sia pieno di busi : nel mezzo del coperchio sara vna candeletta accesa : et alzando in su la mano, quella polue salira in alto, et perchuotera nella candela accesa, di maniera che fara lampi assai bene. Circo al folgore, sara tirato vn filo di ferro lontano a trauerso la scena, che descenda a basso, entro del quale sara aconcio vn rochetto, o raggio, che si sia, ma questo sara ornato di oro stridente, et mentre si fara lo tuono, nel finir di quello sia scaricata vna coda, et nel medesimo tempo dato il fuoco al folgore, et fara buono effetto. Ma s' io volessi trattare di quante cose similimi abbondano, io saria troppo longho ; pero faccio fine quanto alla perspettiua.

APPENDIX H

THE GULL'S HORNBOOK

[Chapter vi from T. Dekker, *The Gull's Hornbook* (1609). There is no entry in the Stationers' Register. Editions are by J. Nott (1812), J. O. Halliwell (1862), C. Hindley (1872, *Old Book Collector's Miscellany*, ii), A. B. Grosart (1884, *Dekker's Works*, ii), G. Saintsbury (1892), O. Smeaton (1904), and R. B. McKerrow (1904, *King's Library* ; 1905, *King's Classics*). I have adopted two trifling emendations ; ' Plaiers are ' for ' Plaiers and ' in the first paragraph, and ' Stage, like time ' for ' Stagelike time ' in the ninth. McKerrow reprints the chapter on the Stage from S. Vincent's Restoration adaptation of the pamphlet in *The Young Gallant's Academy* (1674).]

How a Gallant should behaue himself in a Playhouse.

The Theater is your Poets Royal Exchange, vpon which, their Muses (that are now turnd to Merchants) meeting, barter away that light commodity of words for a lighter ware then words, *Plaudities* and the *Breath* of the great *Beast*, which (like the threatnings of two Cowards) vanish all into aire. *Plaiers* are their *Factors*, who put away the stuffe, and make the best of it they possibly can (as indeed tis their parts so to doe). Your Gallant, your Courtier, and your Capten, had wont to be the soundest paymaisters, and I thinke are still the surest chapmen : and these by meanes that their heades are well stockt, deale vpon this comical freight by the grosse : when your *Groundling*, and *Gallery Commoner* buyes his sport by the penny, and, like a *Hagler*, is glad to vtter it againe by retailing.

Sithence then the place is so free in entertainment, allowing a stoole as well to the Farmers sonne as to your Templer : that your Stinkard has the selfe same libertie to be there in his Tobacco-Fumes, which your sweet Courtier hath : and that your Car-man and Tinker claime as strong a voice in their suffrage, and sit to giue iudgement on the plaies life and death, as well as the prowdest *Momus* among the tribe of *Critick* : It is fit that hee, whom the most tailors bils do make roome for, when he comes should not be basely (like a vyoll) casd vp in a corner.

Whether therefore the gatherers of the publique or priuate Play-house stand to receiue the afternoones rent, let our Gallant (hauing paid it) presently aduance himselfe vp to the Throne of the Stage. I meane not into the Lords roome, (which is now but the Stages Suburbs). No, those boxes, by the iniquity of custome, conspiracy of waiting-women and Gentlemen-Ushers, that there sweat together, and the couetousnes of Sharers, are contemptibly thrust into the reare, and much new Satten is there dambd by being smothred to death in darknesse. But on the very Rushes where the Commedy is to daunce, yea and vnder the state of *Cambises* himselfe must our fethered *Estridge*, like a peece of Ordnance be planted valiantly (because impudently) beating downe the mewes and hisses of the opposed rascality.

For do but cast vp a reckoning, what large cummings in are pursd vp by sitting on the Stage. First a conspicuous *Eminence* is gotten ; by which meanes the best and most essenciall parts of a Gallant (good cloathes, a proportionable legge, white hand, the Persian lock, and a tollerable beard) are perfectly reuealed.

By sitting on the stage, you haue a signd pattent to engrosse the whole commodity of Censure ; may lawfully presume to be a Girder : and stand at the helme to steere the passage of *Scænes* [;] yet no man shall once offer to hinder you from obtaining the title of an insolent, ouer-weening Coxcombe.

By sitting on the stage, you may (without trauelling for it) at the very next doore, aske whose play it is : and, by that *Quest* of *inquiry*, the law warrants you to auoid much mistaking ; if you know not the author, you may raile against him : and peraduenture so behaue your selfe, that you may enforce the Author to know you.

By sitting on the stage, if you be a Knight, you may happily get you a Mistresse : if a mere *Fleet street* Gentleman, a wife : but assure yourselfe by continuall residence, you are the first and principall man in election to begin the number of *We three*.

By spreading your body on the stage, and by being a Justice in examining of plaies, you shall put your selfe into such true *Scænical* authority, that some Poet shall not dare to present his Muse rudely vpon your eyes, without hauing first vnmaskt her, rifled her, and discouered all her bare and most mysticall parts before you at a Tauerne, when you most knightly shal for his paines, pay for both their suppers.

By sitting on the stage, you may (with small cost) purchase the deere acquaintance of the boyes : haue a good stoole for sixpence : at any time know what particular part any of the infants present : get your match lighted, examine the play-suits lace, and perhaps win wagers vpon laying tis copper, &c. And to conclude whether you be a foole or a Justice of peace, a Cuckold or a Capten, a Lord Maiors sonne or a dawcocke, a knaue or an vnder-Sheriffe, of what stamp soeuer you be, currant or counterfet, the Stage, like time, will bring you to most perfect light, and lay you open : neither are you to be hunted from thence though the Scar-crows in the yard, hoot at you, hisse at you, spit at you, yea throw durt euen in your teeth : tis most Gentlemanlike patience to endure all this, and to laugh at the silly Animals : but if the *Rabble* with a full throat, crie away with the foole, you were worse then a mad-man to tarry by it : for the Gentleman and the foole should neuer sit on the Stage together.

Mary let this obseruation go hand in hand with the rest : or rather like a country-seruing-man, some fiue yards before them. Present not your selfe on the Stage (especially at a new play) vntill the quaking prologue hath (by rubbing) got cullor into his cheekes, and is ready to giue the trumpets their Cue that hees vpon point to enter : for then it is time, as though you were one of the *Properties*, or that you dropt out of the *Hangings*, to creepe from behind the Arras, with your *Tripos* or three-footed stoole in one hand, and a teston mounted betweene a forefinger and a thumbe in the other : for if you should bestow your person vpon the vulgar, when the belly of the house is but halfe full, your apparell is quite eaten vp, the fashion lost, and the proportion of your body in more danger to be deuoured, then if it were serued vp in the Counter amongst the Powltry : auoid that as you would the Bastome. It shall crowne you with rich commenda-tion to laugh alowd in the middest of the most serious and saddest scene of the terriblest Tragedy : and to let that clapper (your tongue) be tost so high that all the house may ring of it : your Lords vse it ; your Knights are Apes to the Lords, and do so too : your Inne-a-court-man is Zany to the Knights, and (many very scuruily) comes likewise limping after it : bee thou a beagle to them all, and neuer lin snuffing till you haue scented them : for by talking and laughing (like a Plough-man in a Morris) you heap *Pelion* vpon *Ossa*, glory vpon glory : As first, all the eyes in the galleries will leaue walking after the Players, and onely follow you : the simplest dolt in the house snatches vp your name, and when he meetes you in the streetes, or that you fall into his hands in the middle of a Watch, his word shall be taken for you : heele cry, *Hees such a Gallant*, and you passe. Secondly, you publish your temperance to the world, in that you seeme not to resort thither to taste vaine pleasures with a hungrie appetite : but onely as a Gentleman, to spend a foolish houre or two, because yoe can doe nothing else. Thirdly you mightily disrelish the Audience, and disgrace the Author : mary, you take vp (though it be at the worst hand) a strong opinion of your owne iudgement and inforce the Poet to take pitty of your weakenesse, and, by some dedicated sonnet to bring you into a better paradice, onely to stop your mouth.

If you can (either for loue or money) prouide your selfe a lodging by the water-side : for, aboue the conueniencie it brings, to shun Shoulder-clapping, and to ship away your Cockatrice betimes in the morning, it addes a kind of state vnto you, to be carried from thence to the staires of your Play-house : hate a Sculler (remember that) worse then to be acquainted with one ath' Scullery. No, your Oares are your onely Sea-crabs, boord them, and take heed you neuer go twice together with one paire : often shifting is a great credit to Gentlemen ; and that diuiding of your fare wil make the poore water-snaks be ready to pul you in peeces to enioy your custome : No matter whether vpon landing you haue money or no, you may swim in twentie of their boates ouer the riuer upon *Ticket* : mary, when siluer comes in, remember to pay trebble their fare, and it will make your Flounder-catchers to send more thankes after you, when you doe not draw, then when you doe ; for they know, It will be their owne another daie.

Before the Play begins, fall to cardes, you may win or loose (as *Fencers* doe in a prize) and beate one another by confederacie, yet share the money when you meete at supper : notwithstanding, to gul the *Ragga-muffins* that stand aloofe gaping at you, throw the cards (hauing first torne foure or fiue of them) round about the Stage, iust vpon the third sound, as though you had lost : it skils not if the foure knaues ly on their backs, and outface the Audience, theres none such fooles as dare take exceptions at them, because ere the play go off, better knaues than they will fall into the company.

Now sir, if the writer be a fellow that hath either epigramd you, or hath had a flirt at your mistris, or hath brought either your feather or your red beard, or your little legs, &c. on the stage, you shall disgrace him worse then by tossing him in a blancket, or giuing him the bastinado in a Tauerne, if, in the middle of his play (bee it Pastoral or Comedy, Morall or Tragedie), you rise with a skreud and discontented face from your stoole to be gone : no matter whether the Scenes be good or no, the better they are the worse do you distast them : and, beeing on your feet, sneake not away like a coward, but salute all your gentle acquaintance, that are spred either on the rushes, or on stooles about you, and draw what troope you can from the stage after you : the *Mimicks* are beholden to you, for allowing them elbow roome : their Poet cries perhaps a pox go with you, but care not you for that, theres no musick without frets.

Mary if either the company, or indisposition of the weather binde you to sit it out, my counsell is then that you turne plain Ape, take vp a rush and tickle the earnest eares of your fellow gallants, to make other fooles fall a laughing : mewe at passionate speeches, blare at merrie, finde fault with the musicke, whew at the childrens Action, whistle at the songs : and aboue all, curse the sharers, that whereas the same day you had bestowed forty shillings on an embrodered Felt and Feather, (scotch-fashion) for your mistres in the Court, or your punck in the city, within two houres after, you encounter with the very same block on the stage, when the haberdasher swore to you the impression was extant but that morning.

To conclude, hoard vp the finest play-scraps you can get, vpon which your leane wit may most sauourly feede for want of other stuffe, when the *Arcadian* and *Euphuisd* gentlewomen haue their tongues sharpened to set vpon you : that qualitie (next to your shittlecocke) is the onely furniture to a Courtier thats but a new beginner, and is but in his A B C of complement. The next places that are fild, after the Playhouses bee emptied, are (or ought to be) Tauernes, into a Tauerne then let vs next march, where the braines of one Hogshead must be beaten out to make vp another.

APPENDIX I

RESTORATION TESTIMONY

i.

[Extracts from *A Short Discourse of the English Stage. To his Excellency, the Lord Marquess of Newcastle*, attached to Richard Flecknoe's *Love's Kingdom* (1664), and reprinted in Hazlitt, *E. D. S.* 275. Flecknoe, who died *c.* 1678, was old enough to travel abroad in 1640.]

They Acted nothing here but Playes of the holy Scripture, or Saints' Lives ; and that without any certain Theaters or set Companies, till, about the beginning of Queen Elizabeth's Reign, they began here first to assemble into Companies, and set up Theaters, first in the City, (as in the Inn-yards of the Cross-Keyes, and Bull in Grace and Bishops-Gate Street at this day is to be seen) till that Fanatick Spirit which then began with the Stage, and after ended with the Throne, banisht them thence into the Suburbs, as after they did the Kingdom, in the beginning of our Civil Wars. In which time, Playes were so little incompatible with Religion, and the Theater with the Church, as on Week-dayes after Vespers, both the Children of the Chappel and St. Pauls Acted Playes, the one in White-Friers, the other behinde the Convocation-house in Pauls, till people growing more precise, and Playes more licentious, the Theatre of Pauls was

quite supprest, and that of the Children of the Chappel converted
to the use of the Children of the Revels. . . .

It was the happiness of the Actors of those times to have such
Poets as these to instruct them, and write for them ; and no less
of those Poets to have such docile and excellent Actors to Act their
Playes, as a Field and Burbidge ; of whom we may say, that he was
a delightful Proteus, so wholly transforming himself into his Part,
and putting off himself with his Cloathes, as he never (not so much
as in the Tyring-house) assum'd himself again until the Play was
done : there being as much difference between him and one of our
common Actors, as between a Ballad-singer who onely mouths it,
and an excellent singer, who knows all his Graces, and can artfully
vary and modulate his Voice, even to know how much breath he is
to give to every syllable. He had all the parts of an excellent Orator
(animating his words with speaking, and Speech with Action) his
Auditors being never more delighted then when he spoke, nor more
sorry then when he held his peace ; yet even then, he was an excellent
Actor still, never falling in his Part when he had done speaking ;
but with his looks and gesture, maintaining it still unto the heighth,
he imagining Age quod agis, onely spoke to him : so as those who
call him a Player do him wrong, no man being less idle then he,
whose whole life is nothing else but action ; with only this difference
from other mens, that as what is but a Play to them, is his Business :
so their business is but a play to him.

Now for the difference betwixt our Theaters and those of former
times, they were but plain and simple, with no other Scenes, nòr
Decorations of the Stage, but onely old Tapestry, and the Stage
strew'd with Rushes (with their Habits accordingly) whereas ours
now for cost and ornament are arriv'd at the heighth of Magnificence.
. . . For Scenes and Machines they are no new invention, our Masks
and some of our Playes in former times (though not so ordinary)
having had as good or rather better then any we have now.

ii.

[Extracts from *Historia Histrionica : an Historical Account of the English
Stage, shewing the Ancient Use, Improvement, and Perfection of Dramatick
Representations in this Nation. In a Dialogue of Plays and Players* (1699).
A facsimile reprint was issued by E. W. Ashbee in 1872. The text is also
given in Dodsley[4], xv. I use, with a correction, the modernized text of
A. Lang, *Social England Illustrated* (1903, Arber, *English Garner*[2]), 422.
The *Historia Histrionica* is ascribed to James Wright, an antiquary and
play-collector (1643-1713), who can only have recorded what he learnt
from others. He is, of course, writing primarily of the Caroline, rather
than the Elizabethan or Jacobean period.]

Truman. I say, the actors that I have seen, before the Wars, Lowin,
Taylor, Pollard, and some others, were almost as far beyond Hart
and his company ; as those were, beyond these now in being. . . .

Lovewit. Pray, Sir, what master-parts can you remember the old

' Blackfriars ' men to act, in Johnson's, Shakespeare's, and Fletcher's plays ?

Truman. What I can at present recollect I'll tell you. Shakespeare (who, as I have heard, was a much better Poet than Player), Burbage, Hemmings, and others of the older sort, were dead before I knew the Town. But, in my time, before the Wars ; Lowin used to act, with mighty applause, Falstaff ; Morose ; Vulpone ; and Mammon in the *Alchemist* ; Melancius in the *Maid's tragedy*. And at the same time, Amyntor was played by Stephen Hammerton : who was, at first, a most noted and beautiful Woman-Actor ; but afterwards he acted, with equal grace and applause, a young lover's part.

Taylor acted Hamlet incomparably well ; Jago ; Truewit, in the *Silent Woman* ; and Face, in the *Alchemist*.

Swanston used to play Othello.

Pollard and Robinson were Comedians. So was Shank ; who used to act Sir Roger in the *Scornful Lady*. These were of the ' Blackfriars '. . . .

Truman. Before the Wars, there were in being, all these Play Houses at the same time.

> The ' Blackfriars ' and ' Globe ' on the Bankside. A winter, and summer house belonging to the same Company ; called ' The King's Servants '.
>
> The ' Cockpit ' or ' Phoenix ' in Drury Lane ; called ' The Queen's Servants '.
>
> The Private House in Salisbury Court ; called ' The Prince's Servants '.
>
> The ' Fortune ' near White Cross Street : and the ' Red Bull ' at the upper end of St. John's Street. The two last were mostly frequented by citizens, and the meaner sort of people.

All these Companies got money, and lived in reputation : especially those of the ' Blackfriars ', who were men of grave and sober behaviour.

Lovewit. Which I much admire at. That the Town, much less than at present, could then maintain Five Companies ; and yet now Two can hardly subsist.

Truman. Do not wonder, but consider ! That though the Town was then, perhaps, not much more than half so populous as now ; yet then the prices were small (there being no scenes), and better order kept among the company that came : which made very good people think a play an innocent diversion for an idle hour or two ; the plays being then, for the most part, more instructive and moral. . . . It is an argument of the worth of the Plays and Actors of the last Age, and easily inferred that they were much beyond ours in this, to consider that they could support themselves merely from their own merit, the weight of the matter, and goodness of the action ; without scenes and machines. . . .

Lovewit. I have read of one Edward Alleyn. . . . Was he one of the ' Blackfriars ' ?

Truman. Never, as I have heard ; for he was dead before my time. He was Master of a Company of his own ; for whom he built the 'Fortune' playhouse from the ground : a large round brick building. . . .

Lovewit. What kind of Playhouses had they before the Wars ?

Truman. The 'Blackfriars', 'Cockpit', and 'Salisbury Court' were called Private Houses ; and were very small to what we see now. The 'Cockpit' was standing since the Restoration ; and Rhodes's Company acted there for some time.

Lovewit. I have seen that.

Truman. Then you have seen the other two, in effect ; for they were all three built almost exactly alike, for form and bigness. Here they had 'Pits' for the gentry, and acted by candlelight.

The 'Globe', 'Fortune', and 'Bull' were large houses, and lay partly open to the weather : and there they always acted by daylight. . . .

Truman. Plays were frequently acted by Choristers and Singing Boys ; and several of our old Comedies have printed in the title-page, Acted by the Children of Paul's (not the School, but the Church) ; others, By the Children of Her Majesty's Chapel. In particular, *Cynthia's Revels* and the *Poetaster* were played by them ; who were, at that time, famous for good action. . . . Some of the Chapel Boys, when they grew men, became Actors at the 'Blackfriars'. Such were Nathan Field and John Underwood.

iii.

[Extracts from John Downes, *Roscius Anglicanus, or, an Historical Review of the Stage* (1708), reprinted by Joseph Knight (1886). An earlier reprint is in F. G. Waldron, *Literary Museum* (1792). Downes became prompter to the Duke of York's men under Sir William Davenant at Lincoln's Inn Fields in 1662.]

In the Reign of King *Charles* the First, there were Six Play Houses allow'd in Town : The *Black-Fryars* Company, His Majesty's Servants ; The Bull in St. *John's-street* ; another in *Salisbury Court* ; another call'd the *Fortune* ; another at the *Globe* ; and the Sixth at the Cock-Pit in *Drury-Lane* ; all which continu'd Acting till the beginning of the said Civil Wars. The scattered Remnant of several of these Houses, upon King *Charles's* Restoration, Fram'd a Company who Acted again at the Bull, and Built them a New House in *Gibbon's Tennis Court* in *Clare-Market* ; in which Two Places they continu'd Acting all 1660, 1661, 1662 and part of 1663. In this time they Built them a New Theatre in *Drury Lane.* . . .

Sir *William* [Davenant] in order to prepare Plays to Open his Theatre, it being then a Building in *Lincoln's-Inn Fields,* His Company Rehearsed the First and Second Part of the Siege of *Rhodes* ; and the Wits at *Pothecaries-Hall* : And in Spring 1662, Open'd his House with the said Plays, having new Scenes and Decorations, being the first that e're were Introduc'd in *England*.

APPENDIX K

ACADEMIC PLAYS

[The academic drama only lies on the fringe of my subject, but I have included notes on extant English plays in chapters xxiii and xxiv, and give below, for the sake of convenience, a list of these, and another of those Latin plays which there is any positive evidence for assigning to the period 1558–1616 and to English authorship. Fuller treatment will be found in G. B. Churchill and W. Keller, *Die lateinischen Universitäts-Dramen in der Zeit der Königin Elisabeth* (1898, *Jahrbuch*, xxxiv. 220); G. C. Moore Smith, *Notes on Some English University Plays* (1908, *M. L. R.* iii. 141), and *Plays performed in Cambridge Colleges before 1583* (1909, *Fasciculus J. W. Clark dicatus*, 265); L. B. Morgan, *The Latin University Drama* (1911, *Jahrbuch*, xlvii. 69); and F. S. Boas, *University Plays* (1910, *C. H.* vi. 293, with full bibliography), and *University Drama in the Tudor Age* (1914). Further material from Cambridge archives is in preparation by G. C. Moore Smith. In addition to the plays given in this list, some are incorporated in the description of *The Christmas Prince* (cf. ch. xxiv, s.a. 1607–8.]

ENGLISH PLAYS

Albumazar.
By T. Tomkis.

Antipoe.
By F. Verney.

Birth of Hercules.
Anon.

Caesar's Revenge.
Anon.

Claudius Tiberius Nero.
Anon.

Club Law.
Anon.

Lingua.
By T. Tomkis.

Narcissus.
Anon.

1, 2, 3 Parnassus.
Anon.

Queen's Arcadia.
By S. Daniel.

Ruff, Cuff and Band.
Anon.

Sicelides.
By P. Fletcher.

Timon
Anon.

Work for Cutlers.
Anon.

LATIN PLAYS

Adelphe.
By S. Brooke (q.v.).

Atalanta.
Harl. MS. 6924, with dedication to Laud, President of St. John's, Oxford, 1611–21, signed by Philip Parsons, of St. John's, B.A. 1614, M.A. 1618.

Bellum Grammaticale.
S. R. 1634, April 17. ' A booke called Bellum grammaticale &c by Master Spense ', authorized by Herbert. *John Spenser* (Arber, iv. 317).

1635. Bellum Grammaticale sive Nominum Verborumque discordia civilis Tragico-Comoedia. Summo cum applausu olim apud Oxonienses in Scaenam producta et nunc in omnium illorum qui ad Grammaticam animos appellant oblectamentum edita. *B. A. and T. Fawcet, impensis Joh. Spenceri.*
Editions of 1658, 1698, 1718, 1726, 1729, and in J. Bolte (1908, *Andrea Guarnas B. G. und seine Nachahmungen,* 106).
A performance was given before Elizabeth at Ch. Ch., Oxford, on 24 Sept. 1592, with a prologue and epilogue by Gager, which are printed with his *Meleager.* But the play was not new, for Sir John Harington, who records the 1592 performance in his *Metamorphosis of Ajax* (1596), 127, had already named ' the Oxford Bellum Grammaticale ' as ' full of harmeles myrth ' in his *Apologie of Poetrie* (1591). The ' Master Spense ' of the S. R. entry may be a confusion with the publisher's name. Wood, *Ath. Oxon.* ii. 533, was told by Richard Gardiner of Ch. Ch. that the author was Leonard Hutten, who took his B.A. from Ch. Ch. in 1578, and his M.A. in 1582. He was known as a dramatist by 26 Sept. 1583, when Gager wrote of him (Boas, 256),

> Seu scribenda siet Comoedia, seu sit agenda,
> Primum Huttone potes sumere iure locum.

The source was the Latin prose narrative *Bellum Grammaticale* (1511) of Andrea Guarna. Ralph Radclif (*c.* 1538) seems to have also treated the theme, but not necessarily in dramatic form (*Mediaeval Stage,* ii. 197).

Britanniae Primitiae, sive S. Albanus Protomartyr (*c.* 1600).
Bodl. Rawl. Poet. MS. 215. The Bodleian Catalogue dates the MS. *c.* 1600. The play, described in *Jahrbuch,* xlvii. 75, is a fragment only, probably written in some Jesuit seminary on the Continent, but with an English interest. There seems to be nothing specifically English in the theme of *Sanguis Sanguinem sive Constans Fratricida Tragoedia,* which is in the same MS.

Caesar Interfectus (*c.* March 1582).
Epilogue of a play by Richard Edes (q.v.) at Ch. Ch., Oxford.

Dido (12 June 1583).
By W. Gager (q.v.).

Euribates Pseudomagus.
Camb. Emmanuel MS. 3. 1. 17. ' Authore M[r] Cruso Caii Colle: Cantabr.'
Aquila Cruso entered Gonville and Caius in 1610.

Fatum Vortigerni.
Lansd. MS. 723, f. 1. ' Fatum Vortigerni seu miserabilis vita et exitus Vortigerni regis Britanniae vna complectens aduentum Saxonum siue Anglorum in Britanniam.'
Keller puts the play at the end of the sixteenth century, and thinks it influenced by *Richard III.*

Fortunia (March 1615).
See s.v. *Susenbrotus.*

Herodes.
Camb. Univ. MS. Mm. I. 24, with dedication by William Golding-
ham, B.A. 1567 and Fellow of Trinity Hall 1571, to ' D. Thomae
Sackuilo, Equiti aurato, Domino de Buckhurst '. Sackville became
Lord Buckhurst 1567 and K.G. 1588.

Hispanus (March 1597).
Bodl. Douce MS. 234, f. 15ᵛ. This was ' in diem comitialem anno
domini 1596 ', and the actor-list is composed of members of St. John's,
Cambridge (Boas, 398). The MS. has the note ' Summus histrio-
didascalus Mr. Pratt ' and a possible indication of authorship in
the mutilated name ' orrell ', which may stand for Roger Morrell,
Fellow of St. John's.

Hymenaeus (March 1579).
St. John's Cambridge MS. S. 45 ; *Caius Cambridge MS. 62.*
Edition by G. C. Moore Smith (1908).
The actor-list agrees closely with that of Legge's *Ricardus III,* and
points to St. John's, Cambridge, in 1579 (Boas, 393). The source is
Boccaccio's *Decamerone,* which suggests the possible authorship of
A. Fraunce (q.v.), who used the *Decamerone* for his contemporary
Victoria.

Ignoramus (8 March 1615).
By G. Ruggle (q.v.).

Labyrinthus (March 1603 ?).
By W. Hawkesworth (q.v.).

Laelia (1 March 1595).
Lambeth MS. 838.
Edition by G. C. Moore Smith (1910).—*Dissertation*: G. C. Moore
Smith, *The Cambridge Play ' Laelia '* (1911, *M. L. R.* vi. 382).
The production is assigned by Fuller, *Hist. of Cambridge* (ed.
Nichols), 217, to a visit by the Earl of Essex to Cambridge as
Chancellor of the University in 1597–8. Moore Smith has, however,
shown that it almost certainly belongs to an earlier visit, and took
place at Queens' College on 1 March 1595. The chief evidence is the
reference in Rowland Whyte's account of the *Device* by Essex or
Bacon (q.v.) for 17 Nov. 1595 to ' Giraldy ' and ' Pedantiq ', as played
at Cambridge. These may fairly be taken to be the Gerardus and
the pedant Petrus of *Laelia.* The actors of these two parts are
identified with George Meriton and George Mountaine, Fellows of
Queens', by John Weever, *Epigrammes* (1599), iv. 19.

> Your entertaine (nor can I passe away)
> Of Essex with farre-famed Laelia ;
> Nor fore the Queen your service on Queens day.

Conceivably this may also attribute authorship of the play and the
device. The play is an adaptation of the Italian *Gl' Ingannati* (*c.* 1531)

through *Les Abusez* (1543) of Charles Estienne. It is possible that, directly or indirectly, it influenced *Twelfth Night*.

Leander (March 1598).
  By W. Hawkesworth (q.v.).

Machiavellus (1597).
  Bodl. Douce MS. 234, f. 40ᵛ, dated ' Anno Dmni 1597, Decemb. 9 '.
A note in Douce's hand assigns the authorship to [Nathaniel] Wiburne, who, like the other actors, was of St. John's, Cambridge, in 1597 (Boas, 398).

Melanthe (1615).
  By S. Brooke (q.v.).

Meleager (Feb. 1582)
  By W. Gager (q.v.).

Nero (1603).
  By M. Gwynne (q.v.).

Oedipus.
  By W. Gager (q.v.).

Panniculus Hippolyto Assutus (8 Feb. 1592).
  By W. Gager (q.v.).

Parthenia.
  Emmanuel, Cambridge, MS. 1. 3. 16. Greg, *Pastoral Poetry and Pastoral Drama*, 368, thinks the handwriting later than 1600.

Pastor Fidus (> 1605).
  Cambridge Univ. Libr. MS. Ff. ii. 9. ' Il pastor fido, di signor Guarini . . . recitata in Collegio Regali Cantabrigiae ', with *Prologus* and *Argumentum. T.C.C. MS.* R. 3. 37.
  Greg, *Pastoral*, 247, points out that this must be the ' Fidus Pastor, which was sometimes acted by King's College men in Cambridge ', out of which a contemporary observer thought that Daniel's *Queen's Arcadia* (q.v.) was drawn. It is a translation of Guarini's *Il Pastor Fido* (1590).

Pedantius (1581).
  Caius College, Cambridge, MS. 62. ' Paedantius comoedia acta in collegio Sanctae et individuae Trinitatis authore Mʳᵒ Forcet.'
  T.C.C. MS. R. 17 (9).
  S.R. 1631, Feb. 9. ' A Comedy in Lattyn called Pedantius ', authorized by Austen. *Milborne* (Arber, iv. 248).
  1631. Pedantius Comoedia, Olim Cantabrig. Acta in Coll. Trin. Nunquam antehac Typis evulgata. *W. S. Impensis Roberti Mylbourne.*
  [Engravings of Dromodotus and Pedantius. Introductory lines, ' Pedantius de Se '. The title-page has an engraved border dated 1583, already used for W. Alexander's *Monarchicke Tragedies* (1616).]
  Edition by G. C. Moore Smith (1905, *Materialien*, viii).
  The introductory line, ' Ante quater denos vixi Pedantius annos ',

suggests production in 1591, but the play cannot have been very recent when Sir John Harington, in a note to his translation of *Orlando Furioso* (1591), Bk. xiv, cited a ' pretie conceit ' of ' our Cambridge Comedie Pedantius (at whiche I remember the noble Earle of Essex that now is, was present) '. In his *Apologie of Poetrie*, pre-fixed to the translation, Harington also says (G. Smith, *Elizabethan Critical Essays*, ii. 210), ' How full of harmeles myrth is our Cambridge *Pedantius* ? and the Oxford *Bellum Grammaticale* ? ' Harington, who again cites ' our *Pedantius* of Cambridge ' in his *Metamorphosis of Ajax* (1596), 126, was with Essex at Cambridge during 1578–81, and Moore Smith has shown that the production at Trinity was probably on 6 Feb. 1581, shortly before the defeat of Gabriel Harvey by Anthony Wingfield of Trinity for the Public Oratorship of Cambridge. There can be little doubt that Harvey was the butt of *Pedantius*, and hardly more that Wingfield was concerned in this satire. Nashe has two allusions to the matter. In *Strange News* (1593) he says that Harvey's verses were ' miserably flouted at in M. *Winkfields* Comoedie of *Pedantius* in Trinitie Colledge ' (*Works*, i. 303). In *Have With You to Saffron-Walden* (1596) he says, ' Ile fetch him aloft in Pedantius, that exquisite Comedie in Trinitie Colledge ; where, vnder the cheife part, from which it tooke his name, as namely the concise and firking finicaldo fine School-master, hee was full drawen & delineated from the soale of the foote to the crowne of his head ', and goes on to enumerate the principal traits of Harvey touched off by the actors, who ' borrowed his gowne to playe the Part in, the more to flout him ' (*Works*, iii. 80). So far, we are left a little uncertain whether the main authorship is to be ascribed, with Nashe in *Strange News*, to Anthony Wingfield, or, with the *Caius MS.*, to Edward Forsett, both of whom were Fellows of Trinity in 1581. Moore Smith has, however, shown in *T. L. S.* (10 Oct. 1918) that Forsett refers to ' Pedantio meo ' in the epistle to an unprinted *Concio* of his among the MSS. of St. John's, Cambridge. For an absurd attempt to assign the authorship to Bacon, largely on the ground of some non-existent pigs in the title-page border, cf. E. A. [E. G. Harman], *The Shakespeare Problem* (1909), and *T. L. S.* (27 March, 17 April, 1 May, 1919). Modern ascriptions to Thomas Beard and to Walter Hawkesworth seem to rest on misunderstandings.

Perfidus Hetruscus.
Bodl. Rawlinson MS. C. 787.

Physiponomachia (1609–11).
Bodl. MS. 27639.
Dedicated to John Buckeridge, President of St. John's, Oxford, 1605–11, by Christopher Wren, father of the architect, who took his B.A. from St. John's in 1609.

Psyche et Filii Ejus.
Bodl. Rawl. Poet. MS. 171, f. 60.
This is a Jesuit play, on the heresy of England.

Lugentis Angliae faciem dum Poeta pingeret.

Moore Smith (*M. L. R.* iii. 143), who is responsible for the title, thinks that it was written at the seminary of Valladolid, perhaps in Elizabeth's reign.

Richardus Tertius (March 1580).
By T. Legge (q.v.).

Romeus et Julietta (*c.* 1615).
Sloane MS. 1775, f. 242.
According to H. de W. Fuller in *M. P.* iv (1906), 41, this is a fragment based on A. Brooke's *Romeus and Juliet*, probably a student's exercise, with corrections. It is datable by two poems in the same hand on the royal visit to Cambridge in 1615.

Roxana (*c.* 1592).
By W. Alabaster (q.v.).

Sapientia Solomonis (1565–6).
Addl. MS. 20061. ' Sapientia Solomonis : Drama Comicotragicum.'
This is an expanded version of the *Sapientia Solomonis* of Sixt Birck (1555). A performance is recorded at Trinity, Cambridge, in 1559–60 (Boas, 21, 387), but the prologue and epilogue to this version make it clear that it was acted before Elizabeth and the *inclita princeps Cecilia*, i.e. Cecilia of Sweden, who was in England during 1565–6 (cf. ch. i), by a

> puellorum cohors
> Nutrita magnificis tuis e sumptibus.

These were the Westminster boys, who gave the play in 1565–6 (cf. ch. xii). The elaborately bound and decorated MS. bears Elizabeth's initials in several places, and was evidently the ' book ' officially provided for her.

Scyros (3 March 1613).
By S. Brooke (q.v.).

Silvanus (13 Jan. 1597).
Bodl. Douce MS. 234. ' Acta haec fabula 13º Januarii an. dmi. 1596.'
The actor-list belongs to St. John's, Cambridge, and is headed by the name of [Francis] Rollinson, whose authorship has been unjustifiably assumed.

Solymannidae (5 March 1582).
Lansd. MS. 723. ' Solymannidae, Tragoedia . . . 1581 Martii 5º.'

Susenbrotus or *Foriunia* (March 1615).
Bodl. Rawl. Poet. MS. 195, f. 79. ' Susenbrotus Comoedia. Acta Cantabrigiae in Collegio Trin. coram Rege Jacobo & Carolo principe Anno 1615.'
Bridgewater MS. ' Fortunia.'
The accounts of the royal visit of 7–11 March 1615 do not mention the play, and the date of this visit would be ' 1614 '. It may be the unnamed play given by Cambridge men, not at Cambridge, but at Royston in March 1616 ; the actors are ' extra Lyceum ', cf. ch. iv.

Tomumbeius (> 1603).
  Bodl. Rawl. Poet. MS. 75. 'Tomumbeius siue Sultanici in Aegypto Imperii Euersio. Tragoedia noua auctore Georgio Salterno Bristoënsi.'
  Nothing is known of George Salterne, and a dedication to Elizabeth is hardly sufficient to indicate a production before her at Bristol during the progress of 1574.
Ulysses Redux (5 Feb. 1592).
  By W. Gager (q.v.).
Vertumnus (29 Aug. 1605).
  By M. Gwynne (q.v.).
Victoria (*c.* 1580–3).
  By A. Fraunce (q.v.).
Zelotypus (1606).
  Emmanuel, Cambridge, MS. 3. 1. 17 ; *T. C. C. MS.* R. 3, 9.
  The actor-list points to St. John's, Cambridge, in 1606.

APPENDIX L

PRINTED PLAYS

[*Preliminary Note.*—This is a chronological abstract of plays, printed or entered for printing in the Stationers' Register, of which either the entry or the possible date of production falls in 1558–1616. Some of the later plays are only included in deference to the conjectures of others as to their early origin in whole or in part. The list is little more than an index ; details must be sought in chh. xxiii and xxiv. I think it is nearly self-explanatory. The plays marked T. in col. 1 are those of which the first entry in the Register is in connexion with a transfer of copyright ; the name in col. 4 is then that of the transferrer. Titles of non-extant plays are marked with inverted commas in col. 3 ; some of them (cf. App. M) may not really relate to plays at all. The symbol (s) in col. 6 is used where the imprint indicates, not that a play is printed ' for ' a stationer, but that it is ' to be sold by ' a stationer ; it is not quite clear how far the two formulae are equivalent. The most important notes in col. 7 are those in italics, which indicate direct evidence afforded by the entry or first title-page as to companies by which the plays had been acted. I have added from other sources additional ascriptions which seem certain or reasonably probable, and sometimes omitted even title-page evidence where it obviously relates to production by a company of later origin than 1616. The notes in col. 8 must not be taken as attributions of authorship, but merely as guides to the relevant sections in ch. xxiii or to ch. xxiv. The brackets in this column indicate that the plays, being pre-Elizabethan, are dealt with in App. X of *The Mediaeval Stage.* Some statistics, based on this list, of the output of plays from the Elizabethan press, will be found in ch. xxii.]

Date of Entry. (1)	Date of Print. (2)	Title. (3)	Enterer. (4)	Printer. (5)	Publisher. (6)	Source. (7)	Author. (8)
1557–8	N.D.	Wealth and Health	J. Walley	[No imprint]			[Anon.]
1557–8	N.D.	Youth	J. Walley	J. Walley			[Anon.]
1557–8	1568	Jacob and Esau	H. Sutton	Bynneman			[Anon.]
1558–9	1559	Troas	Tottel	Tottel		Transl.	Seneca.
	1560, Mar. 26	Thyestes		Powell ?		Transl.	Seneca.
1560, June 10	1560	Nice Wanton	King	King			[Anon.]
1560, June 10	N.D.	Impatient Poverty	King	King			[Anon.]
1560, Aug. 14	N.D.	Lusty Juventus	Copland	Copland			[Wever.]
1560, Oct. 30 ?	N.D.	Robin Hood	Copland	Copland			Anon.
	N.D.	Enough is as Good as a Feast	Hacket	J. Allde			W. Wager.
		'Witless'					[Heywood.]
1560–1	1561	Godly Queen Hester	Pickering	⎱ Pickering			[Anon.]
1560–1	N.D.	Free Will		⎰ Hacket		Transl.	Cheke.
1561, May 11	1561	Hercules Furens	Tisdale	Tisdale		Transl.	Seneca.
		'Two Sins of King David '		H. Sutton			[App. M.]
1561–2	1562	Three Laws	Hacket	Colwell			[Bale.]
1562–3	N.D.	Jack Juggler	Colwell	Copland			[Anon.]
1562–3	1575	Gammer Gurton's Needle	Copland	Colwell		Univ.	[Anon.]
1562–3	1661	Tom Tyler and his Wife	Colwell		Kirkman		Anon.
1562–3	1563, Apr. 28	Oedipus	Colwell	Colwell		Transl.	Seneca.
1562–3	N.D.	Weather	Colwell	Awdeley			[Heywood.]
[T. 1582, Jan. 15]	[t.p. lost]	Albion Knight (fragm.)	[Awdeley]				Anon.
1565–6	1565, Sept. 22	Gorboduc	Colwell	Griffith		Inner Temple	Norton.
1565–6	1565, Oct.	King Darius	Griffith	Colwell			Anon.
1565–6	1566	Agamemnon	Colwell	Colwell		Transl.	Seneca.
1565–6	[t.p. lost]	Cruel Debtor (fragm.)	Colwell	Colwell			W. Wager

S.R. Date	Date	Title	Printer(s)	Company	Author
1565–6	1566	Medea	Colwell; Colwell	Transl.	Seneca.
1565–6, 1568–9	N.D.	Patient Grissell	Colwell; Colwell		Phillip.
1566–7	N.D.	Octavia	Denham; Denham	Transl.	Seneca.
1566–7	1581	Hippolytus	T. Marsh; T. Marsh	Transl.	Seneca.
1566–7	1581	Hercules Oetaeus	{ Denham, Denham; Colwell	Transl.	Seneca.
1570–1	[t.p. lost]	Ralph Roister Doister	Colwell; Colwell		[Udall.]
1566–7	1566	'Far Fetched and Dear Bought is Good for Ladies'	Hacket; Hacket		[App. M.]
1566	1566	Repentance of Mary Magdalen	Charlwood; Charlwood		L. Wager.
1566–7		'College of Canonical Clerks'	Charlwood; Charlwood		[App. M.]
	1567	Trial of Treasure	Purfoot		Anon.
	1567	Orestes	Griffith		Pickering.
	1571	Damon and Pithias	R. Jones; R. Jones	Chapel	Edwardes.
	1575	Apius and Virginia	Howe; R. Jones		Anon.
	1568	Like Will to Like	J. Allde; J. Allde		Fulwell.
	[1578 ?]	'Susanna'	Colwell		T. Garter.
	N.D.	The Longer Thou Livest, the More Fool Thou Art	Howe; R. Jones		W. Wager.
[T. 1582, Jan. 15], 1569, Sept. 14		Four Ps	J. Allde; [Awdeley]		[Heywood.]
	N.D.	Disobedient Child	Colwell; Colwell		Ingelend.
	N.D.	Marriage of Wit and Science	T. Marsh; T. Marsh		Anon.
	N.D.	Cambyses	J. Allde; J. Allde		Preston.
	1573	Supposes	Bynneman; R. Smith	Gray's Inn	Gascoigne.
	1573	Jocasta	Bynneman; R. Smith	Gray's Inn	Gascoigne.
	1573	New Custom	Howe; Veale		Anon.
	1575	Glass of Government	Middleton; Barker		Gascoigne.
	N.D.	Minds	[No imprint]	Transl.	Anon.

Date of Entry. (1)	Date of Print. (2)	Title. (3)	Enterer. (4)	Printer. (5)	Publisher. (6)	Source. (7)	Author. (8)
1576, July 26	N.D.	Common Conditions	Hunter	Howe	Hunter		Anon.
1576, Oct. 22	1576	Tide Tarrieth No Man	H. Jackson	H. Jackson			Wapull.
1577, Nov. 25	1578	All for Money	Ward	Ward and Mundee			Lupton.
	1577	Abraham's Sacrifice		Vautrollier		Transl.	Golding.
	1577	God's Promises		Charlwood	Peele		[Bale.]
1578, July 31	1578, Aug. 20	Promos and Cassandra	R. Jones	R. Jones			Whetstone.
1580–1	1581	Ten Tragedies	T. Marsh	T. Marsh		Transl.	Seneca.
1581, July 31	1581	Antigone	Wolf	Wolf		Transl.	Watson.
	1581	Conflict of Conscience		Bradock			Woodes.
1584, Apr. 6	1584	Sapho and Phao	Cadman	Dawson	Cadman	Chapel, Paul's	Lyly.
1584, Nov. 12	1585	Fedele and Fortunio	Hacket		Hacket	Transl.	Anon.
	1584	Arraignment of Paris		H. Marsh		Chapel	Peele.
	1584	Three Ladies of London		Ward			Wilson.
[T. 1597, Apr. 12] 1585, Apr. 1	1584	Campaspe	[Cadman] Cawood	Charlwood	Cadman	Chapel, Paul's	Lyly.
1591, Oct. 4	1592	Galathea	J. Broome	Charlwood	J. Broome	Paul's	Lyly.
	1587 [8]	Misfortunes of Arthur		Robinson		Gray's Inn	Hughes.
	1588	Andria		East	Woodcock	Transl.	Kyffin.
	1589	Rare Triumphs of Love and Fortune		E. A.	E. White	Derby's ?	Anon.
1590, July 31	1590	Three Lords and Three Ladies of London	R. Jones	R. Jones		Queen's ?	Wilson.
1590, Aug. 14	1590	1, 2 Tamburlaine	R. Jones	R. Jones		Admiral's	Marlowe.
1591, Feb. 9	1591	Phillis and Amyntas	Ponsonby	T. Orwin	Ponsonby	Transl.	Fraunce.
1591, July 26	1591	'Hunting of Cupid'	R. Jones				Peele.
1591, Oct. 4	1591	Endymion	J. Broome	Charlwood	J. Broome	Paul's	Lyly.
1591, Oct. 4	1592	Midas	J. Broome	Scarlet	J. Broome	Paul's	Lyly.
	1591	Tancred and Gismund		Scarlet	Robinson (s)	Inner Temple	Wilmot.

S.R. Date	Date	Play	Entered	Printer	Publisher	Auspices	Author
	1591	1, 2 Troublesome Reign of King John		[T. Orwin]	Clarke	Queen's	Anon.
1592, Apr. 3	1592	Arden of Feversham	E. White	E. Allde	E. White		Anon.
1592, May 3	1592	Antonius	Ponsonby		Ponsonby	Transl.	Herbert.
1592, Oct. 6	N.D.	Spanish Tragedy	Jeffes	E. Allde	E. White	Strange's ?	Kyd.
1592, Nov. 20	N.D.	Soliman and Perseda	E. White		E. White		Anon.
[Oxford]	1592	Ulysses Redux		Joseph Barnes		Univ.	Gager.
[Oxford]	1592	Meleager / Panniculus Hippolyto assutus		Joseph Barnes		Univ.	Gager.
1593, July 6	1594	Edward II	W. Jones		W. Jones	Pembroke's	Marlowe.
1593, Oct. 8	1593	Edward I	Jeffes	Jeffes	Barley (s)		Peele.
1593, Oct. 19	1593	Cleopatra	S. Waterson	Roberts and E. Allde	S. Waterson	Closet	Daniel.
1593, Oct. 23	1593	Jack Straw	Danter	Danter	Barley (s)		Anon.
1593, Dec. 7	1594	Orlando Furioso	Danter	Danter	Burby	Queen's / Admiral's / Strange's	Greene.
1594, Jan. 7	1594	Knack to Know a Knave	R. Jones	R. Jones		Strange's	Anon.
1594, Jan. 26	1594	Cornelia	Ling and Busby	Roberts	Ling and Busby	Transl.	Kyd.
1594, Feb. 6	1594	Titus Andronicus	Danter	Danter	E. White (s) and Millington (s)	Derby's / Pembroke's / Sussex's	Shakespeare.
1594, Mar. 5	1594	Looking Glass for London and England	Creede	Creede	Barley (s)	Queen's ? / Strange's	Greene.
1594, Mar. 12	1594	1 Contention of York and Lancaster	Millington	Creede	Millington	Pembroke's ?	Anon.
1594, May 2	1594	Taming of A Shrew	Short	Short	Burby (s)	Pembroke's	Anon.
1594, May 13	1595	Pedlar's Prophecy	Creede	Creede	Barley (s)		Anon.
1594, May 14	1598	Famous Victories of Henry V	Creede	Creede		Queen's	Anon.

DATE OF ENTRY. (1)	DATE OF PRINT. (2)	TITLE. (3)	ENTERER. (4)	PRINTER. (5)	PUBLISHER. (6)	SOURCE. (7)	AUTHOR. (8)
1594, May 14	1598	James IV	Creede	Creede		Queen's ? / Strange's	Greene.
1594, May 14	1594	Friar Bacon and Friar Bungay	Islip		E. White	Sussex's	Greene.
1594, May 14 / 1605, May 8	1605	King Leir	Islip / Stafford	Stafford	J. Wright	Queen's	Anon.
1594, May 14		'John of Gaunt'	E. White				[App. M.]
1594, May 14	1599	David and Bethsabe	Islip	Islip			Peele.
1594, May 14		'Robin Hood and Little John'	Islip			Sussex's	[App. M.]
1594, May 17 / 1632, Nov. 20	1633	Jew of Malta	Ling and Millington. / Vavasour	I. B.	Vavasour	Strange's / Sussex's / Admiral's	Marlowe.
1594, May 24	1594	Wounds of Civil War	Danter	Danter	Burby		Lodge.
1594, June 8	1594	Cobbler's Prophecy	Burby	Danter	Barley (s)		Wilson.
1594, June 10	1595	Menaechmi	Creede	Creede	Burby	Transl.	Warner.
1594, June 18	1594	Mother Bombie	Burby	Scarlet		Paul's	Lyly.
1594, June 19	1615	Four Prentices of London	Danter		I. W.	Admiral's ? / Anne's	Heywood.
1594, June 19		'Heliogabilus'	Danter				[App. M.]
1594, June 19	1594	True Tragedy of Richard III	Creede	Creede	Barley (s)	Queen's	Anon.
1594, July 20	1595	Locrine	Creede	Creede	T. N. and I. W.		Anon.
N.D.		Fair Em			Bankworth	Strange's	Anon.
[T. 1600, June 26 ?]	1594	Battle of Alcazar		E. Allde		Admiral's	Peele.
1595, Apr. 1	1594	Selimus		Creede	Blackwall	Queen's	Anon.
	1594	Wars of Cyrus		E. A.	Woodcock	Chapel	Anon.
	1594	Dido	[Lynley]	J. Orwin	Burby	Chapel	Marlowe.
	1599	George a Greene	Burby	Stafford		Sussex's	Anon.

Date	Title	Entered	Printer	Publisher	Company	Author
1595, Apr. 16	Old Wive's Tale	Hancock	Danter	Hancock (s) and Hardy (s)	*Queen's*	Peele.
1595, May 10	'Ninus and Semiramis'	Hardy				[App. M.]
1595, May 23 / 1600, Mar. 31	'Valentine and Orson'	T. Gosson and Hancock. W. White			*Queen's*	[App. M.]
1595, Sept. 22	Woman in the Moon	Finch		W. Jones	*Admiral's?*	Lyly.
1595, Nov. 24	'Rufus I'	Blackwell				[App. M.]
1595, Nov. 26	Knack to Know an Honest Man	Burby		Burby	*Admiral's*	Anon.
1595, Dec. 1	Edward III	Burby		Burby	*Chamberlain's?*	Anon.
[T. 1602, Apr. 19]	True Tragedy of Richard Duke of York	[Millington]	P. S.	Millington	*Pembroke's*	Anon.
1596, Jan. 20	'1 Chinon of England' [?]	Gosson and Danter				[App. M.]
	'Eunuchus'	Linley			Transl.	Kyffyn
1597, Apr. 21	Richard II	Wise	Simmes	Wise	*Chamberlain's*	Shakespeare.
1597, Aug. 29	Richard III	Wise	Simmes	Wise	*Chamberlain's*	Shakespeare.
1597, Oct. 20 / [T. 1607, Jan. 22]	Romeo and Juliet	[Burby]	Danter		*Hunsdon's*	Shakespeare.
1598, Feb. 25	1 Henry IV	Wise	P. S.	Wise	*Chamberlain's*	Shakespeare.
1598, July 22	Merchant of Venice	Roberts	Roberts	Hayes	*Chamberlain's*	Shakespeare.
1598, Aug. 15	Blind Beggar of Alexandria	W. Jones		W. Jones	*Admiral's*	Chapman.
1598, Oct. 5	'Celestina'	Aspley				[App. M.]
1598, Oct. 5	Virtuous Octavia	Ponsonby		Ponsonby	Closet	Brandon.
[T. 1607, Jan. 22]	Love's Labour's Lost	[Burby]	W. W.	Burby	*Chamberlain's*	Shakespeare.
[T. 1618, Sept. 17]	Mucedorus	[S. Jones]		W. Jones		Anon.
1598 [Cambridge]	Adelphi / Andria / Eunuchus / Heautontimoroumenos / Hecyra / Phormio		Legatt	Legatt	Transl.	Bernard.

Date of Entry. (1)	Date of Print. (2)	Title. (3)	Enterer. (4)	Printer. (5)	Publisher. (6)	Source. (7)	Author. (8)
1599, Aug. 28	1600	1, 2 Edward IV	Oxenbridge and Busby	F. K.	H. Lownes and Oxenbridge	*Derby's*	Anon.
1599, Nov. 17	1599	Warning for Fair Women	Aspley	Simmes	Aspley	*Chamberlain's*	Anon.
	1599	Humourous Day's Mirth		Simmes		*Admiral's*	Chapman.
	1599	Two Angry Women of Abingdon			Hunt and Ferbrand	*Admiral's*	Porter.
	1599	Clyomon and Clamydes		Creede		*Queen's*	Anon.
	1599	Alphonsus		Creede			Greene.
1600, Feb. 20	1600	Old Fortunatus	Aspley	S. S.	Aspley	*Admiral's*	Dekker.
1600, Mar. 28	1603	Patient Grissell	Burby		Rocket	*Admiral's*	Dekker.
1600, Apr. 8	1600	Every Man Out of His Humour	Holme		Ling	Chamberlain's	Jonson.
1600, May 27		'Cloth Breeches and Velvet Hose'	Roberts			*Chamberlain's*	
1600, May 29	1602	A Larum for London	Roberts	Creede	Ferbrand	*Chamberlain's*	Anon.
1600, July 24	1600	Maid's Metamorphosis	Oliffe		Oliffe	*Paul's*	Anon.
1600, July 24		'Give a Man Luck, and Throw Him into the Sea'	Oliffe				
[Stayed 1600, Aug. 4]	[1623]	As You Like It				*Chamberlain's*	Shakespeare.
[Stayed 1600, Aug. 4]	1600	Henry V	[?]	Creede	Millington and Busby (sen.)	*Chamberlain's*	Shakespeare.
[T. 1600, Aug. 14] [Stayed 1600, Aug. 4] 1600, Aug. 14	1601	Every Man In His Humour	Burby and Burre		Burre	*Chamberlain's*	Jonson.

	Year	Play				Company	Author
{ [Stayed 1600, Aug. 4] / 1600, Aug. 23 }	1600	Much Ado About Nothing	{ Wise and Aspley }	V. S.	{ Wise and Aspley }	*Chamberlain's*	Shakespeare.
1600, Aug. 11	1600	{ 1 Sir John Oldcastle / ' 2 Sir John Oldcastle ' }	Pavier	V. S.	Pavier	*Admiral's*	Drayton.
1600, Aug. 11	1605	Captain Thomas Stukeley	Pavier		Pavier	{ *Admiral's* ?	Anon.
1600, Aug. 14		' Tartarian Cripple, Emperor of Constantinople '	Burby			}	[App. M.]
1600, Aug. 23	1600	2 Henry IV	{ Wise and Aspley }	V. S.	{ Wise and Aspley }	*Chamberlain's*	Shakespeare.
1600, Sept. 8	1601	Jack Drum's Entertainment	F. Norton		Oliffe	*Paul's*	Anon.
1600, Oct. 7	1600	Wisdom of Dr. Dodipoll	Oliffe	Creede	Oliffe	*Paul's*	Anon.
1600, Oct. 8	1600	Midsummer Night's Dream	Fisher	Creede	Fisher	*Chamberlain's*	Shakespeare.
1600, Oct. 23	1600	Weakest Goeth to the Wall	Oliffe		Oliffe	*Oxford's*	Anon.
1600, Oct. 28	1600	Summer's Last Will and Testament	{ Burby and Burre }	Stafford	{ Burby and Burre }	*Private*	Nashe.
1600, Nov. 25	1601	Love's Metamorphosis	Wood		Wood	*Paul's, Chapel*	Lyly.
1600, Dec. 1	1601	1, 2 Robert Earl of Huntingdon	Leake		Leake	*Admiral's*	Munday.
[T. 1610, Apr. 19]	1600	Look About You	[Simmes]	Ferbrand		*Admiral's*	Anon.
1601, Jan. 7	1600	Shoemaker's Holiday	Bushell	Simmes		*Admiral's*	Dekker.
1601, Mar. 1	1604	Dr. Faustus	John Harrison	V. S.	Bushell	*Admiral's*	Marlowe.
1601, May 23	1601	' God Speed the Plough '	Burre				[App. M.]
1601, July 3	1601	Cynthia's Revels	E. Allde		Burre	*Chapel*	Jonson.
1601, Aug. 3		' George Scanderbarge '	W. White	W. White		*Oxford's*	[App. M.]
1601, Sept. 16	1616	Englishmen for my Money	W. White			*Admiral's*	Haughton.
	1602	Pastor Fido	S. Waterson		S. Waterson	Transl.	Anon.
1601, Oct. 24	1602	1, 2 Antonio and Mellida	{ M. Lownes and Fisher }		{ M. Lownes and Fisher. / Fisher }	*Paul's*	Marston.
1601, Nov. 11	1602	Satiromastix	John Barnes		E. White	{ *Chamberlain's* / *Paul's* }	Dekker.
1601, Dec. 21	1602	Poetaster	M. Lownes		M. Lownes	*Chapel*	Jonson.

Date of Entry. (1)	Date of Print. (2)	Title. (3)	Enterer. (4)	Printer. (5)	Publisher. (6)	Source. (7)	Author. (8)
1602, Jan. 18	1601	Two Lamentable Tragedies	Busby (sen.)	T. C.	Lawe	Admiral's ?	Yarington.
1602, June 7	1602	Merry Wives of Windsor			A. Johnson	Chamberlain's	Shakespeare.
	1602	Blurt Master Constable	E. Allde		Rocket	Paul's	Middleton.
1602, July 26	1603	Hamlet	Roberts	[Simmes]	Ling and Trundle	King's	Shakespeare.
1602, Aug. 11	1602	Thomas Lord Cromwell	Cotton	Stafford	W. Jones	Chamberlain's	Anon.
	1602	Liberality and Prodigality			Vincent	Chapel ?	Anon.
	1602	How a Man may Choose a Good Wife from a Bad			Lawe	Worcester's	Anon.
[Edinburgh]	1602	Satire of the Three Estaitis		Charteris			[Lindsay.]
1603, Feb. 7 / 1609, Jan. 28	1609	Troilus and Cressida	Roberts. Bonian and Walley	Eld	Bonian and Walley	King's	Shakespeare.
1603, Feb. 23	[t.p. impf.]	Nero	Blount		Blount	Univ.	Gwynne.
[Edinburgh]	1603	Darius		Waldegrave		Closet	Alexander.
[Edinburgh]	1603	Philotus		Charteris			Anon.
	N.D.	Massacre at Paris		E. A.	E. White	Strange's / Admiral's	Marlowe.
1604, Apr. 30	1604 / 1607 / 1607	Croesus / Alexandraean / Julius Caesar	Blount	Simmes	Blount	Closet	Alexander.
1604, July 5	1604	Malcontent	Aspley and Thorpe	V. S.	Aspley	Revels, King's	Marston.
1604, Nov. 2	1605	Sejanus	Blount	Eld	Thorpe	King's	Jonson.
1604, Nov. 9	1604	1 Honest Whore	T. Man (jun.)	V. S.	Hodgets	Henry's	Dekker.
1604, Nov. 29	1605	Philotas	S. Waterson and Blount	Eld	S. Waterson and Blount	Revels	Daniel.
1604, Dec. 4	1605	Trial of Chivalry	Butter	Stafford	Butter	Derby's	Anon.
	1604	Wit of a Woman			E. White		Anon.
1605, Feb. 8		'Richard Whittington'	Pavier			Henry's	[App. M.]

Date	Year	Play	Entered to	Printer	Company	Publisher	Author
1605, Feb. 8	1605	Fair Maid of Bristow	Pavier		*King's*	Pavier	Anon.
1605, Feb. 12	1605	When You See Me, You Know Me	Butter		*Henry's*	Butter	S. Rowley.
1605, Mar. 2 [*cancelled*]	1607	Westward Ho	Rocket		*Paul's*	Hodgets (s)	Dekker.
1605, June 26	1605	Dutch Courtesan	Hodgets	T. P.	*Revels*	Hodgets	Marston.
1605, July 5	1605	1 If You Know Not Me, You Know Nobody	Butter		Anne's ?	Butter	Heywood.
1605, Sept. 4	1605	Eastward Ho	{ Aspley and Thorpe }		*Revels*	Aspley	Chapman.
1605, Sept. 14	1606	2 If You Know Not Me, You Know Nobody	Butter		Anne's ?	Butter	Heywood.
1605, Oct. 16	1606	3 Parnassus	J. Wright	Eld	Univ.	J. Wright	Anon.
1605, Nov. 26	1606	Queen's Arcadia	S. Waterson	Eld	Univ.	S. Waterson	Daniel.
1605, Nov. 26	1606	Gentleman Usher	Simmes	Simmes	Chapel ?	Thorpe	Chapman.
	1605	All Fools			*Revels*	Thorpe	Chapman.
	1605	London Prodigal		T. C.	*King's*	Butter	Anon.
	1606	1 Jeronimo			Chamberlain's ?	Pavier	Anon.
1606, Jan. 10	N.D.	Sir Giles Goosecap	Blount	Windet	*Chapel*	Blount	Anon.
1606, Mar. 12	1606	Nobody and Somebody	Trundle		*Anne's*	Trundle	Anon.
1606, Mar. 12	1606	Fawn	Cotton	T. P.	*Revels, Paul's*	Cotton	Marston.
1606, Mar. 17	1606	Sophonisba	Edgar	Windet	*Revels*		Marston.
1606, May 13	1607	Fleir	{ Trundle and Busby }	F. B.	*Revels*	F. B. (s)	Sharpham.
1606, June 5	N.D.	Caesar's Revenge	{ J. Wright and Fosbrooke }	G. E.	Univ.	J. Wright	Anon.
1606, Nov. 12	1606	Wily Beguiled	C. Knight	H. L.	Paul's ?	C. Knight	Anon.
	1606	M. D'Olive		T. C.	*Revels*	Holmes	Chapman.
	1606	Isle of Gulls			*Revels*	Hodgets (s)	Day.
1607, Feb. 23	1607	Lingua	S. Waterson	Eld	Univ. ?	S. Waterson	Tomkis.
1607, Apr. 10	1607	Claudius Tiberius Nero	Burton		Univ. ?	Burton	Anon.

DATE OF ENTRY. (1)	DATE OF PRINT. (2)	TITLE. (3)	ENTERER. (4)	PRINTER. (5)	PUBLISHER. (6)	SOURCE. (7)	AUTHOR. (8)
1607, Apr. 20	1607	Whore of Babylon	{Butter and Trundle}		Butter	*Henry's*	Dekker.
1607, Apr. 24	1607	Fair Maid of the Exchange	Rocket	E. A.	Rocket		Anon.
1607, May 9	1607	Phoenix	Johnson		Johnson	*Paul's*	Middleton.
1607, May 15	1607	Michaelmas Term	Johnson		Johnson	*Paul's*	Middleton.
1607, May 20	1607	Woman Hater	{Edgar and R. Jackson}	R. R.	Hodgets (s)	*Paul's*	Beaumont.
1607, June 3	1607	Bussy D'Ambois	Aspley		Aspley	*Paul's*	Chapman.
1607, June 29	1607	Cupid's Whirligig	{Busby and Johnson}		Johnson (s)	*King's Revels*	Sharpham.
1607, June 29	1607	Travels of the Three English Brothers	J. Wright	E. Allde	J. Wright	*Anne's*	Day.
1607, July 31	1607	Miseries of Enforced Marriage	Vincent		Vincent	*King's*	Wilkins.
1607, Aug. 6	1607	Puritan	Eld	Eld		*Paul's*	Anon.
1607, Aug. 6	1607	Northward Ho	Eld	Eld		*Paul's*	Dekker.
1607, Aug. 6	1607	What You Will	Thorpe	Eld	Thorpe	Paul's ?	Marston.
1607, Oct. 7	1607	Revenger's Tragedy	Eld	Eld		*King's*	Anon.
1607, Oct. 7	1608	Trick to Catch the Old One	Eld	Eld		*Paul's*	Middleton.
1607, Oct. 12	1608	Family of Love	{Browne and Helme}		Helme	*King's Revels*	Middleton.
1607, Oct. 14		'Jesuits Comedy'	{E. Allde and Johnson}				[App. M.]
1607, Oct. 16	1607	Devil's Charter	J. Wright	G. E.	J. Wright	*King's*	Barnes.
1607, Oct. 22	1608	Merry Devil of Edmonton	Johnson	Ballard	Johnson	*King's*	Anon.
1607, Nov. 26	1608	King Lear	{Butter and Busby (sen.)}	[Okes]	Butter	*King's*	Shakespeare.
T. 1610, Oct. 3]	1607	Volpone	[Thorpe]		Thorpe	*King's*	Jonson.
	1607	Woman Killed with Kindness		W. Jaggard	Hodgets (s)	*Anne's*	Heywood.

Date	Title		Printer		Company	Author
1607, Mar. 22	Sir Thomas Wyatt		E. A.	T. Archer	*Anne's*	Dekker.
1607, Mar. 26	Vertumnus	Bonian	Okes	Blount	Univ.	Gwynne.
N.D.	Your Five Gallants	W. White		Bonian	*Revels*	Middleton.
1608, Mar. 28	'Adams Tragedy'	Moore				[App. M.]
1608, Apr. 12	Law Tricks	Helme		Moore	*Revels*	Day.
	Humour out of Breath			Helme	*King's Revels*	Day.
1608, Apr. 29 / 1630, June 29	2 Honest Whore	T. Man (jun.) / Butter	Eliz. Allde	Butter	Henry's	Dekker.
1608, May 2	Yorkshire Tragedy	Pavier	R. B.	Pavier	*King's*	Anon.
1608, May 20	Pericles	Blount		H. Gosson	*King's*	Shakespeare.
1608, May 20 / 1623, Nov. 8	Antony and Cleopatra	Blount. / Blount and I. Jaggard	W. Jaggard	W. Jaggard and Blount and Smethwick and Aspley	King's	Shakespeare.
1608, June 3	Rape of Lucrece	Busby and / Butter		Busby	*Anne's*	Heywood.
1608, June 5	Conspiracy and Tragedy of Byron	Thorpe	Eld	Thorpe	*Revels*	Chapman.
1608, Oct. 4	A Mad World, my Masters	Burre and Edgar		Burre	*Paul's*	Middleton.
1608, Oct. 6	Dumb Knight	Bache		Bache	*King's Revels*	Markham.
1608, Nov. 25	Mustapha	Butter	H. B.	Butter	Closet	Greville.
1609, Jan. 26 / July 20	The Case is Altered	H. Walley and / Bonian and / B. Sutton	Okes	B. Sutton	*Revels*	Jonson.
1609, Jan. 27	'Bonos Nochios'	Charlton				[App. M.]
1609, Jan. 27	'Craft upon Subtlety's Back'	Charlton				[App. M.]
1610, Mar. 10	Turk	Busby (jun.)	E. A.	Busby (jun.)	*King's Revels*	Mason.
1609	Every Woman in Her Humour		E. A.	Archer	King's Revels ?	Anon.

DATE OF ENTRY. (1)	DATE OF PRINT. (2)	TITLE. (3)	ENTERER. (4)	PRINTER. (5)	PUBLISHER. (6)	SOURCE. (7)	AUTHOR. (8)
1610, Sept. 20	1609	Two Maids of Moreclack	{ Browne and Busby (jun.) }		Archer	*King's Revels*	Armin.
	N.D.	Faithful Shepherdess		N. O.	{ Bonian and H. Walley }	Revels ?	Beaumont.
	{ 1612 ? / 1620 }	Epicoene		Stansby	Browne (s)	*Revels*	Jonson.
1610, Oct. 3	1612	Alchemist	Burre	Snodham	{ Burre / Stepney (s) }	King's	Jonson.
1610, Oct. 31	1610	Histriomastix	Thorpe		Thorpe	Paul's ?	Anon.
1610, Nov. 9	1611	Ram Alley	Wilson	Eld	Wilson	*King's Revels*	Barry.
1611, Sept. 14	1611	Atheist's Tragedy	Stepney		{ Stepney and Redmer }		Tourneur.
1611, Oct. 14	1611	Golden Age	Barrenger		Barrenger	*Anne's*	Heywood.
1611, Nov. 23	1612	Woman a Weathercock	Budge		Budge	*Revels*	Field.
[T. 1635, July 4]	1611	Catiline	[Burre]		Burre	King's	Jonson.
	1611	May Day			Browne	*Revels*	Chapman.
	1611	Roaring Girl			Archer		Dekker.
1612, Feb. 1	1612	Christian Turned Turk	Barrenger		Barrenger	*Henry's*	Daborne.
{ 1612, Feb. 15 / 1653, Sept. 9 }		'Nobleman'	{ Blount / Moseley }			King's	Tourneur.
1612, Feb. 15		'Twins' Tragedy'	Blount			King's	Niccols.
1612, Apr. 17	1612	Widow's Tears	Browne		Browne	*Revels*	Chapman.
1612, Apr. 17	1613	Revenge of Bussy	Hawkins	T. S.	Helme (s)	*Revels*	Chapman.
1612, Dec. 17	1613	Mariam		Creed	Hawkins	Closet	Carey.
	1612	White Devil		N. O.	Archer	*Anne's*	Webster.
	1612	If It Be not Good, the Devil is in It			{ I. T. Marchant (s) / Lightfoot (s) }	*Anne's*	Dekker.
	1613	Silver Age		Okes	Rand	Anne's	Heywood.
	1613	Brazen Age		Okes	R. Barnes	Anne's ?	Heywood.
	1613	Cynthia's Revenge					Stephens.

Year	S.R. Entry	Title	Entered to	Printer	Publisher	Company	Author
1613		Insatiate Countess		T. S.	Archer	*Revels*	Marston.
1613		Knight of the Burning Pestle			Burre	*Revels*	Beaumont.
1614	1614, May 23	Hog Hath Lost his Pearl	Redmer		Redmer	*Prentices*	Tailor.
1614		Greene's Tu Quoque			Trundle	*Anne's*	Cooke.
1615	1615, Jan. 13	Hymen's Triumph	Constable		Constable	*Somerset House*	Daniel.
1615	1615, Feb. 10	Ruff, Cuff, and Band	Partrich	Stansby	Partrich	*Univ.*	Anon.
1615	1615, Feb. 21	Valiant Welshman	R. Lownes	Purslowe	R. Lownes	*Charles's*	Anon.
1615, Mar. 27	[Cambridge]	Melanthe		Legge		*Univ.*	Brooke.
1630	{ 1615, Apr. 18 / 1630, July 20 }	Ignoramus	{ Burre. Edmondson and Spencer }	T. P.	I. S.	*Univ.*	Ruggle.
1615	1615, Apr. 24	Hector of Germany	Jos. Harrison	Creede	Jos. Harrison	*Prentices*	Smith.
1615	1615, Apr. 24	Cupid's Revenge	Jos. Harrison	Creede	Jos. Harrison	*Revels*	Beaumont.
1615	1615, Apr. 28	Albumazar	Okes	Okes	Burre	*Univ.*	Tomkis.
1615	1615, July 4	Work for Cutlers	Meighen	Creede	{ Meighen and T. Jones }	*Univ.*	Anon.
1616	1615, Aug. 14	Honest Lawyer	Redmer	Purslowe	Woodroffe	*Anne's*	Anon.
1616	1616, Mar. 19	Scornful Lady	Partrich		Partrich	*Revels*	Beaumont.
1619	1618, Aug. 7	A King and No King	Blount		Walkley	*King's*	Beaumont.
1618		Amends for Ladies		Eld	Walbancke	{ *Charles's* / *Elizabeth's* }	Field.
1619	1619, Apr. 28	Maid's Tragedy	{ Higgenbotham and Constable }		Constable	*King's*	Beaumont.
1620	1620, Jan. 10	Philaster	Walkley		Walkley	*King's*	Beaumont.
1622	1621, Oct. 6	Othello	Walkley	N. O.	Walkley	*King's*	Shakespeare.
1622		Virgin Martyr		B. A.	T. Jones		Dekker.
1621	1621, Dec. 7	Thierry and Theodoret	T. Jones		Walkley	*King's*	Beaumont.

Date of Entry. (1)	Date of Print. (2)	Title. (3)	Enterer. (4)	Printer. (5)	Publisher. (6)	Source. (7)	Author. (8)
1623, Nov. 8	1623	Tempest	{Blount and I. Jaggard}	[W. Jaggard] at charges of W. Jaggard and Blount and Smethwick and Aspley	{I. Jaggard and Blount}	King's	Shakespeare.
		Two Gentlemen of Verona					
		Measure for Measure					
		Comedy of Errors					
		[As You Like It]					
		All 's Well that Ends Well					
		Twelfth Night					
		Winter's Tale					
		1 Henry VI					
		Henry VIII					
		Coriolanus					
		Timon of Athens					
		Julius Caesar					
		Macbeth					
		[Anthony and Cleopatra]					
		Cymbeline					
1628, Jan. 9	1623	Duchess of Malfi	Blount	Okes	J. Waterson	*King's*	Webster.
1630, Feb. 26	1632	[Six Court Comedies]		Stansby	Blount		Lyly.
1630, Apr. 8	1631	Hoffman	J. Grove	I. N.	Perry	Henry's ?	Chettle.
	1630	Chaste Maid in Cheapside	Constable	{Alsop and Fawcet}	Constable	*Elizabeth's*	Middleton.
1630, Nov. 8	1631	Match Me in London	Seile		Seile		Dekker.
1631, Feb. 9	1631	Pedantius	Milborne	W. S.	Milborne	Univ.	[App. K.]
1631, Apr. 25	1631	Sicelides	Sheares	I. N.	Sheares	Univ.	P. Fletcher.
1631, May 16 ⎫ 1633, Dec. 9 ⎭	1634	Noble Soldier	{Jackman Vavasour}		Vavasour		Dekker.
1631, May 16 ⎫ 1636, Feb. 24 ⎭	1636	Wonder of a Kingdom	{Jackman Vavasour}	Raworth	Vavasour		Dekker.
1631, May 18	1631	Caesar and Pompey	Harper	Harper	{Emondson (s) Alchorne (s)}		Chapman.

1631, Nov. 24	1632	A New Wonder	Constable	G. P.	Constable	Anne's ?	W. Rowley.
	1631	Bartholomew Fair		I. B.	Allott	*Elizabeth's*	Jonson.
	1631	The Devil is an Ass		I. B.	Allott	*King's*	Jonson.
1632, May 9	1632	Roxana	Crooke	Badger	Crooke	Univ.	Alabaster.
1632, Nov. ŗo	1633	Alaham	Seile	E. P.	Seile	Closet	Greville.
	1632	1, 2 Iron Age		Okes		Anne's ?	Heywood.
1633, Jan. 15	1633	Match at Midnight	Sheares	Mathewes	Sheares		W. Rowley.
1634, Apr. 8	1634	Two Noble Kinsmen	J. Waterson	Cotes	J. Waterson	*King's*	Beaumont.
1634, Apr. 17	1635	Bellum Grammaticale	Spencer	{ B. A. and Fawcet }	Spencer	Univ.	[App. K.]
1635, July 17	1636	Labyrinthus	Robinson			Univ.	Hawkesworth.
1635, Aug. 29	1637	Pleasant Dialogues and Dramas	Hearne	R. O.	{ Hearne Slater (s) }	Closet	Heywood.
1637, Mar. 25	1637	Royal King and Loyal Subject	Becket	N. and J. Okes	Becket	*Henrietta's*	Heywood.
1637, Nov. 28	1638	A Shoemaker a Gentleman	J. Okes	J. Okes	Cooper (s)	Anne's ?	W. Rowley.
1638, Mar. 12	1638	Wise Woman of Hogsdon	Shephard	M. P.	Shephard	Anne's ?	Heywood.
1638, Oct. 24	1639	Chabot Admiral of France	{ Crooke and Cooke }	Cotes	{ Crooke and Cooke }	*Henrietta's*	Chapman.
1639, Jan. 22	1639	Monsieur Thomas	J. Waterson.	Harper	J. Waterson	*King's*	Beaumont.
1639, Apr. 25	1639	Wit Without Money	{ Crooke and Cooke }	Cotes	{ Crooke and Cooke }	*Henrietta's*	Beaumont.
1639, Apr. 25	1640	Nightwalker	{ Crooke and Cooke }	Cotes	{ Crooke and Cooke }	*Henrietta's*	Beaumont.
1641, Mar. 23	1641	Parliament of Bees	Ley		Ley	Closet	Day.
1646, Sept. 4 / 1661, Feb. 13	1661	Mayor of Quinborough	{ Robinson and Moseley, Herringham }		Herringham	*King's*	Middleton.
1646, Sept. 4	1647	Captain / Coxcomb / Bonduca / Woman's Prize / Love's Cure / Honest Man's Fortune / Valentinian	{ Robinson and Moseley }		{ Robinson and Moseley }	King's / Revels / King's / King's ? / King's ? / Elizabeth's / King's	Beaumont.

DATE OF ENTRY. (1)	DATE OF PRINT. (2)	TITLE. (3)	ENTERER. (4)	PRINTER. (5)	PUBLISHER. (6)	SOURCE. (7)	AUTHOR. (8)
1660, June 29	1647	Wit at Several Weapons / Four Plays in One	Robinson and Moseley		Robinson and Moseley		Beaumont.
1652, Apr. 12	1652	Widow	Moseley		Moseley	*King's*	Middleton.
1653, Sept 9	1654	Alphonsus, Emperor of Germany	Moseley		Moseley	*King's*	Anon.
		' Jew of Venice '					Dekker.
	1657	' History of Cardennio '			Moseley	King's	Shakespeare.
		No Wit, no Help, like a Woman's	Moseley				Middleton.
1653, Sept. 9	[1824–5]	Second Maiden's Tragedy					Anon.
		' Henry ye first '					Shakespeare.
		' Hen. ye 2d '					Shakespeare.
		' Knave in Print '					W. Rowley.
1654, Apr. 8		' Maidens Holiday '	Moseley			Charles's	Marlowe.
1654, May 13	1654	Appius and Virginia	Marriott		[*No imprint*]	Anne's ?	Webster.
1655, June 20	1655	Fortune by Land and Sea	Sweeting		Pollard and Sweeting	*Henrietta's*	Heywood.
1655, June 20	1655	Lovesick King	Sweeting		Pollard and Sweeting	Provincial ?	Brewer.
1655, June 20	1655	Poor Man's Comfort	Sweeting		Pollard and Sweeting		Daborne.
	1656	Old Law			E. Archer		Middleton.
	1656	Sun's Darling			Penneycuicke		Dekker.
1657, Sept. 14	1659	Blind Beggar of Bethnal Green	F. Grove	Bell	Pollard and Dring	Admiral's	Day.
	1657	Lust's Dominion			F. K. Pollard (s)		Marlowe.
1658, May 21	1658	Witch of Edmonton	Blackmore	Cottrel	Blackmore		Dekker.

Date	Title	Publisher	Printer	Author
[1812]	Faithful Friends	Moseley		Beaumont.
	'History of Madon King of Britain'			Beaumont.
	'Philenzo & Hypollita'			Dekker.
	'Antonio & Vallia'			Dekker.
1660, June 29	'History of King Stephen'			Shakespeare.
	'Duke Humphrey'	King's		Shakespeare.
	'Iphis & Iantha'			Ford.
	'An Ill Beginning has a Good End'			
	'London Merchant'			Ford.
	'Gustavus, King of Swethland'			Dekker.
	'Tale of Joconda and Astolso'			Dekker.
1661	Thracian Wonder		T. Johnson / Kirkman (s)	Anon.
1662	Birth of Merlin		T. Johnson / Kirkman and H. Marsh	W. Rowley.
1662	Grim the Collier of Croydon		R. D.	Anon.

APPENDIX M

LOST PLAYS

[*Bibliographical Note*.—As unknown prints have turned up in the sale of an Irish collection (1907) and the Mostyn sale (1919), and others may yet turn up from time to time, I give a list of plays as to the existence or preparation for publication of which there is some evidence. These are mainly taken either from the Stationers' Register or from the publishers' advertisement lists (Rogers and Ley's in 1656, Archer's in 1656, Kirkman's in 1661 and 1671), analysed by W. W. Greg in an appendix to his *Masques* (1902). One is included in Sir John Harington's catalogue of his library of plays apparently compiled in 1610 (cf. ch. xxii). Probably some of the registered titles, in which the description ' play ' or ' interlude ' is not used, do not relate to plays at all. I might have added a few more of this type from A. Esdaile, *List of English Tales and Romances* (1912, *Bibl. Soc.*), xxxiii. And it must be borne in mind that registration is not proof of publication. In particular, it is pretty clear that the two long series of entries by Humphrey Moseley on 9 Sept. 1653 and 29 June 1660, from which I have taken those conceivably relating to pre-1616 work, represent unaccomplished enterprises. They are fully discussed in W. W. Greg, *The Bakings of Betsy* (1911, *3 Library*, ii. 225), together with John Warburton's (*ob.* 1759) list in *Lansd. MS.* 807, f. 1, of plays which he claims to have possessed in MS., until ' through my own carelessness and the ignorance of my ser[vant] in whose hands I had lodgd them they was unluckely burnd or put under Pye bottoms '. As this list is evidently in some way related to Moseley's entries, I have, for the sake of completeness, cited a few titles which it adds.]

A Bad Beginning Makes a Good Ending.
By Ford (q.v.).

Adam's Tragedy.
S. R. 1608, March 26 (Pasfield). ' A book called Adams tragedie.' *W. White* (Arber, iii. 372).
This is not likely to have been a play.

Antonio and Vallia.
By Massinger (q.v.).

Baggs Seneca.
See ch. xxiii (Seneca).

Bartholomew Fairing.
Comedy in Archer's list as well as Jonson's *B. Fair*.

Battle of Affliction.
Tragedy in Archer's list.

Belinus.
Brennus.
Sir John Harington's catalogue of his plays in 1610 (7 *N. Q.* ix. 382) includes ' Belynus, Brennus '. This might represent either two plays or one.

Bonos Nochios.

S. R. 1609, Jan. 27 (Segar). ' An enterlude called Bonos Nochios.' *Charlton* (Arber, iii. 400).

Cardenio.

Ascribed to Shakespeare (q.v.) and Fletcher.

Celestina.

S. R. 1598, Oct. 5. ' A booke intituled The tragicke Comedye of Celestina, wherein are discoursed in most pleasant stile manye Philosophicall sentences and advertisementes verye necessarye for younge gentlemen Discoveringe the sleightes of treacherous servantes and the subtile cariages of filthye bawdes.' *William Aspley* (Arber, iii. 127).

This was doubtless, like the earlier *Calisto and Meliboea* (*Mediaeval Stage*, ii. 455) and James Mabbe's *The Spanish Bawd* (1631), a version of the Spanish *Celestina* (1499) of Fernando de Rojas, but it can hardly have been Mabbe's, which was entered in S. R. on 27 Feb. 1630, while Mabbe, although born in 1572, is first heard of as a writer in 1611, and appears to have turned his attention to things Spanish as a result of a visit to Spain in that year.

1 Chinon of England.

S. R. 1596, Jan. 20. ' The ffirste parte of the famous historye of Chinan of England.' *T. Gosson and Danter* (Arber, iii. 57).

The Admiral's produced ' Chinone of Ingland ' as a new play on 3 Jan. 1596. Greg, ii. 178, is probably right in relating the S. R. entry to Christopher Middleton's romance, *The Famous Historie of Chinon of England*, printed by Danter for Cuthbert Burby in 1597. But ' Chinon of England ' is in Rogers and Ley's list.

Cleopatra.

An unascribed ' Cleopatra ', in addition to the plays of Daniel (q.v.) and May, is in Rogers and Ley's list.

Cloth Breeches and Velvet Hose.

S. R. 1600, May 27. ' A morall of Clothe breches and veluet hose, As yt is acted by my lord Chamberlens servantes.' *Roberts* (Arber, iii. 161).

This is one of the plays stayed by a note in the Register on the same day (cf. ch. xxii).

College of Canonical Clerks.

S. R. 1566-7. ' An interlude named the Colledge of canonycall clerkes.' *John Charlewod* (Arber, i. 335).

Craft Upon Subtlety's Back.

S. R. 1609, Jan. 27 (Segar). ' An enterlude called, Crafte vppon Subtiltyes backe.' *Charlton* (Arber, iii. 400).

Crafty Cromwell.

A tragi-comedy in Kirkman's list of 1661. Greg, *Masques*, lx, thinks it may be a duplicate entry of *Cromwell's Conspiracy* (1660).

Destruction of Jerusalem.

By Legge (q.v.).

Duke Humphrey.
Ascribed to Shakespeare (q.v.).

English Arcadia.
A comedy in Archer's list, but probably, as suggested by Greg, *Masques*, lxv, an error for Gervase Markham's romance (1607, 1613) of that name.

Eunuchus.
By Kyffyn (q.v.) ?

Faithful Friends.
Ascribed to Beaumont (q.v.) and Fletcher.

Far Fetched and Dear Bought is Good for Ladies.
S. R. 1566–7. 'A playe intituled farre fetched and deare bowght ys good for lades.' *Thomas Hackett* (Arber, i. 331).

Fatal Love.
Ascribed to Chapman (q.v.).

Fortune.
S. R. 1566–7. 'A playe of Fortune to know eche one hyr condicions and gentle manours aswell of Women as of men &c.' *Thomas Purfoote* (Arber, i. 332).
Collier, *Stationers' Registers*, i. 155, suggested that this was a 'lottery, or game', not an interlude, and this receives support from a transfer of his father's copies to Purfoot's son on 6 Nov. 1615 (Arber, iii. 576), which includes 'The little booke of Fortune with pictures'.

George Scanderbeg.
S. R. 1601, July 3. 'The true historye of George Scanderbarge as yt was lately playd by the right honorable the Earle of Oxenforde his servantes.' *E. Allde* (Arber, iii. 187).
There seems no adequate reason for ascribing this to Marlowe (q.v.) or Nashe.

Give a Man Luck and Throw him into the Sea.
S. R. 1600, July 24. 'Two plaies or thinges . . . the other gyve a man luck and throw him into the sea.' *Oliffe* (Arber, iii. 168).

Godfrey of Bulloigne.
See Heywood, *Four Prentices of London.*

God Speed the Plough.
S. R. 1601, March 1. 'A booke called God spede the ploughe.' *Harrison* (Arber, iii. 180).
This is not necessarily the play acted by Sussex's men for Henslowe in Dec. 1593 (ch. xiii), or indeed a play at all.

Guise.
Entered in Rogers and Ley's list as by Marston (q.v.), in Archer's as a comedy by Webster (q.v.), and in Kirkman's of 1661 and 1671 without ascription ; that of 1671 calls it a tragedy.

Gustavus, King of Swethland.
Ascribed to Dekker (q.v.).

Heliogabalus.
 S. R. 1594, June 19. ' An . . . enterlude of the lyfe and deathe of Heliogabilus.' *Danter* (Arber, ii. 654).
 Can this be the play on ' the mad priest of the Sun ' apparently referred to by Greene (q.v.) in *Perimides* (1588) ?

Hemidos and Thelay.
 S. R. 1569-70. ' A boke intituled the Rufful tragedy of Hemidos and Thelay by Rychard Robynson.' *Henry Bynneman* (Arber, i. 411).
 Probably not a play.

Henry I.
Henry II.
 Both ascribed to Shakespeare (q.v.).

Hunting of Cupid.
 By Peele (q.v.).

Impatient Grissell.
 A comedy in Archer's list.

Iphis and Iantha.
 Ascribed to Shakespeare (q.v.).

The Jesuits' Comedy.
 S. R. 1607, Oct. 14 (Jackson). ' A book called the Jesuytes Comedie. Acted at Lyons in Fraunce the 7 and 8 of August 1607.' *Allde and Johnson* (Arber, iii. 361).
 Probably only a narrative of this famous performance ; cf. ch. x.

The Jew of Venice.
 Ascribed to Dekker (q.v.).

Job.
 Ascribed to Greene (q.v.).

Joconda and Astolso.
 Ascribed to Dekker (q.v.).

John of Gaunt.
 S. R. 1594, May 14. ' A booke entituled the famous historye of John of Gaunte sonne to Kinge Edward the Third with his Conquest of Spaine and marriage of his Twoo daughters to the Kinges of Castile and Portugale &c.' *E. White* (Arber, ii. 649).
 Probably not a play but the chap-book source of that begun by Hathway (q.v.) and Rankins for the Admiral's in 1601 (cf. Greg, *Henslowe*, ii. 216). Arber, v. 176, however, describes it as a play printed for White by Islip.

Joseph's Afflictions.
 An interlude in the lists of Archer and Kirkman.

A Knave in Print.
 By W. Rowley (q.v.).

The London Merchant.
 By Ford (q.v.).

Madon, King of Britain.
 Ascribed to Beaumont (q.v.).

The Maiden's Holiday.
Ascribed to Marlowe (q.v.) and Day.

Manhood and Misrule (?).
In Rogers and Ley's list; presumably identical with the comedy of *Manhood and Wisdom* in those of Archer and Kirkman.

The Second Maiden's Tragedy.
Extant in MS. (cf. ch. xxiv).

Marriage of Wit and Wisdom.
By Merbury (q.v.); extant in MS.

Mother Rumming.
A comedy in Archer's list. Greg, *Masques*, xc, suggests an error for T. Thompson's late *Mother Shipton*, which Archer omits. Elinor Rumming, however, might well have made a play-theme.

The Netherlands.
In Rogers and Ley's list.

Niniveh's Repentance.
An interlude in Rogers and Ley's and Archer's lists.

Ninus and Semiramis.
S. R. 1595, May 10. 'The tragedie of Ninus and Semiramis, the first Monarchs of the world.' *Hardy* (Arber, ii. 297).

The Nobleman.
By Tourneur (q.v.).

2 Sir John Oldcastle.
By Drayton (q.v.).

Ortenus.
Archer's list has both *Ortenas*, a tragedy, and *Ortenus*, a comedy.

The Owl.
By Daborne (q.v.).

Philenzo and Hippolyta.
By Massinger (q.v.).

The Queen.
A tragedy in Archer's list. Fletcher's name is given, but Greg, *Masques*, c, says this has 'crept in from another entry'.

Richard Whittington.
S. R. 1605, Feb. 8. 'The history of Richard Whittington of his lowe byrthe, his great fortune, as yt was plaid by the prynces servantes.' *Pavier* (Arber, iii. 282).
The play is referred to in *K. B. P.* ind. 22.

Robin Hood and Little John.
S. R. 1594, May 14. 'A booke entituled a pastorall plesant Commedie of Robin Hood and Little John.' *Islip* (Arber, ii. 649).
Arber, v. 176, describes the play as printed by Islip for E. White, to whom the copy was passed by a cancel. It appears in Rogers and Ley's and Archer's lists of 1656. Greg, *Henslowe*, ii. 190, finds an allusion to its 'merry jests' in Munday's *Downfall of Robin Hood*, iv. 2.

Rufus I.
S. R. 1595, Nov. 24. ' A booke intituled The true tragicall historie of kinge Rufus the First with the life and deathe of Belyn Dun the first thief that ever was hanged in England.' *W. Blackwell* (Arber, iii. 54).

Greg, *Henslowe*, ii. 164, thinks this the *Bellendon* played as a new piece by the Admiral's and Chamberlain's for Henslowe on 10 June 1594 (cf. ch. xiii). The title curiously resembles that of another book, probably, as Greg suggests, a chap-book, entered in S. R. by T. Gosson on 17 May 1594 as ' a book intituled The famous Cronicle of Henrye the First, with the life and death of Bellin Dunn the firste thief that ever was hanged in England ' (Arber, ii. 650). Perhaps this was the source of the play.

A Sackful of News.
S. R. 1557–8. ' These bokes folowynge called . . . a sacke full of newes.' *J. King* (Arber, i. 75).

1582, Jan. 15. Transfer from S. Awdeley to John Charlwood (Arber, ii. 405).

1586, Sept. 5. ' A sackfull of newes, beinge an old copie : whiche the said Edward is ordered to haue printed by Abell Jeffes.' *Edward White* (Arber, ii. 456).

This is less likely to have been the ' lewd ' play suppressed at the Boar's Head, Aldgate, in Aug. 1557 (*Mediaeval Stage*, ii. 223) than the jest-book known to Captain Cox in 1575 (F. J. Furnivall, *Laneham's Letter*, lxvi. 30) and printed from the earliest extant edition of 1673 by W. C. Hazlitt, *Old English Jest Books*, ii. 163.

King Stephen.
Ascribed to Shakespeare (q.v.).

Susanna.
By T. Garter (q.v.).

The Tartarian Cripple.
S. R. 1600, Aug. 14. ' The famous Tragicall history, of ye Tartarian Crippell Emperour of Constantinople.' *Burby* (Arber, iii. 169).
Not necessarily a play.

'Tis Good Sleeping in a Whole Skin.
By W. Wager (q.v.).

Tityrus and Galatea.
Possibly identical with Lyly's *Galathea* (q.v.).

The Twins' Tragedy.
By Niccolls (q.v.).

The Two Sins of King David.
S. R. 1561–2. ' An new interlude of the ij synmes of kynge Davyd.' *Hacket* (Arber, i. 181).

Valentine and Orson.
S. R. 1595, May 23. ' An enterlude of Valentyne and Orsson, plaid by her maiesties Players.' *T. Gosson and Hancock* (Arber, ii. 298).

1600, March 31 (in full court). 'A famous history called Valentine and Orsson played by her maiesties Players.' *W. White* (Arber, iii. 159).

The relation of this Queen's play to that written by Hathaway and Munday (q.v.) for the Admiral's in 1598 is uncertain.

Witless.

S. R. 1560–1. 'Playe of wytles.' *Hacket* (Arber, i. 154).

Probably John Heywood's dialogue of *Witty and Witless*, extant in MS. (*Mediaeval Stage*, ii. 446).

A Yorkshire Gentlewoman and her Son.

Ascribed to Chapman (q.v.).

APPENDIX N

MANUSCRIPT PLAYS

[*Bibliographical Note.*—This list includes only English texts. Most of the Latin plays (cf. App. K) also exist in MS. The English ones so preserved are generally of an academic type; on the general character of the few that are of play-house origin, cf. ch. xxii. Of the fifteen play texts collected in *Egerton MS.* 1994, only three appear to be of plays written before 1616; descriptions of this collection are in A. H. Bullen, *O. E. P.* ii. 417, and F. S. Boas, *A Seventeenth-Century Theatrical Repertoire* (*3 Library*, July 1917). In addition to the plays named below, there are a *Pelopidarum Secunda* in *Harleian MS.* 5110, which may be of any date in the first half of the seventeenth century, and a Welsh 'enterlut', dated 1584 and without ascription or title in *Peniarth MS.* 68 (*H. M. C. Welsh MSS.* i. 2. 467). A full account of the Plots ('plott', 'plotte', 'platt') is given, with the seven texts, by Greg, *Henslowe Papers*, 127. They nave sometimes been taken for '*scenarii*' of impromptu plays, like the Italian 'Commedie dell'arte', although one of them is for the extant *Battle of Alcazar*; but they were probably for the use of the 'bookholder' or the 'tireman', and consist of skeleton outlines of the action, with notes of entrances and exits, and of the points at which properties and music are required. The names of the dramatis personae are generally accompanied by those of the actors who represented them. The paper on which they are written is mounted on pasteboard, and a hole cut near the top probably served to suspend them on a peg in the playhouse. All seem probably belong to companies (Strange's and Admiral's) with which Edward Alleyn was connected. One was utilized for the cover of a Dulwich MS., and G. Steevens, who once owned three of the others, found 'reason to suppose that these curiosities once belonged to the collection of Alleyn'.]

PLAYS

Alaham (Greville). MS. at Warwick Castle.

Alice and Alexis. Bodl. MS. 21745 (Douce MS. 171).

Antipoe (Verney). Bodl. MS. 31041.

Aphrodysial (Percy). MS. formerly in collection of Duke of Devonshire.

Arabia Sitiens (Percy). Ibid.

Birth of Hercules. B.M. Addl. MS. 28722.
Bugbears (Jeffere). B.M. Lansdowne MS. 807.
Charlemagne. B.M. Egerton MS. 1994.
Club Law. St. John's College, Cambridge, MS. S. 62.
Cuck-Queans and Cuckolds Errant (Percy). MS. formerly in collection of Duke of Devonshire.
Cupid's Sacrifice (Percy). Ibid.
Faery Pastoral (Percy). Ibid.
Faithful Friends (Beaumont and Fletcher). Victoria and Albert Museum, Dyce MS. 10.
Gentleman Usher (Chapman). Alleged MS. in Heber collection.
Gismund of Salerne (Wilmot). B.M. Lansdowne MS. 786. B.M. Hargrave MS. 205. MS. in private collection, now unknown.
Hercules Oetaeus (Elizabeth). Bodl. MS. e Museo 55.
Honest Man's Fortune (Beaumont and Fletcher). Victoria and Albert Museum, Dyce MS. 9.
Hymen's Triumph (Daniel). Edinburgh University, Drummond MS.
Iphigeneia (Lumley). B.M. Royal MS. 15 A. ix.
Jocasta (Gascoigne). B.M. Addl. MS. 34063.
John a Kent and John a Cumber (Munday). MS. in collection of Lord Mostyn.
Judith. National Library of Wales, Peniarth MS. 508 (formerly Hengwrt MS.).
Love Feigned and Unfeigned. B.M. I. B. 2172.
Marriage Between Wit and Wisdom (Merbury). B.M. Addl. MS. 26782.
Massacre at Paris (Marlowe). Alleged fragmentary MS.
Mayor of Quinborough (Middleton). A late MS.
Meleager (argument). MS. formerly in possession of Mr. B. Dobell.
Misogonus (Johnson). Formerly in collection of Duke of Devonshire.
Monsieur d'Olive (Chapman). Alleged MS. in Heber Collection.
Sir Thomas More. B.M. Harleian MS. 7368.
Mustapha (Greville). MS. at Warwick Castle. Cambridge University Library MS. Ff. ii. 35.
Narcissus. Bodl. MS. 147303 (Rawlinson Poet. MS. 212).
Necromantes (Percy). MS. formerly in collection of Duke of Devonshire.
Nobleman (Tourneur). Alleged MS. in private collection at Oxford.
Oration of Gwgan and Poetry (Owen). National Library of Wales, Peniarth MS. 65.
Orlando Furioso (Greene). Dulwich MS. i. 138.
Parliament of Bees (Day). B.M. Lansdowne MS. 725.
Parnassus. Bodl. Rawlinson MS. D. 398. MS. formerly in collection of J. O. Halliwell-Phillipps.
Poor Man's Comfort (Daborne). B.M. Egerton MS. 1994.
1 Richard II. B.M. Egerton MS. 1994.
Ruff, Cuff, and Band. B.M. Addl. MS. 23723.
Second Maiden's Tragedy. B.M. Lansdowne MS. 807.
Sicelides (P. Fletcher) Bodl. Rawl. Poet. MS. 214. B.M. Addl. MS. 4453.

Timon.   Victoria and Albert Museum, Dyce MS. 52.
Volpone (Jonson).   MS. as yet unprinted.

PLOTS

Battle of Alcazar.   B.M. Addl. MS. 10449.
Dead Man's Fortune.   Ibid.
2 Fortune's Tennis.   Ibid.
Frederick and Basilea.   Ibid.
1 Tamar Cham.   MS. formerly in the collection of George Steevens,
not now known.
Troilus and Cressida.   B.M. Addl. MS. 10449.
2 Seven Deadly Sins.   Dulwich MS. xix.

MASKS

Ashby Entertainment (Marston).   B.M. Sloane MS. 848.   MS. at Bridge-
water House.
Mask of Blackness (Jonson).   B.M. Royal MS. 17 B. xxxi.
Mask of Queens (Jonson).   B.M. Royal MS. 18 A. xlv.   B.M. Harleian
MS. 6947.
Twelve Months.   MS. formerly in the collection of J. P. Collier, now
unknown.
Ulysses and Circe (Browne).   Cambridge, Emmanuel College MS. 68.
MS. in collection of Mr. H. C. Pole-Gell.

INDEXES

INDEXES

These indexes are selective, not exhaustive. That of *Plays* is, I hope, full. Classical and foreign plays, including plays given by English players abroad, but not Latin plays written in England, are printed in italics; plays not clearly extant in inverted commas. Translations and fragmentary texts are indicated by ' tr.' and ' fr.' respectively, and compositions not properly to be classed as plays are also noted. Duplicate titles which might cause confusion are distinguished by dates or authorship. References to the main notices, in vol. iii, pp. 201–518, and vol. iv, pp. 1–74, and occasionally elsewhere, of plays belonging or conjecturally assigned to the period 1558–1616 are printed in blacker type. Titles are shortened by the omission of such words as ' A ', ' The ', ' King ', and cross-references are only given from the better-known alternative titles. The index of *Persons* gives those connected with the Court and with stage affairs, other as a rule than the players and playwrights, who are alphabetically arranged in chh. xv and xxiii respectively. The index of *Places* includes, besides London localities, all those recorded in Appendix A as visited by Elizabeth, but not, unless for some special reason, those at which travelling players performed. In the index of *Subjects* inverted commas are used for technical terms and for ordinary objects as represented on the stage.

INDEX I: OF PLAYS

A

' A Bad Beginning Makes a Good Ending ', iii. 315 ; iv. 127, 180.
A Woman is a Weathercock, iii. **313**.
A Woman will have her Will. *See* Englishmen for my Money.
Abraham, iii. 322, 514.
' Abraham and Lot ', ii. 95.
Abraham Sacrifiant, i. 249 ; iii. 322.
Abraham's Sacrifice (tr.), iii. **322**.
' Absalom ' (1602), ii. 228.
Absalon (*c.* 1535), iii. 506 ; iv. 246.
' Abuses ', iv. 33.
' Adams Tragedie ', iv. **398**.
Adelphe, i. 131 ; iv. 127.
Adelphi (tr.), iii. **236**.
Aegio (fr.), iii. **209**.
' Aemilia ', i. 131.
' Aeneas and Dido ', iv. 122.
' Aesop's Crow ', ii. 83.
Agamemnon (tr.), iii. **477**.
' Agamemnon ', ii. 169.
' Agamemnon and Ulysses ', ii. 17, 101 ; iv. 101, 160.
Agarite, iii. 16.
' Ajax and Ulysses ', ii. 63 ; iv. 87, 146.

' Ajax Flagellifer ', i. 130, 233.
' Ajax Flagellifer ' (tr.), i. 127.
Alaham, iii. **331**.
Alarum for London, iv. **1**.
' Alba ', i. 130.
' Albere Galles ', ii. 227 ; iii. 341 ; iv. 37.
Albion Knight (fr.), iv. **1**.
Albumazar, i. 131 ; iii. **498**.
Alchemist, iii. 123, 222, 224, **371**, 499 ; iv. 119, 171.
' Alcmaeon ', ii. 15 ; iv. 89, 147.
' Alexander and Lodowick ', ii. 144, 167, 170.
Alexandraean Tragedy, iii. **209**.
' Alexius ', iv. 2.
' Alfonso ', iv. 2.
Alice and Alexis (fr.), iv. **2**.
' Alice Pierce ', ii. 132, 166.
All Fools, iii. 146, **252** ; iv. 119, 171.
' All Fools but the Fool '. *See* ' The World Runs on Wheels '.
All for Money, iii. 23, **411**.
' All is not Gold that Glisters ', ii. 178.
All is True. *See* Henry VIII.
All 's One. *See* Yorkshire Tragedy.

Blurt Master Constable, iii. 142, **439.**
' Bold Beauchamps ', iii. 347.
Bonduca, iii. **228.**
' Bonos Nochios ', iv. **399.**
' Boss of Billingsgate ', ii. 180.
' *Botzario ein Alt Römer* ', ii. 284.
' Bourbon ', ii. 132, 156, 167 ; iv. 50.
' Brandimer ', ii. 122.
' Branholt ', ii. 132, 166 ; iii. 230.
Brazen Age, iii. 109, **345.**
' Brennus ', iii. 183 ; iv. **398.**
Bristol Entertainment (1574). iv. **60.**
Bristol Entertainment (1613), iv. **74.**
' Bristol Tragedy ', ii. 179 ; iii. 304 ; iv. 12.
' Bristow Merchant ', iii. 304.
Britanniae Primitiae, iv. **374.**
' Brute Greenshield '. See ' Conquest of Brute '.
' Buckingham ', ii. 95, 130, 202, 217.
Bugbears, ii. 14 ; iii. 28, **351.**
Bussy D'Ambois, iii. 142, **253.**
' Byron ' (1602), ii. 228 ; iii. 258, 267.
Byron (1608). *See* Conspiracy and Tragedy.

C

Caesar and Pompey (Chapman), iii. **259.**
' Caesar and Pompey ' (*c.* 1582), ii. 394 ; iv. 216.
' 1, 2 Caesar and Pompey ' (1594–5), ii. 143–4 ; iii. 259.
Caesar and Pompey. *See* Caesar's Revenge.
' Caesar Interfectus ', iii. 309.
' Caesar's Fall, or, The Two Shapes ', ii. 179.
Caesar's Revenge, iv. **4.**
Calandra, iii. 9, 13.
Calisto and Melibaea, ii. 30 ; iv. 211, 399.
Calthrop Pageant, iii. **463.**
Cambyses, iii. 37, **470** ; iv. 6, 79.
Campaspe, ii. 17, 39 ; iii. 32, **413.**
Campbell, or, the Ironmongers' Fair Field (show), i. 137 ; iv. **72.**
Captain, iii. **226** ; iv. 127, 180.
' Captain Mario ', iv. 214.
Captain Thomas Stukeley. *See* Stukeley.
' Capture of Stuhl Weissenburg ', ii. 207, 367.
' Cardenio ', ii. 217 ; iii. **489** ; iv. 127, 128, 180.
' 1, 2 Cardinal Wolsey ', ii. 178 ; iii. 266.
' Cards ', i. 268 ; iii. 453 ; iv. 238.

' *Carolus Herzog aus Burgundt* ', ii. 284.
Casina, iii. **5.**
Cassaria, iii. 8, 11.
' Castle of Security ', i. 333.
' Catiline ' (1588), i. 222.
Catiline his Conspiracy (1611), iii. **372.**
' Catiline's Conspiracies ' (*c.* 1579), ii. 394 ; iv. 204.
' Catiline's Conspiracy ' (1598–9), ii. 163, 170.
Caversham Entertainment, iii. **244.**
Cecil House Entertainment, iii. **248.**
' Celestina ', iv. **399.**
' *Celinde und Sedea* ', ii. 284, 289.
Chabot, Admiral of France, iii. **259.**
Challenge at Tilt, iii. **393.**
' Chance Medley ', ii. 169.
Chapman's Mask, i. 173 ; iii. **260.**
' Charlemagne ' (*c.* 1589), iii. 260, 329 ; iv. 5.
Charlemagne (*c.* 1600), iii. 260 ; iv. **5.**
Chaste Maid in Cheapside, iii. **441.**
Chester's Triumph, iv. **71.**
' Chinon of England ', ii. 144 ; iv. **399.**
' *Christabella* ', ii. 286.
Christian Turned Turk, i. 328 ; iii. **271.**
' Christmas Comes but Once a Year ', ii. 227 ; iii. 267.
Christmas Prince (revels), iv. **71,** 228.
Christus Redivivus, iii. 31.
Chrysanaleia (show), i. 137 ; iii. **449.**
Chryso-Thriambos (show), i. 137 ; iii. **449.**
City Gallant. *See* Greene's Tu Quoque.
' 1, 2, 3 Civil Wars of France ', ii. 169 ; iii. 253.
Civitatis Amor (show), iii. **443.**
Claudius Tiberius Nero, iv. **5.**
' Cleopatra ' (Anon.), iv. **399.**
Cleopatra (Daniel), iii. **275.**
Cléôpâtre Captive, iii. 13.
' Cloridon and Radiamanta ', ii. 96 ; · iv. 87, 146.
' Clorys and Orgasto ', ii. 122.
' Cloth Breeches and Velvet Hose ', iv. **399.**
Club Law, iv. **5.**
Clyomon and Clamydes, ii. 286 ; iii. 39 ; iv. **6.**
' Cobler of Queenhithe ', ii. 168.
Cobler's Prophecy, iii. 35, **516** ; iv. 41.
Cockle de Moye. *See* Dutch Courtesan.

INDEX II: OF PERSONS

INDEX OF PERSONS

437

Monarcho, an Italian, i. 48.
Monmouth (title). *See* Carey.
Monox, William, iii. 326.
Monson, Sir Thomas, iii. 240.
Montague (title). *See* Browne.
Monteagle (title). *See* Parker.
Montgomery (title). *See* Herbert.
Montmorency, François, Duc de,
   French ambassador, i. 15, 80, 144,
   157, 162.
Moore, Edward, iv. 64.
Mordaunt, Henry, 4th Lord, iv. 120.
More, Christopher, clerk of ex-
   chequer, ii. 476.
More, Sir George, ii. 486, 503, 506 ;
   iv. 114, 117.
More, Sir William, i. 74, 95, 109 ;
   ii. 476–506 ; iv. 84, 93, 100, 106.
More. *See* Wolley.
Morgan, Meredith, iii. 387, 391.
Morice, Ralph, ii. 460.
Morison. *See* Radcliffe.
Morley, Thomas, musician, cor-
   rector of books, iii. 168, 212.
Morley (title). *See* Parker.
Morrell, Roger, iv. 375.
Moseley, Humphrey, iii. 183 ; iv.
   398.
Mountaine, George, iii. 212 ; iv. 375.
Mountford, Thomas, corrector of
   books, iii. 168.
Mountfort, Thomas, clerk to Sta-
   tioners, iii. 165.
Mountjoy (title). *See* Blount.
Munday, Anthony, on plays, i. 254 ;
   iv. 208.
Muretus, iii. 12.
Murgatroyd, Michael, corrector of
   books, iii. 168.
Murray, Sir James, iii. 254.

N

Najera, Duke of, ii. 454.
Nannoccio, Andrea, iii. 13.
Napton, John, ii. 451.
Nashe, Thomas, on plays, i. 260 ;
   iv. 234, 238.
Necton, William, surveyor of works,
   i. 95.
Needham, John, iii. 212, 402.
Nevers, Duc de, i. 6, 23, 170 ; iv. 15.
Neville, Henry, 3rd Lord Aberga-
   venny, ii. 92 ; iv. 89 ; his men,
   ii. 92.
Neville, Sir Henry, ii. 493.
Neville, Lady Mary, iii. 380.
Neville, Mrs., maid of honour, i. 169;
   iv. 67.
Newcastle (title). *See* Cavendish.
Newdigate, Nicholas, i. 87, 165–6.

Newman, John, ii. 496.
Newport. *See* Hatton, Herbert.
Newton, Katharine Lady, iv. 67.
Nicoll, Basil, ii. 335, 418, 425.
Nicoll, William, ii. 390.
Nidd, Gervas, corrector of books,
   iii. 168.
Nigri, Francesco, de Bassano, iii.
   263.
Niklaes, Henrick, iv. 31.
Noel, Henry, iii. 212, 402 ; iv. 64.
Norfolk (title). *See* Howard.
Norris, Sir Edward, iv. 114, 125.
Norris, Francis, 2nd Lord, after-
   wards Earl of Berkshire, iii. 394 ;
   iv. 127, 129.
Norris, Henry, 1st Lord, i. 112 ;
   iv. 66, 83, 85, 86, 92, 107.
Norris (b. Williams), Marjorie
   Lady, i. 112.
North, Dudley, 3rd Lord, iii. 245,
   246, 394.
North, Edward, 1st Lord, i. 10 ;
   iv. 77, 79.
North, Sir John, ii. 500.
North, Roger, 2nd Lord, treasurer
   of household, i. 35 ; ii. 113 ;
   iv. 95.
Northampton (title). *See* Howard,
   Parr.
Northbrooke, John, i. 253 ; on plays,
   iv. 198.
Northumberland (title). *See* Percy.
Norton, Thomas, city remem-
   brancer, on plays, i. 265, 282 ;
   iv. 273.
Nottingham (title). *See* Howard.
Nowell, Alexander, dean of St.
   Paul's, ii. 16, 70.

O

Offley, Hugh, i. 139 ; iv. 102.
Ogle, wigmaker, ii. 184 ; iv. 33.
Oldcastle, Sir John, i. 324.
Overbury, Sir Thomas, iv. 257.
Oxford (title). *See* Vere.

P

Page, William, clerk comptroller of
   tents and revels, i. 100.
Paget (b. Knollys), Lettice Lady,
   iv. 67.
Paget, Thomas, 3rd Lord, iv. 91.
Paget, William, 1st Lord, secretary
   of state, i. 275 ; iii. 399.
Paget. *See* Lee.
Pakenham, Edmund, clerk comptroller of tents and revels, i. 96,
   100.

INDEX III : OF PLACES

O

Oatlands (Surrey), i. 11, 12, 20;
iv. 77–115 *passim*, 116, 118, 121,
122, 128, 130.
Odiham (Hants), iv. 78, 84, 85, 90,
93, 106.
Olantigh (Kent), iv. 89.
Onehouse (Suffolk), iv. 95.
Orpington (Kent), iv. 89.
Oseburn (Sussex), iv. 106.
Osterley (Middlesex), i. 20, 139;
iii. 267; iv. 81, 82, 83, 86, 90,
91, 92, 94, 106, 108.
Otford (Kent), iv. 77, 89.
Oxenheath (Kent), iv. 89.
Oxford, i. 87, 116, 126, 128–30, 142,
227, 233, 250; ii. 40, 206; iv. 83,
85, 107, 120, 127, 129, 373–9;
plays at, ii. 2.

P

Peckham, West (Kent), iv. 89.
Pendley (Herts.), iv. 86.
Penrhyn (Cornwall), iv. 250, 253.
Pershore (Worcester), ii. 300.
Petworth (Sussex), i. 110, 111; iv.
100.
Philberds (Berks.), iv. 86, 88, 92,
114.
Plymouth (Devon), plays at, ii. 1.
Ponsbourne (Herts.), iv. 100.
Pontefract (Yorks.), iv. 116.
Portsmouth (Hants), iv. 78, 106.
Princes Risborough (Bucks.), iv. 81,
107.
Putney (Surrey), i. 20; iv. 94, 96,
97, 98, 99, 101, 102, 103, 104, 105,
108, 109, 110, 111, 112, 114, 115,
116.
Pyneste (Middlesex), iv. 108.
Pyrford (Surrey), iv. 92, 93, 94, 97,
99, 100, 117.
Pyrgo (Essex), iv. 79, 84, 93, 111.

Q

Quarrendon (Bucks.), iii. 398, 407.
Queenborough (Kent), iv. 79.

R

Ramsbury (Wilts.), iii. 337; iv. 107.
Reading (Berks.), i. 11, 13, 20;
iv. 85, 86, 88, 90, 93, 107, 114,
128, 151; plays at, ii. 2.
Rendcombe (Glos.), iv. 107.
Richmond (Surrey), i. 9, 13, 15;
iv. 77–116 *passim*, 121, 129.
Riddings (Bucks.), iv. 115.

Ridgmont (Beds.), iv. 86, 91.
Rochester (Kent), iv. 89, 98, 99,
121, 128, 129.
Rockingham (Northants), iv. 120.
Roding Abbess (Essex), iv. 87, 95.
Romford (Essex), iv. 84, 96.
Romsey (Hants), iv. 122.
Rookwood Hall (Essex), iv. 87, 95.
Rotherfield (Hants), iv. 78.
Rotherfield Greys (Oxon.), iv. 90, 93.
Royston (Cambs.), i. 13, 131; iv.
116, 129, 130, 378.
Ruckholt (Essex), i. 111; iv. 111,
118.
Rufford (Notts.), iv. 126, 129.
Rycote (Oxon.), i. 111, 125; iv. 66,
83, 85, 86, 92, 107, 127, 129.
Rye (Sussex), iv. 89.

S

Saffron Walden (Essex), iv. 87;
plays at, ii. 2.
St. Albans (Herts.), i. 13; iv. 81,
84, 93, 126, 348.
St. Osyth (Essex), iv. 79.
Salden (Bucks.), iv. 88, 117.
Salisbury (Wilts.), iv. 90, 117, 122,
123, 125, 128, 130.
Sandgate (Kent), iv. 89.
Sandwich (Kent), iv. 89, 98.
Sawbridgeworth (Herts.), iv. 95.
Scadbury (Kent), iii. 419; iv. 110.
Seale (Surrey), iv. 114.
Segenhoe (Beds.), iv. 86, 91.
Sempringham (Lincs.), iv. 83.
Seton (Haddington), iv. 116.
Shardeloes (Bucks.), iv. 81.
Shaw (Berks.), iv. 107, 117.
Sheen (Surrey), i. 9, 13; iv. 105.
Sheffield (Yorks.), ii. 301.
Shelley Hall (Suffolk), iv. 79.
Shenley (Herts.), iv. 83.
Sherborne (Glos.), iv. 90, 92, 107.
Sherborne St. John (Hants), iv. 85,
106.
Shrewsbury (Shropshire), iii. 110;
plays at, ii. 1.
Silchester (Hants), iv. 114.
Sion (Middlesex), iv. 92, 100, 102,
108, 116.
Sissinghurst (Kent), iv. 89.
Siston (Glos.), iv. 128.
Sittingbourne (Kent), iv. 98.
Smallbridge (Suffolk), iv. 79.
Smarden (Kent), iv. 89.
Soberton (Hants), iv. 85.
Somborne (Hants), iv. 90.
Somersham (Hunts.), iv. 118.
Southampton (Hants), i. 387; iv.
78, 85, 106, 117; plays at, ii. 1.

INDEX IV : OF SUBJECTS

Family of Love, iii. 440, 441 ; iv. 11, 16, 29.
' Fee lists ', i. 29.
Fees of household, i. 29, 50 ; of players, ii. 78, 83.
Fencing, i. 289, 305, 361 ; ii. 343, 380, 382, 404, 410, 413–14, 470, 499, 500, 529 ; iv. 54, 79, 121, 205, 206, 270, 277, 283, 289, 293, 294, 324, 337.
Ferrara, plays at, iii. 4, 8.
Finance of masks, i. 207–12.
Finance of stage. *See* Boxholders, Entrance fees, Fees of players, Gallery takings, Gatherers, Gratuity, Henslowe, Highway, Hospitals, Housekeepers, Pensions, Poor, Profits, Rewards, Sharers, Stock, Takings.
Fines of players, ii. 256.
Finestre (windows), iv. 360.
Fireworks, i. 123, 139 ; ii. 455 ; iv. 72, 73, 74, 88, 121, 122, 124, 127.
Flags on playhouses, ii. 546 ; iv. 219.
Folgore (lightning), iv. 365.
Folk-survivals in masks, i. 150.
Fools, at court, i. 48, 53 ; on stage, ii. 327, 339. *See* Clowns.
Foreshortening of space, iii. 25, 33, 37, 38, 41, 43, 50, 99, 117, 137, 150.
Forgeries, i. 59 ; ii. 79, 108, 159, 195, 207, 211, 229, 480, 496, 508, 510, 515 ; iii. 247, 252, 266–7, 274, 292, 421, 423, 425, 426, 428, 434, 459, 490, 512 ; iv. 1, 68, 136–41.
Fortune playhouse, ii. 435–43.
France, players in, ii. 292–4.
Free list, i. 361, 374 ; ii. 387, 406.
French players in England, iii. 19.
Front curtains, i. 231 ; iii. 10, 21, 30, 44, 79.

G

' Gag ', i. 322.
Galleries, of stage, ii. 534 ; iii. 45, 90–8, 119 ; of auditorium, ii. 514, 530–4, 555.
Gallery takings, i. 355 ; ii. 131, 139, 182, 239, 245, 249, 256, 388, 393, 412.
Galliards, i. 6, 198 ; iii. 234, 239, 241, 278, 280, 282, 378, 380, 383, 385, 390, 435 ; iv. 56, 57, 59, 115, 217.
Garden scenes, iii. 55.
Garderoba, i. 55.

Garter, i. 20, 139 ; ii. 61, 160.
Gatherers, i. 356, 371 ; ii. 150, 174, 187, 389, 392, 393, 406, 445, 538.
' Gatheryngs ', ii. 532 ; iii. 504.
Gelosi, ii. 262–3.
Geneva, history of plays at, i. 245.
Gentlemen of Chapel, ii. 24–30 ; iv. 150 ; of Privy Chamber, i. 43, 50.
Gentlemen Ushers of Chamber, i. 44–5, 50, 108, 205, 226.
Germany, players in, i. 342–7 ; ii. 272–92.
' Gests ' of progresses, i. 108 ; iv. 117, 120, 126.
' Get-penny ', i. 373.
' Ghost-names ', ii. 108, 312, 319 ; iii. 495.
Gifts in mask, i. 150, 160, 168, 196 ; iii. 278, 279, 282, 375, 435, 468 ; on progress, i. 113, 116, 125.
Globe playhouse, ii. 414–34.
' Good ' and ' bad ' Shakespearian quartos, iii. 185.
Gowry Day, i. 21.
Grades in household, i. 42.
Gradi (tiers of seats), iv. 355, 358.
Graphic dances, i. 199.
' Gratuity ' to players, i. 339.
Gray's Inn, i. 214, 222 ; iii. 233, 239, 320–1, 348 ; iv. 56, 59, 82, 109, 127, 143, 162.
Great Chamber, i. 13, 216.
Green Cloth, board of, i. 35.
Groom Porter of Chamber, i. 45, 100.
Grooms of Chamber, i. 45, 50, 208, 311, 358 ; of Privy Chamber, i. 43, 50 ; of Revels, i. 93, 100 ; of Stole, i. 53.
Grooms, in playhouses. *See* Attendants.
Groundlings, ii. 527 ; iv. 366.
Guard Chamber, i. 13.
Guilds and plays, i. 289, 296.
Gunpowder Day, i. 21 ; iii. 367.

H

Hall officers, i. 34, 226.
' Hall ' or ' room ', for masks, ii. 189 ; for interludes, iii. 23, 27.
Hall scenes, iii. 63, 86.
Hallowmas, i. 21 ; iv. 237.
Halls of palaces, i. 13, 15, 202, 216.
Hangings, iii. 78, 111, 133, 501 ; iv. 367, 370.
Harbingers, i. 46, 108.
Harlots in playhouses, i. 255, 264 ; ii. 549 ; iv. 203, 209, 211, 218, 223.

i. 158, 192 ; inserted in plays, i. 186–90. *See* Alphabetical, Antimask, Assaults, Banquets, Books, Commoning, Devices, Double Mask, Entry, Finance, Folk-survivals, Gifts, Hall, Honour, Patterns, Perspective, Proscenium, Revels, Scenes, Spectators, Taking out, Torch-bearers, Truchmen.

' Masque ', so spelt by Jonson, i. 176.

Master of Ceremonies, i. 53 ; of Horse, i. 34, 67, 100, 107, 209 ; of Paris Garden, ii. 450–3 ; of Posts, i. 48, 62, 69 ; of Requests, i. 48, 69 ; of Robes, i. 52.

Master of Revels, i. 71–105, 282, 288, 295, 299, 300, 303, 305, 318–22 ; iv. 135–41, 272, 285, 293, 305, 308–9, 325, 338, 340, 342, 343 ; fees of, i. 319 ; ii. 184 ; play-texts altered by, i. 320 ; supposed players of, i. 318 ; ii. 223. *See* Licences.

Masters of Chapel, ii. 23, 27 ; of Eton, ii. 73 ; of Merchant Taylors, ii. 75 ; of Paul's, ii. 8, 21 ; of Westminster, ii. 69 ; of Windsor Chapel, ii. 61.

Masters of companies, i. 379, 386 ; iv. 371.

Masterships in Household, i. 34.

Matachines, iii. 280, 382 ; iv. 162.

Mat-layer, i. 182, 208 ; iii. 262.

May games, i. 4, 6, 20, 120, 135, 303 ; iii. 268, 391 ; iv. 44, 77, 94, 113, 115, 200, 231–3, 247, 311, 338.

Mayors, control of plays by. *See* Justices, Restraint.

Measures, i. 198 ; iii. 234, 239, 241, 278, 280, 282, 375, 378, 383, 385, 386, 434 ; iv. 56, 57, 59.

Men companies, list of, ii. 77.

Merchant Taylors, i. 296 ; ii. 72, 75, 213 ; iii. 394, 493 ; iv. 309 ; children of, ii. 75.

' Merriments ', ii. 325 ; iv. 24.

Messalina engraving, ii. 519.

Messengers of Chamber, i. 45, 69 ; ii. 114 ; iii. 444.

' Mewing ', ii. 549 ; iv. 369.

Middle Temple, i. 222 ; iii. 260 ; iv. 111, 127.

Midsummer bonfires, i. 20 ; watch, i. 4, 135 ; iv. 81.

Mimorum aedes, ii. 538.

Minstrels, i. 48 ; iv. 337.

' Momer ', ii. 324, 332.

Momeries, i. 152.

' Monarke ' at Revels office, i. 87.

' Morals ' written for printing, iii. 179.

Morascos, i. 198 ; iv. 59.

Moresche, i. 195 ; iii. 6 ; iv. 356.

Morley's men, ii. 113, 120, 124, 192.

Morris dance, i. 4, 124, 126, 135, 151, 156, 195, 262 ; ii. 326 ; iii. 362, 391, 453, 513 ; iv. 77, 78, 96, 200, 217, 231, 311, 367.

Mother of the Maids, i. 45, 54 ; iv. 67.

Motions, i. 281 ; iii. 373 ; iv. 271 ; in masks, iii. 382, 387.

' Mouth ', officers for, i. 46.

' Multiple ' staging, iii. 18, 21, 25, 43.

Mumming, i. 150–1.

Music, ii. 541, 556.

Music house, i. 225 ; ii. 542, 557 ; iii. 139.

Music room, iii. 96, 120.

Music tree, ii. 557 ; iii. 137.

Musicians at court, i. 48, 63 ; in masks, i. 201.

N

' ne ', significance of, ii. 122, 141, 145 ; iii. 421.

Netherlands, players in, ii. 273–4, 285, 288, 291, 292.

New Year's Day, i. 19, 213.

Newington Butts playhouse, ii. 404.

Night performances, i. 304 ; iv. 225, 247, 268, 302, 306, 340.

Nîmes, synod of, i. 249.

Nottingham's men, ii. 141–86.

O

Open country scenes, iii. 51.

Orchestra, ii. 530.

Ordinanze di figurette (plots ?), iv. 364.

Original Accounts, iv. 132.

' Originals ' of plays, iii. 193, 227.

Orizonte (vanishing-point), iv. 355–8.

Ostend, siege of, iv. 39.

Out-of-doors action, convention of, iii. 29, 42, 60, 63.

Outer Chamber, i. 42, 45.

' Over the stage ', ii. 534.

Oxford's boys, ii. 100–1.

Oxford's men, ii. 99–102.

P

' Pageanter ', iii. 445.

Pageants, i. 126, 132, 135, 138, 151, 160, 175, 303 ; ii. 90 ; iii. 20, 305,

i. 264; iv. 239; courtiers, iii. 310; French, i. 323; ii. 53; iii. 257, 426; Henri IV, ii. 53; James, i. 325–8; ii. 53; humours, i. 263; lawyers, iii. 365, 475; magistrates, iv. 254; persons of honour, i. 321, 324, 327; ii. 343; iii. 455, 496; iv. 332; Poles, iii. 455; Puritans, i. 261, 262, 294; iii. 372, 476; iv. 229–33, 245, 249; Scotch, i. 323, 326; ii. 51; iii. 254, 286, 354, 432; soldiers, iii. 365; sovereigns, i. 327–8, 493; iv. 247, 254; Spanish, i. 323; Swedish, i. 324; usurers, iii. 286, 288; iv. 239; women, iii. 417; &c., &c. *See* Marprelate, Sedition.

Satyre, iv. 362.
Saxony, players at court of, ii. 288–9.
Scale (steps), iv. 358.
Scena, ii. 539; iii. 3.
Scenae trigemina corona, i. 251.
Scenarii, iv. 404.
Scene, iv. 353–65.
Scenes, as background for stage, i. 233; iii. 12, 129; iv. 366, 370, 371, 372; for masks, i. 155, 170–84; as divisions of play, iii. 50, 125, 131, 199; types of, iii. 50–68, 106. *See* Perspective.
Scenic presentation. *See* Staging.
Schoolboy plays, i. 378; ii. 11, 69–76; iii. 211.
Scotland, players in, i. 341; ii. 78, 265–70.
Scriveners' copies of plays, iii. 193.
Seasons for plays, i. 329.
Seats on stage, ii. 534–8; iv. 366–8.
Secondaries of the Compter, plays licensed by, i. 259.
Secretaries of State, i. 48, 56, 67, 68.
Secretarii, i. 55, 56.
Sedie (seats), iv. 355, 358.
Sedilia, ii. 530.
Sedition in plays, i. 264, 266, 271, 273, 275, 283, 295, 299; iii. 453–5; iv. 322. *See* Politics, Restraints, Satire, Theology.
'Senate houses', i. 231; iii. 44, 58, 95.
Serjeants, i. 34, 42; at Arms, i. 47.
Servitors in playhouses. *See* Attendants.
Setting of plays. *See* Staging.
Sewers for Chamber, i. 46.
'Shadow', ii. 544.
Sharers, i. 352–8, 369; iv. 369.
Sharers Papers of 1635, i. 357; ii. 59, 384, 417, 425, 508–10.

Shepherds, king and queen of, iv. 66.
Ship-board scenes, iii. 116.
Shoes, in play, ii. 326, 365; iii. 362.
Shops on stage, iii. 59, 110.
Shorthand, plays reported by, iii. 185, 343–4.
Shrovetide, i. 20, 213; iv. 237.
Shrove-Tuesday riots, i. 265; ii. 240.
'Side' of stage, iii. 74.
Siege scenes, iii. 38, 54, 96.
Signet, Clerks of, i. 48, 57.
Signet licences for players, i. 306, 338; ii. 260.
Signs of theatres, ii. 362, 400, 424.
Silver mine, satire of, in play, ii. 53.
Sinking curtains, iii. 9, 30.
Size of companies, i. 354.
Small seals, i. 56.
Smoking in playhouse, ii. 548; iv. 367.
'Solace' of queen, i. 267, 292.
'Soundings' in playhouse, ii. 542; iii. 72; iv. 368.
Sovereign, plays licensed by, i. 275.
Spain, players in, ii. 292.
Spanish landings in Cornwall, iv. 251.
Spectators, *rôle* of, in mask, i. 150, 153, 155, 197.
'Split' scenes, iii. 86.
Square playhouse, ii. 439, 524.
Stage, structure of, ii. 528.
Stage-directions, nature of, iii. 180, 193–8; players named in, iii. 196, 227, 271, 285, 295, 330; iv. 32, 43, 45.
Stagekeepers, ii. 109, 541; iv. 38.
Staging, in Italy, iii. 2–12; iv. 353–65; in France, iii. 12–19; at court, iii. 19–46; in 16th century, iii. 47–102; in 17th century, iii. 103–30; in private theatres, iii. 130–54; change of locality the problem of, iii. 18, 99, 121–30. *See* Above, Academic, Alcove, Alternationist, Animals, Arbours, Arras, Atmospheric, Back cloths, Beam, Bears, Bed, Black, Canopy, Castles, Close walk, Counting house, Curtains, Descents, Diagrams, Discoveries, Domus, Doors, Edge, Ἐκκύκλημα, End, Entrance, Excursions, Fore - shortening, Hangings, Heavens, Hell, Houses, Hut, Interior action, Interludes, Juxtaposition, Locality, Machines, Multiple, Out-of-doors, Over, Perspective, Place, Posts, Properties, Rake, Recesses, Rivers, Rushes, Scenes, Senate